Getaways *For* Gourmets *In the Northeast*

By Nancy and Richard Woodworth

Wood Pond Press
West Hartford, Conn.

Prices, menus, hours, and days closed in restaurants and inns vary seasonally and with business conditions. Places in this book are assumed to be open year-round, unless otherwise noted. Readers are advised to call or write ahead to avoid disappointment. Prices quoted were correct as this edition went to press. They are offered as a relative guide to what to expect and are, of course, subject to change.

Lodging rates are for double occupancy and include breakfast, unless specified to the contrary. EP (European Plan) means no meals. MAP (Modified American Plan) means breakfast and dinner.

The authors value their reputation for credibility and personally visit the places recommended in this book. Unlike others, they do not ask the owners to fill out information forms or to approve the final copy. No fees are charged for inclusion.

Readers' comments and suggestions are welcomed.

Cover Photo: Tables for dinner at New Rivers restaurant, Providence, R.I.

Library of Congress Catalog No. 84-51593.

ISBN-13: 978-0-934260-98-5.
ISBN-10: 0-934260-98-2.

Published in the United States of America.

Eighth Edition.

Contents

About the Authors

Nancy Webster Woodworth began her dining experiences in her native Montreal and as a waitress in summer resorts across Canada during her McGill University years. She worked in London and hitchhiked through Europe on $3 a day before her marriage to Richard Woodworth, an American newspaper editor, whom she met on a ski tow at Mont Tremblant in Quebec. In 1972 she started writing her "Roaming the Restaurants" column for the West Hartford (Conn.) News, which led to half of the book *Daytripping & Dining in Southern New England* (1978), since published in two other editions. She co-authored four editions of *Weekending in New England* and is co-author as well of *Inn Spots & Special Places in New England, Inn Spots & Special Places in the Mid-Atlantic, Inn Spots & Special Places in the Southeast, Waterside Escapes in the Northeast, New England's Best, The Ultimate New England Getaway Guide* and *Best Restaurants of New England.* She and her husband have two grown sons and live in West Hartford, where her ever-expanding collection of cookbooks and food and travel magazines threatens to take over the entire kitchen and den.

Richard Woodworth was raised on wholesome American food in suburban Syracuse, N.Y., and except for four years at Middlebury College in Vermont, spent much of his early life in upstate New York. He was a reporter for daily newspapers in Syracuse, Jamestown, Geneva and Rochester before moving to Connecticut to become editor of the West Hartford News and executive editor of Imprint Newspapers. He is proprietor of Wood Pond Press and is co-author of *Best Restaurants of New England, The Ultimate New England Getaway Guide, Inn Spots & Special Places in New England, Inn Spots & Special Places in the Mid-Atlantic, Inn Spots & Special Places in the Southeast, Waterside Escapes in the Northeast* and *New England's Best.* With his wife and sons, he has traveled to the four corners of this country, Canada and portions of Europe, writing their findings – from a cross-country family expedition by station wagon to exchanging houses with a family in England – for newspapers and magazines. Between adventures and writing ventures, he tries to find time for community obligations in winter and maintaining the lawn in summer.

Excerpts from several of the authors' guidebooks may be found online at **www.getawayguides.com.**

Introduction

Between the terrine and the truffles, dining out provides many an adventure. The best of these adventures is what this book is about.

It is written not by food critics who wax poetic or devastate with every precious bite. Rather it is written by travelers who like to eat and explore and who, as journalists and guidebook authors, are in a position to evaluate hundreds of restaurants and share their findings.

Ours is a highly personal guide to the best and most interesting places in 24 of the Northeast's most appealing destination areas for gourmets. They are the "best" as defined locally, by restaurateurs and chefs, and by our tastes.

We don't think haute cuisine should mean haughty cuisine. As journalists, we seek out the new and are skeptical of the old if it rides on pretension or reputation. As diners, we like to be comfortable in restaurants where the food is good and dining an adventure. We don't mind paying a lot if the experience is worth it, but we prefer the unusual or distinctive place and we expect our money's worth.

We also steer you to more than good restaurants. We point out the most choice places in which to stay. We highlight other attractions of interest to food lovers, such as specialty-food shops, kitchen stores, bakeries, wineries, herb gardens and special museums.

Through photographs as well as our reporting, we try to give you a feel for our destinations before you arrive. We want you to know what to expect, and what it will cost.

In the years we have spent researching eight editions of this book, we have eaten in as many restaurants as time and budget have allowed. For those mentioned here in which we have not dined, be assured that we'd like to, having visited and talked with the people involved.

In preparing various editions of this book, we continue to be struck by how young some of the best restaurants and lodging facilities really are. With changing economic trends and rising food awareness, many newcomers have emerged. And prices often have risen, although many restaurants now offer less-expensive café and bistro menus or venues. Diners realize these days that good eating need not be beyond their aspirations or pocketbooks

For this edition in particular, we've noted a trend to more healthful eating. There's a lighter and often a vegetarian accent on many gourmet menus these days. Many restaurants offer small plates and encourage so-called grazing.

The continuing evolution is the nature of the business – and the hazard for a guidebook that aims to keep up with the times rather than stick with the tried and true. We find the food and lodging scene so fluid in the 21st century that we would rather risk a few non-survivors than not share news about promising newcomers.

So here we are, many meals and miles (and pounds) later, having traipsed across the Northeast in sun, rain and snow, from early morn to midnight. Some places we loved; some we tolerated. Some we can't wait to get back to; some may never see us again.

But all had a certain something that earned them a place in this book.

Our hope is that you enjoy the partaking as much as we did the finding.

Nancy and Richard Woodworth

New Year's calling treats are on display for Yuletide at Winterthur.

Brandywine Valley

A Feast for All the Senses

Mention the Brandywine Valley and most people think of gardens, house museums and art, probably in that order. And with good reason, for the region is unsurpassed on the East Coast in its extraordinary combination of the three.

This is an area of unusual visual appeal, especially during spring when the flowering trees and gardens burst into bloom, and in summer, when the renowned mansions and art museums are at their crowded height.

But the area straddling the Delaware-Pennsylvania border from Wilmington to West Chester is more than a treat for the eyes and more than a seasonal tourist destination. It's a feast for all the senses – particularly so during the holiday season, which arrives early and leaves late.

Experiencing a Brandywine Christmas is like coming upon an oasis of color and sensation in the midst of a stark Andrew Wyeth landscape. Simply incredible are the museum treasures within half a dozen miles of each other in this valley that the du Ponts and the Wyeths have made famous. All the museums put on their best holiday spread, and Yuletide at Winterthur is the year's highlight for food lovers, who get to see and smell the feasts recreated from yesteryear.

Most visitors are aware of the valley's museums and gardens. But they may not know the treats they offer those with special interests in food (locally grown mushrooms are a specialty), wine (the area has several wineries), decorating and gardening. And they probably are not aware of the newer inns and good dining opportunities away from the tourist attractions.

Dining

The Best of the Best

Krazy Kat's, Route 100 and Kirk Road, Montchanin, Del.

As distinctive as the posh Inn at Montchanin Village of which it is a focal point, this polished and uniquely styled restaurant occupies the former blacksmith shop in the restored village that once housed workers at the du Pont powder mills.

Owner Missy Lickle chose the unlikely name for an eccentric old maid who once lived there "and was crazy as a cat," in the words of her grandmother. The theme turns up at the entry in a local artist's cartoon-like portrait of a gawky feline with a goofy grin, in cat sculptures clad in Japanese robes in each of the front windows, in gilt-framed portraits of cats attired in royal or military regalia on the walls, and on the brocade vests worn by the wait staff. The theme broadens in the low-slung chairs with zebra-print cushions at tables set with beige over zebra-print cloths and stunning china designed by a Connecticut artist in the colorful jaguar jungle pattern.

The tables seating 55 in two rooms are large and well spaced, the walls radiate a warm salmon color, and a fire burns in one of the original forges up near the ceiling. It's an enchanting setting for exceptional contemporary American fare.

A bowl of four varieties of olives and a basket of breads arrive with the dinner menu. One of us started with the zesty bluepoint oyster gratin teamed with prosciutto, tri-color bell peppers, shallots and parmesan cheese. The other sampled the salad of field greens, a first-rate mélange dressed with toasted pinenuts, stilton blue cheese and a zippy roasted garlic vinaigrette. Main courses range from crispy Atlantic halibut with lemon-brown butter emulsion to pan-seared filet mignon with horseradish-port wine jus. The signature sautéed crab cakes were bound with a shrimp mousseline and served with honey-jalapeño tartar sauce and sweet potato fries. The sautéed Chesapeake rockfish was of the melt-in-the-mouth variety, sauced with bluepoint oysters in a tomato-fennel cream and accompanied by crisp haricots vert and flavorful dark wild rice. Our bottle of Sterling sauvignon blanc (from a well chosen and affordable list honored by Wine Spectator) was poured in the largest wine glasses we've seen, surpassed in size only by the balloon-size globes used here for red wines.

From a dessert recitation that included a walnut-praline tart and crème de cassis crème brûlée, we settled for the intense raspberry and mango sorbets, architecturally presented with enormous blackberries and an edible orchid in an almond tuile.

Although a place for serious dining and undeniably elegant, the feline motif and lack of pretension imparts a refreshing light-heartedness. Both the meal and the setting were among the happiest of our recent travels.

(302) 888-4200. www.montchanin.com. Entrées, $25 to $30. Lunch, Monday-Friday 11 to 2. Dinner nightly, 5:30 to 9:30. Jackets requested.

Dilworthtown Inn, 1390 Old Wilmington Pike, West Chester, Pa.

In the quaint hamlet of Dilworthtown, this old wood, stone and brick inn has a classic continental menu and what is considered to be the area's best wine list. Winner of the Wine Spectator award of excellence, its 900 selections start in the $20s and rise rapidly into the triple digits. We counted more than 110 cabernets from the Napa Valley alone.

The original 1758 inn and its late 18th-century wing were restored in 1972 into a

Zebra-print cushions on chairs contribute to distinctive look at Krazy Kat's.

warren of fifteen small dining rooms seating a total of 220, a bar and a lobby complete with plate-glass windows and plantings in a mini-atrium. Each room features rich, handmade chestnut tables covered with woven mats and flanked by tavern-style chairs. Lighting is from gaslight chandeliers and candles. The dining areas, which use no electricity, have eleven wood-burning fireplaces, including three walk-in hearths and a beehive bake oven. Tuxedoed waiters lend sophistication. In season, diners may eat outside in the ruins of the original stable area, surrounded by the remains of stone walls.

The leather-bound, eight-page dinner menu starts with a dozen appetizers, including two standbys, the house pâté of creamy duck liver with black truffles and port wine syrup, and shrimp cocktail with rémoulade sauce. Executive chef David Gottlieb shows his stuff with goat cheese beignets seasoned with truffles, saffron crayfish risotto and pan-seared foie gras over duck ballotine with framboise sauce. Among the entrées are three kinds of steaks and the chef's duet, filet mignon and stuffed South African lobster tail. Otherwise, expect such contemporary continental updates as saffron-infused sea bass with zinfandel sauce, pan-seared diver scallops with lobster cream sauce and smoked breast of duck with crispy confit.

Many consider the kitchen at its best with its lengthy list of nightly specials: perhaps ginger-crisped lobster drizzled with a Thai apricot sauce and grilled portobello mushrooms with herbed polenta and white truffle sauce for appetizers; grilled mahi mahi with melon and pineapple salsa, medallions of New Zealand venison with juniper berries, and veal osso buco for entrées.

Desserts range from chocolate mousse to crème caramel. They include wonderful homemade sorbets and ice creams of exotic flavors.

Except for the specials, the inn preserves the traditional dishes, according to co-owners Robert Rafetto and James Barnes. That's fine with its steady clientele, who rate it their favorite all-around spot for consistency, charm and service.

Across the street from the restaurant is **The Inn Keeper's Kitchen,** a state-of-the-art culinary demonstration kitchen. It's the site for a cooking school featuring its own staff and visiting chefs.

(610) 399-1390. www.dilworthtowninn.com. Entrées, $23 to $37 Dinner nightly, 5:30 to 9:30, Saturday from 5, Sunday 3 to 8:30. Jackets preferred.

Catherine's Restaurant, 1701 West Doe Run Road (Routes 82 and 162), Kennett Square, Pa.

"What the Brandywine Valley lacks is a good BYOB bistro," was the lament expressed by innkeepers time after time. "These old farmers have plenty of money and will spend it on good food."

Catherine's occupies former general store.

Chef Kevin McMunn, who helped open the Gables at Chadds Ford, and his wife Marybeth Brown, heeded the call. They first opened a snug bistro in a former dairy building on the rural outskirts of West Chester and then moved to larger quarters in a former general store at the main intersection in the hamlet of Unionville. He cooks and she serves, with a polished sophistication that belies the Mom and Pop character of an operation run by a couple in their late thirties and named for her grandmother.

Filled locally by word of mouth, the setting is serene, and the night we were there the lighting was so dim that pen lights were offered to illuminate the menu. All the tables are round and for two, with some joined together to serve four. White cloths cover the tables, which sport flickering candles and a changing array of plants: tulips in spring, artfully twisting bamboo greenery at our fall visit. Stained-glass panels in the windows provide color. The background music is a carefully selected medley of oldies but goodies, in contrast with the atonal jazz typical of many restaurants these days.

Self-taught chef Kevin delivers contemporary American fare with accents from his formative years in the Southwest. Not for timid palates is his signature caesar salad blended with spicy chipotle peppers or the appetizer of blackened sea scallops with pineapple-chile pepper coulis. But his is no Johnny-one-note in fiery fusion. For the main course, he might tame cumin-spiced salmon with cucumber salsa and dijon cream or grill filet mignon with Spanish blue cheese and madeira cream. Even the chicken breast might be finished with chorizo and black bean salsa in an ancho-dijon cream sauce.

An addictive spread of olive oil with tomato and basil that arrives with bread and the menu gets dinner off to an auspicious start. One of us made a meal of appetizers – an ethereal napoleon layered with roasted yellow pepper, spinach and goat cheese, and a lobster crêpe with grilled asparagus and saffron cream. The other wanted the tuna steak, but not blackened and served with raspberry and jalapeño coulis as the menu stated. The chef obliged by grilling it rare with a black mission fig and balsamic reduction, accompanied by a fabulous risotto plus julienned peppers and haricots vert.

Refreshing endings are desserts such as key lime pie, triple chocolate-raspberry torte, butterscotch bread pudding, and ginger-peach sour cream torte, expertly prepared by a friend of the owners.

(610) 347-2227. www.dineatcatherines.com. Entrées, $18.95 to $25.95. Dinner, Tuesday-Saturday, seatings at 6 to 6:30 and 8 to 8:30. BYOB.

State Street Grille, 115 West State St., Kennett Square, Pa.

Another favorite among the BYOB bistros popping up around the Brandywine Valley is this more casual, even funky downtown storefront with a light Victorian interior. The welcome is sincere, the food inspired and the ambiance convivial.

The best seats in the house are at the rear with an up-close view of the cooking action in the open kitchen in the corner. Chef-owner Richard Halka and his wife Evelyn from Long Island raised the culinary bar, reflecting his background at high-end restaurants in the Hamptons. They added an à la carte menu to supplement the traditional prix-fixe dinners ($32 for three courses) that would command up to twice the price elsewhere.

The prix-fixe menu offers four choices for each course. Entrées in the package include pan-seared North Atlantic salmon with sherried crabmeat cream sauce, duck breast with dried cherry-green peppercorn sauce and grilled New York strip steak with wild mushroom ragoût. Appetizers could be the signature pastry shell filled with wild mushrooms in brandy cream, pan-seared scallops on wilted spinach with pear chutney and fried leeks or shrimp wrapped in applewood-smoked bacon. Desserts vary from a classic vanilla bean crème brûlée and key lime tart to banana and chocolate chip challah bread pudding.

The à la carte menu adds favorites ranging from Chilean sea bass over black beans with a mango and peach salsa to veal milanese and pistachio-crusted rack of lamb with port wine demiglace.

The $18.95 Sunday brunch offers an amazing array of breakfast and dinner items.

(610) 925-4984. www.statestreetgrille.com. Entrées, $20 to $31. Prix-fixe, $32. Dinner, Tuesday-Saturday 5 to 9 or 10. Sunday, brunch 11:30 to 2:30, dinner 5 to 8. BYOB.

The Farm House Restaurant, 514 McCue Road, Avondale, Pa.

This once rather ordinary-looking restaurant in the 18th-century farmhouse that doubles as the clubhouse at Loch Nairn Golf Course stands tall in area culinary circles.

Owners Virginia and Hank Smedley have enhanced two small and atmospheric dining rooms off a spacious lounge with barnwood walls, country artifacts, baskets hanging from the beams, candlelight and fresh flowers. We particularly liked the looks of the canopied outdoor patio, glamorously set for dinner with white linens on large tables flanked by heavy wooden chairs. There's also a stunning contemporary function facility that relegates the "farmhouse" image to history.

The chefs know what they are doing. The reputation of the crab cakes preceded our arrival for lunch. We were seated in rather formal surroundings and faced a rather daunting menu strong on dinner-type fare. Yes, there are salads and sandwiches, although caesar salad with pan-fried oysters and sautéed salmon on a warm croissant are not typical golf-club style. A basket of sundried tomato-basil bread and garlicky focaccia staved off hunger as we studied the three dozen choices, augmented by such specials as a sampler of smoked fish from the restaurant's smokehouse. But it was the crab cake we were after. It turned out to be an unpriced special, sautéed to lock in the flavor and then broiled and served over whole-grain mustard sauce. Thick with tender crabmeat, with no filling and absolutely luscious, it came with roasted peppers, snow peas and potatoes, and was well worth the $14 price tag that showed up on the bill. We also sampled the rich mushroom soup and an appetizer of chicken liver pâté with fresh figs, apple slices and crostini rounds. Service was so slow – a frequent problem here – that we ran out of time for dessert. The choice included key lime pie, chocolate mousse torte, crème brûlée and cheesecake laced with grand marnier.

Country artifacts enhance Farm House dining areas.

Dinner is a similarly elegant, leisurely affair served by a tuxedoed staff. The menu pairs some of the luncheon appetizers with more substantial entrées, varying from poached salmon with basil hollandaise to rack of lamb with madeira sauce. The range is indicated by cashew-crusted trout florentine, sautéed breast of chicken with smoked scallops, tenderloin steak au poivre and pan-seared venison rack chop served on roesti potatoes with a confit of tomatoes and herbs.

(610) 268-2235. www.ingolf.com/farmhouse. Entrées, $19.95 to $39.95. Lunch daily, 11:30 to 3, Saturday to 2:30. Dinnre nightly, 5 to 9. Sunday brunch, 10:30 to 2:30.

Simon Pearce on the Brandywine, 1333 Lenape Road, West Chester, Pa.

The original glassblowing workshop, retail store and restaurant of Simon Pearce occupies an old mill along the banks of the Ottauquechee River in Quechee, Vt. A duplicate now draws throngs to the renovated building that once housed the Lenape Inn restaurant along the Brandywine River.

The site lends itself to the Simon Pearce venture, with a wide-open glassblowing studio on the main floor and the retail shop and restaurant on the second. Huge windows in the latter take advantage of a tranquil river view. The two-level restaurant is a tad smaller than the original, and there's no open-air dining. And the food, though excellent, has lost some of its Vermont/Irish "pureness" in the transfer. Many of the traditional Irish specialties are missing here.

Quilts hang on the deep red walls and Simon Pearce glass and pottery is everywhere evident on bare wood tables. The trademark Ballymaloe bread and Irish scones with a glass of hard apple cider proved an auspicious start for lunch. The day's soup was a thick Vermont cheddar. The main events were a pear and baby spinach salad with warm goat cheese crouton and an excellent angel-hair pasta dish with sautéed shrimp, portobello mushrooms and toasted garlic cloves. Sautéed calves liver, crab cake with sherry cream and shepherd's pie were among the choices on the short menu.

The dinner repertoire is more imaginative. Curried chicken spring roll and seared Hudson Valley foie gras with black mission figs might turn up as appetizers. Expect such entrées as miso-steamed red snapper with lemongrass broth, swordfish au poivre, Moroccan-seared Atlantic salmon with a tomato-cumin ragoût, roast duckling with pomegranate glaze and grilled New Zealand venison steak with dried cherry-apple-pecan relish.

Day and night, the stars of the show are the pastry chef's desserts: perhaps a trio of crème brûlées (lavender-honey, vanilla bean and orange-ginger, at our visit), white chocolate mousse cake, anjou pear focaccia with concord grape sauce and cream cheese ice cream, and a chocolate banana "cigar."

(610) 793-0948. www.simonpearce.com. Entrées, $21 to $30. Lunch daily, 11:30 to 2:45. Dinner nightly, 5:30 to 9, Sunday to 8:30. Closed Monday and Tuesday in winter.

The Gables at Chadds Ford, 423 Baltimore Pike, Chadds Ford, Pa.

Once part of a dairy farm, this handsome stone and frame barn is now a stylish restaurant specializing in contemporary American cuisine with French and Asian accents. Jack McFadden, area restaurateur for 30-plus years and known recently for successes at the nearby Marshalton Inn and the Turks Head Inn in West Chester, invested more than $1 million into what he considers his best effort so far. "I call this my grown-up restaurant," he said. His loyal following agreed.

The place is named for the 23 gables added to the barn in an 1897 Victorian facelift. An interior design aficionado who did the architectural renderings himself, Jack scouted up three art deco bronze chandeliers and matching sconces for the bar area, where a grand piano greets arriving customers and the metal milking stools are cushioned with deep red faux ostrich skin. Leaded glass windows separate the bar from the 120-seat dining room, whose acoustics (or lack thereof) raise the noise level. Jack calls the decor "barn chic." The tables are nicely spaced, the floors heart-pine, the walls are white wood and brick and crackle painted with gold tint, and dining is by candlelight. A rear outdoor patio in a recreated barn foundation beside a waterfall is popular in season.

The fairly extensive menu is the kind upon which nearly every item appeals. You could start with a tuna and eggplant terrine or crispy duck confit with a port-poached pear over arugula. "Large plates" range from basil-encrusted tuna with red pepper sauce to grilled venison chop with red wine demi-glace.

On a recent spring weeknight, "small plates" of caramelized sea scallops with a

Grand piano greets patrons in lounge at The Gables at Chadds Ford.

warm chick pea and frisée salad and succulent pistachio-encrusted Chilean sea bass with blood oranges and watercress made a fine dinner for two. The Gables salad of maytag blue cheese, apples, pears and walnuts with mixed greens proved a good starter. For dessert, the fruit sachetti in puffed pastry could have used a lighter touch. The lime-coconut cake or the chocolate mousse bombe might have been better choices.

(610) 388-7700. www.thegablesatchaddsford.com. Entrées, $21.95 to $31.95. Lunch in season, Monday-Friday 11:30 to 2. Dinner nightly, 5:30 to 10 or 11, Sunday 5 to 9.

The Back Burner, 425 Hockessin Corner, Hockessin, Del.

Started as a cooking school, this quickly became a local favorite for interesting American cuisine in a country setting. In a magazine readers' choice poll, it was ranked the best restaurant in Delaware.

The barn-style establishment, casual but sophisticated, is part of the fabulous Everything But the Kitchen Sink culinary complex. "This area was farmland when we opened," said owner Missy Lickle. "We began a cooking school and started serving lunch to get people out here." A full-fledged restaurant was the next step, followed by a thriving café, deli and takeout operation called The Back Burner to Go and, more recently, the **Back Burner Café.** After the restaurant relocated to a new building at the other end of the complex, its former quarters became **Pizzazz,** an Italian bistro with high-style pizzas, pastas and a few Italian entrées.

The new dining room is a beauty, two stories high. Ivy and flowers hang from balconies encircling the space, which is lit by two gigantic electric-candle chandeliers. Cushioned rattan-style chairs are at well-spaced tables.

The menu changes frequently. For dinner, you might start with the specialty pumpkin-mushroom soup, a ragoût of local mushrooms in puff pastry, crab-stuffed crimini mushrooms topped with béarnaise sauce or the signature shrimp lejon, wrapped in applewood-smoked bacon. Entrées range from a jumbo lump crab cake with lime-tarragon butter sauce to grilled Australian rack of lamb with a mint-pesto aioli. Favorites include pan-seared ahi tuna with wasabi emulsion and balsamic glaze, chicken marsala and veal oscar. The signature filet mignon en croûte is sometimes topped with crab imperial and sometimes baked with brie in a whole grain mustard sauce. The mixed game grill recently offered duck breast, venison loin and rack of lamb chop with a wild berry jus.

Desserts could be bread pudding, chocolate-amaretto cake or crème brûlée.

The wine and beer lists are as good as everything else about the place.

(302) 239-2314. www.backburner.com. Entrées, $18 to $26. Lunch, Monday-Saturday 11:15 to 2:15. Dinner, Monday-Thursday 5 to 9, Friday-Saturday 5:30 to 10.

French with Flair

Gilmore's, 133 East Gay St., West Chester, Pa.

Dining is in several small candlelit rooms of a restored 18th-century townhouse at this intimate, wildly popular restaurant opened in downtown West Chester by Peter Gilmore after 22 years as chef de cuisine at Philadelphia's famed Le Bec-Fin. Here he and his wife Susan advertise "French cuisine," although it's anglicized in concept and language and modernized in execution.

The basics of the printed menu seldom change, such are the regular offerings that appeal to a loyal clientele. But the presentations do. Dinner might start with a stellar lobster bisque finished with cream and scotch, veal pâté in puff pastry, artichoke tarte tatin with truffle cream, escargots in puff pastry and – how un-French – "shrimp corn dogs," batter-dipped shrimp with a trio of dipping sauces. Main courses range from sautéed calves liver and onions to butter-poached lobster served on toasted orzo with citrus beurre blanc. Pan-seared salmon with tropical salsa, crispy Thai snapper, magret duck breast with red wine sauce, rack of lamb persillade and venison strip steak au poivre are typical offerings.

Desserts range from warm liquid-center chocolate soufflé and baba au rhum to frozen hazelnut cappuccino and milk chocolate mousse in a candied apple. Francophiles prefer to finish with the artisanal cheese plate.

Susan Gilmore oversees a staff that delivers impeccable service without being pretentious, and the chef tries to visit every table personally during dessert.

Reservations for the 36 seats are accepted three months in advance. Check out the pioneering "availability calendar" on the restaurant's website.

(610) 431-2800. www.gilmoresrestaurant.com. Entrées, $23 to $35. Dinner, Tuesday-Saturday, seatings at 6 and 8:30. BYOB.

More Dining Choices

Half Moon Restaurant & Saloon, 108 West State St., Kennett Square, Pa.

Exciting New American cuisine at remarkably reasonable prices is the hallmark of this hot spot built – literally – by young restaurateur Scott Hammond from an old candy kitchen. With a few helpers, he constructed the 35-seat mahogany bar in the front of the long, high-ceilinged downtown storefront, a popular watering spot for a young crowd. He also built the booths and tables in the rear, where diners gather away from the hubbub to enjoy the inspired fare of chef Lawrence White.

Scott named the place for a favorite after-ski haunt in Montana with the intention of opening a microbrewery called Total Eclipse. The restaurant proved so successful that the brewpub plans were shelved in favor of a large new kitchen and an indoor-outdoor rooftop dining deck. And that deck proved so popular that it was enclosed in glass for year-round dining in 2006.

From an appealing menu made for grazing, we enjoyed the spiced bluefish wrapped in a potato crust with a shrimp and crawfish court bouillon, julienned mixed vegetables and melt-in-the-mouth mashed potatoes, and cashew-encrusted chicken sautéed with chèvre, served with assertive curried vegetables and jasmine rice. With a bottle of Lost Horizon chardonnay, the dinner tab for two came to less than $50.

At least one-quarter of the changing menu is devoted to "grazers," many with a cajun or Southwest bent. Consider the specialty crab nachos, the gator gumbo with crawfish and sausage, the walnut-crusted goat cheese cake, the seafood caesar salad topped with blackened shrimp or a crispy ginger-soy duck salad. Or sample the salmon stuffed with crab imperial, dixie buttermilk fried catfish or slow-roasted barbecued buffalo short ribs. Dessert could be white chocolate-caramel apple cheesecake or chocolate-mocha layered torte.

(610) 444-7232. www.halfmoonrestaurant.com. Entrées, $14.95 to $25.95. Lunch, Monday-Friday 11:30 to 5:30, Saturday noon to 5:30. Dinner, Monday-Saturday 5:30 to 10.

Sovana Bistro & Pizza Kitchen, 696 Unionville Road, Kennett Square, Pa.

Young chef Nick Farrell pioneered in filling the area's bistro niche, launching this jaunty establishment in the Willowdale Town Center shopping complex off Route 82 north of town. He mans the grills and ovens in an elongated open kitchen, nicely separated from the high-ceilinged main dining area by a divider holding wine bottles (stored for regulars) and a prominent horse saddle mounted in front. It's a soaring, stark space with dark colors. Exposed ducts shine beneath a skylight and a large wall mural conveys the local landscape, showing houses from the area.

Nick found the name Sovana in an Italian travel guide and turned to Tuscany for much of the culinary inspiration. The dinner menu has been condensed and the prices elevated, along with the imposition of a corkage fee that distresses some. You might order a first course of tuna tartare, a goat cheese tart or pan-steamed "angry" mussels laced with garlic, chiles and rosemary-carrot brodetto. There's a choice of five salads, often including pear, roasted beet and tuna niçoise. Seven pizzas and four pasta dishes are offered. Main courses could be roasted whole fish with black olive citronette, caramelized dayboat scallops, crispy Lancaster County organic chicken with truffle jus and New York strip "steak frites" with foie gras butter. Dessert could be tarte tatin, mocha truffle torte or a selection of house-made ice creams and sorbets.

Expect similar treats for lunch, or settle for the tasty crab-cake sandwich with dijon mustard sauce

(610) 444-5600. www.sovanabistro.com. Entrées, $23 to $30. Lunch, Monday-Saturday 11 to 2:30. Dinner, Monday-Saturday 5 to 10, Sunday 4:30 to 9. BYOB.

Buckley's Tavern, 5812 Kennett Pike (Route 52), Centreville, Del.

Immensely popular locally is this tavern built in the late 1700s, all spiffed up with a pretty, white-linened interior dining room and an airy garden-room addition. Singles head for the tavern, where snacks and light entrées are available all day, or the open-air bar on two upper levels outside.

The former tavern and dinner menus have been combined into one extensive menu appealing to a variety of tastes, including those who want "small plates" and "big breads," to whom this establishment is catering lately. We ate light at a recent visit. One enjoyed oriental spring rolls and a half serving of an addictive pasta of farfalle with smoked salmon and roquefort. The other liked the caesar salad and porchetta (sliced pork roasted with garlic and rosemary), served on an onion roll with roasted peppers. You also could try, as we did on an earlier occasion, one of the handful of entrées, ranging from shrimp and grits and ruby red grapefruit salmon to jerked pork chop and grilled filet mignon wrapped in applewood bacon and smoked tomato demi-glace. We liked the specialty crab cakes, their flavor heightened by a dill mayonnaise laced with orange, and the linguini with smoked chicken and red peppers. Votive candles cast shadows on bare, rich wood tables flanked by comfortable, cushioned chairs as we lingered over a Hogue Cellars chardonnay.

The special cappuccino-pecan-praline ice cream was a hit among desserts. They included a light lemon-ginger cake and chocolate cups filled with raspberry mousse and served on a pool of crème anglaise. The cheesecake studded with black raspberries and strawberries is to die for.

(302) 656-9776. www.buckleystavern.net. Entrées, $16.95 to $24.95. Lunch, Monday-Friday 11:30 to 5:30, Saturday to 5. Dinner nightly, 5:30 to 9:30 or 10. Sunday, brunch 10 to 3, dinner 3 to 9.

Pizza, with Pizzazz

Pizza by Elizabeths, 4019 Kennett Pike, Greenville, Del.

Two Elizabeths – Greenville residents Betty Snyder and Betsy LeRoy – own this high-style, gourmet pizza parlor in the heart of du Pont country. No ordinary pizza parlor, this. In the midst of a tony shopping plaza called One Greenville Crossing, the place is a beauty in beige and green, with a Mediterranean terra-cotta tile floor, oversize dried flower wreaths on the walls and half a dozen booths and tables. The canopied sidewalk patio is favored in good weather. The pizza toppings are displayed in containers at the pizza bar. Baking in a wood-fired oven makes the crusts crisp and chewy. The beverage list includes not only Evian and cappuccino but also Samuel Adams beer and a connoisseur's selection of wines, priced up to $60.

Pizzas come in regular and mini sizes. You can try some of the owners' favorite creations named after famous Elizabeths, from $10.75 for the basic Barrett Browning to $15.50 for the Crocker (with crabmeat, asparagus and brie). The Taylor combines goat cheese, rosemary, sautéed onions, sundried tomatoes and black olives. Or you can create your own pizza from a selection of six sauces and about four dozen toppings. Seasoned breadstick appetizers with dips, fancy salads and a few rich desserts make up the rest of the menu.

(302) 654-4478. www.pizzabyelizabeths.com. Pizzas, $7.75 to $15.50. Open daily, 11:30 to 9, weekends to 10.

Lodging

The Inn at Montchanin Village, Route 100 at Kirk Road, Box 130, Montchanin, Del. 19710.

The sophisticated yet light-hearted style of its Krazy Kats restaurant (see above) extends to the sumptuous accommodations in this charming complex that evolved from a 19th-century du Pont workers' village. In 1991, preservationists Missy and

Daniel Lickle inherited the twenty-acre village established by her great-great-great grandfather, Eleuthére Irenée du Pont. Rather than sell to developers, they had the vision and resources to restore the site into a lodging and dining destination of distinction.

Guest accommodations were dictated by the idiosyncrasies of a row of turn-of-the-century duplexes, dependencies, a schoolhouse and a railroad station that made this a thriving village for workers who toiled at the nearby du Pont powder mills along the Brandywine, today part of the nearby Hagley Museum.

Most of the planned 37 rooms and suites in eleven stone, stucco and stick-style buildings are one- or two-bedroom suites with sitting areas and wet bars. The recently restored "Barn" holds a guest reception and gathering area with a walk-in fireplace in the soaring great room.

Our quarters in Belin, which turned out to be fairly typical, contained a cozy downstairs sitting room with plump sofa and chair covered in chintz, a TV/VCR atop a gas fireplace and a kitchenette area in the corner with wet bar, microwave and mini-refrigerator, complete with automatic icemaker and stocked with soft drinks and mineral water. Coffee and end tables were charmingly painted with flowers and rabbits. Everything was jolly looking and colorfully decorated in mix-and-match patterns that flow together. Up steep stairs was a skylit bedroom with a king bed dressed in Frette linens, about the most comfortable we've had the pleasure of luxuriating in, and a stunning, huge, all-marble bathroom. The latter came with a chandelier, a deep tub embedded in marble, a separate shower encased in thick clear glass and, if you found the right switch, heated towel racks. Wood-look venetian blinds covered the windows, padded hangers and ironing equipment were in the closet, and a country window had been painted whimsically on the wall beside a real window. The inn's distinctive cowbird logo – a crow perched on the back of a leaping cow – was everywhere (monogrammed on the terry robes, embedded in the marble above the bath). The bed was turned down with chocolates and a copy of the weather forecast, and a thermos of ice water was placed beside. The only downside was traffic noise from the busy intersection out front.

Breakfast the next morning beside the front windows in Krazy Kat's was a feast of fresh orange juice, muffins, and a choice including eggs benedict and an omelet with smoked bacon, brie and chives, tasty walnut-raisin toast, garlicky browned potatoes and garnishes of large blackberries. (Breakfast no longer is included in the rates).

Afterward, Missy Lickle led a tour of the heart of the steeply sloping complex sandwiched between main road and train track (golf carts are lined up to transport luggage from parking areas as well as guests with limited mobility). All is artfully landscaped and full of surprises, from picket fences to pocket gardens to gaslights to porches with wicker rockers. Room sizes and configurations differ, but each appeals in its own right. Some have poster beds and some are kingsize. The Jefferson offers wicker porches front and back and a bathroom walled in travertine marble up to the vaulted ceiling. Missy, who decorated with goods from her huge gourmet emporium known as Everything But the Kitchen Sink, incorporated fine period and reproduction furniture, Staffordshire figurines, colorful fabrics and a welcome sense of whimsy.

(302) 888-2133 or (800) 269-2473. Fax (302) 888-0389. www.montchanin.com. Twelve rooms and sixteen suites with private baths. Rates, EP. Doubles $169 to $209. Suites, $249 to $375.

Spring flowers brighten pond area at Inn at Whitewing Farm.

Inn at Whitewing Farm, 370 Valley Road, West Chester, Pa. (Mail to Box 98, Kennett Square, PA 19348).

Overnight guests can partake of the good life in this stylish B&B fashioned from the former estate of the treasurer of the du Pont Company. Local contractor/architect Edward DeSeta and his wife Wanda moved here in 1992 with their three children and no intention of running a B&B. An innkeeper friend who had overbooked called breathlessly one day to ask the DeSetas to put up her guests in their pool house. "All you have to do is serve them breakfast," Wanda recalls being told. "And I've been serving breakfast ever since." Mighty good breakfasts, we might add, to go with comfortable accommodations, and elaborate common and sporting facilities that would do many a larger establishment proud.

Consider: A sprawling fieldstone and clapboard mansion dating to 1796 and six outbuildings transformed into eleven guest rooms and suites. Forty-three acres of rolling property backing up to Longwood Gardens. A swimming pool with a jacuzzi, a stocked, twelve-foot-deep fishing pond, ducks quacking around lily ponds and a waterfall, a ten-hole chip and putt golf course, a tennis court flanked by a trellised pavilion, a greenhouse and showy perennial gardens for the growing of flowers. The DeSetas use a golf cart to transport guests around the property.

The accommodations are no longer in the mansion but rather in restored outbuildings, and the DeSetas are assisted by a staff of six, who live in apartments in barns across the street. The gathering room is now in the grandly renovated Hay Barn, whose sumptuous demeanor belies its recent status as a wagon storage barn. Not to mention what Wanda calls "Ed's Folly" – a downstairs wine cellar that she envisioned as "a closet" and promptly turned into a two-room showplace opening onto a flagstone terrace. The three-story barn also holds a kitchen, dining area and upstairs library and is open 24 hours with a stocked guest pantry, evening sweets and cordials.

Two guest rooms are in the converted stables, and three in the carriage house. Renovated for the purpose, each has a queensize bed (one is kingsize), modern bathroom (shower only) with marble floor, TV and a veritable library of books. They're decorated in a hunt theme with pale yellow walls, splashy blue and yellow fabrics and thick carpeting. Two simpler rooms were fashioned from the former men's and women's changing facilities in the Pond House, where the decor is garden style, the bed headboard is a picket fence and a patio with wrought-iron lounge chairs faces the idyllic fish pond, with its frogs croaking and its fountain lit at night. Recently upgraded, they have built-in cabinets for the TV and marble floors for the bathrooms. Three luxurious suites were opened recently in another outbuilding. Each with kingsize bedroom, sitting area and fireplace, they include the majestic Clydesdale (the largest with plush chairs and sofas and a row of window seats) and, downstairs, the new English Garden, which opens onto a garden patio and fields frequented by deer.

Our quarters in the Gatehouse Suite included a skylit living room with a fireplace and sofabed, a book-lined den with a plush chair in front of the TV, a skylit bedroom with kingsize bed, a beauty of a bathroom done in marble with a bouquet of rosebuds (this in autumn) reflected in the mirror on the vanity, a modern kitchen and a terrace.

Although the DeSotas claim to be through with inn renovations and expansion, given their track record you have to wonder. Besides his wine cellar, Ed has acquired a 1930 Ford Model A sedan and a 1938 Ford pickup truck in which to taxi guests. They joined two antique carriages and two sleighs kept in a barn across the street. Ed's pride is a horse named "A Little Bit Tipsy," who joins three miniatures and the cow his wife bought him for his birthday. Now there are also six baby belted galloway cows and a pair of swans.

Manager Cathleen Ryan, a former pastry chef at the Inn at Little Washington in Virginia, prepares treats like peppers stuffed with goat cheese and valrhona chocolate chip cookies for afternoon tea. She also prepares and the DeSotas serve sumptuous breakfasts at individual tables in the Hay Barn. Orange juice, cream cheese and raspberry coffee cake, and made-to-order omelets were the fare at one visit. Bananas with coconut twist and ginger-pear pancakes were featured another time. Ed sometimes gets so involved in conversation he forgets to serve. "We have guests who come here and never leave the property," says he. After staying here, we understand why.

(610) 388-2664. Fax (610) 388-3650. www.whitewingfarm.com. Seven rooms and three suites with private baths. Doubles, $135 to $199. Suites $245 to $289. No credit cards.

Hamanassett Bed & Breakfast, 115 Indian Springs Drive, Box 366, Chester Heights, Pa. 19017.

The 19th-century mansion on seven hilltop acres that served as headquarters for the Lima Hunt is now an exceptionally spacious and comfortable B&B. Ashley Mon, an antiques dealer from New Orleans, and her husband Glenn, a sports executive who managed the Super Dome, outfitted the Pennsylvania house with their own furnishings and antiques and incorporated substantial upgrades. The result is one of the more appealing, polished B&B operations in the region, nicely leavened with Southern charm and hospitality.

Energetic Ashley has refurbished the common areas and six sizable guest rooms. Each of the latter is newly equipped with air conditioning and king or queen beds, hardwood floors with oriental carpets, TV/VCRs, English toiletries, bottled water, coffeemaker, plush twill robes, hair dryer, iron and ironing board – "all the things I want when I travel," she says. All beds are triple-sheeted, and the linens are ironed by hand.

The master bedroom is now the Inverness, an elegant space with fishnet canopy bed, loveseat and a second sitting area, and wood-burning cast-iron stove in the fireplace topped by a massive mantel mirror. Another favorite is the Windsor, with a half-tester rosewood bed ten feet high and an antique chest concealing the TV.

Front loggia welcomes guests at Hamanassett.

Ashley is an anglophile who studied architecture at Oxford University. That explains both the names and the English country decor in the Cambridge Room and the newly paneled bath with wainscoting in the Brighton Room. The third-floor Devon Suite comes with a king bed canopied in sheer netting, two chairs with ottomans and a sofa in an alcove. Her interior refurbishing completed, Ashley restored a coachman's house into a child-friendly, two-bedroom cottage and turned another building into an antiques and gift shop for guests.

With the grace of a Southern belle, she goes about making guests feel at home in a house in which her predecessor raised five children. There's plenty of house to enjoy: a formal living room/library with grand piano and fireplace, where cordials are put out on the Empire sideboard in the evening; a period billiards room with another fireplace outlined in Delft tiles, an extensive video library and antique games; a huge solarium with casual seats and tables, plants and wicker hampers ready for picnics; a new side terrace, and a majestic front loggia outfitted with lounge chairs overlooking the gardens.

Elaborate breakfasts are taken by candlelight amid antique china, crystal and silver at two large damask-covered tables overlooking the side terrace. The repast might involve mixed fruit compote, orange croissant french toast and ham one day, and baked pears in cream sauce, eggs florentine and bacon the next. The Sunday specialty is eggs Hamanassett (poached eggs on English muffins with veal sauce) and bananas foster. Ashley, who loves to cook as much as she loves to entertain, wows guests with her baked cheese grits, "though I don't tell people what it is until they try it."

Guests depart well-fed and restored, returning down the winding driveway past forests and gardens to U.S. Route 1, a half mile and another world away.

(610) 459-3000 or (877) 836-8212. www.hamanassett.com. Six rooms with private baths. Doubles, $120 to $215. Carriage house, $300 to $400.

Fairville Inn, 506 Kennett Pike (Route 52), Box 219, Chadds Ford, Pa. 19317.

Fortuitously situated in the heart of museum country, this luxurious B&B is based in what had been a private residence for 130 years. The original 1857 house contains both public rooms and four upstairs guest rooms. The most choice accommodations are the ten out back in the Carriage House, built by an Amish family, and in a nearby barn named the Spring House. They were designed by the former owner's uncle, architect Rodney Williams of Vermont's famed Inn at Sawmill Farm, and bear his wife's unmistakable decorating flair.

Each is the epitome of elegant comfort. Accented with barnwood, beams and occasional cathedral ceilings, eight rooms have gas fireplaces, and all boast decks or balconies looking across three acres of fields toward a pond. Lamps with pierced shades cast pleasant shadows. All possess spacious full baths (our suite had two vanities and a separate dressing area; the towels were thick and matched the decor), king or queen beds, oversize closets, unobtrusive TVs, phones, elegant country furnishings, crisp and colorful chintzes, and flowers from a prolific garden. Each of the two spacious suites has a balcony with wrought-iron furniture, a sitting room with a loveseat, and a bedroom with a kingsize canopy bed and two wing chairs by the fire.

Back in the main hose, breakfast is served in an expanded dining room in space gained from relocating the front office and reception area into new quarters off the living room. In addition to fresh orange juice, cereal, yogurt and pastries, owners Jane and Noel McStay offer an entrée of quiche, scrambled eggs, belgian waffles, vegetable frittata or, the day of our visit, pancakes with strawberry topping, garnished with blueberries and pineapple.

The breakfast cook also bakes the cookies, tortes and scones for afternoon tea, which is a culinary treat as well. It's taken at white-linened tables, each bearing a bud vase with a single white rose.

(610) 388-5900 or (877) 285-7772. Fax (610) 388-5902. www.fairvilleinn.com. Thirteen rooms and two suites with private baths. Doubles, $150 to $225. Suites, $220 to $250.

The Pennsbury Inn, 883 Baltimore Pike, Chadds Ford, Pa. 19357.

This fieldstone and yellow brick house dating to 1714, up against U.S. Route 1 but screened from passing traffic by a high, thick hedge, was opened in 1996 by partners in a nearby furniture and design company as a showcase for their wares. The result was a showplace of decorator-quality common rooms and six guest rooms furnished to the three periods in which the house was built.

Ex-New Yorkers Cheryl Grono and her husband Chip, who were living in the Philadelphia area at the time, acquired the property in 2001 and imparted a personal touch that had been lacking and made the accommodations not only showy but more comfortable.

Listed in the National Register of Historic Places, the B&B has slanted doorways, creaky floorboards, winding staircases and huge open fireplaces. Extensive collections of antiques and old books add to the building's inherent charm

The guest quarters vary widely, from the grand rear Winterthur Room with vaulted ceiling and queensize cherry bed, loveseat, plush armchair and little deacon's bench to the cozy front John Marshall Room with an antique double bed, built-in fireplace and private bath in the hall.

Feather beds with down comforters are the rule, as are modernized baths with pewter or chrome fixtures and splashy but spare decor. The Gronos added a period sofa/daybed in the Lafayette Room, reached via an impossibly steep winder staircase, and turn it into a suite when rented with a parlor beneath.

The main floor offers five comfortable common rooms. One is a library with TV and stereo and another a magnificent garden room off the kitchen with a couple of dining areas and a sofa and chairs facing a huge fireplace. Guests also spread out in a parlor in the oldest section of the house, as well as in a music and game room.

Cheryl offers lemonade or hot spiced cider in the afternoons, depending on the season. In the morning she serves a full breakfast. Two guest favorites are peaches and cream french toast and a scrambled egg wrap – a tortilla filled with creamy scrambled eggs topped with caramelized onions, peppers and grated cheese.

Out back, the Gronos have landscaped four acres with gardens, a reflecting pool, fish pond, fountains and sitting areas. They cut woodland trails in four more forested acres behind.

(610) 388-1435. Fax (610) 388-1436. www.pennsburyinn.com. Six rooms with private baths. April-December: doubles, $145 to $255 weekends, $125 to $235 midweek. January-March: doubles, $125 to $210 weekends, $105 to $185 midweek.

Kennett House Bed & Breakfast, 503 West State St., Kennett Square, Pa. 19348.

Victoriana long reigned in this granite four-square mansion with rust-colored shutters astride a hill at the edge of Kennett Square. It's been toned down a bit since the Scarlett House was purchased in 2001 by Carol and Jeff Yetter. They took the style back to the Arts and Crafts era of its 1910 origin, made the place less museum-like formal and shed the Scarlett House name, a reference to the original owner.

The wide entry foyer remains notable for chestnut woodwork, doors and stairs. Each of two window nooks on either side of the door contains facing benches that are replicas of originals in the old Quaker Meeting House in Kennett Square. Off the foyer are two parlors with fireplaces. The former ladies' parlor has been turned into a traditional living room and the men's parlor is now a library with deep leather furniture to sink into.

Upstairs are another sitting area, this one beside sunny windows full of plants on the stairway landing, plus a suite and three guest rooms. The Yetters added a bath so rooms no longer share. They also made the accommodations more comfortable and homey. All have queen beds and TVs. Carol faux-finished the walls and stenciled the bathroom in the front-corner Wyeth Room, which features Wyeth prints. The rear Longwood Suite offers a mahogany four-poster rice bed in the bedroom and a queen sofabed in a side sitting room. The Delaware Room has a sitting area in what used to be a sleeping porch.

Carol's cooking talents are manifested at breakfast, served in two adjacent dining rooms at the rear of the main floor. Specialties include baked apple french toast and egg casserole. Jeff says her double chocolate-chip banana muffins are not to be missed. In the afternoon, the Yetters offer refreshments in the second-floor sitting area. A mini-refrigerator is stocked with cold beverages, and fruit and cookies are at the ready.

Outside are a broad wraparound porch and English gardens, with a fish pond and a pergola in back.

(610) 444-9592 or (800) 820-9592. Fax (610) 444-7633. www.kennetthouse.com. Three rooms and one suite with private baths. Doubles $145 to $155 weekends, $125 to $135 midweek. Suite, $175 weekends, $155 midweek.

Good Location, Great Value

Mendenhall Inn Hotel & Conference Center, 323 Kennett Pike (Route 52), Mendenhall, PA 19317.

This pleasant hotel in semi-rural surroundings grew from a modest motor inn and sprawling restaurant into a modern, full-service hotel. It's centrally situated for taking advantage of the Brandywine attractions, but it also represents exceptional value.

Fully renovated in 2005, the three-story hotel offers 70 spacious accommodations with kingsize or two double beds off central hallways. Our quiet room facing the countryside to the rear had pine furnishings, a TV in an armoire, and the usual hotel amenities from a small minibar of select brands to a "gift package" of Gilbert & Soames toiletries. The complimentary breakfast buffet the next morning was one of the more varied around, featuring chef-prepared, create-your-own omelets, waffles and breakfast meats on weekdays. The manager hosts a complimentary wine and beer reception Monday-Thursday afternoons. Best of all was the price: $89 a night, with standard discount.

The restaurant that started it all offers an extensive and fancy continental/American menu, priced from $20.95 to $35.95. Lunch and dinner are served daily.

(610) 388-2100. Fax (610) 388-1184. www.mendenhallinn.com. Sixty-six rooms and four suites. Doubles, $129. Suites, $175 to $219.

Museums and Gardens

The area's favorite landmarks are of special interest, partly because of their restaurants and gastronomic appeal.

Winterthur Museum, Garden and Library, Route 52, Winterthur, Del.

Four generations of du Ponts lovingly cared for this noted country estate that today combines art, history, beauty and learning. Henry Francis du Pont, collector and horticulturist, created an unrivaled collection of early American decorative arts, now on display in period settings in the vast mansion-museum, and a matchless 20th-century naturalistic garden. A research library and the Galleries, with special exhibitions on two floors, also are open to the public.

Food lovers find it at its best during the annual **Yuletide at Winterthur,** when the mansion is decorated with Christmas trees, flowers and the appropriate foods of each era represented in the rooms. The tour theme is holiday dining and entertaining of the 18th and 19th centuries, as well as the ways the du Ponts entertained in the home they occupied until 1951. Interestingly, most of the food is so well preserved (some of it freeze-dried by the Smithsonian Institution) that it not only looks real but smells so, too.

Yuletide celebrations are recreated in more than twenty period rooms, from a parlor prepared for an evening musicale to a nursery ready for an infant's holiday christening. When we visited, the du Pont dining room was set up for Christmas meals as the family would have had them in the 1930s and 1940s. Other rooms are set for everything from a Maryland hunt breakfast to a tea party in the Baltimore drawing room. Several rooms are ready for the New Year's Day calling – an occasion when the ladies stayed home to entertain the gentlemen who made the rounds to call (the 300 or so du Ponts in the area continue the family custom to this day, our guide said). Recent highlights were four rooms decorated for 21st-century celebrations by New York designer Thomas Jayne.

If all this makes you hungry, stop after the tour in the **Garden Cafeteria** in the Visitor Pavilion, where breakfast and lunch are available in a large and handsome room, with floor-to-ceiling windows looking onto the gardens. A salad bar has just about everything you could imagine, and we enjoyed the Thursday Mexican fiesta bar where we made our own tacos and salads. Sandwiches and salads and a few items like a hamburger and a smoked salmon plate are available. The restaurant devotes one section to a fancy garden setting where afternoon tea and Sunday brunch are served (reservations 888-4826). The **Cappuccino Café** offers snacks and beverages.

(302) 888-4600 or (800) 448-3883. www.winterthur.org. Open Tuesday-Sunday, 10 to 5, daily during Yuletide. Adults, $15. Yuletide at Winterthur: Late November through early January, reservations required, adults $20.

Longwood Gardens, Route 1, Kennett Square, Pa.

For years the 350-acre private preserve of Pierre S. du Pont, the horticultural legacy he left is the area's single most popular showplace.

The year-round focal points are the Crystal Palace-type conservatories in which spring begins in January and the spectacle changes monthly through Christmas. How appealing they were on the blustery December day we first visited, brightened by 3,000 perfect poinsettias in red, pink and cream, unusually large and grown singly and in clusters. Outdoors after dark, 400,000 lights glitter in Longwood's trees and colorful fountains dance to music of the season. The indoor plants alone – from bonsai to cacti to impatiens to orchids – are so lush and spectacular as to boggle the mind as to what's outside the rest of the year, which, we know from later visits, is plenty.

Longwood's large shop is filled with items for the gardener – small pots of herbs, orchids, tiles, garden chimes, books, placemats and cookbooks, many with an herbal theme. Packets of Brandywine bayberries smell heavenly; tins of various sizes are decorated with flowers and horticultural notes.

Meals are available at the **Terrace Restaurant** (garden admission required). A formal, sit-down restaurant plus a cafeteria that can accommodate 300 at a time, it is done in fine taste in shades of pink and brown, with walls of windows looking onto the gardens and black wrought-iron furniture on delightful dining terraces. The cafeteria does all its own baking and boasts mushroom specialties, chili, deli sandwiches, and local wines and beers. A separate line leads to the desserts, among them a luscious hazelnut torte and, at one visit, a celestial cheesecake topped with almonds, whipped cream and all kinds of fruit, including kiwi, in a decorative pattern. Lunch and brunch (and dinner on the nights the gardens are open) are served in the plant-filled dining room. You could start with double mushroom soup with pernod and tarragon or snapper soup, go on to a Kennett Square mushroom strudel, and for your main course have grilled delmonico steak with spicy ancho and pear barbecue sauce. Finish with a pastry or one of the Terrace sundaes.

(610) 388-1000 or (800) 737-5500. www.longwoodgardens.org. Open daily, conservatories 10 to 5, outdoor gardens 9 to 6, to 5 November-March. Extended hours in December and summer fountain nights. Adults, $12 to $15.

Hagley Museum, Route 141, Wilmington, Del.

The aroma of fresh cookies emanates all year from the wood-burning stove in a typical worker's house, part of this fascinating restoration of the early mill community where E.I. du Pont started the du Pont Company as a gunpowder manufacturer in 1802.

Eleutherian Mills, the first du Pont family home in Delaware, is furnished to reflect the tastes of five generations of du Ponts. We particularly liked the basement keeping room, left as it had been furnished by Louise du Pont Crowninshield, who died in 1958. The formal dining room is remarkable for its scenic American wallpaper, a curious hand-blocked print with Spanish moss adorning trees around Boston Harbor. At Yuletide, it's set for a Twelfth Night celebration. A children's tea set with silver spoons is a highlight of the master bedroom in this house, which impresses because it feels like a home rather than a museum. The French garden outside has been restored with espaliered fruit trees and organic fruits and vegetables – in season, it's not only beautiful, but functional.

In keeping with the period, the simple **Belin House Coffee Shop** on Blacksmith Hill offers sandwiches, beverages and homemade desserts daily from 11 to 4. With lemonade and a piece of pie, you can quite imagine yourself back nearly 200 years in time.

(302) 658-2400. www.hagley.org. Open daily, 9:30 to 4:30, March 15 through December; same hours weekends and one tour at 1:30 weekdays, January to March 14. Adults, $11.

Brandywine River Museum, U.S. Route 1, Chadds Ford, Pa.

This special place made famous by the Wyeth family is extra-special during the holiday season when you not only can gaze at paintings but watch an elaborate model-train layout, enjoy Ann Wyeth McCoy's fabulous collection of dolls, see a ram made of grapevines, magnolia leaves, cattails and goldenrod, and eat roasted chestnuts.

Inside a century-old gristmill with white plastered walls and curved glass windows are three floors of beamed galleries that make up a permanent repository of the works of artists inspired by the Brandywine Valley. The paintings of three generations of Wyeths – Andrew, who lives nearby, his father N.C. and his son Jamie – fill the second floor. The newly restored studio of N.C. Wyeth is a treasure trove for Wyeth fans.

An attractive, newly renovated restaurant has bentwood chairs and little round tables on a floor of old paving bricks in a glass tower that affords a great view of the Brandywine River. It's open from 11 to 3, serving main dishes, salads and wine or beer. The ploughman's lunch brings sausage pâté, cheese and breads.

Museum volunteers put out a marvelous cookbook, named *For the POT* after the Jamie Wyeth painting of a chicken in a pot that graces the cover. It has unusual recipes, many calling for Chester County mushrooms, and several of the Wyeths have contributed their specialties. A raspberry meringue, called "Berried at Sea" from the Andrew Wyeth painting of almost the same name and furnished by Betsy Wyeth, sounds out of this world.

(610) 388-2700. www.brandywinemuseum.org. Open daily, 9:30 to 4:30. Adults, $8.

Gourmet Treats

The main street (Route 52) of Centreville, Del., has several nice shops. **Montrachet Fine Foods,** 5808 Kennett Pike, makes up good sandwiches and gourmet food to go. Across the street is **Wild Thyme,** an exceptional garden and gift shop.

North on Route 52 is **Feasts of Fairville,** a rustic 1810 country house where George Nolan and Kathy Donovan offer a mix of gourmet comfort foods and vegetarian dishes for takeout.

In tony Greenville, Del., you can pick up a sandwich or salad at the deli at **Janssen's,** a fine, family-owned gourmet food market catering to the carriage trade at 4021 Kennett Pike. We liked the Brandywine chicken salad sandwich on a hard roll and another chicken version with almonds and grapes in pita. Nearly adjacent is the **Wine & Spirit Co. of Greenville,** stocking hard-to-find beverages.

Just a shopping complex away in 2 Greenville Crossing at 4001 Kennett Pike is **Pure Bread Deli,** a bakery and café with terrific sandwiches and panini named for dogs, plus soups and salads. The Doberman (smoked salmon on a toasted bagel and the Great Dane (baked ham and brie on grilled herb focaccia) were first-rate. There's pleasant café-style seating inside and out. Across the road at Powder Mill Square is **Brew Ha Ha!** (the first in a regional Italian-style coffee and newsstand chain, with great pastries as well as fancy coffees).

Food Source by Clemens, billed as the ultimate food specialty shop from Philadelphia's Main Line, opened in 2005 in Greenville at 3801 Kennett Pike after first branching out to the Shoppes of Brinton Lake, 925 Baltimore Pike (Route 1) in Glen Mills. Also on Route 1 at 909 East Baltimore Pike in Kennett Square, the old Phillips Place mushroom museum is now the home of **Spring Run Natural Foods,** the area's largest organic market. New in Kennett Square, which bills itself as the mushroom capital of the world, is **The Mushroom Cap,** a small gift and mushroom shop at 114 West State St.

Kennett Square is also home to **La Michoacana,** a most unusual ice cream shop at 231 East State St. Among the nearly 50 flavors of authentic Mexican ice cream, made on the premises, are avocado, cucumber with chiles, mango, tamarind, rice pudding and red bean. The corn with cinnamon powder is the best-seller. "We don't have any weird names for the ice cream," said Noelia Saharon, owner with her husband and another Mexican couple. "We call it what it is so you know what you're eating." They let skeptics sample the flavors "to make sure they like what they get." Ever experimenting, the partners made mushroom ice cream bars for the Kennett Square's mushroom festival, pumpkin ice cream for Halloween, turkey ice cream for Thanksgiving and eggnog ice cream for Christmas.

A Gourmet Mecca

Everything But the Kitchen Sink, 425 Hockessin Corner, Hockessin, Del.

For those with an interest in things culinary, the best destination of all is Hockessin Corner and this incredible complex. It's located in a warren of old warehouse buildings beside the railroad track, just off Route 41 on Old Lancaster Pike. In 1977, Missy Lickle opened a small gift shop in two sections of onetime coal bins. Now she has more than 15,000 square feet to work with, which accounts for The Back Burner restaurant and related food enterprises, a cooking school and room after room of kitchenware, a fabulous array of china, MacKenzie-Childs and Lynn Chase dinnerware, cookbooks, gadgets, gourmet foods, paper goods, table linens and even adorable baby clothes. We've never before seen such an interesting and unusual selection in one place.

(302) 239-7066 or (800) 731-7066. www.thekitchensink.com. Open weekdays, 9:30 to 5, Thursday to 7, Saturday 10 to 5, Sunday noon to 4.

A Pair of Wineries

Six wineries are part of the fledgling Brandywine Valley Wine Trail. Two of the most interesting:

Chaddsford Winery, 632 Baltimore Pike, Chadds Ford, Pa.

Eric Miller explains why he started his winery in this location and why he expends much effort making elegant chardonnays that are finished in French oak barrels and retail for up to $29 a bottle: "Well, this isn't Disneyland, you know. We've got a lot of traveling connoisseurs who know their wines."

The area's first boutique-style winery, opened in a converted 18th-century barn in 1983, imports most of its grapes from vineyards in Chester County and elsewhere. Its production has increased twelve-fold from 3,000 to 37,000 cases a year. It now charges $5 for wine tastings and sells wine by the glass and cheeses in a small café with a pleasant outdoor patio. It also sponsors an outdoor concert series on summer Friday nights on the grounds.

Eric, who comes from a winemaking family (his father owns Benmarl Vineyards in New York's Hudson Valley), and his wife Lee, author of a book about wine, live next door in a house whose image is imprinted on some of the labels that mark their bottles. Their expanding operation includes a private tasting room where they cater dinner parties. A meritage-style cabernet sauvignon/merlot blend called Merican is offered for $39.99, and the winery bottles spiced apple wine ("good with ham," they say) and a sangria (both $10.99). The Chaddsford proprietor's reserve white ($9.99) is great to accompany a picnic lunch on the winery's pleasant outdoor deck.

After hearing the Millers talk about their chardonnay ("it's a good dinner companion and keeps your mouth fresh for the food") and tasting it ("showing honey and vanilla in the nose"), we splurged and laid down a bottle for a special occasion.

(610) 388-6221. www.chaddsford.com. Open daily, noon to 6. Closed Mondays in January-March. Guided tours offered on weekends.

Va La Vineyards, 8820 Gap Newport Pike (Route 41), Avondale, Pa.

For a different kind of wine-tasting experience – one with good food and a refreshing sense of whimsy – head to this working vineyard owned by Anthony Vietri, president of the Brandywine Valley Wine Trail.

Five generations of a farm family named the 75-year-old operation Va La for the tiny village in northern Italy where the founders came from. Theirs is a "true" winery consisting of a wine cellar built into the hillside of the vineyard, seven acres of vines and "one family devoted to each other and to the creation of wine" – small-batch productions of fruity and rustico-style wines to pair with foods. At their Enoteca Va La, they sell pinot grigio, corvina, barbera, chiaretto and viognier, among others, accompanied by Chester County food specialties such as marinated mushrooms, mustards and artisan cheeses. Their Galleria Va La in a loft overlooking the vineyard offers monthly exhibits by local artists.

Area wine experts consider Va La an experience visiting wine connoisseurs should not miss. It's officially open weekends and occasional weekdays "by act of Congress."

(610) 268-2702. www.valavineyards.com. Open Friday noon to 5:30, Saturday and Sunday noon to 6.

Daffodils herald arrival of spring at Black Bass Hotel, Bucks County icon in Lumberville.

Bucks County

Romance along the River

There's something very special about the Delaware River section of Bucks County, Pa., and neighboring Hunterdon County in New Jersey.

In both look and feel, from the sturdy stone houses to the profusion of daffodils marching down to the river in springtime, it's the closest thing this side of Great Britain to the Cotswolds we love so well. There's a welcome sense of remoteness and romance along the River Road, a narrow and winding route that thwarts fast-moving vehicular traffic and invites visitors to take to their feet. There are real country inns, both chic and quaint, and more good dining places than one has a right to expect. And there's the great river with its historic canal and towpath, which shapes the area's character and raises the rationale to laze along, whether by foot, bicycle or canoe.

We're obviously not alone in our love affair with Bucks County, a meandering mosaic of suburbia and seclusion stretching north from the Philadelphia exurbs almost to Easton and the edge of the Poconos. Places like New Hope, the artist colony, are wall-to-wall people on summer weekends. More to our liking is the scenic rivershed area stretching above New Hope to Upper Black Eddy, especially in spring and fall.

Consider Lumberville, Pa., for instance. It's so small that you can drive through in less than a minute and canoe past in a few, yet so interesting that a stroll with stops can take a couple of hours. From our base at Lumberville's 1740 House, we walked the towpath down to Stockton and Phillips Mill, checking out inns and restaurants along the way as we rekindled memories of the British countryside (after all, the area was settled by the English Quakers and names like Solebury, Chalfont and Wycombe persist).

This chapter focuses on the strips of Bucks County and Hunterdon County along the river north of New Hope – and places within walking distance of the river. Thus we stress river towns like Lambertville, which has been revitalized to the point where "there's a restaurant for almost every family," according to one local foodie.

Because liquor licenses are limited, inns and restaurants without them – most of them in Hunterdon County – invite guests to bring their own wines. They can't make a profit on liquor, so to survive they have to be extra good with their food, explained one restaurateur.

And good they are. New restaurants are emerging to compete with the old, and several inns have outstanding dining rooms. At peak periods, dinner reservations often are hard to come by. Most inns require minimum stays on weekends.

So book well ahead and prepare to relax. Here's a perfect place for a gourmet getaway, especially for anyone with an iota of British blood in his body and a bit of romance in his heart.

Dining

The Best of the Best

Anton's at the Swan, 43 South Main St., Lambertville, N.J.

Anton Dodel launched this class act in the Swan Hotel and won a citation from the New York Times as one of the ten best restaurants in New Jersey the year it opened. It has maintained high marks since its purchase by Chris Connors, who had served successively as sous chef and chef under Anton's tutelage.

The transition was so smooth that even regulars, although they had missed Anton's nightly presence, were unaware of the change in ownership. "Everything's the same," assured Chris in his new role as hands-on chef-owner.

Chris's fare is spontaneous and eclectic, like that of his predecessor. His short menu changes monthly. One we liked featured such entrées as sautéed halibut on a curried lentil daal, cumin-crusted swordfish with red beans and rice, roasted duck breast with thyme jus and polenta, and grilled buffalo ribeye steak with truffle-mashed potatoes.

Starters could be a crab cake with sweet and sour red cabbage and tartar sauce, grilled shrimp with coconut rice and spicy peanut sauce, asparagus risotto with aged parmigiano-reggiano and a salad of duck with grilled figs and white beans. Dessert always includes something chocolate and usually a flan, but you might find a cherry brioche bread pudding, orange-ginger crème brûlée or raspberry-lemon tart.

Wall of mirrors and rich wood paneling are backdrops for dining at Anton's at the Swan.

All this good eating takes place in a subdued room with dark woods, paneled wainscoting, a wall of mirrors, and candles flickering in hurricane chimneys atop white-linened tables flanked by windsor chairs.

Chris cooks more casual fare for the Swan's popular bar, where some regulars sup several times a week on fare ranging from a tomato pizza and mussels steamed in white wine and garlic to grilled chicken caesar salad and grilled New York strip steak with scalloped potatoes.

Anton's choice wine list is nicely priced.

(609) 397-1960. www.antons-at-the-swan.com. Entrées, $25 to $34. Dinner, Tuesday-Saturday 6 to 9 or 10, Sunday 4:30 to 8.

Hamilton's Grill Room, 8 Coryell St., Lambertville, N.J.

Former Broadway set designer Jim Hamilton oversees this gem, hidden at the end of an alley in the Porkyard complex beside the Delaware River canal and towpath. Jim, an architect who designs restaurants, installed an open grill beside the entrance and built the wood-fired adobe pizza oven himself. He turned over the contemporary Mediterranean grill concept to executive chef Mark Miller.

Cooking is theater in the front Grill Room, where the chef prepares grilled foods over an open flame in the exhibition kitchen. Our dinner began with a menu standby, grilled shrimp with anchovy butter, and a crab cake on wilted greens and sweet red pepper sauce. Main courses were an exceptional grilled duck on bitter greens with pancetta and honey glaze and a grilled ribeye steak with roquefort cheese. The oversize plates were filled with fanned razor-thin sliced potatoes and grilled zucchini and green and red peppers. The signature grappa torta and the grand marnier cheesecake were fine desserts. Two biscotti came with the bill.

Since Hamilton's is BYOB, the white wine we toted was stashed in a pail full of ice, and red wines and even water are poured in large hand-blown globes made locally.

Patrons dine at a lineup of faux-marble tables in the mirrored Grill Room, beneath angels and clouds surrounding a huge gilt mirror on the ceiling in the Bishop's Room, around a changing decorative focal point in the dining gallery and lately in an airy new garden room formed by enclosing part of the outdoor courtyard.

(609) 397-4343. www.hamiltonsgrillroom.com. Entrées, $23.50 to $32. Dinner, Monday-Saturday 6 to 10, Sunday 5 to 9. BYOB.

The Frenchtown Inn, 7 Bridge St., Frenchtown, N.J.

The food is inventive and good, the service friendly yet flawless, and the setting comfortable in this elegant restaurant with a handsome grill room on the side. Chef-owner Andrew Tomko, a culinary graduate of Johnson and Wales University, was executive chef at the Inn at Millrace Pond in upstate Hope for six years before he and his wife Colleen returned to their home area to buy the acclaimed restaurant.

Arriving for a Friday lunch without reservations, we found the front dining room with its planked ceiling, brick walls and carpeted floors full. So we were seated in the more austere columned Riverside dining room in the rear, outfitted with pink and green wallpaper, crisp white linens and Villeroy & Boch china, two sets of wine glasses and fresh flowers on luxuriously spaced tables. Although we could have been happy ordering anything on the menu, we can vouch for an unusual and airy black bean soup, the charcuterie plate of pâtés and terrines (small but very good), the corned beef sandwich on brown bread and a sensational salad of duck and smoked pheasant with a warm cider vinaigrette on mixed greens. A layered pear-raspberry tart with whipped cream was a perfect ending.

A later visit produced a memorable (and reasonable) dinner in the white-linened Grill Room, where singles were eating at the bar and dinners options might range from fish and chips to a whole quail stuffed with apricot brioche. A salad of baby lettuces and goat cheese, an appetizer of crispy fried rock shrimp with wasabi and mustard oils, and an exotic cavatelli tossed with broccoli rabe and sweet Italian sausage were enough for two to share. With a raspberry sorbet for dessert and a bottle of Preston fumé blanc, we were well satisfied for less than $50.

That was barely half what you'd expect to pay for one of the remarkable dinners in the more formal dining venues just across the hall, where main courses typically range from rare yellowfin tuna with orange-soy-sesame sauce to oven-roasted filet of beef over a toasted brioche topped with crabmeat, bacon and sherry cream. Choices might include pan-seared halibut over a sauté of tomatoes and rock shrimp, pepper-crusted breast of moulard duck and quail stuffed with foie gras, and rack of Australian lamb with port wine jus. The food comes from the same expert kitchen, but the grill represents unusual value for the area.

(908) 996-3300. www.frenchtowninn.com. Entrées, $23 to $34. Lunch, Tuesday-Saturday noon to 2. Dinner, Tuesday-Friday 6 to 9, Saturday 5:30 to 9:30. Sunday, brunch noon to 2:30, dinner 5 to 8. Grill: dinner, Tuesday-Friday 5 to 9, Sunday 3 to 8.

La Bonne Auberge, Village 2, New Hope, Pa.

"Four-star everything," report people who have eaten at this destination restaurant and consider it comparable to the best in New York or Philadelphia. Those doing the reporting happen to be from New York or Philadelphia, where they expect four-star dining and are willing to pay for it. Many of the people around New Hope aren't.

There's no denying the food. The restaurant "seems a strong contender for 'best in Bucks,'" wrote Bon Appétit magazine. "Chef Gerard Caronello, originally from

Skylit dining room is elegant at La Bonne Auberge.

Lyon, makes the kitchen sing. His gracious, soft-spoken wife, Rozanne, sees to things up front. It all translates into some very good French."

There's no denying the setting, either. The pretty 18th-century stone farmhouse is surrounded by nicely landscaped grounds and formal gardens atop a hill at the edge of the Village 2 condominium complex (through which you must pass – and can easily get lost, coming and going). The contemporary, airy, wood-paneled dining room at the rear is gorgeous, its large and well-spaced tables dressed in pink and flanked by upholstered armchairs. Wines are stacked in a corner cabinet, windows look out onto the gardens, fresh flowers are on the tables and salmon-colored napkins stand tall in twin peaks in the wine glasses.

Downstairs is a cozy hideaway bar that even some regular diners don't know about. Nestled in wing chairs in a candlelit corner, couples sipping after-dinner cognacs (at $12 and up a snifter) might think they've died and gone to heaven.

Count on spending upwards of $200 on dinner for two with a bottle of wine. The printed menu rarely changes. Except for melon glacé or avocado vinaigrette (both $10), appetizers start at $14 for escargots provençal. The soups (tomato with basil or leek and potato) are $10. So is the house salad. Big-spenders can go for ossetra caviar ($70).

Entrées are $38 or $39, except for grilled chicken dijonnaise, which is $30. The French classics (sautéed sea bass niçoise, dover sole with lemon and capers, veal medallions with tarragon jus, rack of lamb provençal and entrecôte of beef) are prepared to perfection.

Desserts ($10) are in keeping, and the wine prices sting, starting in the $30 range.

Since 1972, La Bonne Auberge has been doing very nicely with a loyal clientele that appreciates the best.

(215) 862-2462. www.bonneauberge.com. Entrées, $30 to $39. Dinner, Thursday-Saturday 6 to 9, Sunday 5:30 to 8:30. Jackets required.

Manon, 19 North Union St., Lambertville, N.J.

Dining here is reminiscent of the south of France, which comes as no surprise when you learn that young chef-owner Jean-Michel Dumas grew up in Provence. He and his American wife Susan gave a provençal name to the storefront charmer they have run since 1990.

An air of whimsy reigns, from the colorful exterior of burnt orange and blue-green with gingerbread trim to the ceiling painted like Van Gogh's starry night. With a relocated and expanded kitchen, there's more room for Jean-Michel to work his culinary magic. Now there's also space for an extra table for patrons in the intimate, 36-seat dining room in front, as well as a garden terrace with a few tables in back.

Jean-Michel, who was a chef at the Inn at Phillips Mill in New Hope, relies on fresh ingredients cooked simply and served in robust portions. The menu often starts with his trademark anchovy relish and an assortment of raw vegetables, the house pâté, escargots in pernod and salads of mesclun with warm goat cheese or watercress with pear, belgian endive, walnuts and roquefort. Soup of the day could be garlicky mussel or pistou.

Among entrées are red bouillabaisse, roasted monkfish with pernod and tomato fondue, fillet of salmon on a bed of spinach with a lobster-mushroom sauce, calves liver with a honey-shallot confit and bercy sauce, filet of beef with a duck liver mousse and madeira sauce, and rack of lamb with herbs of Provence. Desserts include a classic crème caramel, tarte tatin, chocolate mousse, marjolaine and nougat ice cream with raspberry sauce.

(609) 397-2596. Entrées, $18.50 to $25. Dinner, Wednesday-Sunday 5:30 to 9 or 10. Sunday brunch, 11 to 2:30. No credit cards. BYOB.

The Landing, 22 North Main St., New Hope, Pa.

The only restaurant right in New Hope with a river view is set back from the main street in a small house with windows onto the water and a large brick patio around back. Christopher Bollenbacher, owner since 1976, and his wife Ellen are known for offering some of the best and most consistent food in town.

Inside on either side of a quite luxurious small bar are two small dining areas refreshed following a flood that poured three feet of water inside in April 2005. The front room, welcoming in barnwood, contains booths and two tables for two with wing chairs at each. The rear room has picture windows overlooking the river.

The expansive riverside patio is definitely the place to be in season, the length of which has been extended lately with the addition of patio heaters. It's brightened with colorful planters and umbrellas, dignified by tablecloths at night and made practical by an enclosed bar at one side. A gardener has obviously been at work around the exterior, and there's equal talent in the kitchen.

Umbrellas shade luncheon diners on riverside patio at The Landing.

The changing menu (which arrived in a picture frame when we first ate dinner here) is creative. We would gladly have ordered everything from the lunch menu, so delectable were the choices and so salubrious the ambiance at a patio table beside the river on a recent autumn afternoon. One of us settled for a refreshing soup of golden gazpacho with cilantro pesto and chilled shrimp, paired with a salad of shrimp, crab and artichoke dumplings, greens, bell peppers, roasted corn and horseradish-chive vinaigrette. The other enjoyed the pan-roasted jumbo lump crab cake with julienned summer vegetables, roasted peppers and, rather strangely, mashed potatoes.

At night, entrées range from sautéed red snapper with avocado-tomato relish to herb-roasted rack of lamb. An intriguing dish at one visit was called veal three ways: with emmenthal and fingerling potato stew, pulped grapes and wilted spinach.

Typical starters are pork and shrimp spring rolls with mandarin-sesame dipping sauce, steamed cockles and mussels provençal, prosciutto and brie in puff pastry with cranberry-ginger coulis, and fried calamari with two sauces, a cilantro-lime mayo and spicy tomato sauce. Desserts are luscious: perhaps frozen kahlua mousse, chocolate-cointreau-truffle torte with blood orange syrup, and rose petal crème brûlée with strawberries and white chocolate.

The Landing claims to have the largest wine list in Bucks County.

(215) 862-5711. www.landingrestaurant.com. Entrées, $22.95 to $32.95. Lunch daily, 11 to 4. Dinner nightly, from 5. Closed Monday-Thursday in winter.

No. 9, 9 Klines Court, Lambertville, N.J.

The tiny restaurant space at 9 Klines Court has long been a focal point of Lambertville's culinary constellation, among a lineup of come-and-go restaurants across from a small municipal park and parking lot. Since the hit-player Stars fell by the wayside, a succession of wannabes has tried and failed. Along came Hunterdon County native Matthew Kane, fresh from head chef duties at small restaurants in

New York's Greenwich Village and TriBeCa. In 2001, he and his wife-to-be Colleen took over a space that had seemed destined to fail and turned it into a hit.

Tiny it is, this intimate place now known by its address alone. The square space lacks the glitter and dazzle of previous incarnations. Walls and table coverings are white, and color is added by splashy artworks on loan from local artists. The harvest of onions, tomatoes and pears stashed at the entry is more than decoration – the chef uses it as a pantry and gathers from it liberally throughout the evening because of a shortage of space in the kitchen.

Matthew's menu is short and to the point, its matter-of-factness concealing the assertive tastes that follow. Our meal began with a medley of flavors: an appetizer of potato and goat cheese tart with roasted peppers and grilled onions, and a roasted beet salad with blue cheese and green beans. An appetizer of jumbo lump crab meat on a wild mushroom and brie crostini was ample enough for a main course. The signature pan-seared salmon was accompanied by a stirfry of Asian vegetables, fortunately cooled by a refreshing cucumber and ginger salad. Other entrée possibilities included pan-roasted trout with wild mushrooms, grilled porterhouse pork chop with summer vegetable salsa and grilled hanger steak with blue cheese demi-glace.

Among desserts were lime cheesecake, pear crisp, apple mascarpone tart and chocolate pot de crème.

(609) 397-6380. Entrées, $17 to $24. Dinner, Wednesday-Saturday 5 to 9 or 10, Sunday noon to 8. BYOB.

Marsha Brown, 15 South Main St., New Hope, Pa.

Only in New Hope would a dramatic restaurant like this be found inside a 125-year-old stone church. Its food and decor are designed with enough decadence in mind that they even provide a confessional. Marsha Brown, for those who don't know, owned four Ruth's Chris steakhouses in the Philadelphia and New York areas before deciding it was time to create her version of a refined Creole kitchen and lounge north of the Mason-Dixon Line. She chose the old United Methodist Church in the center of New Hope for a $2.7-million makeover, enveloping a large raw bar and bordello-like private room downstairs and a cavernous, cathedral-ceilinged dining room in the upstairs sanctuary in what she calls timeless Southern luxury.

A Russian artist did the towering mural Redemption in a gilded archway that provides a stunning backdrop for diners at close-together tables flanked by church pews and assorted chairs. At the top of the staircase, where you first get a glimpse of the remarkable scene, is a dark little bar and a service bar in what they say was the confessional.

The extensive menu is a cross between classic Ruth's Chris steakhouse, although executed better, and the New Orleans raw bar and grill of the owner's formative years. The latter trumps the former and sets the restaurant apart.

You might start with a sampling of soups (real gumbo ya ya, turtle, and lobster and shrimp bisque when we were there), crawfish étouffée with dipping sauce, spicy coconut shrimp or lollipop lamb chops with mango chutney. Winning main courses include crab cakes with spicy rémoulade sauce, sautéed Creole catfish, a signature shrimp and crabmeat casserole called eggplant ophelia and a massive cowboy ribeye steak. The duck and andouille sausage jambalaya also tempts. Potatoes, vegetables and "Southern sides" such as okra beignets, turnip gratin and dirty rice are extra.

Former church sanctuary is now home to Marsha Brown dining room.

The sleeper among desserts like crème brûlée and chocolate mousse mountain is "Granmere's comfort custard," a silken vanilla mound ribboned with meringue and crushed saltine crackers.

(215) 862-7044. www.marshabrownrestaurant.com. Entrées, $22 to $38. Lunch daily in summer, noon to 4, Thursday-Sunday rest of year. Dinner nightly, 4 to 10, weekends to 11:30.

Away from the Fray

Three highly regarded restaurants are a few miles removed from the River Road area, a bit "inland" in New Jersey.

The Sergeantsville Inn, 600 Rosemont-Ringoes Road, Sergeantsville, N.J.

This historic restaurant was reopened in late 1999 after being shuttered for two years. Joe and Sandy Clyde closed their highly rated Clyde's in New Brunswick "to get out of the city" and take possession of an old favorite in the tranquil Hunterdon County countryside.

The landmark fieldstone building, where we enjoyed a memorable lunch many years back, appeals more than ever with a new culinary dynamic amid its intimate stone-walled rooms. It seats about 100 diners in a tavern, a couple of fireside dining areas on the main floor and a basement wine cellar plus –beyond and accessible only via stairs up from the wine cellar – the town's original ice house. To serve the last, the staff has quite a trek descending and then ascending from the kitchen.

Chef Joe is known for his game dishes (sliced antelope steak with a wild mushroom demi-glace, grilled filet of kangaroo with a balsamic demi-glace, venison london broil and pan-seared filet of wild boar dusted with cilantro and cumin were on the menu at our October visit). So was farm-raised ostrich. All were teamed with purple mashed potatoes and a root vegetable gratin. Other tastes were tempted by tuna au poivre, shrimp jasmine, poached Atlantic salmon with roasted pepper pesto, and pan-seared breast of duck glazed with sweet soy and served with mashed sweet potatoes.

Each entrée comes with a choice of mesclun salad, soup du jour or Joe's perfectly seasoned tomato bisque, which he considers his signature item. Those with hearty appetites can begin with beef carpaccio garnished with shaved locattelli cheese and drizzled with porcini mushroom oil, tuna tartare, oysters casino or a blackened crab cake with a roasted red pepper puree.

Expect desserts like apple strudel, berries with sabayon and tiramisu. The tavern features a martini and cigar bar.

(609) 397-3700. www.sergeantsvilleinn.com. Entrées, $18 to $28. Lunch, Tuesday-Saturday 11:30 to 3. Dinner nightly, 5 to 10 or 11, Sunday noon to 9.

The Harvest Moon Inn, 1039 Old York Road (Route 179), Ringoes, N.J.

A handsome 1811 Federal stone house surrounded by five acres of landscaped grounds is the setting for some of the area's finest meals. Stanley and Theresa Novak moved here from New Brunswick, where he was executive chef at the acclaimed Frog and the Peach restaurant.

Stanley, who formerly worked at Brooklyn's River Café, is widely known for cutting-edge American cuisine, presented in the architectural style. He teaches cooking classes in his kitchen and seats 120 in two Colonial-style dining rooms warmed by fireplaces. At night, he offers both a restaurant and a tavern menu, and his fans like the fact that both are available in either venue except on Saturday.

The regular dinner menu is complex and wide-ranging. Appetizers might be plantain and crab fritters with a mango salsa, a seafood tartlet with artichokes, lobster and mussel stew in a saffron broth and grilled lamb sausage with curried couscous. Among salads are arugula with crisp duck confit in a creamy lemon vinaigrette and julienned smoked salmon with baby red mustard greens, baby totsoi and crisp wasabi sweet peas.

Typical main courses are cracked pepper-seared tuna with sweet corn and shrimp fritters, roasted pork loin with red wine-shallot demi-glace, grilled pork medallions in a cassis demi-glace and grilled beef tenderloin with diced portobello mushrooms in a sage demi-glace.

Desserts are as varied as assorted sorbets with fresh berries, banana and praline mousse charlotte, and pistachio and milk chocolate roulade with pistachio crème anglaise and milk chocolate ice cream in a pistachio florentine cookie cup.

The wine list is a perennial Wine Spectator award-winner.

The extensive tavern menu offers salads, pastas, pizzas and sandwiches, some of which are repeated on the lunch menu.

(908) 806-6020. www.harvestmooninn.com. Entrées, $24.95 to $35.95. Lunch, Tuesday-Friday 11:30 to 2:30. Dinner, Tuesday-Saturday 5 to 9:30 or 10, Sunday 1 to 8.

The Café, Route 519 at Route 604, Rosemont, N.J.

Lola Wyckoff and Peg Peterson moved their little café from Lambertville to a general store dating from 1885 in Rosemont. They have a lot more room to offer "fresh food at its simple best," as their business card attests.

It's a casual, drop-in kind of place where the floors creek, the chairs tilt and the service, we found on more than one occasion, can be somewhat laid-back. Shelves are filled with the cookbooks the partners use, plus items for sale like gourmet foods, Botanicus soaps and striking ceramics, some done by one of the waitresses. A case along one side displays cheeses, desserts and baked goods. Things get more formal for dinner when candles, cloth napkins and 1940s cloths are on the tables.

For a leisurely brunch we found a couple of omelets – the Russian peasant (with caviar) and the cranberry and brie – worth waiting for. The addictive "potatoes from heaven" were grilled with olive oil, rosemary, garlic, onion and cayenne.

For lunch, we've enjoyed an excellent ham and black-bean quesadilla and a hefty turkey sandwich on whole wheat from a menu that included eggplant and mozzarella boboli, pasta with wild mushroom sauce and roasted red pepper ravioli with olive oil and garlic, most in the $8.50 to $10 range.

At dinner time, you'll find sophisticated entrées like seared salmon with scallion-wasabi sauce, broiled halibut with almonds and olives in a sherry-leek vinaigrette, grilled duck breast with ginger-molasses butter and grilled flank steak with rosemary-pinot noir sauce. Pasta choices might include scallops and spinach in lemongrass-ginger broth or pasta Wilhemina, named for the resident ghost, with chicken, broccoli, mushrooms and garlic. Mocha pot de crème and cranberry flan are popular desserts, and Peg's cheesecakes (maybe rum-raisin or espresso) are also in demand.

The Wednesday night ethnic dinners are a steal, generally $22 for three courses. The foods of Turkey, West Africa and Paris were scheduled in weekly succession at a recent visit. How about the African offerings: coconut and eggplant soup or Liberian cabbage and avocado salad, Ghanaian fish stew or West African chicken in peanut sauce, and Nigerian rice cakes with fruit or Liberian pumpkin cake? Here's a kitchen with reach.

(609) 397-4097. www.cafeatrosemont.com. Entrées, $15 to $25. Lunch, Tuesday-Friday 11 to 3. Dinner, Wednesday-Sunday 5 to 9. Brunch, Saturday and Sunday 9 to 2. No credit cards. BYOB.

Wine Bars and Pubs

The Boat House, 8½ Coryell St. at the Porkyard, Lambertville, N.J.

In the old ice house for the porkyard is an elegant bar, where cocktails are served, fifteen wines are featured by the glass and the walls are paneled with old twelve-foot-high doors. Appetizers are no longer offered, since there's full food service at Hamilton's Grill across the alley. Hamilton's and the Boat House team up to provide food and drinks at the adjacent Wine Bar on Saturdays. Here you might get a glass of Columbia Crest chardonnay for $4 or a Simi cabernet for $6. This is also a good, albeit an expensive, place to pick up a bottle or two of wine for BYOB dinner in a Lambertville restaurant if the liquor stores are closed.

(609) 397-2244. Open Monday-Saturday from 4, Sunday from 2.

The Swan, 43 South Main St., Lambertville, N.J.

This is another great place to have a drink and maybe a salad, a wood-grilled pizza, a cheese plate with apples and bread or a few more elaborate dishes. The public rooms bear the theatrical stamp of designer Jim Hamilton and are filled with art and antiques collected by owner James Bulger. The main bar contains comfortable leather chairs to sink into and a greenhouse wall looking out onto a small garden with a fountain, which is spotlit at night. A pianist entertains on weekends.

You can't beat the prices: our two after-dinner stingers came to about $10. Wines are available by the glass, and there are some exotic imported beers and ales. The grill menu is fulfilled from 5 to 10 or 11 by Anton's at the Swan, the fine restaurant in the other side of the building.

(609) 397-3552. Grill entrées, $15 to $18. Open Tuesday-Saturday 4 to 1, Sunday 3 to 10.

Inn of the Hawke, 74 South Union St., Lambertville, N.J.

Two young sisters took over this oft-changing inn, formerly known as the Wilson Inn and later the Elephant and Castle, a short-lived English pub. Melissa and Doreen Masset made cosmetic changes to turn the huge first floor into what they call a country neighborhood pub, with a long horseshoe-shaped bar in the center room and a couple of dining rooms on either side. One looks onto an outdoor courtyard that's great for sipping some of the twelve draught beers that are featured.

A short menu changes daily. It typically ranges from fish and chips and a ploughman's lunch to roasted pork loin and grilled strip steak. The beers are generally rated better than the food.

Upstairs are six redecorated Victorian guest rooms, four with private baths.

(609) 397-9555. Entrées, $6.75 to $19.95. Lunch daily, noon to 5. Dinner, 5 to 10; late-night menu to midnight. Sunday, brunch 11 to 4.

Left Bank Libations, 32 Bridge St., Lambertville, N.J..

The newest drinking establishment in a town that zealously protects its licensees is ensconced on the ground floor of the restored Lambertville House. Plush sitting areas and tables flank a copper-topped bar in a dark and intimate room with a rich library look. Seats on the ornate front porch overlook the passing street scene. The well drinks are top brands, and priced accordingly.

(609) 397-4745. Open Monday-Thursday 5 to 11:30, Friday and Saturday 2 to midnight, Sunday 3 to 11:30.

Dining and Lodging

EverMay on the Delaware, 889 River Road, Box 60, Erwinna, Pa. 18920.

The culinary tradition at this charming, rural country inn continues under new owner Perry Giovlasitis, a Manhattan antiques dealer and restorationist who planned upgrades following his acquisition of the inn in late 2005. He and Danielle Moffly, the former owner who stayed on as manager, maintained the inn's reputation for inspired contemporary American fare.

Dinner is served only on Friday, Saturday and Sunday nights at one seating, and is in such demand that usually you must book far in advance. The six-course meal costs $74, with little choice except between two entrées.

The main dining room has been enhanced by matching draperies and upholstered chairs. Our favorite is the small rear porch-conservatory, its tables for two set with white over patterned cloths and little electric candles bearing lamp shades. The room is narrow (a bit too narrow, we thought, since you could overhear others' conversations and the waiter's recitation of every course to every table). Also, a chilly evening was made chillier by the stone floors and the wide expanse of windows.

But not to quibble. The meal was one of the best we've had, nicely presented and paced. Hors d'oeuvre of smoked trout salad, sundried-tomato crostini and country pâté with green peppercorns were served first. After these came in order a suave chicken and leek soup, sautéed chanterelles on a saffron crouton, and a salad of

Rear conservancy dining porch overlooks gardens at EverMay on the Delaware.

boston and mache lettuces, garnished with violets and toasted walnuts and dressed with a fine balsamic vinaigrette.

Thank goodness all these courses were small, for we needed room for the main courses: tender lamb noisettes wrapped in bacon and topped with a green peppercorn butter, and Norwegian salmon poached in white wine, served with hollandaise sauce and garnished with shrimp. These came with thin, crisp asparagus from Chile, a mixture of white and wild rice, and sprigs of watercress.

A cheese and fruit course of perhaps St. André, montrachet and gorgonzola cheese precedes dessert. Ours was a perfect poached pear, set atop vanilla ice cream, with butterscotch sauce, golden raisins and pecans. Yours might be white and dark chocolate mousse with chocolate "cigarettes."

About twenty chardonnays are on the well-chosen, primarily California wine list, which contains some not-often-seen vintages.

EverMay is more than a memorable dinner. It's an inn with eighteen rooms (one named for Pearl S. Buck, longtime resident of the area) on the second and third floors, a newer loft suite on the fourth floor, and in a carriage house, cottage and barn. They are furnished in Victoriana, as befits the era when the structure became a hotel (the original house dates from the early 1700s). All have telephones and many have queensize beds. Fresh flowers and a large bowl of fruit are in each room, and at bedtime you may find candy and a liqueur in a little glass with a doily on top.

Two new deluxe rooms in the barn offer kingsize beds, spacious sitting areas with Vermont Castings fireplaces, and baths with whirlpool tubs and separate showers. Another room in a cottage offers a cathedral ceiling and Vermont Castings stove.

A fire burns in the fireplace in the double parlor, and decanters of sherry are placed on tables in front of the Victorian sofas. Afternoon tea with watercress or cucumber sandwiches and cookies is served at 4 p.m. here or on the brick terrace out back.

Although continental, the complimentary breakfast is quite special, with orange juice, flaky croissants and pastries, one with cream cheese in the center, and the pièce de résistance at our visit: a compote of strawberries, red grapes, bananas and honeydew melon, garnished with a sprig of mint and dusted with confectioners' sugar – colorful and tasty.

(610) 294-9100. www.evermay.com. Eighteen rooms and suites with private baths. Doubles, $145 to $275; two-bedroom suite, $355. Two-night minimum stay weekends.

Dinner by reservation, Friday and Saturday at 7:30, Sunday at 6:30. Prix-fixe, $74. Jackets suggested.

The Inn at Phillips Mill, 2590 North River Road, New Hope, Pa. 18938.

Depending on the season, hanging pots overflowing with fuchsias, wooden casks filled with all colors of mums or holiday greenery mark the entrance to this small and adorable yet sophisticated inn. When you see its facade of local gray stone, smack up against an S-turn bend in River Road, with its copper pig hanging over the entrance, you would almost swear you were in Britain's Cotswolds.

Inside, that impression is heightened, as you take in the low-ceilinged rooms with dark beams, pewter service plates and water goblets, and a gigantic leather couch in front of a massive fireplace, on which you can recline while waiting for your table. Candles augment the light from the fireplace, and arrangements of fresh and dried flowers are all around.

At a recent visit, two longtime stalwarts – chef Richard Rohal and pastry chef Thomas Milburn – were back at their early stomping grounds. The classic French menu is concise, the prices reasonable and the results comforting – often exceptional. Smoked salmon with horseradish crème fraîche and a salad of goat cheese and roasted onions on frisée might be among appetizers. We started with a springtime special, Maryland crabmeat in half an avocado. It was indeed special, garnished with shredded carrots and black olives.

Main courses range from coquilles St. Jacques to a trio of mustard-dusted lamb chops. We have never tasted such a tender filet mignon with such a delectable béarnaise sauce (and artichoke heart) or such perfect sweetbreads in a light brown sauce as at our first visit. At our second, the sautéed calves liver in a cider vinegar sauce and the medallions of veal niçoise were excellent, too.

A basket of crusty French bread (with which you are tempted to sop up the wonderful sauces) and sweet butter comes before dinner. Save room for one of the super desserts – once a lemon-ice cream meringue pie, six inches high and wonderfully refreshing, and later a vanilla mousse with big chips of chocolate and fudge sauce.

Sometimes it is hazardous to bring your own wine. The host at a table of four next to ours was wondering where his expensive bottle of Clos du Val had gone when we noticed the waitress on the verge of pouring it into our glasses. We caught her in time and reconciled ourselves to our modest bottle of California zinfandel.

Upstairs are four cozy guest rooms and a suite, cheerily decorated by innkeeper Joyce Kaufman (her husband Brooks is an architect who did the restoration of the 1750 structure). One has its own sitting room. Honeymooners ask for the third-floor hideaway suite, where fabric covers the ceiling. Most beds are four-posters or brass and iron and are covered with quilts. Sometimes the Kaufmans rent a cottage in back of the inn, and share their small swimming pool with house guests.

A continental breakfast (juice, flaky croissants and coffee) is delivered to your room in a basket.

(215) 862-2984 (lodging). Four rooms, one suite and one cottage with private baths. Doubles, $100. Suite, $120. Cottage, $150.

(215) 862-9919 (dining). Entrées, $18 to $28. Dinner nightly, 5:30 to 9:30 or 10. BYOB. No credit cards.

The Mansion Inn, 9 South Main St., New Hope, Pa. 18938.

This Second French Empire/Victorian manor house in the center of town is imposing on the outside and showy on the inside. The wrought-iron gates are locked and you ring a buzzer to enter. You don't get in without a reservation or an appointment – unless you're coming for dinner.

Meal service has been added relatively recently at the sumptuous Victorian B&B, launched in 1995 by restorationists Keith David from New York and Dr. Elio Filippo Bracco, a nutritionist from Milan. As Keith explained it, a guest who spent a night in the inn's garden cottage turned out to be associated with Relais & Châteaux, the prestigious hotel group that includes only inns with dining facilities. Had the Mansion thought about adding food service?

The idea implanted, a wine and tapas bar became "a natural enhancement." The owners turned the front parlor into the **Champagne Room,** a romantic space with glass-topped tables and an Edwardian look. They added a bar in the drawing room across the hall, its walls chock full of framed photos of stars from the Bucks County Playhouse down the street. The food concept proved so popular that the innkeepers set up intimate tables on the wraparound veranda and added a Gallery dining room and a large, enclosed and heated outdoor tent for overflow and private parties.

Tapas quickly gave way to full dinner service and weekend lunch, with seating for more than 100. The menu, which originally reflected Bracco family recipes, has been Americanized since the inn's purchase in 2004 by two couples, Liz and Steve Casper and Christine and Steve Ebersole. They brought on as chef Christopher Tavares, whose entrées range from cedar-planked roasted salmon to filet mignon with bourbon cream sauce. Lemon sole stuffed with seafood, duck à l'orange and roasted veal tenderloin topped with crab imperial illustrate the range. Panko-crusted crab cake with poblano cream is the featured starter, and champagne with bananas, strawberries and two liqueurs the featured cocktail. Desserts include vanilla bean crème brûlée, apple-blackberry crisp and sundried cranberry bread pudding with vanilla crème anglaise.

The entire house is lavishly furnished with fine art and antiques, Schumacher fabrics, and collections of antique clocks, depression-era glass and first-edition watercolors of London street scenes.

"The focal point of each guest bedroom is the bed," the inn's fact sheet points out matter of factly. "A vision in white, each has a featherbed, crisp white ironed sheets, down comforter and an abundance of down pillows, a minimum of six per bed."

That does not do justice to the over-all effect of the accommodations, which include four two-room suites and a "junior suite." Hide out in the third-floor Windsor Suite, stunning in white and rose florals with an enveloping, low-slung canopy over the kingsize rice bed, a double whirlpool tub in the ample bathroom and an elegant sitting room with a fireplace. Retreat to the Kensington Suite on the second floor of the rear garden cottage beside the inn's parking lot. Subdued in beige, cream and white, it comes with a kingsize bed, fireplace, single whirlpool tub and a porch. All told, five suites have gas fireplaces and two have whirlpool tubs. Televisions and telephones are standard. Sherry, bowls of fruit and candy are among the treats, and cookies are presented at nightly turndown.

Rates include a full breakfast served in the dining room. The inn's signature french toast croissant with raspberry sauce and whipped cream or an egg dish with brie, peppers and tomatoes might be the main course. Homemade lemon or banana breads, coffee and the New York Times accompany.

For guests who want to get away from the goings-on out front and in the dining areas, the innkeepers point to the rear garden with its English tea roses, the 1890 gazebo and the swimming pool hidden by hedges. You'd hardly know you were a stone's throw from the busiest intersection in town.

(215) 862-1231. Fax (215) 862-6939. www.themansioninn.com. Two rooms and five suites with private baths. Doubles, $195 to $295 weekends, $155 to $235 midweek.

Restaurant: (215) 862-6260. Entrées, $19 to $34. Dinner, Thursday-Sunday 5 to 9. Lunch, Friday-Sunday 11:30 or noon to 5.

Golden Pheasant Inn, 763 River Road, Erwinna, Pa. 18920.

A more romantic spot than the large solarium of the Golden Pheasant is hard to imagine. Beneath the stars is an array of tables dressed in mauve and white, hanging lamps, green plants and ficus trees, planters of colorful flowers and tiny twinkling lights all around. The place is so dim that we had to ask for an extra candle to read the menu. The canal bank beyond is illuminated at night, and it's all rather magical.

Well-known local chef Michel Faure from Grenoble and his wife Barbara have refurbished the two inner dining rooms to the inn's original 1850s period, brightened with accents of copper pots, oriental rugs and their extensive Quimper collection from Brittany.

The bar is in the front of the wallpapered main dining room, which contains a working fireplace. The inner Blaise Room claims hardwood floors, a beamed ceiling, recessed windows and exposed stone walls. The family live upstairs, and they have renovated six guest rooms to offer "a taste of France on the banks of the Delaware," according to Barbara.

She has decorated the rooms with country touches, antiques and queensize four-poster beds, one so high that you need a stool to climb up. Most have fireplaces and all have TVs. We're partial to the main-floor suite with its kingsize canopy bed, fireplace, bath with jacuzzi tub and a private canal-side porch. All overnight guests may enjoy a rear patio beside the canal.

The geese along the canal don't end up on the menu, though pheasant often does, roasted and flambéed with calvados, shallots and apples. Michel, who worked in a number of well-known restaurants, including Philadelphia's Le Bec Fin and New Hope's Odette's, presents classic French fare rich with sauces.

Start with the pheasant pâté, escargots sautéed in garlic-parsley butter, bay scallops sautéed with saffron sauce, lobster ravioli with a lobster and shrimp sauce or Michel's acclaimed lobster bisque. Entrées vary from poached salmon with a champagne and shrimp sauce to sautéed filet mignon with béarnaise sauce. Lump crab cakes come with a light mustard hollandaise, and venison medallions with a currant and cassis sauce. Cassoulet of seafood bears a lobster sauce. Roasted boneless duck might be sauced with raspberry, ginger and rum.

Desserts include cappuccino cheesecake, pecan pie, crème caramel, homemade sorbets and a specialty, Belgian white chocolate mousse with a raspberry coulis.

A three-course Sunday brunch is available for $22. Michel offers twice-weekly cooking classes in spring and fall.

(610) 294-9595 or (800) 830-4474. Fax (610) 294-9882. www.goldenpheasant.com. Five rooms and one suite with private baths. Doubles, $105 to $175 weekends, $95 to $145 midweek. Suite, $225 weekends, $175 midweek. Two-night minimum on weekends.

Entrées, $22 to $28. Dinner, Wednesday-Saturday 5:30 to 8 or 9. Sunday, brunch 11 to 3, dinner 3 to 7.

Hotel du Village, 2535 North River Road at Phillips Mill Road, New Hope, Pa. 18938.

The French name is a bit misleading, since the chef-owner is Algerian and his hostelry is English Tudor in an early boarding-school setting. The dining room is in the former Lower Campus building of Solebury School and looks exactly like one in an English manor house, with a glowing fire at each end, a beamed ceiling, small-paned windows and a fine Persian carpet on the floor. Crisp linens, candles and fresh flowers add to the luxurious feeling.

Country French cuisine is the forte of Omar Arbani, who arrived in Bucks County in 1976 by way of culinary endeavors in France, Denmark, London and Washington, D.C. Partial to fine sauces, he shuns nouvelle to provide "the kind of home-style country cuisine you'd find in the restaurants of Bordeaux or Burgundy on a Sunday afternoon," in the words of his wife Barbara, a former New Jersey teacher, who manages the dining room, bar, banquet facility and inn.

The menu seldom changes and prices remain among the more reasonable in the area. Favorite appetizers include escargots, shrimp sautéed in garlic butter, clams casino and mushrooms rémoulade, as well as lamb sausage, one of the few additions to the menu since we first dined here in the 1980s. Main courses range from fillets of sole richelieu and frog's legs grenouille to duckling montmorency with cherries and steak au poivre. Our dish of tournedos Henry IV, with artichoke heart and béarnaise sauce, was heavenly. So were the sweetbreads financière, with green olives, mushrooms and madeira sauce. Potatoes sautéed with lots of rosemary, crisp beans and grilled tomato with a crumb topping were worthy accompaniments.

Bread was piping hot and crusty – grand when spread with the house pâté ($6.95 for a small crock as an appetizer). Moist black forest cake, crammed with cherries, and café royale were sweet endings to a rich, romantic meal.

The pre-dinner drinks were huge and one of us, who shall be nameless, ordered a bottle of Mill Creek merlot, which was ever-so-smooth. The trouble was he had forgotten his glasses and when the bill came the price was twice what he had expected. Moral: bring along your glasses.

Accommodations in twenty rather spare rooms in a converted stable in the rear reflect their boarding-school heritage, although most have king or queensize beds and air-conditioning. Guests get continental breakfast and have access to a pool, two tennis courts and pleasant grounds.

(215) 862-9911. www.hotelduvillage.com. Twenty rooms with private baths. Doubles, $130 to $155.

Entrées, $17.95 to $22.95. Dinner, Wednesday-Saturday from 5:30, Sunday 3 to 9. Restaurant closed mid-January to mid-February.

The Black Bass Hotel, 3774 River Road (Route 32), Lumberville, Pa. 18933.

The food has been upgraded and updated lately at the venerable Black Bass, an inn dating from the 1740s and every traveler's idea of what a French countryside inn should look like. The late Harry Nessler, founding innkeeper of the 1740 House just down the road, liked to recall how one of his guests, Pierre Matisse, told him that the Black Bass "looks just like the inns my father painted."

Lunch may be a better bet than dinner here because (1) you should take advantage of the fact the dining room with its long porch and a ground-level dining terrace overlook the river, (2) the food can be inconsistent, although we've had both a good dinner and a good lunch here over the years, and (3) prices at dinner are relatively steep – entrées like the Charleston Meeting Street crabmeat, a fixture on the menu, going for $29.95 at a recent visit.

Wander around the dark and quaint old inn and look at all the British memorabilia as well as the pewter bar that came from Maxim's in Paris. We enjoyed our lunch of New Orleans onion soup and the house salad. The soup, thick with onions and cheese, came in a proper crock; the crisp greens in the salad were laden with homemade croutons and a nifty house dressing of homemade mayonnaise, horseradish, dijon mustard and spices. Famished after a hike along the towpath, one of us devoured seven of the nut and date mini-muffins that came in a basket. The lengthy lunch menu ranges from omelet of the day to oven-roasted cashew-coated grouper with slow-cooked baked red beans and sautéed bananas.

The dinner menu is also extensive, varying from a vegetarian pumpkin stew with chiles, spices and grilled polenta to grilled filet mignon stuffed with saga blue cheese in a wild mushroom demi-glace. If you don't try the crabmeat specialty, which many do, consider head chef John Barrett's lobster bouillabaisse, macadamia-crusted mahi mahi with a cilantro-avocado puree, coffee-lacquered duck with ginger-pear chutney or veal shank osso buco. Start with a warm wild mushroom terrine or seared diver scallops with tasso and a fava bean cream. Finish with a brandy and ginger pear tart with crème fraîche, white chocolate cheesecake with tropical fruit salsa, or homemade ice creams or sorbets.

Lighted stamped-tin lanterns hang from thick beams in the various dining rooms, which are filled with antiques, collections of old china in high cabinets, and fancy wrought iron around the windows. The wooden chairs look as if they've been around since 1740; it's a wonder they don't fall apart.

Upstairs are seven guest rooms sharing two baths and three suites, whose rates have not been increased in years. All come with antique furnishings and some have ornate iron balconies, upon which continental breakfast may be served overlooking the river.

(215) 297-5815 (lodging). www.blackbasshotel.com. Seven rooms with shared baths and three suites with private baths. Doubles, $80 weekends, $65 midweek. Suites, $150 and $175 weekends, $125 to $150 midweek. Two-night minimum weekends.

(215) 297-5770 (dining). Entrées, $25.95 to $42.95. Lunch, Monday-Saturday 11:30 to 3. Dinner, 5:30 to 9:30. Sunday, brunch 11 to 2:30, dinner 4:30 to 8:30.

The National Hotel, 31 Race St., Frenchtown, N.J. 08825.

Eighteen months worth of renovations preceded the reopening in 2004 of the historic National Hotel and its leased restaurant called Lila.

Turned into what new owners Richard Balka and Derek Sylvester envisioned as a boutique hotel, the rambling second and third floors add contemporary amenities to their antique footprint. Their goal was to recreate a turn-of-the-last-century English plantation manor house with ten guest rooms inspired by Colonial, Victorian, West Indies and African decors. The interiors we saw had more of what our guide called a "tropical Chinese" look, with king and queen beds draped in sheer white fabric and TVs hidden in armoires. Three bathrooms have whirlpool tubs and two have large walk-in showers.

Continental breakfast is served in the hotel lobby and taken seasonally on the wide front porches off the first and second floors up against the street. Downstairs is the dark and cozy Rathskellar Pub.

Restaurant Lila, under separate ownership of chef Bill Downes and his wife

Tisha, occupies the bulk of the main floor. The original bar in front retains a tin ceiling. Meals are served here, in the rear dining room and on the front and back porches.

The extensive menu proclaims "innovative American cuisine" that traverses the globe. You can make an interesting meal from a choice among a dozen tapas and a dozen appetizers, ranging from shrimp, white bean and sausage soup to crabmeat-stuffed piquillo peppers. How about a Spanish caesar salad with paprika croutons and manchego cheese or a Maine lobster BLT in a croissant? Assertive pastas come in appetizer or entrée portions. Main courses range from bacon-wrapped monkfish and bourbon-glazed Atlantic salmon to Caribbean jerk-marinated pork loin and mixed peppercorn New York strip steak. Paella valenciana was featured on a recent menu.

Desserts are on the heavy side, with an emphasis on cheesecake and chocolate. Exceptions are the vanilla-bourbon crème brûlée and the "passionfruit-mango paradise."

(908) 996-4500. Fax (908) 996-3642. www.frenchtownnational.com. Ten rooms with private baths. Doubles, $149 to $219 weekends, $129 to $169 midweek.

Lila, (908) 996-4871. Entrées, $17 to $25. Open daily, noon to 9, weekends to 10, Sunday to 8.

Lodging

Lambertville House, 32 Bridge St., Box 349, Lambertville, N.J. 08530.

The 1812 facade of this restored landmark hotel on the National Register is a knockout, with a two-story, wrought-iron trimmed veranda along the stone front and the stucco walls above and beside painted beige with green and burgundy trim.

An elevator serves the 24 guest rooms and suites on the top three floors, each with marble bath and jetted tub/shower (the six suites contain double jacuzzis and separate showers). All but three classified as premium rooms have flick-of-the-switch gas fireplaces. Beds are queen or kingsize. Rooms come with a writing desk and a single wing chair, some with an ottoman. The formal furnishings are period antiques and reproductions. Touch-pad telephones with data ports, TVs hidden in armoires or in cupboards over the fireplaces, waffle-weave robes, granite-top vanities or pedestal sinks, Gilbert & Soames toiletries, make-up mirrors, hair dryers and bottles of San Pellegrino mineral water are among the amenities. Instead of a do-not-disturb sign, a stuffed pussycat hangs on the inside door handle with a little note to "put the cat out" to avoid being disturbed.

Six courtyard suites, two on each floor, are larger and have balconies overlooking the rear courtyard. The one we saw had a queen poster bed with an elegant quilt and a see-through fireplace serving bedroom and bath area, which our guide called "the tub room." It contained a large jetted tub for two and a wicker chair, and opened onto a balcony as well as a bathroom with a glass shower.

A continental-plus breakfast, included in the rates, is offered in a quaint basement breakfast room designed to look like a French kitchen with tiled floor, tiled fireplace, original rafters and wall sconces. Quiches are added on weekends.

Behind the inn, the lovely, landscaped courtyard comes with a goldfish pond and hibiscus blooming in large pots at our October visit. It's a popular place for breakfast or a drink in nice weather.

Two more guest rooms, retail shops and conference facilities are offered in a couple of buildings beyond the courtyard. The inn's main floor contains a reception foyer beside a stone wall, an elegant cocktail lounge called Left Bank Libations and upscale retail shops.

(609) 397-0200 or (888) 867-8859. www.lambertvillehouse.com. Twenty rooms and six suites with private baths. Doubles, $195 to $315. Suites, $350.

The Woolverton Inn, 6 Woolverton Road, Stockton, N.J. 08559.

Built in 1792 as a manor house by pioneer industrialist John Prall Jr., whose mill is nearby, this engaging B&B is on ten bucolic acres – where curious black-faced sheep may mosey up nearly to your car from a field next to the parking area. Its location off a country road, atop a hill away from the river, assures a quiet night.

Three energetic ex-Chicagoans infused the inn with personality and pampering touches. They also upgraded the existing accommodations and added five luxury cottage rooms. "We want this to be welcoming and to capitalize on our rural, farm setting," said Carolyn McGavin, whose original partners left to become inn consultants. She was joined in 2004 by local businessman Bob Haas.

Featherbeds, Egyptian cotton sheets and more comfortable sitting areas were added to the eight bedrooms in the main house. Plush towels, luxurious micro-fiber robes, fresh flowers and bedside chocolates are among the amenities. Letitia's Suite, made from two rooms that shared a bath, claims a fireplace, a jacuzzi tub and a two-person steam shower. Amelia's Suite also has a fireplace, whirlpool tub and two-person shower, and Caroline's Balustrade has a whirlpool tub with a rain shower and a private balcony.

Two former guest rooms in the Carriage House are now the luxury Garden Suite with kingsize bed, sitting area with a sofabed beside the fireplace, whirlpool tub and a separate shower for two.

The most sumptuous and private accommodations are in two rear "cottages" – built to look like rustic barns, a re-creation of the farm outbuildings historically on the property. Each contains two ground-floor guest suites with kingsize featherbeds, gas fireplaces, whirlpool tubs, porches or patios, Bose wave radios and telephones, but no TVs. We liked the woodsy feel of the Hunterdon, topped by a twenty-foot-high cupola for overhead lighting. Its split-level bathroom has a double jacuzzi raised for a view of the fireplace through an opening over the rough-hewn timbered bed. Travel is the theme in the two-level Sojourn Loft. The downstairs contains the bed and sitting area and a multi-tiered fireplace faced in Venetian plaster with Persian motifs. The loft holds another fireplace, a jacuzzi and shower for two, and a long hammock for two, from which some occupants temporarily shun any further travel.

The main inn's large and elegant living room is where afternoon refreshments are offered.

The dining room is the scene of elaborate breakfasts, served from 8:30 to 10. A quiche of onions, apples, Canadian bacon and gruyère cheese was featured at one of our visits, along with homemade muffins and "pineapple upside-up" cake. Vegetable frittata with homemade turkey sausage and grand marnier french toast are among the possibilities. A fruit dish of apple-blueberry streusel baked in parchment paper is a favorite starter.

As you depart, the inn's four friendly sheep – Betty, Pâté, Rita and Lois – might amble up to the fence to bid farewell.

(609) 397-0802 or (888) 264-6648. Fax (609) 397-4936. www.woolvertoninn.com. Eight rooms and five cottages with private baths. Doubles, $150 to $325. Cottages, $350 to $425.

Woolverton Inn features sumptuous accommodations in recently built barn cottages.

Chimney Hill Farm Estate & Old Barn Inn, 207 Goat Hill Road, Lambertville, N.J. 08530.

Three deer were grazing in the back yard one day when we visited this elegant retreat. "There are lots more," said Terry Anderson, owner and innkeeper with her husband Rich. "They ate every chrysanthemum and daisy off our porch this fall. We also have a brood of wild turkeys, rabbits and big fat groundhogs." Not to mention a handful of alpacas, loveable llama-like animals from Peru.

The animals enhance the "farm aspect" at this opulent manor house, sequestered atop a wooded hill beyond a high-rent residential area on the southeastern edge of Lambertville. It was once a working farm, and the restored gardens put in by former owner Edgar W. Hunt, an internationally known attorney, are quite spectacular in season.

The inside of the house borders on the spectacular as well. Vacant when it was acquired by two aspiring innkeepers in 1988, they first put it on display as a designer show house.

The Andersons inherited most of the furnishings for the eight original guest rooms, which they have been enhancing ever since. All but one have king or queensize beds and plump seating, and four have fireplaces. Each is awash in splashy fabrics, all Schumacher or Colfax & Fowler. The smallest room has space enough only for a double bed and two chairs. The rear Tapestry Room is bigger with tapestry fabrics, kingsize bed, a large bath with clawfoot tub and its own balcony. We liked the looks of the Hunt Room master suite, where the covers and canopy on the step-up queen bed match the gently swagged curtains, and the chairs and the oriental carpet pick up the theme.

We also like the looks of the sunken main-floor sun porch, with windows on three sides and floors, fireplace and walls of fieldstone. Warmth and color come from ficus trees and leather loveseats angled around a huge glass cocktail table. The splashy sun porch makes the attractive living room pale in comparison.

Breakfast is served by candlelight at six tables for two in the 1820 dining room that was the original room in the house (the wings were added by attorney Hunt in 1927). Terry offers fresh fruit, cereals and plenty of homemade pastries, from muffins with farm-made raspberry jam to croissants filled with fruit or cream cheese. The main course at our latest visit was vegetable quiche with home fries and bacon. Challah bread french toast with sausage was on tap the next day. In the afternoon, cream sherry awaits in the butler's pantry, where tea, coffee and snacks also are available.

In a major expansion, the Andersons joined a rear carriage house connected by a courtyard to a restored 1800 barn. The carriage house contains a function facility. Much larger is the barn, with a conference/board room and four luxury suites, each more showy than the last. We were comfortably ensconced in one of two on the main floor with queen beds, sitting rooms with loveseats, TVs in armoires, corner gas fireplaces, guest convenience areas with refrigerator and microwave, and baths with bubble-jet tubs and body showers. French doors open onto small patios, from which we could watch some visiting alpacas getting their workouts. Upstairs are two larger, bi-level suites. One has a see-through fireplace facing both a living room with TV and a bath area with a large jacuzzi beneath a brass chandelier in the corner, a bathroom with two-person shower and a spiral staircase to a loft with a Shaker queensize poster bed and another TV/VCR in a cabinet. The crowning glory is Suite 4, otherwise known as "Madelana's Ooh La La," with a stereo steam room in the shower. The surround-sound stereo or CD music lulls guests into a peaceful mood as they steam and bake.

(609) 397-1516 or (800) 211-4667. Fax (609) 397-9353. www.chimneyhillinn.com. Eight rooms and four suites with private baths. Doubles, $189 to $379 weekends, $135 to $299 midweek.

The Inn at Lambertville Station, 11 Bridge St., Lambertville, N.J. 08530.

This architecturally impressive, three-story luxury inn along the riverfront was undergoing a major expansion in 2006 and adding a destination European-style spa. Local developer Dan Whitaker, the inn's founder and co-owner, started construction on 65 new rooms and a spa to open in 2007. These are in addition to the restored Lambertville Station restaurant that launched the complex a couple of decades earlier.

In the existing inn, prized antiques are in the 45 guest rooms, each named for a major city and decorated to match. Ours was the corner New York Suite, high in the trees above a rushing waterfall that lulled us to sleep. There were chocolates at bedside, the bathroom had a whirlpool tub, and around the L-shaped room were heavy mahogany furniture, leather chairs facing the fireplace and TV, handsome draperies, ornate mirrors and fine art. A light continental breakfast with carrot-nut muffins arrived at our door with a newspaper the next morning.

Other rooms that we saw were equally impressive, all individually decorated by an antiques dealer. Though no rooms face the river directly, occupants on the south side beside the woods hear the sounds of Swan Creek spilling down from the canal. Those on the north side view the lights of Lambertville and New Hope glimmering on the river. The large Riverside Room, which faces the river with windows on three sides, is used for the Sunday champagne brunch ($21.95 for quite a spread).

(609) 397-4400 or (800) 524-1091. Fax (609) 397-9744. www.lambertvillestation.com. Thirty-seven rooms and eight suites with private baths. Doubles, $120 to $230. Suites, $165 to $300.

1740 House, 3690 River Road, Lumberville, Pa. 18933.

This new, built-to-look-old motel-type inn was among the first of its genre in 1967 and continued relatively unchanged for 35 years. In 2002, four investors purchased the place from the grandson of Harry Nessler, the inimitable founder who was a presence on site and manned the front desk up to his death at age 92.

The new owners brought the idiosyncratic place into the 21st century – quite nicely, thank you. The exterior facade and the interior configuration remains the same, so the repeat visitor would not suspect the changes: new beds, new furnishings, new decor and – abhorrent to the original owner – television sets, telephones and data ports. Eight "junior suites" were given gas fireplaces and mini-bars. A number of bathrooms were updated. The prices were hiked, of course, and now credit cards are accepted.

Although made more customer friendly, this place backing up to the Delaware River in quaint Lumberville still maintains its charms. Local craftsman Roger Wright made beds and chairs for some rooms, and tiles for the new fireplaces came from the Moravian Tile Works nearby. Each room is different (some have wicker chairs with cushions, while others boast antique wood chairs that are better for show than for sitting). There are kingsize or twin beds, and real wooden coat hangers that detach from the rod. Glass doors open onto your own brick patio or balcony. You can laze in a tiny swimming pool or paddle the canal beneath your room in the inn's canoe, except there's never been enough water for canoeing when we've been there.

A full-service bar was added in 2005 off the living room, open in season to the canopied patio and pool area.

A continental breakfast is served buffet-style in a cheery, flagstone-floored garden dining room, where if it's busy you'll share tables. Guests help themselves to juice, cereal, muffins and cinnamon rolls, and toast their own English muffins or homemade bread. In the afternoon, the staff puts out quite a spread of cakes and cookies along with tea and lemonade.

(215) 297-5661. Fax (215) 297-5243. www.1740house.com. Twenty-one rooms and two suites with private baths. Doubles, $150 to $195. Suites, $195 to $325. Closed in January.

Bridgeton House, 1525 River Road, Upper Black Eddy, Pa. 18972.

The Delaware River literally is the back yard of this comfortable B&B, just beyond a landscaped terrace and on view through french doors and the third-floor balconies. Although smack up against the road, the onetime wreck of an apartment house built in 1836 was transformed by Bea and Charles Briggs and reoriented to the rear to take advantage of the waterside location.

A parlor with a velvet sofa looks onto the canal. Fresh or dried flowers, a decanter of sherry and potpourri grace the dining room, where breakfast is served. Following a fruit course (perhaps baked pears in cream or a fresh fruit plate) comes a main dish: waffles with strawberry butter, eggs roxanne or mushroom and cheese omelets. Fresh lemon breads, muffins and apple cake accompany.

Upstairs are nine guest rooms and suites overlooking the river, each exceptionally fashioned by Charles, a master carpenter and renovator, and interestingly decorated by Bea. Some have four-posters and chaise lounges. All have country antiques, colorful sheets and comforters, feather beds and fresh flowers. All rooms have telephones, and most have TV/VCRs. Our room, one of two on the main floor, included a private porch with rockers and lovely stenciling, a feature throughout the house, done by a cousin who also did the nude paintings scattered about.

What Bea calls Bucks County's ultimate room is a huge penthouse suite with a kingsize bed beneath a twelve-foot cathedral ceiling, a black and white marble fireplace, a marble bathtub, black leather chairs, a stereo/TV center, a backgammon table and a full-length deck looking down onto the river. It shares top billing with the new Boat House, a riverside cottage with cathedral-ceilinged living room, kingsize feather bed, double whirlpool tub and two-person shower, refrigerator, microwave and TV/VCR.

(610) 982-5856 or (888) 982-2007. www.bridgetonhouse.com. Ten rooms, one penthouse and one cottage with private baths. Doubles, $159 to $229 weekends, $139 to $199 midweek. Penthouse and cottage, $329 and $399 weekends, $299 and $349 midweek.

York Street House, 42 York St., Lambertville, N.J. 08530.

This large Georgian brick home was opened as Lambertville's first B&B in 1983 after it had been glamorized as a designers' show house. It wasn't the first time it had received wide publicity – the Massey Mansion was featured in 1911 in House and Garden magazine shortly after a local coal merchant had built it as a 25th wedding anniversary gift for his wife.

Today's visitors are greeted by an imposing brick mansion set back from the street with pillared verandas on the front and side. It's been enhanced lately by owners Laurie and Mark Weinstein, she the innkeeper and he a fulltime physician, who live with their four young sons nearby. "This is my dream," said effusive Laurie, "and he works to support my hobby."

Mercer tiles compliment the working fireplaces in the main-floor common rooms and an original Waterford chandelier glitters over down-stuffed furniture in the living room. Besides the living room, guests spread out on the side porch furnished in wicker overlooking the largest yard on the block.

Crystal knobs open the walnut doors to six large guest quarters on the second and third floors. Each now has a private bath, including newly renovated Room 1 with a two-person jacuzzi beside the window. All with queen or kingsize beds, they are outfitted with TVs and telephones, down comforters and robes. Still a favorite is the second-floor front Room 3 with a step-up fishnet canopy queen bed, two wing chairs in the corner, an extra sink in another corner and – a startling sight in the bathroom – a free-standing toilet amid plants in the front bay window of what once was a dressing room, now equipped with a jacuzzi tub, shower and pedestal sink.

A winding staircase leads to the third floor and two large guest rooms with windows in the eaves and private hall baths. Room 6 has a kingsize wrought-iron canopy bed and an adjoining sitting room with a two-person jacuzzi in which you can relax and watch a flat-screen TV. Room 7 offers a queen canopy bed and pleasant sitting area in front of a fireplace.

A full breakfast, prepared in a kosher kitchen, is served by candlelight at individual tables in the cherry-paneled dining room. The room is notable for a tiled fireplace, a stained-glass window above an oak sideboard and the original lineup of servants' bells above the kitchen door. A fruit course of grapefruit and strawberries marinated in orange liqueur preceded buttermilk pancakes with blueberry compote the morning of our visit. Poached pears in phyllo with raspberry sauce and pecan belgian waffles with caramelized bananas were the fare the day before. Homemade cookies, fruit and an assortment of beverages are available later in the day.

(609) 397-3007 or (888) 398-3199. Fax (609) 397-9677. www.yorkstreethouse.com. Six rooms with private baths. Doubles, $175 to $260 weekends, $125 to $175 midweek.

The Martin Coryell House Bed and Breakfast, 111 North Union St., Lambertville, N.J. 08530.

Mary and Rich Freedman bought one of the finest Victorian houses in Lambertville, launching extensive renovations to turn it into a deluxe B&B. They offer handsome common areas and elegant guest rooms, all with queensize featherbeds, TVs and fireplaces. The couple added three bathrooms in what had been a private residence for a leading local family, installing the jacuzzi tubs and two-person showers much in demand by today's inn-goers.

The guest accommodations on the second and third floors are more spacious and comfortable than those in many a Victorian house. The themes vary, from Emma Lily's Room, light and frilly, to Martin's Suite, dark and masculine, with a queen sofabed in the sitting room. A striking coronet canopy adorns the bed in Camille's Room, which has windows on three sides. The bed in Alice's Suite is ingeniously recessed in a columned alcove to allow more space to access the step-down bathroom. Fine fabrics and coordinated window treatments are the norm.

Hand-painted wall murals, freshly done by a local artist, greet guests in the anteroom off the Italianate front porch and in the foyer beyond. Another mural graces the ceiling of the original wainscoted dining room, where continental breakfast is offered weekdays and a full breakfast on weekends. The weekend fare might be asparagus frittata with scones and hickory-smoked bacon one day, and stuffed french toast with cream cheese and strawberries the next.

Off the foyer are a formal Victorian parlor on one side and a cozy library on the other. The decor is "fancy," Mary concedes, "but not in-your-face Victorian."

(609) 397-8981 or (866) 397-8981. www.martincoryellhouse.com. Three rooms and three suites with private baths. Doubles, $195 to $229 weekends, $155 to $180 midweek. Suites, $234 to $275 weekends, $184 to $220 midweek.

Gourmet Treats

River Road Farms at 905 River Road in Erwinna, Pa., is a complex of buildings centered by a picturesque red wood and fieldstone barn built in 1749. The barn is home to **A Gourmet's Pantry,** an interesting food and gift shop long known as Chachka, chock full of crystal and porcelain, much of it from Portugal. The real draws here, though, are all the "food accents" and the wild and wonderful preserves made by owner Richard deGroot, the "Gentleman Farmer," who lives next door. Most of his preserves, plum-rhubarb with amaretto, pumpkin marmalade with rum, blood orange marmalade with cointreau, banana strawberry with framboise – have you ever heard of such neat combinations? – are in the $8.98 range for ten ounces. They come in Italian jars that can be turned into vases. All are topped with calico bonnets so they make great hostess gifts. Pastas, sauces and condiments like a *very* hot Thai garlic sauce (opened for tasting – we nearly choked) are dotted around. A recent addition to the complex is **Jackson How for the Home & Garden,** an outstanding home furnishings and gift shop.

Open daily for tastings of its 100-percent vinifera wines is **Sand Castle Winery,** run by two brothers from Czechoslovakia, high on a hill above 755 River Road in Erwinna. Joseph and Paul Maxian started with riesling and chardonnay before adding cabernet sauvignon and pinot noir. On weekends, they lead tours ($5 to $15) through their 7,000-square-foot underground wine cellar blasted 30 feet deep into the hillside beneath a new sales building patterned after a 10th-century Czech castle. The 72-acre vineyard, largest in Pennsylvania, yields about 42,000 gallons of wine annually.

Lumberville General Store, River Road, Lumberville, Pa., is a true country store dating to 1770. On jumbled shelves you can find anything from ketchup to chicken soup, with more upscale things like Perrier, Pennsylvania Dutch preserves, antiques and Crabtree & Evelyn goods. At the deli counter you can get good sandwiches.

In New Hope, **Gerenser's Exotic Ice Cream** at 22 South Main dispenses exotica in such flavors as English mincemeat, African violet, Hungarian tokay, Swedish ollalaberry, Polish plum brandy, Greek watermelon, Indian mango, Jewish malaga and ancient Roman ambrosia. All ice creams are made on site, as they have been for more than 50 years. Next door is **C'est La Vie,** which styles itself as a "true Parisian boulangerie and patisserie" and offers an outdoor riverside terrace upon which to enjoy its specialties. Fans says its coffee is cheaper and better than at the new Starbucks nearby at the main intersection in New Hope. **Suzie Hot Sauce** sells sauces, salsas and more at 19A West Bridge St.

A microbrewery offers a variety of handcrafted beers at the new branch of the Princeton-based **Triumph Brewing Co.** in New Hope's new uptown Union Square complex. The brewpub and restaurant serve an extensive menu of contemporary American food (dinner entrées, $13.95 to $26.95). Tours of the brewery are offered Saturdays at 1 and 3.

Across the river in Lambertville, N.J., is the **River Horse Brewery** at 80 Lambert Lane, near the Porkyard complex. The area's first microbrewery produces some highly regarded hand-crafted ales and lagers. It offers a walking tour of its kegging and bottling operation, a tasting room and a shop with items for beer lovers.

Two well-stocked wine shops on the New Jersey side of the river help you handle the BYOB situation at area restaurants. **Welsh's** at 8 South Union St. in Lambertville and **Phillips'** on Bridge Street in Stockton offer shelf after shelf of rare French and Italian vintages plus wines from most California wineries (about 75 percent of Richard Philips's 20,000 bottles are from California, including those from every boutique winery we have ever visited or heard of and many we haven't). A good selection of whites is kept refrigerated in both establishments. Prices are fair and the staffs are well versed to help you choose. Welsh's also has an incredible selection of cognacs, armagnacs and single-malt whiskeys.

Bargain Gourmet

Rice's Sale and Country Market, 6326 Greenhill Road, New Hope, Pa.

For the benefit of weekend visitors, this famed 30-acre outdoor market is now open Saturdays and some holiday Fridays as well as the traditional Tuesdays. It's like no other open-air flea market we've seen, and provided a high point on one of our Bucks County expeditions. Amish specialties, fresh produce, seafood, meats, honeys, spices and kitchenware are available, but foods aren't the best part – the incredible bargains on quality merchandise are. We did all the Christmas shopping (Jantzen and Ralph Lauren sweaters, a set of knives, perfume, a watch and a pretty homemade wreath) that two hours and our checkbook would allow. Many of the 700 purveyors and 15,000 bargain-seekers come weekly to this great flea market, which has been going strong since 1860. It's located off Route 263 northeast of Lahaska.

(215) 297-5993. www.ricesmarket.com. Open Tuesday year-round, 7 to 1:30, and Saturday (except January-February), 7 to 1.

Lineup of front verandas, a Cape May trademark, is on view from Mainstay Inn.

Cape May, N.J.

Two for B&B, Tea and Dinner

Victoriana, bed and breakfast inns, and dining par excellence. That's the combination that makes Cape May a model of its genre and draws visitors in increasing numbers each year from March through Christmas.

Cape May has shed its mantle as a long-slumbering seaside city that time and Atlantic City had passed by. Its potential was recognized in 1976 when it was designated a National Historic Landmark city, one of five in the nation – an honor it had shunned only a few years earlier. Now its Victorian heritage is so revered that Cape May celebrates a ten-day Victorian Week in mid-October, plus a week-long Tulip Festival, a Dickens Christmas Extravaganza, a Cape May Music Festival, Victorian dinners, a Victorian fair, and various inn and house tours. Most are sponsored by the Mid-Atlantic Center for the Arts, a community organization and promoter that runs an annual Cape May Food and Wine Festival.

The B&B phenomenon started here in the late 1970s as preservationists Tom and Sue Carroll restored adjacent Victorian landmarks into museum-quality guest houses, setting a national standard and launching a trend that has inspired the opening of more than 80 B&Bs locally.

Besides enhancing the Victorian structures in which they are housed, some Cape May B&Bs elevate the level of breakfast and afternoon tea to new heights – in formal dining rooms and parlors, or on the ubiquitous front verandas that are occupied everywhere in Cape May from early morning to dusk or later. The sumptuous breakfast and afternoon-tea ritual draws many couples year after year, and has resulted in publication of a number of Cape May cookbooks.

Where upscale B&Bs open, restaurants are sure to follow. Since the late 1970s, more than two dozen restaurants have emerged and, remarkably for a resort town, most of the best have survived. Besides stability, many offer creative food and convivial ambiance. Some are small (make that tiny) and, lacking liquor licenses, allow patrons to bring their own wine. Prices, in many cases, are pleasantly lower than in other resort areas.

The result is that thousands of visitors come to experience the ultimate in bed and breakfast, tea and dinner in this, the culinary capital of South Jersey.

Dining

At peak periods, many restaurants are booked far in advance. Some of the most popular do not take reservations, which may mean a long wait for a table. Some also require a minimum of one entrée per person. Be advised that parking at many Cape May restaurants is difficult to impossible. Parking meters on the street gobble up quarters every half hour until 10 p.m. A few restaurants offer valet parking.

The Best of the Best

410 Bank Street, 410 Bank St., Cape May.

A gumbo of New Orleans, Caribbean and French dishes, many grilled over mesquite wood, is the forte of this Key West-style restaurant that consistently ranks as best in town in the annual New Jersey Monthly readers' poll. The owners' companion Italian restaurant, **Frescos,** is next door and some reviewers think it's even better.

Dining is pleasant in the enclosed garden courtyard, surrounded by plants, tiny white lights and Victorian lamps. If you can't eat there, settle for one of the narrow, vine-covered porches or the small, intimate dining rooms done in Caribbean pastel colors inside the restored 1840 carriage house. Owners Steve and Janet Miller are theater-set designers, so both inside and outside are quite dramatic.

For appetizers, we passed up the menu's crawfish bisque, oyster stew, crab terrine and blackened sea scallops with rémoulade sauce for excellent specials of seviche and mesquite-grilled quail. After those, both our entrées of blackened red snapper with pecan sauce and yellowfin tuna in Barbadian black bean sauce with a hint of sesame and ginger, served with crisp vegetables and rice pilaf, were almost too much to eat. We had to save room for the key lime pie, which was the real thing.

Other favorite entrées include mesquite-grilled mako shark with tamarind-mango sauce, blackened catfish fillet in a lime-jalapeño sauce with bananas and tomatoes, Chilean sea bass creole, cajun shellfish filé gumbo, Florida red snapper sautéed in a light provençal sauce, grilled Jamaican filet mignon with twin island sauces and rasta pudding, and rack of lamb with burgundy demi-glace. A French-style roast is offered nightly.

Patrons dine Key West-style on enclosed outdoor courtyard at 410 Bank Street.

For desserts there are chocolate-pecan pie with amaretto purée, triple-chocolate ganache with grand marnier sauce, hazelnut cheesecake with raspberry purée and a Louisiana bread pudding with hot bourbon sauce that's the best around.

Service is by knowledgeable waiters attired in tropical shirts and bow ties. With the Key West-like atmosphere and a menu like this, who'd guess that the chef, Henry Sing Cheng, is Chinese? Savants consider him the top chef in town.

(609) 884-2127. Entrées, $23.50 to $36.95. Dinner nightly, 5 to 11, May to mid-October. BYOB.

The Washington Inn, 801 Washington St., Cape May.

Far and away the best of the large restaurants in town, this has become even better with the dynamic lent by David and Michael Craig, sons of the founders. Although it offers no lodging, the glamorous and atmospheric establishment has the feeling of an inn. Check out the upstairs ladies' room, which a local innkeeper termed the nicest in the entire state. Beautifully decorated in florals, it has a window seat and fresh flowers on the vanity. Personal touches abound, among them the stunning mahogany bar that founder Arthur Craig crafted for the lounge.

The attractive white 1840 Colonial plantation house is surrounded by colorful banks of impatiens. Inside all is pretty as a picture. The Craig brothers redecorated, picking up the colors from their striking, custom-designed floral china. They seat 130 in five dining areas, including a candlelit wicker-filled front veranda done up in pink, a Victorian conservatory filled with greenery, dark and elegant interior rooms, and a romantic, enclosed brick terrace centered by a fountain trickling over an array of plants. Off a Victorian cocktail lounge is another enclosed, L-shaped veranda.

Executive chef Mimi Wood's American/continental menu blends the traditional with the more creative. Start with her signature sea scallops wrapped in bacon, or perhaps escargots flamed in pernod in puff pastry or a crab cake with a creamy roasted pepper sauce. At a recent visit, we liked the sound of her specials, creamy mustard scallop bisque, shrimp louis and grilled portobello mushroom stuffed with shiitakes, crabmeat and smoked gouda.

For main courses, she might stuff flounder with crab imperial and top it with a lobster and brandy cream sauce, and pan sear sesame-crusted salmon with ginger-mirin beurre blanc and a dollop of wasabi. Blackberry juice might enhance the grilled breast and confit of duck. The grilled Kansas sirloin might be flavored with cambozola, roasted vidalia onions, cracked pepper and red wine reduction. The rack of lamb, rubbed with olive oil and herbs, could be served with a pineapple-mint essence.

The menu ends with "romantic international coffees." Typical desserts are a chocolate mousse tower filled with berries, chocolate lava cake with rum anglaise, vanilla bean crème brûlée, strawberry napoleon and lemon-glazed cheesecake with raspberry sauce.

David Craig likes to show the 10,000-bottle basement wine cellar, which holds an inventory of 850 titles and earns the Wine Spectator Grand Award. The wine list has a table of contents, includes a page of chardonnays, and offers a Virginia red and a Lebanese white, with a number of offerings priced in the teens.

More than 300 recipes are published in the fine *Washington Inn Cooks for Friends* cookbook.

(609) 884-5697. www.washingtoninn.com. Entrées, $21 to $33. Dinner nightly from 5, May-December, fewer days rest of year.

Tisha's, 714 Beach Drive, Cape May.

This little waterside prize in the Solarium Building juts out over the ocean beside Convention Hall. Pretty in pink and white to match the glorious sunsets beyond, it seems to be mostly big windows beneath a high ceiling, with close-together tables and a few art and floral accents on the walls. There's patio dining outside as well.

Such is the summery backdrop for some mighty fine fare, as prepared by chef-owner Paul Negro, whose fisherman-father often provides the day's catch and whose mother, Tisha, persuaded him to open a restaurant in nearby Wildwood before moving into the thick of the Cape May scene.

Interestingly, the contemporary American menus change every two weeks. They're published in booklet form so "you can check your dining date here to see what is offered that evening." What is offered in the way of three appetizers and eleven entrées from fortnight to fortnight doesn't seem to be repeated, making for a remarkable repertoire. In addition, several specials are offered nightly.

Terrific bread and excellent salads, one caesar and one tossed with balsamic vinegar, come with the entrées. At one visit, we enjoyed pork tenderloin with a dijon-caper cream sauce and clams aglio over penne pasta. An autumn dinner produced grilled lamb chops with mint sauce and grilled duck with raspberry sauce.

Walls of windows yield ocean views at Tisha's.

Tiramisu and an apple crisp with ice cream proved worthy endings and, a nice touch at our first visit, the chef sent out complimentary cordials of frangelico.

From smoked salmon parfait to cajun fried oysters, sea scallops sautéed with sambuca to grilled veal chop, profiteroles to strawberry fondue, the choices never fail to impress. Indeed, the guest reviews of local restaurants, as written in one inn's book at a recent visit, were decidedly mixed from one to the next. There was unanimity on only two: Tisha's and the Washington Inn received the most glowing reports, with nary a complaint about either. Now that's high praise.

(609) 884-9119. www.tishasfinedining.com. Entrées, $25 to $31. Dinner nightly, from 5. Closed Tuesday and Wednesday in off-season and Mid-October to April. BYOB.

Daniel's on Broadway, 416 South Broadway, West Cape May.

Meals here have been likened to dining in a private home, but with a difference. It's not your ordinary dining. Nor is it your ordinary home. The owner is a fabulous cook, and the house is a beauty.

Harry and Kristen Gleason saw this when it was a private residence and it was "exactly what we wanted." They opened it as a restaurant that captivated Cape May with its style and charm, winning honors as the best of 1998, in the estimation of Atlantic City magazine, followed by the highest ratings in New Jersey in the Zagat survey. "Stunning in every way– food, atmosphere, service, everything," hailed a Philadelphia Inquirer review.

Harry said he "wanted a change" after running his family's restaurant outside Valley Forge, Pa. The house, which had been home briefly to Swallows restaurant some years earlier, suited his purposes. He built an addition onto the previous kitchen in the oldest portion of the handsome yellow Victorian/Colonial house, which dates to the 18th century and is situated on a nicely landscaped lawn. Six diminutive dining areas on two floors seat a total of 95 amidst swagged windows, antique chandeliers, ornate six-foot mirrors, and splashy floral arrangements. Well-spaced tables are set with cream cloths, large stemware and shaded oil lamps. Framed French posters of different wines and liqueurs grace the walls of the main floor. Upstairs, a corner room comes with a colorful mural on the ceiling. A favorite is the rear room with rustic beams and huge Colonial hearth, accommodating sixteen.

Chef Harry offers contemporary American fare, artfully composed and presented. Homemade breads – perhaps poppyseed rolls with onion and garlic and focaccia with herbs and caramelized onions – are paired with butter and an addictive lemon-dill-garlic-cream cheese spread. They stave off hunger as you study the menu. For appetizers, the chef might sear peppered ahi tuna with white miso vinaigrette and ginger-soy drizzle and accompany with a wasabi and pea shoot sticky rice salad. Or he might serve a black truffle, leek and goat cheese tart with creamy leek sauce and white truffle oil. His Jamaican jerk spiced scallop salad is tossed with greens, avocado, mango, jalapeños and creamy champagne-mustard vinaigrette.

Signature entrées are grouper Charleston (sautéed with lobster, corn, leeks and plum tomatoes in a lobster-sherry broth), duet of duck (caramelized breast and confit of duck strudel with a red currant and port wine reduction) and filet mignon (stuffed with stilton cheese, sauced with shiitake mushrooms in red wine and served with garlicky herb-mashed potatoes and seared spinach). Other possibilities range from red snapper encrusted with horseradish and herbs and sauced with a champagne beurre blanc to macadamia-encrusted rack of lamb brushed with dijon, coconut and green curry sauce.

Desserts are as delightful to look at as they are to taste. Crème brûlée with a cherry compote, frozen grand-marnier soufflé and triple berry napoleon are sure winners.

(609) 898-8770. www.danielscapemay.com. Entrées, $25 to $33. Dinner nightly, from 5:30. Sunday brunch in season, 11:15 to 1:30. BYOB.

Black Duck on Sunset, 1 Sunset Blvd., West Cape May.

The tropical motif of the old Peaches on Sunset has gone the way sunsets do. The nicely restored Victorian house at the head of Sunset Boulevard in West Cape May is now sedate in night and day shades of blacks, whites and grays – like the ducks for which it is named. The formerly pink exterior is now gray, and the traditional peach and green interior is now a couple of crisp white rooms decorated with antique black and white photographs of old Cape May. Dining is al fresco on the porch and a raised deck leading to a back yard gazebo.

The Black Duck's limited promotion touts the cuisine as "darn good." And that's an understatement. For the chef-owner is Chris Hubert, whose inspired cooking we sampled during his seven years at the Ebbitt Room of the Virginia Hotel. He later opened the Union Park dining room in the Hotel Macomber, which he left in 2005 to concentrate on this, his latest venture.

Although not as haute as his earlier fare, it's every bit as innovative. The menu incorporates some of his Ebbitt Room favorites, including a crisp duck confit appetizer with sour cherry poivrade and lobster dumplings with citrus salad and a sesame-soy dipping sauce. The jonah crab spring rolls and the barbecued baby back ribs with a rustic "down-home" slaw are new favorites. The specialty salads – perhaps panko-crusted goat cheese over tomatoes and baby greens or orange-almond with locatelli cheese – are works of art.

The sautéed trout in a polenta crust and the succulent lump crab cakes with baby greens and yukon gold potatoes are among entrées transferred from Union Park.

Pristine white Union Park Dining Room is cool and summery.

Other winners are seafood risotto in a lemon-ginger broth, sautéed local flounder over lobster coleslaw, roast duck with a red wine sauce over sweet-potato risotto and grilled sirloin steak topped with lobster, crab and an ancho chile béarnaise sauce. Those who like their steaks extra hot go for the zesty szechuan spiced beef over udon noodles and a peanut-vegetable stir-fry.

Typical dessert choices are fruit tarts, triple-layered chocolate mousse cake, whiskey bread pudding, bananas foster crêpe, and homemade ice creams and sorbets.

(609) 898-0100. www.blackduckonsunset.com. Entrées, $22 to $29. Dinner nightly in summer, 5 to 10, Thursday-Sunday in off-season, Friday and Saturday in winter. BYOB.

Union Park Dining Room, 727 Beach Drive, Cape May.

Well-known local chef John Schatz, formerly of the late Restaurant Maureen, took over the restored dining room of the 85-year-old beachfront Macomber Hotel in 2005. The ambitious, now year-round venture consists of two dining rooms with fireplaces, cherry and mahogany furnishings, antique fixtures and silver service.

The main room is a stunningly beautiful, high-ceilinged space evocative of the Cape May of the 1930s. It's cool and summery with white-clothed tables and napkins, a white inlaid-tile ceiling, white crinoline covering the windows and cherrywood-backed chairs that innkeepers advised are the most comfortable in town.

The contemporary menu usually begins with the chef's tuna marinated in teriyaki and lime and served with pickled ginger and wakame. Other possibilities include panko-crusted crab cake with horseradish crème fraîche, tuna and scallop seviche with mango salsa, garlic-roasted shrimp with dark rum-tamarind dipping sauce and foie gras, the presentation of which varies nightly. Lobster salad is the star among the salad offerings.

Entrées range from scallops and prawns flavored with sambuca to grilled filet mignon with a red zinfandel demi-glace. Halibut with herb-citrus oil, soy-lacquered duck breast with pomegranate glaze, pesto-crusted rack of lamb and pan-seared elk tenderloin with a ginger-red currant glaze were recent autumn possibilities.

Desserts include tiramisu, crème brûlée, ricotta cheese cake and a flourless chocolate Venetian cake with raspberry coulis and sambuca ice cream.

(609) 884-8811. www.unionparkdiningroom.com. Entrées, $23 to $30. Dinner nightly except Wednesday, from 5:30. BYOB. Closed in January.

Budget Gourmet

Louisa's, 104 Jackson St., Cape May.

Tops on everyone's list for value is this tiny storefront restaurant that packs in the cognoscenti, who covet its twenty seats despite the fact that for years no reservations were taken and long waits were the norm. Lately, reservations for the week have been accepted starting Tuesday at 4 p.m. and are usually gone within two hours.

From a postage-stamp-size kitchen, Doug and Louisa Dietsch – he does the cooking, she does the managing and the desserts – offer some of the most innovative dinners in town. Formerly with the National Geographic Society, he has a natural touch for cooking and a rare way with herbs.

Feeling as if they're sharing their meal and their conversation with everyone in the place, patrons crowd together on molded plastic chairs of vibrant colors at hand-painted tables. Watercolors compete for wall space with photos of New Jersey Devils hockey players.

The changing menu, posted nightly at the door and deceptively simple in terminology, might offer curried carrot soup, smoked fish rillettes, and hot and spicy ginger-sesame noodles to start. Entrées could be soft-shell crabs, scallops with tamari and scallions, grilled salmon, grilled polenta with savory greens and grilled chicken with rosemary, but never a red meat dish.

For dessert, how about plum cobbler, peach oatmeal crisp, chocolate-banana bread pudding or mango upside-down cake?

Some people come for a week to Cape May and contentedly eat almost every night at Louisa's. It's certainly easier now that they can book their tables in advance.

(609) 884-5882. Entrées, $12 to $17. Dinner, Tuesday-Saturday 5 to 9, March-October. No credit cards. BYOB.

More Dining Choices

Frescos, 412 Bank St., Cape May.

New Jersey Monthly magazine once sent two writers to cover what they said "may well be New Jersey's leading center of gourmet restaurants." What did they rate best? Frescos, with three and one-half stars of a possible four. That was one-half star more than their second-best rating, 410 Bank Street. Frescos has slipped a bit in the estimation of locals, but the reviewers' accolades keep it near the top.

Crayons are on the tables for doodling on the paper overlays that cover the white-clothed tables in the restored Victorian summer cottage run as an Italian restaurant by Steve and Janet Miller of 410 Bank Street next door. Faux-marble columns and unusual art involving three-dimensional fish accent the spare white dining rooms, where brown leather chairs flank tables that are rather close together. We prefer the narrow wraparound porch, its tables for two far enough apart for private conversations.

The pasta repertoire is Cape May's most extensive, ranging from three-cheese stuffed rigatoni in a tomato-vodka cream sauce to shrimp with feta and tomatoes over homemade fettuccine. Friends who dined here rated at 9.5 on a scale of 10 both the linguini with white clam sauce and littlenecks, and the fusilli with a sauce of tomatoes, anchovies, black olives, capers and garlic. Seafood and meat choices include grilled Mediterranean sea bass with a crabmeat and smoky tomato sauce, parchment-baked Florida red snapper, pignoli-encrusted salmon in a celeriac-fennel fumé, duck breast with mission figs and port wine demi-glace, and an award-winning osso buco – oven-braised veal shank with farfalle pasta, saffron and peas.

We hear the key lime-cream-filled cannoli is even better than the signature dessert: a layered, rum-soaked sponge cake with imported mascarpone cream and grated chocolate.

(609) 884-0366. Entrées, $20.95 to $29.50. Dinner nightly, 5 to 10, mid-May to mid-October. BYOB.

Island Grill, 311 Mansion St., Cape May.

Eclectic seafood is the hallmark of this new grill, housed in a Civil War-era summer cottage built after the original Mansion House, a huge Cape May hotel, burned in 1857. The restored Mansion House restaurant was run for five years by Perry and Susan Collier, who own the popular Collier's Liquor Store at the other end of the edge-of-downtown block. The Colliers added a trellis-bordered dining porch and a modern kitchen to the small two-story house that now seats about 50 diners.

Chef Harry Gleason of the acclaimed Daniel's on Broadway took over in 2005, offering his Caribbean-influenced cuisine in a more casual setting. The three small dining rooms are likened to a rear Caribbean island restaurant with hot and cool tropical colors and showy paintings with an island theme.

The all-day menu is a mixed bag of soups, salads, appetizers, sandwiches and pasta dishes, with the addition of dinner entrées at night. You could lunch or sup quite nicely on the likes of conch chowder or fritters, Caribbean black bean soup, coconut beer-battered shrimp with tropical fruit salsa, a fried oyster BLT or a Cuban sandwich and jambalaya fettuccine.

These and more are supplemented at night by half a dozen varieties of island fish – yellowtail snapper, grouper, mahi mahi, scallops and the like – offered grilled, sautéed or blackened with a choice among four sauces. You also could order lump crab cakes with a roasted red pepper cream and mustard sauce, macadamia-nut chicken with coconut-curry sauce, chile-crusted pork chop with ancho-orange vinaigrette or grilled flatiron steak with a red-wine demi-glace.

Key lime pie, coconut crème brûlée, chocolate toffee mousse with kahlua and a warm tropical brownie typify the dessert list.

During its inaugural summer, the Island Grill offered an all-you-can-eat Caribbean pig roast on Thursday evenings (adults $20, children $12). Patrons were advised to bring their own rum to add to the tropical fruit punch.

(609) 884-0200. Entrées, $17.95 to $23.95. Lunch daily, 11:30 to 2:30. Dinner nightly, from 5. BYOB.

The Peter Shields Inn Restaurant, 1301 Beach Drive, Cape May.

This Georgian Revival mansion owned by the adjacent Angel of the Sea B&B is the only restaurant in town where you can sit in front of a fireplace and see the ocean. The sea is on view from two large and elegant, high-ceilinged dining rooms, each graced with crystal chandeliers and Victorian wallpapers, as well as from the expansive West Sun Porch. It's the kind of place where one would not be surprised to walk into a fashion show, as we did, literally, one weekday afternoon when we stopped to peruse the menu.

Dinner here is a special occasion for many, according to local innkeepers who recommend the place both for its food and its waterside setting. Executive chef Eric Hegyi's menu might start with an "ahi tower" of rare tuna loin, lump crab and mangos, oysters served in two styles, and seared sea scallops wrapped in salmon. A recent addition was pepper-studded elk carpaccio, served chilled with marinated gnocchi salad and grilled asparagus.

Expect entrées like the signature lobster and crab cakes with a zesty lobster-cognac sauce, dayboat fillet of mahi mahi with a soy-coconut-rum-pepper syrup over pineapple basmati rice, sea scallops with jumbo prawns in cognac sauce, dijon-crusted rack of lamb and roasted veal tenderloin served with lobster risotto, flavored with sharp cheddar and accented with roasted corn and chipotle sundried rouille.

Finish with one of the changing desserts and coffee from the cappuccino bar.

(609) 884-9090 or (800) 355-6565. www.petershieldsinn.com. Entrees, $22 to $34. Dinner from 5:30, nightly in summer, Tuesday-Sunday rest of year. BYOB.

Cucina Rosa, 301 Washington St. Mall, Cape May.

David Clemans, who has a reputation as one of the best cooks in town, opened this authentic and popular Italian restaurant after selling the John F. Craig House, his B&B of many years. Former lodging guests may have lamented his move, but locals applauded since they now get to share the fruits of his culinary prowess. "This is my last permitted insanity, according to my wife," says David, who named it for her late grandmother. Here he teams with his stepson, Guy Portewig, who's the chef.

"We take relatively standard southern Italian dishes and make them very carefully," says David. Everything is done from scratch, from the marinara and meat sauces to semolina bread.

Prices are relatively gentle. Appetizers range from eggplant parmigiana to spicy sausage with peppers, onions and sauce. We enjoyed clams oreganata, the house favorite, and the shrimp Rosa, wrapped in pancetta and baked on spinach and ricotta. That and the zesty seasonal salad made a mighty good meal.

Those with hearty appetites can choose from quite an array of main dishes, from seafood fra diablo to veal piccata or parmigiana. Widely acclaimed is the chicken portofino, stuffed with mozzarella cheese and Italian sausage specially made for the restaurant, rolled and baked with tomato sauce and served with spaghetti. Other treats are shrimp scampi and charbroiled lamb chops, marinated in olive oil, wine and Italian herbs and topped with rosemary butter.

Desserts are David's forte. He makes fruit pies that change daily, lemon cheesecake and a rich chocolate cake. He also offers tartuffo, spumoni and some of the best cannolis ever.

The restaurant is at a corner location along the pedestrian mall, with tables spilling out onto a canopied sidewalk terrace in season. The interior decor is soft and romantic in rose and green tones, with candles flickering on white-clothed tables. An expansion upstairs has added more tables.

(609) 898-9800 or (866) 345-7672. www.cucinarosa.com. Entrées, $17.95 to $25.95. Dinner nightly, 5 to 10, Sunday 4:30 to 9:30. Closed January to mid-February. BYOB.

Virginia Hotel offers fine dining in elegant Ebbitt Room.

Dining and Lodging

The Virginia Hotel, 25 Jackson St., Cape May 08204.

Its gingerbread restored and its interior pristine, the Virginia, built in 1879 as Cape May's first hotel, reopened in 1989 as what owner Curtis Bashaw calls a deluxe boutique hotel, with one of the best dining rooms in town.

Upstairs on the second and third floor are 24 guest rooms that vary widely in size and shape. Like the public rooms, they are furnished in a simple yet sophisticated manner, which we find refreshing after all the elaborate Victoriana one encounters in Cape May.

Bedrooms are equipped with modern baths with new fixtures (a couple with separate glass-enclosed sit-down showers), telephones, and remote-control TVs and VCRs hidden in built-in cabinets. The restful decor is mostly soft peaches and grays. Room service is available, and terrycloth robes, down comforters and Bulgari toiletries are among the amenities.

There are eleven standard-size rooms, eleven deluxe and two extra-premium at the front of the second floor with private balconies. Five come with a plush sofa and two upholstered chairs each, though one premium room with a kingsize bed has room for only one chair. The wraparound balcony on the second floor gave our expansive room extra space and was a pleasant setting the next morning for a continental breakfast of fresh juice, fruit, danish pastries and croissants, delivered to the room at precisely the time specified.

The front of the main floor harbors a pleasant library/parlor as well as a richly appointed piano bar, which opens onto a porch furnished in fancy wicker. The focal point is **The Ebbitt Room,** the hotel's sophisticated candlelit dining room that's elegant in red and gold. Upholstered chairs at crisply linened tables, delicate wine glasses, crystal chandeliers and white urns filled with flowers and greenery enhance the setting.

Named for the original owners of Cape May's first hotel, the Ebbitt Room is known for consistently fine food. In a town where restaurants often get noisy and hectic, this remains an oasis of calm and professionalism.

The tradition of top-notch, progressive American fare continues under executive chef Andrew Carthy, an Ireland native who moved up from sous chef. He favors bold dishes ranging from roast black sea bass with seared foie gras, melted scallions, truffle potato puree and white balsamic reduction to seared venison loin with sauce poivrade, hedgehog mushrooms, swiss chard and roasted turnips.

Dinner starts with exceptional, crisp-crusted hot rolls and an appealing choice of appetizers. Ours were an eggplant and gorgonzola crostini with red onion pesto and a very zesty caesar salad, both served on black octagonal plates. The roast cornish game hen was heavily herbed and rested on a bed of caramelized vegetables on a parsley-flecked plate. The filet mignon was served with pickled ramps, scallion barley and dried tomato-onion relish. On another occasion we liked the shrimp margarita, flamed in tequila and served with avocado cream sauce and roasted tomato salsa, and the pan-roasted quail with grapes and green peppercorns. These came with a medley of zucchini and carrots, and potatoes shaped like mushrooms.

For dessert, we enjoyed an upside-down fig cake and pecan-praline cheesecake. Others are valrhona chocolate cake and crème brûlée. The good wine list leans to the expensive side.

Service by the young waitstaff is graceful, competent and solicitous. And the live music emanating from the piano bar lends a glamorous air.

(609) 884-5700 or (800) 732-4236. Fax (609) 884-1236. www.virginiahotel.com. Twenty-four rooms with private baths. Doubles, $195 to $425 mid-June to Labor Day and weekends Memorial Day to mid-October. Rest of year, $145 to $425 weekends, $85 to $295 midweek. Entrées, $25 to $37. Dinner nightly, from 5:30.

Congress Hall Hotel, 251 Beach Drive, Cape May 08204.

A seaside retreat for four presidents since 1816, one of the nation's most historic hotels reopened in 2002 after two years and $22 million worth of top-to-bottom renovations. Managing partner Curtis Bashaw and team updated the four-story hotel's infrastructure, but retained much of the original fabric and patina, recycling floors, baseboards, doors and knobs, porcelain tiles, plumbing and light fixtures where possible.

Designer Colleen Bohuny orchestrated a simple, minimalist look for the summery guest rooms. The plaster walls are painted in pastels and simple valances and shades screen the windows, which open. Many baths feature pedestal sinks and deep soaking tubs. Some deluxe rooms offer larger baths with separate showers. Some have kingsize beds and private balconies with views across the colonnaded veranda and front lawn to the sea.

Three meals a day are served in the inn's corner restaurant, **The Blue Pig Tavern.** Billed as an American seaside classic, it offers hearty bistro fare and is named for a gambling parlor on the site in the mid-1800s. But for a painting of a blue pig above the fireplace, there's little blue about this rustic refuge of pink and brown – the barnwood walls are painted an eye-popping bubblegum pink above brown wainscoting. The adjacent Brown Room lounge looks more contemporary in chocolate brown with sleek furniture, a zebra-striped carpet, fireplace and a marble and ebony bar.

Both the Blue Pig's main dining room and a smaller, cozy tavern serve what is called "signature American fare – nostalgic, simple and fresh." We sampled an early version during an autumn lunch on the Blue Pig's rear veranda. From an extensive menu, the green gazpacho with fried clams was an interesting novelty, and the soft-shell crab sandwich was quite satisfying. The overly done, dry "black and blue burger" was not.

At night, the dinner menu incorporates many of the lunch items as well as a handful of entrées from potato-crusted cod and mixed seafood grill to half-roasted chicken, braised pork and steak frites.

Hotel facilities include a ballroom, spa, outdoor pool and an arcade of shops.

(609) 884-8821 or (888) 944-1816. Fax (609) 884-6094. www.congresshall.com. One hundred four rooms and five suites. Rates, EP. Doubles, $250 to $430 in summer, $100 to $350 rest of year.

Entrées, $15 to $26. Lunch daily in season, 11 to 3. Dinner nightly, 5:30 to 10.

Lodging

Since bed and breakfast is so integral to the Cape May experience, we concentrate on a few of the more than 80 in town, particularly those with bountiful breakfasts. Most require minimum stays of two to four nights, do not allow smoking inside, and access is only via push-button combination locks installed in the doors. Breakfasts tend to be lighter in summer, more formal and filling the rest of the year. The Cape May ritual is for the innkeepers to serve – and often sit with – guests at breakfast, and later to help with dinner plans as they review the menus during afternoon tea or beverages. So integral is the food element that many inns keep logs in which guests write comments on local restaurants. Some of the reports are scathingly at odds with previous entries.

The Mainstay Inn, 635 Columbia Ave., Cape May 08204.

The Mainstay led the way, and is the most likely to be filled weeks, if not months, in advance. Tom and Sue Carroll began the B&B movement in Cape May in 1971 and when they sold the Mainstay in 2004 to David and Susan Macrae, the Carrolls were the senior B&B innkeepers in the United States.

The showy Italianate villa was built in 1872 for two gentlemen gamblers and, the owners say, is one of the few Victorians in town that went through 100 years with no transitions. It later became a guest house run by a Baptist minister who never got rid of anything, and the collection is there for all to view.

Behind its picket fence, a broad veranda and porch swings beckon. Thirteen-foot-high windows reveal architectural style and haute Victorian luxury that put the Mainstay in a class by itself.

The twelve guest rooms in the main inn and the pleasant 1870 Cottage next door have updated baths, some with copper tubs and marble shower stalls, many lately upgraded with marble floors and Corian shower surrounds – but still in the Victorian style. The rooms are handsomely and formally appointed with lace curtains, stenciling, brass and iron bedsteads, armoires and rockers.

The inn and the cottage, both with wide verandas and rocking chairs, are separated by a brick walk and a handsome trickling fountain; the front gardens are brilliant with flowers. Across the street in the Officers' Quarters, a restored naval officers' building, are four modern two-bedroom suites with queensize beds, TVs and gas fireplaces. Each suite contains a spacious living room with a dining area, kitchenette and a marble bathroom with whirlpool tub and shower. Guests here have tea at the main inn; continental breakfast is delivered to their quarters.

Sue Carroll's recipes for her breakfast and tea goodies were so sought after that she published eight editions of a small cookbook called *Breakfast at Nine, Tea at Four*. In summer, breakfast is continental-plus, served buffet-style on the veranda. Other seasons it is formal sit-down around the table for twelve in the dining room. Strawberry french toast, chicken-pecan quiche, ham and apple pie and California egg puff are among the offerings.

Except in summer, when iced tea is served on the veranda, tea time is inside and formal. The tea is served from a copper container and accompanied by cucumber sandwiches, cheese straw daisies, toffee squares, spiced shortbread, chocolate-chip meringues and the like.

"Young children generally find us tiresome," the inn's brochure advises. Except for the Officers' Quarters, the inn is, as the owners say, "a total Victorian experience."

(609) 884-8690. www.mainstayinn.com. Twelve rooms and four suites with private baths. Doubles, $290 to $345; $155 to $195 midweek mid-October to mid-May. Officers' Quarters suites, $290 to $425; $175 to $325 midweek mid-October to mid-May. Officers' Quarters open year-round; inn closed November-March except December weekends and Christmas Week through January.

The Queen Victoria, 102 Ocean St., Cape May 08204.

Toned-down Victoriana and creature comforts are offered by Doug and Anna Marie McMain in Cape May's largest B&B operation, the only one open every day of the year and one considered an icon by fellow innkeepers.

The inn started with twelve rooms in a meticulously restored corner property dating to 1881 and maintaining a properly historic feeling. In 1989, the Victorian house and carriage house next door were turned into eleven luxury rooms and suites. These rooms and suites offer the niceties that many of today's travelers want: queensize brass or iron canopy beds, bedside clocks and reading lights, sitting areas or rooms, mini-refrigerators, whirlpool baths, television, fireplaces and air conditioning.

In 1995, the former Heirloom 1876 House across the street was renovated and reopened as **Queen's Hotel,** an elegant historic hotel. It has eleven deluxe air-conditioned rooms with TV, telephone, coffeemaker, mini-refrigerator, heated towel bars, whirlpool tubs for two, marble bathrooms, and ocean views from balconies and porches. Hotel guests receive a complimentary European breakfast buffet.

Now with the largest B&B operation in Cape May, the innkeepers still aren't finished. Lately they have enhanced the bathrooms in the original house, some of which are in their third incarnation. These have been updated with large glass-enclosed showers, tile and marble floors, and marble-topped sinks for extra shelf space. Gas fireplaces also are being added where possible, including two in the new Crown Jewel Suite. Billed as the ultimate suite in Cape May, it is two stories of luxury with all the latest bells and whistles from a downstairs library, mini-kitchenette and private patio to a loft with a feather-topped king bed, sitting area and marble whirlpool tub.

Furnishings in both guest and public rooms are not so high Victorian as in other Cape May inns. They are authentic in the post-Victorian Arts and Crafts style. Each house has a living room, one in the original building with a piano and a fireplace and the newer one with TV, games and jigsaw puzzles. Pantry areas are stocked with the makings for popcorn, tea, sherry and such. The library in the original inn contains volumes on architecture, art and history.

Breakfast at a recent visit included choice of juice, homemade granola, blueberry-cinnamon muffins and three kinds of homemade breads, a main course of hash-brown potato bake with ham slices, plus a basket of toasting breads. Baked eggs, cheese strata, spinach or corn casserole and stuffed baked french toast with warm strawberry sauce are other possibilities. The hearty meal is offered in the splendor of two Victorian dining rooms.

Afternoon tea brings crackers and a dip, maybe blue cheese or salmon, plus cookies, cinnamon-walnut shortbread or mint brownies.

Eighty of the house favorites are compiled in The *Queen Victoria Cookbook,* exceptionally good-looking and outstanding in its genre. The recipes, scaled to serve twelve, are geared to entertaining.

(609) 884-8702. www.queenvictoria.com. Fifteen rooms and six suites with private baths. Mid-June to mid-September: doubles $215 to $255, suites $275 to $485. Late spring and fall: doubles $140 to $225, suites $200 to $450. January-April: doubles $100 to $190, suites $145 to $405.

Manor House, 612 Hughes St., Cape May 08204.

This impressive, gambrel-roofed house with warm oak and chestnut foyer and striking furnishings seems almost contemporary in contrast to all the high Victorian B&Bs in Cape May. Guests spread out for punch, cider or tea in a front room with a striking stained-glass-front player piano or a library with two plush loveseats in front of a fireplace. A rear garden patio is a draw in season.

Innkeepers Nancy and Tom McDonald, who had stayed as guests here many times, considered the B&B a model when they acquired it in 1995. They maintained the tradition of good food, and added a secluded lower-level room with kingsize bed and private entrance.

Upstairs are eight guest rooms and a suite, all but one admittedly small room with brass and wood king or queensize beds. They are furnished in antiques, handmade quilts and light Victorian print wallpapers. A third-floor suite stretches across the front of the house with a sitting area and a whirlpool tub by the window in the bathroom. There are handmade "napping" signs for each door knob and Nancy plays "cookie fairy" at night, stocking the cookie jar with treats, including her favorite chocolate chip-pecan hearts.

The McDonalds serve sumptuous breakfasts, employing many of the founding innkeepers' favorite recipes. Among them are "asparageggs" (poached eggs and asparagus on homemade English muffins with mornay sauce), a corn and egg pie with jalapeño cheese and tomato relish, vanilla whole-wheat waffles, a french toast sandwich with raisin bread stuffed with cream cheese, apple crêpes and corn quiche. Juice, fruit and sticky buns, a house signature, round out the meal. Afternoon tea time brings cheese spreads, bean dip, salsa, coconut-macadamia bars and chocolate streusel bars.

(609) 884-4710. Fax (609) 898-0471. www.manorhouse.net. Nine rooms and one suite with private baths. Doubles, $155 to $255.

Rhythm of the Sea, 1123 Beach Ave., Cape May 08204.

Former Maryland restaurateurs run this oceanfront B&B, one of the few in Cape May that can boast a Beach Avenue address with the beach right across the street.

The 1915 summer house, which appeals to those who tire of haute Victoriana, is furnished simply in the Arts and Crafts style with Stickley furniture and Mission-style lanterns, wooden blinds and table linens.

Seven large bedrooms come with queen or kingsize beds and TV/VCRs, and several have gas fireplaces. The look is spare and pure, and the painted walls are done in the rose, pumpkin and olive palettes of the period. Five rooms have ocean views.

Owners Robyn and Wolfgang Wendt relocated here from Rock Hall, Md., where they had run a restaurant and managed the Inn at Osprey. Avid sportsmen who love to sail, they had met at a ski lodge in Colorado. Robyn, a well-traveled New Zealander, is into hospitality. Her German-born husband, a European-trained pastry chef, shows off his baking talents during afternoon tea and cooks four-course dinners for inn guests by reservation, $70 per person. He also teaches cooking classes.

A full breakfast is offered from 8:30 to 9:30 at four tables in the huge dining room. Fresh juices and fruit, perhaps a banana split or a granola parfait with seasonal berries, precede the main course. Eggs oscar, a benedict-style offering with crabmeat and white asparagus, is a guest favorite. Wolfgang bakes his own brioche with a cinnamon swirl, tops it with fresh berries and accompanies it with peppered bacon.

(609) 884-7788 or (800) 498-6888. www.rhythmofthesea.com. Seven rooms and a three-room suite with private baths. Mid-May through October: doubles $210 to $299, suites $295 to $345. Rest of year: doubles $185 to $255, suites $295 to $299.

The Southern Mansion, 720 Washington St., Cape May 08204.

Cape May's largest and most elaborate mansion, the 30,000 square-foot Italianate villa known locally as the George Allen Estate is a showy small hotel in the making. Barbara Bray, barely turned 30, poured sweat equity and millions of dollars into restoring the 100-room house built in the mid-19th century for a Philadelphia department store owner and occupying much of a two-acre square block in the heart of Cape May.

With 30 bathrooms, ten fireplaces, shiny Honduran mahogany floors, twelve-foot-high molded ceilings, cast-bronze chandeliers, 23 gold mirrors and 5,000 square feet of verandas and solariums, this was hardly your typical South Jersey beach house, as Barbara was quick to point out. Amazingly, the original furnishings, chandeliers and artworks were intact, many stored in the basement and ready to outfit ten more guest rooms added in a new wing.

Financing the restoration with house tours and the backing of her father, a Philadelphia physician, Barbara opened in 1995 with the first of fifteen ample guest rooms on three floors of the main house. They vary widely but come with an assortment of ornate, step-up king and queen beds, televisions concealed in armoires, gilt-edged mirrors and chairs, gold damask bedspreads and draperies, and velvet recliners and settees. Some of the bathrooms are small with clawfoot tubs; others have huge walk-in tiled showers with seats. The sink in one room is installed right in the room between two halves of an armoire.

Larger, more deluxe rooms in a new wing are the ultimate with kingsize beds, some with fireplaces, porches and double jacuzzis. One we saw has a poster bed of honduran mahogany matching the rich wood floor, draperies puddling to the floor, oriental rugs, a Victorian settee and a TV hidden in a carved teak armoire. The bathroom has a two-person shower with tiled fish designs and a marble seat. Most deluxe is a bi-level suite with its own solarium.

Beside the wing is an Italianate pool with columns and a waterfall.

The main floor has a catering kitchen, an enlarged solarium restaurant seating 160 for sit-down dinners, and a ballroom with six gold mirrors that "looks like Versailles," as Barbara envisioned it. The bright aqua and butter-yellow ballroom of the main house is now a parlor with sofas, tables bearing vases of long-stemmed roses and end walls of 23-carat gold-leaf mirrors reflecting into infinity. Beyond is a sunken solarium where a full breakfast is offered for house guests. Typical entrées are eggs Chesapeake with hollandaise sauce, strawberry-yogurt pancakes and three-berry belgian waffles. Tea and wine and cheese are served in the parlor in the afternoon.

Barbara's latest venture is Willow Creek Vineyard at 168 Stevens St., West Cape May. She planted 30 acres of vinifera grapes and scheduled her new winery opening for the fall of 2006.

(609) 884-7171 or (800) 381-3888. Fax (609) 898-0492. www.southernmansion.com. Twenty-four rooms and one suite with private baths. Doubles, $230 to $425 in summer, $135 to $385 rest of year.

Gourmet Treats

As the restaurant capital of New Jersey, according to the New York Times, this seaside town now hosts the annual **Cape May Food and Wine Festival** in late September. Sponsored by the Mid-Atlantic Center for the Arts, it involves five days of gourmet lunches, food tastings, a lobster bake luau, a wine cellar tour and tasting, seminars and cooking classes, featuring signature dishes from leading local restaurants. There's even a "restaurant relay." Teams from local restaurants race against the clock and each other to determine who sets the fastest table, folds the fanciest napkin and delivers a cocktail through an obstacle course without spilling a drop. The nightly Chef Dine-Arounds are similar to progressive dinners and wine tastings, with each of five courses at a different restaurant each night ($100 per person).

Throughout the year, MAC sponsors a number of other food and wine events, ranging from gourmet brunch walks and a chocolate fantasy buffet with the pastry chefs at the Washington Inn to wine cellar tours and winemaking classes.

Traditionally, Cape May always seemed to be strangely lacking in specialty-food shops, and our informant at the Visitor Center said someone would make a killing by opening one. Happily, Rhona Craig of the Washington Inn satisfied some of the need. Her **Love the Cook & Company** is an incredible gourmet store and cook shop at 408 Washington St. Mall. Now in expanded quarters, it's still so chock full of more than 10,000 kitchen items that browsers can barely get by on a busy day. From gadgets to cookbooks to dishware to olive oils and a few specialty foods, you can find it here.

For an extensive selection of wines to carry to the BYOB restaurants, most visitors head for **Collier's Liquor Store** at 202 Jackson St., just north of the Washington Street Mall.

La Patisserie, 524 Washington Mall, is the place for lovely fruit tarts, many breads and all kinds of sweets from chocolate croissants to raspberry puffs and cranberry squares.

Mon Frère French Bakery, 315 Ocean St., next to the Acme Market in the Victoria Village shopping plaza, isn't much to look at, but the breads are baked on the premises. Everything from boules and baguettes to fruit tarts is first-rate.

What's a beach town without saltwater taffy? **Fralinger's,** the original taffy emporium from Atlantic City, opened a Victorian candy store at 324 Washington St. Mall. Although we're not into fudge and taffy, we're certainly impressed by its elegant fixtures and wallpaper borders. Also on or near the mall are **Laura's Fudge** and **Morrow's Nut House & Fudge.**

For the ultimate omelet, head for **McGlade's,** a small restaurant with a large deck practically over the ocean (from which on some days you can watch dolphins playing). If you can face lunch after a mammoth plate full of the Uncle Tuse's omelet (with about a pound of bacon, tomatoes and sharp cheddar) plus a load of delicious homefries ($8.50) or the shrimp and garlic omelet ($9.95), you have more appetite than we do (we can't even eat an omelet each here, so choose one to share).

For shopping, we always gravitate to the **Whale's Tale** at 312 Washington St. Mall. A gift shop extraordinaire, it purveys everything from gourmet cookware and nifty coffee mugs to an outstanding collection of cards and children's items.

Our last stop on the way out of town is the **Lobster House Fish Market** at Fisherman's Wharf. Among the largest enterprises around, this includes a restaurant that does one of the highest volumes in the nation, an outdoor raw bar, a moored schooner for lunches and cocktails in season, a takeout counter and one of the best seafood markets we have seen. All kinds of exotic varieties of fresh fish can be packed in ice to travel. We try to take home items like snapper-turtle soup, lump crabmeat, oysters rockefeller or clam pies to remember Cape May by.

Tea Time

The Twinings Tearoom, 1048 Washington St., Cape May.

Think tea and, at least in Cape May, thoughts turn to the Victorian era and B&Bs. So the Mid-Atlantic Center for the Arts, the epicenter of all things cultural and promotional in Cape May, decided to take advantage. Twining's Teas furnished the teapots for the first exhibit in MAC's new Carriage House Gallery, its latest restoration. The association was a natural, so Twinings provided the seed money for MAC to open a tearoom and lunch restaurant at its Emlen Physick Estate. The location at the rear of the 1876 carriage house is perfect. There are 22 seats inside, set amid the old horse stables paneled in dark longleaf yellow pine. Outside are 55 more on a festive brick patio beneath a tent with a rollup canopy for pleasant days and heat to ward off any chill. Here, in Cape May's only tearoom, you can enjoy a leisurely tea luncheon. The $16.50 tab includes a choice of four finger sandwiches and quiches, pasta or potato salad, breads and sweets, along with hot and iced tea, lemonade or coffee. A slightly reduced version of same is available later in the day as "elegant afternoon tea." The flower-bedecked setting is indeed elegant, with crisp linened tables and polished service. The idea was not only to provide visitors a place for lunch or tea, but also educational: a place for tea tastings, pairings of teas and foods, events like mother-daughter teas – "to revive traditions that have been lost," according to a spokesman.

In addition to changing exhibits in the gallery, the gallery shop features teas, unusual teapots, china and silverplate serving pieces and cookbooks.

(609) 884-5404 or (800) 275-4278. Tea luncheon, 11:30 to 2, prix-fixe, $16.50. Afternoon tea, 2 to 4:30, $13.50.

Culinary Institute of America student serves diner at The American Bounty restaurant.

Hudson Valley

Mecca for Gourmands

Barely an hour's drive north of New York City lies an area that represents a different world, one often overlooked by travelers destined for Manhattan's urban attractions.

The central Hudson Valley remains surprisingly rural, at times rustic. It is a mixed-bag area of noted mansions and historic houses, hip boutiques and hippie pursuits, winding country roads and a mighty river with seemingly unending interesting traffic. Steep mountains and rushing streams abound on the west side of the Hudson. The east side, which is our focus here, is a rolling tapestry of pastoral vistas.

It also is an area of fine restaurants, one of which we would go so far as to say could give any restaurant in the country a run for its money. That is The American Bounty, one of four esteemed restaurants at the storied Culinary Institute of America in Hyde Park.

The array of restaurants followed the arrival of the relocated institute in 1972. The CIA created a demand for better food supplies in the area as well as a pool of teaching chefs and a ready entourage of culinary students who needed places to serve their required eighteen-week externships. For its 50th anniversary, the CIA listed 38 food-related places in the area owned by its alumni, running the gamut from gourmet restaurants to McDonald's and Dairy Freeze franchises. Many others have opened since.

Between meals, you will find plenty to do. The Hudson Valley is the nation's oldest wine-growing region, and more than twenty wineries offer tastings and/or tours. The valley is known for its great estates and house museums, from Boscobel to Hyde Park to Montgomery Place. Rhinebeck and Millbrook are villages of particular appeal to visitors.

Following your own pursuits will spur an appetite for the culinary attractions spread across the area.

Dining

The Culinary Institute of America

A former Jesuit seminary high above the Hudson River at Hyde Park became the home of the nation's oldest and foremost school for professional culinary training when The Culinary Institute of America moved in 1972 from New Haven, Conn. It has been a mecca for gourmands ever since, not only for chefs but also for visiting professionals and knowledgeable diners who sample the fare prepared by students in four restaurants at the cutting edge.

This is not a traditional college campus, you find upon arrival as you watch budding chefs in tall white hats scurry across the green, most clutching their knife kits. It couldn't be when you learn the rallying cry for the hockey team is "mirepoix, mirepoix, roux roux, roux; slice 'em up, dice 'em up, drop 'em in the stew!"

The bustling, red-brick classroom building has an institutional tinge, but the aromas wafting from The American Bounty or The Escoffier restaurants at either end of the long main hall are tantalizing, hinting at glories to come.

The restaurants are the final courses in 21 months of study for the institute's 2,000 candidates for associate and bachelor degrees, who arrive and graduate in cycles every three weeks. They work in the kitchens and then serve in the dining rooms.

Casual visitors don't get to see much behind-the-scenes action, except through windows into the kitchens off both restaurants. One-hour tours for the public ($5, by reservation, Monday at 10 and 4 and Wednesday and Thursday at 4) and bus groups afford a glimpse into the mysteries of 36 specialty and experimental kitchens, the pantry and the former chapel, which is now the student dining room and used for large banquets and graduation ceremonies. Visitors may catch glimpses of the General Foods Nutrition Center (first of its kind in the country), the Shunsuke Takaki School of Baking and Pastry, the Conrad N. Hilton Library, the Danny Kaye Theatre and the Colavita Center for Italian Food and Wine.

Open regularly to visitors here is an expanded gift shop and bookstore named after Craig Claiborne, stocking specialty food items and more than 1,300 cookbooks on every culinary subject imaginable. They may inspire you to try at home some of the dishes cooked up in the CIA restaurants.

Or you can dine informally or take out from the CIA's **Apple Pie Bakery Café,** which occupies a former wine room beyond the reception area.

Formal dining experience awaits diners at CIA's Escoffier Restaurant.

Meal reservations for the four major restaurants may be made with the hospitality desk at (845) 471-6608, or through the website at www.ciachef.edu/restaurants. Reservations are more readily available for lunch and dinner on weeknights than on Fridays or Saturdays. All restaurants are closed on Sundays and major holidays. "Business or country club casual dress" is recommended for men.

Keep in mind that this is a school and the always-changing staff is in training. The dining experiences vary accordingly, but we have yet to be disappointed.

The American Bounty Restaurant, The Culinary Institute of America, Hyde Park. Having had lunch at some of the pre-eminent five-star restaurants in New York and elsewhere, our verdict is clear. We like The American Bounty better – at least for lunch. Not only do we think its food more interesting and more attractively presented, but the staff is pleasant and helpful and the cost is less than half.

Opened in 1982 for the presentation of American foods (before they became trendy) and wines, The American Bounty complements the earlier, more formal Escoffier Restaurant.

The high-ceilinged restaurant is the institute's largest. It is stunning, from its etched-glass doors to its cream and green draperies with a floral motif, gathered back from high arched windows. The seminary heritage is evident in the two cloister-style dining rooms, seating 110 people at tables spaced well apart. A recent refurbishing produced a new wine room and a renovated dessert bar/lounge.

A changing array of America's bounty is in front of the window onto the Julia Child Rotisserie Kitchen, through which you can see ducklings turning on the spit as white-clad students near the end of their training.

The menu changes slightly with every meal. Seldom have we had such a dilemma making choices as we did for a springtime lunch, confronting such appetizers as spicy barbecued lamb empanadas with a poblano salsa and New York State foie gras sautéed with concord grape sauce and fried grapes. That dilemma has been mitigated with the welcome menu addition of several choices of samplers – two or three smaller servings among main courses. Enticing rabbit, pork and native American samplers were offered at our latest visit. Ditto for a New England sampler and a trio of quesadillas for appetizers, and a coffee and chocolate sampler for dessert.

We settled for tomato and celery mousse on cold tomato hash, a heavenly dish decorated with a floret of mayonnaise and a sprig of fresh dill, and a sampling of the day's three soups served in tiny cups: chilled strawberry, clam chowder and "New Orleans gumbo Ya-Ya." With these appetizers was passed a basket with at least nine kinds of bread and rolls (bran muffins, corn sticks, cloverleaf rolls and biscuits were among them), served with a crock of sweet butter.

For main courses, we ordered fresh asparagus on sourdough toast with creamed salmon and sweetbreads, and "baked fresh seafood variety, new garden style." The former had perfectly crisp asparagus arranged like a fan on crisp sourdough; the sauce was suave and rich. The seafood was served in an iron skillet and was pretty as a picture, rimmed by tomato wedges. Crabmeat, clams, mussels, salmon and more were topped with butter and crumbs and baked. Vegetables, served family style, were stuffed cherry tomatoes, yellow squash and tiny red potatoes.

Desserts included strawberry and rhubarb cobbler with vanilla bean ice cream, a key lime tart with toasted meringue and coconut sauce and, at another visit, sautéed Hudson Valley apples with praline ice cream in a walnut lace cup and pear-blueberry cobbler with Wild Turkey ice cream. We tried the popular Mississippi river boat, a shell of pastry filled with an intense chocolate mousse with kiwi fruit on top and, weird sounding but very good, fried strawberries – huge fat ones in a sort of beignet, served with a sour cream and orange sauce.

Prices for all this are not unduly expensive. Two people having appetizers, entrées and desserts plus a bottle of wine can have a memorable lunch of dinner-size proportions for $60 to $80.

At night, when dining is by candlelight, typical entrées range from sea scallop casserole with grilled shrimp, fava beans and wild mushrooms to pan-roasted rack of lamb with pink peppercorn jus. Service, of course, is correct and cordial – after all, these students are *graded* for this. But, as you might expect, it can be a bit slow. Not to worry. The food is worth the wait.

Entrées, lunch $16 to $19, dinner $22 to $28. Open Tuesday-Saturday, lunch 11:30 to 1, dinner 6:30 to 8:30.

The Escoffier Restaurant, Culinary Institute of America, Hyde Park.

The great French chef Auguste Escoffier would be pleased that some of his traditions are being carried on in the restaurant bearing his name.

The dining room is pretty in pale pinks and raspberry tones, with comfortable upholstered chairs and elaborate chandeliers and wall sconces. On spacious tables set with ten pieces of flatware at each place, the gigantic wineglasses – globe-shaped for red, hurricane-shaped for white and a flute for champagne – take an inordinate amount of room. With classical background music, it reminds one of a small, select and comfortable hotel dining room and seats about 90.

Menus change seasonally, service is tableside and the prices are the institute's highest. If you come for lunch, expect to spend upwards of three hours and not have any appetite for dinner that evening.

Dining room of St. Andrews Café is bright and airy.

The classic French menu has acquired nouvelle touches since we first lunched here in the late 1970s. Gone are the escargots bourguignonne and onion soup. In their place are such appetizers as foie gras terrine with raspberries, pike quenelle with shrimp sauce and spinach pasta, and smoked salmon and salmon tartare with crispy waffle potatoes. Main courses include a signature dover sole meunière, arctic char with sorrel sauce on a bed of couscous, boneless quail enclosed in chicken mousseline with périgourdine sauce, and seared duck breast with red currant sauce and foie gras raviolis. We remember fondly an entrée of sweetbreads topped with two large slices of truffle and a subtle sauce. Another winner was chicken in a spicy curry sauce, accompanied by a large tray of outstanding chutneys, the tray decorated with white napkins folded to point up at each corner, giving it the appearance of a temple roof.

Overfull diners have been known to moan as the dessert cart laden with noble tortes, rich cakes and more rolls up. But how can one resist at least a taste of a silky coffee-kahlua mousse or an incredible many-layered pastry square, filled with whipped cream and raspberries?

After partaking of the meal, could anyone possibly have room for a full dessert? Our waiter, a former teacher whose wife was putting him through school, replied: "That's nothing. Some people have two or three."

Entrées, lunch $17.50 to $28, dinner $26.75 to $32. Open Tuesday-Saturday, lunch 11:30 to 1, dinner 6:30 to 8:30.

St. Andrew's Café, The Culinary Institute of America, Hyde Park.

For years, the institute's best-kept secret had been this café, transformed from the old Wechsler Coffeehouse and stressing low-fat nutritious food. Dropping in for what we expected would be a quick snack, we were astonished to partake of a memorable three-course lunch, all specially designed to be less than 1,000 calories.

It was a secret, that is, until it moved front and center into the CIA's General

Foods Nutrition Center, behind the main building. All here is state of the art as the CIA seeks to change Americans' eating habits through greater awareness of nutrition and the availability of healthful and delicious meals. That's public-relations jargon for what this café really produces, "good food that's good for you."

The café has gone upscale in decor. Ceramic vegetables on a breakfront in the foyer greet diners, who may see the tiled kitchen through windows behind the bar. Beyond is an expansive, 65-seat room with generally well-spaced tables set with white linens, heavy silver and, surprise, salt shakers that were notably missing in the old coffeehouse. A coffered ceiling, arched windows and upholstered rattan chairs contribute to a light, comfortable setting.

The remarkable appetizers and desserts are what we most remember from two lunches here. The first began with a Mediterranean seafood terrine with the seafood in chunks, on a wonderful sauce, and a smoked duck salad with raspberry vinaigrette, a beautiful presentation including about six exotic lettuces topped with raspberries, ringed by sliced pears. A later visit produced a crabmeat quesadilla with a jícama and citrus salad and an extravagant plateful of carpaccio of fresh tuna and oriental mushroom salad.

Hearty breads like rye, sunflower seed and whole wheat along with butter curls were offered no fewer than four times – surely the fourth would have blown the calorie limit.

Among main courses, barbecue-grilled chicken breast with black bean sauce and roast medallions of lamb with wild mushrooms and a potato pancake came with crisp young asparagus garnished with sesame seeds. These were preceded by salads of fancy greens, including endive, and tender peeled tomatoes. Garnishing the chicken dish was a peeled-back tomatillo filled with fresh salsa.

Desserts were, once, a pumpkin torte with cinnamon sauce and glazed pineapple madagascar, a concoction with rum, honey and peppercorns. The second visit yielded a Hudson Valley pear strudel with amaretto glacé and a remarkable warm apple sauté with graham-cracker crisps and apple pie glacé. The latter was so ample and eye-catching when presented at the next table that we thought it must have been prepared for a visiting dignitary (not so).

All this, with a glass of wine and a beer, came with tip to about $40 for lunch for two. And, according to the computer printout that you can request for a technical but interesting diet analysis, only the cappuccino took our meal over the 1,000-calorie limit.

The dinner menu, which also changes every few days, offers similar style and heartier main courses, many lately with an Asian accent. We figured one couldn't spend more than about $30 for a dinner of Louisiana chicken and shrimp gumbo, grilled tuna with soba noodles and Asian vegetables, and warm apple and cranberry crisp with ricotta glace. Wines by the glass, beers and natural juices are available.

As well as eating delicious food cooked with a minimum of salt, sugar and fat, you are given solicitous service such as is rarely found nowadays. If we lived nearby, we'd be tempted to eat here every week.

Entrées, lunch $16 to $18, dinner $17 to $20. Open Monday-Friday, lunch 11:30 to 1, dinner 6:30 to 8:30.

The Ristorante Caterina de' Medici, The Culinary Institute of America, Hyde Park. She seemed to be the poor stepsister of the CIA's roster of restaurants and was often closed. But you should see her now! Ensconced in the fabulous Colavita

Center for Italian Food and Wine, resembling a Tuscan-style villa, she is Cinderella at the ball. A nearly $7 million facility, encompassing kitchens, classrooms and restaurants, the center opened in 2001 with much fanfare.

The main dining room is a soaring space with handsome appointments, intricate chandeliers of Venetian glass and an olive tree in the center sculpted by a retired chef. There are smaller rooms on either side, one of which is the Al Forno dining room beside the open kitchen, and here walk-ins are welcome and a light menu is served between 1 and 6.

We enjoyed lunch in the main Joseph P. DeAlessandro dining room (everything here is named for a benefactor). The day's aperitif was a strawberry-flavored sparkling wine, a refreshing beginning. An "amuse" of crostini with caramelized red onions, raisins and pinenuts was delicious, as was the rustic bread, especially when dipped in the olive oil (Colavita, of course) poured into a dish. We liked the escarole and white bean soup, which was more like a thick minestrone, and a hearty pasta dish of pappardelle with duck ragu. The day's antipasto came in five little bowls and the trio of sorbets (blackberry, passionfruit and lemon) were intensely flavored.

A similar but expanded menu (written in Italian, with English translations) is offered at dinner. You might find orecchiette pasta with Italian sausage and broccoli rabe, pan-roasted striped bass with soft polenta and tomato-olive sauce, or grilled lamb chops with rosemary, caponata and caramelized spring onions. The wine list is Italian, ranging from $20 to $110, with many available by the glass (and the lunch crowd that day was quaffing lots of it).

An herb garden beside the villa provides herbs, flowers and heirloom vegetables. Our lunch was made even more interesting by the chef-hosted table of visiting Italians beside us, incredibly glamorous and with the best-behaved infant we have ever seen – living up to a magazine tribute as the best place to enjoy Italian cuisine and culture in the Hudson Valley.

Entrées, lunch $17 to $20, dinner $16 to $25. Open Monday-Friday, lunch 11:30 to 1, dinner 6:30 to 8:30.

The Best of the Best

McKinney & Doyle Fine Foods Café, 10 Charles Colman Blvd., Pawling.

The highest accolades go to this café, a fortuitous outgrowth of the Corner Bakery. "Excellent," declared the New York Times critic. "An all-time favorite," swooned the Poughkeepsie Journal. Founders Shannon McKinney and Brian Doyle moved to expanded quarters from a smaller bakery that had attracted national notice. Shannon now mans not only the bakery, but handles the restaurant operation as well.

And a fine restaurant it is. Sophisticated, stunningly executed fare is served in a comfortable, homespun atmosphere. After the bakery closes at 5, the old-fashioned, high-ceilinged storefront undergoes a dinner-time transformation. A curtain screens the bakery cases and a handful of tables are available for cocktails from a full-service bar. The adjacent dining room with upholstered booths takes on a softer, gentler ambiance. Exposed brick walls hold local memorabilia and art displays. Many and changing are the touches of whimsy: words of dining wisdom here and there, wine "racks" hanging from the ceiling, tree branches bearing colorful leaves during fall foliage season, and perhaps a window display with an amusing picture of chefs exercising amid an array of spring-form pans. Shannon lends his decorating skills and laconic wit to a space that exudes personality.

Shannon McKinney and crew have fun at McKinney & Doyle Fine Foods Café.

His kitchen talents and those of his sidekicks are equally diverse. For dinner, you might start with an asparagus-stilton strudel with spicy pecans and red pepper coulis, chicken and ginger spring rolls with ginger-wasabi dipping sauce, grilled Thai shrimp in peanut sauce over angel-hair pasta or lump crab cakes with Carolina coleslaw and rémoulade sauce. The best bread ever with sweet butter and an exceptional house salad of greens with stilton and pears one night, delicate beets and roasted pecans the next, come with. The main event could be pan-seared sesame tuna over mixed oriental vegetables with ginger-wasabi sauce, calves liver with hickory bacon and leeks, pan-roasted muscovy duck breast with applejack-soaked figs and cider sauce, and five-pepper filet mignon with courvoisier demi-glace. Be sure to save room for one of the bakery's fabulous desserts, perhaps valencia orange layer cake with citrus cream cheese filling, bananas foster or the signature "big fat butt cake" with snickers, heath bars, peanut butter and Hershey's chocolate.

Interesting fare also is offered at lunch, perhaps a wonderful bisque of shrimp and scallops in a creamy sauternes-leek broth, duck salad, chicken tostada grande, Shannon's "hogbreath vegetarian chili" with grilled jalapeño cornbread or a sandwich of roasted chicken and apricot salad served on a just-baked baguette. Brunch brings a panoply of egg dishes, banana pancakes, almond french toast, sandwiches and salads, and, at our visit, corned-beef hash served in its own cast-iron skillet with a shirred egg and bakery toast.

The award-winning wine list is affordable, with many available by the glass. The adjacent bakery dispenses all kinds of baked goods as well as a variety of foods to take out under the logo of McKinney & Doyle.

Oktoberfest beer-tasting dinners, wine tastings, a Christmas madrigal dinner, art exhibitions, mail-order – it takes their Word of Mouth newsletter just to follow all that these enterprising folks are up to.

(845) 855-3875. www.mckinneyanddoyle.com. Entrées, $18.50 to $26.50. Lunch, Tuesday-Friday 11:30 to 3. Dinner, Wednesday-Saturday 6 to 9, Sunday 5 to 9. Brunch, Saturday and Sunday 9 to 3.

Le Pavillon, 230 Salt Point Tpke. (Route 115), Poughkeepsie.

An unlikely looking brick Victorian house on the outskirts of town is home to an intimate, country French restaurant run by chef-owner Claude Guermont, who was born in Normandy and apprenticed himself to a French chef at age 14.

After a stintas an instructor at the CIA's Escoffier Restaurant, he opened Le Pavillon in 1980 against the prevailing wisdom that a fine restaurant could not survive in the area. In 1985, he wrote *The Norman Table*, an acclaimed cookbook of 200 regional recipes from his native land. And lately his restaurant vaulted into the upper echelons in the Zagat survey, which called it "a dependable, if pricey, little jewel."

You enter through a vestibule lined with clippings ("Chef has never really left Normandy," headlines one) into a brick and beamed bar. Dining is by candlelight in two intimate dining rooms, each accommodating 30. French posters and art, white service plates bearing a discreet Le Pavillon logo, black candles in small hurricane lamps and white linens contribute to a charming setting.

The French menu is priced from yesteryear, despite the Zagat description. "I try to stay with local products, make everything here and try to be a little contemporary – not entirely classic or nouvelle," Claude says.

Among appetizers, his sautéed frog's legs with garlic sauce and escargots simmered in herb-garlic sauce are highly rated. So are his Normandy-style onion soup, the shrimp and lobster bisque with sherry, the warm duck confit salad with mango vinaigrette and the changing preparation of fresh Hudson Valley foie gras.

The ten or so entrées have been updated lately to include the likes of rare ahi tuna with wasabi-soy sauce with such longtime favorites as sautéed sweetbreads in caper-brown butter sauce, rare roasted squab with cognac sauce, veal kidneys in spicy brandy-mustard sauce and steak au poivre. Trout soufflé, cassoulet, rabbit, quail, pheasant and New Zealand venison might be available as specials.

Desserts are hot soufflés and crêpes suzette, as well as French pastries, profiteroles, homemade sorbets and the like. Le Pavillon's award-winning wine list ranges widely from Hudson Valley vintages to French châteaux.

(845) 473-2525. www.lepavillonrestaurant.com. Entrées, $18 to $25. Dinner, Tuesday-Saturday 5:30 to 9:30.

Terrapin, 6426 Montgomery St., Rhinebeck.

Some of the area's suavest food emanates from this one-time Baptist church at the edge of downtown. It's actually two restaurants in one, a wall having been installed to divide the former sanctuary into a formal restaurant on one side and a lively bistro and bar on the other.

In contrast to local restaurateurs who tout indigenous cuisine, chef-owner Josh Kroner, an ex-New Yorker, favors "the world's most diverse flavors from far-flung origins." That translated at lunchtime to some of the most intense tastes we've enjoyed. The signature roasted garlic soup was comforting yet kicky, embellished with sherry, wine and cream and topped with an ancho chile crouton. The barbecued duck quesadilla, a fixture appetizer on the dinner menu, was light and soothing with a superior mango-avocado salsa. The oyster po-boy in a baguette was a knife-and-fork affair that was enough for two to share. Only the niggardly glasses of fumé blanc wine disappointed.

At night, the fairly extensive menu ranges from half a dozen pastas and several vegetarian dishes to roquefort-crusted filet mignon with port wine sauce. The chef might poach Pacific halibut with enoki mushrooms over dashi broth and udon noodles, enliven pork tenderloin with a Thai orange-coconut curry and spicy jade minted rice, and wrap sliced moulard duck breast and braised confit in crêpes and serve with peking sauce.

Sidewalk tables front Terrapin restaurant.

Start with lobster and shiitake mushroom cakes with citrus aioli or a crispy salmon spring roll with ginger sauce. Finish with a sweet cheese blini, warm chocolate cake with molten center or a selection of house-made sorbets and ice creams.

Similar fare is available in the high-ceilinged bistro/bar, where you can expect tapas, quesadillas, pastas and light entrées from macaroni and cheese to steak frites. In either venue, you will eat creatively and well. The soaring dining room with something of a modern Asian look and well-dressed tables on two levels is quieter and more refined.

(845) 876-3330. www.terrapinrestaurant.com. Entrées, $19.95 to $27.95. Dinner nightly, 5 to 10 or 11.

Bistro, $9.95 to $15.95. Lunch and dinner daily, 11 to midnight or later.

40 West, 40 West Market St., Rhinebeck.

This rustic, two-story space with exposed beams and a wraparound balcony hints of its former life as a blacksmith shop. Co-owners Thomas Turck and chef Wesley Dire, a CIA grad, run a low-profile operation that wins plaudits for some of the most innovative cuisine in the Hudson Valley. One of Wesley's sidekicks touts it as "a very eclectic place for people with a New York City appetite."

The main floor consists of a bar along one side, a tiny kitchen in back and a handful of tables flanked by high-back blond cane chairs with leopard-print seats. Most of the dining takes place in the upstairs lofts, with the waitstaff scurrying up and down narrow stairs to deliver the dinner fare. Muted gray-green walls soften the beams that frame the room and frosted blue lights illuminate the bar.

The seasonal menu combines Asian and Southwest influences. We'd gladly make a meal of such appetizers as a smoked chicken spring roll with Asian radicchio, the house-cured salmon niçoise with quail eggs and haricots vert, the fried oysters with wasabi-lime vinaigrette, and the phyllo-wrapped goat cheese served warm with Lebanese fig jam, toasted crostini and mixed greens.

Equally enticing are main courses ranging from barbecued king salmon with cilantro-lime vinaigrette, zucchini frites and chipotle whipped potatoes to grilled filet mignon with white truffle jus and smoked gouda mac 'n' cheese. Expect the likes of cast-iron roasted sea bass with saffron-tomato fumé, black and white sesame-seed shrimp with stir-fried vegetables and soba noodles, and charbroiled pork scaloppine with pancetta and grain mustard. Duck might be prepared two ways: a chile-honey glazed breast and a barbecued confit tostada, served with chipotle-whipped potatoes, black bean salsa and cilantro sour cream.

Cool the palate with such desserts as crisp almond tuile "cones" filled with lemon mousse and drizzled with raspberry coulis, an old-fashioned cobbler with dried cherries, macerated figs and vanilla ice cream, crème brûlée with papaya and crystallized ginger or pineapple-sambuca granita.

The fairly priced wine list holds some not-often-seen offerings from near and far.

(845) 876-2214. Entrées, $20 to $26. Dinner nightly except Wednesday, 5 to 10 or 11.

More Good Dining

Le Canard Enchaîne, 276 Fair St., Kingston.

Chamonix in the French Alps was home for chef Jean-Jacques Carquillat, who started as a pastry chef at Gaston le Notre Paris in France and trained at The Reserve and Le Bernardin in New York before marrying the daughter of Catskills restaurateurs and launching his own ever-so-French bistro in uptown Kingston. "Welcome to the South of France," proclaimed their opening menu. "Delicious," advised one local connoisseur when asked what she thought of the low-key restaurant. A Kingston reviewer rated it the Hudson Valley's best restaurant.

Jean-Jacques and his wife, Jennifer Madden, employed two side-by-side storefront rooms to create a bistro that looks as if it belongs on the main street of Avignon. They turned one section into Rive Gauche, a plush piano bar and lounge that also serves as an art gallery.

Local folks often drop in for homemade croissants and café au lait, served as it is in France in "a big bowl," Jean notes. Lunch could be a sampling from more than a dozen salads, including the classic salade lyonnaise, or a sandwich, perhaps grilled cajun chicken with watercress on a baguette.

The namesake "enchanted duck" is the specialty at dinner at Le Canard, varying from grilled with orange-fennel sauce on braised endive to roasted with grilled sweet potatoes. Other entrées include trout amandine, grilled tuna with a wasabi coulis, shrimp indochine over Asian rice, roasted organic chicken basquaise, calves liver lyonnaise over roasted garlic potatoes, grilled ribeye steak maître-d with french fries and New Zealand rack of lamb with a balsamic-merlot reduction.

Start with coquilles St. Jacques, a country pâté platter or fricassee of escargots with wild mushrooms flamed in cognac. Finish with crème brûlée, tarte tatin or another of the specialty fruit tarts. Jean-Jacques makes a point of table hopping between stints in the kitchen to say hello to his loyal clientele.

(845) 339-2003. www.lecanard-enchaine.net. Entrées, $19 to $34. Lunch and dinner daily, 11:30 to 10 or 11.

Gigi Trattoria, 6422 Montgomery St., Rhinebeck.

Somewhat hidden along Rhinebeck's main street, the facade is unassuming and easy to miss, except in summer when sidewalk tables catch the eye. The interior is

Robust Mediterranean fare is featured in airy front dining area at Gigi Trattoria.

relatively small and minimalist, with a circular bar in front and a pair of dining areas, one with a high ceiling in front and the other with a low ceiling in back. The rich wood tables are left uncovered. The window ledges are adorned with bottles and foodstuffs, the burnt siena walls are dotted with local artworks, and a couple of high beams and ducts are left exposed.

It is not as showy or over the top as its website might indicate, even though the owner is Laura Pensiero, a cookbook author, nutritionist and culinary consultant. Laura helped turn part of a former automobile showroom in Rhinebeck into an urban-modern trattoria and moved into the limelight following the departure of founding chef Gianna Scappin, her ex-husband.

Subsequent chefs execute the original menu she calls "Hudson Valley Mediterranean," a personal interpretation of traditional Italian dishes made with the bounty of the Hudson Valley. The menu is categorized by traditional Italian courses, such as skizza (flatbread pizzas), antipasti, cheeses, salads, primi, main courses and side dishes. The "Mamma" pizza bears Tuscan-style porchetta ham, fennel salami, tomato and mozzarella. The crispy calamari comes with spicy tomato-serrano pepper-garlic sauce. The barbina salad is composed of baby greens, roasted beets, asparagus and mushrooms, topped with goat cheese and toasted walnuts.

The heart of the menu are the changing pastas and risottos, perhaps rigatoni with spicy sausage, peas, tomatoes and a touch of cream or funghetti, herbed gnocchi with peas, pearl onions and spring mushrooms, topped with shaved pecorino and crispy prosciutto. The handful of main courses include baby chicken roasted under a brick with sausage, pan-roasted salmon with smoked paprika jus, veal scaloppine with wild mushrooms and parmesan shavings, and ribeye steak grilled with rosemary and olive oil, sliced and served with Tuscan fries. Four vegetables are available as side dishes.

Tiramisu, lemon tart brûlée and cantucci, the house-made biscotti with almonds, are typical desserts. The all-Italian wine list represents many regions and is on the pricey side.

(845) 876-1007. www.gigitrattoria.com. Entrées, $22.95 to $36.95. Lunch, Tuesday-Sunday 11:30 to 2:45, Friday-Sunday in winter. Dinner, Tuesday-Sunday from 4:30.

Le Petit Bistro, 8 East Market St., Rhinebeck.

His staff took over where retiring chef-owner Jean-Paul Crozier left off, and their loyal fans report this long-running French charmer – an enduring culinary treasure amid Rhinebeck's sea of new faces – is better than ever. After manager Dan Bleen assumed interim ownership, he was joined by CIA-graduate Joseph Dalu from the late Old Chatham Sheepherding Company Inn kitchen as chef. When Joseph and his wife Jennifer Bell bought the place, Dan and his wife Susan continued to work the front of the house.

Pine walls and floors give the 40-seat dining room and half-circle bar at the side a warm, country-French look. Except for globe lamps inside wooden frames, the decor is simple and the atmosphere convivial and intimate.

The French menu starts with classics like onion soup, pâté maison, smoked trout and escargots bourguignonne. English dover sole, offered meunière or grenobloise, is a house specialty and the priciest item on the value-priced menu. Sea scallops with crushed black peppercorns and cream sauce, duck with chef's choice of sauce, veal scaloppine, frog's legs, rack of lamb provençal and steak au poivre are among the choices.

Regulars tout Joseph's nightly seafood specials, which tend to show a broader Mediterranean influence. Scallops provençal, pan-seared yellow pike, pan-roasted sablefish, and pasta with clams and scallops were posted on the chalkboard at our latest visit.

Desserts include crème brûlée, creamy New York cheesecake, mocha mousse, raspberry frappe and peach melba.

(845) 876-7400. www.lepetitbistro.com. Entrées, $18.75 to $29.95. Dinner, Thursday-Monday 5 to 10, Sunday 4 to 9.

Sabroso, 22 Garden St., Rhinebeck.

Its name means tasty or delightful, and both descriptions fit this new Latin-inspired restaurant in the space vacated by the late Cripple Creek Restaurant. Self-taught chefs Marcia Miller and Erica Mahlkuch and partner Christopher Long created a soft, sunny L-shaped room with buttery colors and pastel accents. It's a pleasant backdrop for food spanning a range of South American countries.

The trio operated Caffe Bocce for ten years in the small village of Scottsville, south of Charlottesville, Va. But their ties to the Hudson Valley drew them here. They offer a novel brand of "Latin world cuisine" inspired by the peoples who settled the continent from Spain, Portugal, France, Italy and Asia, among others. That makes for some mighty interesting dishes, offered as tapas or principal plates.

Grazers are in their element with such tapas as a trio of seviche or a trio of arepas with roasted corn salsa, lime crema and queso blanco. Or you might try littleneck clams with chorizo, tomato and a cilantro-lime pesto; chile-dusted calamari with guafillo sauce and poblano-lime aioli, or sugar-cane skewered shrimp over field greens with hearts of palm, papaya and pomegranate-ginger vinaigrette.

For the main course, the chefs might wrap halibut in a banana leaf, stuff it with tostones (plantains) and serve it in a chipotle-citrus broth. Or they might stuff a whole red snapper with coconut-cilantro rice and finish it with a tomato-mango sauce. The paella bears chicken, chorizo, shrimp, mussels, clams and papaya. Other options include fire-grilled tuna with tropical salsa and a quinoa salad, roast guava-plum duck with a chayote sweet-potato hash and grilled skirt steak with sweet potato fries and chimichurri.

Typical of the desserts is a dense French chocolate cake laced with cointreau and served with banana ice cream.

Sangria, mojitos and wines from Spain, Chile and Argentina are featured at the bar.

(845) 876-8688. www.sabrosoplatos.com. Entrées, $19.95 to $28.95. Dinner nightly except Tuesday, from 5:30.

Calico Restaurant & Patisserie, 6384 Mill St. (Route 9), Rhinebeck.

A perfect five-star rating from the Poughkeepsie restaurant reviewer followed the opening of this snug little hideaway in a twenty-seat storefront across from the famous Beekman Arms. The stars were for the food offered by CIA grad Anthony Balassone, an alumnus of Le Pavillon in Poughkeepsie, and the baked goods of his wife Leslie.

The patisserie in front opens at 8 for croissants and brioche. Come lunch time, the kitchen offers a handful of interesting choices, perhaps seafood chili with cornbread, house-smoked salmon fillet served on a mixture of greens and roasted porcini mushrooms, pizza of the day and sliced flank steak on a toasted baguette. The gratinéed vidalia onion soup laced with Anchor Steam ale makes a good starter. So does the award-winning roasted garlic soup with crème fraîche and an herbed brioche crouton.

For dinner, chef Tony prepares such treats as a classic bouillabaisse, pan-roasted salmon fillet with a light braised shallot and baby spinach cream sauce, sliced pork tenderloin with apple-raisin compote, roast duckling glazed with a honey-peach reduction and grilled New York shell steak with hunter sauce.

Start with a terrine of roasted garlic layered with pesto and Coach Farms goat cheese or a grilled portobello mushroom with sautéed shrimp and pesto sauce. Finish with one of the more than twenty exceptional desserts from the pastry case.

Artifacts and calico items adorn a shelf above the pale blue wainscoting of this pure and simple place beloved by the locals. It has a full liquor license. The wine list features boutique vineyards and good values.

(845) 876-2749. www.calicorhinebeck.com. Entrées, $17.95 to $21.95. Lunch, Wednesday-Sunday 11 to 2:30. Dinner, Wednesday-Saturday from 5:30.

Twist, 4290 Albany Post Road (Route 9), Hyde Park.

Finally, Hyde Park has a good, independently owned restaurant worthy of the name. And it's not run by the CIA, though it has a CIA connection. Benjamin Mauk, who graduated first in his class in two consecutive degree programs at the CIA, and his wife Ellen Henneberry, the manager, took over a former pizzeria in 2004 following the closing of Cripple Creek Restaurant in Rhinebeck, where he had been chef. Several months of sweat equity turned the L-shaped space in a downtown strip plaza up against the street into a colorful, casual American restaurant with a refreshing sense of humor.

Chef Ben puts a creative twist on American food and the neighborhood restaurant genre, which accounts for the name. An open kitchen takes up fully half the space. You can eat on high stools at a counter facing the kitchen goings-on, or opt to sit amidst a mix of pine tables and booths around two sides. A huge mural and tiny hanging halogen lamps provide color.

Instead of bread, a cone of puff-pastry cheese twists is placed on the table. The menu also represents a departure from the neighborhood restaurant norm. Here you'll find starters from twisted caesar (with tortilla strips and asiago cheese) to spicy shrimp skewers with Asian slaw, chicken liver pâté, and crab and corn quesadilla with avocado and tomato salsa. There are half a dozen entrées from miso-rubbed tilapia with soy-mustard sauce to grilled veal chop with roasted shallot sauce. Of equal note are the three steak offerings (cowboy, strip and filet mignon). You mix and match potatoes, vegetables and sauces, choosing one item among four or five in each category. Also available is a "seafood bar," with peel-and-eat shrimp, steamed littlenecks, steamed cockles and fried calamari ordered by the quarter, half or full pound.

Desserts vary from lemon curd with raspberry sauce to an almond and pear tart with caramel sauce.

The wine list is short and modestly priced from $17 to $24.

(845) 229-7094. Entrées, $16 to $24. Lunch, Tuesday-Saturday 11:30 to 2:30. Dinner, Tuesday-Saturday 5 to 9 or 10.

Phoenix Rising, 6423 Montgomery St., Rhinebeck.

The name indicates chef-owner Matthew Fraiman's concept for a progressive eatery serving new comfort cuisine. And the mod 65-seat dining room and lounge certainly have visual style. The with-it establishment in the tony new Montgomery Row shopping center linking Montgomery and Garden streets represents another star in Rhinebeck's galaxy of culinary attractions.

This one's goal is to provide "a warm, casual and fun atmosphere for any time and any mood." It does so with an all-day menu of soups and starters, ample salads (cobb to waldorf), flatbread pizzas, sandwiches (lunch only) and "old-fashioned favorites" featuring local ingredients. The last range from macaroni and cheese and chicken pot pie to trout amandine, Carolina barbecue pork, meatloaf and grilled ribeye steak.

We found the ambiance, frankly, more appealing than the menu. But lunch on the sidewalk patio proved rewarding – and considerably quieter than on the patios of restaurants where passing trucks brake along the main street.

(845) 876-8686. www.phoenixrhinebeck.com. Entrées, $10 to $19. Open daily, 11 to 10; late menu, 10 to close.

Tapas with a Twist

Coast, 69 Broadway, Tivoli.

Tapas from four of the world's coastal regions – the Pacific Rim, Arabian Sea, Mediterranean and Gulf Coast – are featured at this novel eatery what washed up on the Hudson River shores in 2005. Landing in the space of the former Café Pongo, it offers imaginative fare in a funky interior separated into two dining areas by a long bar in the middle, with stools facing the bar on both sides. Map-like paintings of imaginary peninsulas, bays and fjords surrounded by blue seas convey a coastal theme.

You can snack at the bar or make a mighty interesting meal from chef Matt Ifkovitz's array of tapas categorized by their coastal origin. Start perhaps with a trio of Middle Eastern spreads on warm pitas from the Arabian Sea, spicy duck wontons with sweet dipping sauce from the Pacific Rim and the Mediterranean trio of salmon – house-cured salmon, smoked salmon mousse and grilled salmon cake.

Want more salmon? Try the miso-glazed salmon with summer cabbage kimchee. Or continue your explorations with Jamaican jerk pork skewers on pineapple salsa from the (extended) Gulf Coast or the Ethiopian spiced lamb with mint chutney. How about some chicken? You can order spicy chipotle-seasoned flautas from the Gulf region or chicken satay in a Thai peanut sauce.

There are a few rather mundane soups, salads and starches among the selection of tapas, plus a "cabana" menu of burgers, wraps, pastas and chicken tenders for anyone who thinks tapas are for twits. Coast desserts are for big-eaters: perhaps a trio of chocolate chip cookies with vanilla bean ice cream, warm chocolate mousse cake with raspberry-espresso crème anglaise or chiffon cheesecake with mixed berry coulis.

(845) 757-2772. www.coast69.com. Tapas, $6 to $15. Lunch, Tuesday-Saturday 11:30 to 3:30. Dinner, Tuesday-Sunday from 6. Sunday brunch, 11 to 3.

California Spirit

Cascade Mountain Winery & Restaurant, 835 Cascade Mountain Road, Amenia.

Why is a winery listed under dining choices? Because this out-of-the-way place is a gem, known as much for its creative food prepared from local ingredients as for its award-winning wines and a funky, California kind of spirit. In fact, we almost felt we were on a Napa Valley hillside the sunny autumn day we lingered on one of several decks overlooking the apple orchards, enjoying a bottle of seyval blanc and some appealing luncheon fare.

Another time, our party of four enjoyed a thick butternut-squash soup, a gingered carrot soup, a clear leek soup with roasted garlic and a foie gras pâté with cranberry chutney. Then we dug into excellent pan-browned trout with lemon and capers, a Hudson Valley cheese sampler plate, succulent crab cakes with cajun rémoulade sauce and the signature grilled chicken breast – grilled right on the deck – stuffed with Coach Farm goat cheese in puff pastry. An apple-pear crisp, a plum tart with lavender crème anglaise, spiced maple cheesecake with gingersnap crust and a chocolate-raspberry marjolaine ended a leisurely, memorable meal. The bill was written on the back of a wine label.

After lunch, we stepped gingerly around workmen to enter the main winery downstairs. It's an unexpectedly small and primitive affair, considering the merit of the output (it made the strongest showing of any winery east of the Rockies at a couple of wine competitions). The chief workman turned out to be William Wetmore, owner-winemaker and author of four novels, a jack-of-all-trades who produces almost as many red wines as whites because of his grape-planting decisions three decades ago.

A couple of typewritten sheets inside cellophane wrappers pointed out salient facets of winemaking for self-guided tours. Visitors taste wines in the crowded and convivial downstairs setting, where no one takes things too seriously. How could they, at a place where a couple of favorite bottlings are called Heavenly Daze and Pardonnez-Moi? The latter is billed as a dry red wine "for social emergencies," but is also a play on the word chardonnay. The Wetmore family named their beaujolais-style red release Coeur de Lion, meaning heart of the lion, after 60 Minutes documented the drinking of red wine as good for the heart.

Such is the homespun fun of Cascade Mountain Vineyards, a place full of integrity.

(845) 373-9021. www.cascademt.com. Entrées, $12 to $18. Lunch, Thursday-Sunday, noon to 3.

Offbeat Gourmet

The Texas Taco, Route 22, Patterson.

Rosemary Jamison, who hails from Texas, began selling tacos in front of the Plaza Hotel in Manhattan in 1968 "before anyone even knew what they were," she says with a laugh. Within a week she had lines down the block. Moving to Patterson in 1971, she proceeded to fill her small house with flea-market objects and now not an inch is left uncovered and barely a blade of grass outside, either. Even the curbs, paving stones and driveways are painted in wild colors to match the exterior of the house.

Rosemary Jamison at The Texas Taco.

Cooking from her old New York cart that's ensconced in what must have been a dining room off the kitchen, she serves tacos, burritos, tostadas, chili, guacamole and fiesta dogs and that's about it. "Very simple, and I don't have to do a lot of ordering," she explains. With a rhinestone on her front tooth and long green hair ("I change it to fit my mood") at our visit, Rosemary is someone hard to miss.

Tiny dining rooms are filled with small tables, with hundreds of business cards displayed under their glass tops. Old toys, Marilyn Monroe collectibles, posters, jewelry – there's so much to look at you can't begin to take it all in. The bathroom is unique – Rosemary thinks it gives one a feeling of being in an aquarium, with a huge shark on the ceiling.

On the front lawn are a bunch of pink flamingo statuettes and the most motley collection of lawn chairs we ever saw. Even Rosemary's pickup truck is decorated to the max with stickers and jewelry. The Patterson flea-market people understand her tastes and bring to her door things they know she'll buy. Now an icon in the area, she lives in the cellar and rarely goes out except to cater parties. "I have no family," she volunteers, "so this is my life."

Her place sure has character. Her tacos are pretty darned good, too.

(845) 878-9665. Prices, $1.25 to $2.75. Open daily, 11:30 to 9.

Dining and Lodging

Le Chambord, 2737 Route 52, Hopewell Junction 12533.

Here, thanks to the eighteen-hour days of versatile innkeeper Roy Benich, is a distinguished restaurant, a small antique shop and art gallery, and an inn and conference center focused on a pillared, glistening white Georgian Colonial mansion with dark green shutters and an ornate statue on the front patio. The dining rooms are posh, the guest rooms quite European, and romance permeates every nook and cranny. "New Yorkers love this," says Roy, who was previously at the city's Tavern on the Green. "They're only an hour from Midtown but way out in the country."

First things first. The contemporary French food overseen for more than twenty years by executive chef Leonard Mott is superb, from the duck pâté and green salad with all kinds of julienned vegetables that began our dinners to the almond pastry shell filled with whipped cream and luscious fresh raspberries that was the crowning touch.

A complimentary plate of small canapés (two like an egg salad and four of salmon mousse with golden caviar) and a small loaf of sourdough bread came with drinks. For appetizers, expect such exotica as a warm goat cheese and walnut flan with dried cranberry ragoût or lobster raviolis with sturgeon caviar sauce. Among entrées ranging from sautéed sweetbreads to tournedos rossini, the veal chop sautéed with diced onions and a touch of paprika proved a standout. One of us tried the tasting menu, which changes weekly. It brought mesquite-smoked flank steak carpaccio with corn relish, sea scallops in puff pastry with ginger and oregano, medallions of pork in calvados sauce, steamed salmon with carrots, and breast of chicken with broccoli and fennel, plus a trio of chocolate desserts and excellent decaf coffee.

All this was served with polish in one of the two intimate dining rooms, where the tables for two were so large that we had to slide our chairs and place settings closer together to avoid shouting. Lighting is fairly bright from a crystal chandelier as well as candles, plus the lights illuminating each work in a collection of art worth quite a bundle, we were told. The bound wine list, complete with table of contents, starts in the high teens and rises rapidly to $2,200. Roy sold for $4,100 an 1891 port from Portugal, one of the oldest available in the world and one of more than 30 vintage ports he had obtained on trips to Portugal and Madeira and displays proudly on a hallway credenza. Our more modest Parducci chardonnay was poured into champagne flute glasses.

Rack of lamb for two is highly recommended; it might be encrusted with pistachios or topped with a coating of kiwi, grapefruit, honey and cumin, and served with a tarragon sauce. The fish course represents "a new creation every night," says Roy, and the sauce that accompanies the roast duck is ever-changing – plum one night, tangerine and vodka the next – "to keep things exciting." Desserts range from chocolate mousse and tulipe aux framboises to soufflés and crêpes suzette.

Upstairs on the second and third floors are nine spacious and recently refurbished guest rooms, each with television and telephone. They're furnished in different periods with European and American antiques.

Out back in a pillared Georgian Colonial structure that Roy had built and named Tara Hall are sixteen large guest rooms with sitting areas and what he calls a "Gone with the Wind" theme. Imported tapestries adorn the sofas and chairs, the queensize beds include canopies and four-posters, and toiletries await on faux-marble vanities in the large bathrooms. The mahogany furniture includes a European-style desk

Old Drovers Inn Tap Room is a cozy and historic setting for dining.

and a full-length, freestanding mirror in each room. An outdoor terrace with a sitting area goes off the fireplaced lobby.

Guests are served a complimentary continental breakfast (fruit, juices, and croissants and scones baked by the inn's two pastry chefs) in the main restaurant. Downstairs in the cozy Marine Bar at night, exotic coffees and cordials are offered in front of the fireplace.

(845) 221-1941. www.lechambord.com. Twenty-five rooms with private baths. Doubles, $160.

Entrées, $23 to $36. Lunch, Monday-Friday 11:30 to 2:30. Dinner, Monday-Saturday 6 to 10, Sunday 3:30 to 9.

Old Drovers Inn, Old Route 22, Box 100, Dover Plains 12522.

The sense of history is palpable in this out-of-the-way, white wood inn, built in 1750 to serve the cattle drovers traveling to New York City on the post roads. It's been in continuous operation ever since under three long-term owners until it changed hands in 2005 for only the fourth time. David Wilson, who earlier ran inns in New Orleans and Natchez, Miss., and managed restaurants in New York and Boston, took over a going concern, one that had become the world's smallest Relais & Châteaux property. The only major change he made was creating a two-bedroom suite on the third floor out of the former innkeeper's quarters and naming it the Pitcher Suite in honor of Alice Pitcher, who decided to concentrate her energies on her B&B on Cape Cod.

In addition to the suite there are four guest rooms, two with king beds and two with queens. Three have fireplaces. Largest is the Meeting Room, so-called because it served that function for the Town of Dover in the 19th century. Long and fairly wide, it boasts the only known barrel-shaped (rounded) ceiling in New York State. Nightly turndown service brings a plate with an apple, chocolate mints and truffles.

The museum-quality main floor houses a fireplaced parlor/TV room, a long reception hall and the grand Federal Room with five remarkable Edward Paine murals of local and valley scenes. This was the inn's original dining room (the drovers imbibed in the Tap Room downstairs). Now it's the romantic setting in which to order a leisurely, complimentary breakfast off a blackboard menu on weekends (continental during the week).

Few rooms anywhere feel more historic and romantic than the Tap Room, site of the inn's acclaimed restaurant. Forty-two diners can be seated in a stone and beamed room lit almost entirely by candles that fairly sparkle inside hurricane chimneys day and night. Tables, dressed in gray and burgundy linens, are set with red and white service plates bearing pictures of the inn. More hurricane chimneys etched with eagles top the bar and brass utensils adorn the fireplace. An outdoor courtyard also is popular in summer.

Chef Scott Penney's updated American menu is rooted firmly in the past, including two long-time specialties, cheddar cheese soup, served piping hot in a pewter cauldron, and wild turkey hash, its tender potatoes serving as a nest for a poached egg topped with lemon hollandaise.

Hunger is assuaged by a basket of house-made flatbread crisps and mini toasts, crudités, olives and a plate of deviled eggs glazed with a subtle mustard sauce. Contemporary touches are evident in such appetizers as seared crawfish and sesame-crusted shrimp over a chilled noodle salad and a squash blossom stuffed with goat cheese and served over a mushroom ragoût.

Entrées range from pan-seared sea bass with caviar crème fraîche to classic beef wellington. Among the possibilities are wild Alaskan salmon with morel mushrooms, roasted Peking duck breast and braised leg with sweet pomegranate-maple sauce, and rack of lamb with tomato chutney.

Favorite desserts are key lime pie, vanilla bean crème brûlée and warm English chocolate cake perched on a disc of hard sauce flecked with candied ginger.

(845) 832-9311. Fax (845) 832-6356. www.olddroversinn.com. Four rooms and one two-bedroom suite with private baths. Doubles, $210 to $490 weekends, $190 to $315 midweek.

Entrées, $20 to $39. Lunch, Friday noon to 3, Saturday and Sunday noon to 4. Dinner nightly except Wednesday from 5, Saturday and Sunday from 4.

Belvedere Mansion, 10 Old Route 9, Staatsburg (Box 785, Rhinebeck 12572).

Erected in 1900 on a hilltop overlooking the Hudson, this Greek Revival mansion is named for its beautiful view. Formerly a fasting spa, it took on quite a different life in 1995 as an elegant restaurant and an expanding inn and function facility

The restaurant on the main floor gets good reviews under auspices of owners Nikola and Patricia Rebraca, who had run Panarella's restaurant on Manhattan's West Side since 1979. They seat 60 diners in high Victorian dining rooms of the chandelier, fireplace and gilt-framed painting variety. There's also an unusual but romantic table for two or four in a little tea room at the head of the stairway landing.

The contemporary dinner menu is short and straightforward. Appetizers vary from puree of roasted garlic, fennel and potato soup with house-made duck prosciutto to warm wild mushroom tartlets with shaved parmesan and baby arugula. Entrées could include chermoula-marinated red snapper in Moroccan spiced tomato broth, grilled free-range chicken with porcini butter and mustard-thyme juices and pan-roasted filet mignon with cracked black pepper sauce. Expect surprises like pan-seared Alaskan cod served over ratatouille or sautéed ocean perch over purple Peruvian potatoes with fennel and blood orange reduction. Homemade desserts include chocolate truffle cake with mango crème anglaise, raspberry swirl cheesecake with berry coulis and a trio of sorbets.

Upstairs are six guest rooms and a three-bedroom suite of mansion proportions, appointed with the Gilded Age in mind. The rear Roosevelt Room with an English Tudor canopy bed is masculine and mysterious in chocolate brown with gold trim. "There are a lot of pictures to get crooked around here," Patricia noted as she straightened a couple while showing us around. All rooms have marble baths, ceiling fans and matching French Empire queen beds and mirrored armoires.

Behind and to the side of the mansion is a lineup of ten rooms with separate entrances in a carriage house. Euphemistically called cottages, they're decorated differently with as much pizzazz as their simplicity and space would allow (a hand-painted bureau here, a wicker chair there). Six have king beds and four "cozies" each have a double bed tucked away in an alcove, a bathroom and not much more.

More inviting are newer accommodations in a renovated lodge in the Adirondack style beyond the carriage house. Ten rooms here are dressed in Ralph Lauren and Laura Ashley country style. All have bathrooms with slate floors and walls (even the showers), and some have whirlpool tubs. Lighting is low, the chairs cane and the feeling rather Oriental – Nikola calls it "very Zen like." Rooms open off a wraparound cedar porch shared by guests.

The ultimate are four with marble baths and fireplaces in the Hunting Lodge. Two suites here have king beds and whirlpool tubs.

A country breakfast is served from 9 to 10 in the dining room or on the terrace. It generally includes a choice of omelets, perhaps with Coach Farm goat cheese and oven-dried tomatoes, walnut-crusted french toast or Hudson Valley pear pancakes.

The ten-acre property includes a rear pool with cabanas, a tennis court and a pond with a gazebo. A trellised glass conservatory furnished with lounges overlooks an elaborate French garden.

(845) 889-8000. www.belvederemansion.com. Thirty-one rooms with private baths. Doubles, $275 to $350 in mansion, $175 to $450 in lodges, $95 to $195 in cottages.

Entrées, $22.50 to $27. Dinner, Thursday-Sunday from 5:30.

Beekman Arms, 6387 Mill St. (Route 9), Rhinebeck 12572.

Dating from 1766, this is America's oldest continuously operating inn. It passed a milestone in 2002 when Charles LaForge Jr., owner since 1958, turned over the keys to Edward Banta Sr. of Poughkeepsie, owner of Super 8 motels and a steakhouse chain. The retiring innkeeper was the longest lasting of the Beekman's fourteen landlords listed on a plaque at the entry.

The inn's leased restaurant operation was changed. The much-ballyhooed (and over-rated) Beekman 1776 Tavern disappeared along with all vestiges of its owner, New York celebrity chef Larry Forgione, "the godfather of American cuisine." Now known as **The Traphagen Restaurant,** it continues to get mixed reviews, as it has in the past. But at least the kitchen's reach no longer exceeds its grasp. Catering to the tourist crowd, the menu mixes the trendy with the tried-and-true. Expect to find onion soup gratinée and fried calamari marinara among such starters as crispy rock shrimp with sauces of apricot and wasabi, and five-spice duck confit with an apricot-fig demi-glace. For entrées, a burger, country-style meatloaf and "Dutch-style turkey pot pie" are listed alongside pan-seared mahi mahi with a tropical salsa and filet mignon with a forest mushroom demi-glace.

The ambiance is properly historic in the dark and beamed, low-ceilinged Tap Room, the Pewter Room and the Wine Cellar Room, with wooden tables and many private booths, all lit by candles, even at midday. The front greenhouse room facing the center of town, which can be opened to the outside on nice days, feels more sophisticated and contemporary.

Elsewhere in the main inn, history is also evident. A guest log from 1887 is embedded in a coffee table in the far parlor. The thirteen guest rooms upstairs have been remodeled and redecorated with folk art accents lately, but except for their new TVs and telephones remain true to their 18th-century heritage.

More accommodations are found in the Delamater complex a long block up the street from the main inn. The gingerbread-trimmed 1844 Delamater House, one of the few early examples of American Carpenter Gothic residences still in existence, offers a B&B experience. Television sets are hidden in the armoires of its six rooms, sherry awaits in decanters, and front and rear porches are great for relaxing. Behind it are top-of-the-line rooms in the cathedral-ceilinged Carriage House and five other guest houses scattered around the perimeter of the Delamater Courtyard. Each holds four to eight rooms, about half with working fireplaces. Guests here take continental breakfast in a side building with a gift shop and tables overlooking the courtyard lawn.

(845) 876-7077 or (800) 361-6517. www.beekmandelameterinn.com. Sixty-seven rooms and two suites with private baths. Doubles, $140 to $300 in inn; $100 to $250 in Delamater complex.

Restaurant (845) 876-1766. Entrées, $16.50 to $36.50. Lunch daily, 11:30 to 3. Dinner, 5:30 to 9 or 9:30. Sunday, brunch 10 to 2, dinner 3:30 to 9.

The Good (And Social) Life

The Inn at Bullis Hall, 88 Hunns Lake Road, Box 630, Bangall 12506.

A posh country-house hotel in a remote, who-ever-heard-of-it hamlet called Bangall? That was the vision of restorationist Addison Berkey, a former publisher of art books. After designing or restoring a couple of dozen houses over two decades of living in the Hudson Valley, the suave socialite sold his 400-acre farm and turned a decaying Greek Revival structure at the edge of Millbrook hunt country into a small luxury inn "for all my friends and whoever else shows up" – many of them sportsmen and equestrians associated with the Millbrook Hunt.

This tale of an improbable inn and semi-public restaurant involves Addison and the multi-columned structure with quite a history. It began in 1832 as the residence of the Bullis family and expanded on both sides to embrace variously a post office and store, Civil War enlistment center, theater, speakeasy and, lately, a few apartments. The rambling sprawl was "really defiled" when Addison took possession in 2000. He gutted the interior and produced a variety of stunning common areas that bespeak history and affluence, five upscale bedrooms and suites of great style and comfort, and a gourmet restaurant for inn guests and members of its private dining club.

At first blush, the front of the inn smack up against rural County Route 65 does not look the part of the "expansive well-staffed English country house where one is fortunate enough to be a guest for the weekend," as the inn's elaborate website describes it. But the interior and the rear of the building, hidden up a hill with a veranda overlooking lush lawns and gardens, fulfill that vision. The front door opens into an entrance hall, off which on one side is a library equipped with a cigar humidor. The other side opens into an oak-paneled bar/foyer where the latest volume of the Social Register lies discreetly on a table beside a giant antique camera atop a

Addison and Lauren Berkey await guests in front of The Inn at Bullis Hall.

tripod, and a stash of liquors awaits guests who help themselves. Beyond is a dining room with a rustic feel, centered by a table set for ten and, off to the side, a round table for two.

On the second floor, which is at ground level at the rear and serves as the guest entry, are a couple of ever-so-historic-looking Georgian rooms that do double duty as sitting and dining areas. Here also are the guest accommodations. The biggest is the Donald Pierpont Suite with a kingsize bedroom, a casually plush living room, a dressing room with a jacuzzi tub at the side and a large bathroom. A backgammon room leads to the Ethan Emery Room, a quiet hideaway with king bed, jacuzzi and working fireplace overlooking the back lawn. The Peter Berkey Suite has a king bedroom, a library/living room and french doors onto the front balcony. Queen beds are in the Jonathan Underwood, the smallest suite, and the intimate Margaretta Mitchell Room. All the bathrooms are new and all the beds are dressed in Italian linens and down comforters. TVs, telephones and Frette robes are in each room.

Addison and his wife Lauren, who live on the third floor, started cooking dinners for guests who lamented the lack of good restaurants close by. They soon hired a chef, added dinner seating in the hallways, the library and the upstairs living room and can accommodate up to 28 dining guests in a house-party atmosphere inside – and more outside in summer. Inn guests enjoy "a bit of local color," Addison says, since they'll likely be joined by some of the 40 members of the dining club, who pay entrance fees and dues and are "quite protective" of the inn's exclusivity. That exclusivity was enhanced through the hotel's affiliation with the prestigious Relaix & Chateaux group in 2005, when the hotel's restaurant advertised that it was "pleased to accept reservations from the public for the very first time."

After complimentary cocktails, dinner is served at a single seating – communally, or at tables throughout the inn, depending on numbers and preferences. The prix-fixe meal with several choices for each of the four courses might open with a smoked salmon course and escargots in puff pastry. Sautéed grouper, crispy sweetbreads, roasted squab and grilled hanger steak were recent main-course choices. Grand marnier soufflé, chocolate mousse in phyllo, almond crêpes or a cheese plate could be the finale.

Breakfast is continental, featuring fresh juice, homemade muffins and scones, and micro-brewed coffee.

(845) 868-1665. Fax (845) 868-1441. www.bullishall.com. Two rooms and three suites with private baths. Doubles, $325 to $525. Closed February to mid-March..

Dinner by reservation 24 hours in advance, prix-fixe $68, Tuesday-Saturday 7 to 8:30. Jackets requested.

Lodging

Journey Inn Bed & Breakfast, 1 Sherwood Place, Hyde Park 12538.

Two sisters from New York City bought this house across the street from the Vanderbilt Mansion to run as a B&B. Diane and Michele DiNapoli named it the Journey Inn to reflect their travels. They named their six guest rooms for some of their favorite places and furnished each accordingly, if not always obviously.

The house suited their purpose, having been the home of a family with eight children. The bedrooms bear little resemblance to their family status, except for homey touches. They are comfortably furnished and have been frilled, fancied and feminized, complete with leaves and flowers entwined around windows here and a shawl or a blanket splayed on a bench there. Every room opens through french doors onto a balcony that runs along two sides of the house.

The Mombasa Room is suave in shades of brown, with a queen bed and walls hung with photographs the sisters took in Kenya's port city. Equally stylish is the adjacent Tuscany Room. The Kyoto Room has a queen bed and a Japanese motif. The English Country Suite, the original master bedroom, has a king bed, a sitting area with a built-in captain's bed and a two-part bathroom with twin vanities. The rear Vanderbilt Suite comes with a queen bed and a sitting area with a sleigh bed.

The main floor holds a formal living room and a sizable family room/sun room that the sisters employ for breakfast. The fare at our visit was cranberry-apple compote with vanilla yogurt, french toast with caramelized apples and sausage, and banana-walnut cake. "It's nice to do something decadent for breakfast," Diane said of the last. Apple cake was to be the finale to a breakfast of poached pears and croissants à l'orange with ham the next day.

A rear veranda overlooks a wooded back yard that descends to a creek.

(845) 229-8972. www.journeyinn.com. Four rooms and two suites with private baths. Doubles, $105 to $140. Suites, $165 and $185.

Inn at the Falls, 50 Red Oaks Mill Road, Poughkeepsie 12603.

Hard to find but worth the effort is this elegant bed-and-breakfast hotel beside a picturesque stream in a tranquil section of suburban Poughkeepsie. A curving, two-story, residential-style building follows the path of the stream and blends nicely into the landscape. It has 36 rooms and suites, nicely decorated in seven themes from English country to oriental to contemporary. A California artist did the striking paintings that enhance the rooms. Our suite had a comfy sitting room with extra-high ceilings, good reading lights, a dining table and kitchen sink with wet bar, plus two TV sets, three telephones and a canopied kingsize bed. It also had one of the biggest bathrooms we've seen, with an oversize whirlpool tub and a huge walk-in

Breakfast room at Inn at the Falls looks out onto passing stream.

shower. Floor-to-ceiling mirrors, bottles of toiletries and a marble-topped sink added to the imposing effect.

The marble floors of the lobby lead to a large living room with a soaring ceiling, a gigantic chandelier, plush sitting areas and a wall of windows onto the stream. Here, cocktails are available at night and a complimentary continental breakfast is waiting in the morning (you also can have it sent to your room). French doors open to a terrace, where chairs and tables are put out in summer.

The staff pampers guests with nightly turndown service and chocolate mints on the pillows.

(845) 462-5770 or (800) 344-1466. www.innatthefalls.com. Twenty-two rooms and fourteen suites with private baths. April to mid-November: doubles $190, suites $225 to $275. Rest of year: doubles $149, suites $169 to $209.

Olde Rhinebeck Inn, 340 Wurtemburg Road, Rhinebeck 12572.

This rambling, low-slung farmhouse began in 1738 as one room. Fittingly it's the dining area, where Jonna Paolella – proud to have been designated at age 28 as the youngest owner-innkeeper in America – serves up fruit smoothies and lavish breakfasts as up-to-date as today.

Open to her kitchen, the dining room is the heart of the house. It's where she begins tours of a structure that oozes history in almost every inch between wide-plank floors and rough, hand-hewn beamed ceilings.

The dining room focuses on a long trestle table Janna crafted of stained white oak salvaged from Jimmy Cagney's barn in nearby Stannardsville. The chair seats were upholstered in fabric from an old church. An old pig barn on the property furnished the wood for the kitchen cabinets, and the counter tops are made of wood from a carriage barn across the street. The stone floor of a sunken TV/family room off the kitchen came from a nearby gristmill. The woodwork in the living room is patched and weathered and shows its age (1745) and National Register status.

"I'd never even been in an historic house this old," said Jonna, before she saw it in 1998 as the fulfillment of a dream conceived two decades earlier as the daughter of an innkeeper in Brooklyn. "Why, here you can sleep in a place built before Mozart was born."

Her guests sleep in three bedrooms that convey creature comforts amidst antiquity. The floors creak in the Ryefield Suite as you step out of the rare queensize bed, from which six inches had to be cut from the legs for the elaborate carved-wood canopy to fit beneath the chestnut ceiling beams. The queen bed angled in the corner of the light and airy Spirited Dove Room wouldn't fit going up the steep, narrow stairway. "So we blew open the side wall of the room – hence the balcony," says Jonna, referring to the appealing hideaway overlooking a fish pond on the pastoral property.

Each bedroom comes with satellite TV, CD player, terrycloth robes, stocked guest refrigerator and fresh flowers. The Spirited Dove adds a whirlpool tub and a balcony, while the Deer Hill incorporates a separate sitting area and a private covered porch. The Plow & Harrow Suite has a gas fireplace and a two-person shower.

Each also is equipped with a table for breakfast, but most guests prefer to eat communally between 9 and 9:30 in the dining room. The meal starts with a choice of juices or fruit smoothies and an elaborate fruit platter. The main event could be baked french pear pancakes with sides of potatoes and eggs and a maple-pumpkin-walnut mini-loaf. Other possibilities include fluffy German pancakes and sweet potato frittatas layered with spinach, three cheeses and tomatoes.

Welcome amenities might be fruit, fudge made with goat's milk, cookies and assorted pastries. Entertainment is provided out back by Jonna's two pygmy goats. Feedings take place twice a day, and the goats respond with the makings for cheese.

(845) 871-1745. Fax (845) 876-8809. www.rhinebeckinn.com. Two rooms and two suites with private baths. May-November: doubles, $275 weekends, $225 midweek. Rest of year: doubles $225 weekends, $195 midweek.

Veranda House, 82 Montgomery St., Rhinebeck 12572.

Listed in the National Register, this attractive 1845 Federal house started as a farmhouse and once was an Episcopal church parsonage. Yvonne Sarn, originally from England, bought the B&B after 36 years as a hospital administrator on Long Island. She offers five rooms with private baths and telephones.

One room contains an original marble sink like one at the nearby Clermont mansion. Four rooms have a variety of queensize beds, from four-poster Shaker with lacy canopy to antique brass. The side White Heron Room that gets both morning and afternoon sun has twin beds convertible to a king. Two bedrooms, one downstairs in what had been a dining room and the other above, are architecturally notable for their bay windows attached to a five-sided bay.

The main-floor common areas are furnished with period antiques. The living room opens onto a breakfast room as well as a TV room/library with books specializing in history and art. Oriental and Persian rugs dot the original parquet floors and antique porcelain is on display throughout. Yvonne puts out wine and cheese for guests in front of the fireplace or on the wicker-filled wraparound front veranda in season. Dry and sweet sherry are available anytime.

A full breakfast is taken in the dining room or on a terrace outside. It starts with juice, a fruit plate and a homemade pastry, perhaps muffins or maple-walnut coffeecake. Orange-yogurt pancakes, a tomato-sausage tart or assorted blintzes and crêpes could be the main course. Apple or pecan strudel might follow.

(845) 876-4133 or (877) 985-6800. www.verandahouse.com. Five rooms with private baths. Doubles, $150 to $200.

Wine Tastings

Millbrook Vineyards & Winery, 26 Wing Road, Millbrook.

The Hudson Valley's first winery dedicated exclusively to the production of vinifera, Millbrook occupies 130 remote, hilly acres three miles north of Millbrook, somewhere in the back of beyond. It's blessed with dramatic views of vine-covered hillsides, three ponds, a picnic area and an unparalleled vista toward the Catskill Mountains. Owner John Dyson, former New York agriculture and commerce commissioner, converted a former dairy barn into the winery.

He and winemaker John Graziano produce about 8,000 cases of fine wine a year, including award-winning chardonnays, pinot noirs, cabernet sauvignons and merlots (most in the $14.99 to $23.99 range) that some find as spectacular as the setting. Everything is state of the art, from the manmade ponds that help moderate temperatures to a patented "goblet" trellis system that lets pinot noir grapes get more sun and air for better ripening. Dyson, who also owns two California vineyards and one in Tuscany, grows and experiments with about 25 European grape varieties, more than anyone in the East. By example he has proved two claims: that the Hudson Valley can produce world-class viniferas, and that grapes provide a better return for farmers than cows, hay or corn.

You can follow his interesting story during a twenty-minute winery tour. Sample the results in a small sales room holding literature and a tasting counter. Wine tastings ($6) include a sampling of six wines, a souvenir wine glass and samples of extra virgin olive oil from Dyson's Italian estate.

(845) 677-8383 or (800) 662-9463. www.millbrookwine.com. Open daily, Memorial Day to Labor Day 11 to 6, rest of year noon to 5.

Clinton Vineyards, Schultzville Road, Clinton Corners.

With Millbrook and Cascade Mountain, this is the third component of the scenic – and tasty –Dutchess Wine Trail. (A fourth, Alison Wines & Vineyards, recently opened in Red Hook.)

Owner-winemaker Ben Feder patterns Clinton in the tradition of small European estate vineyards. His specialty is a crisp, fruity seyval blanc, which he likens to a sancerre or a Loire Valley muscadet. Clinton was the first in the Hudson valley to produce seyval naturel, a rare domestic champagne fermented in the bottle in the classic méthode champenoise. It also produces a number of fruit dessert wines.

Visitors sample wines in the tasting room and view the champagne cellars and winemaking facility in an old Dutch barn.

(845) 266-5372. www.clintonvineyards.com. Open Friday-Monday 11 to 5.

Gourmet Treats

The Corner Bakery, 10 Charles Colman Blvd., Pawling, was among the first of a new breed of bakeries, featured in a New York Times magazine article and described by Redbook magazine as one of the five finest bakeries in America. Shannon McKinney, who studied with Swiss dean of pastry Albert Kumin, expanded a small bakery into McKinney & Doyle Fine Foods Café and a large takeout-food operation. Using all natural ingredients, he and his staff bake exquisite cakes, pastries and pies (how about eggnog chiffon?), Irish soda bread that was written up in Food & Wine magazine, gingerbread houses and stollen. We can vouch for their blueberry muffins and a scone, which we enjoyed with a latte from the espresso bar. They also bottle their own dijon herb dressing, English mint sauce and preserves, and offer a large selection of soups, salads, appetizers and entrées to go. Open daily from 7 to 5.

At **Adams Fairacre Farms,** 195 Dutchess Tpke. (Route 44), Poughkeepsie, you'll find a farm market like few others – really a one-stop supermarket sprawl of produce, gourmet foods and garden items. The produce section is bigger than many a grocery store, dwarfing even the Adams grocery section. Besides a gift shop and The Chocolate Goose for chocolates and ice creams, there is a Pastry Garden bake shop, where the aromas fairly overwhelm. Fresh rabbit was $2.99 a pound at the Country Butcher shop when we were there. The country deli and cheese shop offers all kinds of interesting goodies. Ralph Adams and company run a somewhat smaller branch along Route 9W near Kingston and a new branch in Newburgh.

In Hyde Park, the **Eveready Diner,** Route 9, a gleaming 10,000-square-foot tribute to yesteryear, serves everything from breakfast to diner classics. The **Hyde Park Brewing Co.,** 514 Albany Post Road, offers four brews plus a restaurant with an interesting menu that includes Asian vegetable salad with grilled chicken and wok-seared salmon fillet to go with. At 4068 Albany Post Road is **The Kitchen Drawer,** billed as the store where restaurant chefs shop for knives.

Recent additions have helped Rhinebeck enhance its reputation as a mecca for food lovers. CIA-trained baker Richard Acher and his wife Cathlyn operate a fine bakery, **Pandemain,** at 18 Garden St. It offers breads, biscotti, savories, soups, light lunches and sweets. **Bread Alone,** an offshoot of pioneering baker Dan Leader's bakery based across the Hudson in Boiceville, also has a retail store and café with a Tuscan country look at 43-45 East Market St. Its organic breads, pastries, soups, sandwiches and coffees are highly rated. **Olde Hudson** offers specialty foods from pastas and Italian oils to cheeses and truffles in its new store in Montgomery Row. Knives as well as cookware, gadgets and hard-to-find tools for the home cook and professional chef are featured in the venerable **Warren Kitchen & Cutlery** store, 6934 Route 9, Rhinebeck.

Mediterranean delicacies and authentic Italian cuisine are featured at **Mercato Tivolio,** 7460 South Broadway in Red Hook. Ebullient Francesco Buitoni from Rome and his partner Michele Platt garnered a receptive following for their panini sandwiches, salads and pastas in a little building behind the Red Hook Inn. There are a few tables for eating inside or outside on a patio with a view of a pond.

The **Hammertown Barn** is an antiques store plus much more at 4027 Route 199 in Pine Plains. Owner Joan Osofsky's expanding sideline is gourmet foods and dishware. We reveled in all the preserves and salsas, the hand-painted pottery, suave placemats and latest cookbooks. The old Gatehouse in front is furnished like a house and everything is for sale. On weekends, its working kitchen is opened for tastings of soups (perhaps mixed bean or potato-leek), salad dressings and mulling juices. Joan's husband Sid, a principal in the nearby **Ronnybrook Dairy** that the New York Times called "the Dom Perignon of Dairy," may offer samples of some of his ice creams. We tasted his yummy green apple and pumpkin flavors.

McEnroe Organic Farm Market, Route 22/44, between Millerton and Amenia, is the area's biggest certified organic produce market, with an almost overwhelming selection. The farm plants 6,000 heads of exotic lettuces a week from March through October, selling them off at about $1 a head. Here is a paradise of produce: mesclun, coriander, garlic, walla walla onions, leeks, fingerling potatoes. A garlic festival was on when we were there. Pies, breads, jellies and vinegars are among the sidelines.

Keuka Lake provides backdrop for wines on Bluff Point.

Finger Lakes

The Pleasures of the Grape

Anyone who has indulged in the pleasures of the grape in the California wine country yearns to return, especially when the harvest is at its height. But Easterners no longer have to go out West. Closer to home, the Finger Lakes region of upstate New York embraces a growing cluster of vineyards and wineries that produce wines of international distinction.

The New York Times headlined an article posted later at many a local winery: "Sorry, France. Too Bad, California. Some New York Wines Outshine Even Yours." At last count, more than 75 wineries were located in an area about the size of Connecticut. It is a landscape of rolling hills, lakes and vineyard vistas that are not only the equal in terms of scenery of most in California but often exceed them because of their proximity to water.

Vine-covered hills descend to the water's edge, where the lakes' extreme depths – some go down 700 feet – moderate the temperatures. The waters don't freeze in winter and they cool the air in summer. With conditions similar to the vineyards of northern Germany and France, the region specializes in cold-climate varieties like riesling and gewürztraminer.

The Finger Lakes wineries range from venerable Widmer's, which attracts hundreds of tourists on busy days, to newish Shalestone Vineyards, a tiny winery with an underground cellar and a tasting room marked by a shale sign and the words, "Red is all we do." Many are clustered along the hillsides that rise sharply from the southern ends of Cayuga, Seneca and Keuka lakes.

The wine boom has spawned related ventures, far beyond the winery visits that beckon more than one million tourists annually to the Finger Lakes, most in the late summer and fall.

Foremost, of course, is the sale of grapes – pick-your-own, or available by the basket or in juice for wine. Grape pie is a staple on some local dessert menus. Fire hydrants are painted purple in Naples for the annual Grape Festival in September.

Although this has traditionally been meat and potatoes country where lobster newburg and veal parmesan were as gourmet as they got, good restaurants – most featuring Finger Lakes wines – have emerged belatedly, particularly in the Ithaca area. So have a handful of new or refurbished inns and B&Bs.

Also emerging lately is a cottage food industry, which is at roughly the same stage of development as the wine scene was 25 years ago. Particularly noteworthy is the local cheese industry. Ithaca was the site for the first annual meeting of the American Cheese Society, and the Ithaca Journal reported the Finger Lakes were "becoming known as the wine and cheese region of the country." Ithaca's Farmers' Market is a model of the genre.

The increasing linkage of food and wine is reflected in the 2006 opening in Canandaigua of the New York Wine & Culinary Center, a $7.5-million promotional showcase for the state's food, wine and agriculture industry.

These days, a tour of the Finger Lakes wine country is much more than a one-day affair, and involves far more than simply touring a winery or two. On a leisurely trip, all the senses are at once heightened and lulled as you sample wines and indigenous foods on a sun-bathed deck overlooking one of the Finger Lakes, particularly in autumn when the grapes are being harvested and the hillsides are ablaze in color.

Tippling Through the Wineries

Canandaigua Wine Co. is the biggest, Widmer's the most picturesque and Bully Hill Vineyards the most controversial of the larger Finger Lakes wineries.

Others are more interesting for visitors with an interest in winemaking and an appreciation for finer wines, especially those who seek personalized, informal tours that follow the dictates not of the leader but of the led.

For a broad overview, start at the **New York Wine & Culinary Center** at 800 South Main St., Canandaigua. The new 19,475-square-foot facility at the northern tip of Canandaigua Lake has an exhibit hall with interactive exhibits, a tasting room offering a rotating selection of New York wines, a wine and tapas bar with an outdoor balcony for light meals and food and wine pairings, a theater-style demonstration kitchen for hands-on cooking classes, professional kitchens and a retail shop. Outside is a demonstration garden where grape vines, fruit trees and vegetables are cultivated.

Otherwise, for orientation purposes, look to the larger wineries, whose guided tours offer a comprehensive if perfunctory look at the winemaking process followed by a quick short course on the proper way to taste wines and a commercialized pitch to purchase your favorites on the way out. Then head for the smaller wineries, where the tours are intimate, the conversations spirited, the tastings more varied and the guide may be the winemaker or the owner. The tastings are sometimes complimentary, although some wineries charge $1 or more, especially for the more prized offerings. Since they tend to be clustered at the southern ends of three lakes, you can visit the wineries along one lake each day. Local brochures group them under the Cayuga and Seneca Lake wine trails and the Keuka Lake Winery Route.

The Finger Lakes specialty has been white vinifera wines, especially rieslings – which are considered among the best in America. Lately, red wines are coming of age.

Restaurant at Glenora Wine Cellars serves meals on deck overlooking Seneca Lake.

Because the wineries are so central to the Finger Lakes and their appeal is so special, we begin with a guide to some of the best or most interesting.

Dr. Konstantin Frank/Vinifera Wine Cellars, 9749 Middle Road, Hammondsport.

This is where the "new" Finger Lakes wine tradition was launched in 1962. Dr. Frank was the first to plant European vinifera grapes successfully in the Finger Lakes and toiled daily in his Keuka Lake vineyards and winery until shortly before his death in 1985 at age 86. His son Willy and grandson Fred continue the tradition. Best known for their rieslings, the Frank wines have been served at the White House and have consistently outscored French wines in blind tastings.

The low-key tasting room along an unpaved side road is the place to go for world-class pinot noir and cabernet sauvignon. "We could spend a quarter of a million dollars and make this a very attractive tourist place," says Willy. "We prefer instead to make the best wine that can be made from our grapes." They produce 10,000 to 14,000 cases a year, exporting internationally to countries as far away as Japan. Wine Report 2005 named Dr. Frank's the "greatest wine producer" in the Atlantic Northeast, having won 32 gold medals in national and international wine competitions in 2004.

Willy also has opened **Chateau Frank** in the cellar of the Frank home for the making of methode-champenoise sparkling wines, including a flagship brut in the French style.

(607) 868-4884 or (800) 320-0735. www.drfrankwines.com. Open daily, 9 to 5, Sunday noon to 5.

Hermann J. Wiemer Vineyard, 3962 Route 14, Dundee.

Hermann Wiemer, whose family has grown grapes and made wine for more than three centuries along the Mosel River in Germany, ranks as today's icon among Finger Lakes vintners.

Wiemer, then the winemaker for the legendary Walter Taylor, acquired an abandoned soybean farm on a slope on the west side of Seneca Lake in 1973 and began planting viniferas as well as the traditional hybrid grapes. Fired by Taylor six years later as disloyal to the hybrid cause, Wiemer set up his own winery and never looked back. His soaring barn winery, renovated to state-of-the-art condition, is low-key and very serious, as befits a producer of award-winning chardonnays and rieslings that command top dollar

Wiemer established a nursery that has become one of the country's most important sources for top-quality grapevines, a sideline that in its way dwarfs his vineyard and winery. He produces 12,000 cases of wine annually, samples of which can be sipped in a rather forbidding tasting room where the solo visitor senses that the staff has other priorities. Prices range from $9.50 for a dry rosé to $39 for the select late-harvest ice wine. In its annual pick of the world's finest wines, Wine Spectator gave Wiemer's semi-dry riesling ($16) the top rating. There are self-guided tours. Private tours may be arranged by appointment.

(607) 243-7971 or (800) 371-7971. www.wiemer.com. Open Monday-Saturday 10 to 5, Sunday 11 to 5. Closed weekends, December-March.

Glenora Wine Cellars, 5435 Route 14, Dundee.

Among medium-size Finger Lakes wineries, this is a pacesetter with a commanding view from the west side of Seneca Lake. Glenora has been winning awards since it opened in 1977 as the first winery along Seneca. Its Johannesburg riesling was rated the best in America two years in a row, and its reserve chardonnay was served at President George H.W. Bush's inauguration. Glenora long ago abandoned variety in order to concentrate on premium white viniferas and French-American varietals, plus premium sparkling wines. Wine Spectator magazine ranks it among the world's 70 top producers of fine wines.

Glenora's merger with the smaller Finger Lakes Wine Cellars of Branchport doubled output to 60,000 cases a year. A large, two-story addition has expanded the production facility as well as the upstairs tasting area and added an impressive new showroom. The expansion continued with a new building housing a restaurant, inn and conference center with a stupendous view. Its principals since purchased Knapp Vineyards along Cayuga Lake and founded the Logan Ridge Estates Winery, which ceased operations in 2005 across Seneca Lake.

After viewing a video presentation, Glenora visitors get complimentary samples of up to five wines. Questioners who linger may get to try a few others, as is the case at most smaller wineries. Glenora offers a line of table wines starting at $8.99, but we always pick up a few of the dry rieslings ($13.99), which are some of the best anywhere. Also great are the brut and blanc de blanc and the merlot. Ever-enterprising, Glenora sponsors food and wine festivals and occasional Sunday afternoon concerts on its lawn.

(607) 243-5511 or (800) 243-5513. www.glenora.com. Open daily, 9 to 9 in July and August, 10 to 6 or 7 in May, June, September and October; 10 to 5 or 6 rest of year.

Wagner Vineyards, 9322 Route 414, Lodi.

This is another favorite among the medium-size wineries, thanks both to its fortuitous location on the eastern slope overlooking Seneca Lake and to the myriad endeavors of owner Bill Wagner, a dairy farmer-turned grape grower-turned winemaker. He started in 1979 with eight wines and now offers more than 30 wines and champagnes, as well as six beers from the new Wagner Valley Brewing Co.'s

Seneca Lake is on view from elegant tasting room at Lamoreaux Landing Wine Cellars.

microbrewery adjacent. One of his early endeavors is the large Ginny Lee Café (see below), but he's proudest that the winery has been ranked among the world's top 70 by Wine Spectator.

Bill Wagner differs from some in that he grows all his grapes ("my philosophy is that good wine is made out in the vineyards, which makes winemakers shudder, but I like that fulltime control over the grapes," says its owner). He also differs in the amount of research ("more than the rest of the wineries put together") and the proportion of red wines, at one point nearly 50-50.

He and his staff host hundreds of visitors on busy weekends in the octagonal building he designed himself, as well as at Friday night musical bashes on the deck of the microbrewery in summer. After guided tours of the winery, visitors taste wines and then browse through a large shop. The limited-release chardonnays and pinot noirs have been much honored; ditto for a couple of dessert ice wines. We came home with a good gewürztraminer for $13.99.

(607) 582-6450 or (866) 924-6378. www.wagnervineyards.com. Open daily, 10 to 5.

Lamoreaux Landing Wine Cellars, 9224 Route 414, Lodi.

In its construction stage, passersby thought this striking structure atop a hill commanding a panoramic view of Seneca Lake was to be a cathedral. It turned out to be a temple – a temple for some of the best wines in the Finger Lakes region.

Owner Mark J. Wagner's "neo-Greek Revival barn" houses perhaps the region's most exciting young, high-end winery. California architect Bruce Corson, a friend whose father was president of Cornell University, designed a four-level masterpiece of open spaces, oak floors, floor-to-ceiling windows and cream-colored walls hung with changing local artworks. A new wing was added in 2005, and classical music wafts from the high-end tasting room onto an outside deck.

Mark, a distant cousin of Bill Wagner of the adjacent Wagner Vineyards, had been growing classic vinifera grapes on his 130 lakeside acres for other wineries before opening his own winery in 1992. The elegant showroom provides a perfect backdrop for the tasting of premium viniferas, including a cabernet franc and a merlot that won gold medals in prestigious wine competitions. The 2000 blanc de blanc, an all-chardonnay sparkling wine, was likened to $40 French champagnes by the New York Times, and the 2003 dry riesling was selected to be served at a wine and seafood pairing event hosted by the American Embassy in Sweden. We savored the barrel-fermented chardonnay ($11.99) and cabernet franc ($16.99). At a recent visit, Lamoreaux had been judged the best winery at the annual Mid-Atlantic Wine Festival.

Mark explains that some of his wines may not be at their best as stand-alone tasting wines, "but I drink wines with food so those are the kind I'm producing here." He plans to remain small and aim for the ultra-premium market.

(607) 582-6011. www.lamoreauxwine.com. Open Monday-Saturday 10 to 5, Sunday noon to 5.

Standing Stone Vineyards, 9934 Route 414, Hector.

Who'd expect a year-old winery open only on weekends to win the Governor's Cup (best of show) at the annual New York Wine and Food Classic? With a red wine, no less? The best-in-state award for its ruby red cabernet franc put Standing Stone quickly on the connoisseur's map.

Owners Tom Macinski, a chemical engineer with IBM, and his wife Marti, a litigation lawyer, commuted on weekends from Binghamton to their home and vineyard along the eastern shore of Seneca Lake. Even before their winery opened in 1994, their first gewürztraminer had won a gold medal at the New York State Fair and their riesling and dry vidal also had won awards. The part-time winemakers won awards for every wine they produced in their first two harvests, and have been reaping more honors ever since for products that are quickly sold out. The Wine Spectator in 2005 called their vidal dessert white a knockout and said that while other area wineries "try to make cabernet sauvignon, the Macinskis actually pull it off."

The rustic winery is in a restored barn and the tasting room is in an old chicken coop enhanced by a covered outdoor deck. The Macinskis have increased their output from 800 cases to nearly 7,000 and now are managing the vineyard here full time. Their stylish chardonnay, riesling, merlot and pinot noir offerings are priced from $7.99 to $27.99.

(607) 582-6051 or (800) 803-7135. www.standingstonewines.com. Open daily, noon to 5, Saturday 11 to 6.

Knapp Vineyards Winery, 2770 County Road 128, Romulus.

A vaguely California air pervades this winery, which began as a family operation on 100 acres of a former chicken farm above Cayuga Lake. There's a large, airy tasting room with a California-like veranda, but the prize addition is the restaurant fashioned from a storeroom at the rear of the winery (see below).

The owners of the expanding Glenora Wine Cellars enterprise took over from founding owners Doug and Suzie Knapp in 2000. Knapp was one of the first wineries to produce "methode-champenoise" brut. It also is one of the growing numbers doing red viniferas, including merlot and cabernet sauvignon. Lately it has moved into producing more semi-sweet and fruit wines and cordials, including limoncello. Recently released was a velvety ruby port, fortified with brandy from the Knapp still. The grappa won a gold medal and, aging slowly in oak, a cognac-style brandy was released.

(607) 869-9271 or (800) 869-9271. www.knappwine.com. Open daily, 10 to 5:30.

King Ferry Winery, 658 Lake Road, King Ferry.

Peter and Tacie Saltonstall (he's a grandson of the Boston Saltonstalls) release 7,000 cases of their award-winning Treleaven wines at their small winery on the former Treleaven farm along the east shore of Cayuga Lake. Aged in oak casks in the French tradition, the chardonnays are highly rated, selling for $12.49 a bottle (the reserve is $16.99). The rieslings and merlots are other good offerings, and the winery's mélange blends merlot and pinot noir. The winery runs a satellite retail outlet in Skaneateles.

(315) 364-5100 or (800) 439-5271. www.treleavenwines.com. Open Monday-Saturday 10 to 5, Sunday noon to 5. Closed in January.

Winery Culinary Treats

The Inn at Glenora Wine Cellars and Veraisons Restaurant, 5435 Route 14, Dundee 14837.

This inn with 30 upscale guest rooms, a restaurant and a conference center occupies a $5 million building straddling a hillside overlooking Seneca Lake, behind and beneath the winery. The view of the lake and vine-covered hillsides here is arguably the most spectacular of any in the Finger Lakes.

Winery principal Gene Pierce sensed the need for an upscale hostelry and restaurant along the lake. "We're right at the stage where the Napa Valley was in 1977 when we started," he said, noting the growth from one winery on Seneca (Glenora) to 32, with more popping up every year. "There's suddenly all this synergy to support a destination inn and conference center."

He designed the low-slung, spread-out board and batten building as a country hotel "to fit in with the architecture of upstate farm country" and to blend into the vineyard. Rooms go off an interior corridor on two floors. Each has a private balcony or patio with a view over vineyards to the lake. The interiors incorporate Stickley mission furniture, an armoire containing an entertainment center and refrigerator, a bureau, a table and two hard-back chairs. Two Adirondack chairs provide more seating on the balcony. Our room was one of ten with a king bed and a corner fireplace, plus a spacious bath with whirlpool tub and separate shower. Others have two queen beds, but no whirlpool tub nor fireplace. Each room comes with a coffeemaker, hair dryer and a chilled bottle of our favorite Glenora riesling.

At one end of the sprawling building is a 150-seat restaurant, a knockout of a space with vaulted ceiling, white walls with wood trim and well-spaced tables decked out in green and beige.

Chef Joseph Sutton has revised the menu to include appetizers like baked shrimp and brie in puff pastry, Atlantic clam fritters and blue crab cakes with jalapeño tartar sauce. Entrées range from Caribbean-seasoned yellowfin tuna on a bed of roasted red pepper coulis to grilled filet mignon with choice of sauces. Limoncello shrimp scampi and veal marsala are sauced with the company's products.

In season, the prime attraction is the spacious rear deck, where we were fortunate

Wine barrels mark entrance to Inn at Glenora Wine Cellars and Veraisons Restaurant.

enough to book a table with an unencumbered lake view. Dinner began with an amusé, tapenade with crackers, to accompany a $13 Glenora chardonnay, selected from a list of Glenora wines plus those from "our neighbors along Seneca Lake." A loaf of bread sliced on a board and a choice of excellent salads (one bearing grapes, toasted pinenuts and shaved ricotta on baby greens) came next. Main courses were excellent Montauk scallops served with a corn salsa and herbed risotto cake and succulent medallions of grilled sea bass, sauced with herbed pinot blanc and served with roasted Israeli couscous. Dessert was a flavorful port-poached pear and ice cream.

At breakfast, we were impressed with the Veraisons poached eggs, topped with crabmeat and hollandaise sauce and served over herbed risotto cakes. Super-sounding salads, interesting sandwiches (smoked salmon, a crab cake po-boy) and entrées like rock shrimp scampi sauté and baked salmon oscar are featured at lunch.

(607) 243-9500 or (800) 243-5513. www.glenora.com. Thirty rooms with private baths. Rates, EP. May-October: doubles, $169 to $259 weekends, $149 to $229 midweek. Rest of year: doubles $139 to $219 weekends, $109 to $199 midweek.

Entrées, $18 to $26. Lunch daily, 11:30 to 3. Dinner nightly, 5 to 9 or 10, to 8 midweek in winter.

Knapp Vineyards Restaurant, 2770 County Road 128, Romulus.

The Knapp family launched one of the earliest and best of the Finger Lakes winery restaurants at the rear of their winery, which they sold recently to the principals of Glenora Wine Cellars.

The culinary tradition continues in an interior dining room that opens onto a trellised terrace where vines grow above, herb and flower gardens bloom beyond, vineyards spread out on three sides, you can see or hear wild turkeys and pheasants, and bluebirds fly all around. It's a delightful setting for some inspired meals. New chef Eric Pierce, son of the one of the winery's owners, changes the menus seasonally to take advantage of local ingredients.

The dinner menu produces a choice of six entrées. They range from baked shrimp tossed with vidalia onions in a chipotle sauce and served with goat cheese toasts and seasonal vegetables to grilled flank steak served with rice pilaf over a bed of roasted corn-pancetta salsa. A specialty is New Zealand rack of lamb, smoked with hickory and rosemary, topped with a mint gremolata, and served with roasted garlic polenta. Starters could be crab cakes with a chipotle dipping sauce or a wild mushroom sauté sauced with a Knapp cabernet bordelaise served with garlic croutons. Desserts vary from cold lemon soufflé to kahlua crème brûlée. Strawberry riesling sorbet with fresh fruit was a special at a recent visit.

Lunchtime brings more basic fare, from a burger or a smoked turkey wrap to a fruit and cheese platter. More substantial options include a fancy blackened chicken salad, limoncello shrimp salad, crab cakes with lemon-chipotle mayonnaise and pasta tossed with mussels, tomatoes, artichoke hearts, spinach and parmesan cheese.

(607) 869-9271 or (800) 869-9271. www.knappwine.com. Entrées, $17 to $23. Lunch daily, 11 to 3:30. Dinner, Thursday-Sunday 5 to 8. Closed November-March.

The Bistro at Red Newt Cellars, 3675 Tichenor Road, Hector.

Local caterer Deb Whiting and her husband Dave, the winemaker, run this winery with a spacious dining area and covered deck in renovated space that once housed the Wickham Winery. Dave had proved his winemaking mettle for a decade at Standing Stone and other Finger Lakes wineries before going on his own. Deb ran the upscale Seneca Savory catering service in nearby Burdett before launching the bistro.

The innovative food is highly rated, presented in a stylish, white-linened dining room and on the adjacent deck with a view of the Seneca Lake valley. The changing menus are brief and intriguing. Among starters all day are phyllo triangles with scallops and water chestnuts, chicken and mushroom empanada with a sherry cream sauce, and quesadilla with cheese, guacamole and pulled pork. Lunchtime might yield a meatloaf sandwich with chipotle mayo on parmesan cheese bread, a grilled chicken and asparagus wrap or a phyllo cup with couscous, leeks, artichokes and roasted red peppers on a bed of spinach.

The dinner menu adds entrées like fillet of sole stuffed with pesto and asparagus, bacon-wrapped pork tenderloin stuffed with spinach and garlic chèvre in a mango-white wine sauce, and grilled beef tenderloin stuffed with porcini mushrooms and topped with gorgonzola butter. Desserts might be rhubarb crumble with whipped cream and chocolate-covered cherry cheesecake.

The winery is named for the Eastern red spotted newt, which the Whitings consider one of nature's more beautiful but obscure creatures. Their spacious tasting room also is a gallery showcasing local art.

(607) 546-4100. Entrées, $20 to $29. www.rednewt.com. Lunch, Wednesday-Sunday noon to 4. Dinner, Wednesday-Sunday 4 to 9. Closed mid-December to mid-February.

Ginny Lee Café, Wagner Vineyards, 9322 Route 414, Lodi.

With its reasonably priced wines and charming setting (a panoramic view of its vineyards and Seneca Lake), the Ginny Lee has long been a treat. Part of the expansive deck has been enclosed to better weather the elements and to extend the season. Now there's a vast interior space with cathedral ceiling, white walls and white garden-type furniture. A large section of the outdoor deck remains. Although the fare has been scaled down from its original heights, the menu has been broadened and Wagner's microbrewery offers a Friday night pub menu.

Wagner wines and Aurora grape juice by the bottle, half carafe and glass are available at winery prices at the café, which was the first at a Finger Lakes winery and was named for the owner's then-infant granddaughter.

The menu ranges from a burger to a grilled chicken sandwich to a crab cake with chipotle cream sauce to a Tuscan wrap to a couple of pizzas. Sunday brunch includes an array of breakfast and dinner entrées for $16.95.

At various visits we've enjoyed a Greek salad, shrimp salad on a croissant, a seafood and cheese pizza, and a fruit and cheese platter with French bread. We won't soon forget the fuzzy navel peach pie, the raspberry praline tulipe and the strong cinnamon-flavored coffee, which after lunch with a bottle of wine was the only way we managed to make it through the afternoon.

(607) 582-6574. Light fare, $5.95 to $8.95. May-October: Lunch, Monday-Saturday 11 to 4; Sunday, brunch 10:30 to 2, lunch noon to 4. Off-season: Lunch, Friday-Sunday 11 to 3. Closed mid-December to mid-March.

Sheldrake Point Vineyard & Café, 7448 County Road 153, Ovid.

Near a point jutting into Cayuga Lake, this winery bottled its first blend in 1998 with plans to plant 75 acres of grapes. A café and tasting bar offers creative fare at the side of the wine showroom and outside under a canopy and umbrellas. Two principals who know their food, managing partner Chuck Tauck and chef Jack Carrington, offer lunch daily as well as dinners on weekends in season.

The crowd was standing-room-only the Saturday afternoon we first stopped by, but a subsequent midweek visit turned up a table for two at the rear of the café. The Santa Fe chicken salad plate and sandwiches like albacore tuna on a croissant tempted. One of us made a light lunch of cream of tomato soup and the signature kalamata olive spread on pita bread. The other was well satisfied with the grilled chicken sandwich with lettuce, tomato and roasted red pepper mayo on a kaiser roll.

The dinner fare is more imaginative. You might start with the kalamata olive spread, herbed Lively Run goat cheese bruschetta or a wood-grilled duck salad. The menu ranges from grilled salmon with citrus cream sauce and seafood ravioli with a roasted red-pepper béchamel sauce to Mediterranean chicken, hickory-smoked grilled duck breast with apricot-merlot demi-glace, and grilled lamb chops with a red currant and rosemary demi-glace.

(607) 532-9401 or (866)743-5372. www.sheldrakepoint.com. Entrées, $16.95 to $23.95. Lunch daily, 11 to 3, May-October. Dinner, Friday-Saturday 6 to 9:30 June-September, 5 to 9 in May and October.

The Stonecat Café, 5315 Route 414, Hector.

The unknowing passerby would likely never stop at this former garage and fruit stand with a garage door in front and funky dining rooms inside. But the local winery crowd cherishes the hip little café next to the obscure Bloomer Creek Vineyard's original tasting room, which was relocated in 2006 to a new building. Ex-Washington, D.C., chef Scott Signori and his wife Jessica dispense their own smoked foods and organic regional cuisine in two laid-back dining areas and a canopied deck where diners enjoy spectacular sunsets across the Seneca Lake valley.

The house-smoked pulled-pork barbecue is the signature item here, slow-smoked with grape and applewood and marinated in the chef's Carolina-style barbecue sauce, and served with black-eyed peas, dill coleslaw and cornbread. Cornmeal-crusted catfish finished with a smoked tomato coulis, house-smoked free-range

Open kitchen is on display at one end of Rosalie's Cucina dining room.

chicken and sausage braised in Northern Italian gravy and served over polenta, and peppercorn crusted strip steak finished with dijon-thyme cream sauce typify other possibilities. Vegetarians hail the grilled smoked tofu served with a red lentil peanut sauce and peach chutney over coconut sticky rice. Start with a smoked fish plate of Alaskan salmon and black tiger shrimp over greens, a roasted organic garlic bulb served with Lively Run chèvre and homemade crostini or a grilled tofu satay. Tapas are on the lunch menu along with salads, sandwiches and cheese boards.

Bloomer Creek wines are featured on the all-Finger Lakes wine list. Live music is offered Wednesday and Saturday nights, with jazz at Sunday brunch.

(607) 546-5000. www.stonecatcafe.com. Entrées, $15 to $23. Lunch, Thursday-Saturday 11 to 3. Dinner, Wednesday-Sunday 5 to 9. Sunday jazz brunch, 10:30 to 3. Closed early December to May.

Dining

The area's best restaurants are concentrated in Ithaca, its largest town and one that claims variously to have more restaurants per capita than New York City and the most restaurants per capita east of San Francisco.

The Best of the Best

Rosalie's Cucina, 841 West Genesee St., Skaneateles.

A plaque on the wall in the rear foyer says this was "built with great love for my sister" and, after listing the architectural credits, adds "with way too much money." Both the love and the money are manifest in the chic Tuscan-style restaurant, wine cellar and bakery – a testament to the late Rosalie Romano from Phil Romano, the restaurant impresario who started the Fuddrucker's and Romano's Macaroni Grill chains.

It seems that Phil, who grew up in nearby Auburn and lives in Texas, still summers on Skaneateles Lake and "wanted a nice place to eat," in the words of co-owner Gary Robinson. "He'd been all over Italy, so he built this the way he wanted it for himself."

His $1.5 million investment includes a stylish 120-seat restaurant backing up to a designer's dream of an open kitchen, a downstairs wine cellar and an upstairs Romano Room for private parties, a bakery, an outdoor bocce court, a small vineyard for show, and an elaborate herb layout and vegetable garden for real.

The result: The hottest culinary establishment in the northern Finger Lakes area. Without advertising, no press kit, barely a tourism listing and not even a website until 2005, the place was mobbed nightly, and up to two-hour waits were the norm on weekends. The bocce court, the wine cellar and a delightful Mediterranean-style courtyard – all holding areas for the waiting crowds, who are given bread, olives and cheese – get quite a workout.

Inside the salmon-colored building identified by a sign so small we missed it on the first pass is a dark and spacious dining area understated in white and black. Black chairs flank well-spaced tables covered with white butcher paper over white cloths. A few columns break up the expanse. The white walls are enlivened with hundreds of splashy autographs of customers, who pay $25 each to charity to enshrine their name and the date for posterity. Most of the color comes from the open kitchen at the end of the room, where cooks work amid hanging ropes of garlic, arrangements of bounty and chickens roasting on the rotisserie.

Seven chefs, most of whom had been executive chefs elsewhere, team up with head chef Marc Albino to vary the menu daily. The specialty is prime meats, as in aged New York strip steak and grilled veal loin chop. The grilled lobster tails with orzo and spinach and the lamb loin with white wine and garlic are done according to family recipes. So are the scampi alla Rosalie (with artichokes and garlic butter) and the veal piccata.

Portions are huge, as we learned upon sampling the signature farfalle con pollo (chicken with pancetta, asiago cream, red onions and peas). That and one of the enormous salads were plenty for two to share. Even so, part of the pasta dish went home in a foil wrap shaped like a swan, along with several loaves of the dynamite bread that begins the meal (extras are freely given at the end of the evening).

Antipasti include carpaccio, pizza margherita, manicotti, steamed mussels and grilled portobello mushrooms. Of the insalatas, the one with arugula, prosciutto, reggiano and lemon is special.

The homemade desserts change daily. The pastries and breads come from **Rosalie's Bakery** at the rear of the establishment, where several varieties of sensational "hand-made breads" and pastries are for sale daily from 6 a.m. to 6 p.m.

A strolling mandolin player serenades tables and adds a touch of Italian charm. Rosalie came in most nights to be hostess before passing on to her eternal reward. The staff continues her legacy in this cucina that love built.

(315) 685-2200. www.rosaliescucina.com. Entrées, $20 to $36. Dinner nightly, 5 to 9 or 10, Sunday 4 to 8.

The Heights Café & Grill, 903 Hanshaw Road, Ithaca.

Ensconced next to Talbots in the Community Corners shopping plaza in tony Cayuga Heights, this storefront operation has matured with age, vaulting into the ranks of best in Ithaca. Starting small and with a decor that was plainer than plain,

Stylish ambiance and imaginative fare are hallmarks of The Heights Café & Grill.

it has expanded to offer three dining rooms seating a total of 100 and now sports crisp, chic decor in white and brown. Each table is topped with flowers and a votive candle, and fresh flowers sprout in wall-mounted vases as well.

Hands-on chef-owners James and Heidi Larounis, who moved here from the Four Seasons Hotel in Philadelphia, are known for imaginative American fare with Mediterranean flair, beautifully presented.

The dinner menu ranges widely, from salmon au poivre and plaki (Greek-style braised codfish and sea scallops) to grilled duck breast and roasted leg with Mongolian barbecue sauce and Mediterranean chargrilled rack of lamb with a lemon-mint demi-glace. Don't be surprised to find a scaloppini of tofu marsala and blue cheese-crusted filet of beef tenderloin on the same page. Know also that James likes to pair rack of lamb with littleneck clams as a main course and with jumbo shrimp as an appetizer. Everything comes with choice of Greek or caesar salad.

Starters could be the Heights antipasto, chicken liver pot pie with paprika cream sauce, semolina-crusted calamari with lemon aioli and banana hot rings, and caramelized sea scallops Greek style. A recent winner was escargots and sweetbreads sautéed with pancetta, asparagus and wild mushrooms in a white wine-herb beurre blanc. Highly rated desserts range from baklava to a roasted pineapple served with coconut sorbet and a crisp tuile. The mini dessert sampler might yield crème brûlée, caramel pecan pot de crème and crème caramel.

The award-winning wine list is deep and varied. So is the roster of single-malt scotches.

(607) 257-4144. www.heightscafe.com. Entrées, $22.95 to $28.95. Lunch, Monday-Friday 11:30 to 2:30. Dinner, Monday-Saturday 5 to 9 or 10.

Renée's, 115 South Quarry St., Ithaca.

Her coterie of fans are happy that Renée Senne is back in the restaurant business – lower profile, perhaps, but on a first-name basis.

After running her vaunted Renée's Bistro in Ithaca for years, she had closed up shop and returned to her first love, baking. The graduate of La Varenne in France and a former cooking instructor with Peter Kump in New York City opened Patisserie

Renée Senne, a French pastry and chocolate shop in suburban Cayuga Heights. She sold that and returned for an encore in a hard-to-find location at the rear of the stately but elderly Quarry Arms Apartment building beside one of Ithaca's ubiquitous gorges.

The new restaurant is about the size of her original, but adds a large covered porch for outdoor dining in season. Although her former restaurant was first called an American bistro, the new Renee's is less of a bistro and more refined, like the building in which it resides. Stressing local ingredients, Renee applies classical techniques honed in Paris to create a contemporary, Americanized version of French cuisine.

Given her pastry background, you might be tempted to eat dessert first. Don't, but be sure to save room. Start instead with the likes of a chèvre flan with smoked salmon, escargots with tomato and garlic butter sauce or the superb four-mushroom vol-au-vent, the puff pastry layered in our case with morels, champignons de Paris, portobello and porcini mushrooms. We also loved her salad of new potatoes served warm with chèvre on baby greens, a menu fixture from the original.

For main courses, Renée might pair diver sea scallops with crab in a tarragon beurre blanc, and serve confit and grilled breast of duck with a fig and red wine sauce. You might find swordfish seared with garlic and olive oil resting on spinach linguini or grilled and served with shrimp-filled ravioli. Other seasonal options could be steak and mushroom pie, venison osso buco with saffron risotto, rack of lamb with green peppercorn sauce, and grilled delmonico steak with caramelized onion, garlic and scallion cream.

And then the dessert trolley rolls to the table. It might hold tarte tatin, lemon soufflé cheesecake, a passionfruit-truffle cake or a fabulous vacherin with lemon curd and raspberries. How about the "petit diable?" The little devil spills forth dark chocolate cake with coffee buttercream, hazelnut succès, chocolate mousse and meringue mushrooms.

(607) 277-4047. Entrées, $21.50 to $29.50. www.reneesfeast.com. Dinner, Tuesday-Saturday 5:30 to 10. Closed first three weeks of January.

Madeline's, 215 The Commons, corner North Aurora and East State Streets, Ithaca.

The downtown space that used to be the main floor of Rothschild's department store is unrecognizable in its latest transformation. The owner of the family-owned Thai Cuisine restaurant (see below) went off on his own in 1997, opening the stylish Madeline's at a prime corner of Ithaca Commons. Sunit ("call me Lex") Chutintaranond and a friend, Phoebe Ullberg, started with a patisserie named for a favorite character from French children's literature. The establishment has since expanded into the city's handsomest restaurant. Slick and urbane, it would appear to be more at home in Manhattan than in upstate Ithaca. The look is modern-minimalist Asian, colorful and vaguely art deco, with a bar and tables spaced well apart on several levels.

Gregarious Lex, the head chef, oversees Pacific Rim fusion fare that dazzles in flavor and execution. "We call it East meets West," he says. In his lately expanded kitchen, "we can do anything." Changing the menu every couple of months, he and his kitchen staff might pair French and Japanese or Italian and Asian. For dinner, they could offer shrimp in a roasted chile and coconut milk sauce over green tea rice or grilled salmon fillet with a honey-chipotle-lime glaze and a Thai cucumber and

Well-stocked bar adjoins dining room at Madeline's restaurant.

sweet corn relish. They might serve grilled pork loin with a sundried cherry and pancetta veal demi-glace, and offer duck two ways: Asian five-spice confit and pan-seared breast with cranberry-port wine sauce. Accompaniments could be five-root salad, purple slaw, Asian greens, steamed baby bok choy, garlic-sesame bean sprouts, spinach ohitashi and chilled steamed napa cabbage.

Starters are as simple as grilled Thai-style calamari over chilled soba noodles and as complex as poke, a Hawaiian seafood preparation, served sashimi-style and seasoned with seaweed, chiles, onions and such. Crisp lobster rolls are served with a roasted chile, carrot and tarragon aioli. Mussels might be steamed in lemongrass with sweet Thai basil and Thai chile broth.

The house-baked focaccia with caramelized onions and kalamata olives is to die for. Ditto for the desserts, which fill sixteen feet of display cases in the restaurant. Pastry chef Teresa Hutchins prepares up to twenty patisserie-style treats a night from a repertoire of more than 50. We've heard their praises sung across the city.

The bar features more than 80 single-malt scotches as well as rare cognacs, grappas and small-batch bourbons.

(607) 277-2253. www.madelinesrestaurant.net. Entrées. $17 to $22. Dinner nightly, 5 to 10 or 11.

Willow, 202 East Falls St., Ithaca.

The late Renee's Bistro gave way in 2001 to this stylish endeavor, the work of Sean O'Brien, a Johnson & Wales-trained chef, and his young wife Amy, a ballerina who looks the part. After working and teaching in Connecticut, they returned to their hometown to establish a restaurant. They refined the decor in the dining room to epitomize clean and classic, the prevailing gray of the walls accented by black metallic chairs at white-clothed tables, each topped with a beaded-glass lamp. The martini bar at the rear features "designer martinis." A wall of windows stretches along the front, and the roar of nearby Ithaca Falls may be heard outside. The willow trees in the adjacent park inspired the name.

Willow's contemporary American menu is short but varied, meaning global. You might start with Pacific Rim tartare – tuna, ginger, cilantro, aioli, sesame crisps and pea shoots – or the signature bruschetta tasting of five kinds. Or how about bacon-wrapped diver scallops with a date-butter sauce, Belgian-style littlenecks in a garlicky beer broth, puree of asparagus soup with roasted mushroom croutons, or a sourdough tart with grilled chicken, smoked mozzarella and sundried tomatoes? There is usually a trio of wonderful-sounding pastas, including trenette of lobster, mushrooms and sugar snap peas in a shallot-brandy sauce. But the entrées entice: perhaps roasted monkfish with a saffron-shellfish nage, sea salt-crusted arctic char with a lemon-caper verjus, roasted cornish game hen with sweet pea risotto and wild mushrooms, and thyme-roasted New Zealand rack of lamb with port wine sauce.

Sorbets and gelatos highlight the exotic dessert list, which might yield a poached pear napoleon or a hazelnut-crusted butternut squash pie with goat cheese and spiced chai anglaise. A surprise at one visit was "coffee and doughnuts" – coffee crème brûlée with cinnamon sugar-coated doughnut muffins. At another it was "more ovaltine please" – chocolate ovaltine pudding with caramelized crisped rice and chocolate caramel.

(607) 272-0656. www.willowithaca.com. Entrées, $19 to $23. Dinner, Tuesday-Saturday 5 to 10. Sunday brunch, 11 to 2.

Pangea, 120 Third St., Ithaca.

Talented young chef Paul Andrews took over the striking Italian trattoria known as Tre Stelle, did some refurbishing and changed the theme to modern American. The sleek dining room, with a mix of art and artifacts on the walls, is light and airy. Canvas table tops hand-painted by a local artist provide interior color. A wraparound terrace offers sylvan courtyard dining beside ivy-covered walls on three sides.

The name Pangea refers to the world as it was before the continents drifted apart and Paul calls the fare "pre-continental cuisine." The seasonal menu favors local products with a vegetarian/organic orientation and is categorized under the elements (earth, water, fire and wind). Many dishes are available in small, medium and large portions, making for an unusual breadth of options. You might order a mushroom fricassee with grilled bread as an appetizer or a main course; ditto for the togarashi-crusted tuna with fennel slaw and pomegranate sauce. The "fire" (meat) dishes come in medium and large sizes. Hostess Nina Hien, the chef's wife, urges diners to mix and match, "sharing and passing dishes around."

The bold-flavored offerings range from forest risotto with wild mushrooms and pinenuts to grilled beef tenderloin with whipped potatoes and collard greens. Start with a grilled asparagus and radicchio salad with feta cheese or sheep's milk ricotta gnocchi in rosemary-lemon broth. Move on to lobster and mussel stew with coconut-lime broth or wood-roasted duck breast with celery-root gratin and caramelized onion jam.

The wood oven is used for flatbreads, smoked foods and for roasting pork loin with piquillo sauce and rack of lamb with rosemary-coriander sauce. It also produces a chocolate lava cake that is Pangea's signature dessert. Other sweets include coconut brûlée and lemon cream napoleon.

Pangea has added a "wine bar and den" for fondues, flatbreads and wood-grilled pizzas.

(607) 273-8515. www.pangearestaurant.com. Entrées, $15 to $26. Dinner nightly except Tuesday, from 5:30.

Sunken dining area looks toward semi-open kitchen at ZaZa's Cucina.

ZaZa's Cucina, 622 Cascadilla St., Ithaca.

Peripatetic Ithaca restaurateur Lex Chutintaranond spent $800,000 to transform a video store into a showplace Italian restaurant that opened with great buzz in 2003. Four designers took four months to ready a space that a fellow restaurateur called "very dramatic – not what you expect to find in Ithaca." The 160-seat restaurant is quite a sight, Lex agreed – "people think it belongs in Manhattan or San Francisco or Florida."

He said the building lent itself to being a replica of an Italian house, with a sunken seating area evoking a Roman bathhouse surrounded by columns in the front, a large fireplace and bar, and a remarkable ceiling mural at the end near the open kitchen. He named it for "a beautiful, mysterious woman who comes in and says, 'Hey, eat your food, eat your pasta.'"

Lex took his chef to Italy to prepare a menu of regional Italian cuisine. So, hey, eat your pasta – you've got a huge selection, from house-made wild mushroom ravioli with walnut sauce to farfalle with prosciutto and vegetables in a parmigiano-reggiano cream sauce to orecchiette with wild boar sausage and broccoli rabe.

To start, how about semolina-crusted fried calamari over baby greens, rosemary-lemon shrimp with a lima bean salad or beef carpaccio with shaved parmigiano-reggiano and truffle oil?

Move on to secondi like grilled swordfish with a lemon-basil sauce, a subtle Ligurian seafood stew in an herbed wine broth, sausage-stuffed pork loin with rosemary sauce, braised veal shank with herbed polenta, grilled New York strip steak Tuscan style and herb-crusted New Zealand rack of lamb with a red pepper-mustard sauce.

Only the seriously hungry have room for the evening's sweets.

(607) 273-9292. www.zazascucina.com. Entrées, $15 to $23. Dinner nightly, 5 to 10 or 11.

Just a Taste, 116 North Aurora St., Ithaca.

This is billed as Central New York's largest wine and tapas bar. Originally opened by Lex Chutintaranond of Thai Cuisine, it was sold to his chef, Jennifer Irwin, and Stan Walton. They continue with a carousel of treats that change daily, sometimes twice a day.

Sleek in gray, black and white with black lacquered chairs, the downtown establishment also has a small outdoor courtyard in the rear.

More than 50 wines are offered by the glass – in two sizes – or by the "flight," a sampling of 1½ ounces in a particular category, say five chardonnays for $7.50 or six local wines for $7.75. There are also Spanish, Italian and sherry flights, as well as a "Big Red" flight of heavy reds, three for $4.75. Assorted beers are available from a beer bar.

We know folks who like to order a couple of flights and a selection of international tapas and while the night away here. We had to settle for a quick lunch, sharing a spicy breaded oyster served on a bed of spinach, a chicken teriyaki kabob with an array of vegetables, and a pizza of smoked salmon and brie (the most expensive item at $5.95). The last was great; the other two were marred by the missing house sauce (so spicy when we finally got it that one of us wished we hadn't) and no semblance of an "array" of vegetables. Cappuccino and a terrific pineapple cheesecake helped compensate.

The dinner hour brings tapas in appetizer and larger sizes, as well as several pastas and entrées. You can order treats like wasabi-crusted swordfish with spicy slaw and mango aioli, pan-seared duck breast with braised bok choy and spicy peanut sauce, and chicken and apple sausage with orange couscous and mint-jalapeño chutney in either tapas or larger sizes. Or try the fettuccine with shrimp, peanuts, scallions, red curry and basil or the grilled ribeye with ancho chile sauce.

For dessert, regulars demand more than "just a taste" of Jennifer's signature warm chocolate soufflé.

(607) 277-9463. www.just-a-taste.com. Tapas, $2.50 to $7.25. Entrées, $11.50 to $13.75. Lunch/brunch daily, 11:30 to 3:30. Dinner nightly, 5:30 to 10 or 11.

Suzanne Fine Regional Cuisine, 9013 Route 414, Lodi.

Take a late-blooming New Jersey cooking instructor and caterer. Have her vacation in the Finger Lakes and fall in love with a 100-year-old farmhouse overlooking Seneca Lake. She and her husband spontaneously decide to buy the place to open a restaurant. She spends her time prepping and cooking, he commutes weekends from New Jersey. And voila! "Here I can live my dream," says Suzanne Stack.

Her little Brigadoon – a "pure" restaurant with an oddball name – reflects a way of life, connecting indigenous food with the land. Suzanne cooks with ingredients from her backyard organic garden as well as from local farmers, cheesemakers and vintners to create a dining experience that captures the flavor of the Finger Lakes.

From the initial amuse-bouche (perhaps a shot glass of creamy tomato soup with a tiny cheese puff) to the final plate of petit-fours, diners are in for a country-chic treat without pretense. The menu is seasonal and modest – generally a couple of appetizers, a soup and two salads and no more than five entrées. You might start with a rich and creamy asparagus soup, poured into a bowl at the table. More complex starters are a charlotte of lump crabmeat, asparagus and fingerling potatoes with a leek vinaigrette and a quartet of pan-seared diver scallops crowned with capers, shallots and almonds atop a swirl of madeira-mirin glaze.

Country-charming dining room is setting for Suzanne Fine Regional Cuisine.

Main courses typically range from Asian-marinated yellowfin ahi tuna with savoy cabbage slaw to filet mignon seared with garlic-mashed potatoes and a port wine sauce. The signature muscovy duck breast might turn out savory with olives, lemon confit and a potato-leek gratin layered with goat cheese from Lively Run Goat Farm in nearby Interlaken. Another time it could arrive sweetened, fanned around the plate in slices with a port wine sauce, pinenuts and currants. The rack of lamb might be sauced with local cabernet wine and accompanied by baked polenta and ratatouille.

Many diners opt for the cheese course ($10), a choice of three from perhaps five local and imported, served with appropriate fruit and bread. Desserts generally combine Finger Lakes fruit and Suzanne's homemade ice cream, as in an apple galette with toasted almonds topped with vanilla ice cream.

Bob Stack put together the wine list – about 30 vintages from the Finger Lakes, and the rest from France, Italy and Australia. He also tends the herb and vegetable garden and assists as a line cook on weekends between five-hour commutes from their home near the Jersey Shore.

The cheery dining room, looking properly farm-like, has ten well-spaced tables. Adjacent is a private dining room with a long pine farm table for ten beside shelves holding Suzanne's collection of provençal pottery and a wall of 300-plus cookbooks. Four bistro tables on the front porch yield a view of the sunset across the lake.

(607) 582-7545. www.suzannefrc.com. Entrées, $19 to $26. Dinner, Thursday-Sunday 5 to 9, June-October, Friday-Saturday off-season. Closed January and February.

Simply Red Village Bistro, 53 East Main St., Trumansburg.

Some of the area's most imaginative food is served up in this storefront diner-turned-spirited-bistro. Red-haired chef-owner Samantha Izzo wears a red baseball

Chef-owner Samantha Izzo strikes playful pose at Simply Red Village Bistro.

cap as she cooks in a snug open kitchen for a convivial crowd at booths and tables in an urbane, "simply red" place from tablecloths to walls to the red-related words painted whimsically around the ceiling. Local artworks and live music often follow the theme.

Self-taught Samantha, a native of South Africa and much traveled for her years, cooked in Boston before moving to the Finger Lakes in 2002 with her husband Gary, a theater producer from Syracuse. Her fare is an eclectic mix of flavors from Provence, Spain, Africa, Mexico and, on Mondays, the American South, reflecting time she spent in Atlanta.

The always-changing menu is short, innovative and sometimes provocative (as in her dessert of "slow ass ginger spice apple cake" on a December night). To start, the soup might be roasted garlic-french onion and the salads could include quail à l'orange or a specialty she calls Mexican flowers featuring chile-lime spiced pumpkin seeds, grilled chorizo, avocado chunks and banana chips tossed with mixed greens and more in an orange-chipotle vinaigrette. Appetizers could be a black truffle mousse, steamed mussels with the works or "killer shrimp" – jumbo shell-on shrimp steamed in Ithaca Beer Co. nut brown ale and a spicy cajun sauce.

Main courses change weekly to allow "the culinary bounty of local producers to inspire the dishes we prepare." There are always a couple of vegetarian dishes (think pad Thai, linguini primavera or stuffed acorn squash). The chef might bake parmesan-crusted monkfish topped with sliced potato and layered with oven-roasted tomatoes in a lemon beurre blanc, roast half an organic chicken with shallots, smoked bacon, red potatoes and apple chunks in a white wine and thyme broth, and offer herb-seared tenderloin medallions topped with a wild mushroom-sherry cream sauce over basil-whipped potatoes.

Typical desserts are cappuccino mousse nestled in dark chocolate cups on a bed of sabayon, blackberry marsala trifle layered with mascarpone custard and chocolate-raspberry torte finished with rum sabayon.

Shrimp and grits, country-style pork ribs and grilled cajun ribeye steak are offered every Monday evening, which features Southern-style food and old-time Appalachian mountain music and turns out to be the busiest night of the week. Live music is offered several other nights as well.

With her newborn daughter at her side, "Sam" expanded the bistro's schedule in 2006 from four to six nights a week, including Mexican Night on Tuesday.

(607) 387-5313. www.simplyredbistro.com. Entrées. $14.95 to $24.95. Dinner, Monday-Saturday 5 to 10. Closed in March.

Daño's on the Move

Daño's Heuriger on Seneca, 9564 Route 414, Lodi.

A classified ad in the New York Times led former Czech ballet dancer Daño Hutnik to Ithaca, where he opened a chic downtown restaurant called variously Daño's on Cayuga and Daño's Vienna that was widely considered the best in the city. His seasonal Viennese-style deli-pub at Standing Stone Vineyards inspired him to bigger things.

He and his wife, artist Karen Gilman, closed their Ithaca bistro to open a larger enterprise in 2005 on property overlooking Seneca Lake south of Wagner Vineyards. The result is America's first heuriger (pronounced hoy-rig-er), patterned after the wine bars outside Vienna.

Visitors pass a kitchen herb garden as they enter the airy and modernistic, architect-designed building with soaring windows onto the lake. Visible through an inside window in front is an open kitchen where Daño does the cooking and Karen the baking. Display cases show what's available beneath a menu written in fancy Viennese script on a black wall. Beyond is an elegant yet casual two-level dining room full of Karen's large paintings, handcrafted tables and earth colors, seating about 90. Outside is a seasonal dining terrace for 50.

Customers pick and choose their meal – as little or as much as they want – at the display counter or from servers who take wine orders and deliver the food. They come in for a snack or linger all evening. Some of the rustic European food is unfamiliar, Karen explains, so people like to see what they're ordering as they assemble meals family-style for sharing. Guests liken the experience to that of Manhattan's ground-breaking Craft restaurant, although with local ingredients and not so fancy nor expensive.

Daño's offers an enticing selection of breads and spreads, salads, charcuterie and rotisserie items, entrées and side dishes (some of them vegetarian) as well as Karen's luscious sweets. Terrines, bratwurst, smoked trout, Hungarian sausage, cold poached salmon, roast pork, chicken paprikash with spaetzle, wiener schnitzel, pan-fried catfish – you name it and Dano's probably has it. Snack on liptauer cheese, the Austrian house specialty, or some of the other seven spreads to dab on the contents of an artisanal bread basket. Perhaps you'd like to try Hungarian goulash or Viennese potato salad. Feast on mussels steamed with Viennese sausage in local wine; a farmer's plate of pork shank, knockwurst and smoked pork chop on a bed of braised sauerkraut with Viennese dumplings, or a Viennese bento box ("a taste of everything" for $17.95).

Display counters face two-level dining areas at Daño's Heuriger on Seneca.

The initial all-Finger Lakes wine list has been supplemented by a few from Austria.

Daño's heuriger was filmed just prior to its opening on a national TV show called Opening Soon on the Fine Living channel here and the Food Network in Canada.

(607) 582-7555. www.danosonseneca.com. Entrées, $12.95 to $17.95. Open daily, noon to 9, April-November; Thursday-Sunday noon to 8, rest of year.

More Dining Choices

Ports Café, 4432 West Lake Road (Route 14), Geneva.

This hot ticket evolved from a grocery/convenience store with a hot dog and ice cream stand. After eight years of doling out snack food to summer passersby, chef David Harvey and accountant Jeff Ritter turned a large section of a grocery/convenience store into a year-round café touting "good food, fine wine."

They still operate the summer snack bar and the grocery specializes in hard-to-fine microbrews and wines. But the star of the show is the convivial café, an assortment of booths and tables in a dark wood interior with a nod to a nautical theme reflecting Seneca Lake across the road.

From the semi-open kitchen at the rear, chef David dispenses an ambitious repertoire of regional and international fare, ranging from a peel-and-eat South Baltimore shrimp boil to garlic-encrusted ribeye steak laden with cracked peppercorns. Fajitas, shrimp sauté with feta, house-smoked Carolina spare ribs, tandoori chicken, hot meatball sandwich, grilled salmon club – you want it, they may have it, and the specials board is where it's at. The adults in our party mixed and matched our way through the rare ahi tuna, chicken and shrimp in Thai peanut sauce, double lamb chops and a killer dinner salad piled high with sirloin steak. The double chocolate-espresso and lemon crème brûlées proved worthy endings. And the kids in the group raved about their burgers and ice cream.

(315) 789-2020. www.portscafe.com. Entrées, $11.50 to $18.50. Dinner, Tuesday-Saturday 5 to 9.

Thai Cuisine, 501 South Meadow St., Ithaca.

The best Thai food in upstate New York – that's the opinion of many knowledgeable

Thai-food lovers. It's served up in a serene, white-linened, L-shaped dining room and a new front solarium in a commercial plaza by a Thai family of cooks and a mainly American staff out front. Following the departure of Lex Chutintaranond to his Madeline's restaurant downtown, this is now owned and run by his younger brother, Noi. As one staffer explained it, nothing really changed: "They learned from the same mother, and she's still in the kitchen."

A large choice of starters at dinner includes a couple of exotic soups, spring rolls, skewered pork and yum talay, a salad of shrimp, clams, scallops, mussels, Bermuda onions, mint leaves and ground chile peppers on mixed greens. There are six rice and noodle dishes, including pad Thai.

You'll have a hard time choosing among such entrées (all served with jasmine rice) as panang neur, sliced beef simmered in panang sauce with sweet basil and pineapple, served with a side of pickled cauliflower, and gaeng goong, shrimp simmered in Thai green curry with coconut milk, sliced eggplant, bamboo shoots, baby corn, chile peppers and kaffir lime. The selection is enormous, with ten shrimp dishes, for example. Almost everything is under $13.95, except for a few of "Mom's favorites."

Sunday brunch is the Thai equivalent of a dim sum meal, offering more than 30 exotic little plates. Thai Cuisine has a fairly good wine list and, of course, Thai beer.

(607) 273-2031. www.thaicuisineithaca.com. Entrées, $9.50 to $19.95. Dinner nightly except Tuesday, 5 to 9:30 or 10. Saturday lunch, 11:30 to 2:30. Sunday brunch, 11:30 to 2.

A Landmark for Vegetarians

Moosewood Restaurant, 215 North Cayuga St., Ithaca.

Once small and plain, this groundbreaking restaurant on the lower level of an old school converted into the quirky Dewitt shopping mall is known to vegetarians around the country because of the *Moosewood Cookbook,* written by a former owner of the co-op operation, some of whose nineteen owners have worked together since its founding in 1973. Now there are ten cookbooks associated with the enterprise. All are for sale along with other Moosewood memorabilia and organic salad dressings, soups and frozen entrées in the Moosewood Bar and Café, which opens off the entry and features juices, coffees and a full bar.

Expansion and remodeling have produced a light look in blond pine, with yellow-sponged walls and wooden banquettes all around. The covered sidewalk café out front is pleasant and obviously popular in season.

Original and natural-food cuisine is featured, although purists are skeptical. ("Beware," warned a printed vegan and vegetarian guide to the area. "This well-known vegetarian restaurant is no longer vegetarian and has virtually no vegan courses" – a charge disputed by the management, which says it always has at least one soup and one entrée that are dairy-less.)

"We're lazy about changing prices," one owner told us, and indeed they are quite modest. Tofu burgers, pasta primavera and Hungarian vegetable soup are frequent choices – the menu changes with each meal to take advantage of what's fresh. Pitas, frittatas, Caribbean stew, a mushroom-cheese strudel, a plate of Middle Eastern salads, cauliflower-pea curry and flounder rollatini are regulars.

The blackboard menu lists an imaginative selection of casseroles, curries, ragoûts, salads and luscious homemade desserts like strawberry cream pie, lemon-glazed gingerbread, peach trifle and a pear poached in wine with whipped cream. We liked the sound of tagine, a Moroccan vegetable stew simmered with lemon and saffron on couscous, at one visit. Also tempting was a Chesapeake platter – baked catfish with old Bay seasoning, salt potatoes and stewed corn and tomatoes. The pasta al calvofiore with cauliflower and Italian cheeses and the Japanese braised eggplant appealed to others. The food varies, depending on which of the rotating chefs is in the kitchen.

Fish is offered most nights, and Sunday nights are devoted to varying ethnic or regional cuisines.

(607) 273-9610. www.moosewoodrestaurant.com. Entrées, $12 to $15. Lunch, Monday-Saturday 11:30 to 3. Dinner, Sunday-Thursday 5:30 to 9, weekends 6 to 9:30. Café, daily 11:30 to 10.

Dining and Lodging

Geneva on the Lake, 1001 Lochland Road (Route 14), Geneva 14456.

If you want to pretend you are in a villa on an Italian lake, stay at this onetime monastery, now a small European-style resort hotel beside Seneca Lake.

Built in 1910 as a replica of the Lancellotti Villa in Frascati outside Rome, with marble fireplaces and symmetrical gardens, the original Byron M. Nester estate was the home from 1949 to 1974 of Capuchin monks. Ithaca developer Norbert Schickel turned it into apartments and then into a resort with 30 rooms and suites in 1981.

The Schickel family sold in 1995 to Alfred and Aminy Audi of Syracuse, who had saved the ailing Stickley furniture company. The Audis financed a much-needed refurbishing and upgrading designed to produce "the crown jewel of all resorts."

Mrs. Audi makes the decorating decisions, employing the vast Stickley collection of furnishings, accessories and art objects. "She has the vision," says general manager Bill Schickel, who oversees every detail. Accommodations range widely from six studio suites with fold-down murphy beds to two-bedroom suites with fireplaced living rooms to two-story townhouses. The bigger ones like the Landmark one-bedroom suite with kitchen and elegant living room in which we stayed are comfortable and luxurious in an understated way. Others are more showy. The Whirlpool Suite in the monastery's former sanctuary is a knockout with cathedral ceiling and a bright red whirlpool tub, big enough for four, in a mirrored alcove off a living room furnished in Stickley Hepplewhite. The premier Classic Suite, with fireplaces in both living room and master bedroom, is 1,100 square feet of luxury, furnished in Stickley Chippendale. The Loft Suite appears more modern in Stickley mission oak. It offers a kingsize bed, a living room with a fifteen-foot ceiling and a balcony sitting area with a view of lake and gardens. Half the suites have two bedrooms, and most come with full kitchens and large living rooms. Complimentary wine is in the refrigerator, a bowl of fruit on the table, and chocolates are at bedside after nightly turndown service.

Manicured grounds outlined in privet and dotted with marble statues stretch to the 70-foot-long swimming pool on a bluff at lake's edge. An impressive colonnade pavilion provides a lovely area for breakfast, lunch or cocktails on the rear terrace.

Guests are treated on Friday nights to a tasting of New York State wines and cheeses in the pavilion. Marion Schickel, widow of the resort's founder, has hosted the event every weekend for more than twenty years.

A light continental breakfast of fresh juice, fruit and croissants is included in the rates. A full country breakfast is available for $12. We can attest that the scrambled eggs with cream cheese and the shirred eggs with Canadian bacon are excellent.

Geneva on the Lake resort accommodates guests in Italian-style villa.

Elegant candlelight dinners with live music are offered to guests and the public nightly in the intimate and romantic Lancellotti Dining Room that could well be in Rome. It's the former foyer with carved wood ceilings, marble mantle and tapestries. Its nine tables are supplemented by five more in an adjacent Garden Room, all graced by extravagant floral bouquets.

The food is fine, the service flawless and the ambiance quite festive as a singer and a pianist or a violinist entertain throughout the meal. The pricey, set menu varies by the night of the week, weekdays prix-fixe for five courses and weekends à la carte.

Diners partake of appetizers like dilled jumbo shrimp cocktail (the recipe featured in Bon Appétit magazine), and entrées like grilled filet mignon chasseur and sesame-crusted yellowfin tuna with soy-ginger glaze. The signature dishes offered by a team of three chefs rarely change. We've enjoyed the chicken jacqueline in port wine and heavy cream with sliced apples and toasted almonds, and sherried shrimp dejonghe, both with crisp beans and mixed rice, followed by pumpkin cheesecake and a grand marnier mousse. Another occasion produced rack of lamb dijonnaise and a tasty special of poached salmon with salsa, teamed with excellent spinach salads with warm bacon dressing. Bananas foster and strawberries romanoff were worthy endings.

Locals shocked by the dinner prices are quite happy with summer lunches on the Colonnade terrace. Options range from vegetable spring rolls to chicken and asparagus crêpes. We liked the garlicky and chunky vegetable gazpacho with a curried chicken and avocado plate and the carrot-ginger soup with a curried chicken in pita sandwich, followed by a cheesecake with blueberries and a delectable frozen grand marnier coupe.

The resort is expensive, but worth it for a special treat.

(315) 789-7190 or (800) 343-6382. Fax (315) 789-0322. www.genevaonthelake.com. Six rooms and 23 suites with private baths. Doubles, $225 to $360 weekends, $205 to $325 midweek. Suites, $350 to $805 weekends, $315 to $730 midweek.

Prix-fixe, $59; entrées, $34. Lunch in summer, Monday-Saturday noon to 2. Dinner, Sunday-Thursday 6:30 to 8, Friday-Saturday 7 to 9.

Mirbeau Inn & Spa, 851 West Genesee St., Skaneateles 13152.

Lavender flourishes at the entry and gorgeous gardens flank a lily pond in a scene straight out of Monet's Giverny. Opened in 2000, this $7-million luxury resort was patterned after a French country estate and notable, in the words of a Syracuse newspaper headline, for "Monet and Money."

Three local residents created the soothing establishment combining the amenities of a boutique country inn and world-class spa facilities with the residential feeling of a French château. Cloistered behind a stone wall off U.S. Route 20, Mirbeau occupies the front portion of a twelve-acre wooded property on the western edge of the village.

Local architect Andrew Ramsgard, one of the three owner-partners, created buildings that take advantage of the sloping lot and the water that flows through the center of the property. Rather than the simple gray stone aspect of Monet's house at Giverny, however, these take on turreted, castle-like proportions, are built of concrete and stucco, and are colored in the earth tones of Provence.

Eighteen guest quarters, a restaurant and the spa occupy the soaring main lodge, which is quite a novelty for upstate New York. Behind and to the side of the lodge are four villa-style cottages of similar French provincial design, each with four guest rooms. All curve around a serene, central landscaped area of tiered lily ponds and gardens with, yes, a replica of the famed Japanese bridge in Monet's garden.

Each of 34 guest rooms comes with a kingsize or two queen beds, fireplace, sitting area and large bathroom with soaking tub, walk-in shower and double vanity. Some rooms open onto hospitality areas and may be joined as suites.

The main lodge is oriented toward the rear, where tall windows overlook ponds and gardens. Near the lobby is one of the waterfalls that trickles through the property and adds to the calming influence of the spa. The rear wing of the lodge holds ten spa treatment rooms, steam and sauna rooms, a weight room and motion studio. Outside are hot and cold plunge pools.

Across the lobby from the spa area is the **Mirbeau Dining Room,** with beamed ceiling, French and American impressionist paintings on the walls, French antiques and a terrace for outdoor dining. Executive chef Edward J. Moro cooked at the Little Nell Hotel in Aspen, Colo., and at the historic Hotel Hershey in his Pennsylvania hometown. Here he offers what is touted as "Mirbeau Estate cuisine," available to the public as well as spa guests. The food and service are impeccable and the terrace setting magical, according to innkeeper-restaurant friends from Ontario. The dinner menu changes seasonally. The meal is available à la carte or prix-fixe, $59 for four courses or $64 for five courses, plus canapés to start and les mignardises to finish. Start with oysters on the half shell with ginger mignonette, house-cured smoked salmon with potato crisps and crème fraiche, or venison carpaccio with romaine hearts, reggiano and a lemon-dijon-caper vinaigrette. Or how about a hearty sweet potato and vanilla soup with jumbo prawn and andouille sausage?

Main courses could be pesto-marinated halibut with wild mushrooms, butter-braised Maine lobster, Hudson Valley duck breast with sundried cherry sauce, garlic-crusted beef tenderloin with bordelaise sauce, and "the year's first lamb chop" with white beans and lamb cassoulet. Desserts range from vanilla crème brûlée with almond biscotti and warm chocolate cake with bourbon ice cream and toasted walnuts to a trio of sorbets with fresh fruit.

Lunch is similarly exotic, from a four-course tasting menu ($32) to a smoked salmon BLT or sautéed beef tenderloin.

Light and airy Mirbeau Dining Room overlooks terrace and garden courtyard.

(315) 685-5006 or (877) 647-2328. Fax (315) 685-0661. www.mirbeau.com. Thirty-four rooms with private baths. Doubles, $205 to $395 mid-May-October, $155 to $350 rest of year.

Dinner entrées, $29; prix-fixe, $59 and $64. Lunch daily, 11:30 to 2:30. Dinner nightly, 6 to 9:30.

Aurora Inn, 391 Main St., Aurora 13026.

Like a Phoenix reborn, the historic Aurora Inn beside Cayuga Lake is riding high again, thanks to a multi-million-dollar renovation in 2003.

The aging Federal-style inn, built in 1833 in the town in which Henry Wells (of Wells-Fargo stagecoach fame and founder of American Express) was to launch Wells College, had deteriorated to the point where it closed in 2000 and stood as a forlorn symbol of a depressed village and a vanished era. To the rescue came philanthropist Pleasant T. Rowland, a 1962 Wells graduate who had created the American Girls Collection of dolls and books. She considered both the inn and the village "a treasure to protect" and formed a foundation with the college to do so.

The three-story brick inn's facade was restored to its original look, complete with white-columned porches and balconies in front and back, some of which had been removed decades ago. Four original fireplaces were uncovered to become focal points of the reception area, parlor, dining room and tavern. Rich woods, antiques, oriental rugs and an impressive art collection enhance the public areas.

Eight guest rooms on the second and third floors blend timeless charm with modern comforts. Each is individually decorated with designer fabrics and furnishings. Frette linens and down pillows dress the queensize Regency-style poster beds. Two additional lodgings with vaulted ceilings are on the fourth floor: a two-room suite with a king bed and a deep-soak whirlpool tub and an extra-large

Umbrella-shaded veranda offers lakeside dining al fresco at Aurora Inn.

room with two double beds, wet bar and a skylit whirlpool bath. The queen rooms open onto balconies furnished with rocking chairs and a swing or a bench. Four have gas fireplaces. All rooms have marble baths, comfortable sitting areas, writing desks wired for high-speed internet access and flat-panel LCD televisions and DVD players hidden inside armoires.

Three meals a day are served at a mix of banquettes, booths and cherry tables in a 55-seat dining room with views onto the lake. French doors open for al fresco dining on a porch and a broad, umbrella-shaded veranda on the roof of the lower-level lakeside function room.

The kitchen is headed by Greg Rhoad, whose cuisine we enjoyed during his seven-year tenure as head chef at Rosalie's Cucina in Skaneateles. He hewed to the inn's traditional American country fare, offering what he called "comfort food at its very best." For dinner that means items like a creamy Boston seafood chowder, an iceberg lettuce wedge salad, roast chicken with "feather" dumplings and the signature slow-cooked pot roast. About the only appetizers in the contemporary idiom on a recent winter menu were a lobster charlotte layered with avocado and mango in a lemon-dill sauce and pecan-crusted shrimp over winter squash risotto. Among entrées were blue-crab stuffed shrimp wrapped in Virginia ham over toasted orzo pasta, seared duck breast with cranberry-pecan stuffing and raspberry demi-glace, delmonico steak charbroiled with garlic butter, and grilled rosemary lamb chops with tzatziki sauce, potato latkes, artichokes and minted tomato relish.

On a lunch menu laden with the tried and true (tuna melt, burger, turkey club sandwich), the slow-roasted lamb enchilada stood out.

Desserts show more imagination. Besides the predictable ice cream sundaes and a classic crème caramel, you might find a caramelized banana tart, a lime bavarian napoleon with pomegranate sauce, warm bourbon-chocolate cake with vanilla cream custard and even an individual pineapple meringue pie.

(315) 364-8888 or (866) 364-8808. Fax (315) 364-8887. www.aurora-inn.com. Nine rooms and one suite with private baths. Doubles, $225 to $350 May-October, $125 to $275 rest of year.

Entrées, $18 to $32. Lunch daily, 11:30 to 2:30. Dinner nightly, 5 to 8 or 9. Sunday brunch, 10 to 2. Restaurant closed Monday and Tuesday from January to early May.

La Tourelle Resort & Spa, 1150 Danby Road (Route 96B), Ithaca 14850.

A French-style country inn or a glorified motel? Although the white stucco building trimmed with brown certainly looked and acted more like the former than the latter, the perennial question is now moot. A major expansion in 2005 elevated it into a resort and spa.

La Tourelle was built with a French accent in 1986 by Walter Wiggins, a partner in the legendary L'Auberge du Cochon Rouge restaurant next door (which was damaged by fire in 1994 and reopened as the John Thomas Steakhouse). The building is set back from the road on a 75-acre hillside sloping to Buttermilk Falls State Park.

The three-story addition off the rear of the original holds nineteen deluxe rooms and suites, each with king bed, fireplace, balcony and jacuzzi bath. Furnishings and decor have contemporary Asian accents, reflecting the East Meets West fusion theme of the new August Moon Spa on the ground floor.

Back in the plant-filled lobby notable for colorful tiled floors, comfortable sofas are in front of a stone fireplace. Guests are greeted with beverages and cookies. Between the lobby and the original Tower building is **Le Petite Café,** a 24-seater offering a buffet breakfast to house guests and spa-oriented cuisine for lunch.

The original 35 spacious rooms are handsomely appointed in elegant country French style. Each has king or queen feather beds, good art, TV/DVDs (movies are available at the front desk), and tiled and marble bathrooms. A decanter of Spanish sherry awaits in each room.

The most memorable are the two round "romantic tower rooms," which must be seen to be believed. Each has a sunken circular waterbed, a double jacuzzi just behind it, a TV mounted over the door and a mirrored ceiling. A room with a wood-burning fireplace has a kingsize poster bed and french doors onto a small balcony.

For dinner, inn guests can walk across the lawn and join the public at the **John Thomas Steakhouse**, where the beef is prime and the prices lofty.

No longer French, the menu ranges from ribeye to T-bone steak. The specialty is porterhouse steak for two ($65). There are Chilean sea bass, broiled salmon, shrimp scampi, jumbo lobster, a vegetarian platter and chicken forestière or pommery for non-beef eaters. Salads, vegetables and the usual side orders cost extra.

Appetizers include smoked trout, baked deviled crab, shrimp cocktail and clams casino. Desserts range from crème brûlée and puff pastry with Italian cream and blueberries to assorted ice creams and triple berry strudel.

(607) 273-2734 or (800) 765-1492. www.latourelleinn.com. Fifty-four rooms with private baths. Doubles, $150 to $325 mid-April to mid-November, $125 to $275 rest of year.

Restaurant: (607) 273-3464. www.johnthomassteakhouse.net. Entrées, $16.95 to $37.50. Dinner nightly, 5:30 to 10 or 11.

Lodging

Morgan-Samuels Inn, 2920 Smith Road, Canandaigua 14424.

Actor Judson Morgan, not J.P. Morgan as was first thought, built this rambling stone mansion in 1810, and eventually it became the home of industrialist Howard Samuels, who ran unsuccessfully for governor of New York a few decades ago. The house was acquired in 1989 by Julie and John Sullivan, who left jobs in nearby Geneseo to convert it into a very special inn. Situated on 46 rural acres, it offers one of the more peaceful, utterly relaxing situations we know of.

One fastidious innkeeper of our acquaintance said she had her best breakfast ever here. Ours certainly was a triumph, and so pretty we wished we'd brought along a camera for a color photograph.

The meal – for some the highlight of a stay at this sophisticated and enchanting B&B – is taken in the beamed dining room, in a glass-enclosed breakfast-tea room with potbelly stove or outside on the rear patio. John oversees the cooking – he or his innkeeper usually makes an early-morning run to the supermarket to pick out the perfect fruit for the first course. We counted 26 varieties exquisitely put together on the silver platter, including local Irondequoit melon, mango, two kinds of grapes, papaya, persimmon, figs, kiwis and prunes sautéed in lemon sauce. Gilding the lily was half a baked grapefruit with port wine and brown sugar. Preceding the platter was fresh orange juice served in delicate etched glasses. Following were huge and delicious carrot muffins and a choice of buckwheat pancakes with blackberries, blueberries or pecans (or all three), scrambled eggs with herbs, french toast or a double-cheese omelet. The last was one of the best breakfast treats we've had. It looked like a pizza with slices of tomato, scallions, red peppers, jalapeño peppers, mushrooms, herbs and parsley. Monterey jack, mozzarella, parmesan and blue cheeses were on top. Spicy sausage patties and sunflower-seed toast accompanied this breakfast worthy of a Morgan, as did hazelnut coffee.

The Sullivans may join guests for hors d'oeuvre and beverages in the late afternoon, which helps break the ice so "everybody is friends when they get together for breakfast the next morning," says Julie. The treats range from John's homemade sauces on chicken wings and piegogi (tenderloin sautéed in a Korean sauce) to cheese and crackers. They accompany hot or iced tea, cider or sparkling grape juice.

John prepares multi-course dinners by reservation for eight or more guests ($65 to $72 per person, depending on the menu). Guests bring their own wine and enjoy togetherness in the dining room or enclosed garden porch or privacy in five separate dining areas. The menu offers a choice of seafood or beef – our filet mignon with a sherry-herb sauce was fabulous.

Although food is obviously a passion here, the five guest rooms and a suite and the common areas are hardly afterthoughts. All eleven rooms in the house come with fireplaces. The Morgan Suite is lavish with early 18th-century French furniture, a kingsize bed, an over-length loveseat in front of the TV and a double jacuzzi in a corner of the bathroom. A fountain sounds like a babbling brook beneath Evie's Chamber, a Victorian fantasy with a rosewood queensize bed, sitting area and balcony. The Antique Rose Room has french doors onto a balcony, a floral carpet and one of the first kingsize beds ever made.

Soft music is piped throughout the house and across the grounds, and candles glow in the common rooms. Besides the aforementioned garden porch where we like to relax, there are a well-furnished living room, an intimate Victorian library with a TV, and fine oil paintings all around. Outside are no fewer than four landscaped patios (one with a trickling fountain and another with a lily pond and waterfall), a tennis court and gardens. Ducks and chickens and a heifer or a horse roam around in the distance. You could easily imagine you were at a house party in the country with *the* J.P. Morgan et al.

In summer, the Sullivans sometimes put up guests in three sumptuous suites at their lakeside home.

(585) 394-9232. www.morgansamuelsinn.com. Five rooms and one suite with private baths. Mid-May through November: doubles $169 to $249, suite $395. Rest of year: doubles $119 to $179, suite $195.

The William Henry Miller Inn, 303 North Aurora St., Ithaca 14850.

In lieu of afternoon tea, dessert and coffee are the gourmet fare at this majestic 1880 mansion at the edge of downtown Ithaca, part of the East Hill Historic District.

Owner Lynnette Scofield, who restored the former residence into a B&B in 1999, treats guests to a dessert buffet when they arrive back from dinner. The fare might be a choice of white chocolate or fudge brownies with cranberries one night, triple chocolate cake and glazed lemon pound cake the next. The treats are put out at 7:30 in a handsome dining room and people adjourn to the front music and reading room which has an organ or to a coffered living room with two pianos.

Lynette, who lives upstairs in the carriage house behind the inn, offers seven guest rooms with crisp decor in a house full of American chestnut woodwork, stained-glass windows and working fireplaces. Dane's Room, an expansive second-story affair with shuttered windows, has a kingsize bed and a large bath with double vanity and whirlpool tub. The Sanctuary, a corner room overlooking church steeples and rooftops, comes with a queen bed, bird-patterned wallpaper, whirlpool tub and separate shower. The Library has a queen sleigh bed, corner fireplace, spacious sitting area and built-in bookshelves. Each room has a telephone and a discreetly located TV.

The main floor of the carriage house in back has a two-room suite with a jacuzzi tub, plus a handicapped-accessible room.

A full breakfast is offered in the dining room, the parlor or in guest bedrooms. Fresh juice and a fruit course (perhaps a baked pear with raspberries and cream) accompany home-baked breads straight from the oven. The main course is usually a choice of sweet and savory: perhaps scrambled eggs with smoked salmon and cream cheese, or pecan waffles with warm syrup, each accompanied by bacon or ham.

(607) 256-4553 or (877) 256-4553. Fax (607) 256-0092. www.millerinn.com. Eight rooms and one suite with private baths. Doubles $145 to $175 weekends, $125 to $155 midweek. Suite, $195 weekends, $165 midweek.

Hobbit Hollow Farm, 3061 West Lake Road, Skaneateles 13152.

This substantial, 100-year-old Colonial Revival on a 320-acre hillside horse farm overlooking Skaneateles Lake offers some of the grandest newer B&B accommodations in the Finger Lakes. Michael and Noreen Falcone, who live lakeside across the street, bought the property to save it from development. They totally rebuilt the original farmhouse and spared no expense in furnishing it in the style of an elegant country house. Forty horses are boarded and roam the pastures.

Guests enter the side door of what looks to be two complete houses joined by a hallway wing in the middle. In the reception foyer is a stunning mural of the house and its setting. On one side of the foyer are a cozy library with TV and a lemon-yellow dining room where breakfast is served at a table for eight. On the other side are two sumptuous living rooms, each open to the other. At the far end of the house, facing the lake, is a nifty porch furnished with chairs so comfortable that "we had to wake up one gentleman there," reported one of the innkeepers.

Upstairs, widely separated from each other because of the layout of the house, are five guest rooms of varying size. Standard are triple-sheeted beds with high-thread-count Italian linens, heavy draperies puddled to the floor, MacKenzie-Childs accessories, telephones, terry robes and hair dryers. The smallest room, basically for overflow, is barely big enough for a double bed tucked in its bay window and has a bath across the hall. Another, with an 18th-century Italian queen bed, has a bath with shower and soaking tub. The other rooms are substantially larger. The Chanticleer, done in French country style, offers a queensize pencil-post bed and a huge bath with a large soaking tub The front-corner Lake View room is aptly named. It comes with a carved oak queen poster bed, a double armoire, gas fireplace, thick oriental rugs, a marble-encased double whirlpool tub and a glass-enclosed, walk-in shower. The Master bedroom occupies the other front corner and is even more grand, with a majestic kingsize poster bed facing a gas fireplace, two plump silk-covered chairs, a double whirlpool tub, and a large screened porch furnished in wicker. Relax there with a view of the lake and you may never want to leave.

But leave you must, if only for the wine and cheese or tea and cookies offered every evening around 6. Chocolate truffles arrive when the beds are turned down. In the morning, breakfast is served amidst sterling, Waterford and Wedgwood. The main course could be a puffed ham and cheese omelet, blueberry pancakes, belgian waffles or cinnamon-roll french toast stuffed with seasonal fruit.

(315) 685-2791 or (877) 746-2248. Fax (315) 685-3426. www.hobbithollow.com. Five rooms with private baths. Doubles, $120 to $270 May-December, $100 to $250 rest of year.

The Halsey House, 2057 Trumansburg Road (Route 96), Trumansburg 14886.

Guests are cosseted in comfort and style in this Federal/Greek Revival-style house built in 1829 on a spacious lot on the outskirts of Trumansburg at the corner of Route 96 and Taughannock Park Road, a pastoral road leading to the Taughannock Falls and the state park. KC and Mitch Clarke, painting and wallpaper contractors in Colorado, undertook several years of restoration, first commuting long-distance from Littleton and eventually moving on site to finish the job.

The spacious house, listed on the National Historic Register, is a beauty. The first floor of the main house has a comfortable parlor, a game room/library and a dining room where breakfast is served. An addition out back holds the kitchen, the owners' quarters and a sunny aviary that's home to the couple's six friendly parrots.

Upstairs in the main house are four guest quarters, each with TV/DVD players and beds bearing pillowtop mattresses, feather pillows and quilts. The largest is Margaret's Retreat, a front-corner expanse with an imposing queensize canopy walnut bed and a bath with two-person whirlpool tub. A kingsize hand-carved mahogany bed is featured in a room with warm gold wallpaper called Serenity. Two rooms are in back, one small and cozy and the other larger with two queen beds.

The hosts serve a full breakfast in the dining room. Southwest egg casserole, banana pancakes or baked stuffed french toast might be the main course.

(607) 387-5428 or (800) 387-5590. Fax (607) 387-5977. www.halseyhouse.com. Four rooms with private baths. Doubles, $160 to $175.

Gourmet Treats

There's a growing regional awareness of what one booster calls the "foods of the Finger Lakes," a reference to the diversity of locally produced foods, from goat cheese to exotic produce.

A national model, the **Ithaca Farmers' Market** is a joy for fresh produce, local crafts and odds and ends (free kittens, bluegrass music, hand-stenciled shirts and such). Fresh egg rolls or falafel sandwiches washed down with homemade raspberry juice are one local innkeeper's Saturday lunch of choice. The cooperative with 150 vendors living within 30 miles of Ithaca marked its 30th anniversary in 2006. The market operates in a pavilion at Steamboat Landing off Third Street on the Cayuga Lake Inlet weekends from 10 to 3 May-October, Saturdays 9 to 3 in April and November-December, and Thursdays from 3 to 7 June-August. It also operates Tuesdays from 9 to 2 May-October in Dewitt Park, downtown across from the Dewitt Mall.

Another market is **The Windmill,** the first rural farm and craft market in New York State and grown in twenty years to more than 250 vendors. Likened to the Pennsylvania farm markets (Amish and Mennonite foods are available), its four buildings, open-air market and street of shops are at 3900 State Route 14A between Penn Yan and Dundee. Wineries are among the booths that operate Saturdays and major holidays from 8 to 4:30, May to early December.

Ludgate Farms, 1552 Hanshaw Road, Ithaca, is where you can get an idea of the variety and magnitude of the local food phenomenon. It is a produce stand without peer, as well as a purveyor of fresh herbs (eight kinds of mint; seven kinds of thyme), edible flowers for garnishes, organic and natural foods, wild game and a potpourri of specialty items. Linda Ludgate and her brother Michael started three decades ago with a card table along the road, selling produce from their father's fields. Today, the stand is an enclosed gourmet market open 365 days a year.

Now You're Cooking at 116 Ithaca Commons carries unusual aprons, many regional and other cookbooks, dishes painted with colorful fruits and vegetables, fine flatware and napkins. Along with classic cookware are hard-to-find gadgets and an enormous collection of cookie cutters.

The Brous and Mehaffey families have cornered a good share of the specialty-foods market in Ithaca since they bought **Collegetown Bagels** at 415 College Ave. in 1981. A downtown branch and **CTB Appetizers,** a gourmet deli and production kitchen in Triphammer Mall, followed. They purchased the **Ithaca Bakery** at 400 North Meadow St. to create a flagship store with the best of all their operations in a single location. Here is a gourmet paradise, where we've often found the makings for a fabulous picnic or a dinner at home. We have a tough time deciding between salads and roasted chicken items, but that's nothing compared to our dilemma in front of the pastry counter.

North Side Wine & Spirits boasts the largest selection of Finger Lakes wines in the world. It may be an idle boast, although the owner says he checked around. The selection is mind-boggling and nicely priced. The toughest part is finding the place, which actually is on the south side of town in the Ithaca Shopping Plaza off Elmira Road (Route 13), where the sign calls it Discount Beverage Center.

The cognoscenti follow the advice of wine writer David Sparrow at **Sparrow's Fine Wines,** 511 North Meadow St.

In an area known for wine, the fledgling **Ithaca Beer Co.** is sharing in "capturing the spirit of the Finger Lakes." Owner Dan Mitchell and brewmaster Jeff Conuel, both Cornell grads, offer eight different beers and one soda (root beer) on tap and by the bottle at the microbrewery at 606 Elmira Road, Ithaca. They have tastings daily and tours on Saturday. Open Monday-Saturday 11 to 6.

A supermarket for gourmets? The new **Wegmans** in Ithaca, a mega superstore at 500 South Meadow St., is heaven on earth for food lovers. This even has a demonstration kitchen and a school of culinary arts. The Market Café and coffee bar at the entry set the stage for the wonders to come. We sipped latte as we watched sushi chefs rolling their treats, ogled breads and French pastries, visited the wokery (one huge table of just Chinese prepared food) and the Mediterranean snack bar, and pondered the choices at the gourmet salad bar, not to mention all the pizzas and pastas. With selections like these to eat here or to go, who'd ever cook at home? But if you want to, Wegmans will oblige. The 30 checkout counters at the front await.

Canandaigua, home of the New York Wine & Culinary Center, offers two special shops long of interest to gourmands. **Renaissance – the Goodie II Shoppe** at 56 South Main St. stocks all the socially correct gifts, from jewelry to porcelain dolls, Portmerion china and lovely Christmas ornaments. Cookbooks (we picked up Linda McCarthy's for a vegetarian son) and nifty paper plates and napkins abound. At **Cat's in the Kitchen,** 367 West Ave., Laurel Wemett has collected, from tag sales and auctions, all the things our mothers and grandmothers used in the kitchen. She specializes in the Depression era to the 1960s, and it's fun to check the old canisters, cookie jars, china, pots and pans and more. New items are mixed in.

Skaneateles has become a mecca for shoppers lately, and the shops backing up to Skaneateles Lake are manifestly upscale. **Rhubarb** at 59 East Genesee St. is a small but select kitchen and garden shop, where everything from gadgets and gourmet foods to espresso makers is chosen with great taste and nicely displayed. **Pomodoro,** our favorite gift shop here for many years, occupies a ramble of rooms in a house at 61 East Genesee. Cookbooks, a few specialty foods, dishes and placemats are among the wares. Friendship pays, says owner Kay DiNardo, for her **Vermont Green Mountain Specialty Co.** at 50 East Genesee is the only retailer to whom Albert Kumin sells his famed Green Mountain Chocolate Co. candies. His luscious chocolates vie for attention with Green Mountain coffees and Vermont specialty foods at this most unlikely place for a Vermont shop.

At **Patisserie** at 4 Hannum St., in a carriage house behind the Sherwood Inn, Hawaiian baker Chris Uyehara and his wife Kelly create fabulous sweets and artisan breads in a retail shop that also supplies inn owner Bill Eberhardt's varied restaurant operations. The delectable pastries – blueberry turnovers, cranberry scones, marzipans, fancy cakes – are to die for. We departed with a loaf of sundried tomato ciabatta, described as "the Italian slipper bread" and looking the part.

Goats and Gelati

Skyland Farm Craft Gallery & Café, 4966 Route 414, Hector.

Display and cutting gardens, a labyrinth and farm animals lure passersby to a showy 200-year-old golden brown hemlock barn with all kinds of delights inside and out. A new portion of the barn is built around the trunk of a two-story-high white oak tree, with a spiral staircase winding through the branches from a café and bakery up to a second-floor craft gallery featuring works by 300 artisans. The chief artisan is Skyland owner Barbara Hummel, whose husband Greg designed and built the place and whose mother named it Skyland because she felt the setting turned the sky and land into paradise on earth. Barbara works in her potter's studio in back when she's not helping customers in the ground-floor gift shop, which features everything from specialty foods to cutting boards shaped like the leaves of grapes associated with favorite wines. The Garden Room Café offers light lunches, tea, fabulous dessert pastries and – most in demand – 20 varieties of Italian gelato imported from New York City and colorfully displayed in a glass cooler. You can eat at handcrafted booths beside windows looking down the hillside to Seneca Lake. Browse through the gallery and find stained glass, framed fiber art featuring grape leaves with their tentacles, colorful brooms, mirrors crafted from Seneca Lake stones, jewelry and art made of Finger Lakes beach glass, wire sculptures, organic soaps and lotions, bath soaps, even Finger Lakes popping corn. You and/or the youngsters can walk with the goats, cut bouquets from the garden, meditate in the inspirational labyrinth modeled after one at the Chartres cathedral in France, feed the sheep and chickens, and dig for dinosaur eggs in the oversize children's sandbox. And, of course, savor those to-die-for baked goods and gelati.

(607) 546-5050. www.skylandfarm.net. Open 11 to 5, Wednesday-Sunday from Memorial Day to Labor Day, Friday-Sunday in fall and daily week before Christmas.

Color This Fanciful

MacKenzie-Childs Ltd., 3260 State Route 90, Aurora.

You may have seen the fanciful hand-painted majolica pottery by MacKenzie-Childs in fine gift shops and department stores across the country. Be advised that their design and production studio is on a wonderful Victorian farm estate on 75 acres above Cayuga Lake, a mile north of the Wells College town of Aurora. The venture founded in 1983 by ceramists Victoria and Richard MacKenzie-Childs was acquired in 2001 by Pleasant T. Rowland, a Wells alumna who raised its profile as she began spearheading the revival of the lakeside village. A long brick driveway leads visitors past ever-changing gardens, hay fields, a duck pond, barns, a herd of 25 grazing Scottish Highland cattle and an ornate, Gothic Revival-style "chicken palace" that is home to about 100 ducks, chickens and guinea fowl.

The destinations for most are the production studio in a former dairy barn, the restored Second Empire farmhouse that's now a MacKenzie-Childs showhouse, and a vast barn of a retail shop. The shop sells the MacKenzie-Childs pottery, furniture, painted floor rugs and trimmings, all noted for their intricate stripes, dots, checkerboards, fish and pastoral landscapes. Seconds are available, but also command high prices.

Artisans lead enlightening, 90-minute tours of the production studio where 150 artisans work. Visitors get a behind-the-scenes glimpse of how terra cotta clay is molded, painted and fired into decorative dinnerware and watch master craftsmen hand-decorate fine furniture layered with remarkable detail.

Daily tours of the newly restored Farmhouse at MacKenzie-Childs are also available. The 1840s homestead was renovated on all three floors to showcase MacKenzie-Childs products in a home-like setting. Some fifteen rooms reflect how the company's pottery, glassware, tiles and home furnishings can be paired with a variety of styles. That farmhouse tour also includes a look at the former Restaurant at MacKenzie-Childs, a stunning three-story space attached to the retail shop. Striking for a round hole in its ceiling open to a colorful roof sporting flags and pieces of "Happy Accidents," the second-floor dining area was a whimsical blend of Adirondack lodge and MacKenzie style. Alas, the restaurant was closed in 2004 with no plans for reopening. A hot-dog cart offers light refreshments in the summer.

(315) 364-7123 or (800) 640-0546. www.mackenzie-childs.com. Tours twice daily mid-May to mid-October: studio tours Monday-Friday at 9:30 and 1:15, farmhouse tours daily at 11 and 3. Rest of year: studio tour Monday-Friday at 1:15, farmhouse tour Monday-Friday at 10.30, Saturday-Sunday at 2. One tour, adults $10; combination tour, $18. Store open daily, 9:30 to 6.

Niagara-on-the-Lake

Wine, Orchards and Shaw

There is no single area in the East where food and wine meet naturally in such fertile surroundings as in Niagara-on-the-Lake.

It was not always thus. When we first met the place in the 1960s, Canadians referred to it as Sleepy Hollow. With a set of parents in tow, we had driven to Ontario from our home in Rochester, N.Y., so a visiting father could see "The Devil's Disciple" by one of his favorite playwrights, George Bernard Shaw. After a matinee performance at the Court House Theatre, we browsed through the few shops worth browsing, ate dinner at the quaint Oban Inn and headed home under a full moon. It was the historic night when man first landed on the moon, and that extra-terrestrial feat remained etched in our consciousness long after the Niagara outing had been forgotten.

Now, many moons later, we regard Niagara-on-the-Lake far more favorably. This Sleepy Hollow has awakened, spread its wings and come of age. The opening in 1973 of the Shaw Festival Theater – coupled with the launch in 1975 of Canada's first cottage winery – sparked a renaissance in the performing arts, viticulture and tourism on a scale unmatched in eastern North America.

It was quite a change for this charming, tree-lined town located where the Niagara River meets Lake Ontario. Founded by British Loyalists escaping the American Revolution, it served as the first capital of what was called Upper Canada and played a pivotal role in the War of 1812 – still called "the war" in local circles today. But the capital was moved to safer ground in Toronto and business languished as the Welland Canal bypassed Niagara to the west.

Spared the onslaught that an economic boom can wreak, Niagara's Old Town was an architectural treasury of early buildings awaiting revival. The homegrown Shaw Festival provided that impetus, attracting visitors who wanted good lodging, good food and good shopping.

Geography has afforded the area natural advantages that won it recent acclaim as Canada's prettiest town. Old military reserves and fertile farmlands yield a greenbelt around the Old Town. The Niagara River Parkway cuts through 35 miles of some of the most picturesque parklands and scenery you'll ever see. The Niagara fruit belt yields an abundance of fresh fruits and vegetables. And wineries flourish in Eastern North America's largest and most concentrated wine-growing region, described by Canadians as "the Napa of the North." As its wineries escalate to world-class status, demand grows for world-class food. The marriage of local produce and wines has inspired the development of a regional cuisine of distinction.

Success was assured by its location at the start of the Golden Horseshoe, Canada's largest population corridor, which curves around the southwestern end of Lake Ontario into Toronto.

Niagara's burgeoning success now threatens its appeal, however. Crowds of visitors choke the Old Town in summer to the extent that residents avoid downtown for weeks on end. A Chinese entrepreneur acquired and upgraded the town's largest hotel properties and began attracting a clientele that has, old-timers scoff, more money than taste.

Yet there are no chain stores or hotels, beyond a large Crabtree & Evelyn branch that seems very much at home and a newer Dansk outlet that does not. There is

Dining room at On the Twenty Restaurant looks onto wooded ravine.

only one traffic light (at the edge of town). A clock tower in the middle of Queen Street is the dominant landmark in a downtown swathed in showy flowers.

Come along and see why Niagara-on-the-Lake is such a choice getaway for the gourmet.

Dining

More than in other wine regions, the area's best and most appealing restaurants are associated with wineries. Like the wineries themselves, they are of relatively recent vintage and multiplying exponentially.

The Best of the Best

On the Twenty Restaurant, 3836 Main St., Jordan.

Ontario's first full-service winery restaurant draws food lovers from miles around. Housed in the old Jordan Winery dating to 1870, the restaurant at Cave Spring Cellars has a sophisticated country air and food to match.

"You can't imagine what it's like for a cook to come into an area like this," said founding chef Michael Olson, who for nearly a decade ran the ambitious food and catering venture launched in 1993 by the owners of the adjacent Cave Spring Cellars and wrote the fine *Inn on the Twenty Cookbook.* Before leaving to teach culinary classes at Niagara College, he and Angelo Pavan, Cave Spring's winemaker, set about matching foods and wines for adventuresome palates. Executive chef Kevin Maniaci followed in their footsteps.

Like most of the other winery restaurants, the lunch menu would serve as dinner almost anywhere else in terms of content and price (entrées, $16 to $24). You could start with a galette of artisanal cheese with warm quince and a Niagara vegetable salad or lobster taglioni in brandied cream. The seven main courses typically range from a curried lamb burger with ratatouille to grilled veal medallions with gaie bleu cream on a fresh fig, purple potato and fine bean salad.

At dinner, our party of four was impressed with both the tastes and presentations. A bruschetta of toasted sourdough bread with herbed tomatoes barely made it around the table, so good was each morsel. Among other starters, the mushroom bisque with chardonnay cream and sourdough croutons was a work of art and the salad of roasted bell peppers on greens with baked olives and feta cheese was sensational. The pan-fried chicken livers with sour cherries atop greens and toasted pumpkin seeds was an interesting if not wholly successful combination, and the chilled cucumber soup with smoked trout and chives turned out a bit bland. For main courses, we were delighted with the Pacific halibut with sweet corn salsa, grilled trout with golden plum and mint salsa, pancetta-wrapped rack of lamb with spicy salsa verde, and fresh spaghettini with roast chicken, leeks and apricots in a riesling-olive oil sauce. Each plate came with the chef's trademark decoration, squiggles of puréed beets blended with yogurt, as well as exotic accompaniments.

The night's desserts included blueberry-sour cream cake with maple hard sauce, chocolate-espresso torte with caramelized orange glaze and cardamom cream, and a selection of ice creams. We passed in favor of a sample of Cave Spring's riesling ice wine, which winemaker Angelo correctly described as "dessert in a glass" – a heavenly ending to a most pleasing meal.

Dining is at white-linened tables in a couple of high-ceilinged rooms with wooden beams, sponged pastel walls, floors and columns of travertine marble, striking art works and floor-to-ceiling windows onto a garden terrace atop the ravine shielding Twenty Mile Creek from view below.

Cave Spring wines are featured at little markup. The restaurant has a full liquor license and carries the best of other local winery offerings. It also sells some of the kitchen's preserves, including peach-pepper relish, late harvest drizzle and chocolate-merlot sauce.

(905) 562-7313 or (800) 701-8074. www.innonthetwenty.com. Entrées, $31 to $40. Lunch daily, 11:30 to 3. Dinner nightly, from 5.

Hillebrand's Estates Winery Restaurant, 1249 Niagara Stone Road, Niagara-on-the-Lake.

Big money went into the restaurant at Hillebrand Estates Winery, and it shows. Interesting architectural lines delineate the handsome, high-ceilinged establishment on two levels. A wall of windows opens onto the barrel-aging cellar along one side, while taller windows in back yield views of the vineyards. Cushioned wood chairs are at well-spaced, white-linened tables, each topped with a different potted herb. A few dramatic artworks and the odd ficus tree add color. Canvas umbrellas top the tables seating 80 more on the sunny outside patio.

Prominent chef Frank Dodd arrived in 2006 from the five-diamond Langdon Hall, a Relais & Chateaux property in Cambridge, Ont., to oversee the kitchen following the departure of founding chef Tony de Luca. Menus neatly bound with grapevines detail some exotic fare. To start, a changing array of breads comes in a grapevine basket with a daily spread – at our lunch, an unusual black bean concoction to soothe an assertive olive focaccia, cornbread with peppers and fennel seed bread. One of us sampled the day's cold cucumber soup, "garnished" with an awkward-to-handle hunk of smoked salmon, and the salad of arugula and radicchio with a confit of tomatoes, smoked scallops and dill. The other was impressed with the penne pasta tossed with caramelized vidalia onions, smoked chicken and roasted garlic with a spicy tomato sauce. At $12, it was the least expensive among main courses

Hillebrand Estate Winery dining room overlooks umbrellaed patio and vineyard.

priced up to $23 for grilled lamb loin brochette with a warm basil and mascarpone tart. The highly touted mango and cardamom crème brûlée with fresh berries lacked the traditional crust and any hint of mango or cardamom, but the trio of homemade ice creams and sorbets listed as "frozen tarts" were more assertive.

Dinner fare is similarly elaborate. You might start with a terrine of lobster, smoked salmon and king crab with sweet pea salad or petite lamb and foie gras sausages with cabernet butter. Main courses range from pan-roasted pickerel fillet with green herb broth and organic arctic char to Ontario lamb loin lavishly wrapped in chanterelles and sweetbreads with wild leeks, asparagus and rhubarb. The "tour of Niagara," a sampling of entrée selections for $42, is generally a winning choice.

Besides turning up in some of the sauces, Hillebrand wines make up the entire wine list, nicely varied (particularly among whites).

(905) 468-7123 or (800) 582-8412. www.hillebrand.com. Entrées, $30 to $42. Lunch daily, 11:30 to 5. Dinner nightly, 5 to 11.

Peller Estates Winery Restaurant, 290 John St., Niagara-on-the-Lake.

Handsome murals and big windows onto the vineyard distinguish the large and elegant restaurant that's the centerpiece of the Peller Estates Winery, the 2001 addition to the Peller-Hillebrand family and its culinary showcase. An outdoor patio and wine garden harbor the tables of choice in season.

Chef Jason Parsons offers a concise but ambitious, bordering-on-pretentious menu of "regional wine country cuisine." At lunch, that might range from an omelet of house-smoked chicken and Quebec brie to "surf and turf" – pan-seared scallops on a salad of rabbit confit and red potatoes with house-made tartar sauce.

We enjoyed a leisurely midday repast of Pacific salmon tartare with cucumber and peppercorn chutney and a Quebec duck breast salad with celery root, duck confit and belgian endive. Dessert was coffee brûlée with hazelnut jaconde, espresso poached pear and granite with cardamom sauce anglaise in a side espresso cup – very good and very precious, like the rest of the meal.

For dinner, expect such entrées as pan-seared diver scallops with ginger essence, West Coast black cod with smoked oysters and red wine sauce, rosemary-roasted pheasant breast, and the Peller version of "tournedos rossini" – roasted veal tenderloin with foie gras and cabernet truffle gastrique.

Typical appetizers are a trio of salmon (smoked salmon bisque, salmon supreme with grape mustard crust and salmon pastrami panini), roasted quail with a poached quail egg, braised rabbit and veal sweetbread terrine, and seared foie gras with an apple and aged cheddar tarte tatin. For salad lovers, there's something described on the menu as "a gathering of shoots and seedlings, cardamom-spiced ver-jus."

Desserts include chilled cherry consommé accompanied by a cherry shortcake, dark milk chocolate pâté with icewine-preserved apricots and a trio of fruit soufflés.

(905) 468-4678 or (888) 673-5537. www.peller.com. Entrées, $32 to $42. Lunch daily, noon to 3. Dinner nightly, 5 to 8:30 or 9.

Terroir La Cachette, 1339 Lakeshore Road, Niagara-on-the-Lake.

This "hideaway" at the rear of the Strewn Winery building moved from Elora to capitalize on larger crowds in the Niagara region. Owners Alain Levesque, the chef from Quebec City, and his wife, Patricia Keyes, produced a handsome wine bar leading to a long and narrow, 75-seat restaurant with big windows onto greenery hiding Four Mile Creek. Colorful in burnt siena, mustard and blue, and with French music playing in the background, it's a soothing setting for provençal-style cooking paired with an all-Ontario wine list. Small votive candles light up the insides of opaque-glass wine bottles employed as centerpieces on each white-clothed table. A small patio offers outdoor dining.

At lunchtime, Terroir offers more of a lunch-style menu than do most winery restaurants in the area. One of us delighted in the luxurious fish soup dotted with wild mushrooms and the country-style pâté served with fruit chutney nested in a delicate pastry shell. The other was well satisfied with the provençal tart laden with braised onion, roasted pepper and chèvre, paired with a side salad. Desserts were citrus cheesecake and butter-pecan pie with Niagara maple ice cream. Two candies arrived with the bill.

At night, the fish soup and the provençal tart are featured among such appetizers as steamed mussels with a chardonnay and grain-mustard cream sauce, escargot and root vegetable roll with ginger and sesame broth, and house-smoked duck with rhubarb and sour cherry confiture. The menu expands to include entrées ranging from prosciutto-wrapped pickerel fillet with thyme and beet coulis and seared arctic char with lemon-truffle vinaigrette to fennel-seed crusted rack of lamb with lentils and cabernet reduction.

(905) 468-1222. www.lacachette.com. Entrées, $25 to $34. Lunch daily, 11:30 to 2:30. Dinner nightly 5 to 9. Closed Monday and Tuesday in winter.

Vineland Estates Winery Restaurant, 3620 Moyer Road, Vineland.

When Ontario liquor authorities finally permitted wineries to open on Sundays, accept credit cards and serve food on the premises, Vineland Estates – which with its hilly country setting is the Beamsville Bench area's most picturesque winery – was the first to oblige. It enclosed the front porch of its original 1845 estate house and opened a small, limited-service bistro. The side deck was later expanded to seat

Colorful dining room at Terroir La Cachette has view of creekside greenery.

100 under cover and outside, where on a clear day you can see Lake Ontario and discern the Toronto skyline through the grapevines.

A subsequent major kitchen expansion allowed the winery to offer lunch and dinner year-round. Another deck was added, the original was enclosed and the tasting room relocated to make way for the expanding restaurant operation. Its team of chefs is in the vanguard of a distinctive regional cuisine. Every morning, they bake their own sourdough bread and baguettes and make their own pastas and gelatos. What local farmers can grow dictates the dishes they create.

The fare has become far more sophisticated than in the early bistro days, when we relaxed over platters of cheeses and pâtés for lunch and, more recently, a supper of bruschetta, caesar salad with Canadian bacon and a platter of smoked salmon.

Nowadays, lunch is apt to involve the likes of smoked chicken minestrone, cold smoked arctic char and semolina-crusted salmon cake with sambal rémoulade. And those are just for starters. Main courses run to cioppino, duck confit over risotto and braised lamb shank with herbed polenta and euro lardons. Dessert could be white chocolate mousse with a stewed fruit compote.

The dinner menu substitutes more substantial entrées: soy-braised monkfish, mustard-crusted pork tenderloin with apple chutney, estate-cured duck breast with quince preserve, szechuan pepper-crusted lamb loin and dry-rubbed ribeye steak with smoked mushroom jus. The pastry chef thinks outside the box with desserts like tarte tatin with black walnut gelato, honey crème brûlée with a sweet potato tartlet and carrot foam, and a mascarpone and apple short stack with egg yolk ice cream and apple-raisin beignets.

A five-course tasting menu is available for $70, or $100 with wine.

Sit outside at a beige-clothed table, sip a fine wine and watch the sunset paint a changing palette across the western sky.

Though the food and service are urbane and the interior dining areas stylish, the setting could not be more bucolic. If you linger, you may want to stay the night. The little stucco cottage down the driveway is a B&B called **Wine 'n Recline.** It harbors a fully equipped kitchen, living room, bathroom and sleeping accommodations for four. You can barbecue on the deck, and the refrigerator is stocked with a bottle of wine as well as the fixings for the next day's breakfast.

(905) 562-7088 or (888) 846-3526. www.vineland.com. Entrées, $30 to $40. Lunch daily, 11 to 3. Dinner, 5 to 9. B&B, $135.

Restaurant Tony de Luca, 160 Front St., Niagara-on-the-Lake.

Celebrated chef and cookbook author Tony de Luca moved in 2006 from the Hillebrand Estates Winery Restaurant, where he was the founding chef after making his mark in Toronto, to operate his own eponymous restaurant in the venerable Oban Inn.

The inn's former lounge was renovated to produce in conjunction with an adjacent solarium a 70-seat dining room with fireplace, tumbled marble floors and sand-colored walls, terra cotta tile floors and a fireplace. Unique in town is a chef's table, which a party of four to six can reserve for a dinner of multiple courses introduced by Tony, plus a tour of the kitchen.

Dinner is prix-fixe, $55 to $85 for three to six courses. The chef puts his personal stamp on the food here, as in starter courses of "one soup, two ways," a terrine of icewine-marinated foie gras, oysters tempura with six dipping sauces and dungeness crab cakes with serrano ham.

Main courses on the opening menu included a Pacific salmon sampler with fresh noodles and winter mushrooms, scallops topped with pan-seared foie gras, Canadian lamb sirloin with French mint glaze, and poached beef tenderloin with foie gras dumplings.

Dessert could be blood orange-vanilla parfait with coconut anglaise or banana soufflé with crème fraîche and bitter chocolate sauce. A selection of international and Canadian cheeses from de Luca's Cheesemarket and Deli may be carved tableside.

(905) 468-7900. Prix-fixe, $55 to $85. Lunch daily, 11:30 to 2:30. Dinner nightly, 5 to 9:30.

Other Dining Choices

The Queenston Heights Restaurant, Queenston Heights Park, 14276 Niagara Pkwy, Queenston.

Operated by the Niagara Parks Commission, this restaurant is a cut above – in culinary aspiration, as well as in location, commanding a panoramic view down the Niagara River toward Lake Ontario.

The menu mixes traditional with contemporary regional cuisine. One of us made a wonderful lunch of two appetizers: a tomato and eggplant salad, served on a black octagonal plate brightened by corn kernels and colorful bits of peppers, and smoked-salmon carpaccio, garnished with shavings of romano cheese, herbs and tiny purple edible flowers. The other enjoyed smoked turkey with cranberry mayonnaise on a whole-wheat croissant. From the dessert cart we picked a super chocolate-strawberry charlotte with curls of chocolate and savored both it and the afternoon sunshine on the capacious outdoor terrace.

At night, you might be tempted by main courses like the signature sea scallops and tiger prawns with banana-mango curried cream sauce or the veal rack bordelaise. The pork tenderloin might be stuffed with leek mousse, sauced with port wine, served on spinach spaetzle and vegetables, and accompanied by a Quebec goat cheese turnover. One of the interesting starters could be shrimp and peppered salmon tempura bonded with nori seaweed, creamy teriyaki and ginger sauce. Desserts include profiteroles with mint-chocolate chip ice cream, cabernet-poached bosc pear in a brandysnap basket, and mascarpone semifreddo with raspberry coulis.

The extensive wine list is strong on Niagara whites and reds.

The formal main dining room is Tudor in feeling with a high timbered ceiling, armchairs at well-spaced tables and a painting of Niagara Falls above a huge stone fireplace. The view down the length of the river, while sitting at a table by the expansive windows, almost gives one the sense of being on an airplane. There's a large outdoor dining patio at the side, but here trees block much of the view.

(905) 262-4274 or (877) 642-7275. www.niagaraparks.com. Entrées, $19.95 to $32.50. Lunch daily, 11:30 or noon to 3, summer Saturdays from 11. Dinner nightly, 5 to 9, summer Saturdays to 10. Sunday brunch, 11 to 3. Closed January to late March.

The Grill at the Epicurean, 84 Queen St., Niagara-on-the-Lake.

The Grill is the latest venture of Ruth and Scott Aspinall, Old Town Niagara-on the-Lake's culinary leaders, who turn their daytime cafeteria-style eatery known as the Epicurean into a full-blown restaurant at night.

The dinner menu mirrors the innovative pattern set by the midday spread and represents good value. Favorite starters include mussel and saffron soup, house-made pâté with pear chutney, and scallop seviche with a cherry tomato salad. From the grill come such treats as Atlantic salmon with Thai coconut sauce and baby bok choy, black tiger shrimp with shiitake mushrooms and black bean broth, sea scallops with saffron cream sauce, and New York strip loin with peppercorn sauce and frites.

Dining is at bistro tables in a colorful blue and buttercup yellow dining room or out back on a garden patio shaded by a leafy butternut tree.

By day, the Epicurean is popular for its extensive lineup of creative fare posted on an immense blackboard and doled out from deli cases below. Soups could be Mexican chicken or gazpacho, or you might order chicken and feta pie or seafood quiche. Focaccia sandwiches range from tuna to seafood and avocado or eggplant with roasted peppers and chèvre. We sampled a medley of three salads ($8.50), served with homemade bread, and cleared our own table afterward on the patio.

Wines are available by the glass, or you can bring your own bottle and pay a corkage fee.

Between meals, check out the fine selection of specialty foods and culinary books in Ruth Aspinall's **Kitchen Accents** store, newly relocated from the front of the Epicurean to larger quarters at 46 Queen St.

(905) 468-0288. www.epicurean.ca. Entrées, $19 to $30. Lunch daily, 11 to 5:30. Dinner nightly, 5:30 to 9 or 10.

Stone Road Grille, 238 Mary St., Niagara on the Lake.

Disguised beneath a makeshift "REST" sign in the outlying Garrison strip plaza is this trendy newcomer, beloved by locals for its imaginative menu and refreshing takeoff on pretentious dining.

The refreshment starts with the unlikely sign, as explained in a printed handout given to curious customers. It seems that as renovations ended the night before the opening, owners Perry and Heidi Johnson asked a waiter to peel off the letters of the old sign, Mina's Restaurant & Bar, and leave just the restaurant portion. "I'd had a couple of cocktails and went too far," explained Kevin the instigator after he warmed to the task. When ordered to stop, all that was left was REST. The saving grace was that REST was at least a word and that it was somewhat centered across the front. The owners planned eventually to get the sign redone. But the idea stuck and that's the way they left it.

The colorful interior seats 38, plus six at the bar, at cushioned banquettes and chairs facing heavy wood tables amid crazy art and beneath a giant hanging sculpture. Hosta leaves in red glass vases were the table centerpieces at our visit and the ice water was infused with lemon and cucumber.

Novel touches extend to young chef Ryan Crawford's food as well. The lunch menu offers a "ham and cheese" sandwich, this consisting of slow-roasted pork loin with fresca peppata cheese and chipotle aioli. Another offering is a pair of mini bison burgers, one with caramelized onions and blue cheese and the other with house-smoked bacon and cheddar cheese.

Appetizers at both lunch and dinner include smoked salmon salad with a poached egg, dungeness crab spring rolls, moules frites, a charcuterie plate and an "unclassic shrimp cocktail" yielding gulf, black tiger and fresh water shrimp.

Main courses at dinner could be salmon "osso buco" (braised salmon steak and marrow with wild mushrooms), duck three ways (pan-seared breast, confit ravioli and peking consommé), a mixed grill of lamb and local sausage, and grilled flatiron steak with béarnaise sauce and frites.

Desserts are takeoffs on Canadian classics, among them our favorite Nanaimo bars, s'mores, a butter tart with homemade bourbon ice cream, an unusual candy floss, and poached rhubarb with cloudberry panna cotta and icewine must.

Little wonder that, despite its hidden location, REST plays to turn-away crowds.

(905) 468-3474. www.stoneroadgrille.com. Entrées, $19 to $25. Lunch, Tuesday-Friday 11:30 to 2. Dinner, Tuesday-Sunday 5 to 10.

Shaw Café & Wine Bar, 92 Queen St., Niagara-on-the-Lake.

You can't miss this striking circular restaurant jutting onto the downtown sidewalk, part of a Victorian shopping complex built by local hotelier Si Wai Lai, who knows and likes good food. It is flanked by flowers and statuary, fountains and dining terraces, looks like something out of modern-day Italy and is mobbed by tourists day and night.

The interior is unexpectedly trendy for little old Niagara-on-the-Lake: a prominent pizza oven, an open kitchen, a deli case loaded with sophisticated offerings, a dessert and gelato counter, an upstairs loft area with paneled wine bar overlooking the scene, and dining tables all around, inside and out.

The all-day menu has been condensed and downscaled lately as its prices soared. Typical choices are smoked salmon or portobello mushroom sandwiches, a goat cheese blini, a potato and artichoke salad, and steamed mussels in an anchovy cream sauce. Shaw's version of meatloaf is a blend of pork and lamb, served with a potato galette and truffled mushroom ragoût. The pan-seared salmon, drizzled with a ginger and lime butter sauce, comes with baby bok choy and an herbed scallion-potato galette.

Desserts from the patisserie are a strong point. Typical are grand marnier cheesecake, white chocolate mousse surrounded by raspberries, vanilla mille-feuille, and kirsch and blackberry mousseline. Espressos and lattes, wines and beers round out the offerings.

(905) 468-4772. Entrées, $16 to $22. Open daily, 10 to 9, weekends to midnight.

Escabèche in Prince of Wales Hotel offers opulent setting for dining.

Niagara Culinary Institute Dining Room, 135 Taylor Road, Niagara-on-the-Lake. Budding chefs are trained at the Niagara Culinary Institute at the Niagara College's new Glendale campus. Working with chef-instructors (some from regional restaurants), they use herbs and produce grown by horticulture students in the adjacent greenhouse and serve wines made by students at the college's Teaching Winery.

The results are evident in the circular 80-seat restaurant, flanked by walls of glass and open to the public for lunch and dinner by reservation. The cooks – second-year students in the training program – prepare à la carte or prix-fixe meals with recommended wine pairings at reasonable prices (three-course lunch for $20 or four-course dinner, $35).

A typical dinner might begin with butternut squash bisque with clove-scented honey and smoked salmon cheesecake on citrus-dressed greens. The main course could be roasted butterfish fillet with seafood cream sauce or grilled mignon of beef strip loin on wilted greens. Dessert could be tarte tatin or eggnog crème brûlée. Much the same fare is available for lunch, at even lower prices.

Days of operation vary with college schedules.

(905) 641-2252, Ext. 4619. www.niagarac.on.ca/dining. Entrées, lunch $11 to $14, dinner $17 to $19. Lunch by reservation, Tuesday-Sunday 11:30 to 2. Dinner by reservation, Wednesday-Saturday 5 to 9 or 9:30.

Dining and Lodging

The Prince of Wales Hotel & Spa, 6 Picton St., Niagara-on-the-Lake L0S 1J0. Here is the ultimate showcase for the taste, energy and opulence of Niagara-on-the-Lake hotelier Si Wai Lai, an iconic figure who as a teenager fled mainland China by swimming for 36 hours to Hong Kong and later proved equally fearless as she bought up much of Niagara-on-the-Lake.

Using her own resources and those of her twin brother Jimmy Lai, a Hong Kong publisher and clothing magnate, she quickly acquired the town's leading hotel properties and built a local empire of Vintage Inns – that is, until she and brother Jimmy unexpectedly parted company. He installed his representative in Canada, a venture capitalist from Toronto, in charge of the three biggest Vintage Inns properties in 2005. Si Wai retained the Oban Inn and the Shaw Café & Wine Bar.

Her legacy is manifest at The Prince of Wales, which after $25 million worth of renovations is opulent Victorian, in the high British or continental style.

The riches begin in the lobby, where the wallpaper is embossed gold to match the carved molding, a stained-glass mural is backlit and Italian statues preside here and there. The former bar was converted into a drawing room. Here the wall sconces match three glittering crystal chandeliers and afternoon tea is served on a 24-carat gold china service for $32 per person. In the Secret Garden Spa, the tiled indoor saltwater pool is flanked by murals of princes of Wales watching over any swimmers who can get through all the frou-frou – not that anyone was swimming at our July visit.

The 114 guest rooms ramble through a square block of buildings behind a meandering brick facade that looks more residential than commercial. Their exaggerated luxury comes in 23 color schemes and all have Italian marble baths. Plush fabrics, delicate crystal, velour bathrobes and towel warmers are standard, creating in the publicity jargon "an atmosphere of refinement and pure serenity."

The hotel's restaurants spread across three rooms with thick carpeting, white linens, and sparkling crystal and china. One is a Cigar Room. Beyond is Churchill's Lounge, a huge space with the look of a gentleman's library and quite a stash of wines and champagnes offered by the glass.

The main restaurant was renamed **Escabèche** (for a popular marinated fish dish in southern France). Executive chef Andrew Dymond trained at Relais & Châteaux hotels in England before returning to the Niagara area where he grew up.

The contemporary Canadian cuisine is straightforward yet distinguished, as in our appetizers of beignets of Atlantic salmon with cucumber-radish salad and horseradish cream and seared scallops with shiitake mushrooms, asparagus tips and a madeira vinaigrette. Entrées included a superior roasted breast of muscovy duck with cherry jus, Washington rack of lamb with black olive and chive jus, and pan-seared venison loin with smoked bacon, quince jam and black peppercorn reduction. Desserts were hazelnut parfait with chocolate ice cream and a trio of pears – poached with stilton, pitherier and sorbet. A plate of mignardises with a red rose accompanied the bill.

A chef's tasting menu brings five courses for $85 ($115 with wine).

Lighter fare is offered for lunch and dinner in Churchill Lounge.

(905) 468-2195 or (888) 669-5566. Fax (905) 468-5521. www.vintageinns.com. One hundred ten rooms and suites. Rates, EP. May-October: doubles $245 to $345, suites $455 to $555. Rest of year: doubles $150 to $230, suites $360 to $440.

Entrées, $26 to $44. Lunch, Monday-Friday noon to 2. Tea, 2 to 5. Dinner nightly, 5:30 to 9, weekends 5 to 10. Sunday brunch, 11 to 2.

Queen's Landing Inn and Conference Resort, 155 Byron St., Niagara-on-the-Lake L0S 1J0.

Built in 1990, this three-story, Georgian-inspired hotel backing up to the Niagara River has matured nicely. Si Wai Lai revived it after two previous owners had failed, making it Niagara's first four-diamond establishment for both dining and lodging.

Curved ceiling and columns grace Tiara dining room at Queen's Landing Inn.

The rear of the brick hotel looks across the busy Niagara-on-the-Lake Sailing Club marina onto the Niagara River. Inside all is placid and sumptuous, especially the two-story entrance foyer with a marble floor and a stained-glass ceiling. There are large mirrors, reproduction antique furniture and flowers everywhere (one bouquet alone contained 120 long-stemmed roses). A couple of shiny elevators take guests to their rooms, which contain plush furnishings, minibars, and tiled and marble bathrooms, some with whirlpool tubs. Three dozen rooms offer gas fireplaces.

The lower floors, built into the side of a slope, offer a restaurant and lounge, business center, twenty conference rooms, a health facility and a light, airy area with a large indoor swimming pool, a whirlpool and a lap pool.

Most noticeably improved is the dining situation. The Bacchus Lounge bar menu is considered good value and its outdoor dining terrace positively idyllic, for those not distracted by the looming statue of David clad only in a small fig leaf. The pillared **Tiara** restaurant is a majestic oval of soaring windows onto the marina beneath a curving ceiling accented with stained glass. On two levels, it is spacious and serene in cream and mauve, with tables well separated.

Executive chef Stephen Treadwell, known for strong flavors and complex cooking, is credited with some of the best food in town. Four of us sampled the night's eight-course tasting menu ($85), paired with appropriate wines (the steward's recommendations from the all-Niagara wine list can rapidly run up the tab). The four-hour feast, from foie gras terrine through the signature "symphony of desserts," proved exceptional.

The regular menu might start with crisp-skin arctic char with salt-roasted potato and caviar crème fraîche or coriander-glazed king prawn with enoki, shiso leaf and tokyo red onion. Our tasting menu yielded two of the main courses, szechuan-crusted sea scallops with a carrot emulsion and charred yellowfin tuna with chile gazpacho and vodka-lime goat cheese. Other treats were sesame-grilled quail with Niagara peach preserve and mustard greens, a feature on the lunch menu, and pan-roasted veal loin with chanterelles, zucchini blossoms and truffle essence. A plate of imported cheeses with oven-dried fruit and date-walnut bread followed the veal course.

The dessert sampling indicated that any of the pastry chef's choices would suffice. We'd happily settle for the trio of intense fruit sorbets served in macadamia nut petals.

(905) 468-2195 or (888) 669-5566. Fax (905) 468-2227. www.vintageinns.com. One hundred thirty-seven rooms and five suites. Rates, EP. May-October: doubles $225 to $325, suites $435 to $535. Rest of year: doubles $130 to $210, suites $340 to $420.

Entrées, $32 to $45. Lunch, Monday-Saturday noon to 2:30. Dinner nightly, 6 to 9, weekends 5 to 9 or 9:30.

Riverbend Inn & Vineyard, 16104 Niagara River Pkwy., Box 1560, Niagara-on-the-Lake L0S 1J0.

The Wiens family, original owners of the Prince of Wales Hotel here, re-emerged in 2004 with this luxury inn in a handsome 1860s Georgian mansion with later additions. The inn is nicely situated back from the parkway in the midst of thirteen acres of grape vines close to the Niagara River.

John Wiens, his wife Jill and his father Henry Wiens are actively involved in running this endeavor, as they had been at the Prince of Wales. Here they offer 21 sizable rooms and suites and a small, elegant restaurant serving three meals a day.

Guest rooms on three floors are furnished in formal Georgian style, with queen or two double beds, sitting areas with gas fireplaces, flat-screen TVs hidden in armoires, and standard bathrooms. Seven rooms, including one massive affair near the board meeting room, come with stand-up Juliet balconies or decks.

The restaurant is at the rear of the mansion's main floor. It includes an elegant 1890s salon/bar separated by marble pillars from a cheery yellow 26-seat dining room with windows onto the Peller Estates vineyard and a lovely, 40-seat dining patio.

The contemporary regional menu is as creative as those of its winery dining peers. Expect entrées like butter-poached sea scallops with purple kohlrabi slaw and a blue cheese croquette, sage-candied tenderloin of wild boar with chile-seared jumbo shrimp and faro, and pistachio-crusted rack of Ontario lamb with wilted braising greens and a sweet-potato scone with garlic marmalade. Typical starters are crawfish and sweet basil ravioli with kaffir-lime butter, and spiced pork and hubbard squash en croûte with chiogga beet coulis. Sweet endings include a creamy caramel, toffee and pecan cheesecake and vanilla bean crème brûlée with warm berry compote.

An appealing lounge menu ($9 to $14) is available all day in the grill or on the terrace.

The inaugural wines from the inn's grapes were being produced by the neighboring Reif Winery under the inn's own label.

(905) 4688-8866 or (888) 955-5553. Fax (905) 468-8839. www.riverbendinn.ca. Twenty rooms and one suite with private baths. Rates, EP. May-October: doubles $255 to $325, suite $370. Rest of year: doubles $160 to $235, suite $260.

Entrées, $25 to $36. Lunch daily, noon to 2:30. Dinner nightly, 5 to 9. Lounge menu, 11 to 11.

Gate House Hotel, 142 Queen St., Niagara-on-the-Lake L0S 1J0.

This sleek, mirrored hotel in black and white was the first glitzy hotel in Niagara-on-the-Lake. It emerged in 1988 from the simple, old Gate House Inn – tastefully on

Expansive windows bring outside in at Ristorante Giardino in Gate House Hotel.

the outside, contemporary Italian and showy on the inside. A marble entry leads to the reception desk, where guests are directed to the two-tiered dining room or upstairs to guest rooms on the second floor. We were shown a very modern, deluxe room done in teal and black with two double beds, German and Italian furnishings, and a bathroom with double sinks, a bidet and Auberge toiletries. Two rooms have queensize beds and the rest have two double beds. Rooms come with TVs and all the usual amenities in high-tech European style. A continental breakfast is included.

The hotel's **Ristorante Giardino** is the gem of the operation. Huge windows in the ultra-chic dining room look onto the gardens and lawns (and passersby look in as well). Generally well-spaced tables are set with black-edged service plates, white napkins rolled up in black paper rings, pink carnations in heavy crystal vases, votive candles and two long-stemmed wine glasses at each place. All the plates and water glasses are octagonal. Masses of flowers brighten the room's dividers, and good art hangs on the walls here and in the halls.

The modern Italian fare is on the expensive side and service may be delivered with attitude. Dinner possibilities range from an appetizer of salmon carpaccio rolled in baby green beans to a dessert of cold Italian chocolate grand marnier soufflé. Main courses could be mushroom-stuffed Atlantic salmon with a Sicilian caponata, lamb osso buco braised in Guinness beer or grilled veal chop scented with sage and lemon.

Not wishing to break the bank, we settled for lunch, which – as is usually the case at high-end establishments – is a better value. A plate of crusty Italian bread arrived along with two glasses of the house Inniskillin wine (brae blanc and brae rouge). One of us started with an intensely flavored and silken shrimp bisque, followed by a rolled pasta with spinach and ricotta cheese. The other sampled a trio of pastas: spaghetti with pancetta and parmesan-cream sauce, tagliatelle sautéed with salmon and chives, and a house specialty, eggplant Giardino, baked with mozzarella, basil and tomato sauce.

Dessert was a slice of carrot cake with vanilla ice cream and fresh strawberries – imported from California, which seemed strange, given all the peaches, pears and plums in season at the time around Niagara. Good cappuccino and coffee finished a fine repast. The extensive wine list is especially strong on Niagara and Italian vintages.

(905) 468-3263. Fax (905) 468-7400. www.gatehouse-niagara.com. Ten rooms with private baths. Doubles, $225 to $245 June-October, $145 to $210 rest of year.

Entrées, $26 to $38.50. Lunch daily, 11:30 to 2:30. Dinner nightly, 5 to 9:30. No lunch in off-season. Closed early January to mid-March.

The Charles Inn, 209 Queen St., Box 642, Niagara-on-the-Lake L0S 1J0.

With a verdant residential setting beside the Niagara-on-the-Lake Golf Club, this was reborn from the aging Kiely House as the latest project of Susan Murray, owner of several other hostelries in town. Extensive refurbishing in 2004 enhanced a dozen guest rooms in the Georgian house built in 1832 for barrister Charles Richardson, a member of Parliament.

Rooms in the main house and the Victorian-era servants' wing vary in size and decor. Each is individually decorated with good art works. Beds are dressed with 300-count linens, down duvets and pillows. Many have wood-burning or gas fireplaces, and baths with multi-head showers or clawfoot tubs.

The largest is the Verandah Room, with a frilly four-poster canopy bed, large sitting area beside the fireplace, a bath with whirlpool tub and a rainforest shower, and a private veranda. Others vary from the Poppy Room, sleek in gray and black, its contemporary decor accented by the Georgia O'Keeffe poppy print above the fireplace that gives the room its name, to the third-floor Safari Room, with a kingsize netted canopy bed and accents of drum tables and tribal masks. Large paintings of apples or sunflowers serve as colorful headboards for the queen beds in the two smallest rooms.

Dinner is available in a formal and ornate, crystal-chandeliered dining room fashioned from the original double parlor. Chef William Brunyansky's changing menu offers appetizers ranging from a blue crab cake with a roasted red pepper and garlic aioli to carpaccio of bison tenderloin garnished with a celery root and apple salad. Typical entrées include pan-seared Chilean sea bass over braised salsify, roasted breast of muscovy duck sauced with seasonal berries, and herb-crusted loin of lamb with curry-spiked lamb jus. Dessert could be double chocolate mousse, pecan bread pudding or New York-style cheesecake.

Afternoon tea and after-dinner drinks are served in the wine bar or on the side veranda overlooking the oldest golf club in North America.

(905) 468-4588 or (866) 556-8883. Fax (905) 468-2194. www.charlesinn.ca. Twelve rooms with private baths. May-October: doubles, $200 to $310 weekends, $170 to $275 midweek. Rest of year: doubles, $170 to $270 weekends, $99 to $205 midweek.

Entrées, $18 to $29. Lunch, 11 to 4 spring through fall. Dinner nightly, 5 to 8:30.

Lodging

The Oban Inn, 160 Front St., Box 94, Niagara-on-the-Lake L0S 1J0.

This Niagara icon, facing Lake Ontario across a strip of golf course, has been around since 1824 and looks it. Which is quite remarkable, given that it was destroyed by fire on Christmas Day 1992 and was rebuilt to its original specifications for reopening eleven months later.

A favorite of traditionalists, it was the latest to be acquired by Si Wai Lai, who

Horse and carriage arrive for Christmas festivities at Lakewinds.

changed its focus into a wellness retreat and spa after she and the Vintage Inns parted company. Now devoting full time to the Oban, she added a spa facility in the front portion of what had been the restaurant, built a new exercise facility and two deluxe guest rooms, and enlarged a dining porch off the lounge into a restaurant, which she leased in 2006 to celebrity chef Tony de Luca.

Upstairs on the second and third floors, nineteen rooms go off narrow corridors adorned with a multitude of ornate paintings. Those in front looking toward the lake are larger and have queen or twin beds, antique furnishings, gas fireplaces and plush armchairs or a loveseat facing a TV set. Vivid wallpapers, terrycloth robes, a clock-radio and a phone in each room are the rule. Guests enjoy a library/sitting room upstairs with TV, gas fireplace and lots of books and games.

The best accommodations are considered to be a new room and a suite behind the inn, each with two double beds, and six overlooking the golf course and lake in the adjacent Oban House and the Greenview Estate, transformed from the former owner's residence. One is a suite with a queen bedroom, a loft with twin beds, a full kitchen, sunroom and living room.

The new O Spa offers a range of holistic treatments, wellness seminars and state-of-the-art exercise facilities, a steam room and a lap pool.

(905) 468-2165 or (866) 359-6226. Fax (905) 468-4165. www.obaninn.ca. Twenty-five rooms and four suites with private baths. Rates, B&B. April-October: doubles, $265 to $395 weekends, $245 to $325 midweek. Rest of year: doubles, $195 to $295 weekends, $150 to $250 midweek.

Lakewinds, 328 Queen St., Box 1483, Niagara-on-the-Lake L0S 1J0.

Pristine white with dark green trim, this substantial Victorian manor sits amidst an acre of trees and gardens facing Lake Ontario across the golf-course fairways. Besides a scenic residential location, it offers Niagara-on-the-Lake's most elegant B&B accommodations and culinary treats, and was the setting for a country-inn scene in the Bette Midler movie, "That Old Feeling."

You'd never suspect that "the house was falling down," as owner Jane Locke put it, when she and her husband Stephen from nearby Hamilton bought it for their home in 1994 with the idea of turning the front section into a B&B. "We were trying to make a silk purse out of a sow's ear."

The main floor is devoted to a formal living/dining room in which the Lockes serve breakfasts to remember, an ample games room for billiards or cards, and an airy solarium that becomes a working greenhouse in the winter to produce the seedlings for the lavish flower, vegetable and herb gardens that grace the grounds. The solarium opens onto a flagstone-flanked swimming pool much enjoyed by guests.

The second floor holds four guest quarters, three with queensize beds and one with a king. The Venetian suite with double whirlpool tub and separate shower is so named for all the silver and glass and the hand-painted mirrored furniture. Others bear furnishings appropriate to their names: Florentine, Singapore and the Algonquin, in which we enjoyed the most comfortable of beds. Entries in the guest diary embellished on three themes: sumptuous surroundings, delicious breakfasts and personable hosts.

The transformation to silk purse culminated in the conversion of the third floor into two king-bedded suites. A large handcrafted angel watches over Heaven, a secluded hideaway with loveseat and window seat offering a bird's-eye view of the lake and golf course, a stereo system, and bath with a jacuzzi tub and an antique marble-top vanity. French country decor enhances the cathedral-ceilinged Sans Souci, with a fireside sitting area, TV, balcony and a double jacuzzi with separate shower.

Guests are welcomed with tea, and help themselves to mixers in a bar area off the solarium. The Lockes, whose family quarters are in the rear of the house, often mingle with guests and provide turndown service at night.

The highlight is the morning repast, a communal sit-down affair at 9 o'clock. Ours began with apple-cassis juice, cantaloupe harboring port and berries, and five varieties of breads, from orange-date muffins to muesli baguettes to croissants. The main event was a melt-in-your-mouth leek and sage quiche with roasted red pepper coulis, teamed with a crostini bearing sautéed mushrooms, pesto, tomato and goat cheese. On tap the next morning was honeydew melon marinated in lime and gin, followed by orange-cointreau french toast. Crêpes, often incorporating asparagus or smoked salmon, are a specialty. Five of Jane's recipes are included in the Canadian edition of the *Rise and Dine* inn cookbook.

Jane, who was preparing a batch of rhubarb-ginger jam at our initial visit, challenges herself by inviting top local chefs for dinner. She attributes her cooking talents to training in a private yacht club and corporate travels around the world with her husband, Stephen, who now devotes full time to Lakewinds and heads the local B&B Association. Both love to entertain, and treat their guests royally.

(905) 468-1888 or (866) 338-1888. Fax (905) 468-1061. www.lakewinds.niagara.com. Three rooms and three suites with private baths. Doubles, $195 to $295 May-October, $165 to $195 rest of year. Two-night minimum weekends. Closed mid-December through New Year's.

Harbour House Hotel, 85 Melville St., Box 760, Niagara-on-the-Lake L0S 1J0.

All is sumptuous and high end at this deluxe new boutique-style urban hotel, located near the mouth of the Niagara River. As designed by owner Susan Murray's husband, an architect, the newly constructed, shingled Cape Cod-like structure with a gambrel roof is turned inward to cosset guests away from the sights and sounds of a busy marina across the street.

The place exudes style, from the restful Library Lobby with oriental rugs and a fireplace to the beautiful conservatory dining room beside a garden patio. Decor is understated nautical with a lighthouse table here, a ship's painting there. Rooms on the second and third floors have kingsize feather-top beds dressed with 300 thread-count linens and down duvets, gas fireplaces, TV/DVD players in armoires and marble bathrooms. Most have California whirlpool tubs, except for a few that have oversize glass showers with multiple jets. One second-floor corner suite with a harbor view has a sofabed in the living room, three TVs and a double whirlpool tub.

Guests enjoy a complimentary wine tasting daily at 4 in the library lobby. An extensive European-style breakfast in the conservatory is complimentary. It might include crunchy granola, croissants and scones, a selection of cold meats and cheeses, and perhaps quiche, cheese and meat strata or bread pudding.

(905) 468-4683 or (866) 277-6677. Fax (905) 468-0366. www.harbourhousehotel.ca. Twenty-eight rooms and three suites with private baths. May-October: doubles $285 to $375, suites $395 to $430. Rest of year: doubles $199 to $310, suites $310 to $370.

Inn on the Twenty, 3845 Main St., Jordan L0R 1L0.

Plush accommodations in this expanding inn – fashioned from an old sugar storage warehouse – complement the Cave Spring Cellars winery, restaurant and shopping complex across the street. Formerly the Vintner's Inn and looking the part, it's the kind of place you'd expect to find in the French wine country.

Helen Young, wife of winery owner Leonard Pennachetti, offers rooms and suites with sitting areas, gas fireplaces, TVs, whirlpool tubs and kingsize or two double beds. Eight are double-deckers with sitting areas and powder rooms downstairs and loft bedrooms and baths up. The skylit deluxe loft adds a wet bar, refrigerator and a down-seated settee so deep you can barely get up. Three garden suites on the lower floor offer columned sleeping alcoves and bathrooms with heated floors, plus large windows facing demonstration gardens. The deluxe garden suite opens through french doors onto a private garden.

Handsomely decorated in restful Mediterranean tones, each suite contains a colorful painting (for sale) by local artist Jane Kewin, whose works adorn the restaurant. You'd never guess that some of the furnishings took on new life after resting in Buffalo junk shops. Helen mixed refurbished castoffs with antiques, chintz fabrics and old marble vanities to create "an eclectic country look," simple but stylish.

The prime accommodations are two suites in a nearby house renamed the Winemaker's Cottage. Here we luxuriated on the private garden patio off a pleasant living room, a kingsize bedroom and a huge bath with a jacuzzi tub and separate shower. A complimentary split of Cave Spring cabernet/merlot preceded dinner, and chocolates accompanied turndown service.

The treats continued the next morning at the inn's companion On the Twenty restaurant across the street. Assorted fruits and pastries on the buffet are augmented by a light entrée, in our case a tomato-chicken-spinach crêpe with lemongrass sauce and salmon hash topped by a poached egg.

Lately, the inn expanded with three suites in the adjacent Vintage House, where a full-service spa is available. In 2005 the owners were renovating the old Jordan

Hotel to add fourteen simpler guest rooms and a pub. They also opened **Twelve,** a classy but casual waterfront grill on the Port Dalhousie riverfront in St. Catharines.

(905) 562-5336 or (800) 701-8074. Fax (905) 562-0009. www.innonthetwenty.com. Twenty-nine rooms and suites with private baths. Doubles, $239 to $369 May-October, $169 to $325 rest of year.

Shannaleigh, 184 Queen St., Box 1357, Niagara-on-the-Lake L0S 1J0.

Fine architectural details grace this 1910 Tudor mansion on a substantial property with a one-acre garden. Consider leaded windows, tiger oak doors, mahogany fireplace mantels and paneling, and three kinds of intricate moldings in the dining room. They're quite a backdrop for the museum-quality Native Art paintings displayed throughout by owners Carole and John Holmes, who show them for his brother, a Toronto art dealer. They make the large living room into a low-key gallery, where plush seating abounds and the house TV is hidden in an armoire. The gardens outside make the large side screened porch furnished in wicker seem like an open-air solarium.

Understated luxury prevails in the five upstairs guest rooms, reached by a sweeping staircase flanked by barley twist spindles. A kingsize carved mahogany canopy bed is the focal point of the master bedroom, decorated in English country style. It has a settee beside the fireplace. French provincial is the theme in the other front corner bedroom, with a queensize brass bed, wicker sun porch and a bathroom with its original cast-iron soaking tub and rain-head shower. Three attractive, slightly smaller rooms are in back. The bedrooms bear the names of her nieces, but Carol told her daughter she would name the inn for her. "Well, of course, Mother," was the reply.

The formal dining room with wine-colored walls, leaded windows and leather banquette and the adjacent sun porch are the settings for three-course breakfasts. "I cook and John schmoozes," says Carol. The repast begins with fruit and yogurt. Next might come a sweet pepper frittata or a cheese soufflé with grilled tomatoes and herbed potatoes. Lemon-yogurt waffles or blintzes and raspberries might follow.

(905) 468-2630 or (866) 511-1263. www.shanna.ca. Five rooms with private baths. Doubles, $195 to $275, off-season $159 to $269. Two-night minimum weekends. Closed November to early April.

The Old Bank House, 10 Front St., Box 1708, Niagara-on-the-Lake L0S 1J0.

Nicely located across from a park and facing Lake Ontario, this historic B&B dates to 1817. It has been vastly upgraded since our first stay here when it was one of the few fulltime B&Bs in town.

Owners Judy and Michael Djurdjevic offer nine comfortable bedrooms furnished in elegant European style with king or queen beds or two double beds and TVs in armoires. Three rooms have direct views of the lake through the park, and three rooms have access to a balcony. Everyone enjoys the flower-bedecked front veranda and a huge living room. The foyer is brightened with the stunning artworks of Adrian Milankov, a friend of the family.

Breakfast is served at individual tables in a sunny conservatory that opens onto a side patio. The morning of our visit yielded a fruit cup with ladyfinger biscuits in crème anglaise and omelets laden with cheese, mushrooms and ham.

(905) 468-7136 or (877) 468-7136. www.oldbankhouse.com. Nine rooms with private baths. Doubles, $175 to $225 May-October, $125 to $165 rest of year.

Grand Victorian, 15618 Niagara Pkwy., Niagara-on-the-Lake L0S 1J0.

Across the parkway from the river and screened by trees is this large B&B that's a work in progress. The imposing white stucco landmark – very grand and very Victorian – is next to the Reif Estate winery, whose wines the innkeeper, ex-Torontonian Eva Kessel, pours for guests in the late evening.

Five second-floor rooms have fireplaces and ornate, oversize beds. The River Room yields a view of the river and has a king canopy bed reached by a small step ladder. The Porch Room offers a screened porch onto the side yard and river. The main-floor North Suite has a step-up bed canopied in beige brocade and buried in pillows, plus a sitting area and a bath with clawfoot tub.

Breakfast is served in a round conservatory. The fare could be quiche, orange french toast or waffles with fruit.

There's plenty of space for guests to spread out in the main-floor common rooms and the flower-bedecked front veranda. In back are a pool and a tennis court and proliferating gardens that are Eva's pride and joy. The facility lends itself to the weddings and corporate seminars that Eva seeks to attract to build her business.

(905) 468-0997. Fax (905) 468-1551. www.grandvictorianbandb.com. Five rooms and one suite with private baths. Doubles, $170 to $200. Suite, $225.

The River Breeze, 14767 Niagara Pkwy., Niagara-on-the-Lake L0S 1J0.

Exceptional landscaping beautifies this substantial gray brick house, set well back from the parkway on an acre of gardens and trees, several miles south of town. Bert and Mimi Davesne, originally from France, designed and built the French-look house in 1975 and have shared it with overnight guests since they became empty-nesters.

All four guest rooms have queen beds. Three offer views of the Niagara River, and two have balconies. Ours, one of the latter, was rather confining, so we were glad to have the extra balcony space.

Repeat guests, who are legion, come back for his wife's breakfasts, says Bert. The fare ranges from quiche to crêpes to rolls and croissants, prepared and served in the French manner. Ours began with orange juice and fruit cup, included asparagus quiche and ended with cinnamon buns "for dessert."

Guests gather in a handsome living room or on the back terrace, atop a bluff with a view onto the river. They also enjoy a swimming pool surrounded by tropical plants and potted palms that give it a Caribbean air.

(905) 262-4046 or (866) 881-7536. Fax (905) 262-0718. www.theriverbreeze.com. Four rooms with private baths. Doubles, $120 to $150.

Touring the Wineries

Geographically, one would not think of Canada as a wine-producing country. The Niagara Peninsula has changed that perception big time.

Shortly after New York's Finger Lakes region started proving that European viniferas could be grown in the Eastern climate, Niagara scrapped acres of concord and niagara grapes in favor of chardonnays, rieslings and pinot noirs. Today, vineyards are everywhere around Niagara-on-the-Lake, interspersed among more orchards of diverse fruit trees than we've ever seen in close proximity. Both are the area's distinguishing features, yielding mile after mile of beauty and bounty.

Vineyards proliferated in recent years to the point where Niagara-on-the-Lake

Dining patio at Riverbend Inn looks across vineyards toward Peller Estates Winery.

boasted a Group of Seven, borrowing a well-known name from the Canadian art world. That since has become a group of sixteen. Altogether, the Niagara Peninsula has 60 wineries and counting.

Such has been their success that some have grown to California-size proportions, dwarfing in size their counterparts in New York's nearby Finger Lakes area – a factor due in part to the region's proximity to Canada's largest customer base, metropolitan Toronto.

The grape-growing region is wedged between Lake Ontario to the north, the Niagara River to the east and the picturesque Niagara Escarpment to the south. The escarpment – a long, tiered ridge shaped something like a bench – separates the flatlands along Lakes Erie and Ontario. The land along the seat of the bench is considered the most fertile, giving rise to the local phenomenon of "the Bench," whose growers dismiss the flatlands below as "the Swamp." The escarpment is responsible for making such a prolific fruit belt, both in terms of the rich minerals eroded into its soil and the micro-climate created by its sheltering effect and the moderating influence of Lake Ontario.

Its location near the 43rd-degree latitude places Niagara in the same position as such wine-growing regions as northern California, southern France and northern Italy. Some increasingly acclaimed wines, particularly rieslings, are the result. "For an area our size," says Cave Spring Cellars winemaker Angelo Pavan, "we probably win more awards in international competitions than any other region in the world."

The Niagara region also has become the world's leading maker of icewine (eiswein), a rare, sweet, almost chewy dessert wine whose minuscule production formerly was centered in Germany and Austria. Riesling and vidal grapes for icewine are left to freeze on the vine and are pressed frozen in winter to yield a wine that will age for ten or fifteen years. The limited supply fetches $30 to $50 or more a half bottle, and one wine writer predicted icewine could become "as Canadian as ice hockey."

Connoisseurs enjoy following the scenic, well-marked Wine Route, spending a day touring the wineries in the flatlands around Niagara-on-the-Lake and another day touring those along the Bench.

Inniskillin Winery, Line 3 Road off Niagara Parkway, Niagara-on-the-Lake. This is the one that started Canada's wine industry, and still leads the pack. Since 1975, Karl Kaiser, winemaker who learned the art in Austria as a monk, and Donald Ziraldo, promoter, have been at the helm of what some consider to be Canada's finest winery, seller of more than 150,000 cases annually, nearly half from its own 120 acres of vineyards.

Co-founder Ziraldo was profiled as one of the top 25 Canadian CEOs of the 20th century in a National Post magazine article for his leadership in the Canadian wine industry. Now he is overseeing Inniskillin's Millennium Project, uniting the original production facility with new construction and outdoor design elements to create "a world-class winery experience."

In the meantime, visitors may take a twenty-station self-guided tour or a 45-minute guided tour and taste wines in a 1920s barn said to have been inspired by Frank Lloyd Wright, the ground floor of which has been transformed into a retail store and tasting area. A menu at the door showed that Inniskillin's cabernet sauvignon reserve was served at former Prime Minister Mulroney's 1993 dinner for Mikhail Gorbachev. The 1997 icewine made by Karl Kaiser from vidal grapes won a record three gold medals in a row, culminating in the Civart Award of Excellence at Vinexpo in France. In 1999, Inniskillin produced Canada's first sparkling icewine. Otherwise, it continues to concentrate on premium viniferas, particularly pinot noir, here and at its newer winery in the Okanagan Valley of British Columbia.

Tastings are featured for $4 to $7, the fees based on the retail prices of the wines. Older vintages are periodically available to taste, as are the three internationally known icewines sampled ($10) at a new icewine tasting bar, another Inniskillin first.

(905) 468-3554 or (888) 466-4754. www.inniskillin.com. Tours daily at 10:30 and 2:30 May-October, weekends rest of year. Wine boutique and visitor center open daily, 10 to 6 May-October, to 5 rest of year.

Jackson-Triggs Niagara Estate Winery, 2145 Niagara Stone Road, Niagara-on-the-Lake.

A name first made famous on Canada's West Coast, Jackson-Triggs in 2001 added a Niagara location to its less than decade-old presence in British Columbia's Okanagan Valley. And what a presence the Eastern location is for Canada's largest single wine brand.

Set in a 26-acre vineyard, the exterior of the modernist/minimalist winemaking facility looks like a cross between a World's Fair pavilion and an airport terminal. A semi-open, two-story-high atrium or Great Hall separates the sleek retail and tasting center from the high-tech production facility. A new amphitheater is used for concerts and special events.

Visitor education is a Jackson-Triggs hallmark, from the "demonstration vineyard" labeling its seven varietals in front of the entrance to private, close-up guided tours through the grape-pressing areas and underground barrel cellars that produce 100,000 cases of premium wine a year. Five-course Savor the Sights epicurean food and wine tastings ($135) are staged on one Saturday night a month from November to June, moving like progressive dinners through various locations around the winery.

Transient visitors enjoy complimentary tastings of three wines in the wine boutique and may adjourn to the multi-windowed Tasting Gallery, a V.I.P.-looking area where flights of wine are paired with such light fare as cheese plates or barbecued oysters ($15 to $20).

In 2004, the winery was named best Canadian wine producer for an unprecedented fourth time (since 1999) at the International Wine and Spirit Competition in London, England. In 2005 at the San Francisco Wine Competition, its Okanagan property was honored as International Winery of the Year, ranking it above more than 1,000 competing wineries across the world – a first for Canada.

(905) 468-4637 or (866) 589-4637. www.jacksontriggswinery.com. Tours daily, 10:30 to 5:30. Open daily 10 to 6:30, to 5:30 in winter.

Hillebrand Estates Winery, 1249 Niagara Stone Road (Highway 55), Niagara-on-the-Lake.

Billed as Canada's most award-winning winery and top producer of premium Vintners Quality Alliance (VQA) wines, this is the nation's largest estate winery, producing more than 300,000 cases a year and running more than 100 retail stores across Ontario.

The frequent tours are said to be the most lively and informative of any Niagara winery. Indeed, Hillebrand was the first winery to give regular tours year-round and they last an hour or longer.

A welcome center and gallery provides directions to the expanding complex, which includes a 110-seat restaurant. Complimentary tastings are offered in the large retail boutique, which purveys a selection of regional gourmet foods, Hillebrand's restaurant specialties and wine-related items as well as wines. The superb Trius chardonnay goes for $16.95 a bottle.

A vineyard jazz and blues concert series is scheduled on certain summer weekends.

(905) 468-7123 or (800) 582-8412. www.hillebrand.com. Tours daily on the hour, 10 to 6. Showroom daily, 10 to 6, summer and fall to 8.

Peller Estates Winery, 290 John St. East, Niagara-on-the-Lake.

Nestled into 26 acres of vineyards within a stone's throw of the Shaw Festival Theatre, this elaborate cathedral of wine is the chateau-like showcase for the rapidly growing wine enterprise run by John Peller, head of the company that owns Hillebrand Estates Winery and Andrés Wines Ltd. in Grimsby.

Here he focuses on chardonnay and three premium reds, cabernet franc, sauvignon and merlot, as well as Cristalle, a methode-champenois sparkling wine accented with a touch of icewine. His stated goal: to produce "big, bold, new world wines – the best reds in Canada."

Until then, the annual production of 25,000 cases a year is window-dressing for the winery's hospitality business, which includes guided and self-guided tours of the underground barrel-aging cellar, an extensive retail area and an acclaimed restaurant. Tour options range from a complimentary open cellar tour to in-depth tours and tastings (starting at $5) that focus on areas of specific interest.

(905) 468-4678 or (888) 673-5537. www.peller.com. Open daily, 10 to 6, summer and fall to 8. Tours hourly on the half hour.

Château des Charmes, 1025 York Road, Niagara-on-the-Lake.

This was touted by a leading Finger Lakes winemaker as Niagara's "best of the

Deck at Vineland Estates Winery Restaurant yields distant view of Lake Ontario.

bunch" and owner Paul Bosc Sr., the French-born patriarch, has been dubbed the "Baron Philippe Rothschild of Ontario." The winery is known for estate chardonnays, aged in oak barrels imported from France for $550 each. Its brut sparkling wine is widely considered to be Canada's best, and its recent riesling, cabernet and merlot releases are quite good. The winery was Canada's first to experiment with the French barrels. Its 60-acre vineyard was the first in Canada planted entirely with European vinifera vines. And lately, it was the first to install gas-powered reverse windmills to blow cold air away from tender grape vines.

Another 85 acres have been planted around a rather pretentious, $6 million French chateau erected in 1994 beneath the St. David's Bench. The stone mansion houses the winery, a champagne cellar, a banquet facility and a showroom and reception area.

(905) 262-4219. www.chateaudescharmes.com. Tours daily at 11 and 3. Showroom daily, 10 to 6.

Vineland Estates Winery 3620 Moyer Road, Vineland.

This expanding winery is Niagara's most picturesque – situated in the rolling countryside along the Bench, with a view of Lake Ontario to the northwest. Lots of trees and hills make for a pleasant break from the sameness of the flatlands scenery below (follow Route 81 and the Niagara Winery Route along the Bench and you may think you're in the upper vales of California's Napa Valley).

German wine grower Hermann Weis wanted to prove to skeptical Canadian growers that his riesling grapes could be cultivated so far north, so he established a vineyard of his own here. Today, his original 45 acres produce 12,000 cases annually of mostly riesling and some chardonnay. Subsequent owners acquired 50 more acres, planting cabernet, merlot and pinot noir vines, and increased production to 50,000 cases. They vastly expanded the restaurant in the original 1845 estate house and restored a rear carriage house with soaring windows and Napa-style views for craft shows, themed wine dinners and private functions. One of Ontario's last log-construction heritage barns was converted into a beauty of a wine shop and tasting room.

Vineland's premium dry rieslings are decisive proof that Niagara rieslings are "better than anything outside the Rhine-Mosel axis itself," one writer proclaimed. Brothers Allan and Brian Schmidt, the winemakers, are also known for gewürztraminers, pinot noirs and icewines. Theirs was the first Canadian winery to win the top winery award at the Vinitaly International Wine Competition in 2003 in Verona, Italy.

(905) 562-708 or (888) 846-3526. www.vineland.com. Tours daily at 3, May-November, weekends only in winter. Showroom daily, 10 to 8 in season, to 5 rest of year.

Cave Spring Cellars, 3836 Main St., Jordan.

Serious, prize-winning wines from vinifera grapes are the specialty of this much-honored boutique winery on the Bench, housed in a lineup of buildings that comprised the defunct Jordan Winery, Ontario's oldest winemaking facility. The expanded wine-tasting and sales room is as stylish as the owners' On the Twenty restaurant at the other end of the complex and their inn across the street.

Chardonnays and rieslings are featured here, the elegant and oaky chardonnay reserve selling for $19.95 and the smooth, award-winning riesling icewine commanding $59.95 a half bottle. The venture also produces cabernet, merlot, gamay and pinot noir varietals among its 60,000 cases annually. The bone-dry riesling reserve is winemaker Angelo Pavan's favorite.

Winery president Leonard Pennachetti was a founder in 1988 of the Vintners Quality Alliance (VQA), Ontario's appellation of origin system and served as its board chairman.

Besides pioneering with its restaurant and inn, Cave Spring has inspired more than a dozen one-of-a-kind shops (from clothing to Inuit native art to gardening, antiques, and Nantucket and Santa Fe styles) leased to the owners in its buildings along both sides of Jordan's Main Street. They help make Jordan a special destination.

(905) 562-3581. www.cavespringcellars.com. Tours, daily at noon and 3, Friday-Sunday at 3 October-May. Showroom, Monday-Wednesday 10 to 6, Thursday-Saturday to 7:30, Sunday 11 to 6.

Henry of Pelham Family Estate Winery, 1469 Pelham Road, St. Catharines.

Here is a small but growing winery with quite a history. Located in the heart of the Bench, the hilly 80-acre vineyard has been owned by a single family since Henry Smith planted the first grapes in 1794. Some 190 years later, Paul Speck Sr. ripped out the original vines and replanted with French hybrids and viniferas. In 1993, when his quickly successful winery had reached his goal of producing 20,000 cases, its founder died and the business was left to his sons' care.

Since then, Paul Jr., Matthew and Daniel Speck increased annual production to 45,000 cases. Their chardonnays, rieslings and icewines are considered some of the best in Canada. The brothers have experienced success with red wines, too. At the prestigious Cuvée 1999 awards in Niagara-on-the-Lake, the winery's baco noir was named the best red hybrid, while its cabernet-merlot was honored as top red wine over-all.

We sampled a variety, from the house Loyalist cabernet-foch to an elegant reserve chardonnay, in the stone basement of a stone inn and tollgate built in 1842 by Henry Smith, the brothers' great-great grandfather, who licensed the inn under the name Henry of Pelham. The building houses a wine boutique, tour center and a gallery of Canadian art collected by the brothers' parents. The Specks renovated a barn on the property to house new wine-tasting facilities and special events, such as their popular Shakespeare in the Vineyard series.

Chef Erik Peacock offers light lunches, sweets and wine pairings with cheese in the winery's new **Coach House Café and Cheese Shoppe,** open daily from 11:30 to 5 from late May through October.

(905) 684-8423. www.henryofpelham.com. Tours daily at 1:30, late May-October. Showroom daily, 10 to 6, to 5 November-April.

Other wineries worth a visit:

Stratus Winery, 2059 Niagara Stone Road, Niagara-on-the-Lake, is a new ultra-modern, gravity-flow winery with a difference. Its owner, Toronto furniture design bigwig David Feldberg, created an eco-friendly winery that marries Old World winemaking with forward-thinking environmental design – a combination that's of as much interest to architects and designers as to oenophiles. The latter are well served, however, by winemaker Jean-Laurent Groux, a Frenchman who developed the prized line of Trius wines during fifteen years at Hillebrand. Here he creates distinctive wines based on the principle of "assemblage," incorporating not one but several grape varieties. Simply labeled Stratus reds or whites, each blends up to seven varieties and are sampled in flights of three wines ($10). They're served in crystal stemware in a chic, four-story-high tasting room full of glass, natural light and innovative details. The inaugural blends retail for $36 to $40 a bottle. Open daily 11 to 5, May-October; rest of year, Wednesday-Sunday noon to 5.

Strewn Winery, 1339 Lakeshore Road, Niagara-on-the-Lake, is really into things culinary. The sparkling estate winery occupies what was once the tumbledown warehouse of an old fruit cannery. President-winemaker Joe Will developed it in 1998 as the core of an operation that includes the leased Terroir La Cachette restaurant and his wife Jane Langdon's Wine Country Cooking School. The school offers hands-on cooking classes during culinary weekends from March through November, as well as customized five-day culinary vacations. Strewn's small state-of-the-art winery and tasting room delivers fine cabernets and rieslings. Open daily, 10 to 6; free tour at 1 p.m.

Reif Estate Winery, 15608 Niagara Pkwy., Niagara-on-the-Lake, the closest to the river, is known for wines in the German style. All North American grapes were uprooted in favor of European vinifera and premium French hybrids on the 135-acre estate behind the winery. Klaus W. Reif, descendant of a winemaking family in Germany, selects only the best 40 percent of the harvest for his own wines, selling the rest to other wineries. The dry riesling and gewürztraminer are standouts here. The winery stages functions in conjunction with the Grand Victorian B&B next door. Open daily, 10 to 6, winter to 5. Tours daily at 1:30, May-September.

Creekside Estate Winery, 2170 Fourth Ave., Jordan Station, claims one of Canada's largest underground barrel cellars where premium wines outside the Ontario mainstream are produced. The winery was founded in 1998 by Peter Jensen and Laura McCain Jensen, she of the McCain Foods empire. Their early concentration was on a signature sauvignon blanc, pinot noir, cabernet sauvignon and a pioneering shiraz that won a Cuveé gold medal in 2004. Lately they added a

Wine Deck and Grill offering weekend lunch beside 16 Mile Creek. Open daily 10 to 6, May-September, to 5 rest of year. Tours daily at 2 in season.

Creekside also produced the initial wines in partnership for the new **Mike Weir Estate Winery,** planned for opening in 2006 in Niagara-on-the-Lake. Canada's leading golfer, a wine enthusiast who had spent summers in the area at the home of his grandparents, earmarked net proceeds from his winery venture to fund children's charities. Its inaugural chardonnay and merlot offerings were well received by fellow PGA golfers and fans.

Marynissen Estates Winery, 1208 Concession 1, Niagara-on-the-Lake, specializes in red wines from Canada's oldest cabernet vines. Winemaker John Marynissen, a Dutch immigrant who started planting vinifera grapes in 1974, won amateur winemaking competitions for years before his daughters convinced him to open an estate winery in 1991. His wines were judged by local winemakers as the "Best Red" two years in a row at Cuvée 1996 and 1997. Among leading Marynissen wines are cabernet franc, cabernet sauvignon, pinot noir, gamay and petit syrah. Open daily, 10 to 6, to 5 in winter.

Sunnybrook Farm Estate Winery, 1425 Lakeshore Road, Niagara-on-the-Lake, is Canada's first fruit winery, producing wines made from fruit grown in Gerald Goertz's orchards. Fruit wines tend to be sweeter than grape wines because of a higher sugar content, but among his two dozen varieties Gerald ranks his empire apple and damson plum wines up there with the best. He finds his bosc pear wine an excellent match with cheeses, and "more civilized than the fruit itself – no peel to deal with." Open daily 10 to 6, May to mid-October, to 5 through December and March-April, and Thursday-Monday 10 to 5, January-February.

The most ambitious winery yet may be **Le Clos Jordan,** a joint undertaking by Don Triggs, president and CEO of Vincor International (Jackson-Triggs, Inniskillin), and Jean-Charles Boisset of Boisset, La Famille des Grands Vins of Nuits-Saint-Georges, France. They snagged Canadian-born superstar architect Frank Gehry to design what he calls "a cathedral for wine" as his first Canadian project, a $30-million venture unveiled in 2002 on the Jordan Bench. The 77-acre parcel surrounding the winery was planted with chardonnay and pinot noir vines shipped from Burgundy as the principals set out to create "the best wine in the world." Because vineyard damage in subsequent winters resulted in insufficient quantities of quality grapes for wine production, the project was delayed. Ground-breaking for the winery was rescheduled for 2006 or 2007 and the opening reset for 2008.

Fruit Stands

In harvest season, the fruit fairly drops off the trees, evidence of how prolific the Niagara Peninsula orchards are. They represent 90 percent of the fruit raised in Ontario, and Niagara is a major fruit bowl for much of Canada. Country markets, some of them run by local Mennonites, stand chock-a-block between orchards along every road. Prices naturally are lower the farther you get from the Queen Elizabeth Way and population centers. Some of the best are around Niagara-on-the-Lake.

Harvest Barn Country Market, 1822 Niagara Stone Road at East-West Line, is a large country market selling everything from fresh produce to home-baked breads, pies, cornish pasties, and steak and kidney pies; two of the last made a good dinner back home. We also made a picnic lunch out of the fantastic salad bar (priced by the

Roadside stands testify to nature's bounty all around Niagara fruit belt.

pound, supermarket style), with ever-so-fresh ingredients set out on ice in about 50 separate dishes.

Kurtz Orchards Country Market, 16006 Niagara Pkwy. at East-West Line, is the biggest and most commercial market, but don't be fazed by the tour buses out front. Jean and Ed Kurtz started more than 25 years ago with one table under an umbrella and maintain the family touch. There are varieties of jams, maple syrups, honeys and plum butter with crackers for sampling, many specialty foods, baked goods like almond-raisin bread (a local specialty with marzipan in the middle) and butter tarts, drinks like cherry cider and peach nectar, and salad and sundae bars. Items are labeled in English and Japanese, to serve the prevailing bus-tour crowds.

Gourmet Treats

Imagine an entire store in a prime downtown corner location devoted to jams. **Greaves Jams & Marmalades,** 55 Queen St., looks just as it must have when it began in 1927. This is where the Greaves family retails its jams, marmalades and preserves. Bins of jams, shelves of jams, boysenberry, peach, raspberry, red and black currant – you name it, they have it, and they use no pectin, preservatives or coloring. We picked up six mini-jars for $6.30, as well as some special mustards (these they don't make).

Niagara is known for fudge. **Maple Leaf Fudge** at 114 Queen St. is where you can choose from many kinds, made with "real butter," including chocolate-ginger studded with chunks of fresh ginger.

The **Niagara Home Bakery** at 66 Queen St., the oldest surviving business in town, operates as it did nearly a century ago. The bread is still baked in an old stone oven and the Easter chocolate is made by hand. Scones, tea biscuits, bridies, almond tarts, sausage rolls, quiches and more are for sale.

Taylor's Bakery & Ice Cream at 69 Queen is the place to stock up for an old-fashioned picnic. You could get a submarine, but why not try a schnitzel on a bun or a cornish pastie? Sandwiches come on a choice of breads or "balm" cakes, which are large rolls. Have a date square or an Empire biscuit for dessert, or one of the more than 50 flavors of ice cream, including Laurentian vanilla.

More contemporary tastes are served at restaurateur Ruth Aspinall's **Kitchen Accents** store at 46 Queen St. Check out her fine selection of specialty foods, kitchen wares and culinary books.

L'Esprit Provence, 106C Queen St., is a haven of food, kitchen gadgets, cuisine posters, pottery, serving bowls and much more from the South of France. It now has a thriving catalog and website operation.

Two wine shops feature tastings and sales of local wines. **Wine Country Vintners** at 127 Queen St. is the local retail outlet for Hillebrand & Peller wines. Around the corner on King Street is **Ontario Wine Merchants,** featuring Vincorp's Inniskillin and Jackson-Triggs wines.

Chiefly Cigars at 32 Queen St. specializes in Cuban cigars, pipes and smoking accessories.

"Have a sweet day," says the sign near the entry of **Willow Cakes & Pastries,** 22 Mary St., which has a more conspicuous location than its hidden neighbor, the Stone Road Grill. But the two enterprises share the same serious commitment to product. We ogled owner Catherine O'Donnell's breakfast items, exotic breads, quiches, a goat cheese tart and a fabulous looking raspberry charlotte before leaving with a sensational strawberry cake to conclude a dinner party back home.

More nifty gourmet items are served up at **de Luca's Cheesemarket and Deli,** in the outlying Forum Galleries antique center at 2017 Niagara Stone Road. Noted local chef Tony de Luca opened this as he transitioned from heading the kitchen at Hillebrand Estates Winery to opening his own restaurant in the Oban Inn. His stock ranges from pâtés and olives to Quebec foie gras, and his staff makes up panini sandwiches for $7.50. His cookbook, *Recipes from Wine Country,* is on prominent display.

Gourmet Theater

Shaw Festival, Box 774, Niagara-on-the-Lake L0S 1J0.

No report on Niagara-on-the-Lake would be complete without mention of the Shaw Festival. Ten productions of George Bernard Shaw and his contemporaries are staged in three theaters from April through November. Artistic director Christopher Newton and one of the world's largest permanent ensembles of actors explore classic plays in a modern way for contemporary audiences. The 869-seat Festival Theater, built in 1973, contains the larger epic works. The 327-seat Court House Theater where the festival began in 1962 presents smaller Shaw works and the more intimate American and European dramas of the period. The 328-seat Royal George Theater houses musicals and perhaps an Agatha Christie mystery.

(905) 468-2172 or (800) 511-7429. www.shawfest.com. Performances, Tuesday-Sunday at noon, 2 and 8. Tickets, $45 to $86.

Stately Gideon Putnam Hotel is a Saratoga icon in midst of Saratoga Spa State Park.

Saratoga Springs

The Summer Place to Be

The party's really hopping these days in that grand dowager of American resorts, Saratoga Springs. The small town that mineral springs, horse racing and society summers made famous had nearly died in the 1950s and 1960s. It re-emerged slowly in the 1970s and now is back on track, as it were, with a five-and-a-half-week racing season that extends through Labor Day, live performances almost nightly in July and August at the Saratoga Performing Arts Center, and a summer social scene that revives the good old days. Little wonder that Saratoga proclaims itself "the summer place to be."

A culinary renaissance has added dimension to what U.S. News and World Report termed "the August delirium of Saratoga, for generations America's symbol of high living." The result is a uniquely Saratoga spirit and panache, one that gives it an odd parochialism as if encased in its own cocoon with a north-south focus on Albany and New York, oblivious to points east and west.

The romance of the old Saratoga was evident in its grand, long-gone hotels with their sprawling porches along Broadway, the wide main street. Herbert A. Chesbrough, longtime executive director of the SPAC, which was instrumental in the city's rejuvenation, says "the romance of the new Saratoga is in the small cafés, unusual restaurants and the boutiques that have opened in some of the community's oldest buildings."

Food has become a big – and expensive – business in Saratoga, and some restaurants stay open in August until 3 a.m. to accommodate the after-the-concert or after-the-race crowds. In fact, scoffs one restaurateur, "even the clothing stores sell food. Everything and anything becomes a restaurant for two months." In a bit of local hyperbole, she claimed the town has more restaurants and bars per capita than any other in the United States.

Much of the year, Saratoga is "very low key," says Linda G. Toohey, executive vice president of the local Chamber of Commerce. "We think we're the best-kept secret in the world."

The pace picks up in late June with racing at the Saratoga Race Course harness track, the Saratoga Jazz Festival and performances by the New York City Ballet at SPAC, and the opening of the party season that culminates in socialite Marylou Whitney's grand entrance at her annual ball at the Canfield Casino.

Come August, the crowds converge for the height of Saratoga's storied racing season, the Saratoga Chamber Music Festival and the Philadelphia Orchestra series at SPAC. Prices double and even triple, but many are the people who are willing to pay.

Where else would a Holiday Inn switch from a rack rate of $139 to $249 for much of the year to a base of $309 to $549 in August?

That's Saratoga for you, a curious anomaly of a world-class resort with a shiny gold sheen and a hand out for the big bucks. Especially in season.

Dining

Serving days and meal hours vary widely in Saratoga, especially off-season. To avoid disappointment, check ahead.

The Best of the Best

Chez Sophie, 534 Broadway, Saratoga Springs.

Ever since it opened in 1969, the French restaurant Chez Sophie has been on the move. Sophie and Joseph Parker started small at their home in the Adirondack foothills town of Hadley. From there, they moved to Saratoga Springs, back to Hadley and back to Saratoga before settling in the former Sam's Place diner in Malta Ridge in 1995. In 2006, the family relocated back to downtown Saratoga to larger quarters in the Saratoga Hotel & Conference Center.

LXR Luxury Resorts, which bought the former Prime Hotel on Broadway in 2005, sought out Chez Sophie because it was renowned in the area for its cuisine and could fulfill its desire to improve the hotel's dining offering. It produced a new state-of-the-art kitchen and a 100-seat dining room designed to the Parker family specifications, plus a wine cellar with storage for 7,000 bottles and a sculpture garden for patriarch Joseph Parker to display his art.

Thus the legacy of legendary French-born chef Sophie Parker will continue as son Paul and his wife Cheryl Clark carry on the family business they acquired following her death in 2001.

With the extra room the new space allows, Cheryl Clark said they wanted a sculpture garden to feature the works of her father-in-law, whose paintings and fantastic wire sculptures had been mainstays of their previous decor. The restaurant

Hosts Paul and Cheryl Parker say farewell to old as Chez Sophie moves into new home.

hours and menu also will be expanded to accommodate breakfast and lunch service. The dining room features a two-sided fireplace in the center and four round tables in glass alcoves overlooking the sculpture garden. A jazz composer plays a baby grand piano in the elegant bar.

Otherwise, Cheryl said, Chez Sophie would remain the same as it has for decades, only larger and more versatile.

Chef Paul cooks in his mother's classic French style – although, Sophie once demurred about hers, "I don't even think of it as French. I just think of it as good food." So good that the New York Times called her bistro in a diner "perfect" and lionized it in a cover story in its food section. Sophie's cuisine was based on fresh ingredients and straightforward preparations, but each dish seemed touched with something otherworldly.

The spirit of Sophie's food shows up in the escargots bourguignonne, the house-cured smoked salmon, farmstead goat cheese in puff pastry and, when available, a dynamite rabbit pâté with prunes and armagnac and a coulis of blueberries, an odd combination that tastes wonderful. The menu changes daily, but expect such main courses as black sea bass steamed in parchment with aromatic herbs, a pair of grilled quail with truffle butter and red wine sauce, and rack of lamb with rosemary and garlic. The duck breast with apricot and green peppercorn sauce and the local rabbit braised with olives in Belgian beer are house favorites.

Dessert could be a dynamite crème brûlée, rich chocolate cake, fresh lemon cheese tart or our old favorite, vacherin, a meringue filled with vanilla ice cream and served with dark chocolate ganache and whipped cream.

(518) 583-3538. www.chezsophie.com. Entrées, $25 to $45. Lunch daily, 11:30 to 2. Dinner nightly, from 5 in summer, from 5:30 rest of year.

43 Phila Bistro, 43 Phila St., Saratoga Springs.

Consistent winner of culinary honors in downtown Saratoga is this suave American café-bistro run by Michael Lenza, an ex-South Jersey chef who cooked locally at Sperry's before launching his own venture in 1993. "I might as well own a place if I'm working so hard," he figured.

Sixteen-hour days have paid off for Michael, who spent eight months gutting and remodeling a former café. He and executive chef John Winnek earn rave reviews for their contemporary fare served with finesse. Wife Patty Lenza oversees the 90-seat dining room, lovely in peach and terra cotta. The bar and banquettes are custom-made of bird's-eye and tiger's-eye maple. Caricatures of local businessmen brighten one wall. Tables – most of the deuces rather close together – are covered with white linens topped with paper mats bearing the 43 Phila logo (a curious but attractive touch that we far prefer to glass). Atop each are fresh flowers, a lucite pepper grinder and a bottle of red wine – a different label at each table.

Arriving almost as we were seated for dinner was a dish of assorted spicy olives marinated in olive oil – the oil useful for soaking the accompanying bread from Rock Hill Bakery, an area institution. The signature starter was a crab martini, jumbo lump crabmeat served with citron vodka, romaine lettuce and an olive in a chilled martini glass. Others were panko-fried shrimp with a mango salsa, marinated duck breast layered with roasted vegetables on crostini and, our choices, a smooth chicken liver pâté served with crostini and cornichons, a terrific trio of smoked seafood (with capers in a little carrot floret and roasted red-pepper crème fraîche) and an enormous pizzetta on Italian bruschetta, a meal in itself.

Had we eaten more than a sliver of the pizzetta we never would have made it through the main courses, a choice of up to a dozen ranging from classic paella and coq au vin to grilled tuna with ginger-scallion mojo and filet mignon with brandy-gorgonzola cream sauce. Our Tuscan chicken pasta with roasted peppers, olives and white beans was a lusty autumn dish; ditto for the jerk chargrilled swordfish with papaya-lobster salsa and a Thai red curry sauce. A bottle of our favorite Hogue Cellars fumé blanc accompanied from a varied, well-chosen wine list.

The pastry chef is known for distinctive desserts, including an acclaimed 43 Phila chocolate cake soaked in kahlua and covered with a brandied chocolate ganache, deep-dish peach crumble pie, and white chocolate cheesecake topped with blueberry compote, sweet red cherries, whipped cream and a star cookie. We settled for plum-port sorbet, a refreshing ending to an uncommonly good meal.

(518) 584-2720. www.43philabistro.com. Entrées, $20 to $36. Lunch daily, 11:30 to 3. Dinner nightly, 6 to 10 or 11. Closed Sunday in off-season.

Dine, A Restaurant, 26 Henry St., Saratoga Springs.

The chef lists 350 dishes over the course of three months in his changing, rapid-fire menu scrawled on blackboards at this sleek, cosmopolitan restaurant transformed from the old Freihofer's wholesale bread outlet. The offerings change every two days, which is why there's no menu posted at the door (and a sampling only recently turned up on the restaurant's ahead-of-the-times website).

The restaurant's "mission" is in global comfort foods. And "a culinary safari in Asian, French and American cuisines" is how chef Keith Landry and new owners Corinne Chauvin and Emily Hopeck describe it.

The modern European-style dining room seats 60 at white-linened tables, with a bar along one side and a backdrop of windows and walls of taupe. The most adventurous seats are at the chef's table for eight in "a Moroccan-style gentleman's pantry" off the kitchen, where he produces a succession of four to ten small courses for $50 and up per person.

Back in the dining room, Saratoga's most ambitious menu might begin with a coconut-lemongrass scallop chowder, a lobster chèvre sandwich, Hong Kong shrimp,

Showy glass chandelier and sleek "sconces" enhance decor at Dine.

grilled duck sausage with braised fennel, calamari "cigars" with ginger-carrot sauce or pheasant salad with candied orange on rosemary shortbread. Main courses range from pan-seared escolar with lobster to royal Thai duck breast and espresso-rubbed filet mignon with a burgundy demi-glace. A dish called "three little pigs" – a sixteen-ounce frenched pork chop with Asian mizuni sauce – intrigued at one visit. But some of the fare could be as comforting as "Lena's pot roast" or "chicken and sausage a la rocco" or even "meatloaf wellington."

Desserts follow suit, from Cuban sugar cookies to sticky date pudding and from soufflés to pumpkin dumplings with caramel sauce.

(518) 587-9463. www.dinesaratoga.com. Entrées, $27 to $42. Dinner, Wednesday-Sunday from 5:30.

Springwater Bistro, 139 Union Ave., Saratoga Springs.

The executive chef from the posh Sagamore Resort on Lake George left to open a restaurant of his own in Saratoga. David Britton purchased what for a dozen years had been the off-again, on-again Springwater Inn, renamed it a bistro, made a few cosmetic changes and vaulted the enterprise into Saratoga's top echelon.

"The menu reflects my travels," says David, the chef, whose 25-year cooking career began with a three-year apprenticeship through the American Culinary Federation at the Arizona Biltmore in Scottsdale. His culinary pedigree includes stints at hotels in California and Hawaii as well as at the five-star Inn at Little Washington in Virginia.

The high-style menu, printed daily, reflects several continents and many countries.

Appetizers are categorized as hot and cold bistro fare. The cream of carrot soup might be elevated with mussels, lemongrass, ginger and coconut milk, and the smoked Hawaiian marlin embellished with pea shoots and caviar dressing. A terrine of rabbit could be served with a baby romaine and fried garlic caesar salad.

More exotic fish turn up in the entrée section called Hawaiian Fish Collection: perhaps sesame-crusted tuna mignon with wasabi and ginger and grilled opah with champagne butter. Other possibilities might be roasted Long Island duck with balsamic poached cherries, rabbit cacciatore, grilled ribeye steak with watercress butter and grilled veal london broil with lemon butter.

In typical bistro style, there's often a "plat du jour." At our visit, it was tandoori-grilled prime boar chop with curry and long-grain rice.

Desserts are as extravagant as the rest of the offerings. Typical are a trio of crème brûlées, warm chocolate ganache cake with double chocolate ice cream and chocolate fondue, orange meringue tart, a crispy anjou pear beignet and walnut bread pudding with golden raisins, nutmeg and red wine-honey caramel.

All these good tastes are served up in a couple of pleasant dining areas with black walnut tables and booths set with white napkins and shaded oil lamps. The artistry turns up not in the decor but on the plates, which is as it should be.

(518) 584-6440. www.springwaterbistro.com. Entrées, $23 to $31. Lunch in racing season, Thursday-Sunday 11:30 to 2. Dinner nightly, from 5:30; closed Tuesday in off-season, also Monday in winter.

Chianti Il Ristorante, 208 South Broadway, Saratoga Springs.

A former fast-food eatery is the hottest restaurant in town – according to both its ebullient Italian chef-owner and his avid following. Chianti is lovingly tended by David Zecchini from Rome, whose grandparents run a restaurant there.

David, who claims to have been the youngest maitre-d' in California at age 22, went on to open La Fontana, a highly rated restaurant in Newport Beach. He sold it at age 29 to move to his former wife's hometown, where he transformed a Long John Silver's seafood franchise into a place of earth tones and Mediterranean beauty. "I built this restaurant piece by piece," he said. He made the handsome tabletops with Italian tiles, hand-painted the ceiling a burnt siena color, hung remarkable iron light sculptures and installed an open kitchen with a shiny copper effect at the rear. He also created the prototype for the colorful new service plates custom-made for the restaurant. With a subsequent expansion that added a bar in front and a new side dining room, Chianti seats 140 at close-together tables inside and an additional 40 on the front patio.

David's labor of love includes a passion for food, although lately he has turned over cooking duties to a chef from Italy. The offerings are creative, robust and considered good value. Among antipasti are bruschetta topped with garlic and tomato, six versions of carpaccio (one marinated in truffle oil and topped with gorgonzola), fried calamari with spicy marinara sauce, and grilled scampi tossed with wild greens. Can't decide? Consider the chef's-choice antipasto sampler for two.

Two risottos, one with porcini mushrooms and the other with crab and scampi, come highly recommended. So do pastas like rigatoni with Italian tuna, olives and garlic, and angel hair with jumbo shrimp in a lobster-grappa sauce.

Favorite main courses are scampi marinated with mint in a balsamic-citrus sauce, chicken with artichokes in a lemon-wine sauce, veal scaloppine with porcini mushrooms in a white wine sauce, and filet mignon with gorgonzola sauce.

Desserts range from lemon or orange sorbet to profiteroles, tiramisu and a light lemon torte finished with pinenuts and powdered sugar.

The award-winning, predominantly Italian wine list starts in the thirties and includes many in the triple digits.

Lately, David has branched out, opening the lively **Luna Lounge** nightclub at 17 Maple Ave. and the casual yet stylish **Forno Toscano Bistro** at 541 Broadway. The latter is an affordable place for salads, pizzas and pastas for lunch and dinner, with arguably Saratoga's most inviting dining patio overlooking Broadway.

(518) 580-0025. www.chiantiristorante.com. Entrées, $16 to $28. Dinner nightly, from 5:30. Closed Monday in off-season.

Sargo's, 458 Union Ave., Saratoga Springs.

The artistic culinary displays in the entry foyer to the dramatic clubhouse indicate that the Saratoga National Golf Club is serious about food. So do the reviews and its award as the best new restaurant in upstate New York, as bestowed in 2002 by the New York State Restaurant Association.

Here is one beautiful restaurant, part of the top-rated Saratoga National golf course that Tom Newkirk and Bob Howard from Albany opened on a former horse farm east of town. Something of a cross between a stone castle and an Adirondack lodge, the clubhouse is devoted to food and drink in the plushest of surroundings.

Prepare to be awed as you stroll through the long, two-story high "lobby" toward a sumptuous lounge outfitted with plush leopard-skin chairs in the rear and a spacious, soaring beamed dining room at the side. Both open onto an idyllic cobblestone patio beside what our guide called "a negative-edge pond" with a waterfall and fountain splashing near and far, a life-size statue of a grazing horse and the verdant golf course beyond.

Little wonder that Sargo's lured so many customers for its lavish Sunday international jazz brunch, a phenomenon that is such a tradition in Saratoga. The setting is stunning, and the food well received (more than 70 dishes and six chef's stations for $24).

Executive chef Larry Schepici, a veteran of Vermont resort dining rooms, oversees an extensive menu of contemporary American cuisine as well as enough special culinary events – from gourmet pasta nights to Tuscan wine dinners to Swedish Christmas smorgasbords – to keep the 96-seat dining room busy.

There's a light fare menu to appeal to golfers and casual diners, but the real culinary extravagance shows up on the dinner menu. Where else locally would you find dover sole flown in from England, beef tournedos and seafood neapolitan, veal and lobster lorenzo, and even lobster savannah (for a cool $48)? Expect to pay big bucks for the likes of wood grilled swordfish with a ragoût of shrimp and flageolets, veal chop Michelangelo (here with the works) and rack of lamb with a minted star anise jus. The moulard duck might be served three ways: juniper-encrusted breast, confit and pan-seared liver with a wildberry-duck glace.

Oysters mignonette, dungeness crab cakes, quail stuffed with Hudson Valley

Distinctive windows and chandeliers provide backdrop for dining at Sargo's.

foie gras, and duck and shiitake spring rolls are typical appetizers. Desserts range from tortes and pies from a pastry tray to flambéed baked alaska.

(518) 583-4653. www.golfsaratoga.com. Entrées, $22 to $48. Lunch, Monday-Saturday 11 to 4 in season, Saturday 11 to 3 off-season. Dinner nightly in season, 5 to 9 or 10; Wednesday-Saturday in off-season. Sunday, brunch 10 to 2, dinner (light fare only) 3 to 7.

Wine Bar Plus

The Wine Bar, 417 Broadway, Saratoga Springs. (518) 584-8777.

A shared interest in wine and travel inspired Judith Evans and her daughter Melissa to open this wine and tapas bar. "We thought it was something Saratoga would enjoy," explained Melissa. "There was a niche here."

The Evanses gutted a former hair salon to produce one of Broadway's most beautiful buildings, inside and out. The contemporary interior in grays and mauves is elegant and stylish – a cross between New York and San Francisco, in Melissa's words. Tables on the main level flank a long granite bar, and a glass-enclosed room with a humidor serves as a smoking lounge.

More than 50 wines by the glass are offered. They may be upstaged by the first-rate food, as prepared by chef Mark Graham and offered in "small plate" and entrée sizes. You could make a satisfying meal of "beginnings" like a trio of soups, lobster and sweetbread strudel, foie gras with wine-poached nectarines and an ice wine vinaigrette, a shortrib tart and a smoked salmon salad with heirloom radishes, shaved fennel and nectarine. Entrées are available in main-course or tapas portions, the latter at half price. Typical are seared dayboat scallops served with baby beets, white asparagus and a celeriac-potato puree, Cuban spiced pork tenderloin served with crispy plantains, duck breast with a duck confit "stir fry" and a fermented black bean-orange vinaigrette, and rack of lamb with a warm olive sauce and a napoleon of eggplant, tomato and chèvre.

Assorted cheeses are offered, as are desserts like warm plum soup with sour cherry ice cream and almond brittle, chèvre panna cotta with honey-walnut-fig compote, a granita sampler and a "s'mores" tart.

(518) 584-8777. www.thewinebarofsaratoga.com. Small plates, $7 to $17. Entrées, $18 to $30. Dinner, Tuesday-Saturday 4 to 10, also Sunday during July and August.

One for the Season

Siro's, 168 Lincoln Ave., Saratoga Springs.

Imagine a fancy restaurant next to a racetrack, open a mere five weeks a year (for the racing season) and considered an institution. Only in Saratoga could such a place survive. Siro's has not only survived since the 1930s but thrived.

Siro's occupies a little white house that sports blue awnings and canopies. There's a tent at the side for jazz, a prominent bar inside the front entry and a couple of medium-size dining rooms dressed in white linens with white candles standing tall.

Expect to spend more than $200 for dinner for two with wine. The menu changes nightly, but the contents are always inventive, the product acclaimed and the delivery polished.

High-rollers like to start with exotic hors d'oeuvre, perhaps flash-seared Maine scallops with sesame-wakame salad and tobikko or seared Hudson Valley foie gras with caramelized onion and peach and black currant glace. The lobster tortilla with corn relish and peppered guacamole is a menu staple. So is a service of Beluga caviar, $90 for 42 grams.

Then it's on to a "first course," say lump crab gazpacho, Wellfleet oysters and tasso cream over linguini, local beefsteak tomato salad with fresh mozzarella, or Siro's romaine salad with anchovy, reggiano shards and caesar dressing.

Typically, the dozen or so main courses run from a signature crusty baked fluke with caramelized banana and mango-melon salsa or pan-roasted Hawaiian opa with mango-ginger emulsion to roasted rack of lamb with rosemary jus and garlic polenta cake or broiled veal chop with porcini jus.

For dessert, many opt for Siro's mosaic, perhaps warm apple tarte tatin, petite crème caramel and vanilla gelato with ginger and caramel sauces.

(518) 584-4030. www.sirosrestaurant.com. Entrées, $30 to $48. Dinner nightly, 6 to 11, late July to Labor Day.

More Dining Choices

Sperry's, 30 Caroline St., Saratoga Springs.

Only in Saratoga could what "looks like a gin mill" (a local booster's words) pass itself off as a good restaurant. Everyone we talk with, from top chefs to hotel desk clerks, mentions Sperry's among their favorites.

It's certainly not for the speakeasy-look decor – peek through the window and you might not venture inside. A long bar with a black and white linoleum floor takes up about half the space. At either end of the room are dark old booths and tables covered with blue and white checked cloths. On one side is a small dining addition, similarly outfitted and used for overflow. Beyond is an enclosed (and heated) patio for outdoor seating in season.

Chef-owner Eldridge Qua is known for consistently good food – with Asian and Louisiana accents – at reasonable prices. The menu rarely changes, but the preparations and lengthy list of specials do.

For lunch, one of us enjoyed a great grilled duck-breast salad with citrus vinaigrette and the other a cup of potato-leek soup with an enormous open-face dill-havarti-tomato sandwich, served with a side salad. Service on a slow day, unfortunately, was so leisurely as to be interminable. We had to go to the bar to request – and later to pay – the bill.

At night, when we assume service is better, the menu ranges widely from jambalaya to steak au poivre. Pesto-crusted black grouper sauced with white wine and butter, fillet of sole sautéed with malt vinegar, sautéed shrimp and scallops in a saffron beurre blanc over linguini, and New Zealand lamb chops stuffed with figs and wrapped in prosciutto were among choices at a recent visit. The day's pasta was sautéed rock shrimp, escarole, snow peas and roasted red peppers over linguini. The salad du jour produced beer-battered catfish over mesclun greens with spicy salsa and a New Orleans rémoulade dressing.

Appetizers like escargots, sautéed soft-shell crabs, Malpeque oysters on the half shell, a smooth chicken liver pâté and grilled portobello mushrooms with chèvre and garlic toast are better than run-of-the-gin-mill offerings. Desserts include tortes, cheesecakes, seasonal fruit tarts, crème caramel, and lemon and chocolate mousses.

(518) 584-9618. Entrées, $16.95 to $25.95. Lunch in season, Monday-Saturday 11:30 to 3. Dinner nightly, 5:30 to 10 or 11, Sunday from 5.

Eartha's Restaurant, 60 Court St., Saratoga Springs.

Ever since it opened as Eartha's Kitchen in 1985, the intimate Court Street bistro has been a major player on Saratoga's dining scene. Its fortunes have risen and fallen with a succession of owners and chefs and an aborted move to larger quarters in 2003, but it reopened in 2005 in its original haunt with an edgy new dining concept.

Adam Madkour, president of Saratoga Spring Water Co., earlier had purchased Eartha's to restore it to its glory days. He installed in the kitchen his son Shane as chef, who launched an oddball menu of pint-size options categorized as spring rolls, romaine lettuce wraps, crispy ravioli, grilled skewers and create-your-own mini-burgers, with nothing priced over $6. All these for dinner, mind you. And that was all.

They found a receptive following among health addicts and diet-watchers for the likes of a shrimp spring roll with chile mayo, a falafel and tomato lettuce wrap, Asian-style pork and vegetable ravioli in a ginger-infused soy sauce, and an assortment of mini-burgers and toppings. Those with heartier appetites had to be satisfied with grilled skewers of vegetables with a choice of shrimp, chicken, pork, lamb or filet, each with a side of chickpea salad.

The idea was to offer a diverse array of tastes and textures in small portions to allow flexibility in ordering. It was billed as both a tasting menu of cultural fusion and a phenomenon of "dining as a social event." The latter has been facilitated, no doubt, by the small, close-together wood tables lined up in three rows running the length of the snug storefront, with barely space for servers or customers to squeeze between. Perhaps the tastes are enhanced by the enforced conviviality.

(518) 583-0602. www.earthas.com. Menu items, $2.50 to $6. Dinner, Tuesday-Sunday 5:30 to 10:30.

Longfellows Restaurant, 500 Union Ave., Saratoga Springs.

The famed Caunterbury restaurant complex has given way to this well-regarded restaurant with an inn-turned-hotel adjacent.

The principals are Steve and Yvonne Sullivan, owners of the Olde Bryan Inn restaurant downtown. Here, on the far outskirts of town, they gave two 1915 dairy barns a facelift and toned down the Caunterbury's eye-popping Disneyesque theme to create a pleasing Federal-style restaurant and grill.

It's still quite an eyeful, this grand barn of a space with an open courtyard centering an amazing variety of venues for dining. There are dining rooms on several levels behind the facades of "village houses" set around what had been an interior lagoon. One room has a wooden footbridge crossing a pond full of goldfish. Other rooms are smaller and more standard. The tavern and wine cellar with a fireplace is favored in winter. All told, the place seats 425 – if there's a wait, check out the enormous upstairs cocktail lounge with its lighted ficus tree.

A mesquite grill produces a variety of steaks and other items, perhaps swordfish steak with melon-lime salsa, bourbon-glazed salmon fillet, chili-glazed chicken breast with sweet and spicy pineapple, and twin pork chops with an apple cider-black currant glaze. Slow-roasted prime rib is a specialty. Other possibilities range from sashimi tuna au poivre to pistachio-encrusted rack of lamb with a port wine sauce.

The menu also offers a trio of pastas and appetizers from a signature lobster and asparagus tart to cajun chicken strudel with andouille sausage and creole vegetables. Cheesecake, triple chocolate terrine, apple-walnut pie and crème brûlée might be on tap for dessert.

(518) 587-0108. www.longfellows.com. Entrées, $17.95 to $28.95. Dinner, 5 to 10 or 11, Sunday 4 to 9.

Tiznow, 84 Henry St., Saratoga Springs.

Tiznow, in case you didn't know, is the name of the colt that won back-to-back Breeders Cup Classics. Restaurateur John Costanzo, an inveterate racing fan from New York City, bet money on him. So when he moved to Saratoga to open a restaurant in 2004 he had a ready explanation: "I wanted to ride him a third time."

He envisioned a niche for a trendy bistro like those he enjoyed in the Big Apple and found an offbeat setting in a former machine shop at the edge of downtown. It's an urban, high-ceilinged space with exposed beams, chocolate brown and mustard-colored walls accented by black woodwork and black-framed mirrors, and soft pendant lighting. There's leather banquette seating at close-together tables covered with white butcher paper over white cloths, with a convivial twenty-seat black wood bar at one side. The front windows come out so the outdoors can come in on summer evenings.

Costanzo bills the place as a bistro serving "French and Asian cuisine, Belgian beers and Latin music.'" The global menu begins with the likes of onion soup gratinée, tuna seviche, beef tartare, duck spring rolls and salade niçoise. Three mussels dishes (Belgian with frites, Portuguese and Thai) come in appetizer or main-course sizes. A trio of steak offerings (au poivre, Tuscan and Cuban filet sofrito) illustrate the kitchen's range. Other main courses could be cumin-dusted Caribbean salmon with rum-mango salsa, hazelnut-crusted Chilean sea bass in a chai tea broth, Asian Moroccan chicken, duck madeira and lamb tenderloin with a blue cheese demi-glace. Desserts are few but select, perhaps Asian five-spice chocolate torte, a classic lemon tart or crème brùlée.

The full menu is available at the bar, a late-night spot favored by racing fans.

(518) 226-0655. www.tiznowrestaurant.com. Entrées, $23 to $34. Dinner, Tuesday-Sunday from 5, nightly during racing season, Tuesday-Saturday in winter.

Chameleon on the Lake, 251 County Road 67, Saratoga Springs.

A taste of Key West in Saratoga is the billing for Richard Rodriguez's funky and festive new eatery near Saratoga Lake. The former maitre-d'hôtel at the posh Sagamore Resort on Lake George downscaled when he left as a partner in Saratoga's Springwater Bistro to open his own place at a marina alongside Fish Creek.

"I'm all about changing colors," he says of the name. That goes for the menu, the floor plan, the staff uniforms, the linens. "Sometimes I put the dining room in the bar." Otherwise, there's somewhat formal dining at well-spaced tables in a large room, casual dining in the bar/lounge and creekside dining on the expansive deck, plus champagne cruises and food and wine dinners on a pontoon boat.

The food comes highly rated, somewhat unexpectedly given the not-exactly-high-end setting. The menu changes frequently, but you could start with a trio of bruschetta, a crabmeat and brie quesadilla, mussels provençal, salt cod fritters or fried calamari. Main courses might be paella, tilapia en papillote, pan-seared yellowfin tuna, roasted balsamic-glazed chicken, grilled spiced steak topped with piquilla peppers, and Moroccan lamb loin topped with mango salsa, served with couscous, Moroccan vegetables and fried plantains. Profiteroles are featured for dessert.

(518) 581-3928. www.chameleononthelake.com. Entrées, $19.95 to $25.95. Dinner, Wednesday-Saturday 5:30 to 9:30, Sunday 4 to 8.

A Sweet Homecoming

Mrs. London's, 464 Broadway, Saratoga Springs.

The pastries made famous by Michael and Wendy London came back in style to the town in which they got their start on Phila Street in the 1970s.

The Londons acquired a more prominent storefront location along Broadway to purvey their Rock Hill Bakehouse breads and pastries in what Michael likened to a French patisserie and espresso bar. A larger retail area than before, a stylish café setting in the Neo-Classical style of New York of the 1820s, and a pastry and demonstration kitchen occupy the main floor. The unusual café decor displays Federal period pieces and the Londons' collection of early American silk embroideries. The kitchen is a showcase for Michael and Wendy, who were happy to get back to baking, and is a teaching facility for their licensees. The onetime Skidmore College professor-turned-world-class-baker revives memories of such Mrs. London's favorites as lemon tarts and chocolate whiskey cake as rich as fudge, with bitter chocolate curls on top.

In the decade after their Phila Street bake shop closed, the Londons had concentrated on baking sourdough and natural grain breads at their farmhouse outside Greenwich, producing a ton of bread a day for delivery to restaurants and stores around the East. They also licensed bakers to produce Rock Hill breads across the country, and now produce Rock Hill reserve breads from a unique, enormous wood-fired oven made of volcanic rock in a new bakehouse addition in Greenwich.

The Saratoga operation offers espresso, teas and high-end sandwiches (croques, panini and such) as well as their trademark pastries, which Food & Wine magazine rated among the best in the world.

The adjacent storefront was being readied in 2005 for son Max London's planned Max's restaurant.

(518) 581-1834. www.mrslondons.com. Café menu, $6.50 to $12.50. Open Tuesday-Sunday, 7 to 6; Friday and Saturday to 10.

Left Bank, Saratoga Style

Ravenous, 21 Phila St., Saratoga Springs.

Fellow chefs say the pommes frites here are the best in the world. Ditto for the sweet and savory crêpes. Which is as it should be, given that this tiny hot spot is run by chef Francesco D'Amico from Belgium and his wife, Lauren Wickizer.

Sit at the counter facing the open kitchen, the counter at the window or at a communal table for ten in the corner storefront and enjoy the biggest variety of crêpes you're likely to find this side of Brussels. Start with the frites, served as in Belgium in a paper cone and as addictive as they come. You can order from a choice of nine dipping sauces – the aioli and the horseradish mayo proved tasty, but these fries don't really need add-ons. These are great even with the vinegar that comes free.

The Left Bank crêpe of ham, melted gruyère and tomato is like those you get on the streets of Paris, served with a perfect mixed green salad. Also super was the Taj Mahal, full of curried chicken, cauliflower, apples, raisins and zesty Indian spices. Next time we'll try the Upper West Sider with salmon, cream cheese and scallions. Finish with a banana crêpe, the merry berry or the lemon squeeze.

Coffees, teas and the Ravenous pink lemonade go with.

(518) 581-0560. Savory crêpes, $7.95 to $9.75. Open daily, 11:30 to 8, Friday to 9, Saturday 10 to 9, Sunday 10 to 3. Closed Monday in off-season.

Lodging

Saratoga Arms, 497 Broadway, Saratoga Springs 12866.

Saratoga's most versatile innkeepers have turned their attention to the growing boutique hotel they opened in downtown Saratoga. Noel and Kathleen Smith restored a Second Empire brick hotel built in 1870 by Gideon Putnam's grandson, transforming what had become a derelict rooming house into a place of charm and beauty. "It was horribly neglected but never abused," said Kathy. "We found the original chandeliers, fireplaces and woodwork beneath layers of subsequent renovations."

To that in 2005 they added a three-story wing that blends seamlessly with the original and provides fifteen more guest rooms with high-end amenities.

The Smiths, who moved from their former Saratoga Bed & Breakfast and motel into quarters in the hotel, keep the front entrance locked to ensure privacy for guests. A wraparound front porch, outfitted in wicker and colorful with enormous hanging baskets of impatiens, overlooks the Broadway scene.

The main floor of the original building holds a formal sitting room with a black floral carpet and two prized chartreuse chairs in front of the fireplace. "We're clean-cut Victorian – not goofy Victorian," Kathy points out. Beyond are not one but two dining rooms. "We have a lot of guests to feed for breakfast," she explains.

A modern elevator takes guests to fourteen rooms on the second and third floors of the original hotel. All have tiled baths (some with whirlpool tubs, others with

Wide front veranda of stately Saratoga Arms boutique hotel faces Broadway.

clawfoot tubs), telephones and TVs. Six have restored gas fireplaces. Beds are king, queen or twin-size. Each room has at least one fine piece – an armoire here, a full mirror there – along with antique and reproduction furnishings and the splashy decor that is Kathy's trademark.

Rooms differ in style and size. A third-floor room with kingsize poster bed is decorated in black and white French toile, from wallpaper and draperies to bed coverings and shower curtain. Another with two queen beds is colorful in moss green and lavender florals and adds a small sitting room just big enough for two chairs. A colorful wooden piece serves as a headboard above the king bed in another room. Light from tall windows lends a bright and airy look to each high-ceilinged room. Expect to find coordinated fabrics, hand-painted dressers, and custom-made Kleenex boxes and wastebaskets hand-painted by a local artist.

Two premier rooms are situated on the walkout lower level, opening onto a sunken front terrace. Each with a fireplace and cool ceramic tile floors, they come with kingsize beds, two-person jacuzzi tubs and separate showers. One has a small kitchenette and, with a separate outside entrance, is like a maisonette apartment.

The new wing harbors two suites, whose bathrooms are unusual for the TV screens embedded in half of the mirrors, as well as six rooms with Juliet balconies. The wing also has a fitness room and an executive conference room. Massages and facials are offered as well.

The aforementioned artist has inscribed a local quote or factoid onto a tile at eye-level in each shower bath. The most notable carries the blessing of Marylou Whitney, "the Queen of Saratoga," with a crown slightly askew. The inscriptions make for good ice-breakers as guests swap secrets at the breakfast table in the morning.

Breakfast is a hearty affair. Noel handles the cooking while Kathy converses with guests. The fare was vegetable or cream cheese and herbed omelets the day of our visit. Irish scones often accompany.

(518) 584-1775. Fax (518) 581-4064. www.saratogaarms.com. Thirty-one rooms with private baths. Doubles, $175 to $375 mid-May-October, $295 to $595 racing, $150 to $300 rest of year.

The Batcheller Mansion Inn, 20 Circular St., Saratoga Springs 12866.

Saratoga's most spectacular, conspicuous and architecturally fanciful landmark is now an urbane city inn. Built in 1873 and patterned after a Bavarian castle, the 28-room edifice sports Moorish minarets and turrets and reflects what has been variously called flamboyant French Renaissance and High Victorian Gothic styles.

Guests enter through arched mahogany front doors. Off one side of the hall is a living room with gilt-edged mirrors and an enormous crystal chandelier. Off the other side is a mahogany-paneled library with plump red velvet sofas beside the fireplace and towering ficus trees by the tall windows in the bay. The dining room is large enough to hold a long table for twelve and four side tables for two. The dream of a kitchen is a breathtaking space, long and narrow and 26 feet high – contemporary and stark white except for an extravagant display of colorful culinary artworks and three soaring, twenty-foot-high arched windows that bring the outdoors in.

All nine guest rooms on the second and third floors come with private baths, queen or kingsize beds, fancy wallpapers and coordinated fabrics, oriental rugs atop thick carpeting, writing desks, television sets, telephones, mini-refrigerators, monogrammed bathrobes, thick towels and Haversham & Holt toiletries. Some have gas fireplaces. They vary widely in size from two small front rooms with hall baths to the enormous third-floor Diamond Jim Brady Room, outfitted with a billiards table in the middle, a kingsize iron canopy bed, a sitting area and a huge bathroom with an oversize jacuzzi, large stall shower and mirrored wall.

On weekdays, an elaborate continental breakfast is set out buffet style on the kitchen counters, It includes fresh fruit (perhaps melon wrapped in prosciutto), cheeses, cereals and homemade granola as well as muffins, scones and croissants. On weekends, a full breakfast is cooked to order.

(518) 584-7012 or (800) 616-7012. www.batchellermansioninn.com. Nine rooms with private baths. Doubles, weekends $180 to $295, midweek $120 to $235. Racing, $265 to $400.

Fox 'n' Hound Bed & Breakfast, 142 Lake Ave., Saratoga Springs, NY 12866.

She had owned and operated a Victorian B&B for seven years in California's Mendocino County. So Marlena Sacca knew what to do when she acquired this majestic 1904 Victorian in 2002. She named it to reflect the theme of her collection of hunt prints that dot the common rooms and set about blending her special brand of European hospitality with the warmth of home.

The Romanian-born innkeeper had scoured the Northeast for the appropriate site to move back East and open a B&B. "The minute I walked in the door I knew this was it," the ex-New Yorker said of the house with a large entry foyer paneled with birds-eye maple, a sweeping spiral staircase and a large, stained-glass window.

Two parlors (one full of plush velvet furniture and ornate carved burl paneling), a large dining room, a butler's pantry and a kitchen – all bearing fine Victorian woodwork and detailing – contributed to her decision. The attributes of five upstairs guest rooms sealed the deal.

Stunning wallpaper and handmade window treatments and bed canopies lend themselves to Marlena's furnishings. That's particularly evident in the Crown Room, named for the large purple and gold satin canopy that crowns the kingsize bed. Purple satin draperies puddle to the floor, adding to the regal feel of a room graced by an armoire that looks as if it had been there forever. The angels on the wallpaper border inspired the name for the rear Cherub Room, an L-shaped space with a kingsize carved oak bed nicely angled in the corner of the ell, a matching armoire, a fainting couch in the far alcove and a large bath. The Lilac Room, richly dressed in eggplant colors against a prevailing white backdrop, has a kingsize bed draped in sheer fabric and sports a private balcony. Queensize beds and whirlpool tubs are features of the Saratoga and Springs rooms in front.

Guests avail themselves of the wraparound porch and side lawn with gardens, statuary and a swimming pool.

Marlena, who was a chef-instructor at the Culinary Institute of America in Hyde Park before moving to California, serves a multi-course breakfast in the formal dining room. "My philosophy is that you can cook healthier without sacrificing flavor," she says. So she uses spices and herbs in place of fats and sweets, and markets every morning for fresh vegetables, herbs and fruits. She frequently makes frittatas using vegetables of the season and makes her own salsas to serve with the egg dishes. Still, her Romanian cheese pancakes with cream sauce and raspberry jam are the guests' favorite. Shrimp benedict, omelets, dried cranberry scones, poached pears and pancakes with caramelized apples and raisins are others.

Cookies, snacks and beverages are available at all hours in the butler's pantry. "People can help themselves," says Marlena. "I want everyone to feel at home."

(518) 584-5959 or (866) 369-1913. Fax (528) 584-2594. www.foxnhoundbandb.com. Five rooms with private baths. Doubles, $160 to $245. Racing, $295 to $400.

The Westchester House, 102 Lincoln Ave., Box 944, Saratoga Springs 12866.

One of Saratoga's oldest guest houses, this Queen Anne Victorian structure has been taking in guests for more than 100 years. But never so lovingly as in the nearly fifteen years since Bob and Stephanie Melvin of Washington, D.C., realized a dream by restoring the abandoned house into an elegant yet welcoming B&B in which guests' comfort is paramount.

All seven guest rooms have handsomely tiled private baths, telephones and king or queensize beds except for one with two three-quarter beds. Each is attractively furnished to the period. On the chest of drawers you'll find fresh flowers and chocolates embossed with the raised Westchester House logo. Handsome woodwork, blue tiles, two elaborate fireplaces and distinctive wainscoting are all original. The Melvins collect antiques, which are scattered throughout the house, along with "old" and modern art.

Guests gather on a wraparound porch overlooking old-fashioned gardens for tea and cookies or wine and cheese. The side and rear gardens contain six distinct sitting areas, where guests also can relax. Or they can enjoy two main-floor parlors, one with a great suede sofa and a grand piano (upon which Stephanie practices, when no guests are around, for her performances as an opera singer).

The Melvins serve a continental breakfast stylishly amid fine linens, china, crystal mugs and stemmed glasses in the dining room or on the porch. Juice, fresh fruit salad, baked goods from the nearby Bread Basket and sometimes cheese are the fare, enhanced by Stephanie's homemade peach butter and apple preserves. After

Dining room is stylish setting for breakfast at The Westchester House.

breakfast, Bob snaps photos of guests, which are forwarded to their homes with a thank-you note to remind them of their stay.

(518) 587-7613 or (800) 581-7613. Fax (518) 583-9562. www.westchesterhousebandb.com. Seven rooms with private baths. Doubles, $115 to $225. Racing, $240 to $445. Closed December-February.

The Mansion, 801 Route 29, Rock City Falls 12863.

About seven miles west of Saratoga in an old mill town is a 23-room Venetian, villa-style mansion that has been carefully turned into an elegant B&B. Built as a summer home in 1866 by industrialist George West, known as the Paper Bag King for his invention of the folded paper bag, the imposing light purple Victorian house with cupola on top has been upgraded and expanded since its acquisition by Jeffrey Wodicka, head of a Saratoga insurance firm, and partner Neil Castro.

The house is full of striking details, including original brass and copper gas chandeliers with Waterford glass shades, six fireplaces with massive mantelpieces, parquet floors of three woods, wooden indoor window shutters and etched-glass doors. Brass doorknobs detailed with classical heads – including a dog with one paw outstretched – greet you at the front door.

Guests luxuriate in grand parlors, seven bedrooms and three suites amid priceless Victoriana, and enjoy a pond and three acres of grounds across from the mills. Off the central hall with its cheery yellow walls and an unsigned Tiffany chandelier is a double parlor with recessed pocket doors and extravagant floral arrangements. Across the hall is the library/lounge, where the rosewood piano – once owned by Mamie Eisenhower – was obtained on eBay and Jeffrey was told he could sell the wood for more than the piano. Not that he's about to. It's the focal point for complimentary cocktails for guests in the late afternoon.

Beyond the piano lounge in this house that keeps unfolding to the rear is the George West Room. It features a French chestnut queen bedroom set, matching marble dresser, mirrored armoire and ornamental fireplace. The bed is topped by a distinctive tapestry-type comforter like those throughout the house.

In the rear is the Saratoga Room, reconfigured from a kitchen and a room in which we stayed when the Mansion opened as a B&B back in the 1980s. Today it's a beauty with a kingsize carved poster bed, period wallpaper, a whirlpool tub and a private porch.

Upstairs are five spacious guest rooms and three suites with fourteen-foot-high ceilings. The most impressive may be the side Excelsior, whose cheerful yellow walls and white marble fireplace are the backdrop for a queen bed and matching bedroom set with hand-painted floral and gold-leaf design and marble tops. The adventurous may go for the seasonal High Rock Room in the cupola, barely big enough for a queen bed amid a 360-degree panorama of windows, with a sitting alcove and bathroom on the level below.

All rooms are outfitted with small TVs, telephones, Croscill bed linens and French toiletries by L'Occitane.

An elaborate breakfast is prepared by Rick Bieber, a Cordon Bleu-trained chef hired by the inn to cater its growing numbers of weddings (an enormous side deck was built for the purpose off the 60-foot-long Victorian side porch overlooking gardens and fountain). The feast varies from frittata to crêpes to french toast stuffed with berries – the three choices varying "according to chef's whim."

(518) 885-1607 or (888) 996-9977. www.themansionsaratoga.com. Seven rooms and three suites with private baths. May-October: doubles, $100 to $250. Racing: $160 to $300. November-April: $95 to $180.

Union Gables, 55 Union Ave., Saratoga Springs 12866.

Locally known as the Furness House, this three-story mansion with a corner turret has been enhanced by new owner Tom Fox, a landscaper by avocation and owner of an apartment house across the street for long-term stays.

Union Gables offers ten bedrooms with private baths in the circa 1901 Queen Anne Victorian with a corner turret and a great wraparound veranda filled with wicker, part facing lavish side gardens maintained by Tom. The rooms – spacious, airy and uncluttered – have been redecorated with partial-canopy beds and colorful fabrics. Each is named for a member of the former owner's large family.

Annie, a front-corner turret room, has a painted sideboard, interesting periwinkle glaze-painted walls and a white floor painted with ribbons, a partial-canopy bed and a single wicker chair. Edward also has a king canopy bed and two armchairs. Bill offers a king bed, seating area and its own small porch overlooking Union Avenue. Kate's room is dark and horsy; a horse's collar is wrapped around the mirror in the bath, and a great wreath hangs above the queensize bed. The Tom is frilly and feminine, for some reason, while the Bruce has twig furniture and an Adirondack lodge feeling. The queen-size Cindy has its own porch and adjoins a twin room to make a suite.

All rooms but one come with pillow-top kingsize beds, TV/HBO and telephones, mini-refrigerators stocked with a sampling of Saratoga's sparkling waters and a Victorian country decor. There's an exercise room, and outside are a tennis court and a hot tub. Across the street at Tom's house is a new swimming pool for guests.

Rich paneling abounds throughout, especially in the large foyer and the huge living room/dining area. The continental breakfast spread includes fresh fruits, yogurt, cereals and pastries from the Bread Basket in the morning. It can be taken at a table for eight or outside on the great veranda with 80 feet of frontage on storied Union Avenue.

The house, designed by noted Saratoga architect R. Newton Brezee for a local manufacturer, blends Richardson and shingle styles. The variety of exterior surfaces (limestone, sandstone, pressed brick, wood shingles and slate) and their diverse planes produce an ever-changing play of lighting effects enhanced by the deep red, beige and dark green color scheme.

(518) 584-1558 or (800) 398-1558. Fax (518) 583-0649. www.uniongables.com. Ten rooms with private baths. May-October: doubles, $160 to $230. Racing: $360 to $410. Rest of year: $140 to $210.

Longfellows Hotel, Conferencer Center and Restaurant, 500 Union Ave., Saratoga Springs 12866.

Situated on knoll east of town is this pair of elaborate tan dairy barns with bright red roofs built in 1915 as part of a 1,000-acre dairy farm. One barn has long been a restaurant. The second – previously used for storage for the restaurant – was converted by owners Steve and Yvonne Sullivan in 1998 into a stylish eighteen-room inn with a Saratoga theme and creature comforts.

Thus began what is now a rural hotel and conference center, thanks to a subsequent addition with 32 more guest rooms and suites.

Each room comes with a kingsize or two queen beds, TV, telephone and a modern bath with jetted tub and separate glass-enclosed shower. Bath amenities include Caswell-Massey toiletries, hair dryers and antique mirrors. The decorative theme is country Shaker with hints of Victorian Saratoga, as in the tasseled window shades. Vivid hunter green and beige wallpaper borders run atop the wainscoting beneath walls accented with Saratoga photos, each room reflecting a different variation on a local equine theme.

Original beams are used to good advantage beneath the vaulted ceilings of the eight second-floor loft suites. These have sitting areas with sofa and chair, wet bars and TV here as well as upstairs in the kingsize loft bedrooms, which have skylights over the beds.

Guests are welcomed with baskets containing a pair of the locally ubiquitous blue bottles of Saratoga water and a box of Saratoga Sweets chocolates.

A deluxe continental breakfast – with pastries baked by the restaurant's pastry chef – is put out with fruits and cereals in the Rose Room of the restaurant.

(518) 587-0108. www.longfellows.com. Forty-six rooms and four two-bedroom suites. May-October: doubles $125 to $295. Racing: doubles $229 to $495. Rest of year, doubles $95 to $185.

A Hotel in the Park

Gideon Putnam Resort and Spa, 24 Gideon Putnam Road, Saratoga Springs 12866.

Set amid stately pines deep in the heart of the Saratoga Spa State Park, the majestic, red-brick and white-columned Gideon Putnam Hotel – its front outdoor café almost walled in by colorful hanging plants and window boxes – looks as if it's been there forever. It's owned by the state, operated by the nation's largest parks concessionaire and on its way up. About $5 million invested in the hotel in recent years has produced new and renovated bathrooms, better air-conditioning and heating, and new carpeting and lighting.

Each of the 120 guest quarters has at least a glimpse of part of the 1,500-acre park. Rooms are furnished in Colonial reproductions and wicker in rose or blue color schemes. Because two double beds didn't fit well, most rooms have one queensize and an extra-long twin bed. All have enormous closets, television sets and telephones. Guests who spend the season usually snap up the eighteen parlor and porch suites. The latter come with large screened porches furnished in bamboo overlooking a forest.

The Sunday buffet brunch ($21.95 each, $24.95 with unlimited bloody marys, mimosas or margaritas) draws mobs of people. We know traditionalists who come here regularly for lunch, savoring the quiet and majestic setting through large windows overlooking the manicured grounds, the sensitive refurbishing and the restored murals of local scenes in the main **Georgian Room,** the modestly updated menu and service by "real" waitresses. Nachos supreme, taco and chicken caesar salads, vegetarian melts and grilled reubens are the fare, and old-timers lament the passing of such standbys as welsh rarebit and chicken pot pie.

At night, the menu takes on international overtones. Expect the (for the Gideon) unexpected: pan-roasted salmon with a pickled ginger-tomato coulis, roasted teriyaki duck breast with star anise-infused mango puree, pan-seared veal tournedos wrapped in bacon, and paprika-rubbed grilled tenderloin with pomegranate sauce. The **Saratoga Grill** offers more casual fare.

The canopied **Café in the Park** outside the front portico is particularly popular before and after events at the nearby Saratoga Performing Arts Center.

(518) 584-3000 or (800) 732-1560. Fax (518) 584-1354. www.gideonputnam.com. Ninety-eight rooms and 22 suites with private baths. Rates, EP. April-October: doubles $165 to $195, suites $249 to $299. Racing: doubles $310 to $355, suites $495 to $555. November-March: doubles $130 to $160, suites $180 to $225.

Entrées, $19.95 to $34.95. Lunch, Monday-Saturday 11:30 to 2. Sunday brunch, 10:30 to 2. Dinner nightly, 6 to 9.

The Breakfast Tradition

Breakfast is a Saratoga tradition, from the buffet at the Saratoga Race Course thoroughbred track to Sunday brunch at the Gideon Putnam Hotel. On the porch outside the historic clubhouse at the track, watch the horses take their morning exercise as you sip the Saratoga Sunrise – a concoction of vodka, orange and cranberry juices, and a slice of melon – and pick your way through a selection of à-la-carte breakfast items. Breakfast is served from 7 to 9:30 every racing day.

The Bread Basket at 65 Spring St. is where many innkeepers in town obtain their breakfast breads. Proprietor Joan Tallman bakes daily "from scratch – no mixes used" in a basement bakery beneath her retail showroom. There's also a front room with help-yourself coffee, tables and chairs, and a new addition for more retail and eating space. Besides at least 30 varieties of breads, Joan offers muffins, walnut sticky buns, coffee cakes, apple-raspberry and peach pies, coconut-apricot dessert bars, raspberry mousse brownies, assorted cookies and a triple-layer chocolate cheesecake that's to die for. There's an off-price bin for "yesterday's temptations." Plus – would you believe? – dog biscuits.

Wonderful coffees and pastries are featured at **Uncommon Grounds,** 402 Broadway, a long cavern of a room with bags of coffee beans inside the entrance and more than 40 bulk coffees and teas. Pick out a cranberry-orange muffin or a slice of English toffee cheesecake or peanut-butter mousse pie to go with a café au lait or iced latte. Enjoy with the day's newspapers at one of the many tables.

Gourmet Treats

One of the best gourmet and specialty-food stores between Manhattan and Montreal is **Putnam Market.** Sisters Cathy Hamilton and Gloria Griskowitz turned an old beer warehouse into a wondrous emporium called the Putnam Street Market Place. It since has moved to a more visible location at 435 Broadway, retaining part of its name. You'll find juice and coffee bars, delectable sandwiches, salads and prepared entrées to go, baked goods, cheeses, imported chocolates, a butcher shop, gift baskets and even an "olive tasting bar." Adjacent is the excellent **Putnam Wine Store.**

Also on Broadway is **Compliments to the Chef,** a kitchen and cutlery shop, and the atmospheric **Eugenio's Café Gelato,** which offers 30 flavors of homemade Italian gelatos to accompany (or upstage) its Italian sandwiches, pastries and entrées.

At 33 Phila St. in the heart of Restaurant Row is **Four Seasons Natural Foods Store & Café,** providing health foods and vegetarian fare inside and out. The evening dinner buffet, which looked to us like a glorified salad bar, is highly regarded and charges by the pound. Up the street is **Hot Stuff of Saratoga,** purveying hundreds of sauces, salsas and other fiery food items.

If you're into gourmet pizzas, check out **Bruno's,** a transformed 1950s roadhouse full of character and good aromas – not to mention pizzas, pastas, burgers and salads – at 237 Union Ave. Closer to downtown, **D'Andrea's** offers take-out deep-dish pizzas, stuffed breads (one is chicken cacciatore, $4.50 a loaf), and hot and cold focaccia sandwiches in a colorful old paint store at 33 Caroline St.

Worth a side trip is **Sutton's Market Place,** Lake George Road (Route 9), Queensbury, a favorite upscale shopping destination. It has an abundant selection of gourmet foods, delectable baked goods, handmade chocolates (even a chocolate sheep with a white chocolate bow), zillions of cookbooks, a line of Adirondack coffee cups that look as though they're made of birch bark, Crabtree & Evelyn bath items, and all kinds of fine gifts and accessories. Hearty, homemade food is served in the large, contemporary café at down-to-earth prices. We sometimes take out a couple of Sutton's hefty deli sandwiches for a picnic. Breakfast, 7:30 to 11:30 (to noon on Sunday); lunch, 11:30 to 3.

Taking the Cure

Roosevelt Baths & Spa, 37-39 Roosevelt Drive, Saratoga Spa State Park.

Reopened in 2004 after extensive renovations, the Georgian-style Roosevelt Bathhouse is a good place in which to relax after over-indulging in Saratoga's good life. The historic structure now houses a 13,000-square-foot spa, 42 private rooms with bathtubs for experiencing the resort's effervescent mineral baths, a salon, fitness center and Vichy shower. Stress and pain float away as you sink into a deep tub of hot, bubbly, beige mineral water in a private room, $18 for twenty minutes, followed by a half-hour's nap while wrapped in hot sheets. For $40 more, a massage therapist will massage you from head to toe for half an hour. Other wrap, facial and spa treatments are available by appointment. This and the other two architecturally grand mineral baths that drew thousands to Saratoga in years past for the cure are being upgraded by the concessionaire that runs the Gideon Putnam Hotel.

(518) 226-4790 or (800) 732-1560. www.gideonputnam.com. Open daily in summer, 9 to 7, reduced hours rest of year.

Montreal

A Tale of Two Cities

What can one say that hasn't already been said about Montreal, that changing, cosmopolitan slice of the continent just north of the Canadian border?

It's the city and the heritage in which one of us was raised, and it's been a home away from home ever since. But it's very different from the Montreal we once knew, the French-Canadian majority having asserted itself to give the city and the province in which it is located a singular, strong sense of place.

More than any other, Montreal is a city of duality. Which side one sees depends on the eye of the beholder.

The reigning duality is, of course, the "French fact." After Paris, Montreal is the world's second largest French-speaking city, and Canadian bilingualism translates in Quebec into French, down to the street names, store signs and restaurant menus.

Its English heritage has given parts of Montreal a British character. The mix of British and French in North America makes Montreal unique – solid, sedate and sophisticated but also surging, swinging and sensual.

We do not aspire here to give a definitive guide to Montreal, which has been well defined since it hosted two international extravaganzas, the Expo 67 World's Fair and the 1976 Summer Olympics. Instead, we share our personal observations of a city that always surprises our friends as being so near, yet so far – never more than a six-hour drive or an hour's flight from where we've lived but a world apart from the one most Americans know.

As a destination for fine dining for every taste and pocketbook, Montreal takes a back seat to no city in North America. Haute cuisine competes side by side with more casual fare in thousands of cafés and bistros. Although Montreal claims the densest concentration of French restaurants in North America, its ethnic enclaves span the spectrum of the world's cuisines. There's also a sampling of the hearty regional Quebeçois fare.

To the casual visitor along the main streets, all Montreal appears to be one vast emporium of food and drink, from boucherie to bistro. There are four principal concentrations of restaurants: for urban sophisticates, the downtown hotels and the Crescent-Mountain street area off Sherbrooke Street West; for tourists, the charming mix of haute and honky-tonk that is Old Montreal; for the young and young at heart, the swinging Left Bank bistro row along lower St. Lawrence Boulevard and St. Denis Street, and for the real thing, the chic spots in the Plateau Mont-Royal and Outremont, where many of the savvy, affluent French-Montrealers go.

Be advised: you don't need to know French (almost everyone can speak some English). But it certainly helps – if only to read visitor brochures, signs and menus. In the mysteries of translation, "essence de col-vert en surprise" in one hotel dining room becomes "duckling consommé."

Be advised also that prices in Montreal, as elsewhere, run the gamut from bargain to rip-off (liquor and wine prices are astonishingly high). When the currency exchange rate is in Americans' favor, as it has been in recent years, food items can be reasonable – American money stretches 15 to 20 percent farther than the Canadian prices quoted here. Much of that difference may be negated by Canada's wide-ranging Goods and Services Tax, however.

Christine Lamarche and Normand Laprise (inset) are co-owners of Toqué! which moved to expanded quarters in downtown Montreal.

Finally, be advised to look beyond the Basilica-museum-calèche on Mount Royal tourist circuit of the Montreal of yore. Look beyond the glittering skyscrapers, shiny shopping concourses, the underground city and subways that are the monuments of new Montreal.

Savor the spirit and style of the real Montreal, the joie de vivre that makes it so special. Especially when it comes to culinary pleasures.

Dining

Most restaurants offer several-course, table-d'hôte meals that are good values compared with the à-la-carte prices if ordered separately. On Montreal menus, "entrées" are appetizers, "pâtes" are pastas and "plats" are main courses. Wine prices at the better restaurants usually start in the $50 range.

The Best of the Best

Toqué! 900 Place Jean-Paul Riopelle.

There's near universal agreement as to Montreal's foremost restaurant. Chef-owner Normand Laprise and Christine Lamarche, his former sous chef from the old Citrus restaurant on St. Lawrence Boulevard, started small. They opened Toqué! in the heart of the St. Denis Street restaurant row in 1993, updated and expanded twice in the 1990s, and moved downtown in 2004.

The first Montrealer invited to cook at the James Beard Foundation in New York,

Normand is hailed by the North American food press as the hottest chef in town. His 95-seat restaurant is the highest-rated not only in Montreal but in all of Quebec province, setting the standard by which others are judged.

Toqué! is suave, stylish and serious – all the more so following its relocation to larger quarters on the main floor of a new office building in the Financial District near Old Montreal. The interior of the glass-walled structure is as sleek as the facade of the Palais des Congrèss convention center across the plaza. The high-ceilinged corner room angles around on several levels, with large, well-spaced tables draped in Egyptian cotton cloths embossed with the restaurant's logo. A mirrored wine bar along one side and a glassed-in wine cellar in the center are focal points.

The name – a play on the name for a chef's hat – means crazy or nuts when it takes on the accent, advised Christine, the engaging and omniscient hostess and co-owner. It also reflects the daring that established Toqué! as one of Canada's leading restaurants.

The quality and presentation of food are foremost to Normand, who is known for his imaginative approach and devotion to regional products. Indeed, at one late-afternoon visit, he was shopping at the fish market and would send that night's dinner menu to the computer at 5:15. He works with a kitchen brigade of fourteen in a custom-designed, state-of-the-art kitchen.

The short menu, available in English as well as French, changes nightly. Ours detailed a tantalizing choice of six first courses and six main courses. Those really out for a meal to remember can select a "mystery menu" ($88, with wine $144), seven sampler portions "to be discovered one after another, each more surprising than the last."

As we were seated, our waiter suggested a kir royale and a champagne as well as "the chef's proposal" – a poached Pearl Bay (B.C.) oyster with clementines and tarragon. It proved a worthy if pricey ($3) little indulgence. A custom-made wooden bread cart laden with breads and rolls (including a stellar olive and feta cheese bread) arrived at the table and stayed there, except when it was quietly replenished. Appetizers were a tasty arctic char tartare with avocado and chives, ginger-marinated parsley root and taro chips, and a sensational rare yellowfin tuna tempura with pickled yellow beets, sevruga caviar, two spears of seemingly extraneous asparagus, and an almond and Cortland apple compote. The chef sent out a taste of shrimp tempura with yellow beets and russet apples, as well as a sample of his seared scallops with risotto, fried leeks, pomegranates and truffle sauce.

For main courses, the Atlantic halibut might be accompanied by Jerusalem artichokes, cauliflower purée and wilted wild daisy leaves. The farmed veal could be paired with sautéed Quebec chanterelles, "Mr. Daignault's organic carrots" and garlic puree.

We tried the sweetbreads, grilled simply with apple juice flavored with cinnamon and paired with gnocchi stuffed with wild mushrooms, sautéed Japanese artichokes and parsley root. Equally good was "Mr. Leroux's barbarie duck" roasted with licorice and caramelized kumquats, fanned in slices around the plate and accompanied by polenta with duck confit and dried fruits, wilted field greens and artichoke hearts. The duck was pronounced the best ever by a Toronto relative, who was so enthusiastic that he ordered a cheese plate even though we were too sated for dessert.

Dessert could have been a chocolate and mango puree feuilleté with natural ice

La Chronique dining room is suave in scarlet, gray and white.

yogurt, a caramelized fig tart with lemon-thyme ice milk, or the signature warm molten chocolate cake with red wine reduction, spices and berries. Like the rest of the meal, the presentations of those we saw were as dazzling as the ingredients. Seamless service was provided team style by an ever-changing cast of waiters in black pants and natty mint green dress shirts. They didn't miss a beat.

(514) 499-2084. Entrées, $35 to $45. www.restaurant-toque.com. Dinner, Tuesday-Saturday 5:30 to 10:30. Closed last week of December and first week of January.

La Chronique, 99 Laurier Ave. West.

A small pumpkin or gourd on each table typified the season at a recent visit to this inspired bistro that's considered one of Montreal's finest. Belgian-born chef-owner Marc de Canck, who trained at Michelin restaurants in his native land, moved to Quebec and worked at our old favorite in the Eastern Townships, Hovey Manor in North Hatley, before opening his own place in Outremont in 1994.

Behind an unassuming storefront facade that you might well pass by lies an intimate interior suave in scarlet, with double layers of white cloths on the tables, gray patterned banquettes, and black and white art photos (many taken by the chef himself) on the walls. Marc calls his fare "fine fusion cuisine," a blend of French, Asian and Latin American in particular, and presents it in the trendy architectural style. He shares some of his secrets in a fancy French cookbook, titled simply *La Chronique.*

At a table-d'hôte lunch, our party of four sampled each of the appetizers included in the tab: a subtle cream of asparagus soup, a coarse pâté with green salad and tasty coulis, a terrific mesclun salad dressed with the chef's signature vinaigrette and a dumpling of fresh tuna. Each was quite satisfactory, but the main courses were far more impressive. The succulent fillet of vivaneau (a variation of the snapper family) arrived atop a julienne of vegetables. Also architectural were the "conjugaison" of sweetbreads wrapped in smoked salmon with miso sauce, resting on a tempura (nest) of straw potatoes. The duet of barbarie duck and shrimp won over the resident skeptic, who sliced the duck breast like steak and called it the best he ever tasted. His spouse found her less exotic (and less costly) order of seafood fettuccine a model of its genre. Served in paper coffee filters in spring-form pans were bread slices and toasted melbas, so good we asked for seconds.

We ended an exceptional meal by polishing off a sampling of three good sorbets (coconut, mango and strawberry) before continuing on our rounds, leaving our guests to relax and savor "the best lunch ever" as they finished their wine.

The chef likes to tinker with the format of the dinner offerings. The latest was an à la carte approach on weekdays, a four-course prix-fixe menu ($68) on weekends and, every night, a seven-course tasting menu ($95) designed around a different theme every month – at one October visit, an intriguing month-long special incorporating oysters in all courses except dessert. The rest of the dinner menu features a number of longtime holdovers. Among them are the aforementioned sweetbreads and the duet of duck and shrimp, as well as medallions of grilled tuna, venison with cabernet sauce and rack of Quebec lamb with lamb jus and truffle oil. Recent additions were roasted dover sole dusted with Southwestern spices and medallions of Alberta beef loin in a foie gras sauce.

You might start with a traditional South of France fish soup garnished with croutons, rouille and saffron or an unusual yam soup with bocconcini cheese and coriander. Other starters include a sashimi of salmon, duck foie gras with tomato chutney, and agnolotti with wild mushrooms and foie gras mousse.

Finish with a trio of crème brûlées (star anise, chocolate and coffee), chocolate marquise or the chef's signature pecan tart flambéed in bourbon.

(514) 271-3095. www.lachronique.qc.ca. Entrées, $32 to $45. Lunch, Tuesday-Friday 11:30 to 2:30. Dinner, Tuesday-Saturday 6 to 10.

Le Club Chasse et Pêche, 423 St. Claude St.

Call this the Club. To the uninitiated, that's what it looks like, more than the hunting and fishing lodge theme conveyed by the name. And call it refreshing. The chef-owned restaurant simplified its cuisine, stressing fine products, straightforward presentations and affordable prices. Shortly after opening in 2005, the Montreal Gazette reviewer called it the most exciting new restaurant in the city.

Chef Claude Pelletier and manager Hubert Marsolais, former partners at Restaurant Cube, turned the former Le Fadeau temple of haute gastronomy in Old Montreal into a citadel for contemporary tastes. One side is a 30-seat salon and bar for casual dining. The other side is a dark and clubby, 50-seat dining room with low ceiling, windows set in stone and leather club chairs at white-linened tables. The moose antler and flying fish logo on the wine glasses conveys the hunting and fishing theme.

So does the leather-bound menu, which changes from week to week. It's a short and simplified recitation of what Hubert calls "humble and essential cuisine." Gone are the complex, over-the-top presentations of the architectural style. In their stead are more straightforward entrées such as crisp-skinned striped sea bass with asparagus and sorrel, glazed magret duck with cauliflower and spelt, suckling pig risotto with foie gras shavings, and kobe beef with vidalia puree and mushroom ravioli.

Appetizers are meant to be shared. The single-side roasted scallops – a mainstay on the menu – turn out to be three perfect beauties seared golden brown on one side, then roasted and served with puréed fennel. Another must-have is the gnocchi with white truffles, the Italian truffle shaved tableside by the waiter. The asparagus salad comes with smoked venison, and the yuzu juice seviche with grapefruit granité. Duck foie gras is served two ways: seared and parfait.

Semi-open wall divider separates salon dining areas at Le Club Chasse et Pêche.

The Japanese pastry chef's exotic desserts employ ingredients like sweet potato, rose water and honey jelly. One of the more novel items to emerge from the kitchen is a jellied saffron soup with rice, dried figs and apricots topped with ice cream.

(514) 861-1112. www.leclub-mtl.ca. Entrées, $25 to $29. Lunch, Tuesday-Friday 11:30 to 2. Dinner, Tuesday-Friday 5 to 10, Saturday 6 to 11.

Brunoise, 3807 St. André St.

Hot-shot chef Michel Ross and master host Zach Suhl moved from Mediterraneo in 2004 to launch this with-it restaurant with an appealing formula: contemporary Quebec market-based cuisine at a reasonable price. Theirs is a simple bistro-style establishment in white and gray, with a mirror at the far end making the place look bigger.

Brunoise earns raves partly because of its price point and partly because of its welcome, Zach working the room to ensure that customers are happy. And partly because Michel knows how to make his salmon and his sweetbreads taste as good as filet mignon and foie gras, neither of which is on the menu.

Dinner is prix-fixe, with six choices for each of three courses and the price varying with the choice of entrée. An amuse-bouche – perhaps three tiny fiddleheads with shredded celeriac – is served as diners peruse the offerings. Typical first courses are a bourride of mussels in saffron foam, house-smoked fish with mujjol caviar and olive oil on brioche, and a ballotine of rabbit and boudin, served with a poached quail egg and green bean salad.

Main courses might be seared scallops with caramelized artichokes and fennel, roasted sweetbreads and braised veal cheeks with cumin and hazelnuts, and beef tenderloin with porcini-red wine sauce. The seared salmon takes on complexity with lobster caramel, shiitake mushrooms, crab ravioli and five-spice sauce.

The chef and pastry chef collaborate to produce signature desserts like vanilla

French-born chef André Besson in front of his classic bistro Laloux.

panna cotta with basil coulis and passionfruit, a frozen pistachio parfait with bitter chocolate sorbet and raspberry nage, and cherry clafoutis with sour cream ice cream and cherry milkshake.

(514) 523-3885. www.brunoise.ca. Prix-fixe, $35 to $48. Dinner nightly, 5:30 to 10:30.

Laloux, 250 Pine Ave. East.

Nicknamed "Paris on Pine" for its French ambiance, this classic bistro is considered tops in the city for food and style. It's run by French-born chef André Besson, who trained with Paul Bocuse and proclaims his membership in the Academie Culinaire de France.

The decor is modern Parisian bistro, simple and stark yet sophisticated: high ceilings, bare floors, white linens, black banquettes and chairs, hanging globe lamps and a wall of mirrors – not even flowers to intrude on the generally black and white theme against a yellow backdrop.

The cuisine is a blend of traditional and nouvelle, and the chef's reach far ranging. Changing three-course, table-d'hôte dinners with soup or salad, beverage and dessert du jour are priced typically from $23.75 for fillet of doré with nouilles and riesling to $28.95 for sweetbreads with truffles and port wine cream sauce. Friends sampled both items at a recent visit and found them wonderful.

Ordered à la carte, the half dozen main courses range from supreme of red snapper with olive and basil tapenade to loin of Quebec lamb in a honey, rosemary and sherry sauce. Others could be porgy fillet in muscat and red wine emulsion, duck breast in a red wine sauce and caribou tenderloin with a peppered red currant sauce.

Appetizers run from a dynamite French onion soup and fish soup with saffron to a duo of duck foie gras, one served cold with an apple and currant compote and the other as a warm pan-seared terrine with sauternes and grapes. The scallop and scampi fricassee with baby vegetables and coriander, the crab en papillote with lime and coconut, and the shrimp and chicken tempura with mangoes and mint intrigue. Salads might be papaya and watercress, mesclun and grapefruit, or "toute verte" (all green).

Desserts are delectable: perhaps pernod crème brûlée, a pear charlotte with mascarpone cream, genoise with pralines, chocolate and crème anglaise, and an acclaimed chocolate mousse topped with coconut, ginger and chocolate shavings. André suggests the sweet or frozen feast, a selection of several and "better to share." He also touts his platter of assorted Quebec and French cheeses.

The wine list is comprehensive and pricey. Many wines are available by the glass.

(514) 287-9127. www.laloux.com. Entrées, $25.95 to $36.95. Lunch, Monday-Friday 11:30 to 2:30. Dinner nightly, 5:30 to 10:30 or 11:30.

Area, 1429 Amherst St.

Small and trendy, this restaurant with an obscure name (which translates to "rest area" in French on its website) is located on the slightly seedy edge of Montreal's revitalized Gay Village. A catering operation gone public, it was an instant hit upon opening. Twenty-five-year-old chef Ian Perrault was one of only two Canadian chefs to make Condé Nast Traveler magazine's 2001 "Hot List" for the world's top new tables. He and co-owner Denis Lévesque prompted food reviewers to sit up and take notice for their over-the-top fusion fare and affordable pricing. Such "high-level cuisine is a steal at these prices," gushed one, although a wine list starting in the $40s takes away any pangs of guilt.

We were impressed at lunch, which was discontinued in 2005 (except in December) but gave us a representative taste of the chef's repertoire. To start, the assertive bite of the delicate curried shrimp tempura with corn salsa testified to the artistry in the kitchen and the lack of salt on the tables. Salt, however, would have benefited the steak tartare, served with chopped beets and toasts. (When requested, several kinds of salt were presented in an unusual chrome sculpture, not unlike that in which the breads had arrived at the start of the meal.)

One offering was a fabulous pasta – raviolis stuffed with ricotta, asparagus and roasted pinenuts and served in a broad bowl with light cream and parmesan shavings. Another was lamb shanks with polenta and wild mushrooms, one of the more robust dishes we've had.

Desserts included the best lemon meringue tart ever and a mascarpone tarte with California dates, cinnamon butter and ginger cream.

Similar taste treats await at dinner, which was expanded from five to seven nights a week and joined the small-plate phenomenon. Main courses were dropped in favor of appetizer-size portions referred to as "areas" and categorized as sea, sky, earth and vegetables. The offerings are tempting and the choices difficult. The chef has a way with flavor enhancers in risky combinations that usually work. He might serve scallop tartare with pistachio oil, soya-braised spareribs with lemongrass and satay of Quebec lamb. Expect such treats as a chilled yellow tomato soup enlivened with a wasabi-filled ice cube, smoked guinea fowl with hoisin sauce, and deep-fried sweetbreads in a hot quince dipping sauce.

Most of this culinary adventure takes place along two sides of black and pearl gray leather banquettes down the middle of a long and narrow room with brick walls. Individual tables are placed around the perimeter. Slim horizontal mirrors, a black streak along a stucco wall, a potted tree and a small aquarium serve as accents. "Zen-like" and "very feng shui," some call it. The artistry is on the plate, rather than in the decor.

(514) 890-6691. www.rest-area.qc.ca. Tapas, $9 to $20. Lunch in December, Tuesday-Friday 11:30 to 1:30. Dinner nightly, 6 to 11.

Les Caprices de Nicolas, 2072 Drummond St.

Les caprices reflect the whims of the ingredients and cooking style of its founding chef, the late Nicolas Jongleux, the baby-faced wunderkind who ranked among the best in Montreal. Subsequent chefs have found his legacy of exciting French haute cuisine a tough act to follow.

Located on the ground level of a swank downtown townhouse, the handsome, sophisticated restaurant seats 50 at large tables spaced well apart – a rare attribute in Montreal – in a garden atrium, an intimate library/salon with lipstick red banquettes and a serene dining lounge with a stunning abstract painting above a cream-colored banquette across from an antique marble and oak bar. In fact, the ambiance was so appealing and the menu so enticing that when we dropped by to check it out, we decided on the spot to stay for lunch (since discontinued except in December, but indicative of the restaurant's style as masterminded by owner Dan Medelsy, the genial host).

Garden atrium at Les Caprices de Nicolas.

The seats of choice are beside a trickling fountain in the garden courtyard, an idyllic space soaring three stories to a skylight, with vines hanging down the sides.

The food is said to have slipped a bit from its heady days when the artistry was in the kitchen rather than on the walls. But visitors without Montreal memories can still do well here. You might start with the signature wild salmon and abitibi caviar potato crêpe with a yuzu butter sauce, roasted quail with caramelized apple and a poached quail egg or chile-pepper roasted scallops with crème fraîche, salmon roe and green apple tartare with a yuzu vinaigrette. Duck foie gras is offered "caprice du moment." Main dishes at a recent visit included fillet of daurade with mussels and cauliflower emulsion, caramelized veal sweetbreads with veal and apple cider jus, roasted milk-fed piglet with a braised flank and lentil-truffle vinaigrette, and lacquered caribou medallions with brandied cherry chutney and wild mushroom jus.

Few can resist the cheese board, considered one of the city's best. But save room for the sweets – those we sampled may be surpassed by the latest repertoire. How about almond and lime "moelleux" with warm autumn fruits and clove ice cream; roasted apples with vanilla cake, Jack Daniels-caramel sauce and maple ripple ice cream, or caramelized Guanaja chocolate ganache with candied kumquats and a chai milkshake? Perfect café filtre follows.

The peerless wine list carries Wine Spectator's best of award of excellence. It's full of caprices reflecting attention to detail in a place that cares.

(514) 282-9790. www.lescaprices.com. Entrées, $34 to $43. Dinner nightly, 6 to 10.

Les Chèvres, 1201 Van Horne Ave.

Trend-setting Montreal restaurateur Claude Beausoleil oversees this new vegetarian-oriented Outremont establishment with two of the city's leading chefs. A risk-taker who gave Toqué! chef Normand Laprise his first stand-alone restaurant at Citrus and later opened Chez L'Epicier in Old Montreal, he teamed here with Chef Selio Perombelon and pastry chef Patrice Demers.

Their main dining room is cheery in lime, lilac and orange, reflecting the garden-based vegetables and fruits that are their specialty. Adjacent is the bar section called **Le Chou,** a bistro offering a separate menu of small plates categorized in two sections, salty and sweet.

The menus, written in French, may prove obscure to English-speakers. To simplify matters, some choose the $74 dégustation menu or the $48 three-course seasonal table d'hôte menu.

Ordering à la carte, one might start with avocado soup with lime, fennel, orange, and Australian olive oil; roasted white asparagus with almond velouté, or scallop carpaccio with pureed avocado and tobiko crab salad. Besides vegetarian offerings, main courses include several fish and meat options, perhaps truite de mer poêlée, sweetbreads and roast Quebec lamb.

Desserts are a highlight. Typical are chocolate pot de crème, chocolate mousse with caramel froth topping and rhubarb shortcake with vanilla crème.

Diners with smaller appetites or budgets enjoy the chef's creations in the bistro. Here you'll find a short list of savory tapas for $8 each and sweets for $6.

(514) 270-1119. www.leschevres.com. Entrées, $27 to $37. Dinner nightly, 5:30 to 10:30, bistro to 11.

Brontë, 1800 Sherbrooke St. West.

Arguably the best of Montreal's hotel dining rooms is this newcomer in Le Meridien, an apartment tower-turned-hotel. It's the bastion of local chef-owner Joe Mercuri, who at age 27 opened what En Route magazine called Canada's best new restaurant of 2004, citing a dining experience "as ambitious, adventurous and avant-garde as you'll find in Canada."

The interior of the main-floor dining room, with tall windows in front and along the side, is sleek in grays and beiges. Color is provided from illuminated columns with glowing amber and blue centers. Tall-backed white circular banquettes provide intimate dining enclosures facing the sideways bar in front, with a bevy of white-clothed tables in the back.

Like the ultra-modern decor, the market-based cuisine is at the cutting edge and centered on bold and beautiful plate presentations. The latter are distinctive, the food usually lined up on the diagonal across a square plate. Consider an arugula and gorgonzola salad with figs, hazelnuts and raspberries carefully arranged in a straight line across the plate, or an appetizer of limoncello-cured salmon framed on the diagonal in a sea salt tuile.

Entrées on the ever-changing menu could be a mélange of rabbit and lobster with extras like gnocchi, chanterelles and basil scattered along the diagonal, Tasmanian trout and beef two ways, filet mignon and braised beef cheeks.

Desserts include a peach and blackberry mille feuille and a caramel tart with coffee ice cream.

(514) 934-1801. www.bronterestaurant.com. Entrées, $32 to $38. Dinner, Tuesday-Saturday 6 to 11.

Chez L'Épicier, 311 St. Paul St. East.

The name means grocery, and that's the first thing you see upon entering this establishment in the heart of Old Montreal. Restaurateur Claude Beausoleil and chef Laurent Godbout created the restaurant and wine bar and yes, a grocery, although not your typical kind. This is a high-end specialty foods boutique, with shelves of regional products and the chef's private-label creations lining the brick walls of two high-style dining rooms.

The menu is printed on a paper bag and water is served in old milk bottles. The young chef helped create the concept of food entertainment in Quebec – an example is his bloody caesar served on a plate. He gives comfort food a new twist, whereby the traditional shepherd's pie becomes a snail pie, and offers tasting plates of different dishes based on a single ingredient.

His regular menu features Quebec "products from the land" with French and Asian accents. Appetizers might be "recreated calamaris," arctic char in verrine and terrine, and poached scallops in a lemongrass broth and spicy lobster oil. For main dishes, the salmon might be simmered in a mustard and mint sauce, the roasted pavé of halibut enhanced by mango and chive caviar and ginger salsa, and the beef tenderloin served with blue cheese polenta and veal broth. Dessert could be a chocolate club sandwich with pineapple fries or a medley of four crème brûlées.

The chef offers his take on Mediterranean cuisine at his ambitious new **Version Laurent Godbout,** 295 St. Paul East, billed as Canada's first "boutique restaurant." Looking rather like a high-end china and tableware shop, it's a restaurant where you can eat while you shop, or shop while you eat. You can purchase most of the components of his fanciful culinary vision, including the plates they are served on.

(514) 878-2232. www.chezlepicier.com. Entrées, $22 to $35. Lunch, Monday-Friday 11:30 to 2. Dinner nightly, 5:30 to 10. Grocery open daily, 11:30 to 10.

Version Laurent Godbout, (514) 871-9135. www.version-restaurant.com. Entrées, $19 to $30. Lunch, Tuesday-Friday 11:30 to 2. Dinner, Tuesday-Saturday 5 to 10 or 11.

This 'Pig's Foot:' Bold and Brash

Au Pied de Cochon, 536 Duluth St. East.

With frying pan in hand, a toque-topped chef riding an upright pig serves as the logo for this brash brasserie – generally considered *the* restaurant to try if you want an authentic taste of Quebec cuisine. The chef is Martin Picard, known locally as a culinary enfant-terrible, a passionate young chef who does things his way. After three years at Le Club des Pins in Outremont, where he was revered for his bold take on southern French cuisine, he resurfaced in his own place in the heart of the Plateau. Here the theme is big, rustic, bold food slow-cooked in the Quebec tradition. He named it "a pig's foot." And yes, he actually roasts the meat of pig's feet in the huge wood brick oven near the front and serves it as a side dish with potatoes (employing the same cheese curd and garlic that he puts into the French-Canadian favorite, poutine). He goes through two sides of pork a week for his house boudin (sausage), his thick pork chops, his pork salad, his happy pig's chop and the like.

Martin is hardly a one-note chef, however. He serves farmed Quebec venison (steak, ribs, tartare) in winter, and northern Quebec seafood (sliced mackerel, salmon, arctic char) or an assorted shellfish platter from the Magdalen Islands in summer. In fact, he likes nothing better than to cook a whole piece of meat or fish (perhaps guinea hen, goat or cod) and serve it family-style on platters for the entire table.

Illuminated orchids float in glass bowls as centerpieces on tables at Bonaparte.

This is obviously a place to try different Quebec dishes and tastes. Start with smoked sausage, a classic French onion soup, scallop seviche, even one of six styles of foie gras – terrine, flan, poutine, hamburger, tartlet or stuffed in a pig's foot. At our autumn visit, the French menu proclaimed that les huitres sont arrivées! The oysters were being offered in various combinations and styles, including with lamb steak and lotte bonne femme.

The possibilities go on and on: pickled venison tongue, beet and goat cheese salad, duck carpaccio, duck magret with wild mushrooms, lamb shank confit. Desserts are more traditional (cheesecake with fruit, crème brûlée, apple tart), except for one called "pouding chômeur," translated as a pudding for the unemployed from the Depression. Made with maple sugar, it's one that true Quebeçois cannot resist.

Martin and crew make their own preserves, ratatouille, tomato sauce and pickled mackerel to sell from a deli case in front of the restaurant. The rest of the long and narrow storefront consists of an open kitchen along the side and a row of rustic tables against a mirrored wall that makes the place seem bigger. But the Cochon is not as big in size as it is in character.

(514) 281-1114. Entrées, $12.50 to $24. Dinner nightly except Monday, 5 to midnight.

Nouvelle in Old Montreal

Bonaparte, 443 St. Francois Xavier St.

A dining-room addition and a talented chef have restored Bonaparte to its position of pre-eminence in the shadow of famed Notre Dame Basilica in the Old City. Add the stylish new 31-room auberge on the upper floors. The result is a destination for gourmands.

The new dining room, in what had been a bakery, doubles the size of the restaurant. Here, a miniature statue of Napoleon stands guard on the fireplace mantel amid potted plants and rich mahogany details. The two-level original room is dark and intimate. Pinpoint lights illuminate orchids floating dramatically in glass bowls on white-clothed tables. Seats of choice are a handful up a few steps by the front windows, whose occupants watch horse-drawn buggies pass by and fancy themselves in Paris. Other popular tables are in a glass-enclosed atrium terrace in the rear.

The setting is an elegant foil for chef Gérard Fort's take on classic French cuisine. Reviewers rave about the menu dégustation ($57), a six-course parade of nicely paced, flawless delights starting with an aromatic lobster bisque flavored with ginger and saffron and ending in a "symphony" of homemade desserts. Standouts are the mushroom raviolis perfumed with a delicate sage sauce and a fish course of shrimp and scallops. Four choices are offered for the main course: grilled salmon in a citrus butter sauce, roasted duck flavored with maple syrup and blueberries, veal filet sauced with morel mushrooms and cream, and filet mignon laced with five peppercorns and cognac. Desserts include mandarin-orange crème brûlée and a towering triumph of chocolate and hazelnut called Palais Royal.

Many of these treats also are available à la carte. That option gives access to a couple of house specialties, beef tartare, served with fried potatoes, and lobster stew, flavored with vanilla and served with spinach fondue. Other possibilities are tuna steak sauced with raspberry vinegar and mushrooms, duck breast flavored with maple syrup and berries, rack of lamb with port wine sauce, and filet of wild boar with red wine sauce and pasta. The grand marnier and calvados-cinnamon soufflés are dessert specialties.

Value-seekers are well served by table-d'hôte menus priced from $24.50 to $28.50.

(514) 844-4368. www.bonaparte.ca. Entrées, $21.50 to $32.50. Lunch, Monday-Friday noon to 2:30. Dinner nightly, 5:30 to 10:30.

Les Remparts, 97 Commune St. East.

This establishment in the basement of Auberge du Vieux Porte is a charming hideaway. Literally. The entrance from the hotel is an antique spiral staircase descending from the lobby into the heart of the dining room (there's a small entrance from the street, as well). The stone-walled room contains the cornerstone of a rampart, discovered when the basement was excavated to make the ceiling higher. Dating from the days when Montreal was a fortified city, it is now cordoned off like a museum piece from the well-spaced, white-clothed tables seating 55 amidst a comforting backdrop of barn beams, copper pipes, upholstered chairs and table-top oil lamps with delicate fabric shades. A seasonal terrace on the hotel's roof doubles the capacity in summer, and is one of the best places in town to view Montreal's summer fireworks shows.

In the kitchen is the one of the city's young wunder-chefs, Janick Bouchard. Originally from the Lac St. Jean area, he moved to Montreal in 1989 to train with two of the city's top chefs, Normand Laprise of Toqué! (then at Citrus) and James MacGuire at the recently departed Le Passe-Partout. He left the latter in 1997 to take over his own kitchen here at the ripe young age of 25. He calls his cuisine "a cross between Laprise and MacGuire" – the best blend of contemporary and classic.

His short menu is à la carte and choice in the idiom of those in the vanguard of the new Quebec cuisine. Expect the freshest and best ingredients, as in "Mr. J.R. Paquin's garden salad," duly credited as one menu's lead-off item. Ditto for the salmon and lobster salad with avocado puree, the marinated octopus with coriander and ginger, and the ravioli of duck confit with caramelized apples.

Elegant dining room at Les Remparts retains vestiges of fortified city.

Ask Janick what he recommends. "I come here to eat and have this," he says, citing appetizers of escalope of foie gras with apples and caramelized onions in a leek papillotte and an assiette of yellowfin tuna served with endive and apple salad and fennel vinaigrette. For the main course, he cites his signature herb-encrusted Pacific sea bass fillet with pesto coulis and sundried tomato vinaigrette and the butter-roasted deer with wild mushrooms and gooseberry jelly. Other options include lightly smoked Gaspé char with scallops and calamari with a saffron beurre blanc, and roulade of guinea hen with seared foie gras and thyme jus.

The treats continue with a coffee crème brûlée, a puff pastry of strawberries and rhubarb with mint glacé, a "soupe" of fruits and banana genoise with blueberry ice cream, and apple beignets with a coulis of cassis and vanilla ice cream. The wine list is choice and expensive, with a supplemental reserve list.

At lunch, the all-inclusive table-d'hôte menu ($15 to $18) represents good value.

(514) 392-1649 or (888) 660-7678. www.restaurantlesremparts.com. Entrées, $28 to $36. Lunch, Monday-Friday noon to 3. Dinner nightly, 6 to 10.

Gastronomic Landmarks

Chez la Mère Michel, 1209 Guy St.

For four decades we've been directing friends heading for Montreal to this welcoming downtown restaurant we first visited during the summer of Expo 67, not long after it opened. None has been disappointed, nor have we on subsequent trips. With the closing of the famed Les Halles in 2005, it remains one of the last vestiges of a bygone area.

Inside a typical Montreal gray stone townhouse are three cozy dining rooms, plus a massive downstairs wine cellar and a skylit atrium courtyard that's exceptionally pleasant for dining year-round.

Decor is elegantly rustic: high ceilings with dark beams and stuccoed arches, shiny hardwood floors, stained-glass windows, walls of showy fabric above mottled gray and copper pots here, there and everywhere. White lace over bright red linens and lovely arrangements of roses and lilies grace the tables, and candles inside graters cast fascinating shadows. Brilliant enamel paintings add to a colorful scene. The crowning glory is the courtyard, lovely with banquettes and high-back chairs, antique tables, a Delft-tiled fireplace and a sixteen-foot enamel mural.

Seasonal and contemporary specialties enhance the traditional fare from the kitchen of Micheline Delbuquet. She bestowed her childhood nickname Michel on her "little house" in the city and her French Riviera restaurant background on her cuisine, which has become progressively lighter and more refined with time.

Micheline Delbuquet at Chez la Mère Michel.

Over the years, we've enjoyed as appetizers a light and fluffy sweet onion pie, a robust pâté en croûte with pistachios, baked pheasant and mushrooms au gratin, and asparagus and sweetbreads in puff pastry.

Each of the dozen or so entrées comes with garnishes and vegetables – purées of celery root and carrot at one visit, brussels sprouts and carrots with rosettes of potatoes, whipped and then sautéed at another. At dinner, many dishes are finished tableside and served on piping-hot plates. The veal kidneys flamed in armagnac are as good as when we first had them here in the 1960s. We've also liked sweetbreads with wild mushrooms en croûte, noisettes of lamb with tarragon sauce, the specialty lobster soufflé nantua and, at a fall visit, an interesting special of skate fish and a tender caribou steak with sauce poivrade.

Such desserts as a smashing strawberry napoleon, grand-marnier soufflé, fresh fruits with kirsch and black-currant sorbet are refreshing endings. The chocolate delice with grand marnier, kiwi and raspberry sauce is a work of art. So is a whole poached pear, its cavity filled with sorbet and served atop an almond tuile.

The wine list is handsome and extensive, as you'd guess when you look at Micheline's husband René's wine cellar, which he ranks among the best in the city.

Micheline and René, a widely traveled photographer, are caring hosts. They've had only two chefs over the years, and the tuxedoed staff welcomes returning customers by name. The cozy French provincial ambiance, consistently fine food and value combine to make La Mère Michel a good bet for visitors in this city where more trendy establishments can be pricey, pretentious and perhaps short-lived.

(514) 934-0473. www.chezlameremichel.com. Entrées. $25 to $39. Lunch, Tuesday-Friday noon to 2. Dinner, Monday-Saturday 5:30 to 10:30.

Les Chenêts, 2075 Bishop St.

This relative old-timer, with an awesome wine cellar and a collection of copper that's out of this world, also is one of the coziest, warmest restaurants we've seen.

It's doubly so on a wintry Yuletide afternoon, when the copper pots and pans that cover every available bit of wall space reflect the glow of candles and even the Christmas tree behind the reception table is trimmed mostly in copper.

Chef-owner Michel Gillet, a Frenchman who opened the restaurant in 1973 after a stint at Le Chambord in Westport, Conn., employs one person full-time just to keep all that copper gleaming. Copper service plates top the white-linened tables in two lavishly decorated dining rooms, and there's a mix of semi-circular banquettes and chairs upholstered in velvet.

Wine connoisseurs marvel at two weighty tomes of wine selections mounted on a bookstand behind the reception table. They list some 2,800 choices representing 48,000 bottles at prices up to $15,000 for an 1890 Château Lafite-Rothschild. The pricier bottles are too old to drink, our waiter advised; instead, they are sold as collector's items. He led us upstairs (yes, up) to the wine cellar on the second floor, where he hoisted himself to the top shelf to retrieve the 1890 Lafite, which, we must say, looked much like any other. Michel, who's partial to white wines himself, also has an outstanding collection of cognacs – more than 800 labels, we're told – that has been recognized by the Guinness Book of World Records.

His menu is quite traditional – classics like lobster thermidor and châteaubriand bouquetière – but the preparation is often innovative. The soup du jour might be a delicate cream of watercress swirled with crème fraîche and centered with croutons. The seafood feuilleté comes in puff pastry shaped like a little fish. The terrine of rabbit is enhanced by anisette. House specialties are fish with two sauces (salmon with beurre blanc and halibut with hollandaise and a dollop of caviar, the two separated by a puree of broccoli over slivered carrots) and pheasant with morels accompanied by a pastry barque filled with beans, carrots and potato sticks.

Main courses vary from chicken in wine sauce and rabbit in mustard sauce to filet mignon with goose liver. The best bet may be the lunch menu gastronomique, five courses with choice of beef filet or saddle of rabbit for $45. That includes such desserts as grand marnier parfait, chocolate profiteroles, pear belle hélène and raspberry mousse cake. The evening menu gastronomique is $350 for two, wine included. Or perhaps you'd like the nine-course menu for six, $6,000, wine included.

Although this is considered a place for a splurge, you also can find good value. The $16, three-choice lunch special is one of the best bargains in the city.

(514) 844-1842. www.leschenets.com. Entrées, $22.50 to $52. Lunch, Monday-Friday 11:30 to 2. Dinner nightly, 5:30 to 11.

The Ultimate Bistro

L'Express, 3927 St. Denis St.

No sign identifies this quintessential French Montreal bistro – only the name discreetly embedded in white tiles on the front sidewalk. But L'Express, as authentic a French bistro as they get, is generally packed day and night with Montreal's trend-setters, media types, restaurateurs and wannabes. Everybody who's anybody seems to turn up to see and be seen – a phenomenon enhanced by the squeezed-together tables and the mirrors on the walls.

So we were surprised to have the place completely to ourselves for a weekday continental breakfast of café au lait, flaky croissants and a couple of slices of grilled brioche. With jam and cheese on the side, the bill came to a rather continental $15-plus, but, hey, isn't this the good life in Montreal?

The waitress was chatty, the white paper tablecloths were rolled out like gift wrap and were printed with Perrier bottles, and the no-smoking signs were appreciated. The fare is simple and ever so French. The only egg dish at breakfast was basic egg with sausage or ham. No one comes to be dazzled by the food, although it is quite good.

They come for the Gallic ambiance, the conviviality and a short menu of well-turned-out bistro standards, all available à la carte. The menu strikes the adventurous as somewhat old-hat, as in appetizers of soupe paysanne, jellied egg, celeriac rémoulade and quiche du jour. But reviewers consider the chicken-liver mousse with pistachios the city's best. Ditto for the terrine of duck foie gras (at $21.50 the most expensive item on the menu, except for the three caviars).

Bistro interior glitters at L'Express.

More substantial dishes start with a cold roast beef sandwich, served with legendary fries that set the standards to which others aspire. Pickled duck salad, fillet of doré amandine, grilled salmon on a bed of spinach, pot au feu, pan-fried veal livers with tarragon, steak tartare, roast lamb with rosemary and grain-fed chicken in mustard sauce are among the standbys. Specials are simply inserted along the sides of the plastic-covered menus diner style, as in "six oysters."

Desserts include a floating island that our waitress called "the bombe," chocolate mousse cake, raspberry charlotte and a couple of "frozen logs" made of pear and raspberry sorbets or black cherry and chocolate ice creams with crème anglaise.

The wine list is extensive, and the selection of eaux de vie exceptional.

(514) 845-5333. Entrées, $12.35 to $22.50. Open daily 8 a.m. to 2 or 3 a.m., Saturday and Sunday from 10 a.m.

A New Montreal Classic

Joe Beef, 2491 Notre-Dame St. West.

Homegrown star chef David McMillan of Montreal's glamorous, see-and-be-seen restaurant scene always dreamed of opening a little place where he could cook whatever he felt like cooking and cook it simply. He's doing it now with cohort Frédéric Morin at this 28-seater in the gentrifying Little Burgundy neighborhood near the Atwater Market.

It sounds like a steakhouse, this humble haunt reviving the nickname of an iconoclastic ex-Brit whose legendary 19th-century riverfront tavern was known across North America. Joe Beef's Canteen survived until 1982. Now it's more bistro than bar, and the specialty is seafood – especially oysters, shucked expertly behind the long wood raw bar by resident oysterman John Bill, who imports them himself from around the world. The menu, chalked on a large blackboard, cites four appetizers and four main courses determined by the whims of the chefs, who walk daily to the Atwater Market to pick what's new and fresh.

Those who find the off-the-beaten-path place rave about the lobster spaghetti, pan-fried haddock, a halibut dish with shellfish and vermouth, roasted rabbit and the sirloin steak – a hefty portion spilling off the plate and served with sides of sautéed spinach, fried artichoke hearts and smashed potato homefries. Appetizers vary from a watercress salad with cheese and apples to foie gras, the presentation changing nightly. The night's desserts might be a lavish pot de crème with red concord grape jelly or sourdough bread pudding flavored with ripened pears, drizzled with chocolate sauce and served with chocolate ice cream.

The atmosphere is laid-back and convivial, and the decor retro and eclectic – rustic cutlery and plates, thick blue and white cloths for napkins, and long burgundy banquettes for seating. Fans of David McMillan's other local restaurant ventures (Globe, Rosalie et al) predict Joe Beef may join L'Express and Au Pied du Cochon in the realm of indigenous Montreal classics.

(514) 935-6504. Entrées, $18 to $32. Dinner, Tuesday-Saturday to 9:30.

Great Values

Le Poisson Rouge, 1201 Rachel St. East.

This corner storefront facing Lafontaine Park is a find – both for food and ambiance. Not to mention the bottom-line tab, since it's one of the growing number in the Plateau Mont-Royal area that encourage patrons to bring their own wine.

The most astonishing surprise of all is the man behind the stove: Pascal Gellé, one of the famed "Group of Six" chefs who launched the new Quebec cuisine in the 1980s. Former owner of Montreal's much-acclaimed La Chamade and later of Bagatelle (both now defunct), he resurfaced here in 1999 after a few years of wanderlust. "This is easier to run and the rent is much lower," he advised.

It has to be a labor of love. Pascal and "two and one-half" assistants in the kitchen and a host/manager and servers out front represent a rather high staff-to-patron ratio for a 34-seat gourmet restaurant whose tables turn at most twice an evening. The menu is both table d'hôte ($35 for four courses) and à la carte. As in the past, fish is the specialty, including signature main courses like shark au poivre and noisettes of skate au beurre, plus perhaps dore with saffron cream, grouper with beer sauce and arctic char with rhubarb.

Our party of three can vouch for Pascal's appetizers of mussels au lait du coco, a mussel and zucchini gratin glazed with crayfish bisque and a chicory salad adorned with croutons topped with warm goat cheese. The usual good French bread – you really can't get bad French bread in Montreal – was great for mopping up the sauces.

Main courses were tilapia with red wine and mustard oil, a duo of blue marlin and arctic char with lemongrass and ginger, and a special of halibut with saffron sauce. These came with far more interesting accompaniments than the bland rice served with the quenelles Val de Loire, a Gellé trademark, that we sampled at a previous visit.

For dessert, we enjoyed Pascal's ethereal "gâteau des crêpes" (layers of crêpes and hazelnut mousse), a cranberry-raspberry clafouti, and heavenly chestnut ice cream over a hot chocolate sauce.

These treats and more, plus your own bottle of wine, can be enjoyed in a convivial and colorful room with rag-painted orange and yellow walls, green bistro lights hanging from the ceiling and an abundance of plants. Green runners and yellow napkins top the pine tables, which look to have been handcrafted in Quebec but actually came from Ikea. Large windows open onto the street to create an al fresco feeling in summer. A good thing, too, for the inside can get noisy, as we found when seated next to a party of eight trying to out-shout each other in two languages.

(514) 522-4876. Entrées, $26. Dinner, Tuesday-Sunday 5:30 to 10:30. BYOB.

La Gaudriole, 825 Laurier Ave. East.

This hideaway in a nondescript yellow building in a transitional block at the eastern edge of the Plateau Mont-Royal was the home of Da Marcello, the premier Tuscan restaurant in Montreal, until the death of its owner. It resurfaced as a market-fresh French restaurant under chef-owner Mark Vézina, who struck out on his own after years of teaching cooking.

Tiny and true, the new incarnation is simple but unexpectedly stylish. A gray wall divided horizontally by a long mirror is the backdrop for about fifteen tables dressed in pale blue over white and flanked by modern rattan chairs.

The excitement here is on the plate. The ingredients are exotic, the preparations adventurous, the presentations artistic and the prices out of the past. The format is table-d'hôte at both lunch and dinner.

For $10 to $15, you can dine at midday on the likes of mushrooms in puff pastry, chicken breast stuffed with avocado and brie, and a dessert of crêpes with caramelized fruits. One of us made a great lunch of a cheese quiche with lardons, lamb tenderloin with mint couscous and a superb almond cake. The other found the creamy vegetable soup rather boring but liked the salad with goat cheese crouton and the fruit sorbet.

The bargains for the budget gourmet continue at night. The price of the three-course dinner is determined by the entrées, ranging from a vegetarian offering to hare strip loin with "gingerbread" sauce. Other possibilities: shrimp sautéed with whiskey and tonka beans, mahi mahi with smoked bell pepper and sundried tomato coulis, and roast wild boar with sage and mushroom jus. A signature dish is grilled lamb filets nestled between thin strips of grilled eggplant, refried flageolet beans and couscous, surrounded by a sauce of purple basil flowers.

Typical starters are snapper rillettes with wasabi tapioca and kidney bean salsa, grilled quail on oriental green papaya salad and homemade ravioli stuffed with venison, porcini pesto and monterey jack cheese. For a $9 supplement, you can order duck foie gras with cider vinegar sauce – a generous dollop that would probably cost up to three times as much elsewhere.

For dessert, there are trios of chocolates, ice creams and sorbets, as well as almond polenta filled with fresh fruits and drizzled with orange sauce. The star of the show is the "caprice de Patrice" – a delicate chocolate mousse filled with ginger pot-de-crème, atop a round of spicy carrot cake surrounded by twisted carrot chips.

The markup on wines is about half that at most Montreal restaurants, with most priced from $19 to $50.

(514) 276-1580. www.lagaudriole.com. Table d'hôte, $27 to $34. Lunch, Tuesday-Friday 11:30 to 2. Dinner nightly, 5:30 to 9:30.

Première Rue, 355 St. Paul St. West.

This little-known establishment at the western edge of Old Montreal is packed at noon with business types from the nearby Financial District. They know a good thing but go home at night, leaving the twenty-table dining room to regulars and visitors who stumble across the place and are taken by the charm.

A warm welcome is provided by host/waiter Claude Ferran – "I'm the little owner," he advises. "My wife (the chef) is the real owner." The interior is a mix of stone, dark blue and red walls. Ladder-back chairs face small tables covered with brown butcher paper over white cloths. The tables for two are nicely angled for privacy, French music plays quietly in the background and the ambiance is relaxing in an era of urban chic.

The menu is chalked in French on a large blackboard on a side wall. There are nominal surcharges for some appetizers, such as escargots, smoked salmon or goat cheese salad. A choice of a modest salad, a smooth country terrine and soup du jour, perhaps cauliflower with a dollop of beet purée for color or, at our autumn lunch, a comforting cream of vegetable, come with. So do desserts, a bit more lavish: among them, pear crêpes with raspberry sauce, profiteroles and, in our case, pear clafouti with raspberry coulis and a classic crème caramel.

The main dishes are traditional French and executed to perfection. We were impressed with the veal sweetbreads dijonnaise and the succulent rabbit with two mustards, both of which are signatures on lunch and dinner menus. Other choices at our visit were fillet of tilapia andalouse, seafood in puff pastry prepared Gaspé style, tagine of lamb Madras style and entrecôte of beef with blue cheese sauce. Appropriate starches and vegetables accompany. Even the wine choices are posted on the blackboard. They're humanely priced, about a dozen in the high $20s range, with liters of perfectly good house wine for $23.

How can you afford *not* to eat here?

(514) 285-0022. Table-d'hôte, $21.80 to $25.80. Lunch, Tuesday-Friday noon to 2:30. Dinner, Thursday-Saturday 6 to 10.

Lodging

Of the multitude of choices, we suggest a few with special appeal:

Traditional Hotels

The Ritz-Carlton, 1228 Sherbrooke St. West, Montreal H3G 1H6.

Splendidly posh and comfortable in the Old World sense, Montreal's venerable hotel (1912, and the original Ritz, as envisioned by Cesar Ritz), is still favored by many knowledgeable travelers over the more glitzy newcomers. In a city that becomes more French every year, the Ritz is a nostalgic reminder of the days when Sherbrooke Street West ("The Golden Mile") was a bastion of anglo institutions, tastes and affluence.

Renovated and grandly updated over the years, the hotel has preserved much of its cherished interior even as all 229 high-ceilinged guest rooms and suites have been redone. Lately, it has added an exercise room to keep up with the times and each suite comes with three telephones and high-speed internet. Twenty rooms contain fireplaces and many have original moldings, embossed ceilings and chandeliers.

Ritz Garden is a traditional favorite for outdoor dining at The Ritz-Carlton.

Though not what they used to be, the hotel's restaurants have been favorites of anglo-Montrealers for years. One of us remembers having the businessman's lunch in the Ritz Café for about $3.95 for three courses back in the late 1950s. It was there she was introduced to such an unfamiliar dish (because her mother certainly never cooked it) as calves brains in black butter.

The main restaurant is known as the **Café de Paris** in winter and the **Ritz Garden** in summer. The latter in particular, utterly charming, has been the scene of family celebrations. Tables on a covered terrace on two sides of a courtyard look out over an oasis of lawns, flowers and a duck pond. Here, Sunday brunch is an event, as it should be for $60.

Afternoon tea from 3:30 to 5 is a tradition seasonally in the Ritz Garden. More than a dozen loose-leaf teas are offered (Imperial Gunpowder, Scottish Breakfast and Spiced Orange are some). "English Tradition" finds your tea presented with tea sandwiches, scones with devonshire cream, petits fours and sweets, while the "Royal Tea" adds a glass of champagne and a bowl of strawberries.

Live music accompanies the locally famous Saturday evening seafood buffet in the Café de Paris.

A martini hour in the Grand Prix piano bar offers a selection of seventeen kinds of martinis with complimentary snacks and more substantial hors d'oeuvre.

(514) 842-4212. Fax (514) 842-3383. One hundred eighty-one rooms and 48 suites. Doubles, $295 to $445. Suites, $445 to $4,000.

Hotel Omni Mont-Royal, 1050 Sherbrooke St. West, Montreal H3A 2R6.

If the Ritz is Montreal's grand, understated hotel, the Omni is arguably its most sumptuous high-rise.

Built by the Four Seasons chain for the Summer Olympics in 1976 and until recently known as the Westin Mont-Royal, it was acquired by the Omni chain and underwent major renovations. It has 300 large, tastefully appointed rooms and suites with kingsize or two twin beds, an indoor-outdoor pool, saunas and a full-service health club. Each guest room has a stocked minibar, most have sitting areas with sofas, and the bathrooms offer bidets, hair dryers and terrycloth robes.

The hotel's showy Mediterranean restaurant called **Opus II** is very visible with its skylit, glass-enclosed bistro adjunct beside the sidewalks along Sherbrooke and Peel streets. Its food fortunes rise and fall with the comings and goings of the chefs. Those in the know head downstairs to **Restaurant Zen** for a more authentic dining experience. The first North American venture for the Hong Kong-based Zen chain, the two-tier, circular space is as dramatic as the Asian-inspired fare.

(514) 284-1110 or (800) 843-6664. Fax (514) 845-3025. Two hundred seventy-one rooms and 29 suites. Doubles, $159 to $329. Suites, $299 to $1,840.

Sofitel Montreal, 1155 Sherbrooke St. West, Montreal H3A 2N3.

France's Sofitel luxury hotel chain opened its first in Canada in 2002, a minimalist monument of glass and metal. A sixteen-story office tower built in 1975 was gutted to produce 250 rooms and suites of considerable comfort. The landmark glass canopy in front helps make the place resemble a crystal by day and a lantern at night.

Rooms are notable for floor-to-ceiling windows, furniture of exotic wood called anegre (a South American teak), feather beds and goose down duvets, and unusual square modern chairs with ottomans beside a circular wood barrel-shaped table. Some of the white-marble bathrooms have rainforest showers without tubs; others have baths and separate showers. About a third of the deluxe rooms have two double beds. The rest are kingsize.

The main floor holds a soaring lobby with a wall of windows and furniture of Quebec cherry wood that follows the Danish modern style. Alongside is the high-ceilinged restaurant **Renoir**, a large and informal bar and eatery opening onto an outdoor terrace. The French-trained chef features Provençal-inspired cuisine that is highly rated.

(514) 285-9000 or (877) 285-9001. Fax (514) 289-1155. Two hundred forty-one rooms and seventeen suites. Doubles, $180 to $460. Suites, $325 to $2,000.

Boutique Hotels

In the last few years, Montreal has experienced an explosion of boutique hotels that qualify as hip enough to be sought out by the film stars and celebrities who have turned the city into an international destination. Four opened in one year alone in Old Montreal. Although all are considered "designer" hotels, the design in some like the Hotel Gault and the St.-Paul Hotel may come at the expense of comfort.

Hôtel Le St.-James, 355 St. Jacques St., Montreal H2Y 1N9.

An $11 million restoration turned a former bank into Montreal's most sumptuous, over-the-top hotel – a description solidified by its becoming the sole Canadian member of Leading Small Hotels of the World.

Opened in 2002 for a clientele that wants "nothing but the best," according to proprietor Karen Anthony-Rémillard, the twelve-story hotel at the western edge of Old Montreal is "a place where people can feel as if they are in the comfort and privacy of their own home." Some home.

The bank's soaring trading floor is now the majestic Grand Salon, one of the few that lives up to the name. White-linened tables are flanked by plush sofas for guests to take breakfast and light meals (smoked salmon napoleon or duck foie gras) in a living-room setting. Staircases sweep up to mezzanines on either side, where there are more tables as well as more privacy.

Mezzanines overlook dramatic Grand Salon at Hôtel Le St.-James.

Elevators with doors from the original Waldorf-Astoria in New York ascend to guest accommodations that qualify for house-museum status. Each of the 61 rooms and suites is different, although all are furnished luxuriously in contrast to the minimalist motif of several of Montreal's new boutique hotels. The usual high-tech amenities are surrounded by what a bellhop described as "old-fashioned comforts." Think fine art and estate furniture, lamps for reading, French linens and Penhaligon toiletries from Great Britain, and truffles at turndown. The all-marble bathrooms come in different colors. A kingsize executive suite sports fabric wallpaper that matches its chairs. The four Heritage Collection "board-room" suites have three flat-screen TVs for living room, bedroom and bath. A 4,600-square-foot penthouse suite with a wraparound terrace is available for $5,000 a night.

The front of the hotel's main floor contains a masculine-looking library and cigar lounge with three elaborate chandeliers. The lower level holds an exercise room with stone and brick walls and onyx floors and a candlelit spa for private massages.

(514) 841-3111 or (866) 841-3111. www.hotellestjames.com. Forty-nine rooms and twelve suites. Doubles, $400 to $675. Suites, $925 to $5,000.

Le Place d'Armes Hotel & Suites, 701 Côte de la Place d'Armes, Montréal H2Y 2X6.

Opened in 2000 and much expanded in 2005, this is the first hotel owned by the Antonopoulos family, Greek immigrants who started in 1970 with a 50-seat deli in Old Montreal. The hotel began in a seven-story Beaux Arts office building with a soaring entry and a lobby bar that doubled as a breakfast area. The original 44 rooms and four suites are contemporary in pale yellow, with duvet covers on kingsize beds and bathrooms with brick walls and black and white tiled floors, many with corner whirlpool tubs and glass-enclosed showers. Mezzanine suites added pleasant living rooms and loft bedrooms with sitting areas.

In 2005 the hotel expanded into two adjacent buildings, adding 39 rooms and 48 suites as well as a spa and fitness center. Outfitted with all the latest amenities from Frette bathrobes to flat-screen TVs, they feature electric fireplaces in every room and a few offer private balconies with views of Old Montreal.

The hotel's 2,000-square-foot spa has four treatment rooms, a Vichy shower room, a relaxation room and Montreal's first Hammam, a steam room steeped in Middle Eastern traditions.

Downstairs in the original hotel is **Aix Cuisine du Terroir,** a contemporary restaurant in soothing earth tones serving dinner. On the rooftop, the new **Aix La Terrace** features an open kitchen and grill, offering sandwiches, salads, pastas and main courses for lunch and a grazing menu with cheese plates, antipasti and light fare at night.

For the winter of 2006, the rooftop turned into **Grey Goose Sub Zero,** Montreal's first ice bar. The walls, chairs and even the glasses were made of ice.

Continental breakfast and afternoon wine and cheese are included in the rates. The ice bar levies a $10 cover charge, which includes a drink.

(514) 842-1887 or (888) 450-1887. www.hotelplacedarmes.com. Eighty-three rooms and 52 suites. Doubles, $190 to $330. Suites, $365 to $1,200.

Hôtel Nelligan, 106 St. Paul Street West, Montreal H2Y 1Z3.

This stylish yet welcoming and comfortable hotel is named for Quebec poet Émile Nelligan, whose verses are inscribed on some of the brick and stone walls of 63 rooms and suites spread between two 1850 office buildings. Opened in 2002, it is the third hotel owned by the Antonopoulos family.

Rooms on four upper floors go off corridors and alcoves surrounding an open atrium. Goose duvet comforters, each artfully topped by a throw, cover the kingsize or two double beds in 35 standard rooms, some of them small and prone to noise emanating from windows onto the atrium below. Larger and quieter are 28 outside rooms with king beds, fireplaces and baths with double jacuzzis and separate showers. These have sofabeds and club chairs with ottomans, as well as large work desks.

The hotel has a small fitness center with a massage room. A rooftop terrace and bar yields a glimpse of the St. Lawrence River. Continental breakfast is offered here in season, and light meals are served in good weather.

The main floor holds a double salon with fireplace and library, a garden atrium containing tables and chairs amid plants and a fountain, a bar-salon and a clubby restaurant called **Verses,** which features contemporary Quebec cuisine. Continental breakfast is offered in the skylit atrium, which becomes a tearoom later in the day. Wine and cheese are complimentary in the afternoon.

(514) 788-2040 or (877) 788-2040. Fax (514) 788-2041. www.hotelnelligan.com. Sixty-one rooms and two suites. Doubles, $190 to $295. Suites, $295 to $2,000.

Le Saint-Sulpice Hôtel, 414 Rue St-Sulpice. Montreal H2Y 2V5.

They call it an "urban resort," this new six-story building erected in a U-shape around an interior courtyard. The precise reason is unclear, unless it is for the resort-style balconies offered by fifteen suites overlooking a beautiful courtyard with the city skyline and the majestic Notre-Dame Basilica in the background.

They also call it a condominium hotel, a reference to its financing (108 individually owned suites with common furnishings and management) and to its condo-like accoutrements (stocked kitchenettes, living rooms on the outside with windows that open, separated by french doors of frosted glass from interior bedrooms).

The chic boutique hotel differs from others in that it's all new (and solidly built to feel, if not look, old), as opposed to an historic renovation. Except for the spaciousness and accessories of its suites, you'd never know it was a condo. They range in size from 500 to 1,700 square feet and each is outfitted similarly with stone walls, rich woods, modern furnishings, supple leather chairs, contemporary artworks and the usual hotel amenities. Studio suites have pull-down murphy beds and sofabeds. Deluxe suites add fireplaces, separate bedrooms with feather duvets and baths with unusual curving glass vanities. Staying in one of the huge two-bedroom, two-bath executive suites with private terraces is like having your own house.

A large and inviting lobby opens onto the landscaped, open-air courtyard. The hotel's stylish restaurant, known simply as **S,** serves three meals daily.

(514) 288-1000 or (877) 785-7423. Fax (5214) 288-0077. www.lesaintsulpice.com. One hundred eight suites. Doubles, $249 to $489.

Inns and B&Bs

Auberge Bonaparte, 447 St. Francois Xavier St., Montreal H2Y 2T1.

An outgrowth of the Restaurant Bonaparte, this 31-room inn emerged with great style in 1999 in the shadow of Notre Dame Basilica in Old Montreal. Owner Louis Ladouceur teamed up with B&B impresarios Daniel Soucy and Michael Banks from neighboring Les Passants du Sans Soucy (see below), who helped design and still manage the place.

You'd never guess that the four floors above the restaurant had been a rundown apartment and rooming house. The owner gutted the interior and dressed up the 1886 facade, graced with granite and wrought-iron trim work in front and brick in back. It's now the place of choice for those seeking prime yet historic accommodations at reasonable rates in the Old City.

A variety of rooms, each rather different, go off central corridors notable for their walls of French yellow and floors covered with showy oriental runners. The shiny maple floors in the rooms are left bare. Expect to find TVs hidden in armoires, tiled bathrooms with pedestal sinks and double showers or whirlpool tubs, a cushioned chair or two, closets with automatic lights, and – blessed wonder in today's cocooned urban society – windows that open (the air-conditioning shuts off automatically). Rooms that we saw had antique iron sleigh beds in queen or king sizes, dressed in colorful fabrics. Eight others have one double bed and more basic bathrooms. Private balconies are attributes in two, one of them a suite. The latter encompasses a living room with sofabed, a queen bedroom and a bath with double jacuzzi.

A complimentary full breakfast, prepared in the Sans Soucy style, is served in the Bonaparte restaurant.

(514) 844-1448. Fax (514) 844-0272. www.bonaparte.com. Thirty rooms and one suite with private baths. Doubles, $150 to $210. Suite, $325.

Les Passants du Sans Soucy, 171 St. Paul St. West, Montreal, H2Y 1Z5.

The first real B&B in Montreal, located at the quieter western edge of Old Montreal, is cheery, comfortable and as authentic as all get-out. Engaging innkeepers Daniel Soucy, a French-speaking Quebecker, and Michael Banks from Ontario offer eight bedrooms and a suite on three floors of an old fur trading warehouse dating to 1723.

Each has the requisite beamed ceilings, brick and stucco walls, and European ambiance you'd expect, as well as all the comforts of home and then some. All rooms have marble baths (four with whirlpool tubs), bedside telephones and TVs ensconced in armoires made by a Quebec craftsman and painted a distressed green. Beds (most of them queensize) are made up in the European fashion, with pillows showing. The buffed wood floors are left bare, but colorful bed covers, draperies and, in some rooms, paisley sofas add warmth.

Petunias brighten the window boxes facing the street, and we loved the colorful Parisian glass sconces in varied colors in the halls and bedrooms. They're $500 a pair, and Michael says he has sold quite a few.

A ground-floor suite contains a living room with sofabed, a queen bed in the rear bedroom and a marble bath with jacuzzi.

You enter through a lobby also serving as a gallery showcasing Quebec art and crafts. To the rear is an open, skylit living room with a fireplace and a convivial dining area, where Michael serves a breakfast cooked to order by Dan. A choice of seven kinds of juices, huge flaky croissants (some with chocolate filling), smoked-salmon and ham and cheese omelets (several fillings are offered), bottled mineral water and café au lait served in big bowls made ours a breakfast to remember.

(514) 842-2634. Fax (514) 842-2912. www.lesanssoucy.com. Eight rooms and one suite with private baths. April-December: doubles $155 to $185, suite $215. Rest of year: doubles $115 to $130, suite $145.

La Maison Pierre du Calvet, 405 Bonsecours St., Montreal H2Y 3C3.

Montreal's oldest private house (1725) open to the public is this charmer, which had four years as a restaurant under its belt before adding B&B accommodations in 1995. The sense of history is palpable in the residence of Calvet, a wealthy merchant and patriot, located in the heart of Old Montreal across the street from the historic Notre-Dame-de-Bonsecours Chapel. Behind the Breton-style facade of thick stone walls, French windows and heavy chimneys lies a complex of nine baronial guest quarters.

The accommodations are large, luxurious and decidedly masculine except for the 18th-century costumes on a hook here and an old pram in a corner there. Otherwise they're all fieldstone walls, rich walnut paneling, dark wood floors and high, step-up queensize canopy beds with oversize bedding made up in the European style. Expect gas fireplaces, Canadian art and tapestries on the walls, a mix of sturdy Quebec antiques and apparent hand-me-downs, and, in at least two cases, carved bed headboards fashioned from church pews. Lord & Mayfair toiletries enhance the marble bathrooms.

A hearty breakfast of fruit, croissants, and bacon and eggs is served in an appealing plant-filled Victorian solarium with three talkative parrots or outside in a tiny garden courtyard.

The public may join guests for dinner by candlelight in the plush main-floor restaurant of the same name. It's an elegant, living-room-like affair with leather sofas grouped around a fireplace in the center and tables around the perimeter. Classic French cuisine is offered à la carte (ten choices from $32.95 to $38.95) or table d'hôte (three courses from $44.95 to $49.95, depending on choice of four entrées), nightly 5 to 11.

(514) 282-1725 or (866) 544-1725. Fax (514) 282-0456. www.pierreducalvet.ca. Eight rooms and one suite with private baths. Doubles, $265 to $295.

Auberge du Vieux-Port, 97 de la Commune East, Montreal H2Y 1J1.

Leading innkeepers Daniel Soucy and Michael Banks always wanted to have an inn on the waterfront in Old Montreal, but satisfied themselves with Les Passants du Sans Soucy (see above) in the interim. Their chance came in 1996, when they gutted a five-story leather factory and created a deluxe 27-room auberge facing the St. Lawrence River. They sold in 1999 to their partners, Greek brothers Costa and Tony Antonopoulos, after helping win a Montreal design award for the stunning architectural restoration.

Terrace dining atop Auberge du Vieux-Port.

More than half the rooms with brick and stone walls, exposed beams and tall casement windows in this urbane European-style hotel have kingsize brass beds. The rest are queens or two doubles. All but four come with single or double jacuzzis in the bathrooms. Each has a TV and a minibar in the armoire, Canadian pine doors and handsome maple floors "with as many knots as we could find," in the words of a manager. Hair dryers and irons are among the amenities.

Guests have a choice of bagels with cream cheese, omelets or waffles with all the trimmings for breakfast. Complimentary wine and cheese are offered in the afternoon. Downstairs is **Les Remparts** (see above), a hidden French restaurant serving some of the best food in the city. Upstairs is a rooftop terrace yielding a great view of the river. The promotion calls a light meal with wine here "the height of romance."

(514) 876-0081 or (888) 660-7678. Fax (514) 876-8923. www.aubergeduvieuxport.com. Twenty-seven rooms with private baths. Doubles, $199 to $290 May-October, $175 to $235 rest of year.

Gourmet Treats

More than any place we know, all Montreal seems passionate about food. In a city where there is a bakery or specialty food shop or charcuterie or café issuing forth delectable aromas at almost every corner and in between, we can do no more than cite a few favorites.

The quaint **St. Viateur Bagel Shop,** 263 St. Viateur St., is home to the best bagels in a city known for great bagels. Some are produced here, but most come from the nondescript bakery at 158 St. Viateur.

There is probably not a Montrealer who hasn't at some time in his or her life had a smoked meat sandwich at **Bens Delicatessen,** 990 Maisonneuve Blvd. West. Although it has expanded and now has a liquor license, it hasn't changed much since one of us, who attended nearby McGill University in the 1950s, would stop in late at night after parties to sit with other students under dreadful fluorescent lights that turned faces green and nosh on the inch-high smoked-meat creation (now $3.95). Bens has been upstaged by **Schwartz's Hebrew Delicatessen** at 3895 St. Lawrence Blvd., a favorite of the younger generation. Look for the sign Charcuterie Hebraique and a line out the door. Once inside you'll share communal tables to enjoy the kitchen's trademark stack of spicy smoked beef sandwiched between rye bread ($3.75), with a giant dill pickle and vinegary, neon-green coleslaw. The recipes, from Romanian Jewish emigrés, are a family secret.

Connoisseurs say some of the best breads, pâtés (ten kinds) and especially foie gras emanate from **Marché de La Villette,** a Parisian-style boucherie and charcuterie at 324 St. Paul St. West in Old Montreal. Nicole and Jean-Pierre Marionnet make everything on the premises. Stop in here for a local treat or even the soup and sandwich lunch, $9.95 including beverage and tax. Across the street is **Olive & Gourmando,** a bakery and café evocative of the villages of Provence. Here you can choose from a delectable array of pastries, salads, paninis and sandwiches.

Self-described as "the Disney World of Gastronomie" is **Marché Mövenpick** at 1 Place Ville Marie. An offshoot of the Swiss original, it's an enormous, cafeteria-style restaurant based on a festive, open Mediterranean market concept. After you are shown to a table, you take a tray to food stations throughout the "market" and pay as you leave – probably with some flowers, baked goods or pottery, which are displayed to good advantage at the front of the market.

Optimum, 630 Sherbrooke St. East at Union, is billed as Montreal's largest all-natural supermarket and department store. It's full of a wondrous variety of natural foods, a takeout counter, vitamins, minerals, healthware appliances, juicers and such – the biggest selection we've seen in Canada.

Also of interest to those into healthful eating is the local chain called **Le Commensal,** specializing in "gastronomie végétarienne." We were surprised by the number of lunchers lined up at the cafeteria-style buffet on the second floor of the sleek downtown outlet, a glass-enclosed solarium running for nearly a block at 1204 McGill College St. From couscous to vegetable pizzas to ginger tofu, the midday spread has something for everyone. It's open daily from 11:30 to 10.

Two huge indoor/outdoor markets in Montreal, **Jean Talon Market** in the East End and **Atwater Market** on the southwest edge of downtown, are well worth a visit. Recently renovated, Jean Talon is bigger and has more produce stands and Italian items; Atwater has more indoor shops and butchers. Two of the best destinations are on opposite sides of the Jean Talon. **Fromagerie Hamel** is perhaps the biggest cheese shop of the old school that you'll ever see. With more than 475 varieties to choose from, regulars ask owner Marc Picard for his current favorite. **Le Marché des Saveurs du Quebec** is a sophisticated, contemporary market purveying only Quebec food and beverages, from tourtière to fiddlehead ketchup to an enormous selection of wines, far more than we realized the province produced. Connoisseurs of indigenous products could easily spend a bundle here, and we departed with sauces, salad dressings and cheese soaked in port.

Although the Jean Talon is more authentic, we are more familiar with the Atwater Market, and frequently fill our cooler with things like stuffed quail or boned rabbit, and exotic cheeses and olives, as well as the most impeccable of vegetables, to take home to Connecticut for a dinner to remind us of "La Belle Province."

Another suave food emporium is **Le Marché Westmount Square** at St. Catherine

Street West and Greene Avenue in uppercrust Westmount. Starting as an underground retail complex in the 1960s, it has evolved into a first-rate market and food court. The freshest produce, baked goods, seafood (including sushi) and ready-to-heat take-out items, from delectable looking pizzas to vegetarian tortes, are close at hand from several vendors. Pick out your treats and find a table in one of the little alcoves, or take something out for a picnic or dinner.

Across the street at 1250 Greene Ave. is **Les 5 Saisons,** an anglicized version of the original at 1180 Bernard Ave. West in Outremont. We've shopped both, but are partial to the Outremont store for exotic vegetables, fresh salmon pies, pastas, beautiful steaks and seafood, a salad bar with hot soups and café filtre, a charcuterie with fantastic pâtés, and a pastry shop with adorable animals made out of marzipan. Here is the ultimate gourmet paradise.

Or so it seems until you find **Patisserie de Gascogne.** There are four, but the most accessible for us is at 4825 Sherbrooke St. West (a newer, non-anglicized version is at 237 Laurier Ave. West in Outremont). From platters loaded with delectable little tea sandwiches, to the fanciest ice-cream desserts we have seen, this is a treasure. Brioche, croissants, an incredible selection of cheeses (some made with raw milk), quiches with all kinds of fillings, pâtés, mini-pizzas, pastries – no wonder Westmount's elite love this place. There are a coffee bar and a few little tables where you could have one of the made-up sandwiches or a fancy dessert and a café au lait. We took home one of the vacuum-packed dinners for two – poached salmon in a citrus sauce with rice, about the best salmon dish we have ever had. And all we had to do was stick it in the microwave.

Gourmet Chic

For the authentic French experience, tour the shops along Laurier Street in Outremont. Before you get there, you can smell the coffees at **Café GVH (Gerard Van Houtte)** at 1042 Laurier, a large grocery store specializing in coffees, health foods, gourmet items and cookware; it also has a bakery and a café. The tiny smoked-salmon rolls and kiwi cakes are delicious. There are GVH cafés all over Montreal. **Anjou Quebec** at 1025 is about the most authentic charcuterie/boucherie we've seen, a paradise of terrines, wild mushrooms, exotic fruits and more. The tiny haricots vert are flown in from France. **La Maison d'Emile** at 1073 is an excellent kitchen and bath shop. **La Pâtisserie Belge** at 1075 has display cases full of pastries, and the windows are full of exotic breads at **Au Pain Dore** at 1145, one of a local chain. An overpowering aroma of Belgian chocolates emanates from **Daskalides** at 377 Laurier, a high-ceilinged space that is as much a treat to the eyes as it is to the nose. Newest in a local chain of five, the chocolatier also offers coffees and a salon de thé (tea). Be sure to check out **Patisserie de Gascogne** at 237 Laurier, newest in its chain (see above). Across Park Avenue at 222 Laurier is **La Petite Ardoise,** a contemporary boutique gourmande with fabulous-looking desserts, salads and sandwiches, recently expanded with a café one storefront away. **Olive & Olives,** 1389 Laurier East, is devoted solely to olives and olive oils, mostly from Spain. The bottles of oil are arranged by geographical origin, similar to a wine shop.

Not far away is **La Tomate** at 4347 de La Roche St. in Plateau Mont-Royal, a cheerful place where staff in red lab coats offer up a variety of tomato products. Big baskets of ripe tomatoes were scattered around the shop at our May visit, along with salsas, chili, juices, aspics, olive oils and sea salt, all attractively packaged.

Burlington's Church Street Marketplace is a smorgasbord of carts and cafés.

Burlington

A Culinary Sense of Place

Few areas exude such strong feelings of pride and place as Vermont, and nowhere are these more pronounced than in Burlington, the state's Queen City, poised along a slope above Lake Champlain. From a university town that once had little more than college hangouts and greasy spoons, Burlington has blossomed into the culinary mecca of northern New England.

More than a dozen restaurants of distinction have opened in the last decade or so in the city, as well as south along the lake toward Shelburne. "They seem to spring up every other day here," reports the manager of one of the better ones, the Daily Planet. "This town is ripe."

At the edge of downtown Burlington, in one short block of Church Street one finds a lineup of side-by-side eateries that run the gamut from Tex-Mex to vegetarian and multi-Asian.

The main shopping area, the Church Street Marketplace pedestrian mall, is a smorgasbord of carts and cafés dispensing everything from chicken wings to chimichangas. Coffee à la Carte pours espressos and lattes as long as the temperature does not fall below 20 degrees.

Ben Cohen and Jerry Greenfield, the gurus of fancy ice cream, got their start in Burlington in 1978. Since 1979, the New England Culinary Institute in nearby Montpelier has focused attention on regional cuisine, and moved closer to the action when it opened restaurants in the Inn at Essex in suburban Burlington and, until the NECI Commons closed unexpectedly in 2005, on Church Street itself.

South of town in Shelburne, the Webb family's Shelburne Museum is renowned as a remarkable "collection of collections" of Americana. Another part of the Webb family operates Shelburne Farms, which is known for its farm programs and cheddar cheeses, and has received wide recognition for its majestic Inn at Shelburne Farms.

The area claims the Lake Champlain Chocolates factory, New England's largest cheese and wine outlet, the Harrington ham company headquarters and a showplace bakery, plus countless gourmet food shops and growers or producers of Vermont-made products.

Almost every restaurant in the Burlington area offers al fresco dining in season, and tables spill onto sidewalks and decks at every turn. This is a casual, outdoors city, where people go for interesting food with a Vermont-made theme.

Dining

The Best of the Best

Café Shelburne, 5573 Shelburne Road (Route 7), Shelburne.

This prize among small provincial French restaurants has been going strong since 1969, but never better than under chef-owner Patrick Grangien, who trained with Paul Bocuse and came to Vermont as part of the short-lived Gerard's Haute Cuisine enterprise in Fairfax.

Chef Patrick Grangien at entry to Café Shelburne.

Talk about happy circumstance: after twenty years, owners André and Daniele Ducrot offered the café for sale in 1988, Patrick was suddenly available, and he and his wife Christine bought it and moved in upstairs. They built on a tradition of inspired French food and good value.

The copper bar and the dining areas with their black bentwood chairs and white-linened tables topped with tiny lamps retain much of the original ambiance. Patrick covered and screened the rear patio, a beauty with lattice ceiling and grapevines all around. It's a good choice for dinner on a pleasant evening.

Patrick calls his cuisine "more bistro style than nouvelle." Seafood is his forte (he won the National Seafood Challenge in 1988 and was elected best seafood chef of the year). His prize-winning fillet of lotte on a bed of spinach and mushrooms in a shrimp coulis is a fixture on the menu. Try his salmon medallion with a fennel sauce, sautéed sea scallops with a curried mussel risotto and light curry sauce, or the panache of assorted steamed seafood with champagne-chervil sauce. Other entrées might be duck breast with a white wine sauce, roasted lamb loin with a red wine sauce, filet mignon with a creamy port wine and green peppercorn sauce and, a staple on the menu here, steak tartare, seasoned at tableside.

Soups are a specialty, and all of the night's four offerings are usually winners. In summer they could be chilled pea garnished with prosciutto, creamy mussel perfumed with saffron, lobster bisque and the two vichyssoises – creamy leek and potato and cold asparagus soups served in the same bowl. Tempting appetizers include a warm salmon mousse served with a chive and shiitake mushroom sauce, a baked tomato filled with garlicky mussels and vegetables, and escargots with prosciutto, mushrooms, almonds and croutons.

Crème brûlée is the favorite dessert. Others from the changing but always delectable repertoire include three-chocolate fondant with a vanilla sauce, lemon mousse, profiteroles, assorted fruit sorbets and a trio of chocolate ice creams – semi-sweet, white and cacao.

The heavily French wine list, priced from the twenties to the triple digits, harbors considerable variety. Quite a few wines are available by the half bottle.

(802) 985-3939. www.cafeshelburne.com. Entrées, $20 to $25. Dinner, Tuesday-Saturday 5:30 to 9.

Smokejacks, 156 Church St., Burlington.

"Bold American food" is the billing for this innovative restaurant run by chef-owner Leslie Meyers. She and her chefs share a fondness for smoked foods, robust tastes, a martini bar and an extensive cheese tasting menu. They smoke their own salmon, duck, turkey, mushrooms and more in the restaurant's smoker in the basement. They even smoke peanuts in the shell for munchies at the bar.

Their fare lives up to its billing for boldness, starting with the focaccia and sourdough breads served with sweet butter. At lunch, the maple-cured smoked salmon with pickled red onions and horseradish cream made a fine appetizer. A crispy gruyère cheese risotto square, served with sautéed spinach, was an assertive main course. The star of the show was a grilled wild mushroom bruschetta, emboldened with roasted garlic and served on sautéed greens. A lemon curd upside-down cake with strawberries and whipped cream and white chocolate bread pudding with a rhubarb and sour cream compote and toasted almonds were memorable desserts. A watery cappuccino was the only disappointment.

The dinner menu is categorized by small plates (incorporating many of the lunch dishes) and main courses. Typical of the former are seared yellowfin tuna with tobikko caviar vinaigrette, skillet-roasted mussels in a spicy cilantro broth and a "big bold black angus burger," served with Cabot cheddar on onion focaccia with bacon-roasted potatoes. Main dishes include smoky grilled Atlantic salmon with roasted yellow pepper sauce, smoke-roasted chicken breast with basil butter, smoked brown-sugar-cured pork loin with maple-pecan glaze and herb-crusted leg of lamb with tapenade vinaigrette. Indicative of the kitchen's experimentation was an autumn offering called "pork-o-buco" – braised pork shanks with pumpkin grits and cilantro-apple red cabbage.

Signature items on the interesting weekend brunch menu are smoked turkey hash with scrambled eggs, smoked ham and cheddar grits and brioche french toast with applewood-smoked bacon.

Patrons gather for lunch amid exposed ducts and plants at Smokejacks.

The menu includes an entire page of exotic cheeses (most from Vermont), each served with dried apricots, candied hazelnuts and crostini. They are recommended as a sampler with a glass of wine or beer, as an appetizer or as a savory ending to a meal.

All these bold tastes are served up in a long, narrow storefront room painted silver gray from floor to ceiling. Exposed ducts, candle chandeliers over the bar, tiny purple hanging lights and splashy artworks provide accents.

(802) 658-1119. www.smokejacks.com. Entrées, $19 to $24. Lunch, Monday-Friday 11:30 to 3. Brunch, Saturday 11:30 to 3, Sunday 10:30 to 3. Dinner, Monday-Saturday 5 to 9:30 or 10:30, Sunday 5 to 9.

A Single Pebble, 133 Bank St., Burlington.

Steve Bogart, who started redefining what Chinese food meant to New Englanders at the old China Moon in Warren, moved into the city in 2002. He took over the space vacated by the late Sài-Gòn Café and Vietnamese market and won a place on Vermont magazine's cover in 2004 and its accolade as "the best restaurant in the great, green state of Vermont."

The new setting was ready-made by the previous owner, who had connected two houses by enclosing the driveway between them and offering three dining rooms on several levels. The former Victorian residential look took on modest Chinese overtones, with beige-clothed tables holding chopsticks and lazy susans that permit sharing in the classic szechuan dining style.

The latest restaurant takes its name from John Hersey's book about a trip up the Yangtze River and the dishes are classics from the upper reaches of the Yangtze. Steve, a China aficionado who spends his off-hours reading recipes in Chinese and procuring ingredients from a supplier in New York's Chinatown, tantalizes the taste buds with every offering.

His menu is categorized by small, medium and large dishes. Dinner might start with imperial spring rolls filled with shrimp, scallops and squid or "meat buns," steamed wheat buns filled with seasoned pork and served with hoisin and peanut sauce. Some of the most intriguing possibilities are among medium dishes. The Peking duck is four pancakes enclosing crispy duck, cucumbers and a scallion brush. The mock eel is braised shiitake mushrooms in a ginger sauce. Fiery dry-fried green beans are sautéed with flecks of pork, black beans and preserved vegetables.

Among big dishes are lemon-sesame shrimp in a ginger glaze, crispy scallops served over shiitake mushrooms and red peppers with a ginger-shallot sauce, and spicy szechuan shredded pork, wok-fried in a spicy chungdu sauce tossed with carrots, celery, bamboo shoots and pressed tofu. The red pine chicken, topped with ground pork, braised in star anise and served over spinach, is a Bogart original.

A carefully selected wine list, beers from China and Thailand, and six blends of tea go nicely with the spicy dishes.

(802) 865-5200. www.asinglepebble.com. Entrées, $15.25 to $18.25. Lunch, Monday-Friday 11:30 to 1:45. Dinner nightly, from 5.

Pauline's Café & Restaurant, 1834 Shelburne Road, South Burlington.

One of the earliest of the Burlington area's fine restaurants, this unlikely-looking roadside place has been expanded by Robert Fuller, the regional restaurant impresario who later bought Leunig's Bistro in Burlington and opened Bobcat Café, a brew pub in Bristol, in 2002.

Dining setting is elegant upstairs at Pauline's.

The original downstairs dining room is now an attractive, clubby café paneled in cherry and oak. A side addition adds bigger windows for those who like things light and airy. The original upstairs lounge is now a ramble of small, elegant dining rooms. All is serene in sponged yellows and greens. The walls are hung with handsome artworks, heavy draperies obscure the view from the windows of busy Route 7, and the nicely spaced tables are topped with small oil lamps and, at our spring visit, vases of tulips. Off the second-floor entry is a hidden brick patio enveloped in cedars and a latticed pergola decked out with small international flags and tiny white lights.

These are versatile settings for some of the area's best food. Both the café and dinner menus are offered in the café and on the patio, which makes for unusual range and variety.

With the café menu you can make a mighty good meal of appetizers and light entrées such as fettuccine with smoked salmon, seafood mixed grill with a tangy Thai vinaigrette, maple-mustard pork medallions, chicken with Shelburne Farms cheddar-cream sauce and grilled flank steak.

The changing dinner menu is the kind upon which everything appeals. You might start with roasted garlic soup or a warm caponata salad with Vermont chèvre. Main courses range from potato-encrusted arctic char with watercress sauce to veal florentine.

Our spring dinner began with remarkably good appetizers of morels and local fiddleheads in a rich madeira sauce and a sprightly dish of shrimp and scallops with ginger, garnished with snow peas and cherry tomatoes. A basket of oh-so-good steaming popovers and so-so bread accompanied, as did salads with zippy cream dressings and homemade croutons.

The entrées were superior: three strips of lamb wrapped around goat cheese, and a thick filet mignon served with spring vegetables and boiled new potatoes. The glasses bearing the house Père Patriarche white wine, generous and good, were whisked away for the proper globes when it came time for a Rutherford Hill merlot. A honey-chocolate mousse from Pauline's acclaimed assortment of desserts (Bon Appétit magazine requested the recipe for the bananas foster) and a special coffee with cointreau and apricot brandy ended a fine meal.

(802) 862-1081. www.paulinescafe.com. Entrées, $14.95 to $25.95; café, $10.95 to $14.95. Lunch, Monday-Saturday 11:30 to 2. Dinner nightly, 5 to 9:30 or 10. Sunday brunch, 11 to 2:30.

L'Amante Ristorante, 126 College St., Burlington.

Chef-owner Kevin Cleary and his wife Kathleen earn accolades with their contemporary Italian newcomer in a sleek downtown office building. The couple moved from the Boston area to Vermont after selling their pint-size restaurant of the same name in Gloucester, Mass. Having trained at the New England Culinary Institute in Montpelier, they knew Burlington as a potential place to open a larger restaurant. They transformed a former Chinese eatery into an urban-chic space in shades of olive green with dark wood trim. A 57-seat dining room, separated by a window divider from a fourteen-seat bar, is notable for lots of glass, sleek dark wood chairs and starched white tablecloths.

The simple yet stylish decor extends to the food, where Kevin lets the local ingredients speak with an Italian accent honed from the couple's frequent travels in Tuscany. He bakes the breads, makes the pastas and desserts, and does much of the cooking himself. Kathi handles the front of the house as sommelier and hostess.

The contemporary menu is short and straightforward. Squash blossom fritters stuffed with taleggio and drizzled with honey and truffle oil is the signature starter. Others range from Tuscan white bean and escarole soup and grilled marguerita flatbread to a caramelized onion tart and grilled calamari with radicchio and pancetta. Pastas like orecchiette with caramelized parsnips, turnips, pancetta and swiss chard or gnocchi with slow-roasted pork and dried cherries come in small and large portions.

Expect main courses at down-to-earth prices. Typical are potato-crusted sea bass with sautéed greens and citrus beurre blanc, roasted chicken with truffled mashed potatoes, grilled leeks and rosemary jus and roasted duck sauced with marsala or

Contemporary Italian cuisine is served in stylish dining room at L'Amante Ristorante.

balsamic vinegar. The grilled flatiron steak with a red wine sauce comes with roasted tomatoes and a potato-shallot tart.

Desserts could be pear and apple strudel or crème brûlée. The daily selection of homemade ice cream included basil ice cream with strawberries and balsamic at our winter visit. The primarily Italian wine list is particularly strong on reds.

(802) 863-5200. www.lamante.com. Entrées, $21 to $23. Dinner, Monday-Saturday from 5:30.

Five Spice Café, 175 Church St., Burlington.

This spicy little prize occupies two floors of a former counter-culture restaurant at the edge of downtown. Since 1985, chef-owner Jerry Weinberg has won a host of followers for his multi-Asian menu of unusual, tantalizing dishes from Thailand, Vietnam, Indonesia, China and Burma.

Lately expanded to 80 seats in a main-floor bar area and two upstairs dining rooms, the place exudes character – much of it that of the talkative owner, who at our latest lunch in the bar area was sitting at a nearby table off the kitchen making dim sum and chatting up customers heading to the dining room. Ever the promoter, he ended each sales spiel with the words: "Save room for dessert."

Our meal began with a bowl of hot and sour soup that was extra hot and a house sampler of appetizers, among them siu mai dumplings, hunan noodles, szechuan escargots and spicy cucumbers. The less adventurous among us passed up the Thai red snapper in black bean sauce for a blackboard special of mock duck stir-fry in peanut sauce (the vegetarian dish really does taste like duck, just as, we were assured, the mock abalone really tastes like abalone). Sated though we were, we simply had to share the ginger-tangerine cheesecake.

Chef Weinberg's wizardry in the kitchen is apparent on a chatty, wide-ranging dinner menu that boasts that some of the items and spices have been imitated locally but never matched. Main courses range from spicy hunan noodles and Southeast Asian chicken curry to Thai red snapper flamed in brandy and an eye-opening shrimp dish called Thai fire shrimp ("until this dish, we had a three-star heat rating. Now we have four.")

A drunken chocolate mousse laced with chambord and a blackout cake drenched with triple sec are among favored desserts. The aforementioned ginger-tangerine cheesecake won Jerry a first prize somewhere, and the ginger-honeydew sorbet is extra-appealing. A dessert sampler teams the chocolate mousse with three other sweets. End your meal with one of Jerry's homemade liqueurs – his maple scotch gives quite a kick.

Oil lamps flicker on each table even at noon. Beige cloths and flowers in green vases comprise the decor. Above the serving sideboard is a collection of Five Spice T-shirts emblazoned with fire-breathing dragons and the saying, "Some Like It Hot." Yes, indeed.

(802) 864-4045. www.fivespicecafe.com. Entrées, $16.50 to $17.99. Lunch, Tuesday-Saturday 11:30 to 2:30. Dinner, Monday-Saturday from 5. Sunday, dim sum brunch 11 to 2:30, dinner 3 to 9.

More Good Dining

Leunig's Bistro, 115 Church St., Burlington.

The garage doors go up in the summer to open this European-style bistro and café to the sidewalks along the front and side. People pack the tables day and night, sipping drinks and espresso and savoring the appetizers and desserts, but increasingly they also come for full meals.

Robert Fuller, who also owns Pauline's Café & Restaurant in South Burlington, aimed for a Parisian look and ambiance to give credence to Leunig's slogan as "the soul of Europe in the heart of Burlington." The high-ceilinged interior with tile floors and marble bar is pretty in peach with black trim.

The fare is international with a French accent, as in soup au pistou, onion soup gratinée, duck cassoulet salad and grilled quail salad. Possibilities on the varied menu range from grilled chive polenta, fried calamari with spicy chipotle aioli and grilled asparagus topped with Vermont chèvre to mussels Tuscan style, Portuguese chicken and innovative pasta dishes.

Dinner entrées are as classic as coquilles St. Jacques, duck confit and white bean cassoulet, grilled marinated quail, veal forestière and steak au poivre. Others are as au courant as panko-crusted halibut with a spicy peanut sauce, grilled yellowfin tuna with raspberry vinaigrette and rack of lamb with Vermont chèvre medallions.

Homemade desserts include French tarts, fresh fruit crisps and crème brûlée.

(802) 863-3759. Entrées, $15.50 to $19.50. Breakfast, Monday-Friday 7 to 11. Lunch, 11:30 to 3. Dinner nightly, 5 to 10. Weekend brunch, 9 to 3.

The Daily Planet, 15 Center St., Burlington.

Creative food at down-to-earth prices is the forte of this quirky place, advertised in the alternative press as an "inner city playground."

The name reflects its "global fare – ethnic and eclectic," in the words of the staff. Casual, innovative and a favorite local watering hole among knowledgeable noshers, it has a large bar with a pressed-tin ceiling, a solarium filled with cactus and jade plants plus a jukebox, and a lofty dining room where the pipes are exposed, the tables are dressed with white linens and the walls are covered with works of local artists.

There's artistry as well in the kitchen, a stage for chefs who trained at the Culinary Institute of America or the California Culinary Academy. Their output sparkles with appetizers like rum-soaked grilled shrimp with mango-red onion salsa, mussels steamed in lager or a trio of Mediterranean treats to be spread over grilled focaccia. Entrées might include Greek seafood pasta, Moroccan grilled salmon, Jamaican chicken and grilled Yucatan-style pork. When was the last time you saw black pepper-crusted strip steak for $19, enhanced with a bourbon-shallot sauce and served with a mushroom-bacon baked potato and blue cheese roasted tomatoes? Or how about nine-spice rack of lamb for $23, or $18 for half? Have you ever tried pork vindaloo, an Indian hot and sour pork loin sautéed with tomatoes and chickpeas and served with a scallion flatbread? Vegetarian and vegan options are available, too.

Desserts intrigue as well. Among them are mocha pots de crème, pear-blueberry pie, white-chocolate/apricot cheesecake, fresh plum ice cream and Southern nut cake with bourbon crème anglaise.

The wine list, though small, is well chosen and offers some incredible steals.

(802) 862-9647. www.dailyplanet15.com. Entrées, $17 to $23. Dinner nightly, 5 to 10 or 11.

Trattoria Delia, 152 St. Paul St., Burlington.

An old-world ambiance and an updated menu characterize this authentic Italian establishment. Tom Delia, who used to cook at Mr. Up's in Middlebury, and his wife Lori took over the old What's Your Beef steakhouse and transformed it into a trattoria. The dark beamed and timbered room is comfortable and good-looking in deep red and green, with a long bar along one side.

Homemade pastas are featured as primi courses. Tagliatelle with porcini mushrooms, spaghetti with gulf shrimp and pappardelle with sea scallops and wild mushrooms are typical. Among secondi are wood-grilled fish of the day with a garlic-pepper sauce, salt cod simmered with raisins in a sweet tomato sauce, wild boar shoulder braised in red wine and served over soft polenta, veal saltimbocca and osso buco. A mixed grill might yield a lamb chop, grilled veal involtini and home-made wild boar sausage, served with creamy polenta. A house favorite is filet mignon sautéed in barbera wine and perfumed with white truffle butter from Alba.

Antipasti include bruschetta, deep-fried calamari, carpaccio and the traditional sampling of imported Italian meats, cheeses and roasted vegetables. Among desserts are profiteroles filled with gelati, semifreddo and tiramisu.

The award-winning wine list is extensive and fairly priced. Digestives at the end of the dinner menu include sweet Italian dessert wines.

(802) 864-5253. www.trattoriadelia.com. Entrées, $17 to $26.50. Dinner nightly, 5 to 10.

The Iron Wolf Café, 86 St. Paul St., Burlington.

A small iron wolf over the entry identifies this European-style restaurant, which turned over its tiny Lawson Lane hideaway to Opaline (which ultimately closed in 2005) and relocated into vastly larger quarters.

German chef Claus Bockwoldt and his Lithuanian wife Danny, the hostess, renovated an old bank to produce a sleek room in black and gray, with a semi-open kitchen in the rear and glass shelves holding fine vintages from their adjacent wine shop along one side. The dining experience is different – it's too big to be like "going to a friend's house for dinner," as was the earlier incarnation. But the food is the same and Claus, who cooked all across Europe, prepares every dish from scratch.

He calls his fare "basically classic French," with an emphasis on sauces. Typical entrées are monkfish with tomato coulis infused with salmon and shrimp, scaloppine of ostrich with mango and onion confit, noisettes of lamb sautéed with garlic and rosemary, and filet of beef marchand de vin.

Appetizers are more numerous, among them carpaccio, scallops in puff pastry, lobster bisque, roasted red peppers marinated with goat cheese and caramelized garlic, and a watercress and endive salad with roquefort and caramelized walnuts. Dessert could be profiteroles, baked apple tart with crème fraîche, soufflé glacé au mocha or assorted sorbets.

(802) 865-4462. Entrées, $21 to $28. Dinner, Tuesday-Saturday from 5:30.

Dining and Lodging

The Inn at Shelburne Farms, Shelburne 05482.

It's hard to imagine a more aristocratic inn or a more spectacular setting than the 19th-century brick mansion built by Dr. William Seward Webb and his wife, Lila Vanderbilt Webb, high on a promontory surrounded on three sides by Lake Champlain.

Their 1,400-acre Shelburne Farms agricultural estate was planned by Frederick Law Olmsted, the landscape architect who designed New York's Central Park. The focal point is their incomparable summer home, a lakeside landmark completed in 1899 for $10 million and converted in 1987 into an inn and restaurant of distinction.

The rambling, towered and turreted, Queen Anne-style mansion contains 24 bedrooms and suites, seventeen with private baths. It retains the original furnishings, although Old Deerfield Fabrics created for the inn a Shelburne House line of fabrics and wall coverings from original designs dating to the turn of the last century.

Most guest rooms on the second and third floors are awesome in size, some with non-working fireplaces and three windows onto the water. Each is done in its own style, but four-poster beds, armoires, settees, lavishly carved chairs, writing tables and such barely begin to fill the space. Fresh flowers adorn the bathrooms, mostly original and some with skylights. Guests' names are on the doors and bowls of fruit in the rooms upon arrival.

For their spaciousness and aura of royalty, we would choose to stay in Lila Webb's south corner sitting room with its twin pencil-post beds and a fine view of forests and lake from mullioned windows, or Dr. Webb's room with William Morris wallpaper setting off a massive double bed, a two-story bathroom and spiral stairs up to his valet's quarters (now the White Room full of wicker and containing one of the inn's few queensize beds). Other choices would be the Overlook bedroom in between, or the Rose Room with a canopy bed, silk moiré wallpaper and a view of sunsets over mountains and lake that defies description. Although they represent good value, most would not happy in some of the smaller rooms with shared baths and hard-to-climb-in double beds up against the wall.

The newest accommodations are two modest bungalow cottages, one the Pottery Shed and the other the Treehouse.

Dinner is served with a view of Lake Champlain on veranda at Inn at Shelburne Farms.

The inn's main floor is a living museum reflecting the graciousness of another era. There are porches full of wicker, a library with 6,000 volumes, several sitting rooms (one for afternoon tea and pastries), a dark and masculine game room harboring an 1886 billiards table, and a formal dining room in which breakfast and dinner are served. Telephones in the guest rooms, TV sets on request and a tennis court are among the few concessions to modernity.

Meals are quiet and formal at twelve well-spaced tables dressed with white linens and Villeroy & Boch china in the spacious Marble Room, quite stunning with black and white tiled floors and walls covered in red silk damask fabric. Favored in summer are outdoor tables on the adjacent veranda with views of Lake Champlain. The public may join house guests by reservation.

Executive chef Rick Gencarelli, a Culinary Institute of America grad, added Mediterranean influences to the menu when he joined the inn in 2005 after opening Olives in New York City's W Hotel for his mentor, Todd English. He incorporates produce from the farm's organic gardens and uses local purveyors in keeping with the Shelburne Farms mission of sustaining local agriculture.

Dinner begins with complimentary canapés, perhaps truffle mousse or salami with Shelburne Farms cheddar. Then there could be a choice of roasted butternut squash soup with maple crème fraîche, crispy fried oysters with pickled cippolinis, confit of Vermont quail and handmade garganelli with Shelburne Farms lamb bolognese, mint and shaved sheep's milk cheese. Hand-chopped beef tartare could be served with röesti potato, truffle vinaigrette and a quail egg.

Typical main courses are roasted wild Alaskan halibut with escargot butter, organic chicken cooked under a brick with mushroom vinaigrette, slow-roasted suckling pig with chestnut-honey-truffle glaze, and leg of lamb crusted in black olives and feta cheese.

Desserts vary from seasonal fruit cobblers and assorted fruit sorbets to a compote of summer berries with champagne sabayon and a chocolate mousse torte with hazelnut ganache, cherry amaretto, white peach brandy and raspberry sauces.

Breakfast for overnight guests is à la carte and available to the public. The choices might include eggs benedict florentine and Irish oatmeal with caramelized bananas and brown sugar.

Guests walk the grounds, enjoy the superb gardens, swim at a small beach, play croquet on a manicured lawn and hike up Lone Tree Hill for a 360-degree view of the lake and mountains, says Alec Webb, president of Shelburne Farms and great-grandson of the original owners. The quiet and sense of privacy are overwhelming.

The house was opened as an inn "to preserve the structure and generate revenues," explains Alec, who spent summers in the house as a teenager before his father bequeathed it to a non-profit foundation. "It's an appropriate use since it was basically a guest house originally."

(802) 985-8498. Fax (802) 985-1233. www.shelburnefarms.org. Seventeen rooms with private baths and seven with shared baths, plus two cottages. Rates, EP. Doubles, $210 to $380 private, $100 to $190 shared. Cottages, $215 to $325. Two-night minimum weekends. Open mid-May to mid-October.

Entrées, $24 to $32. Breakfast, Monday-Saturday 7:30 to 11:30. Dinner nightly by reservation, 5:30 to 9:30. Sunday brunch, 8 to 1.

The Inn at Essex, 70 Essex Way, Essex Junction 05452.

"We have a chef for every room," says the manager of this elegant small country hotel and "culinary resort" that emerged along the Route 289 circumferential highway on the outskirts of Essex Junction. That's because the founding innkeeper approached the New England Culinary Institute for advice on a leasee for the planned food and beverage operation at the very time NECI was seeking a teaching kitchen in the Burlington area. NECI decided to run the inn's two restaurants with faculty and students.

The white, three-story main structure is one of several built around what the developers liken to a New England village green. Furnishings and wallpapers in each room are different, and decor varies from Shaker to Queen Anne, from canopy to pencil-post to brass beds. Vermont artist Susan Sargent recently redecorated some of the rooms in vibrant colors with Scandinavian flair. Each room has a sitting area with comfortable upholstered chairs, a TV hidden in the armoire and a modern bath. Thirty have working fireplaces.

An attractive outdoor swimming pool beckons beneath a large fountain/rock sculpture chiseled on the property by a Vermont artist.

At one end of the main inn are two restaurants: the formal, 50-seat **Butler's** with a Georgian look in pale green and lavender, upholstered Queen Anne chairs, heavy white china and windows swagged in chintz, and the more casual **Tavern,** where woven mats on bare tables, dark green wainscoting and small lamps with gilt shades create a Vermont country setting. There's considerable creativity in the enormous professional kitchen, thanks to fifteen teaching chefs and 175 student assistants.

The Tavern was where we had a fine Christmastime lunch: sundried-tomato fettuccine with scallops and a wedge of pheasant pie with a salad of mixed greens. Although the portions were small and the service slow, we saw signs of inspiration, on the menu as well as in a dessert of chocolate medallions with mousseline and blueberries in a pool of raspberry-swirled crème fraîche, presented like a work of art. Two pieces of biscotti came with the bill, a very reasonable tab. Lunch since has been discontinued in favor of a light-fare menu starting at 2 p.m.

The Inn at Essex is home for two New England Culinary Institute restaurants.

Dinner in Butler's, NECI's temple to haute American cuisine, is a study in trendy food prepared and served by second-year students. Dinner is prix-fixe ($34 to $42 for three courses, depending upon choice of entrée), the menu changing daily, although there were à-la-carte options the summer night we dined. Piano music emanated from the lounge as one of us made a meal of three starters: a subtle duck and chicken liver pâté garnished with shredded beets and wild mushrooms, pan-seared scallops with potato-garlic coulis and a salad of organic greens with a cilantro-lime dressing. The other enjoyed an entrée of crispy-skin salmon with wilted greens, tomatoes and risotto. A complimentary canapé of mushroom duxelles in pastry preceded, and a scoop of honeydew melon sorbet appeared between courses. From the delectable looking desserts on display at the entry we shared the trio of sorbets – mango-passionfruit, strawberry daiquiri and peach champagne – spilling from a cookie cone, and splurged for an eau de vie for a bargain $6. Four little pastries and candies accompanied the bill, about $90 for a highly satisfactory experience.

Because of its NECI connections, the inn offers a number of hands-on culinary programs to live up to its recent billing as a culinary resort. A former guest room was turned into a Dacor Kitchen, an intimate culinary-theater that is the venue for interactive demonstrations and dining experiences.

(802) 878-1100 or (800) 727-4295. Fax (802) 878-0063. www.vtculinaryresort.com. Ninety-seven rooms and 20 suites with private baths. Doubles, $179 to $239. Suites, $209 to $499.

Butler's, prix-fixe $34 to $42. Lunch, Monday-Saturday 11:30 to 2. Dinner, Monday-Saturday 6 to 9:30 or 10. Sunday brunch buffet, 10 to 2.

The Tavern, entrées $8.25 to $15.95. Light fare and dinner daily, 2 to 11.

Lodging

The Willard Street Inn, 349 South Willard St., Burlington 05401.

Enter the handsome cherry-paneled foyer of this 1881 brick mansion in the city's Hill Section to reach Burlington's first historic, B&B-style inn. It was opened in

1996 by restaurateur Beverly Watson, who sold in 2005 to concentrate on her catering business.

Fourteen guest rooms on three floors are furnished in traditional style with period antiques and reproductions, plus TVs and telephones. Rooms vary widely, from a large first-floor bedroom with kingsize bed, armoire and floral wallpaper to second-floor corner bedrooms with handsome ornamental fireplaces, and small rooms on the third floor. One of the last, the Tower Room, is among the favorites. Beyond the simple bedroom with a queen bed and country decor is a wicker sitting area in the turret, with a view of Lake Champlain in the distance. Settle here and you may never want to leave.

There are other attractions, however. Guests share a high-ceilinged living room, a formal dining room and a spectacular, plant-filled rear solarium with a marble floor. It's furnished with six tables for breakfast and there's a plush sitting area as well. From here a marble exterior staircase descends to the ornate English gardens in back. They are showy enough to have been featured on a benefit garden tour.

Breakfasts have become more elaborate under new owners Larry and Katie Davis, whose daughter Kerrie continues to serve as manager. Homemade peanut butter-apricot granola with fresh fruit and yogurt is a staple. You might find corned beef hash with poached eggs and hollandaise sauce and whole wheat pancakes with spiced peaches one day. The next day's choices could be cranberry-pecan bread pudding with vanilla custard sauce and an unusual spinach, pear, gorgonzola and sausage omelet garnished with edible flowers.

Afternoon tea and cookies are offered in the solarium.

(802) 651-8710 or (800) 577-8712. Fax (802) 651-8714. www.willardstreetinn.com. Fourteen rooms with private baths. Doubles, $125 to $225.

Lang House, 360 Main St., Burlington 05401.

A restored 1881 Eastlake mansion just above downtown became another urbane B&B in 2000, thanks to Beverly Watson of the Willard Street Inn and Bobbe Maynes, Vermont's former director of tourism and until recently owner of the Heart of the Village B&B in nearby Shelburne. They joined forces here to bathe guests in Victorian grandeur and contemporary amenities before selling to Kim Borsavage, innkeeper with her sister, Patricia Redalieu.

Blessed with a corner turret, the three-story white clapboard house with white shutters holds nine guest rooms, one on the lower level claiming the only double whirlpool tub. A rear carriage barn adds two more guest rooms.

All rooms have queen or kingsize beds flounced with pillows, wing chairs, oriental rugs, armoires (the original closets were converted into bathrooms), TVs and telephones.

Front rooms like the king-bedded Allen Room are spacious; some others are smaller with only one chair and the bathroom vanity in the room. Decor is elegant and unfussy. The front-corner Captain Lyon Room has a sitting area in the turret, a kingsize bed with prim canopy and a colorfully wallpapered bathroom. Its turret yields a partial view of the lake in the distance. The sitting area in the turret of the third-floor Van Ness Room gets a full lake view.

On each dresser is a gaily decorated container marked "noise abatement program." Inside are ear plugs. The house adjoins the University of Vermont's Fraternity Row and, we're advised, weekend nights can get somewhat rowdy.

Breakfast is served at individual tables in the dining room or sunroom. The fare at our visit included a choice of scrambled eggs with prosciutto and asparagus in a popover or orange-macadamia nut pancakes.

(802 652-2500 or (877) 919-9799. Fax (802) 651-8717. www.langhouse.com. Eleven rooms with private baths. Doubles, $145 to $225.

Heart of the Village Inn, 5347 Shelburne Road, Box 953, Shelburne 05482.

An understated Queen Anne Victorian, built by a local merchant in 1886, is now the centerpiece of a thriving B&B. New owner Pat Button is continuing the tradition launched by Shelburne resident Bobbe Maynes, formerly Vermont's commissioner of tourism, who opened the B&B in 1997.

What had been a private home was converted into a five-room B&B, with plenty of main-floor common space. A rear carriage barn produced four more spacious, quieter accommodations away from the road.

The main house has two living rooms, a wraparound porch and a large dining room where four tables are set for breakfast, available from 8 to 10 o'clock. The sideboard is laden with muffins, fresh fruit, juices and granola. From the kitchen comes the day's main dish, perhaps maple toast cups holding a baked egg, garnished with dill and hollandaise sauce, or baked puff pancakes with Vermont maple syrup. Innkeeper Janice Carte employs recipes contained in Pat Button's *Heart of the Village Inn* cookbook.

The second floor of the house, listed on the National Register, holds five bedrooms. They range in size from the front Van Vliet master bedroom with king bed, armoire, bath in a former closet and sink in the room to a small rear room with the largest bath. TVs and telephones are available in each.

More deluxe quarters are available in the carriage barn. The king-bedded Bostwick is housed in an old horse stall in which you can see where the horses chewed around the windows. It is also notable for its original dark bead-board barn walls. Upstairs is the spacious Webb, with queen bed and a two-person whirlpool tub.

(802) 985-2800 or (877) 808-1834. Fax (802) 985-2870. www.heartofthevillage.com. Eight rooms and one suite with private baths. Doubles, $130 to $225, foliage $150 to $245.

Gourmet Destinations

Shelburne Museum, Route 7, Shelburne.

The incredible collections of Electra Havemeyer Webb, wife of a Vanderbilt heir, became the Shelburne Museum, and the resulting 39 exhibit buildings spread across a 45-acre heritage park fascinate young and old. The almost overwhelming display of Americana, unrivaled in New England, spans three centuries and a multitude of interests. People into things culinary will enjoy the kitchens in four restored homes, each with large open hearths full of gadgets that our ancestors used. The Weed House has a remarkable collection of pewter and glass, and the dining-room tables in the side-wheeler Ticonderoga are set with Syracuse china.

Altogether there are more than 80,000 pieces of Americana in this national treasure described by the New York Times as "Vermont's Smithsonian."

(802) 985-3346. www.shelburnemuseum.org. Open May-October, daily 10 to 5. Adults $18, children $9.

Shelburne Farms, 1611 Harbor Road, Shelburne.

The 1,400-acre agricultural estate of Dr. William Seward Webb and Lila Vanderbilt

Webb is open for the public to enjoy its farm landscape and historic buildings. Blessed with one of the more spectacular lakeside-mountain settings in the Northeast, Shelburne Farms combines an active dairy and cheese-making operation, a children's farmyard, walking trails, a bakery, a market garden, furniture-making and other leased enterprises in a working-farm setting that has a Camelot-like quality.

Ninety-minute guided tours leave from the Welcome Center after a multi-media slide introduction. Visitors board an open-air wagon to view the enormous Farm Barn, the Dairy Barn, the formal gardens and the Shelburne House, where they stop to tour a few of the public rooms. You may see grazing along the way the choice herd of brown Swiss cows, descended from stock raised for making cheese in Switzerland. Their Shelburne Farms farmhouse cheddar (the extra-sharp is one of the best cheddars we have ever tasted) is sold in the visitor center and farm store, where a fine shop also stocks other Vermont farm products and crafts and is open daily year-round.

Tea tours ($15) are scheduled Tuesday and Thursday afternoons for those with a special interest in the Shelburne House inn and gardens. Following tours, which include all public areas and the gardens, tea is served in the Tea Room.

(802) 985-8686. www.shelburnefarms.org. Open mid-May to mid-October, daily 10 to 5. Guided tours daily at 9:30, 11:30, 1:30 and 3:30, adults $9. Day pass, adults $6, children $4. Visitor center and walking trails open year-round.

Gourmet Treats

In Burlington, **Lake Champlain Chocolates** at 750 Pine St. produces some of the best chocolates in the Northeast. It's an outgrowth of Jim Lampman's original Ice House restaurant, where partner Richard Spurgeon was the baker who produced truffles that generated such demand that they branched into the chocolate enterprise in 1983. The relocated and expanded production area adjoins a showroom that smells like chocolate heaven. Production starts with Belgian chocolate but the addition of Vermont heavy cream and sweet butter and intense natural flavoring puts their creations "on a par with the best in the world," according to one food magazine. Among the latest treats are "Vermints," and factory seconds are offered at 40 percent off. A sampling is available downtown at 65 Church St., where a couple of guys making chocolate-covered strawberries attracted quite a crowd of passersby at our latest visit.

"Custom-built coffees" are the trademark of **Speeder & Earl's,** a high-tech, high-ceilinged space in black and white at 412 Pine St. Its boutique roastery and coffee bar are located here, while a small Speeder's coffee bar is situated downtown at 104 Church St. You'll find rare coffee roasts that are served plain, with foam and/or with flavored syrups. What are custom-built coffees? The menu answers: "Simply put, if you want hazelnut Italian syrup in a nonfat latte, with nonfat whipped cream topping, sprinkled with mint-flavored sugar, don't be shy. Just ask." Ask also for teas, Italian Italian sodas, biscotti and pastries.

The **Cheese Outlet/Fresh Market** at 400 Pine St. has evolved into a gourmet emporium with a café, bakery, a section of local produce, a specialty deli featuring good-looking salads, a European-style charcuterie, an olive bar and a case of all kinds of pasta, some with interesting fillings, where you can take as much or as little as you want. It remains northern New England's largest cheese and wine warehouse, with a selection of pâtés and cheeses, quiches and cheesecakes at bargain prices.

Desserts and pastries that turn up at the best parties in town come from **Mirabelles,** 198 Main St., a terrific bakery and deli created by Alison Lane and Andrew Silva and named for the golden plums grown on the Continent, where both had worked. Sandwiches are inspired, perhaps black forest ham and brie, artichoke pesto with vegetables or goat cheese with Mediterranean tapenade and vegetables, served on homemade wheat, sourdough and honey oat breads or a baguette. The ploughman's lunch is a sampling of cheeses, breads, fruits and a sweet. Finish with a raspberry butter tart, chocolate-raspberry mousse cake or a slice of cappuccino-truffle cake.

Another good spot for breakfast or lunch is **Penny Cluse Café,** housed in the quarters where Ben & Jerry's got its start at 169 Cherry St. Charles Reeves and Holly Cluse offer an extensive variety of tempting creations. Come here for huevos rancheros, breakfast burritos, tofu scramble, polenta and eggs or sourdough french toast. Flank steak on a grilled baguette is a lunchtime favorite.

The best breads in town come from **Klinger's Bread Company**, headquartered at 10 Farrell St. in South Burlington and with a small downtown sidewalk kiosk at Church and College streets. Designed to resemble a European village courtyard, complete with murals and a tiled roof, the bakery's Disneyesque display area dispenses countless varieties of breads, sandwiches and salads.

Those fabulous American Flatbread pizzas, produced for the gourmet trade in the Sugarbush Valley, are available now in Burlington. The first licensed **American Flatbread-Burlington Hearth** restaurant franchise is at 115 St. Paul St. Open daily for lunch and dinner, it features flatbreads fresh from the wood-fired clay oven as well as tasty homebrews made on site by brewmaster/co-owner Paul Sayler.

Overlooking the lakefront at 125 Battery St. is the **Burlington Bay Market & Café,** an upscale convenience store with a selection of deli salads, quiches, sandwiches and takeout dinners – even sushi. There are tables inside beside windows overlooking the lake, and four picnic tables outside. Down the street is the new **Cobblestone Café, Market and Deli,** billed as a place where yesterday and tomorrow meet for breakfast and lunch. The BLT&G (guacamole) proved an early favorite.

Turkish coffee, Italian espresso and homemade Bosnian breads and pastries are among the offerings at **Euro Gourmet,** a funky new Eastern European market and café at 61 Main St. The owners feature salads, panini and Balkan specialties, to eat here or to go.

Bennington Potters North, a multi-level emporium at 127 College St. in downtown Burlington, carries everything from the popular Vermont pottery to aprons to egg cups. Housed in an old warehouse restored with taste, it's enormous, and so is the selection.

A great downtown **City Market** at 82 South Winooski Ave. is run by the Onion River Co-op. The slick, high-ceilinged space is a supermarket of natural foods, produce categorized as "organic" and "conventional," baked goods, meats, wines and more. A deli offers sandwiches and a soup and salad bar.

Shelburne is home to the **Shelburne Country Store,** opposite the village green. It still sells penny candy but now also offers an upscale assortment of country things, accessories, kitchenware, homemade fudge and Vermont specialty foods, including its own line of chowders and finnan haddie.

"The world's best ham sandwich" is advertised at **Harrington's of Vermont,** Route 7, next to Café Shelburne. Headquartered in nearby Richmond, this has a café as well as everything for the kitchen from cookbooks to Cuisinarts. It sells a panoply of gourmet foods, including every kind of cracker imaginable.

Woodstock and Hanover

Quintessential New England

Woodstock, which has been called one of America's prettiest towns by National Geographic, is the quintessential New England village. Across the New Hampshire state line is Hanover, a quintessential New England college town.

Put them together and you have an extraordinary destination area for those who seek a New England potpourri, relatively unspoiled, even if highly sophisticated. Happily, both towns have escaped the commercial trappings that so often accompany tourism. The Rockefeller interests have enhanced much of Woodstock, even burying the utility wires in the center underground for a picture-perfect Currier and Ives look. Dartmouth College sets the character for Hanover. Both towns exude an aura of culture and class.

The attraction of the area is epitomized by historic Woodstock, where America's first ski tow was installed in 1934, propelling it into a winter sports mecca called "the St. Moritz of the East – without the Ritz." There's still no Ritz, although the Woodstock Inn and Resort built in 1969 by Rockefeller interests and the Twin Farms luxury hideaway that emerged in 1993 could qualify.

Also in 1934, Woodstock benefactor Laurance S. Rockefeller married Mary Billings French, granddaughter of railroad magnate Frederick Billings. Now the town's largest landowner and employer, until recently he lived about two months of the year in the mansion north of town that was once the home of conservationist George Perkins Marsh, the 19th-century ambassador and a founder of the Smithsonian. The Rockefellers are preserving the family heritage – and that of Vermont – in their Billings Farm & Museum. Their home and 550 acres of surrounding gardens and woodlands have been given to the National Park Service for preservation as the Marsh-Billings National Historical Park, the first to focus on conservation history and the changing nature of land stewardship in America.

A generation ago, chowders, boiled dinners and pumpkin pies were the fare served at the White Cupboard Inn – which closed in 1967 – and at the old Woodstock Inn, which was razed to make way for the flagship of RockResorts. "Had a patron requested chocolate mousse he probably would have been told that the pharmacy didn't carry those but they did have maple sugar candies shaped like Indians," a local magazine once wrote.

Today, the Woodstock and Hanover region abounds with restaurants and inns appealing to diverse tastes.

Dining

The Best of the Best

Barnard Inn Restaurant, 5518 Route 12, Barnard, Vt.

Its red-brick facade accented by four white pillars and surrounded by mighty trees, the Barnard Inn is a handsome, two-story structure dating to 1796. It really is out in the country, ten miles north of Woodstock almost at the "back of beyond." But its fans consider the distance a trifle to be put up with for a meal at a restaurant they tout as one of the best in Vermont.

Innovative new American cuisine is its forte under new owners Will Dodson and

All is elegant and historic in Barnard Inn's main dining room.

Ruth Schimmelpfennig, Culinary Institute of America graduates who had operated two neighborhood restaurants – one Italian and one French – in the Russian Hill section of San Francisco.

The husband-and-wife team lightened up the decor in four cozy, elegantly Colonial dining rooms and added a tavern menu to the charming Max's Tavern in back, named for their first-born son. They also made the menu less daunting, while retaining continental overtones. "Our whole style about a restaurant is approachability," Will explained.

Dinner is prix-fixe ($55 to $65 for three or four courses) in the main dining rooms and à la carte in the tavern. From the kitchen comes the inn's longtime specialty, roast duckling, the presentation varying but on a recent winter menu pairing medium-rare breast of muscovy duck and a duck leg confit with a classic glace de volaille accented with maple syrup. Other entrées included pan-seared escolar with lemon-caper-herb butter, sesame-seared ahi tuna with ginger-soy glaze and filet of beef with cabernet demi-glace.

Dinner might begin with tomato bisque flavored with Vermont cheddar, butternut squash soup laced with crabmeat and herbs or a Greek salad. The second course could yield Asian pork dumplings with ponzu sauce, soft-shell crab with cilantro-lime mayonnaise or duck pâté on toast points.

Finish with Ruth's signature Tahitian vanilla crème brûlée, frozen grand marnier soufflé with blackberry sauce, a dark and white chocolate bread pudding with butter-pecan ice cream, or a trio of grapefruit-campari, lemon zest and mango sorbets.

Dinner in the tavern is a pleasant mix of the innovative and comfort food, from crab and scallop cakes with jalapeño mayo and Thai chili sauce to yankee pot roast ("the real deal") and von Schimmelpfennig wiener schnitzel.

The 200-choice wine list is as well considered as the rest of the fare.

(802) 234-9961. www.barnardinnrestaurant.com. Prix-fixe, $55 to $65. Dinner by reservation, Tuesday-Saturday from 6, Thursday-Saturday in off-season. Tavern (no reservations), entrées, $13 to $21, Tuesday-Saturday 5 to 8:30.

The Prince and the Pauper, 24 Elm St., Woodstock, Vt.

Walk up the brick walkway alongside one of the area's oldest buildings, open the green door, pass the cocktail lounge with the shiniest wood bar you ever saw and enter the intimate, L-shaped dining room. You're in what is considered to be the best restaurant in Woodstock proper.

Oil lanterns cast shadows on beamed ceilings and pink-clothed tables are surrounded by Hitchcock chairs or tucked away in high, dark wood booths, the ultimate in privacy. Antique prints decorate the white walls, one of which has a shelf of old books.

Chef-owner Chris Balcer calls his cuisine "creative contemporary" with French, continental and international accents. The prix-fixe menu ($44, for appetizer, salad and main course) changes frequently. The soup of the day could be billi-bi or Moroccan lentil, the pasta perhaps ravioli stuffed with house-smoked duck and ricotta cheese, and the crêpes stuffed with lobster and seafood in a nantua sauce. Other appetizers could be maple-cured smoked rainbow trout with raifort sauce and crispy Vietnamese vegetable spring rolls with soy-ginger dipping sauce.

The six entrées range from prosciutto-wrapped baked halibut with a sundried tomato-basil beurre blanc to filet mignon au poivre. Crisp roast duckling with a sauce of kiwi and rum and sautéed veal medallions finished with applejack brandy and crème fraîche are typical options. The specialty is boneless rack of New Zealand lamb baked in puff pastry with spinach and mushroom duxelles.

Save room for dessert – maybe a fabulous raspberry tart with white chocolate mousse served with raspberry-cabernet wine sauce, cappuccino cheesecake, or a homemade sorbet like Jack Daniels-chocolate chip. Finish with espresso or an international coffee. The award-winning wine list is particularly strong on California chardonnays and cabernets.

A bistro menu is available in the elegant lounge. Grilled rainbow trout, curried chicken and lamb shanks osso buco are typical offerings. Also offered here are five kinds of hearth-baked pizzas.

(802) 457-1818. www.princeandpauper.com. Prix-fixe, $44. Dinner nightly, 6 to 9 or 9:30. Bistro, entrées, $17 to $20, nightly 5 to 10 or 11.

Carpenter & Main, 326 Main St., Norwich, Vt.

As a teenager in Norwich, Peter Ireland pushed donuts at Lou's Bakery, washed dishes at Café la Fraise and sold gourmet mustards at Bentley's across the river in Hanover. Following graduation from Williams College, he trained at leading restaurants in New York, Chicago and a Michelin three-star in Vonnas, France. But he returned to his roots to open a restaurant.

He had a ready-made void to fill in the Norwich-Hanover area. The space that once housed the beloved Carpenter Street Restaurant was available following the demise of La Poule à Dents, a high-style French restaurant that suffered from Texas braggadocio. Peter and his wife Rebecca toned down the Victorian decor to let the building speak for itself and brought the French fare back down to earth, favoring ingredients from the local terroir.

Although his background is in French cuisine, he says his "heart and soul are pure Vermont." He infuses classic French dishes with local flavor, as in a spring appetizer of house pâté with pickled ramps and candied rhubarb and main courses of free-range chicken glazed with maple syrup and Vermont-raised veal with morels and asparagus.

Recessed alcove holds table for two in fireplaced dining room at Carpenter & Main.

He necessarily goes farther afield in other seasons. A fall menu offers appetizers like quail confit with pickled peaches and shaved fois gras, a fricassee of escargots with a pair of garlic and parsley purees, and a fallen potato soufflé with a cheese custard center and a mesclun salad. Main courses range from poached halibut with eggplant caviar, tomato compote, green olive tapenade and sautéed spinach to bourbon-glazed pork tenderloin with creamy garlic polenta and broccoli rabe. A traditional Marseilles bouillabaisse and Vermont grass-fed beef are menu staples. Vegetarians are well satisfied with a baby pumpkin filled with chestnut custard, sautéed spinach with caramelized onions, quinoa and roasted cauliflower.

Rebecca Ireland oversees the wine list and prepares the extravagant desserts. Typical are coffee pots de crème with candied fall fruits, warm chocolate cake with rum ice cream, a terrine of homemade sorbets with citrus tuiles, a plate of exotic cookies and a couple of updated childhood revivals: ice cream sandwiches (with chocolate cookies and three ice creams) and a vanilla ice cream sundae with valrhona chocolate sauce, walnut praline, brandied cherries and whipped cream.

All these treats are served in three comfortable dining areas set with fine linens. A handsome oak bar flanks a casual, post-and-beam, bistro-style dining area with vivid persimmon walls accented with modern art. Two smaller dining rooms are more formal, one painted butterscotch and the other a soft café au lait with white trim. The latter harbors a couple of romantic recessed alcoves, just big enough for two.

Most of the night's appetizers show up with light entrées on an appealing tavern menu, offered in the bar area.

(802) 649-2922. www.carpenterandmain.com. Entrées, $23 to $26. Dinner, Thursday-Monday 6 to 9. Tavern menu, $8 to $13, Thursday-Monday 5:30 to 10.

Hemingway's, 4988 U.S. Route 4, Sherburne, Vt.

The restored, 19th-century Asa Briggs farmhouse has been earning culinary accolades since Linda and Ted Fondulas moved over from Annabelle's in Stockbridge in the early 1980s.

Antiques, locally crafted furniture, fresh flowers from Linda's gardens and original oil paintings, watercolors and sculpture enhance the decor in each of three dining rooms. A European feeling is effected in the formal, peach-colored dining room with dark upholstered chairs and sparkling chandeliers. A colorful accent here is the life-size painting of Ted relaxing at table, his prize for winning the Robert Mondavi Culinary Award of Excellence for 2001. A fire is often blazing in the hearth in the smaller garden room done up in white and pink with brick floors, pierced lamps on the walls and ivy adorning the windows overlooking patio and herb garden. Most unusual is a charming, secluded wine cellar with stone walls and four tables set with hand-crocheted cloths and elaborate candlesticks.

These are diverse settings for ever-changing, new American fare that made Hemingway's the first four-star, four-diamond restaurant in northern New England. An additional accolade came when Food & Wine magazine ranked it among the top 25 restaurants in America. Hemingway's also is known for its monthly food and wine tastings featuring wine experts as guest speakers. The Fondulases stock more than 175 wine selections, at prices from $20 to $200.

Dinner is prix-fixe, $65 for three courses. Also available are a four-course vegetarian tasting menu ($55) and, with prior notice, a vegan tasting menu.

Four or five choices are available in each category for the main option. You might start with the signature cream of garlic soup, a fallen Vermont goat cheese soufflé with mache and endive, roast quail with Chinese sausage and baby bok choy or a risotto of pheasant, exotic mushrooms and truffles.

The main course could be wild bass with lobster essence, slow-roasted breast of duck with duck confit strudel, pork tenderloin with cheddar polenta or sirloin of beef and braised ribs with a thyme-scented potato pie.

Typical desserts are venetian chocolate cake with caramel sauce, autumn fruit soup with cranberry-orange sorbet, warm apple tart with almonds and maple cream or "local anything," says Linda, whose husband oversees the kitchen. The chef gets his herbs from a garden out back, and scented geraniums might turn up as a garnish.

(802) 422-3886. www.hemingwaysrestaurant.com. Prix fixe, $65. Dinner, Wednesday-Sunday 6 to 10. Closed mid-April to mid-May and early November.

Simon Pearce Restaurant, 1760 Main St., Quechee, Vt.

Irish glassblower Simon Pearce's intriguing mill complex includes a restaurant serving Irish and eclectic regional specialties with global accents in a smashing setting beside the Ottauquechee River.

The interior dining areas, vastly expanded over the years, reflect the exquisite taste of the entire complex. Sturdy ash chairs are at well-spaced wood tables dressed with small woven mats by day and white linens at night. The heavy glassware and the deep brown and white china are made by Simon Pearce and his family at the mill. Plants, dried flowers in baskets and antique quilts lend a soft counterpoint to the brick walls and bare wood floors. Through large windows you get a view of the river, hills rising beyond. An enclosed terrace with retractable full-length windows opening to the outside is almost over the falls and offers the tables of choice year-round.

Arched windows give diners view of waterfall outside Simon Pearce Restaurant.

The chefs train at Ballymaloe in Ireland, and they import flour from Ireland to make their great Irish soda bread and Ballymaloe brown bread. They change the menu periodically, but there are usually such specialties as shepherd's pie and beef and Guinness stew (which we tried at lunch – for $12.50, a generous serving of fork-tender beef and vegetables, plus a small side salad of julienned vegetables). We also liked a pasta salad heaped with vegetables and a superior basil-parmesan dressing and a Mediterranean lamb burger with a roasted pepper and feta salad. One of us nearly always orders the mouth-watering smoked salmon with crème fraîche. For dessert, the walnut meringue with strawberry sauce and whipped cream is unsurpassed. A menu fixture, it's crisp and crunchy, yet melts in the mouth. Irish apple cake, profiteroles and white chocolate mousse cake with raspberry sauce are other possibilities.

At night, dinner by candlelight might start with Maine crab and scallop mousse cakes with mango lychee relish and red miso vinaigrette, crispy ginger calamari with wasabi drizzle or grilled pheasant sausage with a lingonberry-pomegranate sauce. Entrées range from pan-seared wild salmon sauced with grain mustard to grilled filet mignon with cassis-port wine sauce. Other choices might be horseradish-crusted cod with crispy leeks, roast duckling with mango chutney and peppercorn-seared rack of venison with cherry-brandy sauce.

The wine list has won Wine Spectator's best of award of excellence. Naturally, you can get beers and ales from the British Isles. You also can buy loaves of the restaurant's wonderful breads and flavored vinaigrettes.

(802) 295-1470. www.simonpearce.com. Entrées, $25 to $38. Lunch daily, 11:30 to 2:45. Dinner nightly by reservation, 6 to 9.

More Dining Choices

Three Tomatoes Trattoria, 1 Court St., Lebanon, N.H.

Pizzas from a wood-burning oven, pastas, and entrées from a wood and charcoal grill at wallet-pleasing prices. These are the hallmarks of a sleek but casual, New

Yorkish place that became an early dining sensation of the Upper Valley, across from the green in oft-overlooked Lebanon.

Occupying the key front corner space of a new downtown commercial complex, this was the brainchild of James Reiman, who was formerly at the Prince and the Pauper and opened Spooner's in Woodstock, and Robert Meyers, a builder whose experience was pivotal in putting the space together. And it's quite a space. Seats for 100 are at tables placed well apart under mod California spotlights, their neon-like rims echoing the neon encircling the exposed metal grid beneath a high black ceiling. Tall windows, a black and white tiled floor, a few indoor trees, a mural along one wall, a tin mobile and plants hanging on pillars complete the minimalist decor.

Excitement is provided by the totally open kitchen, where the owners sometimes join the cooks at the grills, wood-burning oven and work counters amidst garlic ropes hanging from on high. Theirs is what Robert calls "strictly ethnic Italian cooking, priced for the times." You'll find pastas like linguini with shrimp and sweet peas or fusilli with chicken and artichoke hearts, and pizzas from the namesake sweet tomato pie to one with fresh clams.

Entrées include grilled chicken with herbs, skewers of marinated lamb, rainbow trout stuffed with bay shrimp and crabmeat, and, our choice, grilled swordfish with basil pesto, served with a side salad of red potatoes, peas, leeks and garlic.

We thoroughly enjoyed the cavatappi with roasted chicken, plum tomatoes and arugula, a memorable concoction served with two slices of herbed sourdough bread and cheese sprinkled liberally from a hand grater. The enormous clam pizza, its thin crackly crust weighted down with clams and mozzarella, proved too much to eat at one sitting. We had to forego the delectable desserts, which included chocolate-espresso cake, cannolis and dacquoise.

Success here led the partners to open carbon copies in downtown Burlington and Rutland, Vt.

(603) 448-1711. Entrées, $8.95 to $14.95. Lunch, Monday-Friday 11:30 to 2. Dinner nightly, 5 to 9 or 9:30.

Canoe Club, 27 South Main St., Hanover, N.H.

There's no sign, they don't advertise and yet folks of all ages flock to this sprightly newcomer in a section of the Dartmouth Co-op building. "It's all word of mouth," says owner John Chapin, a prominent Hartford area restaurateur who "retired" in 1989 to raise his family and serve as a lobbyist in Connecticut. He resurfaced fifteen years later in Hanover, opening a multi-faceted restaurant, lounge and jazz club that's a larger-scale reprise of his hugely popular Hartford restaurant, Shenanigans, and its musical successor, Lloyd's.

Two large rooms – a bar/lounge and a dining room with a music stage near the front window – seat a total of 130. Blue-clothed tables topped with white butcher paper are surrounded in an updated lodge look by memorabilia from the owner's Hartford Canoe Club affiliation and from the summers his children were camp counselors at nearby Vermont lakes Fairlee and Morey.

The average age of his clientele "drops eight years an hour from 6 to midnight," John calculates, as octogenarians yield to Dartmouth College graduate students. They come for the live music offered 363 days a year as well as for the eclectic food served at lunch, dinner and Sunday brunch.

"I want the food to surprise people," says John, whose food was always well received in Connecticut. His kitchen staff produces such grown-up appetizers as a

Restaurateur John Chapin awaits patrons in main Canoe Club dining room.

shrimp and baby corn cake with smoky rémoulade, artichoke and cheddar fondue with onion crostinis, a wild mushroom tart with pear essence and brie, and Vermont baby quail stuffed with cranberries, barley and wild rice.

Not for a college drinking crowd are main courses ranging from Atlantic salmon with cranberry cream and tarragon basmati to New Zealand venison chops with a juniper demi-glace. Others could be crispy duckling with a shallot-pear glaze, organic chicken stuffed with artichokes and gruyère, and top sirloin of lamb with roasted fennel jus.

Artisanal cheeses vie for attention with homemade ice creams and sorbets on the dessert list. Options could be Vermont goat cheese cheesecake with huckleberry sauce, vanilla bean crème brûlée, warm apple galette, and spiced poached pear with orange crème fraîche, candied ginger and toasted almonds. The sweet treats include house-made biscotti and hand-rolled truffles.

Twenty-four draft beers, a dozen varieties of martinis, small-batch bourbons and single-malt scotches tend to overshadow a short but well-chosen wine list.

(603) 643-9660. www.canoeclub.us. Entrées, $20 to $29. Lunch, 11:30 to 2. Dinner nightly, 5:30 to 9:30 or 10.

Bentleys, 3 Elm St., Woodstock, Vt.

This casual, engaging and often noisy place at the prime corner in Woodstock caters to every taste at every hour. It serves lunch, dinner and Sunday brunch, has dancing on weekends, and there's a great bar to visit in cold weather for a hot buttered rum or a Bentley burner (hot apple cider, brandy, ginger and cinnamon).

On two levels, the eclectic space is filled with jungles of plants, bentwood chairs, oriental rugs, antique lamps and cozy alcoves with Victorian sofas. At lunch it offers all kinds of burgers, sandwiches (some in croissants), chili, Mexican dishes and salads. We enjoyed the specialty French tart, a hot puff pastry filled with vegetables in an egg and cheese custard, and a fluffy quiche with turkey, mushrooms and snow peas, both accompanied by side salads. From the dessert tray came a delicate chocolate mousse cake with layers of meringue, like a torte, served with the good Green Mountain coffee in clear glass cups.

At brunch, try a bellini (champagne with the essence of peaches) before eggs benedict, a woodlands frittata with wild mushrooms and shallots, or salade niçoise.

Appetizers, salads, sandwiches and light entrées such as sausage crespolini and cold sliced marinated flank steak make up half the dinner menu. The other side offers more hearty fare from fillet of Alaskan salmon with a dill-aioli crust to maple-mustard chicken to pepper-crusted sirloin steak flamed tableside with Yukon Jack bourbon.

Partners Bill Decklebaum and David Creech also run **FireStones,** featuring a wood-fired oven, in Waterman Place at Quechee. Transformed from their former Rosalita's, a Southwestern bar and grill, this offers flatbreads, pastas and grills ($13.95 to $18.95) in an Adirondack lodge atmosphere and on an outdoor rooftop deck.

The owners also operate **The Willows at Barnard,** a stunning new function facility north of Woodstock.

(802) 457-3232 or (877) 457-3232. www.bentleysrestaurant.com. Entrées, $14.95 to $21.95. Lunch. Monday-Saturday 11:30 to 3 (late lunch menu, 3 to 5). Dinner nightly, 5 to 9:30 (late dinner to 11). Sunday brunch, 11 to 3.

Tuscan Treat

Osteria Pane e Salute, 61 Central St., Woodstock, Vt.

This true little osteria got its start as an Italian bakery named for "bread and health." But the weekend dinners that Caleb Barber and his wife Deirdre Heekin offered as a supplement proved to be the tail that wagged the dog. They gradually phased out the bakery and stopped serving lunch to expand their dinner business to five nights a week.

Caleb, who apprenticed at a bakery south of Florence, does the baking and cooking, while his wife manages the front of the house and sells fresh breads and pizzas to go.

The menu of Italian country fare changes weekly, offering a handful of choices for each of four courses (prix-fixe, $36, or à la carte). A meal typically begins with assorted vegetable antipasti and perhaps grilled onions with ricotta cheese and toast or an endive salad with gorgonzola and walnuts. The main course could be tiger shrimp steamed with zucchini, Sicilian veal and pork stew or handmade pasta with portobello and porcini mushroom sauce. Dinner might end with pears poached in pernod, an apple-almond tart, profiteroles or the house selection of three cheeses.

Fifteen versions of Tuscan pizzas are available, as are beer and wine.

The couple have published some of their favorites in *Pane e Salute: Recipes and Recollections from a Classic Italian Osteria,* a small but choice cookbook with essays on life in Tuscany.

(802) 457-4882. Prix-fixe, $36. Entrées, $18 to $20. Dinner, Thursday-Monday 6 to 9.

Dining and Lodging

Home Hill French Inn & Restaurant, 703 River Road, Plainfield, N.H. 03781.

In the mood for France but have neither the time nor the desire to fly? You can get

Fireplace warms dining room at Home Hill Country Inn & Restaurant.

a taste of Provence at this lovable place along the undulating Connecticut River south of West Lebanon. Inspired by the country auberges found in the South of France, Marseilles native Stephane du Roure and his American-born wife Victoria run a Relais & Châteaux inn that's as close as you can get to the real thing without being abroad.

On 25 rural acres with a swimming pool and reflecting pond, Home Hill is quiet, refined and polished. It was so quiet that we slept far past our planned awakening in the Maxfield Parrish suite in the 1818 Federal house with two blazing gas fireplaces and a living room as big as the bedroom. And, as Stephane advised, people come here to get away "so there are no TVs or telephones anywhere to disturb them." Otherwise, there are all the comforts of a well-endowed home in five upstairs accommodations furnished with antiques in rather formal country French style. The queensize beds are triple-sheeted and dressed with fabric crown canopies that coordinate with the window treatments. Oriental rugs grace the hardwood floors. One bathroom still contains an original toilet and a bidet. Frette towels and linens and L'Occitane toiletries cast a European spell.

Out back in the expanded carriage house are six more rooms, three with fireplaces. La Piscine, a seasonal cottage with queen bed and white wicker-decorated sitting room, is situated behind the swimming pool. The property also includes a tennis court, bocce court, putting green and restored gardens, as well as a corral for the owners' horses and polo ponies.

A basket of fresh fruit and bottled water welcome guests upon arrival. A country French continental breakfast is served in the morning, as is tea in the afternoon.

The main floor of the recently expanded inn contains a fireplaced living room, a library/lounge with another fireplace and a reception room with a small gift shop specializing in provençal toiletries and handmade dishes like the monogrammed chargers custom-designed for the inn by a Frenchman in Moustier Ste.-Marie.

The soul of the operation is the new dining room, gorgeous in provençal reds and yellows with a large fireplace and a vaulted ceiling. Chef Victoria, who trained at the Ritz Escoffier in Paris and with celebrity chef Bradley Ogden in California, offers contemporary French cuisine with California accents. Her seasonal menus are as ambitious as they come, reflecting her determination to serve nothing but the best, even having fish sent overnight from France for her classic bouillabaisse. Dinner is available à la carte, but most people order one of the prix-fixe dinners, the six-course vegetarian tasting menu for $59 or the chef's six-course dégustation menu for $89 ($154 with wines). A new bistro menu of country French classics ($16 to $18) is available in the lounge and a private dining room.

Our dinner began with a couple of complimentary canapés with drinks – caramelized fennel and tapenade with fromage blanc. One appetizer was chilled belon oysters interestingly counterpointed with warm savoy cabbage, periwinkles and littleneck clams. Another was delicious house-made raviolis of artichokes, goat cheese and aromatic vegetables. Seared foie gras enriched a salad of baby arugula with braised fennel and warm grapes poached in olive oil.

A dollop of homemade green apple sorbet prepared the palate for the main courses, which ranged from seared sea scallops on a bed of oxtail ragoût with roasted root vegetables to roasted breast of squab and confit legs finished with zesty whole grain mustard sauce. We were well satisfied with the house cassoulet of duck and rabbit confit, braised lamb leg, country sausage and white beans, and the juniper-scented venison with creamy parsnip puree and black truffle sauce.

After sampling a couple of French and local cheeses as we finished a bottle of côtes du rhone from a pricey, predominantly French wine list, we adjourned to the library/lounge for dessert and espresso. The former was a masterful tarte tatin with crème fraîche. Instead of brandy, Stephane suggested Glenmorangie single-malt scotch aged in port wood. For a Frenchman to recommend that over cognac, he said, it has to be very good. It was. So is Home Hill.

(603) 675-6165. Fax (603) 675-5220. www.homehillinn.com. Ten rooms, one suite and one cottage with private baths. Doubles, $235 to $425. Suite and cottage, $425.

Entrées, $34 to $38. Dinner, Wednesday-Sunday from 6.

The Jackson House Inn, 114-3 Senior Lane, Woodstock, Vt. 05091.

Elaborate accommodations. Fabulous appetizers with complimentary champagne. Extravagant breakfasts. We didn't think a B&B could get much better than this. But recent owners turned it into an inn – adding four luxury rooms, an acclaimed dining room open to the public, and a higher level of service.

The pride of the expanded Jackson House is its restaurant, housed in a rear addition with a cathedral-ceilinged dining room harboring big windows onto four acres of gardens. Well-spaced tables are flanked by chairs handcrafted by Charles Shackleton, a local furniture maker. The focal point is a soaring, see-through open-hearth fireplace of Pennsylvania granite. A stone mason laid it slab by slab, a laborious process that took three weeks and appears so natural one wonders how it's held together.

Executive chef Jason Merrill, who returned to his native state from chef stints in Arizona, added contemporary flair to the New England regional cuisine. Dinner is prix-fixe ($55 for three courses and $70 for four), with several choices for each course. The chef's seven-course tasting menu goes for $95.

Open-hearth granite fireplace is focal point of dining room at The Jackson House Inn.

A typical dinner might start with sweet corn and leek chowder or tempura-fried soft-shell crab. Main courses range from East Coast wild striped bass with a charred tomato vinaigrette to Ninan Ranch grilled tenderloin with red wine demi-glace and chanterelle mushroom ragoût.

Dinner actually begins for inn guests in the elegant living room and library, where complimentary champagne and wine accompany an elaborate buffet of hors d'oeuvre. And we mean elaborate. One occasion produced California rolls, curried grilled chicken with diced green apple on a chickpea flour crisp and prosciutto-wrapped black mission figs. Our latest yielded a remarkable seared salmon and frisée salad atop a wafer, alsatian-style onion tarts, and phyllo-wrapped brandade and root vegetable mash.

Later, the tasting dinner in the candlelit dining room opened with appetizers of pan-seared diver scallops with belgian endive and parsnip purée, and pheasant confit and wild mushroom crepinette with a young field green salad. The main courses, designed to showcase a masterful 1996 echezeaux from Labouré-Roi in Burgundy, were slow-braised short ribs of beef with an oxtail croquette and achiote-rubbed lamb loin with black beans, roasted poblano and chayote squash. These riches were topped off by a warm liquid-center chocolate cake with white chocolate ice cream and cardamom-ginger crème brûlée.

Fortunately, we had only to toddle off to Clara's Corner in another wing, where more chocolates awaited on the pillows. It's one of four large deluxe rooms there with corner gas fireplaces, sitting areas and modern bathrooms with whirlpool or massage therapy tubs, separate showers and cherry floors. The queensize Sheraton poster bed was topped with red and gold Anichini fabrics and a sheeted duvet.

Antique pots and vases graced the shelves, and an array of antique pillboxes topped a lace doily on a side table. There were fresh flowers, assorted fruits for nibbling and replacement towels at turndown. The staff even produced a new toothbrush for the one that had been forgotten.

Each of the deluxe rooms is different, as are nine second-floor rooms in the original inn, where the eclectic decor varies from French Empire to British Oriental to old New England. The third floor has been converted into two large one-room "suites" with queensize cherry sleigh beds, Italian marble baths and french doors onto a rear balcony overlooking the spectacular gardens.

The treats continue in the morning. The buffet might be laden with homemade granola, spiced pear yogurt and an array of sliced fruit. Juices, scones, croissants and muffins come next. The main course in one case was a scrambled egg and country sausage tart with goat cheese. Others could be ricotta pancakes, brioche french toast or – one we'll never forget – poached eggs on dill biscuits with poached salmon and hollandaise sauce.

After all this, settle into a deep wing chair in the library or retire to a lounge chair around the pond in the landscaped back yard for a morning nap. Or work it off in a small spa located on the lower level. It includes exercise equipment and a steam room.

(802) 457-2065 or (800) 448-1890. Fax (802) 457-9290. www.jacksonhouse.com. Nine rooms and six suites with private baths. Doubles, $195 to $260. Suites, $295 to $390. Prix-fixe, $55. Dinner by reservation, Wednesday-Sunday 6 to 9.

Woodstock Inn & Resort, 14 The Green, Woodstock, Vt. 05091.

The biggest institution in town, this is a full-service resort for those who want everything from sumptuous accommodations to the best recreational facilities. The inn faces the village green, a covered bridge and mountains, and the back looks across a pool and putting green and down the valley toward the resort's golf course and ski touring center. Other leisure facilities include the Suicide Six ski area, ten tennis courts, lighted paddle tennis courts, and an indoor sports and fitness center.

Built by Rockresorts in 1969 after Laurance Rockefeller found the original Woodstock Inn beyond salvation, the interior contains a lobby warmed by a ten-foot-high stone fireplace around which people always seem to be gathered, a comfy library paneled in barnwood, and a wicker sunroom and lounge where afternoon tea is served. The 144 guest accommodations are among the more comfortable in which we've stayed: spacious rooms with handmade quilts on the beds, upholstered chairs, three-way reading lights, television, and large bathrooms and closets. The most luxurious rooms are 34 in the newer rear brick tavern wing, 23 with fireplaces and three with sitting-room porches overlooking the putting green. They are notable for graceful reading alcoves, TVs on wheels hidden in cupboards, mini-refrigerators and double marble vanities in the bathrooms.

The long, semi-circular main dining room, lately doubled in size, has large windows onto a spacious outdoor terrace overlooking the pool, putting green and gardens. Dinner is served nightly, the contemporary fare ranging from grilled ahi tuna steak with black trumpet mushrooms to port-glazed duck breast with summer truffles and pistachio-crusted lamb loin with roasted garlic pan jus. The elaborate Sunday buffet brunch is enormously popular. The stylish **Eagle Café** offers a more casual lunch or dinner. We've enjoyed interesting salads and, most recently, smoked chicken and green onion quesadillas and a grilled chicken sandwich with melted jack, roasted

Spring flowers brighten entrance to Woodstock Inn & Resort.

peppers and herbed mayonnaise on toasted focaccia. Stop for a drink or light fare in the sophisticated Richardson's Tavern, as urbane a nightspot as you'll find in Vermont.

(802) 457-1100 or (800) 448-7900. Fax (802) 457-6699. www.woodstockinn.com. One hundred thirty-three rooms and nine suites with private baths. Rates, EP. Doubles, $255 to $434. Suites, $564 to $664. March-April and November to mid-December: doubles $139 to $278, suites $360 to $460.

Entrées, $21.95 to $31.95. Lunch, 11:30 to 2. Dinner, 6 to 9. Sunday brunch, 10 to 1.

The Hanover Inn, Main Street, Box 151, Hanover, N.H. 03755.

As its advertising claims, this venerable inn is really "an elegant small hotel." Facing the Dartmouth College green, the five-story, 19th-century brick structure contains 92 Colonial-style rooms decorated with period furniture, handmade lampshades and eiderdown comforters. Hand-tied quilts, coordinating window treatments and Crabtree & Evelyn bath amenities are the norm.

The older East Wing has been remodeled to make the rooms larger and more comfortable, like those of the West Wing. An expanded lobby and a new front entrance are the latest in a continuing series of renovations.

Veteran executive chef Michael Gray, whose credentials include the old Rarities in Cambridge and Seasons in Boston, oversees a menu of contemporary American cuisine, described as "simply prepared but with adventurous twists."

Dining is in the elegant Daniel Webster Room or the more intimate **Zins Winebistro,** a warm and mellow wine bar and bistro transformed from the rather New Yorkish-looking former Ivy Grill. The two-level grill has interesting angles, curves, arches and alcoves to go with a menu of "wine-friendly food."

The Zins menu changes weekly, even daily. A chilly autumn day's offerings appealed enough to entice us in for lunch, despite an alert from previous visitors that the menu reads better than it delivers. Alas, they were right. The staff was in training and had to depart for answers to every question, which did not help matters. We asked for bread – and bread we eventually got, two slices that looked like Wonderbread (a waiter later advised that he had gone AWOL to scrounge up some rolls from the neighboring Daniel Webster Room but they had run out). From the cup of "white bean soup with vegetables" that tasted like lukewarm water with a few beans in it to "Sunja's vegetable roll" that was burnt to a crisp, one meal was a travesty. The other was marginally better, the lobster and crab ravioli at least tasting of seafood but upstaged by the tasty julienned vegetables in the middle. For dinner, the menu offers an interesting selection of "apps and salads," small plates, dinner plates, pastas, flatbreads and burgers.

More formal meals are served in the gracious, gray and white **Daniel Webster Room,** a vast space in the Georgian style with potted palms, brass chandeliers, and changing food and wine displays at the entry. While Zins is designed for a modern crowd, this is the dining venue of choice for Dartmouth alums of a certain age, although again the menu tells a different story. Typical among dinner entrées are soy-seared tuna with wasabi, sautéed sweetbreads with a lemon-caper beurre blanc, rabbit two ways (braised leg and macadamia-crusted loin), and grilled venison with dried cherries and port wine sauce.

The wine list is among New Hampshire's more extensive.

In season, meals from both restaurants are available on a shady outdoor terrace overlooking the Dartmouth green. Canvas umbrellas, planters and tiny white lights in the trees make it a most engaging spot.

(603) 643-4300 or (800) 443-7024. Fax (603) 646-3744. www.hanoverinn.com. Ninety-two rooms and junior suites with private baths. Doubles, $260 to $310.

Daniel Webster Room, entrées $23 to $30. Lunch, Monday-Friday 11:30 to 1:30. Dinner, Tuesday-Saturday 6 to 9. Sunday brunch, 11:30 to 1:30.

Zins, entrées $15.50 to $19.25. Open Monday-Saturday 11:30 to 10, Sunday 5:30 to 10.

Kedron Valley Inn, Route 106, South Woodstock, Vt. 05071.

This historic inn in the hamlet of South Woodstock, the heart of Vermont's horse country, has long been a favorite of the equestrian set as well as others seeking a rural setting. New innkeepers Jack and Nicole Maiden redecorated the public rooms, installed a long bar in the tavern to make it more of a pub and started updating the guest rooms.

Accommodations include thirteen rooms in the three-story inn dating to the 1830s, seven in the old tavern building, and six out back in the motel-style log lodge rechristened the Country Cottages. Most rooms have canopy beds covered with antique quilts or down duvets. Twenty have fireplaces or wood stoves, and five have whirlpool tubs. All have TV/VCRs and Bose radios. The largest rooms and suites generally are in the tavern building, where day beds or pullout sofas can accommodate the families who flock to the place. A full country breakfast, from omelets to blueberry pancakes, is served in the sunny terrace room. Above the inn is a spring-fed pond for swimming. Lawn chairs are scattered about to take in the view of cows grazing on the hillside. Equestrians can rent horses in nearby stables, and the inn can arrange horse and buggy rides or horse-drawn sleigh rides.

The new owners redecorated the main dining room in Polo/Ralph Lauren equestrian decor and created an inviting tavern/pub with a tavern menu. Guests relax on plush sofas and chairs beside a fireplace in the tavern before or after dinner, which is served at white-clothed tables lit by candles in hurricane lamps in the beamed dining room and outside on a porch in season. Chef Mark McInnis oversees a changing menu that ranges from prosciutto-wrapped cod to grilled filet mignon with a roasted garlic-wine demi-glace. The inn's signature salmon stuffed with an herbed seafood mousse and wrapped in puff pastry is superb. We also were impressed with a special of baked pheasant stuffed with local chèvre and topped with roasted macadamia nut butter. The tavern menu offers five kinds of burgers and a handful of entrées like fish and chips and turkey pot pie.

(802) 457-1473 or (800) 836-1193. Fax (802) 457-4469. www.kedronvalleyinn.com. Twenty-one rooms, six suites and one cottage with private baths. Doubles, $133 to $223. Suites, $250 to $299. Foliage and holidays: doubles $201 to $291, suites $317 to $365.

Entrées, $22 to $29. Dinner, Thursday-Monday 6 to 9, nightly August-October. Tavern from 5, entrées $8.50 to $15.95.

Twin Peaks

Twin Farms, Barnard, Vt. 05031.

For the ultimate in food and lodging, jet-setters from across the world converge on the pastoral, 300-acre farm once owned by writers Sinclair Lewis and Dorothy Thompson, now the East's most sumptuous small country resort. One of a kind, it offers ten suites and ten cottages, superb dining and a staff of 80 to pamper up to 40 guests in style. The tab – if you have to ask, you can't afford it – includes meals, drinks and all kinds of recreational activities, from a private ski area and a creekside pub to a fitness center with spa treatment rooms and Japanese furo soaking tubs.

In the main house, three living rooms, each bigger than the last, unfold as resident innkeeper Michael Beardsley welcomes guests for the owners, the Twigg-Smith family of Honolulu and Barnard. Upstairs are four guest rooms bearing some of the Twin Farms trademarks: plump kingsize feather beds, tiled fireplaces, comfortable sitting areas, fabulous folk art and contemporary paintings, satellite TV/VCR/stereos, tea trays with a coffee press and Kona coffees from the family-owned corporation, twin sinks in the bathrooms, baskets of all-natural toiletries, terrycloth robes, and unbleached and undyed cotton towels. They impart a feeling of elegant rusticity, but come with every convenience of the ultimate home away from home.

Less antiquity and even more convenience are found in the stone and wood guest cottages, each with at least one fireplace, a screened porch or terrace, an incredible twig-sided carport and its own private place in the landscape.

The Perch, for instance, is situated above a small stream and beaver pond. It harbors luxuriant seating around the fireplace, a dining area, a bed recessed in an alcove and shielded by a hand-carved arch of wooden roping and a wicker-filled porch where a wood sculpture of a shark hangs overhead. Its bathroom has alcoves harboring a copper tub the size of a small pool and a separate shower, both with windows to the outdoors. The soaring Treehouse is furnished in Adirondack twig, while a Moroccan theme turns the Meadow Cottage into a desert king's traveling palace.

The ultimate is the 3,000-square-foot Chalet, which has a two-story-high living room with birch tree rafters, floor-to-ceiling stone fireplace and windows, a bedroom with second fireplace, and his and hers bathrooms, one with a circular mosaic deluge shower and the other with a skirted soaking tub beside the window. An enclosed porch adds a hot tub.

Vaulted ceiling, chandeliers and fireplaces enhance dining room at Twin Farms.

Four more suites were created in 2005 in the newly built Farmhouse at Copper Hill, across the road above the Copper Pond. The farmhouse and the racy new bi-level Aviary cottage that's billed as geometric and sexy were part of a $9 million upgrade that expanded the dining facilities and added a new cabana at the refurbished waterfront along the pond.

Good food and drink (from well-stocked, help-yourself bars) are among Twin Farms strong points. Guests meet at 7 o'clock for cocktails in a changing venue – perhaps the wine cellar, one of the living rooms or, the night before our visit, in the Studio cottage. A set, four-course dinner is served at 8 at tables for two in a baronial dining hall with chandeliers hanging from the vaulted ceiling and fieldstone fireplaces at either end or in a new dining room addition with a terrace grill.

The kitchen brigade of six is headed by veteran chef Neil Wigglesworth. Dinner might open with medallions of lobster with avocado relish and angel-hair pasta, followed by warm red cabbage salad with slices of smoked chicken. The main course could be veal mignon with timbales of wild rice and xeres sauce or five-spiced duck with nut-brown cabbage and golden beets. Fresh figs with French ice cream and peach-caramel sauce might be dessert. In summer, guests often round out the evening with armagnac and s'mores around a campfire before they toddle back to their cottages for the night.

A visit to the glittering professional kitchen is instructive – and Neil says he likes to have guests in to "talk and dabble." We enjoyed seeing the three patterns of Wedgwood china (one each for breakfast, lunch and dinner), the pantry wall of table linens in every color and material (there were about 25 sets of placemats and it was like being inside a well-stocked linen shop), the Fiestaware used exclusively for picnics, the fine sterling-silver pieces, the pottery from Miranda Thomas and the glassware from Simon Pearce.

Breakfast is continental if taken in the guest rooms and cooked to order in the dining room from a small menu – raspberry pancakes or eggs benedict with lobster when we were there. The property is a registered American natural organic farm, and the kitchen staff make its own oils, vinegars, breads and preserves, some from the raspberry bushes planted by Dorothy Thompson some 70 years earlier.

Lunch is a movable feast, depending on the day and guests' inclinations. It could be a sit-down meal in the dining room, a picnic of lobster and champagne anywhere, or a barbecue beside the inn's pond or at its own ski area, where there's never a lineup for the pomalift. Afternoon tea is a presentation worthy of the Ritz, complete, perhaps, with little edible gold leaves on one of the five kinds of tea pastries.

The creekside pub, incidentally, is nearly a museum piece with its collection of beer bottles from around the world. Beer-bottle caps cover the light shades over the billiards table, outline the mirror and sconces above the fireplace, and cover the candlesticks on the mantel. Even a pub chair is dressed in beer caps – a dramatic piece of pop art from the Twigg-Smiths' renowned art collection.

Such are some of the delights and surprises encountered by guests at Twin Farms.

(802) 234-9999 or (800) 894-6327. Fax (802) 234-9990. www.twinfarms.com. Ten suites and ten cottages with private baths. Suites, $1,050 and $1,200. Cottages, $1,650 to $2,700. All-inclusive, except for 15 percent service charge and 8 percent state tax. Two-night minimum on weekends, three nights on holidays. Closed in April.

Lodging

The Maple Leaf Inn, Route 12, Box 273, Barnard, Vt. 05031.

Guests are showered with hospitality at this four-diamond-rated inn built from scratch by Texans Gary and Janet Robison. They couldn't find the perfect old New England inn in their search among existing buildings. So they built it – a brand new, meant-to-look-old Victorian structure with the requisite gingerbread and gazebo – in a clearing amid sixteen acres of maples and birches in tiny Barnard.

Crackers with a mango-chutney cheese spread or a homemade Texas chili cheese log – incorporating pecans grown in her yard by Gary's aunt and sent as "a CARE package from home" – are served arriving guests on the wraparound front porch with its corner gazebo and Tennessee oak rockers, or inside in the library or fireplaced parlor. Light suppers of soup, bread, salad and dessert are served by request in winter. Two chocolates are placed at bedside at nightly turndown. A small bottle of maple syrup, a packet of wildflower seeds or a personalized maple leaf wood Christmas ornament is hung on the doorknob with a thank-you note for being their guests. And effervescent Janet is apt to send you on your way with a farewell package of pumpkin bread or muffins for midday sustenance. Between arrival and departure, guests are cosseted with unusual warmth and creature comforts, the latter the result of "being able to build what we wanted from the ground up," in Gary's words.

Most of the seven luxurious bedrooms are positioned to have windows on three sides. All have kingsize beds, modern baths (four with whirlpool tubs and two with two-person soaking tubs), sitting areas with swivel club chairs, TV/VCRs secreted in the armoires, ceiling fans and closets. Five have wood-burning fireplaces with antique mantels. Janet spent a week in each room doing the remarkable hand stenciling. She stenciled an elaborate winter village over the fireplace and around the doors and windows in the Winter Haven room in which we stayed. Birds are the stenciling theme in the Spring Hollow Room; foliage the theme in Autumn Woods.

The Robisons' attention to detail continues throughout, from the maple leaf engraved in the window of the front door to the "pasta-hair angels" that Janet fashioned from angel-hair pasta and placed atop bud vases as centerpieces in the dining room.

The love stamps that she needlepointed and framed on the dining-room walls were anniversary gifts to Gary and, by extension, to their guests, who take breakfast by candlelight at individual tables near the fireplace.

And what a breakfast! Ours began with buttermilk scones garnished with flowers. The accompanying orange and cranberry-apple butters were shaped like maple leaves, and the preserves were presented in leaf dishes. The fruit course was sautéed bananas with Ben & Jerry's ice cream, an adaptation of bananas foster at Brennan's in New Orleans. The main event was stuffed french toast with peach preserves and cream cheese, garnished with nasturtiums. A savory favorite is a dijon egg puff sprinkled with Italian cheese and confetti bell peppers.

(802) 234-5342 or (800) 516-2753. Fax (802) 234-6456. www.mapleleafinn.com. Seven rooms with private baths. Doubles, $160 to $230, foliage and holidays $190 to $260. Deduct $30 midweek most of the year and weekends March-May.

The Charleston House, 21 Pleasant St., Woodstock, Vt. 05091.

This handsome, 1835 Greek Revival townhouse is named for the hometown of a former owner. Owners Dixi and Willa Nohl spent a weekend here in 1997, learned the place was for sale and started the purchase process on the spot.

"It was serendipitous," said Willa. Dixi was general manager of Burke Mountain ski area and grew up in the lodging business in St. Anton in his native Austria. He and his wife wanted to stay in Vermont but distance themselves a bit from the skiing world.

Listed in the National Register of Historic Places, the B&B is elegantly furnished with period antiques and an extensive selection of art and oriental rugs. Four guest rooms upstairs in the main house have queen beds and one has twins. A substantial recent addition – nicely secluded in back – contains three deluxe guest rooms with queen beds, jetted tubs, fireplaces, TVs and porches that look onto a wooded area. Another favorite room is the Summer Kitchen, downstairs between the original house and the addition. It is cozy and romantic with a four-poster queen bed, TV and two wing chairs angled beside the fireplace.

Breakfasts by candlelight here are such an attraction that the former owners put together a cookbook of recipes, called *Breakfast at Charleston House*. Willa continues to serve some of those favorites along with her own. Among specialties are baked french toast, a cheese and grits soufflé, macadamia-nut waffles with papaya and strawberries, and Charleston strata, an egg dish with sausage and apples.

At our latest visit, the main dish was peach puffed pancakes – so "light and mouthwatering," according to a guest, "that where ordinarily I would have one I ended up having three." A tea aficionado, she was impressed with the Nohls' collection of teas – "some that I hadn't even heard of."

(802) 457-3843 or (888) 475-3800. www.charlestonhouse.com. Nine rooms with private baths. Doubles, $135 to $240, foliage and holidays $155 to $276.

The Trumbull House, 40 Etna Road, Hanover, N.H. 03755.

Lights in the windows welcome guests year-round to this rambling white Colonial house built in 1919 on a hillside four miles east of Hanover. Hilary Pridgen operates it "with the able assistance" of her children. "The whole family is involved." Her eldest son receives guests and carries their bags, a younger son lights the fireplaces, and her teen-aged daughter helps with breakfast.

The family, who originally occupied the front of the house, live in the attached barn at the rear. Their guests have the run of the front, including an enormous living room with oriental rugs and several seating areas and tables for breakfast overflow. Breakfast is served whenever the guests want it, in the dining room at a table for six or in the living room. They are offered a choice of entrées, following a fruit course of perhaps honeydew melon with prosciutto or pineapple with cinnamon. "Fat and puffy omelets" are Hilary's specialty, although her menu also includes raisin bread french toast, a portobello mushroom and brie omelet, Mexican eggs with salsa and scrambled eggs with smoked salmon.

Upstairs are four guest rooms and a suite. All have TV/VCRs, telephones, sitting areas with good reading lights, plush carpeting and king or queensize beds with feather comforters and all-cotton sheets. Spacious and extra-comfortable, the rooms are named for the prevailing colors of their décor. Two offer sofabeds for extra occupants and two others add window seats. A second-floor suite has a living room with a queen sofabed and a window seat, a king bedroom with two club chairs, an enormous bathroom with jacuzzi tub, double vanity and separate water closet, plus a second bathroom with a shower.

Guests also may stay in a recently opened cottage in the rear with king bed, sitting area with sofabed, gas fireplace, wet bar and deck.

Behind the house are sixteen acres containing a trout-stocked swimming pond, hiking and cross-country ski trails, and a paved basketball half-court.

(603) 643-2370 or (800) 651-5141. www.trumbullhouse.com. Four rooms, one suite and one cottage with private baths. Doubles, $160 to $235. Suite and cottage, $275 to $290. Off-season: doubles $135 to $195, suite and cottage $240 to $250.

Gourmet Treats

Woodstock is chock full of elegant stores – just stroll along Central or Elm streets. The most fun shop of all is **F.H. Gillingham & Co.** at 16 Elm, a general store owned by the same family for more than a century and reputed to have been a favorite of Robert Frost's. It's now run by Jireh Swift Billings, great-grandson of the founder. His is a sophisticated and varied emporium, with everything from spa dessert sauces produced in nearby Norwich to trapunto aprons (embroidered with blue jays, rabbits or squirrels). Fresh fruits (even baskets of lichee nuts) and vegetables, wines, cooking equipment, Blue Willow dinnerware, dozens of mustards, cloudberry preserves from Scandinavia, Black Jewel American sturgeon caviar – you want to cook with it? They probably have it.

Next door is **The Village Butcher** with wines, a deli and gourmet items. Across the street is **Bentleys Coffee Bar and Florist Shop,** which has lovely flowers and twelve flavors of cappuccino, which you can drink at little marble tables amid the plants. **Aubergine,** a good kitchenware shop, is a few doors away. You'll probably find a thermos of the day's coffee flavor to sample, as well as a lineup of jams, relishes and salsas to try on various crackers. We like the majolica pottery here.

Not the usual transient farmers' market, the **Woodstock Farmers' Market,** west of the village, is a permanent fixture where you can find not only fruits and vegetables, but "famous" deli sandwiches, salads, Vermont food products, baked goods, seafood – all the "right" things are here.

The historic **Taftsville Country Store,** an 1840 landmark in tiny Taftsville, has the requisite general store and post office in back. Up front are all kinds of upscale Vermont foodstuffs, including jams, chutneys, mustards, wines and maple syrups from South Woodstock. The selection of cheeses is exceptional, and the cheddars are cut to order off 38-pound wheels.

You can sample (and buy) thirteen flavors of cheese and four grades of maple syrup at **Sugarbush Farm,** 591 Sugarbush Farm Road, Woodstock. A video shows how the staff taps 6,000 maple trees and turns the sap into maple syrup and candy. The farm shop also sells Vermont preserves, mustards, cheese spreads and the like.

The old mill built in Quechee has been turned into a nationally known glass-blowing center and shop known as **Simon Pearce.** Simon Pearce, the Irish glassmaker, moved here in 1981 and headed the growing company until turning over the CEO reins in 2002. It's worth a visit just to observe how space is used in his tremendous mill, but it's also fascinating to watch the glass blowers by the fiery furnaces on the ground floor (the main production facility has been relocated to nearby Windsor). You can see the water roar over the dam outside from a floor-to-ceiling window on the second floor, and you can buy the handsome glass pieces (and seconds that are a bit more gently priced), as well as pottery and woolens from Ireland. The table settings are to be admired.

The Baker's Store at King Arthur Flour, 133 Route 5 South, Norwich, has grown from a modest shop for local customers to a destination for amateur and professional bakers with a working kitchen, on-site bakery and education center open seven days a week. The shop stocks not only baking products, ingredients and equipment but local products and Vermont specialty foods. Breads, pastries and sandwiches are available. So are samples.

Classy Co-ops

Hanover Consumer Cooperative Society, Hanover and Lebanon, N.H.

To our minds, the area's best supermarkets are off the tourist path and run by this member-owned co-op. The Hanover original at 45 South Park St., long favored by the Dartmouth and medical intelligentsia, is notable for its automotive service center as well as its enormous selection of prepared foods cooked daily in its kitchens. We picked up the makings here for a grand dinner for our weekend hosts at a nearby lake.

The co-op opened a huge store in the Centerra Marketplace off Route 120 between Hanover and Lebanon. This is the ne plus ultra, a state-of-the-art establishment that emulates some of the co-op supermarkets found in the Pacific Northwest. Here you'll find bulk foods, fresh fish and meats, local produce, wines, a sampling station, a café, more than 200 cheeses, and the largest selection of ethnic and imported foods in northern New England. And, nice touch, the store even has a map and alphabetized directory. You'll need it to negotiate your way around.

Hanover: (603) 343-2667. 45 South Park St. Open daily, 8 to 8.
Lebanon: (603) 643-4889. 12 Centarra Pkwy. Open daily, 7 a.m. to 9 p.m.

Pristine white facade of Equinox resort hotel is symbolic of Southern Vermont.

Southern Vermont

Old Inns, New Style

As verdant as the Green Mountains and as New England as they come. That's the area of Southern Vermont slicing from Dover to Dorset, names that have an English ring to them, but that are the heart of old New England – or is it old New England, new style?

The fairly broad area embraces such storybook Vermont towns as Newfane, Weston and Manchester. It ranges from unspoiled Dorset, a hamlet almost too quaint for words, to changing West Dover, where inns and resorts congregate in the shadow of Mount Snow ski area.

This is a land of mountains and lakes, ski and summer resorts and, because of its fortuitous location for four-season enjoyment within weekend commuting distance of major metropolitan areas, a center for fine inns and restaurants.

Some of the East's leading inns were established here before people elsewhere really thought of the idea. In an era in which new inns and B&Bs seem to be popping up everywhere, most of those featured here have been around a while, the better to have established themselves in the lodging and culinary realm.

The food here is far more than Vermont cheddar and maple syrup, as adventuresome diners have known for years. Many of the area's top dining rooms are found in inns. Several restaurants are dining destinations as well.

Dining and Lodging

The Inn at Sawmill Farm, Crosstown Road, Box 367, West Dover 05356.

As country inns go, the Inn at Sawmill Farm was a pioneer among the more sophisticated. Founded by architect Rodney Williams and his interior-decorator wife Ione and built around a converted barn, it is the epitome of country elegance and was a member of the prestigious Relais & Châteaux for 25 years until it dropped its affiliation in 2005.

Admiring the old barn and farmhouse during ski expeditions to Mount Snow, the

Williamses bought the property in 1967 and turned it into a decorator's dream. It is now run by a second generation, their daughter Bobbie Dee and son Brill, the talented chef.

The rates here are MAP and such that, for many, this is a special-occasion destination. The indulgences lavished in any of the 21 accommodations are considerable – queen and kingsize beds, comfortable upholstered chairs with good reading lights, little gold boxes of Lake Champlain Chocolates, terrific dinners, incredible breakfasts, and afternoon tea with nut bread and ginger cookies. Not to mention a splashy decor of color-coordinated fabric and chintz.

The most deluxe are eleven outlying rooms and suites with fireplaces in four buildings called cottages. Six sport new whirlpool tubs and separate showers as the inn keeps up with the times. A luxury suite does it up in spades with a cathedral-ceilinged living room with a stone wall including a fireplace and built-in TV and sound system, king bedroom with antique Federal mahogany headboard, bath with jacuzzi and glassed-in shower, and a wraparound deck overlooking the grounds, which include a pool, tennis court and two trout ponds.

The large brick fireplace in the inn's cathedral-ceilinged living room, festooned with copper pots and utensils, is the focal point for guests who gather on chintz-covered sofas and wing chairs and read magazines that are spread out on a gigantic copper table. Other groupings are near the huge windows, through which you get a view of Mount Snow. Upstairs in a loft room are more sofas, an entire wall of books and the main inn's lone television set, which does not seem often to be in use.

The restaurant – billed as "Sawmill's crown jewel" – draws the public with a choice of à la carte, prix-fixe ($44) and weeknight table d'hôte bistro options ($29.95).

The three attractive dining areas display the owners' collection of folk art. One, off the living room, has a cathedral ceiling, with large wrought-iron chandeliers and Queen Anne-style chairs contrasting delightfully with barnwood and fabric walls. We like best the Greenhouse Room in back, with its indoor garden and rose-papered and beamed ceiling.

You can pop into the cozy bar between the dining rooms for a drink before dinner; crackers and cheese are set out then. The dining rooms at night are dim and romantic: tables are set with heavy silver, candles in pierced-silver lamp shades, napkins in silver napkin rings, fresh flowers and delicate, pink-edged floral china.

Quite a selection of appetizers and entrées awaits, warranting the National Restaurant Association's selection of Brill Williams as Vermont's top chef in 1999. The menu is larger and appears more traditional – shrimp in beer batter, veal piccata, sautéed breast of pheasant forestière, sirloin steak au poivre – than one might expect, with many favorites remaining year after year by popular demand. But Brill does not rest on reputation and adds the occasional au courant item, such as an appetizer of grilled rare tuna with mango salsa and an entrée of Key West red snapper with lobster risotto and saffron sauce.

Diners are served canapés and a basket of hot rolls and crisp homemade melba toast. That will hold you while you choose from Brill's remarkable and quite costly wine compendium (selected annually by Wine Spectator as winner of its grand award, ranking it as one of the best in the world). The house wine is French, bottled specially for the inn, and the côtes du rhône rouge we tried has been acclaimed better than many a châteauneuf du pape. Those with a special interest can descend to the wine cellars, where more than 1,250 selections and 30,000 bottles reside. Brill

Main dining room at The Inn at Sawmill Farm is country elegant.

says he does this "more as a hobby than a business," but manages to sell $5,000 to $7,000 worth of wine a week.

For starters, we liked the thinly sliced raw prime sirloin with a shallot and mustard sauce, and the sauté of chicken livers with onion brioche and quail egg. Among entrées, we found outstanding both the hearty rabbit chasseur and the sautéed sweetbreads with white truffle butter sauce on a bed of fried spinach.

Dessert lovers will appreciate chocolate whiskey cake with grand marnier sauce, fresh strawberry tart, bananas romanoff, and ice cream with chocolate-buttermilk sauce. The espresso is strong, and better-than-usual decaffeinated coffee is served in a silver pot.

Breakfast lovers will be in their glory in the sun-drenched greenhouse, watching chickadees at the bird feeders and choosing from all kinds of fruits, oatmeal and fancy egg dishes (eggs buckingham is a wonderful mix of eggs, sautéed red and green peppers, onions and bacon seasoned with dijon mustard and worcestershire sauce, placed on an English muffin and topped with Vermont cheddar cheese and baked). Scrambled eggs might come with golden caviar, and poached eggs with grilled trout. Don't pass up the homemade tomato juice. Thick and spicy, it also serves as a base for the inn's peppy bloody marys.

(802) 464-8131. Fax (802) 464-1130. www.theinnatsawmillfarm.com. Fourteen rooms, four suites and three one-room cottages with private baths. Rates, B&B. Doubles, $250 to $375 weekends, $175 to $325 midweek. Suites and cottages, $450 to $750 weekends, $350 to $600 midweek.

Entrées, $28 to $39. Dinner nightly by reservation, 6 to 9. Jackets preferred.

The Four Columns Inn, 21 West St., Box 278, Newfane 05345.

Facing a Newfane green unchanged since the 1830s, this venerable inn has upgraded its accommodations while maintaining its reputation as a culinary landmark in Southern Vermont.

New owners Deb and Bruce Pfander from California took over a going concern,

Tables are set for fine dining at The Four Columns Inn.

their predecessors having refurbished the dining room, expanded the rear lounge, added creature comforts and opened several new guest rooms that are the ultimate in luxury. Most deluxe are above the main inn's foyer with vaulted ceilings and see-through fireplaces between bedrooms and large tiled baths, complete with two-person whirlpool tubs and separate showers. Top of the line is now cathedral-ceilinged Suite 4, with king bed and double-sided fireplace. Its bath has a two-person whirlpool and marble shower with twelve-head massage spray, and a wall of arched windows beneath the cathedral ceiling looks across the tops of maple trees onto the town green. Altogether, eleven accommodations now have gas fireplaces and nine have whirlpool or soaking tubs for two. All but one have king or queensize beds.

The 150-acre property includes a swimming pool, hiking trails, lovely gardens and spacious lawns on which to relax in country-auberge style.

Through all the upgrades, chef Gregory Parks has led the inn to a four-diamond AAA rating for dining. Starting here more than 25 years ago as sous chef under René Chardain, then the famed chef-owner, he enjoys free rein in the kitchen, where he turns out exemplary contemporary American fare.

The inn's sophisticated dining room is in a white building behind the white clapboard 1832 structure containing some of the guest rooms and the four Greek Revival columns that give the inn its name. It combines beamed ceilings and a huge fireplace with stylish window treatments, pristine white table linens, shaded oil lamps and new stemware. The expanded and refurbished lounge is decorated with a stunning impressionistic mural of 1850s Newfane progressing through the seasons.

The lounge opens onto a side deck with umbrellaed tables overlooking gardens and a trout pond, a pleasant spot for a cocktail.

Chef Greg's appetizers are some of Vermont's most exotic: perhaps tuna carpaccio with cucumber salad and citrus-ginger vinaigrette; grilled quail with lentils and celery root rémoulade, and chicken and truffle mousse with baby lettuce salad.

Entrées range from pistachio-crusted swordfish fillet with a saffron-citrus sauce to black angus tenderloin with garlicky escargot and creamy gorgonzola sauce. Others could be moulard duck breast with a rhubarb demi-glace, rack of lamb with rosemary-garlic sauce and venison loin with sundried cherries and a merlot reduction.

The dessert repertoire here has long been famous. It might include a silky chocolate torte with mango-rum sauce and local raspberries, pumpkin spice cheesecake, a warm Italian plum crisp with walnuts and ice cream, and maple-pecan pie with bourbon-scented whipped cream. You can stop in the lounge to enjoy one from the cart, even if you haven't dined at the inn.

The longtime breakfast cook prepares a healthful country breakfast. The buffet table contains fresh orange juice, ample fruit, yogurt, homemade coconut-laden granola, hot oatmeal in winter and an assortment of homemade muffins, scones and croissants. The apple turnovers and various quiches are first-rate.

(802) 365-7713 or (800) 787-6633. Fax (802) 365-7713. www.fourcolumnsinn.com. Six rooms and nine suites with private baths. Doubles, $185 to $210 weekends, $160 to $185 midweek, $195 to $225 foliage and holidays. Suites, $315 to $365 weekends, $265 to $315 midweek, $325 to $385 foliage and holidays.

Entrées, $27 to $33. Dinner nightly except Tuesday, 6 to 9.

The Inn at Weston, Route 100, Box 66, Weston 05161.

Orchids, fine dining and luxury accommodations are the hallmarks of the venerable Inn at Weston, grandly reborn after having been abandoned unexpectedly in 1998.

The orchids are grown in a state-of-the-art greenhouse alongside the inn by owners Linda and Bob Aldrich from New Jersey. Bob, a cardiologist, and Linda, a nurse, took over an inn that had been upscaled by a short-term owner. They redecorated with fine antiques, artworks and glass, added featherbeds and high-thread-count linens, and placed some of their prized orchids around public and guest rooms.

The front of the original 1848 farmhouse holds a parlor and cozy library with fireplace and some of the books the couple brought in 48 boxes with them to the inn. It's truly a library – the Aldriches lend books to guests along with videos from their extensive collection. Bob's framed photographs of Vermont adorn the walls here and throughout the inn.

The main floor also holds a lovely, 50-seat dining room, its walls enlivened with red floral wallpaper over white wainscoting. A pianist plays the grand piano on weekend evenings. Beyond is a cozy, pine-paneled pub. Outside is a dining deck with a gazebo, complete with crystal chandelier. It's surrounded by orchids and plants and holds a single table "for very romantic dining," according to Bob.

Said dining is delivered by chef Michael Kennedy, who flavors his contemporary American cuisine with international accents. His appetizers usually include sushi, perhaps an avocado maki roll with seared ahi tuna. Other starters might be mussels in consommé with lemongrass, water chestnuts and tofu triangles, a crispy pesto pizza bearing grilled chicken and mozzarella, and a confit of duck salad.

The chef likes to mix things in his entrées, as in pan-seared catfish with Mexican bay scallops. A wild boar sausage and tiger shrimp sauté combines olives, artichokes, squash and red pepper over porcini fettuccine in a tarragon-saffron vodka. A mixed grill of stuffed quail and venison loin is a house favorite. The veal osso buco, double-cut pork chop and spice-encrusted tournedos of beef are more straightforward.

Dessert could be cherry cobbler with house-made maple ice cream or chai-spiced crème brûlée with a shortbread biscuit. Linger by the fire over a cordial or single-malt scotch in the amiable pub.

The Aldriches have integrated their personal collection of wines assembled over three decades into the inn's award-winning yet affordable wine list.

Upstairs in the main inn, the original eleven guest rooms have been reconfigured to five. All have king or queen beds and all but one fireplaces and TV/VCRs. Three have whirlpool tubs and two offer thermal massage tubs with separate showers. The most deluxe are two new rooms in a carriage house with king beds, TV/VCRs, wood stoves, whirlpool tubs, steam showers, pine floors with Persian rugs, and private entrances and decks. Across the street in the Coleman House are three rooms with kingsize beds and fireplaces, and three with queen or twin beds. All rooms come with telephones, plush linens and Ralph Lauren comforters, European toiletries, Saratoga sparkling water and Lindt chocolate truffles.

A gourmet breakfast is served by the fireplace in the skylit dining room or outside on a stone patio beside the greenhouse. The feast culminates in a choice between sweet and savory, perhaps sweet potato and walnut pancakes with crème fraîche or smoked trout and gouda omelets.

Everyone takes a tour of the greenhouse, where Bob grows more than 500 varieties of orchids, most of them fairly rare. "There's always something in bloom," he says.

(802) 824-6789. Fax (802) 824-3073. www.innweston.com. Thirteen rooms with private baths. Doubles, $185 to $325; $235 to $375 foliage and holidays.

Entrées, $27 to $34. Dinner nightly, from 5:30.

Windham Hill Inn, 311 Lawrence Drive, West Townshend 05359.

Gourmet dining is part of the appeal of this elegant inn atop a remote hill overlooking the West River Valley. Once here, you tend to stay here, which is why innkeepers Marina and Joe Coneeny go out of their way to make their guests' stays so comfortable and satisfying.

Five-course dinners of distinction are served nightly to guests and the public in the inn's expanded restaurant. Patrons gather for drinks and hors d'oeuvre in a bar off the inn's parlor. Then they adjourn to an enlarged dining room dressed in pale pink, with oriental scatter rugs, upholstered chairs at well-spaced tables, and views onto lawns and Frog Pond.

Dinner is available prix-fixe ($50) or à la carte, with four to six choices for most courses on chef Jennifer Cayer's menu that changes monthly.

Appetizers are few but select. At our latest visit they were pan-seared diver scallops with English pea puree, mint and crispy beets; a warm eggplant, roasted pepper and fontina cheese terrine with crispy prosciutto, and house-made morel mushroom ravioli with leek puree and sautéed asparagus.

An orange sorbet over raspberry sauce refreshed the palate for the main course. Choices ranged from grilled halibut with a red grapefruit beurre blanc to pan-seared beef tenderloin with herbed compound butter. The chef stuffed a roasted chicken with morel mushrooms and offered grilled loin lamb chops with balsamic syrup.

Dining room at Windham Hill Inn looks onto lawns and pond.

Desserts were individual lemon meringue tartlet, warm chocolate truffle cake, caramelized banana and walnut napoleon and a trio of sorbets.

The inn hosts monthly wine dinners. The innkeepers are as proud of their award-winning wine selection as they are of the accommodations, which have been considerably expanded and upgraded since we stayed here some years back.

All but one of the 21 rooms have king or queensize beds and sixteen have fireplaces or Vermont Casting stoves. They're furnished with a panache that merited a six-page photo spread in Country Decorating magazine. We've always been partial to the five rooms fashioned from nooks and alcoves in the White Barn annex, particularly the two sharing a large deck overlooking the mountains, and the renovated Taft Room with fireplace, bay window and floor-to-ceiling bookshelves. Three deluxe rooms have been carved out of the former owners' quarters in the south wing. These come with kingsize beds, two armchairs in front of the fireplace, and jacuzzis or freestanding soaking tubs. The most lavish accommodations are three extra-spacious rooms in the third-floor loft of the barn. Each has a king bed, fireplace and private deck facing the mountains. Two have double soaking tubs and the other a double jacuzzi. The one in the middle has a winding staircase up to the cupola with a window seat and a 360-degree view.

The staff pamper guests with gourmet touches, from complimentary juices and Perrier in baskets in each room to candy dishes at bedside and Mother Myrick's chocolates on the pillows at nightly turndown, when small votive candles are lit.

Besides the new bar room off the living room, common areas include another sitting room and a large and sunny game room with windows on three sides. Outside are a heated gunite swimming pool and clay tennis court, as well as 160 acres of woods and trails.

Full breakfasts are served amid a background of taped chamber music, antique silver and crystal. You'll find fresh orange juice in champagne flutes, a buffet spread of granola, breakfast pastries and fresh fruits, and a main dish such as lemon pancakes with blueberry syrup or scrambled eggs with chives and sausages.

(802) 874-4080 or (800) 944-4080. Fax (802) 874-4702. www.windhamhill.com. Twenty-one rooms with private baths. Doubles, $195 to $380; $245 to $430 foliage and holidays. Closed Christmas week and first week of April.

Entrées, $28 to $31. Dinner nightly by reservation, 6 to 8:30.

The Inn at Weathersfield, 1342 Route 106, Perkinsville 05151.

What a Los Angeles Times travel writer once extolled as "the perfect Vermont inn" is back from the brink. Jane and David Sandelman rescued the abandoned inn from bankruptcy, renovated and upgraded the accommodations, and restored the restaurant to its traditional rank as one of the premier dining establishments in Vermont.

The task was not without considerable work and expense for the New Jersey transplants who left the corporate world at mid-life. The out-of-the-way rural inn on 21 acres dates to 1792, when it began as a stagecoach stop. Its age and subsequent abandonment required massive infrastructure upgrades and renovations to more than half of the twelve guest rooms and suites. The accommodations were furnished with creature comforts in mind. Those renovated have kingsize or queen featherbeds so comfortable that guests want to buy them, upholstered chairs beside working fireplaces, updated baths with whirlpool tubs or oversize spa showers with wall jets, towel warmers, small TVs and telephones, plush robes and fine toiletries. Our quarters in the main-floor Lincoln Room came with access to a pillared front veranda that gives the front of the inn a Southern ante-bellum look, plus a spacious common parlor that turned out to be private because most guests opted for the larger common room at the far end of the inn.

The 21st-century comforts blend well with the aura of history of an 18th-century inn without lace and fussiness. The combination makes an appealing self-contained destination for inn-goers. So do the down-to-earth warmth and welcome of the enthusiastic owners, whose hands-on hospitality turns nearly every evening into a house party. Best of all is the dining experience, offered formally in a beamed and barnwood room illuminated entirely by candlelight, casually in the rear Lucy's Tavern named for the Sandelmans' friendly black poodle or privately at a chef's table in a charming new wine cellar.

Executive chef Jason Tostrup moved East with his fiancée after seven years in Aspen and cooking with celebrity chef Thomas Keller in the Napa Valley. He wanted "to be closer to the seasons, the products and the farmers" – and skiing. He nicknamed his fare "Verterra," short for Vermont terra or cuisine of the land. He bakes bread in a beehive oven, roasts meats in a brick fireplace in the front entry and buys from local purveyors, whom he credits on the menu. He produces nearly everything in house, from the cranberry cassis liqueur that went into the kir royale aperitif mixed by bartender Jane Sandelman in the convivial tavern area to the sorbet sampler that ended a superior meal.

The concise menu varies weekly, with à la carte, prix-fixe tasting or light-fare tavern options. The former provided a winning appetizer called "Three from the Sea," served as were the dessert samplers on stunning long white plates with individual compartments, obtained from a Chinese restaurant supplier in New York. The tuna bruschetta, salmon tartare and shrimp seviche were tasty morsels, as intricate as they were exotic. The hot date-marinated rack of lamb was served with cauliflower flan, pickled carrot salad and curried flageolet beans. Dessert was the aforementioned sorbet sampler – intensely flavored green apple, cassis, brown buttered cranberry and persimmon, plus a dollop of chocolate ice cream and a few tiny cookies.

The five-course "sampling of the season" taste menu was equally rewarding. Ours began with the chef's amuse-bouche, three little palate-pleasers of bison broth with truffle jus, heirloom apple cider with pomegranates and a goat-cheese

Dining room is illuminated entirely by candles at The Inn at Weathersfield.

croquette. A tureen of lobster curry and butternut squash soup with a sea scallop and pomegranates was served on a plate laden with aromatics. Wild striped Atlantic bass came with a Jerusalem artichoke barigoule. The highlight was sliced pheasant breast with black mission figs and a potato pie à la mode (the mode turning out to be garlic foam), followed by a duet of locally raised rabbit: a grilled loin placed upon a braised leg with wild mushroom agnolotti and truffle emulsion. Dessert was an architectural-style "twisted apple" paired with chocolate bread pudding.

If all this sounds rather esoteric, it was. Yet it was not at all pretentious, thanks to the warmth of the servers and the appearances of the engaging chef as he made the rounds during and after dinner. A pianist playing show tunes throughout the meal contributed to the ambiance.

Breakfast was served at individual tables in the spacious sun room the next morning. After the epicurean triumphs of the night before, we anticipated more than a selection of juices, spiced zucchini-walnut bread and a choice between scrambled eggs with hash browns and buttermilk pancakes with bacon. Yet it was only a minor letdown in an otherwise first-rate culinary treat.

Those treats are embellished for parties of six to twelve at the chef's table in the wine cellar and at the inn's monthly wine dinners.

(802) 263-9217. Fax (802) 263-9219. www.weathersfieldinn.com. Nine rooms and three suites with private baths. Doubles, $155 to $205 weekends, $140 to $175 midweek, $175 to $225 foliage. Suites, $175 to $250 weekends, $155 to $225 midweek, $195 to $285 foliage.

Entrées, $28 to $32; tasting menu, $55; tavern $7 to $18. Dinner, Thursday-Sunday 5:30 to 8:30, nightly except Tuesday foliage and holidays.

Three Mountain Inn, Route 30, Jamaica 05343.

When Ed and Jennifer Dorta-Duque from Annapolis, Md., scoured the Northeast in search of the perfect inn, they found this venerable 1790s inn to be a ready-made fit. The accommodations had already been upgraded by David Hiler in partnership with his mother, Heide Bredfeldt, and his stepfather, Bill Oates, well-known inn consultants, who had used the inn partly as a training ground for prospective innkeepers. Ed, who had opened hotels for the Ritz chain, and Jennifer kept things virtually the same, but as hands-on innkeepers infused the place with hospitality and enthusiasm.

Their predecessors' deft touch is apparent in recent refurbishing and upgrades. All but two of the inn's fifteen accommodations now have fireplaces, four have whirlpool tubs and all but one have queen or kingsize beds. The paintings in the rooms are Vermont originals, as are most of the period accessories.

The seven rooms in the Robinson House annex next door were reconfigured, enlarged and decorated with style. The premier Jamaica Suite, main floor rear, has a queensize poster bed, a sitting room with a gas fireplace and a loveseat that opens into a twin bed, a private patio and a bath with double whirlpool tub and rainforest shower. The last two amenities also are found in the Weston and Wardsboro rooms in the upstairs rear, each with queen bed and soaring picture windows onto a mountain view.

The seven accommodations in the main house vary from a couple of simple, cozy rooms to the corner Windham room with private balcony, kingsize four-poster bed and TV/VCR. Similar attributes enhance the Sage Cottage in the rear, rebuilt to offer a cozy, cathedral-ceilinged space with a queensize sleigh bed beneath a skylight, a double whirlpool tub in one corner and two comfortable chairs beside a gas fireplace in the opposite corner. Wicker chairs on the front porch look onto the gardens, pool area and two life-size fiberglass cows grazing in the yard.

The inn's common rooms include a large keeping room with an original Dutch oven fireplace, a spacious library that doubles as a conference room, an atmospheric pub and two small dining rooms with fireplaces.

Executive chef Tim Rieben, a Culinary Institute of America grad, took over the kitchen upon the Dorta-Duques' arrival. He offers contemporary regional fare.

Dinner is available prix-fixe ($55 for four courses) or à la carte from the same menu, and begins with a complimentary amuse-bouche. Starters might be a potato-leek soup with a brie crostini, a salmon rillette with caper berries and cornichons, and sweet potato ravioli with carrot-ginger cream sauce.

The night's six entrées, one of them vegetarian, could include a scallop casserole with smoked cheddar mornay, roasted pork tenderloin with maple redeye gravy, sautéed duck breast with pineapple gastrique and grilled filet mignon with toasted herb demi-glace.

Desserts sound ordinary but take on added dimension, as in pumpkin cheesecake with raspberry coulis, candied ginger and whipped cream or key lime pie augmented with seasonal berries.

Guests are treated to a sumptuous breakfast buffet. Pecan waffles, french toast, local sausage and eggs, homemade biscuits and blueberry muffins are typical fare.

(802) 874-4140 or (800) 532-9399. Fax (802) 874-4745. www.threemountaininn.com. Thirteen rooms, one suite and one cottage with private baths. Doubles, $145 to $235. Suite, $295. Cottage, $325.

Entrées, $26 to $34. Dinner, Wednesday-Sunday 6 to 8:30.

Doveberry Inn, Route 100, West Dover 05356.

Glowingly described by a fellow innkeeper as "a diamond in the rough" in its early stages, the Doveberry has upgraded its accommodations and matured into what Condé Nast Traveler ranks as one of America's 25 top inns with super chefs.

Michael Fayette, the young chef-owner who trained at Paul Smith's College in New York and 21 Federal in Nantucket, and his wife Christine, the baker, offer acclaimed northern Italian fare. They also added a wine bar in the common room, and attract the public for dessert and cappuccino as well as dinner in the evening.

They seat 30 guests in a two-part, beamed dining room with mint green walls and swag curtains. The tables are covered with Christine's mother's handmade quilt overcloths that change with the seasons. Michael's menu changes weekly, and in summer incorporates produce from the Fayettes' organic garden. Typical starters might be pan-seared scallops tossed with roasted peppers and pinenuts atop homemade spinach pasta, grilled shrimp with tomatoes and olives over creamy polenta, and foie gras served with duck confit, mushrooms, sundried tomatoes and juniper berries. A salad of field greens tossed in a balsamic vinaigrette is included with the main course. Choices range from shrimp and scallop penne with a light pink sambuca sauce to wood-grilled veal chop with wild mushrooms. Rare grilled ahi tuna with white truffle oil over creamy risotto, grilled pork loin with a cranberry-apple-maple demi-glace and rack of lamb with a black cherry demi-glace are among the possibilities. Christine might prepare orange-cinnamon crème brûlée, banana semifreddo, mascarpone cheesecake or a plum napoleon for dessert.

Overnight guests are nicely accommodated in a variety of rooms with king, queen or two double beds. All have TV/VCRs, and some with skylights convey a contemporary air. Two rooms were enlarged and renovated and three deluxe newcomers emerged in a three-story addition to the south end of the building. The three new rooms come with whirlpool tubs, fireplaces and balconies or decks – "anything and everything that anybody ever asked for in the past," in Michael's words. The renovated Blue Room with queen bed gained a whirlpool tub, and the Green Room became a suite with king bed and twin and a fireplace stove. Christine decorated all the new rooms with wallpaper above painted wainscoting, country accents and lots of pillows.

Overstuffed dark blue sofas and armchairs are grouped around the open brick hearth that warms the large common room. Tea and cookies are served here in the afternoon.

Guests order a complimentary breakfast from a full menu. Choices range from belgian waffles to eggs benedict with a crab cake.

(802) 464-5652 or (800) 722-3204. Fax (802) 464-6229. www.doveberryinn.com. Eleven rooms with private baths. Fall-spring: doubles, $125 to $215 weekends, $105 to $145 midweek. Summer: doubles, $95 to $135 weekends, $78 to $95 midweek. Two-night minimum weekends

Entrées, $21 to $33. Dinner, Thursday-Sunday 6 to 9. Closed two weeks in mid November and early May.

Inn at West View Farm, 2928 Route 30, Dorset 05251.

Ex-New Yorkers Christal Siewertsen, the innkeeper, and her husband Raymond Chen, the chef, have imbued the restaurant at the old Village Auberge with flair. Ray, who had been a chef in Manhattan, cooks in the new American style with international flourishes, and his food is rated best in town. Indeed, the inn won the American

Institute of Wine and Food's Epicurious award for best new restaurant shortly after he took over. Ray redecorated the dining room and set the white-clothed tables in the European style, with heavy silver cutlery face down.

Wild mushroom and mascarpone raviolis with spinach, parmesan cheese and white truffle oil is a signature starter. Others include a panko-crusted Maine crab cake with chipotle vinaigrette and arborio-crusted sweetbreads with fried spinach and sauce gribiche. The wine-braised beef short ribs are so popular that Ray cannot take them off the menu. Other entrées could be diver scallops and oyster mushrooms in puff pastry, halibut with root vegetables in a ginger-carrot broth, roast duck and confit with port-soaked cherries, rabbit with a sage-niçoise olive sauce, and coriander-crusted venison with chanterelles and port wine sauce. Dessert could be warm valrhona chocolate cake with vanilla ice cream or a trio of strawberry, citrus and mango sorbets. Gourmet magazine requested the recipe for the buttermilk panna cotta with caramelized bananas and blackberries. The wine list has been honored by Wine Spectator.

The inn's accommodations also have been upgraded, the bar/lounge and waiting area expanded, and a large living room with a fireplace and an attractive enclosed side porch full of white wicker sofas and chairs added for the comfort of overnight guests. The four original guest rooms upstairs have been redecorated, and six tidy rooms with full baths have been added. All but two with a pair of twins have queensize beds. They are nicely furnished with country antiques. One queen room, billed as a suite, has the inn's only in-room TV.

Breakfast is served to overnight guests in the cheery, plant-filled bay window end of the dining room. A ham and cheese terrine, pancakes, croissants and pain perdu with various fillings are among the offerings.

(802) 867-5715 or (800) 769-4903. Fax (802) 867-0468. www.innatwestviewfarm.com. Ten rooms with private baths. Memorial Day to Labor Day: doubles, $125 to $170. Foliage: $150 to $200. Rest of year: $110 to $155.

Entrées, $22 to $29. Dinner, Thursday-Monday from 6.

The Dorset Inn, 8 Church St., Dorset 05251.

Vermont's oldest continuously operated country inn dates back to 1796 and feels it, from its homey public rooms to its old-fashioned guest rooms.

Under the aegis of chef-owner Sissy Hicks, the inn is best known these days for its high-style comfort food. The main dining room is handsome in hunter green with white wainscoting and trim. Out back are a tavern with dining tables and a large oak bar, and in front, an enclosed garden porch that's especially pleasant for lunch.

Renowned for her home-style American cuisine, Sissy has changed the previously separate tavern and dining room menus into one that serves both areas. Now you'll find a burger and turkey croquettes on the same menu as grilled Colorado loin lamb chops with roasted shallots and garlic confit. At least four vegetarian items – including baked eggplant crêpes and mushroom stroganoff – are usually offered.

Among appetizers, we found the crabmeat mousse with a cucumber-mustard dill sauce and a few slices of melba toast enough for two to share. Although the duck confit with plum chutney and the grilled skirt steak with Spanish-style adobo sauce tempted, we couldn't pass up the calves liver, which we'd heard was the best anywhere. Served rare with crisp bacon and slightly underdone slices of onion, it was superb. The trout, deboned but served with its skin still on, was laden with sautéed leeks and mushrooms.

Pies, bread pudding with whiskey sauce and chocolate terrine with raspberry sauce are on the dessert menu. We chose a kiwi sorbet, wonderfully deep flavored, accompanied by a big sugar cookie.

Rooms on the two upper floors have been redone with carpeting, modern baths with wood washstands, print wallpapers and antique furnishings. Two of the nicest are the third-floor front corner rooms, one with twin sleigh beds, two rockers, Audubon prints and floral wallpaper, and the other with a canopy bed, marble table and wallpaper of exotic animals and birds. A second-floor corner suite overlooking the green includes a sitting room with TV, telephone and refrigerator and a bedroom with double brass bed. A second suite also has a TV, as do a couple of rooms at the rear of the ground floor.

The inn serves a hearty, prix-fixe breakfast and interesting lunches, with enough choices to appeal one autumn day to all in our party of seven youngsters and adults.

(802) 867-5500 or (877) 367-7389. Fax (802) 867-5542. www.dorsetinn.com. Twenty-eight rooms and two suites with private baths. Doubles, $120 to $220 B&B, $220 to $330 MAP.

Entrées, $17 to $31. Lunch daily, 11:30 to 2. Dinner nightly, 5 to 9.

A Grand Resort Reborn

The Equinox, Route 7A, Manchester Village 05254.

In a class by itself is the grand old Equinox, a resort hotel dating to 1769 and renovated twice in the last two decades to the tune of more than $32 million. A partnership whose majority owner is Guinness, the beer company that owns the noted Gleneagles Hotel in Scotland, applied the finishing touches: renovations to the hotel's 141 guest rooms and eleven suites, a dramatic new lobby, a vastly expanded Marsh Tavern and the formal Colonnade dining room.

Now a RockResort, the classic, columned white facade embraces a world of lush comfort. All bedrooms have been winterized, equipped with modern baths, TVs and telephones, and dressed in light pine furniture, new carpeting, and coordinated bedspreads and draperies. Rooms come in five sizes, and anything smaller than deluxe could be a letdown.

If you really want to splurge, settle into one of the suites in the Equinox's nearby **Charles Orvis Inn,** the famed fisherman-innkeeper's former home and inn renovated in 1995 for $2.8 million. From the fly-fishing gear framed in the "lift" to the game room with not one but two billiards tables next to the cozy Tying Room Bar, it elevates club-like luxury to new heights. The three sumptuous one-bedroom and six two-bedroom suites come with king or queen beds, stereos and TVs in armoires in both bedroom and living room, gas fireplaces, marble bathrooms, full cherry-paneled kitchens, and rich colors and furnishings in the English style. Charles Orvis "would have approved," according to the inn's elaborate brochure.

The barrel-vaulted ceiling in the resort's enormous **Colonnade** dining room was stenciled by hand by a latter-day Michelangelo who lay on his back on scaffolding for days on end. It's suitably formal for holiday dinner buffets and Sunday brunch.

Everyday dining is in the 1769 **Marsh Tavern,** fashioned from the old lobby and quite sumptuous in deep tones of green, red and black. The tavern is four times as big as before with a handsome bar and well-spaced tables flanked by windsor and wing chairs and loveseats. We found it too bright one winter's night with lights right over our heads, although the hostess said that was a new one on her – most folks thought the place too dark. And our elegant and rather pricey "supper" from the tavern menu was best forgotten. The experience has improved since the tavern became the resort's main dinner venue. Nowadays, expect straightforward contemporary American entrées ranging from cornmeal-crusted trout with tomato vinaigrette to pan-seared New York strip steak with red wine demi-glace. Appetizers might be a tad more inspired, as in lobster cakes with corn custard and baby greens or pan-seared buffalo skewers with mango relish. Desserts include a fine maple crème brûlée, warm chocolate truffle cake and apple-caramel bread pudding. A trio plays here most nights after 9:30.

There's no better setting for lunch than the seasonal **Dormy Grill** on the veranda at the golf-course clubhouse. The evening lobster fest and cookout here is a draw on summer weekends.

Work off the calories at the full-service, state-of-the-art Avanyu Spa in an adjacent building. It contains an indoor pool, sauna and steam rooms, an exercise room with Nautilus equipment, massage and spa therapy, aerobics programs, the works.

(802) 362-4700 or (800) 362-4747. Fax (802) 362-4861. www.equinoxresort.com. One hundred seventy rooms and thirteen suites and townhouses. Rates, EP. Doubles, $239 to $429. Suites and townhouses, $559 to $759. Orvis suites, $629 to $929.

Marsh Tavern: (802) 362-7833. Entrées, $24 to $29. Lunch, Monday-Saturday noon to 2:30; dinner nightly, 6 to 9. Dormy Grill, lunch daily, 11:30 to 4, late May to mid-October; lobster fest dinner on summer weekends, 5:30 to 8. Colonnade, Sunday brunch noon to 2:30.

Dining

Chantecleer, Route 7A, East Dorset.

Ask anyone to name the best restaurants in the Manchester area and the Chantecleer usually heads the list – absolutely tops, says an innkeeper whose taste we respect. One of Swiss chef Michel Baumann's strengths is consistency, ever since he opened his contemporary-style restaurant in an old dairy barn north of Manchester in 1981. The rough wood beams and barn siding remain, but fresh flowers, oil lamps, good art, hanging quilts, shelves of bric-a-brac, and navy and white china atop white-over-blue calico tablecloths lend elegance to the rusticity. A pig tureen decorates the massive fireplace.

The contemporary menu features French provincial and Swiss cuisine. Except for staples like rack of lamb, it changes bi-weekly.

Our party of four sampled a number of offerings, starting with a classic baked onion soup, penne with smoked salmon, potato pancakes with sautéed crabmeat and a heavenly lime-butter sauce, and bundnerfleisch, the Swiss air-dried beef, fanned out in little coronets with pearl onions, cornichons and melba rounds. Artichokes stuffed with crabmeat and a terrine of eggplant and roasted peppers with goat-cheese mousse are other favorites among appetizers. Caesar salad is prepared tableside for two.

Entrées range from whole dover sole meunière to grilled venison and wild boar chop with truffle butter demi-glace. We savored the specialty rack of lamb roasted with fine herbs, veal sweetbreads with morels, sautéed quail stuffed with duxelles and the night's special of boneless local pheasant, served with smoked bacon and grapes. Fabulous roësti potatoes upstaged the other accompaniments, purée of winter squash, snow peas and strands of celery.

Grand marnier layer cake, bananas foster, Swiss tobler chocolate mousse and

Window tables overlook Bromley Brook outside Mistral's at Toll Gate.

trifle were memorable endings to a rich, expensive meal. A number of Swiss wines are included on the reasonably priced wine list. Yodeling may be heard on tape as background music.

(802) 362-1616. Entrées, $28 to $39. Dinner by reservation, nightly except Tuesday from 6.

Mistral's at Toll Gate, Toll Gate Road, Manchester Center.

The other great restaurant in the Manchester area is Mistral's, a delightful French restaurant with a difference.

Long gone is the haute demeanor of the old Toll Gate Lodge, one of Vermont's original Travel-Holiday award winners with a tuxedoed staff and sky-high prices. In its place is a less intimidating dining room, a simpler menu and the hospitality of chef-owners Dana and Cheryl Markey. Both local, they met as teenagers at the Sirloin Saloon, worked their way through area restaurants and ended up here in 1988, living upstairs in the rustic structure that looks like Grandmother's house in the woods.

Although the two dining rooms seating 80 are country pretty with dark woods, lace curtains, blue and white linens, and gold-edged white china, it is the views through picture windows looking onto the trickling flume of Bromley Brook that are most compelling. After dark, when the brook and woods, accented in summer by purple petunias and brilliant impatiens, are illuminated, the setting is magical.

The menu offers a choice of about ten starters and a dozen entrées, most classic French with some nouvelle and northern Italian touches. Tempting starters include French onion soup gratinée, frog's legs persillade, beef carpaccio with frisée salad, smoked salmon blini and escargots bourguignonne en croûte.

Main courses range from breast of chicken paillard with lemon-caper sauce to grilled filet mignon with roquefort ravioli. Homemade bread and a house salad with choice of dressings accompany. The options could be halibut stuffed with spinach and crabmeat, crispy sweetbreads dijonnaise, roast duckling with cherry kirsch sauce and medallions of venison with black truffle cabernet sauce. The specialty châteaubriand béarnaise and rack of lamb rosemary may be ordered for two.

The signature dessert is coupe mistral (coffee ice cream rolled in hazelnuts with hot fudge sauce and frangelico). Others include a complex chocolate godiva cake, praline cheesecake and assorted fruit sorbets.

While Dana is in the kitchen, Cheryl oversees the front of the house and a growing wine list, honored by Wine Spectator.

(802) 362-1779 or (800) 279-1779. Entrées, $24 to $34. Dinner nightly except Wednesday, from 6.

Bistro Henry, 1942 Routes 11 & 30, Manchester Center.

Some of the area's most exciting food is offered by Henry and Dina Bronson, who met in the kitchens of top Manhattan restaurants and moved to Vermont to pursue their dream. They first opened Dina's, a contemporary American dining room in an inn north of town, and then resurfaced in a motel dining room they called Bistro Henry. In 2003, they moved up the road to a green farmhouse they could call their own.

With seating for about 100, it's the perfect spot for what Henry calls "a restaurant for today," as well as a home for Dina's growing Vermont Baking Co. business. Dining is in cheery bistro-style rooms with salmon-colored walls accented with framed European posters. Tables are topped with white butcher paper over white linens and centered with bottles of S. Pellegrino water.

Henry executes a contemporary Mediterranean bistro menu, based on the food the couple enjoyed while living and working in France. He has elevated the classics to 21st-century tastes, and his food sparkles with authenticity. Recent examples were grilled rare tuna with wasabi and pickled ginger, Moroccan grilled chicken with couscous, merlot-braised lamb shank, steak frites and grilled veal chop with mushroom sauce. As always, the menu was supplemented by tempting specials, among them soft-shell crab sauté, red snapper with orange-basil butter, organic Pacific salmon with pinot noir sauce and beef wellington with truffle sauce.

Start with a classic onion soup gratinée or the more innovative sweetbread éclair with madeira cream. Finish with one of Dina's great desserts, perhaps her ever-famous fruit crisp, grand marnier crème brûlée, bananas foster cheesecake or lemon sorbet. She sells them retail and wholesale from her bakery.

(802) 362-4982. www.bistrohenry.com. Entrées, $21 to $36. Dinner, Tuesday-Sunday from 5.

Asta's, 3894 Main St. (Route 30), Jamaica.

Swiss cuisine and European ambiance are the hallmarks of this restaurant opened by chef Michel de Preux and his wife Bonnie, who named it for a favorite great aunt from Estonia. The couple took over an abandoned pizzeria in what earlier had been the Brookside Inn and turned it into a charming restaurant and small village "hotel," as old-world European as they come.

Colorful alpine geraniums hanging from planters along the second-floor porch welcome summer guests in the Swiss style. Dark European decor prevails inside the 40-seat restaurant, where a small dining nook faces the bar in front. The rear dining area opens onto a porch overlooking a brook.

Michel, who moved here after serving as executive chef at Ivana's at the Trump Plaza in Atlantic City and the restored Capital Hotel in Little Rock, features the

French-German-Italian cuisine of his native Valais region of Switzerland. Entrées include a house salad, but you might want to start with his escargots, truffle mousse pâté or Nordic fish sampler.

Among main courses are specialties such as choucroute garni, chicken cordon bleu, wiener schnitzel and veal zurichoise. Those with Americanized palates like the salmon glazed with maple teriyaki and served over angel-hair pasta and the garlicky grilled lamb chops. Apple strudel and black forest cake are dessert specialties.

With advance notice, two or more can make a leisurely meal of such Swiss specialties as raclette and beef or cheese fondue, $22 to $26 per person. These include a Swiss dinner salad, cornichons, pickled onions, potatoes and condiments.

Upstairs are three guest rooms, two with fireplaces, renting for $98 to $179.

(802) 874-8000. Entrées, $15.95 to $27. Dinner nightly except Wednesday, 5 to 9 or 10. Sunday brunch, noon to 2. No credit cards.

Two Tannery Road, 2 Tannery Road, West Dover.

The first frame house in the town of Dover has quite a history. Built in the late 1700s and moved "stick by stick" from Marlborough, Mass., it was the summer home in the early 1900s of President Theodore Roosevelt's son and daughter-in-law, and the president is said to have visited. In the early 1940s it was moved again to its present location, the site of a former sawmill and tannery. It became the first lodge for nearby Mount Snow and finally a restaurant in 1982.

Along the way it also has been transformed into a place of considerable attractiveness, especially the main Garden Room with its vaulted ceiling. It's a many-windowed space so filled with plants and so open that you almost don't know where the inside ends and the outside begins. A wall of windows looks onto the Garden Room from the Fireplace Room, which along with two smaller interior dining rooms has beamed ceilings, barnwood walls and wide-plank floors dotted with oriental-patterned rugs. Charming stenciling and folk art are everywhere. A pleasant lounge contains part of the original bar from the Waldorf-Astoria. A light tavern menu is offered here Friday-Sunday from 6 to 9.

Longtime chef Brian Reynolds has spiced up the continental/American fare with starters like Acadian pepper shrimp and grilled cajun steak tips, two items that proved so popular they now are also available as entrées. We enjoyed the garlicky frog's legs as well as the duck livers with onions in a terrific sauce. Nearly two dozen entrées plus nightly specials range from pecan-stuffed shrimp to spice-crusted lamb chops with apple-currant chutney. "Tannery Three" might pair jumbo Acadian shrimp with cajun steak tips and andouille sausage. Veal is a specialty, so we tried veal granonico in a basil sauce as well as grilled New Mexican chicken with chiles, herbs and special salsa, accompanied by a goodly array of vegetables – broccoli, carrots, parsley and boiled new potatoes in one case, rice pilaf in the other.

A four-layer grand marnier cake with strawberries – enough for two to share – testified to the kitchen's prowess with desserts. They include a renowned mud pie, frozen black and white mousse with raspberry sauce, apple crêpes and homemade peanut-butter ice cream.

Colombian-blend coffee and espresso end a pleasant meal. And if the dining room is a wondrous garden retreat with rabbits running around the lawn in summer, think how lovely it must be when the lawn is covered with snow in winter.

(802) 464-2707. www.twotannery.com. Entrées, $24 to $32. Dinner, Tuesday-Sunday 6 to 10.

Le Petit Chef, Route 100, Wilmington.

Although the renovated 1850 Cutler Homestead looks tiny from the outside, it is surprisingly roomy inside, with three dining rooms and an inviting lounge. The chef is Betty Hillman, daughter of Libby, the noted cookbook author and food writer. Betty studied in France for a year and her formerly classic French menu has become more contemporary of late.

Appetizers include a signature tomato, basil and goat cheese tart, grilled sea scallops on tropical fruit salsa, lobster and guacamole salad garnished with crisp wontons and fricassee of escargots and wild mushrooms.

Typical main dishes are shrimp en brochette grilled on a rosemary branch and served on a tomato and feta risotto, Mediterranean bouillabaisse, sliced moulard duck with red onion marmalade, grilled veal chop with a balsamic reduction and beef tournedos on a crouton garnished with merlot sauce and a ragoût of wild mushrooms. A classic rack of lamb is available for two.

Homemade lemon sorbet and ice creams, fresh fruit tarts, apple cake, crunchy meringue and chocolate torte are among desserts.

The dining rooms are notable for grapevine wreaths on the walls, oriental rugs on the floors, and cabinets filled with antique china and glass. Tables are topped with white linens, handsome and heavy white china and cutlery, and oil lamps.

(802) 464-8437. Entrées, $25.50 to $34. Dinner nightly except Tuesday, 6 to 9 or 10.

Peter Havens, 32 Elliot St., Brattleboro.

"Established 1989," says the logo of this highly regarded but low-key restaurant that borrows the first and middle names of chef-owner Gregg Vaniderstine's father. The handsome white dining room has high ceilings, cane and chrome chairs, beige-clothed tables with pottery lamps crafted in Marlboro, and track lights aimed at stunning artworks by an artist-friend. A large plant hangs from a recessed skylight.

The short menu emphasizes fresh seafood, perhaps sea scallops provençal, jumbo shrimp sautéed with pernod and fire-roasted red peppers, and poached grouper with lemon-cilantro béchamel sauce. Filet mignon usually is fired with a green peppercorn-bourbon cream sauce, and roasted duck might be sauced with sour cherries, black currants and port wine. Escargots, clams casino, duck-liver pâté and smoked salmon with a popover and horseradish-dill sauce are typical starters. Among desserts are chocolate truffle cake, pot de crème, white chocolate mousse cake with raspberry sauce and assorted cheesecakes. The chocolate-butternut sauce that tops the ice cream has proved so popular that the owner bottles it to sell at Christmas.

(802) 257-3333. Entrées, $24 to $28. Dinner, Tuesday-Saturday from 6.

T.J. Buckley's, 132 Elliot St., Brattleboro.

"Uptown dining" along a side street in Brattleboro is how chef-owner Michael Fuller bills this choice little black, red and silver diner with intimate tables for up to twenty lucky patrons. The setting is charming; the food, creative and highly regarded. The city slicker from Cleveland, who came to Vermont more than two decades ago to ski and to apprentice with René Chardain at the Four Columns Inn in Newfane, does everything here himself, except for some of the prep work and serving.

He usually offers four entrées a night at a fixed price of $30 to $35, which he's quick to point out includes rolls, vegetables and a zippy salad of four lettuces,

Chef Michael Fuller answers phone in open kitchen facing dinner tables at T.J. Buckley's.

endive, radicchio and marinated peppers dressed with the house vinaigrette. At one visit, Michael was preparing a neat-sounding shrimp and clam dish with a purée of roasted plum tomatoes and dill oil with shaved fennel and slices of reggiano, to be served with polenta. Other choices were roasted halibut with wild rice risotto and a lobster stock reduction, roasted guinea hen, and grilled beef tenderloin with portobello mushrooms and red wine sauce.

Typical appetizers include an elaborate country pâté of veal and pork garnished with all kinds of fruit, a smoked trout tart with chèvre and a four-cheese tart that resembles a pizza. For dessert, look for a lime-macadamia tart that's very tart, a rich but not terribly sweet chocolate-hazelnut torte and a trio of sorbets: kiwi, blood orange and pineapple.

Red roses grace the linen-covered tables in wintertime, and other flowers the rest of the year. They add a touch of elegance to this tiny charmer.

(802) 257-4922. Prix-fixe, $30. Dinner, Wednesday-Sunday 6 to 10. No credit cards.

Thirty-Nine Main, 39 Main St., Brattleboro.

Funky, hip and eclectic. How else to describe this converted storefront that's billed as an international tapas-style restaurant "for right brain satisfaction?" It's colorful in pale greens and purples, with matching tile tables and booths topped by small aquariums and a skylit ceiling that nurtures exotic plants.

Chef-owner Matthew Miner calls himself a frustrated artist – which helps account for his sculptured food presentations. Working from a partly open kitchen facing a wraparound bar, he offers innovative fare that the uninitiated consider far-out. His menu is categorized by small plates and bigger plates. The former include a green rice roll with bamboo shoots, avocado and Asian slaw; salmon tartare with a chilled cucumber julienne and wasabi sorbet, and a dish deceptively called "eggs" – quail benedict with foie gras and shaved truffle alongside lobster flan. More conventional are a three-cheese tart with fig salsa and minted crème fraîche, a bruschetta of roasted garlic, goat cheese, black olive tapenade and tomato concasse, and a butternut squash risotto with toasted pinenuts and panna granada.

Bigger plates yield the likes of grilled escolar with porcini mushrooms, kale and savory grits, roasted monkfish with caramelized fennel and cilantro-goat cheese pesto, and pan-seared sea scallops with truffled tapioca, spinach and tabiko caviar. The flank steak might be flavored with a port wine-olive reduction and the cider-glazed venison chop served with apple and pomegranate relish and turnip gratin.

Desserts could be an apple custard tart, bread pudding with rum-flavored bananas, and warm bittersweet chocolate torte with raspberry and mango coulis.

Matthew knows his wines and prices them to move.

In 2005, he launched food service for the **Flat Street Brew Pub** in the Latchis Hotel complex across the street.

(802) 254-3999. www.thirty9main.com. Entrées, $14 to $16. Dinner, Thursday-Sunday from 5:30.

Capers Restaurant, 51 S. Main St., Brattleboro.

Fine cooking and affordable prices draw the locals to this sprightly downtown establishment lovingly run by Laurie Merrigan and Steve Berger, who between them had 50 years in the area restaurant business before opening their own in 2005. "We modeled it after restaurants we love in Europe," said Laurie, who was managing the front of the house the night we were there but alternates in the kitchen with Steve.

Their crispy decorated corner storefront looks more like modern California than old Europe, with tall windows onto the street, pale yellow walls, and blond wood tables and chairs and floors. A few plants and blue water bottles provide color.

The international dinner menu is short, healthful and priced from yesteryear. The entrées at our visit – all under $20 – were seared sea scallops with lemon-lime-thyme aioli, coq au vin, curried lamb with garam masala and ginger, and veal marsala. Vegetarians savored a vegetable pot pie and spinach tortellini stuffed with ricotta cheese and roasted garlic cream sauce.

You could start with smoked salmon with mascarpone or truffle mousse pâté served with the proper condiments and toast points. Desserts were warm triple ginger cake with apple compote, a rich chocolate-raspberry torte, mocha pots de crème and maple bread pudding with golden raisins.

The wine list is reasonably priced and harbors some unusual finds.

(802) 251-0151. Entrées, $16 to $19. Lunch, Wednesday-Saturday 11:30 to 2. Dinner, Wednesday-Saturday 5:30 to 8:30. Sunday brunch, 11 to 3.

Lodging

The Inn at Ormsby Hill, 1842 Main St. (Route 7A), Manchester Center 05255.

Chris and Ted Sprague, who turned the dining room at their Maine inn into a destination for gourmands, now lend their considerable innkeeping talents to this expanded B&B backing up to Robert Todd Lincoln's Hildene estate.

Chris, who cooked six nights a week in Maine, found she could not keep up the pace. "The change rejuvenated me," she advised after they acquired the Ormsby Hill in her native Vermont. "I'm able to do more creative breakfasts here, and we've reached a level of elegance that would have been impossible in Maine."

The elegance comes in five new luxury rooms they added in an unfinished wing of this sprawling manor house long owned by Edward Isham, an Illinois state legislator and senior partner in a Chicago law firm with Abraham Lincoln's son, whom he entertained here. Each has a gas fireplace, whirlpool tub and handsome decor. Rooms come with interesting angles – "we don't like squares," says Chris – and novel touches, a see-through fireplace between the bedroom and corner jacuzzi in one, a jacuzzi accessed through cupboard doors in another, and shuttered doors that open to reveal fireplaces in a couple more.

The main house already offered five comfortable guest rooms, all with fireplaces and two-person whirlpool baths and separate showers. All contain king or queen canopy or four-poster beds, plush armchairs, antique chests, artworks and oriental rugs. We stayed in the main-floor library room, beamed and dark with well-stocked bookshelves and a wood-burning fireplace.

Some are partial to the Tower suite, a three-level affair located in the tower section of the inn. There's a writing desk in the foyer, which leads to a raised bedroom with fireplace, sitting area and a tiger maple queensize canopy bed. The top level has a tiled bathroom with an oversize whirlpool tub in the corner and an oversize shower that doubles as a steam shower for two.

The best part may be the common rooms and the culinary treats. The main foyer leads to a front parlor furnished with antiques. From here one looks to the rear through a spacious library with fireplace into a conservatory dining room extending 40 feet back. At first glance, the total depth, in what is a strikingly wide house, is breathtaking. So is the view across the terrace, back yard, gardens and Hildene property to mountains through the many-paned windows.

Breakfast is usually a lavish buffet, taken in the conservatory or on the outdoor terrace. The sideboard holds three kinds of cereal including homemade granola (which inspired the Ormsby Hill cereal in a bag distributed nationally by a subsidiary of Kellogg), a bowl of assorted fruit, a basket of English muffins and two kinds of pastries (perhaps espresso or chocolate coffee cake and blueberry-lemon pound cake). The main dish could be a bacon and egg risotto, basil-scrambled eggs on portobello mushrooms, blueberry bread pudding, leek-bacon-gorgonzola polenta or a baked pancake dish that looks like a top hat. Dessert – yes, dessert – is the icing on the cake, so to speak: perhaps apple-cranberry crisp with vanilla ice cream or peach crisp with white chocolate sauce.

From welcoming madeleines and almond crescents upon arrival to a doggy bag of white-chocolate pound cake to take on your way, food is the star at this winning B&B.

(802) 362-1163 or (800) 670-2841. Fax (802) 362-5176. www.ormsbyhill.com. Ten rooms and suites with private baths. Doubles, $275 to $335 weekends, $215 to $275 midweek. Foliage and holidays: $330 to $390.

1811 House, Route 7A, Manchester Village 05254.

Bowls of popcorn and no fewer than 65 single-malt scotches – the biggest selection in Vermont, they say – are available in the intimate pub of this elegant B&B full of antiques, oriental rugs and charm. The pub (open nightly from 5:30 to 8) is where owners Marnie and Bruce Duff offer McEwan's ale on draught or one of their rare scotches, $4.50 to $20 a shot or three for $10 for a wee dram of each, if you're into testing. Although it's supposed to be a reproduction of an early American tavern, to us it looks like a Scottish pub with its McDuff tartan seats and horse brasses, and a McDuff coat of arms above the polished wood bar. A warming fireplace, a regulation dart board and Waterford glasses add to the charm.

Nearby are the elegant yet comfortable parlor and library. Each has a fireplace, dark wood paneling, fine paintings and porcelains, and stenciled flowers of the British Isles (the thistle, shamrock, rose and daffodil). Decanters of port and sherry await guests. Downstairs is a game room with both a ping-pong and a regulation billiards table.

Guest quarters in the nationally registered Federal house are air-conditioned and, except for one with a double bed, are quite spacious. Four have fireplaces, including a corner main-floor suite with a sitting room and kingsize canopy four-poster bed. The fabrics in the draperies and bedspreads are exceptionally tasteful. The bedroom of Mary Lincoln Isham (Abraham Lincoln's granddaughter, who lived here for a short time) contains a marble enclosure for the bathtub that she had put in. The Henry and Ethel Robinson Room with kingsize canopy bed offers a private porch overlooking the grounds, pond and mountains.

An addition in a rear cottage has produced three deluxe rooms with kingsize beds and fireplaces. The largest takes up the entire second floor. It has a vaulted ceiling, and two oversize leather chairs facing the fireplace.

In the big kitchen with a commercial stove, Marnie Duff and her daughter and son-in-law, Cathy and Jorge Veleta, whip up hearty English breakfasts, perhaps including scones, fried tomatoes, eggs any style or special french toast soaked overnight with pecans. The Sunday specialty is eggs benedict. Guests partake in the dining room or pub amid Villeroy & Boch china and the family sterling.

(802) 362-1811 or (800) 432-1811. Fax (802) 362-2443. www.1811house.com. Eleven rooms and two suites with private baths. Doubles, $140 to $260. Suites, $280. Two-night minimum stay weekends, holidays and foliage.

The Four Seasons Inn, 145 Route 100, Box 2540, West Dover 05356.

Expatriate Brits Ann and Barry Poulter had enjoyed renovating houses in their spare time, but this was something else: a rundown, 24-room ski lodge and restaurant that catered to the bus group trade. The couple spent three years and several million dollars renovating what a fellow innkeeper termed "a dump" into an almost all-new, fifteen-room generally upscale inn that the aforementioned innkeeper calls "the best rooms in the Mount Snow valley."

The main entry opens into a foyer with a wood-paneled bar that proved so inviting it doubles as the reception area. Across the way is a stunning living room with massive fieldstone fireplace, plush dark brown sofas and chairs in one section and lighter furnishings in the front section. Dividers topped by colorful teapots separate the two sections from each other and from the expansive rear breakfast room, sunny and elegant with individual tables draped in yellow and white. It opens onto a lovely back deck overlooking the North Branch of the Deerfield River .

Several more small common rooms are scattered here and there through the various wings of the inn. The most deluxe guest rooms are six above the main-floor common areas in the South Wing, plus two in North Wing. All have step-up king or queen canopy or poster beds, gas or wood-burning fireplaces and modern baths with jacuzzi tubs. Five have private balconies. Each is individually decorated by Ann, who is partial to subtle floral wallpapers, 300-count bed linens, down comforters, Molton Brown toiletries from England and TV/DVD players concealed in armoires.

The Poulters serve a full breakfast, ordered from a menu. Choices include challah french toast, buttermilk pancakes with "blueberries we pick ourselves," eggs any style and the house specialty, baked eggs in ham crisps.

(802) 464-8303 or (877) 531-4500. Fax (802) 464-3373. www.thefourseasonsinn.com. Sixteen rooms with private baths. Doubles, $145 to $380 in foliage and winter, $135 to $275 rest of year.

Light Fare

The Little Rooster Café, Route 7A south of Manchester Center, started as an offshoot of the Chantecleer restaurant, and the chef continues the tradition. For breakfast, the Rooster tops an English muffin with poached eggs, Canadian bacon, creamed spinach and smoked salmon in a light mustard sauce. The french toast triple-decker, layered with smoked ham and pineapple, is served with raspberry butter. For lunch ($6.50 to $9.95), we've enjoyed the crab cake baguette, the leg of lamb sandwich and the grilled tuna niçoise salad. There's a wine list, plus the usual coffees. Open daily except Wednesday, 7:30 to 3.

Across the street is **The Buttery at the Jelly Mill,** on the second floor of a fun, four-story collection of shops selling gourmet foods and kitchenware, among other things. It purveys many sandwiches, including smoked salmon on a toasted croissant with capers. The shrimp-stuffed artichokes are famous. Snacks like nachos, soups, salads and specials such as a tomato, bacon and cheddar quiche are offered, and you can end with neapolitan mousse torte or amaretto bread pudding. Open daily, 9 to 3; weekend brunch, 10 to 1.

Up for Breakfast, Main Street, Manchester Center, is just what its name says: upstairs above a storefront, and open for breakfast only. Although reports on the food lately have been mixed, you'll find pain perdu, cajun frittata, huevos rancheros and belgian waffles in the $5 to $8 range. We chose "one of each" – one eggs benedict and one eggs argyle (with smoked salmon). These proved hearty, as did the heavy Irish scone, both dishes garnished with chunks of pineapple and watermelon. Only after we'd eaten did we see the blackboard menu around the side, listing some rather exotic specials like rainbow trout with eggs and mango-cranberry-nutmeg pancakes. Open weekdays 7 to noon, weekends 7 to 1.

Gourmet Treats

Long known for its high-fashion designer outlets, Manchester Center is branching out lately with factory stores of food interest. Besides the predictable **Mikasa, Dansk** and **Harrington Hams, Vermont Kitchen Supply, Godiva Chocolatier, Baccarat** and **Mary's Kitchen** ("celebrating the art of cooking") caught our eye.

Peltier's Market on the Green in Dorset has been the center of Dorset life since the early 1800s. A true country store with all the staples, it also caters to the upscale. You might pick up a sandwich from the refrigerator – perhaps smoked salmon or avocado, cheese and tomato. Caviar, good wines, Vermont products like cheese from Shelburne Farms, Peltier's own pancake mix and flavored horseradish spreads, exotic vegetables and prime meats can be found here. So can worms and night crawlers, close by the pesto and sundried tomatoes in the chilled produce case.

Billed as "a true factory store," **The Kitchen Store at J.K. Adams Co.** woodworkers on Route 30 just south of Dorset has a fine selection of cheeseboards, spice racks, butcher blocks, and the like made of native hardwoods. On the second floor, seconds are sold at substantial savings. There's a smell and sound of woodworking in the air, and you can see some of the action through a factory-viewing window.

"Not your average...we cater to all cuisines," advertises the **Flat Road Diner,** 709-A Depot St. (Routes 11/30), Manchester Center. A handbill cites truck and trailer parking, and gives directions off the ramp from the Route 7 bypass. But many customers seem to be outlet shoppers, feasting on breakfast specialties like crab benedict, cilantro breakfast burrito and Japanese scrambled eggs with tofu. Not your usual truck stop fare are offerings like beefalo burger, portobello sandwich with goat cheese, cobb salad and croque monsieur. You can stop for a beer and a burger at the counter, enjoy a full dinner with a bottle of wine, or just check out the hub-cap collection. Open daily for breakfast and lunch, 6 to 6, dinner Wednesday-Saturday 5:30 to 9:30.

Fine produce, fruit, plants, fresh pies and more are featured at **Dutton Farm Stands,** a fixture along Route 30 in Newfane and with an expanded second location along Routes 11/30 in Manchester Center. Wendy and Paul Dutton grow the produce on their 105-acre Newfane farm and apples on a 30-acre orchard in Brattleboro. In melon season they offer slices of many kinds to sample – an instructive touch, and refreshing, too.

Mozzarella and More

For superior fresh mozzarella, drop into **Al Ducci's Italian Pantry,** Elm Street, Manchester Center, and meet Al Scheps, who has been making his own since he was eight years old. The name of the little Italian grocery is a takeoff on Balducci's in Manhattan. "We have a lot of fun here," says Al, who jokes back and forth with customers. A one-pound ball of mozzarella runs $4.99 and, as Al suggests, it is delicious cut into cubes and mixed with ripe tomatoes, red onions, fruity olive oil, balsamic vinegar and cubes of homemade Italian bread, all of which he sells. Good sandwiches ($4.50 to $8) are also made with the bread; you can have additions like grated carrots, sundried tomatoes and roasted peppers. Homemade sausage, cannoli and sfogliatelle (a flaky pastry with ricotta cheese) are other goodies. Pasta salads and dinner entrées are available to go. Open Tuesday-Saturday 8 to 6, Sunday 9 to 4.

Gourmet Sweets

Mother Myrick's Confectionery, Route 7A, Manchester Center.

Here is paradise for anyone with a sweet tooth. Jacki Baker and Ron Mancini have operated Mother Myrick's (named for a famous midwife and the nearby mountain) since 1977, although they downsized in 2005, closing their café and ice-cream parlor and relocating to a small showroom across and down the road from the original. Their chocolates and candy are known across the East.

Using old-fashioned equipment wherever possible (like a two-foot cream beater from the 1940s for fondant), they make a myriad of chocolates, truffles, fudge, apricots hand-dipped in dark chocolate, fancy molds and their most popular candy, buttercrunch, rolled in roasted almonds and cashews, $28 in a one-pound gift box and worth every penny. The best fudge sauce we have tasted (even better than mom's) comes out of Ron's production kitchen. Holiday stollen, pies, cakes, cookies and much more are for sale.

(802) 362-1560 or (888) 669-7425. www.mothermyricks.com. Open daily 10 to 6.

Blantyre, a replica of a castle in Scotland, symbolizes the good life in the Berkshires.

The Tri-State Berkshires

A Tradition of High Tastes

Country inns may seem more historic in Vermont, but they have reached their pinnacle in the Berkshires, an area whose name is inseparably linked in the national perception with country inns and summer tradition.

That may be a result of Norman Rockwell's depiction of the Red Lion Inn and Main Street in Stockbridge, a scene that has come to epitomize the essence of New England for anyone west of the Hudson River.

Indeed, when friends from Switzerland visited one foliage season and asked to "see" New England in a day, we headed off to the Berkshires and Stockbridge so they could sense what New England is all about. They shot two rolls of color film before departing for Texas.

Had their visit been in the summer, we would have taken them to Tanglewood in Lenox, where the elaborate picnics complete with tablecloths and candelabra on the lawns beside the Music Shed are as delightful a tradition in which to partake (and observe) as the Boston Symphony Orchestra is to hear.

The inns in the Berkshires are keeping up with the times, both in quality and in numbers. Indeed, two country-house hotels were Andrew Harper Hideaway Report grand award winners: Wheatleigh in 2002 and Blantyre in 2005. And although the area has had good restaurants longer than most resort regions, thanks to its early status as a destination for summer visitors, new restaurants pop up every year.

As with the inns, the dining situation reflects the sophisticated tastes and often the prices of a noted resort and cultural area close to metropolitan centers.

But there also are rural, rustic charms to be discovered amid the luxury of Lenox or Lakeville and the sophistication of Stockbridge or Salisbury. Seek them out as well, to savor the total Berkshire experience.

Dining and Lodging

The Berkshires are such a popular destination that three-night (and even four-night) stays are the minimum for weekends in summer and foliage season at many inns. Restaurant hours generally vary from daily in summer and foliage to part-time the rest of the year.

The Old Inn on the Green, 134 Hartsville-New Marlborough Road (Route 57), New Marlborough, MA 01230.

What many consider to be the best dining experience in the Berkshires is offered at this restored 1760 stagecoach inn that blends a patina of antiquity with inspired contemporary cuisine.

The inn quickly achieved star status as a destination for gourmands with the arrival of top Berkshires chef Peter Platt, who took over after sixteen years heading the kitchen at Wheatleigh in Lenox. He and his wife, Meredith Kennard, purchased the inn from its founders in 2005 and extended their hospitality beyond their dining rooms to their lodgings.

Although it offers à-la-carte menus during the week in the fireside tavern or on the canopied outdoor terrace in summer, the Old Inn's culinary claim to fame continues to be its Saturday night prix-fixe dinners, served totally by candlelight in as historic a setting as can be conceived. About 50 people are seated in the tavern room, a formal parlor or at the harvest table in the dining room. In each, the original wainscoting, stenciling, antiques and windows draped in velvet are shown to advantage. The handmade wreaths of branches and bark are fascinating, the large mural of cows grazing on the New Marlborough green is wonderful to see, and it's easy to imagine yourself transported back a couple of centuries for the evening.

Chèvre and almond puff-pastry sticks might accompany drinks, served in delicate stemmed glasses. From a mushroom and herb soup that is the essence of mushroom to the final cappuccino with shredded chocolate on top, things go from great to greater.

A recent autumn meal began with a choice of mussels with julienned vegetables in orange-saffron sauce, Maine peekytoe crab salad with diced mango and sliced avocado, and a warm salad of pan-roasted Hudson Valley squab with a foie gras flan and smoky corn salsa.

The main-course options were seared fillet of line-caught striped bass sauced with olive oil and aged balsamic vinegar, roast breast of normandy duck with caramelized shallot sauce and roast rack of Colorado lamb with rosemary-infused balsamic jus.

Dessert was bittersweet chocolate sorbet in toasted almond cups with coffee sauce, blueberry and nectarine croustade with crème fraîche, or a sampling of New England and European cheeses.

A short and with-it à la carte menu is offered other nights in the tavern beside the hearth or outside on the canopied, candlelit terrace overlooking a Colonial flower and herb garden. Entrées typically range from pan-roasted fillet of Maine cod with sweet corn chowder sauce to roast tenderloin of veal with porcini mushroom sauce.

Although best known for its dining, this inn also attracts overnight guests with a variety of charming accommodations. That is due as much to the warmth of the owners/innkeepers as to its quiet location out in the boondocks of the southern Berkshires.

Mural of scene outside graces dining room at The Old Inn on the Green.

Upstairs in the inn are a newly renovated suite and four queensize bedrooms, authentically furnished with antiques and country furniture. The suite comes with a fireplace, TV/VCR, whirlpool tub and a separate shower. The second-floor veranda across the front of the inn is a serene spot from which to view the passing scene – what little there is of it – across the village green.

The grandest lodgings are next door in the restored 1821 Thayer House, which had been owned for 40 years by the late sister of editor Ben Bradlee. Also facing the village green, it's a luxurious refuge of six bedrooms, three of them kingsize, with a common parlor, a fireplaced den, a library and a courtyard terrace with a swimming pool. A mural of the village green as it appeared in the 19th century graces the foyer. All but one Thayer House rooms include fireplaces, whirlpool tubs and TV/VCRs.

Overnight guests enjoy a substantial continental breakfast at the main inn. "We bake our own pastries, croissants and brioche and make our own granola," says Peter, who does the cooking while Meredith serves. Eggs or pancakes are available for an extra charge.

(413) 229-7924. www.oldinn.com. Ten rooms and one suite with private baths. Doubles, $205 to $325 in inn, $325 to $365 in Thayer House.

Dinner by reservation, prix-fixe $65, Saturday 5:30 to 9:30. À la carte, $26 to $38, Sunday-Monday and Wednesday-Friday 5:30 to 9:30. Closed Monday as well as Tuesday November-June.

Wheatleigh, Hawthorne Road, Lenox, Mass. 01240.

Understated European-style opulence and luxury are offered in this exotic Italian palazzo built in 1893 as a wedding gift for the Countess de Heredia and lately refurbished and embellished to the tune of many millions of dollars by owners Susan and Linwood Simon.

The setting on 22 sylvan acres is grand, even palatial, but as refashioned by a New York design team the interior decor is unexpectedly minimalist, producing what the New York Times Magazine called the most European small hotel in America. "The most sophisticated country house hotel in America" is how Andrew Harper described it in his Hideaway Report.

The imposing entrance of the beige brick building framed in wrought iron leads into a soaring Great Room with modern and traditional sitting areas, a majestic staircase rising to the second floor, parquet floors and fine art all around. A portion of the basement has been transformed into a state-of-the-art fitness room with computerized equipment that tallies how you're doing as you watch the overhead TV. Outside are a tennis court, a heated swimming pool hidden in a sylvan glade and tranquil grounds within walking distance of Tanglewood.

To enhance the classical Renaissance architecture, the guest-room style is a light European look in muted beige and taupe colors with a mix of English and French antiques and European-modern furnishings. Bedrooms have French-designed bedspreads of imported silk, and more comfortable seating than in the past. Bathrooms were redone in imported English limestone or Italian marble, with silver-plated fixtures from England and Bulgari toiletries from Italy. Each room now has a TV/VCR and a portable telephone for those who want to be in touch wherever they are. Here and there on the walls are large and splashy canvases by painter Daniel Cohen.

Of the nineteen guest accommodations, eight are spacious, seven medium-size and four small (one with a built-in double bed is, frankly, tiny – ten-by-twelve feet to be precise). Nine of the best have fireplaces and six add private terraces or balconies.

The most exotic is the Aviary Suite, an unusual two-story affair joined by an outside spiral staircase enclosed in glass. Its upstairs has a kingsize bedroom with large windows onto a garden, dark chestnut ceiling and pale brick walls. Adjoining is an expansive "wet room" with an open shower, one of Wheatleigh's original deep soaking tubs and a separate water closet. The sitting room on the main floor is surrounded by glass and opens onto a terrace.

Also relatively new is the main-floor Terrace Suite, formed by enclosing part of a portico that matches the dining portico. It has a king bed with fabric headboard and two curved loveseats facing each other in the portico, which is enclosed in glass, bronze and brick. A pot of hot spiced cider, served by one of the staff clad in black, warmed our arrival here on a chilly autumn afternoon.

One of the best meals of our lives unfolded that evening in Wheatleigh's main-floor restaurant. Dinner is served in a handsome chandeliered dining room and in a large and glamorous glass-enclosed portico, pristine in white and with floor-to-ceiling windows on three sides. Their round tables are set with white linens, service plates in three patterns, delicate wine glasses, flickering oil lamps and vases of fresh flowers. Off the dining room is the intimate Library lounge, a sleek misnomer (shelves of china rather than books) that offers a light menu for lunch and supper.

Executive chef J. Bryce Whittlesey credits stints at L'Espalier in Boston, the Chanticleer in Nantucket and Michelin two-star restaurants in France for his disciplined French technique. He and a kitchen brigade of fifteen prepare three prix-fixe tasting menus each evening – three-course regular and four-course vegetarian (both $95) and six-course fish menu ($125).

Wheatleigh's kitchen uses exotic ingredients and is said to be labor-intensive. You know why when you see the night's regular offerings. Start as we did with the golden ossetra caviar and oyster "progression," the first of several that evening and yielding three choice oysters in various dress. Other starters, these from the

Dining in glass-enclosed portico at Wheatleigh is almost like being outdoors.

fish tasting menu, were truly exceptional bay scallops served with apple relish and blood orange vinaigrette in large scallop shells and Maine sea urchins with dungeness crab salad and pearl tapioca froth. These, mind you, followed an amuse-bouche of parsnip mousse with hamachi-soy sauce and preceded another amusé of mallard duck with cranberry sauce as what the staff called "little extras" kept appearing at each table. A fish course featured head-on prawns with hazelnut foam (the prawns turned out to be the size of a baby lobster and were tasty yet messy enough to require a finger bowl). Next came a whole roasted lobster with cardamom and star anise butter (fortunately, by this time, the whole was served in a half portion), to be followed by line-caught dover sole roasted on the bone and served with sautéed chicken oysters and poultry jus. Our other main course from the regular menu was described simply as "local young lamb with variation on butternut squash." That turned out to be two simultaneous "progressions" – lamb shoulder, confit and rack, each of the three with a different version of squash, about the only vegetables we saw all evening.

Two more amusés preceded dessert: one a buttermilk panna cotta and the other grapefruit sorbet inside a grapefruit. The main desserts were an ethereal lemon soufflé with limoncello sauce and apple tart normande, two small apple custard tarts flanking crème fraîche and calvados-cider sorbet.

If the preparations were labor-intensive, so was the service – deftly provided by the young international staff clad in black and working in "teams." Courses not only arrived but were eventually removed simultaneously. With each course came a complete change of silver service and stunning, sometimes clever plates – different shapes, sizes and brands, fitting perfectly with the food being served.

Never have we experienced such presentation and service. If it all sounds precious, it was, but in the best sense – not pretentious nor with attitude. Food portions, though appearing small, were ample in sum. At meal's end, the truffles that sent us into our Terrace Suite dreamland were almost too much.

Breakfast the next morning was another extravagance and began – a first in our experience – with another amuse-bouche. This one was a caramelized apricot topped with crème fraîche, so good that we asked the chef for the particulars – he readily obliged (he also offers day-long, hands-on cooking classes for day guests in the Wheatleigh kitchens in winter). The main courses were poached eggs Wheatleigh (rather like eggs benedict, but with wild mushrooms in the hollandaise sauce) and a souffléd omelet of smoked salmon and cheese. Each was accompanied by asparagus spears and roësti potatoes – more "vegetables" at breakfast than we'd experienced at dinner the night before.

Such indulgence exacts a price. Those with the wherewithal find the sybaritic experience as good as it gets.

(413) 637-0610. www.wheatleigh.com. Seventeen rooms and two suites with private baths. Rates, EP. Doubles, $645 to $1,250. Suites, $1,400 to $1,750.

Prix-fixe, $95. Dinner nightly by reservation, 6 to 8:30; closed Monday-Wednesday in winter. Library, entrées $19 to $29, lunch daily, noon to 2; dinner, 6 to 9:30. Sunday brunch, 9:30 to 1.

Blantyre, 16 Blantyre Road, Lenox, Mass. 01240.

Past a gatekeeper and up a long, curving driveway in the midst of 85 country acres appears the castle of your dreams. In fact, the 1902 Tudor-style brick manor built as a summer cottage for a millionaire in the turpentine business as an authentic replica of the Hall of Blantyre in Scotland used to be called a castle. It's full of hand-carved wood ornamentation, high-beamed ceilings, crystal chandeliers and spacious public rooms, plus turrets, gargoyles and carved friezes – just as in the English country-house hotels that its membership in the prestigious Relais & Châteaux group reflects.

Faithfully restored by the Fitzpatrick family of the Red Lion Inn in nearby Stockbridge, Blantyre houses guests in eight elegant rooms and suites in the mansion, twelve more contemporary quarters in a distant carriage house and four scattered about the property in small cottages.

The public rooms and guest rooms are so luxurious in a castle kind of way as to defy description – take our word or that of those who pay up to $950 a night for the Paterson Suite with a fireplaced living room (complete with a crystal chandelier over a lace-covered table in the middle of the room), two bathrooms and a large bedroom with a kingsize four-poster bed. A typical bathroom has a scale, a wooden valet, heated towel racks, embroidered curtains and more toiletries than one ever hoped to see.

Newly renovated rooms in the carriage house have hand-painted tiles and marble floors in the bathrooms, balconies or decks and wet bars. Some have lofts or sitting rooms, and all are near the pool. The newest of the four cottages, the Ice House, is the grandest yet. Upstairs is a king-bedded suite with fireplaced sitting room, kitchen, bath with whirlpool tub and a screened porch. The main floor has a downstairs bedroom with a king bed and patio. They are available individually for the night for $1,100 and $550 respectively, or $1,600 for the two.

A continental breakfast of croissants and muffins is served in Blantyre's sunny conservatory. Tables topped with mustard jars full of flowers are set beside windows overlooking gnarled trees and golf-course-like lawns. Additional breakfast items can be ordered for a charge.

Country-house cuisine, lately lightened up in style and made more contemporary by British-born executive chef Christopher Brooks, is available to house guests and the public in the formal dining room or two smaller rooms. The tables are set with different themes, the china and crystal changing frequently as Jane Fitzpatrick and her daughter, Ann Fitzpatrick Brown, add to the collection. Investing in its kitchen, Blantyre added a barbecue for grilling purposes and new and adventurous dishes for a savvy clientele with high expectations. Dinner is prix-fixe, $85 for three courses with many choices.

A typical dinner starts with a "surprise," perhaps foie gras or veal sweetbreads with sauternes and carrot sauce. Just a couple of bites to whet the appetite for what's to come – Maine lobster with smoked potato and lobster hash, poached quail eggs and hollandaise sauce or pan-seared sweetbreads with braised carrots, chestnuts and a licorice sauce. Main courses could include roasted arctic char in an apple-horseradish broth, pecan-crusted Texas antelope with cranberry sauce and, on a recent autumn night, rack of lamb with braised lamb shank, turnips and that ever-so-British bubble and squeak.

For dessert, how about bitter Swiss chocolate cake with sour orange compote and blackberry sorbet, white chocolate mousse and plum roulade with ginger-lime sauce, or lemon meringue tart with blueberry compote and passionfruit coulis? The wine list is strong on California chardonnays and cabernets and French regionals, priced into the triple digits. After dinner, guests like to adjourn to the Music Room for coffee and cordials, Blantyre having the atmosphere of a convivial country house.

Lunch in summer on the terrace ($42 for three courses or $18 to $26 à la carte) is a sybaritic indulgence. Walk it off around the gorgeous property. Play tennis on one of four Har-Tru courts or croquet on the only bent-grass tournament lawn in Massachusetts.

The oversize guest book in the entry hall is full of superlatives written by pampered patrons. The consensus: "Perfect. We'll be back."

(413) 637-3556. www.blantyre.com. Twelve rooms, eight suites and four cottages with private baths. Doubles, $500 to $750. Suites, $650 to $950. Cottages, $800 to $1,600.

Prix-fixe, $85. Lunch in summer by reservation, Tuesday-Sunday 12:30 to 1:45. Dinner by reservation, nightly in summer and foliage season, 6 to 8:45, otherwise Tuesday-Sunday. Jackets and ties required.

Mayflower Inn & Spa, 118 Woodbury Road (Route 47), Washington, Conn. 06793.

"Stately" is the word to describe this renovated and expanded inn, as styled by owners Robert and Adriana Mnuchin of New York. They took a venerable inn, once owned by The Gunnery school and hidden away on 28 wooded acres, and – with a Midas touch – renovated and expanded it into one of the premier English-style country-house hotels in North America.

Mayflower Inn dining room is appointed in English country-house style.

No expense was spared in producing accommodations that are the ultimate in comfort and good taste. Fifteen rooms are upstairs on the second and third floors of the main inn. Ten more are in two guest houses astride a hill beyond.

Fine British, French and American antiques and accessories, prized artworks and elegant touches of whimsy – like the four ancient trunks stashed in a corner of the reception foyer – dignify public and private rooms alike. Opening off the lobby, an intimate parlor with plush leather sofas leads into the ever-so-British gentleman's library. Across the back of the inn are three handsome dining rooms serene in white and mauve. Along one side is an English-style tap room and piano bar.

The setting for meals is exceptional, especially the outdoor terrace overlooking a Shakespeare garden with a view of manicured lawns and imported specimen trees. Executive chef Timothy Au, formerly of California's Lodge at Torrey Pines, changes the menu seasonally. A recent autumn visit produced the likes of parmesan-crusted halibut with a citrus butter sauce, roasted free-range chicken with madeira jus and rosemary-crusted Colorado rack of lamb with black currant sauce. Specialty starters are house-smoked salmon with tomato-caper relish and togarashi-seared ahi tuna sashimi with mustard-soy sauce. Desserts are extravagant, from maple crème brûlée to the "chocolate symphony" – a chocolate mousse pyramid, chocolate-caramel tart, chocolate truffle and white chocolate ice cream. The perennial house favorite is the plate of Mayflower cookies, a tasty assortment including perhaps macaroons, thick butter shortbreads and chocolate chip with cocoa.

Lighter fare ($9 to $29) is offered in the tap room. Spa cuisine is available throughout and in the dedicated Spa Dining Room.

Each guest room is a sight to behold and some are the ultimate in glamour. We like Room 24 with a kingsize canopied four-poster featherbed awash in pillows, embroidered Frette linens and a chenille throw. An angled loveseat faces the fireplace and oversize wicker rockers await on the balcony. Books and magazines are spread out on the coffee table, the armoire contains a TV and there's a walk-in closet. The paneled bathroom, larger than most bedrooms, has marble floors, a double vanity opposite a glistening tub, a separate w.c. area and a walk-in shower big enough for an army. Even all that didn't prepare us for a second-floor corner suite with a spacious living room straight out of Country Life magazine, a dining-conference room, two bathrooms, a bedroom with a kingsize canopied four-poster, and a porch overlooking the sylvan scene. The rear balconies and decks off the rooms in the two guest houses face the woods and are particularly private.

Across from the entrance to the main inn, a magnificent tiered rose garden tiptoes up a hill to a heated swimming pool and a tennis court. On the inn's lower level is a state-of-the-art fitness center.

Such amenities, along with a pampering staff of 85, contributed to the inn's speedy elevation to the ranks of Relais & Châteaux, the prestigious international hotel group whose clientele expects the finest.

The Mnuchins' daughter, Lisa Hedley, joined them to expand the estate's wellness facilities and to help Adriana to open a luminous, 20,000-square-foot spa in 2006.

(860) 868-9466. Fax (860) 868-1497. www.mayflowerinn.com. Seventeen rooms and eight suites with private baths. Rates, EP. Doubles, $400 to $600. Suites, $650 to $1,300. Entrées, $21 to $36. Lunch daily, noon to 2. Dinner nightly, 6 to 9. Taproom, noon to 9.

The Boulders, East Shore Road (Route 45), New Preston 06777.

This venerable inn across the road from Lake Waramaug has been grandly refurbished in Adirondack lodge style under new ownership to appeal to a more sophisticated, moneyed clientele. The new look is evident in the main-floor public rooms that sprawl across the front of the substantial Dutch Colonial residence built in 1890. The luxurious living room has been redecorated in cool taupe and beige, with six oversize lodge chairs facing windows onto the lake.

Boulders remain integral to the decor, comprising the massive fireplace chimney in the living room and jutting out from the walls of the interior dining room. Both the intimate interior room and the airy, six-sided Lake Dining Room with windows onto Lake Waramaug have been redecorated. The latter is pristine in cream and white, with upholstered chairs covered in gray-beige fabric. Interestingly, the best "view" tables are those for two placed neatly around the perimeter – their positions dictated by individual pinpoint spotlights overhead. Three tiered patios add seats for outdoor dining in season.

These are varied settings for some of the area's better meals. Chef Paul Bernal's innovative contemporary American style is illustrated by two recent autumn offerings: roasted Alaskan halibut with seafood gumbo and a cheddar-crayfish beignet, and pan-roasted mignon of beef "benedict" with quail eggs and a tomato béarnaise sauce. Other entrées range from crispy skinned black pearl salmon with a provencal vinaigrette and sweet garlic-crusted Chatham cod brushed in basil oil to muscovy duck breast with a bourbon-maple-blueberry glaze and sautéed venison medallions with green peppercorn sauce.

Typical appetizers are a plantain-crusted crab and corn cake with mango salsa and pan-seared scallops. Desserts include white and dark chocolate mousse in a tuile cup and an ethereal cheesecake with candied ginger crust.

Five accommodations with king or queen beds are upstairs in the main house. Three rooms facing the lake offer large, cushioned window seats to take in the view. The most luxurious are seven rooms (four of which may be joined to become a pair of suites) in a rear carriage house with plush chintz seating in front of stone fireplaces. Favored for romantic getaways are eight more contemporary rooms with fireplaces in four hillside duplex cottages called guest houses. Renovated and upgraded with king or queen four-poster beds, the guest houses have new decks in front and back facing woods and lake, and five have whirlpool tubs. All rooms have TV/DVDs and telephones.

The Boulders offers a spa program and a state-of-the-art fitness facility. A full breakfast is included in the rates.

(860) 868-0541 or (800) 455-1565. Fax (860) 868-1925. www.bouldersinn.com. Seven rooms, three suites and eight cottages with private baths. Doubles, $350 to $410. Suites, $395 to $875.

Entrées, $23.50 to $33.50. Dinner, Wednesday-Saturday 6 to 9:30, Sunday 5 to 8.

The Red Lion Inn, 30 Main St., Stockbridge 01262.

The granddaddy of them all, this big white wood structure immortalized by Norman Rockwell in his painting of Stockbridge's Main Street is the essence of an old New England inn. For more than two centuries, it has dominated the street, its guests rocking on the wide front porch – which seems a block long – or sipping cocktails in the homey parlor. Antique furniture and china fill the public rooms, and the Pink Kitty gift shop is just the ticket for selective browsers. Also here is **Country Curtains,** the original in the retail chain launched by Jane Fitzpatrick, who took over the inn in the late 1960s with her state-senator husband and has restored it with taste.

Rooms and suites in the rambling inn and eight nearby guest houses are furnished in period decor. All room styles feature queen or twin beds with luxurious Italian linens and feather duvets. Rooms in the main building are equipped with TV/DVDs, telephones and wireless Internet service. Twenty-six suites come with a queen bed or two twins and a separate sitting area. A deluxe suite in the former firehouse has a kingsize poster bed and jacuzzi bath upstairs and an open sitting room with dining area and kitchen downstairs. The Red Lion also rents a two-bedroom apartment called Meadowlark, part of sculptor Daniel Chester French's summer studio at Chesterwood.

The dining room is enormously popular with visitors and pleasant in an old hotel kind of a way, and the food situation has improved under executive chef Brian J. Alberg. He launched five-course regional tasting menus on weekends in the off-season, and imparted new takes to regional favorites on the regular menu. Entrées run the gamut from roast turkey with the trimmings and prime rib with a popover to – don't these sound au courant? – grilled salmon fillet with roasted tomato tapenade and arugula vinaigrette and maple-cured venison loin with a celery root puree and confit of root vegetables. You could even order a lump crab martini with crispy wonton chips and espresso crème brûlée at a recent visit. Traditionalists can still start with New England clam chowder and finish with apple pie à la mode for a meal from yesteryear.

More intimate dining takes place in the dark-paneled **Widow Bingham Tavern,** everyone's idea of what a Colonial pub should look like. In season, the shady outdoor courtyard lined with spectacular impatiens is a colorful and cool retreat for a drink, lunch or dinner. The same menu is served inside and out. A smaller menu is available downstairs in the **Lion's Den,** which offers entertainment at night.

(413) 298-5545. Fax (413) 298-5130. www.redlioninn.com. Fifty-three rooms and 25 suites with private baths and 30 rooms with shared baths. Rates, EP. Mid-June to late October: doubles $190 to $215, suites $285 to $441. Rest of year: doubles $89 to $210, suites $175 to $420.

Entrées, $24 to $32. Lunch daily, noon to 2:30, Sunday to 4. Dinner nightly, 5:30 to 9 or 10.

Canopied sidewalk tables lure diners into interior of West Street Grill in Litchfield.

Dining

The Best of the Best

West Street Grill, 43 West St., Litchfield, Conn.

Two of the best meals we've ever had were served at this jaunty establishment, which offers some of the most exciting food in Connecticut. It's the subject of universal adulation from food reviewers and is the perfect foil for the Litchfield Hills trendoids who make it their own at lunch and dinner. The two dining rooms were full the winter Saturday we first lunched here, and the manager rattled off the names of half a dozen celebrities who had reserved for that evening.

Lunch began with a rich butternut-squash and pumpkin bisque and the signature grilled peasant bread with parmesan aioli that was absolutely divine. Main dishes were salmon cakes with curried French lentils and a special of grilled smoked-pork tenderloin with spicy Christmas limas. Among the highly touted desserts, we succumbed to an ethereal crème brûlée and a key lime tart that was really tart. With two generous glasses of wine, the bill for lunch for two came to a rather New Yorkish $60.

That was nothing, however, compared to the special tasting dinner that Irish owner James O'Shea presented to showcase the new summer menu. The meal began with beet green soup, grilled peasant bread with parmesan aioli and roasted tomato and goat cheese, corn cakes with crème fraîche and chives, roasted beet and goat cheese napoleons with a composed salad, and nori-wrapped salmon with marinated daikon, cucumbers and seaweed. A passionfruit sorbet followed. By then we felt that we had already dined well, but no, on came the entrées: tasting portions of pan-seared halibut with a beet pappardelle, spicy shrimp cake with ragoût of black beans and corn, grilled ginger chicken with polenta and ginger chips, and grilled leg of lamb with a ragoût of lentils, spicy curried vegetables and fried greens, including flat-leaf spinach. A little bit here, a little there, and next we knew came a parade of desserts: a plum tart in a pastry so tender as not to be believed, a frozen passionfruit soufflé, a hazelnut torte with caramel ice cream and a sampling of sorbets (raspberry, white peach and blackberry). How could we be anything but convinced, if ever there were a question, of West Street's incredible culinary prowess?

The talented chefs de cuisine come and go, often moving on to open their own restaurants. But James continues to orchestrate both the menu and the style.

The long, narrow dining room is sleek in black and white, with a row of low booths up the middle, tables and mirrors on either side, and a back room with trompe-l'oeil curtains on the walls. Lavish floral arrangements and artworks add splashes of color. Two tables on the sidewalk out front catch passersby in summer.

(860) 567-3885. Entrées, $25 to $35. Lunch daily, 11:30 to 3, weekends to 4. Dinner nightly, 5 to 9 or 10. Closed Monday and Tuesday in winter.

John Andrew's, Route 23, South Egremont, Mass.

"Innovative and spectacular" are words that area chefs and innkeepers employ when describing this culinary star fashioned by Dan and Susan Smith. The Smiths met in Florida while he was cooking at the Ritz-Carlton in Naples. She wanted to return to her native Berkshires and named their restaurant in a rural late 19th-century New England clapboard residence after her grandfather, John Andrew Bianchi.

The sponged walls are a romantic burnt red, the ceiling green and the striking chairs that came from the Copacabana in New York have been reupholstered and repainted green. Metal wall sconces and a tiled fireplace add warmth. At night, the walls "positively glow – like copper," says Susan. The enclosed rear porch, mod in cane and chrome, overlooks an outdoor dining deck and gardens beyond.

Chef Dan favors Northern Italian and Mediterranean cuisine on his straightforward menu, which changes seasonally and represents good value. Favorite starters include tuna sashimi with soy and ginger, crisp sweetbreads with duck liver crostini, and smoked duck breast with a cornmeal pancake and apple salad.

The homemade pastas might pair fettuccine with wild mushrooms and pinenuts, or gnocchi made from Old Chatham Sheepherding ricotta, prosciutto, spinach and parmigiano-reggiano.

Main courses range from pan-seared yellowfin tuna with Thai curry to grilled organic ribeye steak with extra-virgin olive oil and shaved parmesan. The pan-roasted cod might come with clams and chorizo, and the grilled leg of lamb with a red wine and roast garlic sauce. Dan's cassoulet combines duck confit, house-made pork sausage and braised lamb with white beans.

Desserts include plum crisp with vanilla ice cream, fresh berry lemon tart, chocolate torte with white chocolate chip ice cream and caramelized apple tart with cider crème anglaise.

The 160-bottle boutique wine list is particularly strong on California and Italian reds.

An appealing bar menu ($8 to $18) ranges from a grilled lobster sandwich with shoestring potatoes to pot roast with mashed potatoes and beans.

(413) 528-3469. www.jarestaurant.com. Entrées, $19 to $28. Dinner nightly in summer, 5 to 10. Closed Wednesday rest of year.

Sponged walls and tile fireplace add warmth to John Andrew's dining room.

Bistro Zinc, 56 Church St., Lenox, Mass.

French authenticity and nuances are everywhere evident in this chic bistro and bar opened by young Lenox native Jason Macioge in partnership with Charles Schultz.

The gracefully curving mahogany bar in the rear cocktail lounge is topped with polished zinc, the restroom doors are made of lettered wood wine crates and the tables in the mirrored front dining room are as close together as any in Paris. The mustard on the tables is dijon, and water is poured from antique glass bottles inscribed in French with the date 1895.

The menu has been updated from the early days when it was so authentic as to be ho-hum, as real French bistro menus tend to be. The food, though rather minimal in portion, is not at all ho-hum. We lunched in the bar on a lovely French onion soup gruyère, a salad of goat cheese, arugula and roasted tomato, and a special entrée of cumin-crusted lamb with couscous. The salad was mostly goat cheese, and cried out for bread upon which it could be spread (the bread was doled out as sparingly as the few leaves of arugula and a single tiny roasted tomato). The lamb was sensational, fanned around couscous that never before tasted so delectable. A not-so-classic tarte tatin was nonetheless delicious, paired with vanilla ice cream drizzled with caramel sauce. The bill was presented in a Zinc folder with a postcard.

The bar seats 50 at tables and stools, the same number as can be served in the main dining room, full of cherry trim, mosaic tiled floors and white-clothed tables. The abbreviated menu sampled at lunch is similar but much expanded at night. Expect such starters as steak tartare, mussels marinière, peking duck rolls, prosciutto-wrapped quail and salads, perhaps one of frisée with pancetta and a poached egg.

Walls of mirrors and windows convey bistro look in front dining room at Bistro Zinc.

Typical entrées are hazelnut-encrusted halibut with leeks and creamed spinach, yellowfin tuna dusted with star anise, wood-roasted free-range chicken with herb jus, steak frites, and grilled Australian lamb loin with red wine sauce. Desserts at our visit included vanilla crème brûlée, profiterole with mocha ice cream and a platter of petits fours, a lemon tart and cookies.

In addition to an all-French wine list, the bar book touts American single-barrel bourbons and single-malt scotches from Scotland. "There were a lot of high-end restaurants but no bars in town," said Jason. "We tried to fill a niche, and so far it's gone over very well."

Lately, he set out to fill another niche, opening the 40-seat **Fin Sushi & Sake Bar** around the corner in a former diner refashioned by his architect father at 27 Housatonic St. His brother, Nick, is one of the sushi chefs.

(413) 637-8800. www.bistrozinc.com. Entrées, $24 to $32. Lunch daily, 11:30 to 3. Dinner nightly, 5:30 to 9:30.

Aubergine, Intersection of Routes 22 and 23, Hillsdale, N.Y.

This classic country inn is the worthy successor to the famed L'Hostellerie Bressane, a culinary landmark since 1971. When French chef-owner Jean Morel and his wife Madeleine decided in 1995 to retire, they approached David and Stacy Lawson to uphold their tradition. David, a native Minnesotan who had trained in London in the French tradition with Albert Roux, had earned his spurs in the Berkshires as executive chef at the Old Inn on the Green and at Blantyre. There was only one remaining step – a restaurant he could call his own. He found it in this rosy brick inn, built in 1783 by a Revolutionary War soldier in the Dutch Colonial style, across the Massachusetts/New York state line at the crossroads of Hillsdale.

With a change in name to the easier-to-pronounce Aubergine and some dramatic changes in the entry, the establishment barely skipped a beat. The lightened-up foyer now focuses on a stunning display (at one late summer visit) of huge sunflowers in a vase, and eggplants, runner beans and squashes on a table. The walls of the men's room are still papered with wine labels and the four smallish, fireplaced dining rooms retain a quaint, somewhat old-fashioned look. The fare continues to reflect the French tradition, but the menu is in English and blends contemporary nuances and techniques that quickly earned it a four-diamond AAA rating as a destination restaurant. Smoker dinners for cigar aficionados, wine tastings and cooking classes are among special events.

Three accomplished cooks assist David in the kitchen, while Stacy oversees the dining rooms. The silver forks and spoons are set upside down in the European style beside Limoges service plates on tables spaced decently apart. Fresh flowers, pretty wallpapers and curtains, and ladder-back or round-back velvet chairs in a plum color convey French country charm. A few tables are set up for overflow in the lounge with its copper bar, where we were seated.

Chef David Lawson visits wine cellar at Aubergine.

Dinner begins with a complimentary amusé, perhaps a slice of rich country pâté, served on a crouton with cornichons, or triangles of duck confit and scallions wrapped in an Algerian feuille-de-bric. Among starters are a classic caesar salad garnished with crispy fried onions, seared diver scallops au poivre on a parsnip puree and fondue of leeks, and crispy veal sweetbreads and chicken livers with pancetta and shallots. Salt-cured Hudson Valley duck foie gras with roasted plums, toasted hazelnuts and arugula from the large kitchen garden in back was a recent treat. Soups (perhaps creamy mushroom bisque with croutons or onion with madeira and cognac) are served from a silver tureen at tableside.

Typical main courses range from a bouillabaisse of monkfish and mussels with rouille croutons to grilled New York sirloin steak with black olive tapenade and a rich red wine sauce. Others could be spice-rubbed Atlantic salmon with minted yogurt sauce, roasted loin and confit leg of local rabbit with sautéed apples and grainy mustard sauce, and roasted breast of squab with honey-vinegar jus.

The most exemplary desserts here have always been the soufflés, hot or cold. We'll never forget the frozen coffee soufflé with kirsch, ringed by figs and candied chestnuts. David continues to offer grand marnier and hazelnut soufflés, "as much for theater as anything else." He prefers profiteroles, pumpkin crème brûlée or what he calls a Roux Brothers' lemon tart "in the style of my mentors."

Stacy has developed the wine cellar so the wines will "compliment the food, rather than serving as trophies in themselves," according to David.

Aubergine offers two plain but comfortable guest rooms, each with queen bed and private hall bath, on the second floor. On the third are two more luxurious bedrooms with private baths. One is done in soft lavenders with a queensize bed and one is in coral shades with twins. Coffee is complimentary in the morning, but there's no breakfast. As David explains, this is not an inn: "we're adamantly a restaurant with rooms."

(518) 325-3412. Fax (518) 325-7089. www.aubergine.com. Entrées, $22 to $28. Dinner, Wednesday-Sunday from 5:30. Four rooms with private baths. Doubles, $95 and $120.

Verdura, 44 Railroad St., Great Barrington, Mass.

Copper-toned walls and square farm-style tables with comfortable chairs convey a Tuscan look to this cucina rustica, the hottest restaurant in Great Barrington lately.

Chef-owner Bill Webber became enamored with Tuscan-style trattorias while living among the vineyards of California's Napa Valley. After cooking locally at Wheatleigh in Lenox, he opened his own place in 2001 in Great Barrington, where visiting New Yorkers contend that his food is better than what they can find at home. He recently expanded next door with **Dué Enoteca,** a more casual "little cousin" serving Italian and Spanish tapas ($5 to $11) in a wine-bar setting

A wood-fired stone oven in the spacious open kitchen imparts distinctive flavors to thin-crust pizzas and roasted meat and vegetable dishes. Any ingredients that are purchased are local, seasonal and organic whenever possible. The rest is made in house: the pastas, the pizza dough, gelato, sorbet and other desserts. Bill smokes his own salmon and mussels and churns his own butter.

His short Tuscan menu makes for appetizing reading and agonizing choices. The ever-changing bruschetta is a memorable starter, topped with smoked goose breast, local goat cheese and port-braised shallots at a recent visit and with mascarpone, prosciutto, figs and arugula at another. Other primi possibilities range from the house tagliatelle with lobster and salsify to quail saltimbocca and free-range duck confit with pickled mustard seed. The wild mushroom pizza with leeks, chèvre and white truffle oil may be the best you've had.

Typical main courses are free-range chicken under a brick with pesto vinaigrette, and braised lamb shanks with black olive-citrus jus. The roast wild cod might be teamed with cockles, watercress and braised fennel in cioppino broth and the wood-roasted quail with sweet potato gratin, swiss chard and hen jus. The signature wood-grilled beef tenderloin is sauced with balsamic vinegar, extra virgin olive oil and black truffle butter.

Dessert specials could be wood-grilled peaches in a silken vanilla-scented sauce or a belgian chocolate panna cotta with brûléed bananas. Verdura obtained a full liquor license just so it could offer more than twenty kinds of grappa. They make a fitting end to a memorable meal.

(413) 528-8969. Entrées, $23 to $29. www.verdura.net. Dinner nightly, 5 to 9 or 10.

Thomas Moran's Petite Syrah, 223 Litchfield Tpke. (Route 202), New Preston, Conn.

Chef Thomas Moran worked around the world for the Four Seasons hotel chain and then cooked for six years for the demanding Relais & Châteaux clientele at the Mayflower Inn nearby. Although not exactly a household word, his name carried weight locally when he and his wife embarked in 2003 on their first solo venture, an intimate bistro in a small white dormered house that long housed the French restaurant Le Bon Coin in the Woodville section of New Preston.

Chef-owner welcomes guests at copper bar in Thomas Moran's Petite Syrah.

His theme is "California Meets New England," a reference to the light, creative California style with Asian accents he imparts to local ingredients. Appetizers like Maine jonah crab spring roll and a duck confit quesadilla with spicy Chinese sambal are examples.

The short menu changes nightly. At a recent visit, you could start with saku tuna tartare with pickled ginger or seared foie gras with pear compote and baby greens. Main courses ranged from Maine diver scallops with steamed cockles, shrimp wontons, Thai noodles and ponzu soy broth to venison medallions with sautéed potato cake and cranberry-chestnut essence. The Florida tilapia fillet was sauced with rice wine-garlic-chile vinaigrette and served with mashed potatoes and baby vegetables. Desserts included a classic crème brûlée and chocolate decadence cake with praline ice cream.

The chef claims "a love affair with the California wine country," which accounts for naming his restaurant for a wine indigenous to California. His small lounge with a copper-topped bar is painted a wine red. He renovated the entry so the lounge is partly open to the beamed dining room appointed in white and brown. The open feeling extends to the guest experience. The exuberant chef tries to meet and greet diners upon arrival "and then do what I like best – cook for fun."

In late 2005, the Morans took on more cooking, opening a second restaurant, **Forsythia,** serving lunch and dinner at 31 Bank St. in nearby New Milford.

(860) 868-7763. Entrées, $22 to $29. Lunch, Saturday and Sunday 11:30 to 3. Dinner, Thursday-Monday 6 to 11.

Church Street Café, 65 Church St., Lenox, Mass.

Marking its 25th anniversary in 2006, this is the casual, creative kind of American bistro to which we return time and again for an interesting meal. Co-owners Linda Forman and Clayton Hambrick, once Ethel Kennedy's chef, specialize in light, fresh café food, served inside by ficus trees and eclectic paintings and outside in season on a large canopied deck.

The kitchen has lately been tripled in size, the better to produce the blackboard specials that supplement the seasonal menus. Virginia-native Clayton once worked at a creole restaurant in Washington, a background that shows in his Louisiana gumbo and a special of blackened redfish. Lately, the fare has acquired Southwest and oriental accents, as in an appetizer of a New Mexican-style tortilla stuffed with ten-hour smoked brisket, grilled onion and jack cheese in a smoky crema sauce or a main dish of seared duck breast chinois with a hoisin-orange roasted leg, szechuan pan sauce and sesame greens. These join such traditional favorites as sautéed Maine crab cakes with dilled tartar sauce, coq au vin, and rack of lamb with red wine sauce. One of the pasta dishes might incorporate garlic-roasted shrimp and vegetables with Thai noodles and a peanut-curry dressing. The provençal vegetable bouillabaisse employs many vegetables, saffron broth, roasted pepper rouille and Mediterranean couscous.

Our latest lunch here included a super black bean tostada and the Church Street salad, a colorful array of greens, goat cheese, chickpeas, eggs and red pepper, with zippy balsamic vinaigrette dressing. The whole wheat-sunflower seed rolls were so good that we accepted seconds.

Clayton's chocolate mousse loaf was written up in the first issue of Chocolatier magazine. We're partial to the apple-walnut crisp and the sensational chilled cranberry soufflé topped with whipped cream.

There are fresh flowers on the white-linened tables and white pottery with colorful pink and blue flowers in three dining areas. Track lights illuminate colorful artworks on the walls at night.

(413) 637-2745. churchstreetcafe.biz. Entrées, $21.50 to $28.50. Lunch, Monday-Saturday 11 to 2. Dinner nightly, 5:30 to 9. Sunday brunch in summer and fall. Closed Sunday and Monday in off-season.

Pastorale Bistro & Bar, 223 Main St., Lakeville, Conn.

This handsome white house dating to 1765 has housed many an upscale restaurant. One that should last is the authentic French bistro opened in 2003 by chef-owner Frederic Faveau and his wife Karen Hamilton. Frederic's masterful cooking impressed us first at Litchfield's West Street Grill and later at the Birches Inn on Lake Waramaug. His food here is every bit as brilliant but less contrived – "more bistro-like, with a more laid-back presentation," he says – and also less expensive than at similar establishments. His emphasis here is on local and organic ingredients.

The main floor houses an atmospheric bar/lounge with booths for dining and a small dining room. Up a staircase passing a window onto the kitchen is the main dining area, a mix of booths and tables covered with white linens and white butcher paper. An outside patio is popular in season.

Starters entice, from an ahi tuna and savoy cabbage egg roll to seared sweetbreads with pancetta, bordelaise sauce and arugula. The watercress and duck confit salad is a classic of its genre.

Gallic accents embellish entrées like mussels marinière, beef bourguignonne and steak frites. The menu also offers a cheeseburger with Irish cheddar on a sourdough roll, several pasta dishes and grilled seafood. The specialty is grilled leg of lamb in a port wine reduction, served perhaps with mustard greens and a casserole of flageolet beans, roasted tomatoes, roasted garlic and preserved lemon.

Chef Frederic Favreau takes a break from kitchen duties on patio at Pastorale Bistro.

Desserts reflect the chef's French heritage as well: the specialty cherry clafoutis from Burgundy, profiteroles, tarte tatin and chocolate marquise. The crème brûlée might bear an Asian accent of ginger and lemongrass.

(860) 435-1011. www.pastoralebistro.com. Entrées, $16.50 to $24. Dinner, Tuesday-Saturday 5 to 9. Sunday, brunch noon to 3:30, dinner noon to 8.

More Good Dining

Castle Street Café, 10 Castle St., Great Barrington, Mass.

The locals cheered when Michael Ballon, who used to cook at the Williamsville Inn in West Stockbridge, returned to the Berkshires to open his own café after several years at upscale restaurants in New York City.

Other restaurants had not had much luck in this space beside the Mahaiwe Theatre, but Michael succeeded first with his bistro, especially on nights the theater was busy, and more recently as well with his Celestial Bar adjacent, featuring live music on weekends. Artworks are hung on the brick walls of the long narrow room with white-linened tables and windsor chairs. Michael puts out goodies like pâté and cheese at the bar at the rear. The wine bar dispenses a number of choices by the glass from a selection cited by Wine Spectator.

With appetizers like grilled shiitake mushrooms with garlic and herbs, fried shrimp dumplings with dipping sauce, an olive sampler with focaccia, and a mesclun and goat-cheese salad and entrées like a Castle burger with straw potatoes or portobello mushroom ravioli, there is something for every vegetarian and carnivore. Other main courses could be broiled halibut with wasabi sauce, sesame-crusted chicken breast glazed with ginger and soy, steak au poivre and rack of lamb with garlic and rosemary sauce.

The dessert list is headed by the world's best chocolate-mousse cake, as determined by the late New York Newsday. Others include caramelized banana tart with banana ice cream, frozen lemon soufflé with raspberry sauce and samplers of three sorbets or three cookies.

A bar menu ($5 to $12) offers light fare, from appetizers and an open-faced grilled portobello, tomato and goat cheese sandwich to meatloaf with mashed potatoes.

Michael makes a point of buying from Berkshire farmers and purveyors, whom he acknowledges on the back of his menu.

(413) 528-5244. www.castlestreetcafé.com. Entrées, $19 to $28. Dinner nightly except Tuesday, 5 to 9:30, weekends to 11.

Spigalina, 80 Main St., Lenox, Mass.

Fresh out of the Culinary Institute of America, Lina Aliberti got a job as garde manger at Wheatleigh and awaited the day when she could open her own restaurant in the house her father had bought in the center of Lenox and leased out for commercial purposes. That day came when the main floor was transformed into a Mediterranean-style bistro and bar focusing on a large center fireplace with a Count Rumford oven. Forty-two diners can be seated at well spaced tables inside, with an equal number on the front porch that quickly became a popular gathering spot to sit and watch the passing parade.

The restaurant is a play on the chef's name (she originally called it Semolina, but had to drop it for trademark purposes). The new name means wheat stalk in Italian and Spanish.

The menu is Mediterranean in spirit: perhaps paella or Spanish seafood stew, grilled free-range chicken marinated in Moroccan preserved lemon and herbs, veal saltimbocca and pan-seared beef tenderloin with red wine-shallot sauce. The chef might serve herb-stuffed sole fillets over Israeli vegetable couscous and roast pork tenderloin wrapped in prosciutto with sautéed spinach, dates and almonds.

Expect such starters as a luscious lobster and crabmeat profiterole with blood-orange vinaigrette, organic salmon tartare, a Mediterranean salad and crispy kataifi-wrapped goat cheese on field greens. The vegetarian antipasto might yield hummus, three-grain salad, beet salad, tzatziki, muhammara dip, Moorish apple salad, Spanish urgelia cheese and pita bread.

Desserts vary from spiced apple and pear strudel with crème anglaise and lemon mousse cake with hazelnut praline to a duo of coffee and caramel pots de crème. The desserts, incidentally, are prepared by the Swiss baker and maître d'hotel, Serge Paccaud, whom Lisa recently married. The couple close the restaurant for part of the winter to go to Switzerland.

(413) 637-4455. www.spigalina.com. Entrées, $24 to $32. Dinner, Thursday-Monday 5 to 9. Closed mid-February through March.

The Old Mill, Route 23, South Egremont, Mass.

In the charming and oft-overlooked hamlet of South Egremont, the Old Mill (which really is an old gristmill and blacksmith shop) has been impressing regulars since 1978. The atmosphere is a cross between a simple Colonial tavern and a European wayside inn, warm and friendly, yet highly sophisticated.

The large, L-shaped main dining room has wide-planked and stenciled floors, beamed ceilings, pewter cutlery and bottles of olive oil as centerpieces on the nicely spaced tables, and a collection of old mincing tools on the cream-colored walls. Reflections of candles sparkle in the small-paned windows. An addition to a

Old mincing tools decorate walls of beamed dining room at The Old Mill.

sunken rear dining room provides views through large windows onto Hubbard Brook.

Owner Terry Moore – a Brit who trained as a chef on the Cunard Line ships – adds a few nightly specials to supplement the ten entrées on the seasonal menu. Appetizers and smaller portions of some of the entrées turn up on a bar menu, available in both bar and dining room except on Saturdays.

The black-bean soup is a treat – hot and thick with pieces of spicy sausage. Other starters might be chicken liver and foie gras mousse with red onion jam and grilled peasant bread, frog's legs provençal, steamed mussels in Thai coconut-curry sauce, and saffron risotto bearing shrimp, sweet peas and rosemary. Three kinds of rolls are served in a handsome basket. The house salad is a mixture of greens and sliced mushrooms.

Of the entrées, which always include the freshest of fish, we have enjoyed broiled red snapper, sesame-crusted mahi mahi and baked bluefish with ginger and scallions. The grilled veal chop with wild mushroom sauce and truffled potato gratin was sensational, and the calves liver with caramelized onions and apple-smoked bacon superior. Other possibilities range from panko-crusted rainbow trout with citrus-caper brown butter to rack of lamb with mint pesto.

The mocha torte and the meringue glacé with cointreau and strawberries are heavenly desserts. Others are profiteroles au chocolat, maple crème brûlée and chocolate-ginger truffle tart with espresso ice cream.

The interesting wine list, reasonably priced, is split in origin between California and France, with nods to Italy and Australia. There's a cozy parlor bar for drinks while you wait for a table, a not unlikely occurrence since reservations are not taken for less than five.

The Old Mill's 65 seats may turn over four times on busy nights. No wonder the guest book at the entry is full of praise for the food, hospitality and ambiance.

(413) 528-1421. Entrées, $20 to $26. Dinner, Tuesday-Sunday from 5.

Bizen, 17 Railroad St., Great Barrington, Mass.

This true Japanese restaurant and sushi bar opened in 1994 to such acclaim that it doubled in size three years later and in 2005 added a kaiseki teahouse restaurant next door. All are the inspiration as well as the handiwork of Michael Marcus, a Berkshires potter who apprenticed in Japan, where he became enamored not only of its ancient pottery style but of its cuisine. "I am obsessed by quality," says Michael, and it shows.

Some of his "chef-associates" work at the large marble and cherry sushi bar in the original space, which holds two Japanese-looking dining rooms of modest proportions. Others man the robata charcoal grill in the newer section. Here are three elegant tatami areas and a crisp and contemporary sake lounge visible from the street. It looks as if it would be more at home in San Francisco, say, than in Tokyo, but dispenses an ambitious selection of estate sakes from ancient Japanese microbreweries. And two others work in the new kaiseki kitchen that serves a half-dozen small tea rooms, each enclosed by shoji doors and seating up to eight each. Kaiseki is the seasonal meal that accompanies a traditional Japanese tea ceremony.

The fare throughout is authentic Japanese, served on the museum-quality pottery made by Michael in a multi-chambered, wood-fired climbing kiln at his celebrated Joyous Spring Pottery in nearby Monterey. The dramatic fire- and ash-detailed bowls and platters showcase the food because, in artist Michael's words, "eating is a form of theater."

In the robata bar and sake lounge, choose grilled items to snack on, perhaps grilled corn, jalapeño kabob or grilled baby abalone with choice of sauces. Squid, cod roe, tiger shrimp and clams are other options. Of course, there's a great selection of sushi by the piece, rolls (the Bizen combines lobster and avocado) and combinations (a sushi dinner for $21.75). Dishes from the charcoal grill, with miso soup or salad and rice, might be Canadian sea scallops on fried sweet potatoes or unjyu, Asian grilled river eel. Noodles, tempuras and many appetizers like spring rolls and grilled Japanese yellowtail cheek teriyaki are available. You might start with a deluxe seafood soup and end with blackberry sorbet or ginger ice cream.

Or go all-out with one of the prix-fixe kaiseke dinners, available Wednesday-Sunday evenings. Meals of six to eleven small courses vary in price from $40 to $100. Waitresses in kimonos serve you privately in your own zashiki, a special tea ceremonial room lined with tatami mats. Reserve one that has a well under the table for your legs, unless you're prepared to enjoy a two-hour meal in the lotus position.

(413) 528-4343. Entrées, $13.95 to $18.95. Lunch daily, noon to 2:30, weekends to 3. Dinner nightly, 5 to 9:30 or 10.

Oliva, 18 East Shore Road (Route 45), New Preston, Conn.

Chef Riad Aamar moved from Doc's up the road to take over this ground-level café, a snug, grotto-like setting with fieldstone walls, bleached barnwood and a huge, warming fireplace for chilly evenings. In summer, folks spill out from the 30-seat interior to tables on a jaunty, flower-bedecked front terrace nurtured by Riad's wife, Joanna Lawrence.

Here, in a kitchen even smaller than at Doc's, the personable Moroccan-born chef produces dynamite pizzas, super appetizers and a dozen robust pastas and Mediterranean entrées that earned the New York Times reviewer's highest rating. Typical among the latter are linguini with garlicky shrimp, prosciutto and gorgonzola, sautéed tilapia served over roasted vegetables with saffron-lemon cream, Moroccan-

Canopied front terrace doubles dining capacity of Oliva in summer.

style roasted chicken stuffed with prunes and pinenuts, veal stew and Moroccan lamb tagine.

The menu is printed daily. You might start with the house antipasto (roasted vegetables, mixed cheeses and often prosciutto), seared sea scallops wrapped in grape leaves or a spinach and goat cheese tart over baby greens. Many choose one of the thin-crust pizzas, perhaps the artichoke with prosciutto, olives and mozzarella with spinach and sundried tomatoes. Pizzas are served in small and large sizes, and like the appetizers can be ordered "assaggi" style (a sampler of any two).

Desserts could be a caramelized pear and marzipan tart, chocolate pot de crème, panna cotta with raspberry sauce, coffee-espresso ice cream or chocolate macaroons.

(860) 868-1787. Entrées, $12.75 to $23.75. Lunch, Saturday and Sunday noon to 2:30. Dinner, Wednesday-Sunday 5 to 9. BYOB.

Rouge Bistro, 3 Center St., West Stockbridge, Mass.

French chef William Merelle and his wife, Maggie, a wine distributor, opened this small place to wide acclaim for its food and refreshing prices, although some report service and attitude to be a problem. True to its name, the place is identified by a bright red door and canopy in front of an olive green shingled building up against the sidewalk.

The front bar holds a handful of close-together tables in the bistro style. There's a bit more space in colorful side and back rooms, where square red tables are set with yellow or blue service plates and blue glasses against a backdrop of sponged Mediterranean yellow walls. A rear deck adds four tables for two in season.

William, who cooks in the contemporary French style with Asian twists, graduated from cooking school in France at age 17. The couple met in Provence while she was spending a college semester abroad. He worked at Wheatleigh and John Andrew's before opening his own venture.

When we were there, jalapeño tapas kicked off a menu particularly strong on appetizers. Among the choices: fried calamari with harissa aioli, a brochette of escargots and roasted garlic with crispy polenta, mussels steamed in rice wine and lemongrass, tuna tartare with mache and cucumbers, and a charcuterie plate of imported ham, French sausages and Spanish olives. The sautéed foie gras and shredded celery root came with granny smith apples, raspberries and black fig sauce.

Main courses ranged from pan-seared salmon with cranberry-lime sauce to steak au poivre with cognac sauce and frites. Seared tuna encrusted with peppercorns and ginger was served with ratatouille and Moroccan couscous. An escalope of veal might be encrusted in parmesan-reggiano and topped with shiitake and oyster mushrooms. Free-range lemon chicken, barbecued baby back ribs and braised duck were among the offerings. Lighter fare is offered on tapas and bar menus.

Rouge royale was the house aperitif on a select French wine list overseen by wife Maggie.

(413) 232-4111. www.rougerestaurant.com. Entrées, $19 to $24. Dinner, Wednesday-Sunday 5 to 10.

Lodging

The Inn at Stockbridge, 30 East St. (Route 7), Box 618, Stockbridge, Mass. 01262.

The B&B based in this lovely pillared, Georgian-style mansion on twelve secluded acres with colorful flower gardens and a swimming pool has been enhanced and expanded by owners Alice and Len Schiller from New Jersey. They first upgraded the eight original bedrooms in the mansion, and later added eight luxury rooms in two new buildings in back.

Each of the original bedrooms now has a telephone, CD player and TV/VCR. All but two have kingsize beds. There are fans over the bed in the Madame Butterfly Room, with original headboards and oriental accents, and vintage rose wallpaper and two posh chairs in the Rose Room. The main-floor Terrace Room overlooking a reflecting pond and swimming pool features a private deck and a circular whirlpool tub in the skylit bathroom. The toiletries bear the inn's private label.

In back is the Cottage House with four spacious rooms called junior suites. Each has a gas fireplace and TV/VCR. Two add large whirlpool tubs. A giraffe sculpture occupies a corner of the room aptly named Out of Africa, and three black masks grace the wall. An interesting wall hanging of five golf clubs linked horizontally by leather cords is a focal point in the St. Andrews Room, also notable for a high, plump fishnet canopy bed. The largest Provence Room on the end has windows on three sides and is decorated in mauve and white toile florals.

Four top-of-the-line rooms occupy a new building called the Barn, complete with open cupola in the common entry. Each spacious, cathedral-ceilinged room has a king bed, corner gas fireplace, double whirlpool, TV/VCR and private deck. They range from one of Shaker simplicity to the richness of the Shakespeare and Wharton rooms. The barn also contains a fitness room for guests.

Back in the main house, guests meet over complimentary wine and cheese in an expansive living room and adjacent library. The table in the elegant dining room is set for sixteen, with eight more seats available in a smaller room beyond. Breakfast is by candlelight from 9 to 9:30, starting perhaps with juice and a fresh fruit plate, orange-cranberry compote or baked pears. The main course could be baked eggs with havarti and dill, sausage soufflé, portobello mushroom strata, lemon-cottage cheese pancakes or vanilla french toast. Orange-blueberry bread, apple crisp or apricot-cheese bread could accompany.

Pillared Georgian-style mansion houses The Inn at Stockbridge.

The Schillers have a culinary background, she having worked with the New York Restaurant School and he taking classes at Peter Kump's New York Cooking School. After jointly attending a cooking school in Tuscany, they offered periodic cooking classes followed by dinner.

(413) 298-3337 or (888) 466-7865. Fax (413) 298-3406. www.stockbridgeinn.com. Sixteen rooms with private baths. Doubles, $170 to $360 June-October, $140 to $260 rest of year. Three-night minimum summer and holiday weekends.

Applegate Bed & Breakfast, 279 West Park St., RR 1, Box 576, Lee, Mass. 01238.

A pillared porte cochere hints of Tara at this majestic, sparkling white Georgian Colonial, built by a New York surgeon in the 1920s as a weekend retreat. Surrounding it are six tranquil acres bearing venerable apple trees, towering pines, flower gardens and a beckoning swimming pool.

Inside are elegant common rooms, eight guest rooms and an effervescent welcome by Gloria and Len Friedman, she a retired educator and psychotherapist and he a retired computer executive.

Off a lovely entry foyer are a fireplaced dining room, where three tables are each set for breakfast for four, and a large living room equipped with a grand piano. To the side of the living room is a sun porch, newly enclosed for use as a reading and TV room. Off the dining room is a screened back porch facing the pool and gardens.

A carved staircase leads to eight guest rooms, one the master suite with a kingsize poster bed, family photos on the mantel above the working fireplace, a sitting area with a sofabed and two chairs, and a great steam shower. The other second-floor rooms, slightly less grand in scale, hold queensize beds. One has Shaker-style pine furniture, another a walnut sleigh bed and a third an antique white iron bed and white and blue wicker furnishings. Two newer rooms are situated in a far wing of the house. One is a sunny corner space swathed in pale lavenders and greens with a tiger-maple four-poster, a sitting area and the best view of the grounds. The other is a smaller room done up in Victorian style with an antique bed and matching marble-topped dresser.

The premier accommodations are now four luxury rooms, each with kingsize bed, fireplace, double whirlpool tub or soaking tub, wet bar, sofa and TV/VCR. Two are on the third floor of the main house, each with a private balcony overlooking the grounds from on high. Most in demand is Room 8 with a step-up kingsize bed, a TV secreted behind a picture above the fireplace, and a "wow" of a bathroom with a double whirlpool tub encased in marble beneath a palladian window.

The other two luxury rooms are located on the ground floor of the former garage and carriage house and come with private patios. The carriage house also had a second-floor apartment for the chauffeur. It has been converted into a cottage apartment with two queensize bedrooms, living room with TV/VCR, kitchen facilities and bath with whirlpool tub.

The beds are dressed with 400-count linens and the robes are microfiber. Also in each room are decanters of brandy and Grenada chocolates from a nephew's chocolate factory in the West Indies. "You name an amenity and we try to fit it in," says Gloria. They recently created a guest pantry where popcorn and beverages are available all day.

The Friedmans offer wine and cheese around 5 p.m. The continental-plus breakfast, including cereal and yogurt, is served amid stemware and Wedgwood china in the dining room.

(413) 243-4451 or (800) 691-9012. Fax (413) 243-9832. www.applegateinn.com. Eight rooms and two-bedroom cottage with private baths. Doubles, $155 to $360 June-October, $120 to $270 rest of year.

Stonover Farm Bed & Breakfast, 169 Undermountain Road, Lenox 01240.

Los Angeles record producer Tom Werman and his wife Suky returned to their East Coast roots to restore a 110-year-old stone "cottage" that served as the farmhouse to the Stonover Estate. It's now a luxurious B&B offering both creature comforts and charm on eight acres of sylvan tranquility not far from Tanglewood.

The Wermans reconfigured the interior of the house and joined it to the stable, wrapping around an idyllic courtyard terrace looking onto a spring-fed duck pond. A California decorator friend furnished the place in a light and airy, uncluttered style. All is embellished by an eye-popping collection of contemporary art gathered by four artisans whom Suky, a former museum educator, represents.

Guests are comfortably housed in three second-floor suites, the outlying Rock Cottage and a suite in a restored 1850 school house. Beds are king or queensize, dressed in Frette linens and fabric duvets. The typical sitting room has a Shaker desk with a Bose radio, telephone, a sofabed and a rocker. It opens into a bedroom with an entertainment center concealing a 27-inch flat-screen TV and DVD player. One suite has a gas fireplace and a bath with jacuzzi tub and separate shower. Other bathrooms, all full of slate, tile and marble, contain walk-in showers for two. One has a soaking tub.

A stone fireplace warms an enormous living/dining room in the four-room cottage, which has a kingsize bedroom on the main floor, twin beds upstairs in an aerie called the sleeping turret and a full kitchen. The School House Suite beside the pond has a sitting room with gas fireplace, a kingsize bed and a spacious bath with two-headed shower and whirlpool tub for two.

The hospitable hosts offer wine and imported cheeses in the afternoon, by the fire in the living room or library, or outside on the courtyard terrace. A lavish breakfast is served at a table for ten in the former creamery with windows on three sides and a vaulted ceiling rising to a cupola. Fresh-squeezed juice, cut-up fruit salad, breads, bagels, muffins, Suky's homemade granola, yogurt and cereals are offered buffet style. Tom does the cooking for both healthy and hearty options on his AGA stove, serving up guests' choice of omelets, french toast or pancakes, with thick sliced bacon. His goat cheese omelet with sautéed mushrooms is a breakfast favorite.

(413) 637-9100. www.stonoverfarm.com. Four suites and one cottage with private baths. July-October: doubles $375 to $485, cottage $515. Rest of year: doubles $275 to $450, cottage $385 to $465.

Gedney Farm, Route 57, New Marlborough, Mass. 01230.

Bradford and Leslie Wagstaff parlayed an abandoned 1760 inn on the old Hartford-Albany stage route into the centerpiece of a growing complex that included sophisticated lodging complexes on either end of the off-the-beaten-path village.

The success of the Old Inn on the Green led the couple to develop luxury rooms and suites in a great Normandy-style barn called Gedney Farm on the eastern approach to town. They followed that by opening a country-house hotel and spa in their latest acquisition, the gilded-age estate called Mepal Manor on a hilltop west of town. They sold the Old Inn in 2005 to concentrate on their more recent holdings and the new spa.

The Gedney Farm restoration – the inspired re-use of a former cattle barn – is a sight to behold. The lower floor houses public areas for functions and weddings, along with a mini-art gallery leading to a sculpture park on the grounds outside. Beneath the barn's soaring, 30-foot ceiling is a lineup of guest rooms and six two-level suites, their second floors fashioned from the old hayloft and reached by private staircases. Most have sitting rooms with granite fireplaces, and some open onto indoor balconies looking onto the barn interior. The modern baths are outfitted with Neutrogena amenities; some have deep, two-person whirlpool tubs under glass ceilings open to the roof structure. Leslie has decorated each room with panache in styles from French provincial to Moroccan. Oriental and kilim rugs are on the floors, woven or fabric coverlets are on the beds, exotic wreaths adorn the walls and country antiques abound.

Twelve guest rooms are available in the restored **Mepal Manor**, an imposing, stone Berkshires cottage/castle off by itself on rolling grounds with super vistas of the Berkshires. The operative words here are large and grand, from the fireplaced great hall, library, oak-paneled dining room and patio terrace to the best of the Victorian-era guest rooms, individually decorated in rich fabrics and furnishings appropriate to the Gilded Age.

The manor was built in 1906 by New York City banker and sportsman Hildreth Bloodgood. He named it after his prize-winning Hackney show horse, "Star of Mepal," the first of 100 horses he imported from England to his horse farm here.

The Wagstaffs ingeniously turned an unlikely looking gymnasium building into a spectacular spa and fitness center. Four serene rooms for body treatments, massages and facials are nicely tucked away next to a large, quiet meditation space with a whirlpool and cleansing steam room. A radiant-heated maple floor provides year-round comfort in the yoga/pilates movement studio.

A generous continental breakfast – including fresh fruits, cereals, hard-boiled eggs, pastries, toasting breads and homemade preserves – is put out for guests at Gedney Farm. A more spa-oriented, health-conscious continental breakfast is offered guests at Mepal Manor.

Mepal Manor serves lunch for spa guests and the public in a majestic dining room notable for a large white-stone fireplace and scenic mountain views to the west. The prix-fixe menu changes daily, $19.50 for three set courses. A typical lunch might begin with a roasted beet and fennel salad over mesclun greens, followed by an entrée of pan-seared Hudson Valley chicken breast with a roasted shallot-farro risotto. Dessert could be a cinnamon poached pear with vanilla ice cream.

The ambiance at Mepal could not be more tranquil. Windows in most guest rooms as well as the dining room are oriented toward the mountain views. From them not a sign of civilization can be seen or heard.

(413) 229-3131 or (800) 286-3139. Fax (414) 229-8236. www.gedneyfarm.com. Sixteen rooms and suites with private baths. Doubles, $225 to $325.

Mepal Manor: Twelve rooms with private baths. Doubles, $225 to $395. Lunch, Thursday-Sunday noon to 2 in summer, Saturday and Sunday in winter.

The Huckleberry Inn, 219 Kent Road, Warren, Conn. 06754.

One of New England's more sumptuous, charming and personality-driven B&Bs fills a niche in northwestern Connecticut – the gap between the small, makeshift B&B in someone's house and the larger, high-end inn staffed for the purpose. That's the way Andrea DiMauro planned it.

After twelve years as a personal chef for affluent families in suburban New York, the perky, 33-year-old blonde and her contractor husband Sam restored a 1779 farmhouse to create three plush bedrooms and three distinctive common areas, all decorated with great style. They also gutted a former blacksmith shop/garage into an idyllic, two-level cottage in which celebrities like to hide out.

The handsome yellow house came with the patina of age: hand-hewn beams, wide-plank chestnut floors, intricate woodwork and warming fireplaces. The couple created luxurious baths with whirlpool tubs, tumbled marble showers and heated marble floors. They furnished with plump, oversize beds, pressed linens and goose down comforters, TV/VCRs, exotic toiletries and showy art.

Guests watch Andrea cook organic breakfasts, while sipping espresso and cappuccino made with the special Huckleberry blend from her shiny Capresso "coffee center" machine on a sideboard in the dining room. They view the proceedings when the pocket shutters open to reveal a wide pass-through window in her showplace country kitchen. The blackboard menu posts the morning's offerings: at our visit, citrus fruits with cardamom glaze and pomegranate seeds, cranberry-pumpkin bread, baby bella and fontina omelets with sausage links, and the grand finale – a smidgen of ginger crème brûlée. The four-course repast is taken at tables in the dining room or the adjacent stone-floored sun porch.

The breakfast dessert is "a little extra the guests don't expect," says Andrea. Others are the complimentary Hopkins Vineyard wine in the rooms and the array of liqueurs stashed in a remarkable mahogany liquor cabinet (made during Prohibition to look like a radio) in the cozy, fireplaced living room. The personal touches and over-all welcome account for a large repeat clientele.

(860) 868-1947 or (866) 868-1947. Fax (860) 868-6014. www.thehuckleberryinn.com. Three rooms and one cottage with private baths. Doubles, $205 to $285. Cottage, $365.

Gourmet Treats

This entire area is a hotbed of culinary activity, with Great Barrington increasingly the focal point. Its railroad station is the site of a farmers' market Saturday mornings in season.

Focus on Great Barrington

Guido's Fresh Marketplace at 760 South Main St. is a branch of the flagship store established in 1979 along Route 7 at the Pittsfield-Lenox line by brothers Chris and Matt Masiero. It's a fascinating complex of small owner-operated food markets, to which we'd gladly repair to turn marketing chores into fun. The brothers and their father Guido knew produce and groceries, but turned to others with experience in fish, meat, cheese and prepared foods. That's explains the presence of Mazzeo's Meat Center, Masse's Seafood and Bella Flora here. We always head to **The Marketplace of the Berkshires,** a kitchen and catering operation that moved its retail gourmet takeout store to Guido's. You'll be tempted to take home some of their terrific breads (the olive bread is sensational), salads (perhaps lo mein with shiitake mushrooms), quiches, dinner entrées like Thai-basil chicken and moussaka, and desserts. We couldn't resist picking up a special of lamb rolled with pinenuts and spinach, new potatoes with dill and grilled vegetables for a fancy dinner at home.

For a taste of Provence, head to **Bizalion's Fine Food,** a charming new charcuterie, cheese shop and café-of-sorts at 684 South Main St. Francois Bizalion and his Irish wife Helen charm regulars with their salades and assiette platters, panini, fondues, espresso and more, to enjoy at a long communal table in front or a couple of tables outside or to take away for a picnic in the countryside.

Main and Railroad streets in downtown have become the happening retail sites lately in the Berkshires. "We're what's cooking," advertises proprietor Rob Navarino of **The Chef's Shop,** which relocated to expanded quarters at 31 Railroad St. The well-equipped cooking equipment store also offers cooking classes with leading local lights. Billing itself as "Provence in the Berkshires," **Mistral's** offers a fine selection of tabletop kitchenware along with perfumes and bed and bath accessories.

The funky **Berkshire Coffee Roasting Co.** at 286 Main St. offers all the right coffees, teas, fresh juice, muffins and croissants at a handful of tables or to go. Adjacent is **Baba Louie's Sourdough Pizza Co.,** where the wood-fired oven produces organic and San Francisco sourdough pizzas.

Rubiner's Cheesemongers and Grocers occupies what once was an imposing bank at 264 Main St. After six years at the famed Formaggio Kitchen in Cambridge, Matthew Rubiner opened his version of the perfect food store, seeking quality products from around the world "to suit my palate." He stocks about 100 rare cheeses (we left with a couple of versions of our favorite époisse), gourmet specialties from Spanish bonito tuna to Bolude smoked salmon, homemade chicken and veal stocks, artisanal olive oils, canisters of Catalan sundried tomatoes, French brandied cherries, cornichons, Celtic grey sea salt and more to warm the finicky cook's heart. He even sells homemade fruit lollipops. In the rear of the building, **Rubi's Coffee and Sandwiches** offers hot and cold sandwiches and salads incorporating the grocery's stock of exceptional ingredients.

Locke, Stock and Barrel, just north of Great Barrington at 265 Stockbridge Road (Route 7), is more than a large gourmet and natural food store with a nifty name. Sophisticated as all get-out, it supplies a great selection of English cheeses, salsas and a remarkably extensive supply of preserves, conserves and jellies from all over the world (as in apricot jam from Lebanon). Owners Pat and Locke Larkin must have a lot of fun finding the dozens of hot sauces (oink ointment is a barbecue sauce), the hundreds of olive oils, the exotic cheeses and hams, rice from Thailand, the glazed violets, the chutneys, the nutmeg syrup – you get the picture. Locke sells granola made from his own recipes, too. At a recent visit, we came out with a couple of good bargains from his eclectic wine selection.

Lenox's Little Luxuries

In Lenox, **Mary Stuart Collections,** 81 Church St., carries exquisite accessories for bed and bath, hand-woven rugs, imported needlepoint designs, potpourris and fragrances, jewelry, fine china and glass, clothing, adorable things for babies, beautifully smocked dresses for little girls and hand-painted stools. Owner Judith Macioge knows her food. Her son runs Bistro Zinc across the street.

For an ice cream fix, head to **SoCo Creamery,** 38 Housatonic St., or at 5 Railroad St. in Great Barrington. Beverly Mazursky opened the establishment here as Bev's Homemade Ice Cream, after graduating from the Culinary Institute of America in 1989. She and her son Dan used to make the wonderful flavors in machines behind the counter, but most come now from Dan's new production facility at 955 South Main St., Great Barrington. They're known for their raspberry-chocolate chip and their margarita sorbet, served in sugar cones. You can order gelatos, frappes, smoothies and even a banana split, as well as espresso, cappuccino and café latte. Soups and sandwiches are available except in summer, when their popular Jamaican patties (different kinds of Caribbean breads with such fillings as beef, mixed veggies and broccoli-cheese) are about the only things that get in the way of the ice cream.

Next door at 26 Housatonic is **Betty's Pizza Shack,** the third effort of young restaurateur Jason Macioge (of Bistro Zinc and Fin). A potted palm tree at the entry sets the stage for a "shack" like you never thought you'd see: A riot of blues, reds, purples and orange. Walls and ceiling of corrugated silver. A decor of surfboard and sharks and different colored lights. A curving counter with seats of cushion-topped garbage cans. Oh, yes. The food is a hip collection of pizzas, salads, "samiches" and "bevvies" for the hip young crowd that frequents the place.

The lately reinvented Lenox Shops along Route 7 north is home to **Chocolate Springs,** a chocolate and pastry café. Chef-owner Joshua Needleman returned to his home area after training at pastry boutiques in New York and Paris. Here he produces exotic chocolates and delectable dessert pastries, served with coffee or tea in a sleek retail showroom and salon-style dining area. One taste of his champagne-cognac bonbon and we were hooked.

Seldom have we seen so many kitchen resources, so enticingly displayed, as at **Different Drummer's Kitchen,** on the north side of Lenox at 374 Pittsfield Road (Route 7). Everything you could ever want for kitchen or dining room is here, from the best cookware to gadgets galore. We came away with a little gizmo for making gyozas and a practical thing for peeling garlic cloves, a tube that you put the garlic into, roll it and the skin comes right off.

Two for Tea

Harney & Sons, Main Street, Railroad Plaza, Millerton, N.Y.

Tea sommelier and master blender John Harney, a former Connecticut innkeeper, parlayed a family tea business into one of the top gourmet success stories in America. His concept: produce great tea at a price that would make it an everyday luxury as compelling as fine coffee and wine, and even put it to use as a flavoring for food. John and younger son Paul create custom tea blends, tea and food pairings

Michael, John and Paul Harney are ready for tea in tasting room at Harney & Sons.

and occasional tea cocktails from artisanal tea leaves found by son Michael on annual excursions across the Far East during spring tea harvest. They sell exotic teas by the bag or tin in a tasting room recently relocated from their packing factory in Lakeville, Conn., to the refurbished McArthur's Smokehouse building across the state line in Millerton. All the teas – ordered through a catalog by discriminating customers and purveyed to Williams-Sonoma and leading restaurants across the country – can be sampled here. Loose teas, flavored iced teas and tea bags, as well as accessories like solid black walnut tea chests, thermometers and permanent tea filters, even a "tea-shirt" are on display. So are preserves, mixes for scones and lots of information about tea, including the Harneys' book on tea-leaf reading and his latest, a quasi-cookbook called *Eat Tea* revealing recipes flavored with tea.

When he's not traveling, John is a genial host as he shows novices the proper way to taste tea from canisters arranged along counters in his tasting room. He makes it more fun to sample teas than we could have imagined. And the teas come in an amazing variety of flavors and hues (display cabinets contain more than 200 varieties in gold-labeled black canisters). After sampling three or four, meticulously timed by little timers to just the right flavor and served in small handle-less white cups, we left with some Indian spice tea and some wonderful (and pricey) Japanese green tea. At our close-to-Christmas visit, local folks kept coming in for a stash of holiday tea, spiced with citrus, almond, clove and cinnamon.

(518) 789-2121 or (888) 427-6398 (800) 832-8463. www.harney.com. Open Monday-Saturday 10 to 5, Sunday 11 to 4.

Chaiwalla, 1 Main St., Salisbury, Conn.

Tea lovers like Chaiwalla (which means teamaker in Sanskrit) and flock in for owner Mary O'Brien's pots of rare tea. They sit at gate-leg tables with mismatched chairs in her dining room and a counter facing the open kitchen. Mary serves morning fare ("offered whenever it is 'morning' for you"), tiffin (midday fare) and tea all day. A stunning selection of perfectly brewed teas, using local spring water, is served in clear glass pots on warmers and poured into clear glass mugs. You also may try Chaiwalla's own granola, eggs en cocotte, fruit-filled french toast, perhaps a soup like corn chowder or tomato-kale, pot stickers or a sandwich like "scholar's delight," roast beef with watercress and homemade herb mayonnaise. At teatime, Scottish shortbread, crumpets and scones with lemon curd are among the goodies. When we stopped in, plum kuchen and three-berry cobbler were among the desserts.

(860) 435-9758. Open daily, 10 to 6.

Connecticut's Cornucopia

Fine table-top items and Simon Pearce glassware are among the choice home furnishings and gifts on display on two floors of an 1832 house called **Perfect Pear,** a super shop at 2 Main St. in Salisbury. **Holly's Place** is a delightful little café for breakfast, lunch and takeout in a former bakery and deli at 10 Academy St.

You can sample many kinds of coffee, pastries and panini sandwiches down the road at **Riga Mt. Roast** in Lakeville.

You'll find select cookware, table-top pieces and a few specialty food items at **New Preston Kitchen Goods** at 11 East Shore Road (Route 45) in New Preston. Owner Martin Rook, a former pastry chef at New York's La Grenouille restaurant, knows his stuff. He scouts out for the home kitchen basic items favored by the professionals, things like enameled cast-iron Staub cookware from France, de Buyer copper pans, all-steel pots by Iittala, Bespoke porcelain tableware and stainless-steel flatware with colorful patterned plastic handles. We found a handy propane tank pressure gauge we hadn't come across before.

More fine cookware and tableware is available at **Kitchenworks & Gourmet Gifts,** facing the green at 23 West St. in Litchfield.

A chic destination in tiny Washington Depot is **The Pantry,** a winning specialty food shop and café off Titus Road in the center of town. Tables are set amidst high-tech shelves displaying condiments, kitchenware and table settings. Owners Michael and Nancy Ackerman dole out at lunchtime an extensive repertoire of innovative soups, salads, sandwiches, entrées and desserts, as well as wine and beer, for here or to go. At a recent visit the chef was dishing up a special muffaletta sandwich, as well as Asian chicken and Thai snap pea salads, a Greek pasta and the best-looking pecan tarts and petits fours we ever saw.

Two Northwest Connecticut wineries are of interest to visitors. **Hopkins Vineyard** in New Preston is run very personally run by ex-dairy farmers-turned-winemakers Bill and Judy Hopkins and their offspring. Their rustic red barn offers a self-guided tour, an attractive showroom and tasting area, and the country-sophisticated Hayloft Wine Bar upstairs, where on weekends you can order a cheese and pâté board and wines by the glass and savor a view of Lake Waramaug. The gift shop sells wine-related items like baskets, grapevine wreaths and stemware. On nice days, sip one of the eleven varieties of award-winning wines – perhaps a hearty cabernet franc or an estate chardonnay – in a small picnic area overlooking the lake. The winery is open Monday-Saturday 10 to 5, Sunday 11 to 5, May-December; Wednesday-Sunday in March and April, weekends in winter.

Haight Vineyards and Winery near Litchfield, the first farm winery in New England's biggest wine-producing state, is Connecticut's largest. The Haight family take pride in their covertside white and merlot award-winners as well as their chardonnay and riesling labels. There's an informative vineyard walk and guided tours are available in the Tudor-style winery, which is open Monday-Saturday 10:30 to 5 and Sunday noon to 5.

Rural pond with swan and geese is an attraction at Stonehenge inn and restaurant.

Ridgefield

An Enclave of Elegant Eateries

For its size, no town in Connecticut – perhaps even in all New England – enjoys the reputation that Ridgefield has for fine dining. "Some people think that Ridgefield was put on the map by our restaurant," claims the brochure for Stonehenge. The same could be said by a couple of other restaurants after the rural charm of Ridgefield was discovered by New Yorkers in the post-war era.

For three decades or so, Stonehenge, the Inn at Ridgefield and The Elms had things pretty much to themselves. In recent years, more first-rate restaurants have sprouted in Ridgefield and environs as affluent newcomers punctuate the bucolic landscape with oversize McMansions.

That there is such a concentration of top-rated establishments in one small area does not surprise the restaurateurs. "It's like opening a fine shoe store," said one. "You don't want to be the only good store around."

Lately, the early emphasis on haute has been superseded by a proliferation of bistros and cafés that specialize in everything from Southwest fare to sushi. "This town has really taken to gourmet takeout," said one merchant who added a café to cater to the busy lunch trade as well as to the takeout phenomenon.

That trend was noted by the folks from Hay Day, the Westport-based, country-chic farm market, who opened a market with an extensive takeout section, a coffee bar and a café in Ridgefield. Successful beyond expectations, it served as a prototype for the expanded Westport operation. Hay Day recently became part of the Maryland-based Sutton Place Gourmet market group, which in turn merged with Balducci's of New York.

The Hay Day/Balducci concept was tailor-made for Ridgefield. This is, after all, a town where a sidewalk vendor dispenses gourmet hot dogs and a store called Bone Jour advertises gourmet treats for pets.

The burgeoning of the restaurant business extends to lodging, with a fine B&B next to the original Inn at Ridgefield, and upgraded and expanded accommodations at Stonehenge and The Elms.

But food remains foremost in Ridgefield, an enclave of creative cuisine.

Dining

The Best of the Best

Bernard's, 20 West Lane, Ridgefield.

Two young chefs who worked in New York area restaurants were looking for a country inn and a house of their own. Bernard and Sarah Bouissou found both in the glamorous but fading Inn at Ridgefield, nestled in a grand residential section. They moved with their four daughters into a house in back, added spectacular formal gardens and a dining patio, lightened up the decor in the dining rooms and freshened the contemporary French fare.

And voilà! The reinvented Inn at Ridgefield – now called Bernard's – is the culinary gem of northern Fairfield County.

Bernard, born in the South of France, and his wife met while working at Le Cirque in New York. He became chef at La Panetière in Rye, N.Y., and she launched a high-end catering business. "This is what we wanted," said Sarah of the move from the city to Ridgefield. "Here we both do everything," working side by side in the inn's big kitchen, he for the restaurant and she mainly for the catering business.

Fresh flowers from their gardens designed by noted landscape architect Andrew Grossman grace each table in three elegant dining rooms and a small bar. Busy fabric wallpapers have given way to painted walls of pale yellow or green and the formerly tuxedoed staff is now clad in burgundy shirts and black pants. A grand piano takes center position in front of a fireplace near the entrance, where a pianist entertains Friday and Saturday evenings and during Sunday brunch.

The menu, printed in straightforward English, is free of the pretensions of the past. For lunch on a pleasant autumn Friday, we were one of only four couples in the hushed dining room. The food more than made up for the unexpected solemnity. The thick French onion soup gratinée was perfection in a bowl, a hearty meal when paired with an appetizer of sautéed sweetbreads with green pea raviolis, cepe mushroom sauce and watercress. A main course of portobello-crusted halibut, succulent as could be, was served atop wild mushroom risotto. It was sauced with a balsamic mushroom reduction, flanked by spears of asparagus and crowned with a sprig of thyme. Although Sarah's trio of crème brûlées (banana, apricot and vanilla) tempted for dessert, we settled for her pineapple tarte tatin with ginger ice cream – a fine ending to an extravagant lunch.

Bernard's new garden menu offers a three-course prix-fixe lunch with choices for $24.

Bernard and Sarah Bouisson pause on staircase at Bernard's.

At night, an amuse-bouche begins a dinner pageant that uniformly earns reviewers' highest accolades. Many start with Bernard's signature foie gras trio: sautéed with calvados sauce, torchon with sauterne jelly and smoked with horseradish aspic. Another superb appetizer is sea scallops baked in their shell, with shaved black truffles and leek fondue beneath a puff pastry seal.

Half of the main courses involve seafood, perhaps baked baby black sea bass filled with a compote of tomatoes, black olives and capers or braised New Zealand john dory and cockles over basil linguini. Roasted free-range chicken gets royal treatment here, served crisp-skinned and moist with a sage sauce amid an array of potato-sage gnocchi, butternut squash and baby bok choy. Roasted veal tenderloin wellington with truffle sauce, sautéed venison medallion with grand veneur sauce, and a duo of beef – braised short ribs and roasted sirloin with red wine sauce – typify the other possibilities.

Bernard's collection of more than 1,300 wines from around the world is categorized by country, grape and region. It has earned Wine Spectator's Best of Award of Excellence since 2001.

(203) 438-8282. www.bernardsridgefield.com. Entrées, $26 to $36. Lunch, Tuesday-Friday noon to 2:30. Dinner, Tuesday-Saturday 6 to 9 or 10. Sunday, brunch noon to 2:30, dinner 5 to 8.

Elms Restaurant & Tavern, 500 Main St., Ridgefield.

They were high-school sweethearts at Ridgefield High, Class of 1976. Twenty years later, they returned to take over the restaurant in Ridgefield's oldest (1799) operating inn.

It was a happy homecoming for Brendan and Cris Walsh. The pioneer in new

Chef-owner Brendan Walsh and wife Cris relax in dining room at the Elms.

American cuisine had got his start "flipping crêpes" at Stonehenge and was a waiter at The Elms and the nearby Le Château while attending the Culinary Institute of America. At age 26 after working in the California kitchen of Jeremiah Tower, he made a national name as opening chef at Arizona 206 in New York City.

Three Long Island restaurants of his own and three children later, he got a phone call from his old boss, Robert Scala, of The Elms: "I'm retiring. Do you want the restaurant?"

It was a godsend, recalls Cris. "All our family was still here." They negotiated to take over the restaurant operation, added a more casual tavern concept and launched a new, flag-waving American cooking style.

Brendan, the master of innovative Southwestern cooking who helped create the trend of small plates called "grazing," took inspiration from 18th-century food associated with New England. He elevated stews, roasts, spoon breads and puddings to new culinary heights and quick acclaim in the national media. His renowned "food of the moment" now is refreshingly familiar, its presentation new and exciting.

For starters, consider the signature shepherd's pie, masterfully done here with lobster, peas and chive-mashed potatoes. Macoun apples enhance the curried apple and buttercup squash soup, with a crème fraîche swirl on top. Braised lamb, celery root and goat cheese embellish the corn cake, and the duck confit salad comes with seasonal mushrooms and a roasted green apple.

Among main courses, the tasty skillet-roasted free-range chicken might be accented with a sausage made of its leg and paired with sweet potato spoon bread, creamed collards and truffle-whipped potatoes. The Connecticut seafood stew is a mélange of lobster, mussels, shrimp, sole and scallops in a tomato-fennel broth. The grilled Montauk swordfish with charred tomato salsa is as good as swordfish gets. Other seasonal favorites are grilled cervena venison with maple-thyme glaze, thyme-roasted pheasant and buffalo ribeye steak with cheddar-green chile soufflé.

Desserts are new twists on traditional themes. The apple pandowdy with granny smith apples is teamed with Tahitian vanilla yogurt. The pumpkin mousse comes with cranberry granité and cinnamon cookies, and the pear-ginger charlotte with a spiced wine glaze.

Cris Walsh, an interior decorator and graphic artist, stenciled the four small dining rooms in 18th-century patterns, painted the walls white with "lantern-glow yellow" trim, cloaked the well-spaced tables in white over 18th-century fabric, and added simple Colonial plaid curtains for the windows. It's a stylish, updated setting for food that's the last word in New England Yankee dining.

A more casual tavern menu is offered for lunch and dinner in the handsomely refurbished, Tudor-look Grill. Atmospheric as all get-out, it has a beamed ceiling, sturdy dark wood tables seating 30, a neat birdcage bar with four seats, a big fireplace with a roaring fire in season and windows onto an expansive, covered terrace with a cottage garden in one direction and a park in the other. Here you can order "one-dish meals" like bangers and mash, chicken pot pie, spice-rubbed hanger steak with potato cake and wilted spinach or an alderwood-smoked salmon sandwich that an admiring local chef says is to die for.

(203) 438-9206. www.elmsinn.com. Entrées, $22 to $32. Dinner by reservation, Wednesday-Sunday 5 to 9 or 10. Tavern, $9.95 to $18.95, Tuesday 5 to 9, Wednesday-Sunday 11 to 9.

Stonehenge, Route 7, Ridgefield.

The famed Swiss chef Albert Stockli of Restaurant Associates in New York put Stonehenge on the culinary map back in the 1960s. Since his death, owner Douglas Seville has survived changing eating habits and a disastrous fire, adding a variety of settings for dining as well as upgrading and expanding the overnight accommodations.

Rebuilt following a 1988 fire, the restaurant could not be more sophisticated in a country way. Modeled after the original early 19th-century, Colonial white edifice, it has a new side entrance and a layout that gives almost every table a view of the property's tranquil pond. The main dining room is light and airy in a peachy coral and white color scheme. Fresh flowers and small lamps are on the widely spaced tables flanked by upholstered Chippendale-style chairs. Handsome swagged draperies frame the large end window onto the pond, and french doors open into an enclosed Terrace Room adding 60 seats for overflow on the former flagstone cocktail terrace. More masculine is the cozy tavern in hunter green, where English sporting prints cover the walls and the sconces are made from hunting horns.

The ambiance is sheer luxury, but not pretentious. The over-all dining experience is said to have slipped a bit of late, according to locals who recall better days.

Generous drinks are served in pretty, long-stemmed goblets. The half American, half French wine list is short and rather pricey, starting at $35 and rising to $4,000.

Chef Raymond Peron has updated and condensed the contemporary continental fare. Stonehenge's famed beer-batter shrimp was retired after 30 years' service in favor of such appetizers as tuna carpaccio with sesame-seaweed salad and crab cake with saffron aioli. We found the snails baked with hazelnut and garlic butter and the wild mushrooms in puff pastry with port wine cream sauce out of this world.

The short list of entrées ranges from navarin of sea scallops and shrimp with basmati rice, and organic chicken breast stuffed with goat cheese and spinach to roquefort-crusted black angus steak with bordelaise sauce and lobster "of the evening, out of the shell." Specialties include dover sole meunière and roast rack of lamb Mediterranean with rosemary sauce and an artfully created pastry basket, complete with handle and holding diced tomatoes, zucchini and other vegetables. We can vouch for the tournedo of seared salmon with ginger-chive beurre blanc and the veal scaloppine with truffle sauce and savoy cheese.

Desserts are luscious. House favorites are the three versions of soufflés (perhaps chocolate, pineapple-coconut and grand marnier), tarte tatin, and warm chocolate cake with white chocolate ice cream. Ours was a strawberry tart with an abundance of fresh berries on a shortcake crust and topped with a shiny glaze. We're also partial to the ginger crème brûlée.

(203) 438-6511. www.stonehengeinn-ct.com. Entrées, $22 to $38. Dinner, Monday-Saturday 6 to 8:30 or 9.

Le Château, Route 35 at Route 123, South Salem, N.Y.

Drive through the gate and up the winding, dogwood-lined road just across the state line from Ridgefield. You'll reach the baronial stone mansion built by J. Pierpont Morgan on a hilltop in 1907 for his former minister and enjoy one of the most majestic views of any restaurant – a sylvan panorama across the northern Westchester valley. The entry hall is paneled in rare chestnut, hand-hewn and held together by butterfly pieces. Dining is in high-ceilinged rooms, a couple facing onto the garden patio and all with expansive views. No wonder Le Château does such a lively wedding and function business.

Window table yields view at Le Château.

Despite the numbers, dining is correct and quiet. It's well regarded locally, a credit to Monique and Joseph Jaffré, daughter and son-in-law of the original owners who came here from Le Coq au Vin in New York in 1974, and their longtime staff. The fabulous array of appetizers and desserts, on display buffet-style on either side of the entry foyer, are enough to make the most diet-conscious succumb.

Chef André Molle has imparted more colorful and dramatic presentations to the contemporary continental fare, which received a rare excellent rating from the New York Times. The menu is of manageable size and, curiously, printed in English with French translations in small print below. Entrées range from almond-crusted Pacific salmon with champagne truffle to roasted rack of lamb crusted with mustard and basil. The pan-seared arctic char is served with a ragoût of morels and a chive coulis. The medallions of veal come with a fricassee of crimini mushrooms and artichokes.

Some of the appetizers bear Manhattan prices. Those with the wherewithal are rewarded with fine renditions of a lump crabmeat napoleon with poire william vinaigrette, sautéed foie gras with pineapple and mango chutney or a terrine of duck foie gras on toasted country bread. Desserts include grand marnier soufflé and a creamy chocolate-kahlua terrine.

Birch divider separates bar from main dining room and sushi bar in background at Koo.

It's idyllic in summer to have cocktails on the lawn, enclosed by gray stone walls as in a castle. And it's great any time to tarry at the bar, its windows offering the best view around.

(914) 533-6631. www.lechateauny.com. Entrées, $29 to $38. Dinner, Tuesday-Friday 5:30 to 9, Saturday seatings at 6 and 9, Sunday 2 to 9. Jackets required on weekends.

Koo, 470 Main St., Ridgefield.

"Neo-Japanese cuisine" is the theme in this ultra-sleek newcomer at the rear of the lower level of a downtown building known as Yankee Ridge Center. Restaurateur Alex Poon transformed the space formerly occupied by Bully's Steakhouse into a very un-bullylike arena as neo as its cuisine.

Visually, the space is a stunner. Two dining areas – one in the front and one up a step in back – have curved banquettes and circular tables and red or yellow walls accented with circular back-lit glass panels. The front dining area is separated by a divider of upright white-birch branches from an American-style bar on one side and is open to a sushi bar on the other. Most striking is the ceiling, accented with gray netting and from which hang sculpted wire fixtures bearing tiny colored lights.

Into this designer's dream comes food overseen by an executive chef who hails from the Four Seasons Hotel in Singapore. It's called neo-Japanese because of its Malaysian, French and Latin American nuances. The menu, like the one at the flagship Koo in Rye, N.Y., is straight-forward in English – a good thing, too, for the staff is Japanese and better versed in their native language.

Seafood prevails, especially the various sushi and sashimi specialties incorporating the highest quality of raw fish – 30 varieties at last count. The spicy mango lobster roll is a favorite among such choices as rolls of white tuna and jalapeño, king crab California, sundried tomato and avocado, and crispy duck confit. The omakase sashimi platter brings about twenty pieces of five kinds of raw fish for $30.

The predictable miso soup, gyoza, shumai, tempuras and seaweed salads are among two dozen choices on the list of starters. Entrées include broiled black cod

Colorful mural of Tuscan countryside wraps around skylit dining room at Toscana.

glazed in saikyo miso sauce, grilled salmon wrapped in spinach with soy-ginger sauce, jumbo shrimp with mangos in a Thai sweet chili sauce, roasted duck breast with crispy duck ravioli and hoisin duck sauce, and grilled ribeye steak with truffle-mushroom sauce.

The wine list is small. The sake repertoire is more interesting, with eleven types (some rarely available outside Japan), priced from $13 to $55 a bottle. The chocolate ganache cake ranks best among desserts.

(203) 431-8838. www.ridgefieldkoo.com. Entrées, $19 to $26. Lunch, Monday-Saturday 11:45 to 2:45. Dinner nightly, 5 to 10.

More Dining Choices

Toscana, 43 Danbury Road, Ridgefield.

You don't expect to find an Italian restaurant in Ridgefield housed in a pillared house of Greek Revival vintage. Nor do you expect to step inside and find such stylish and relatively minimalist decor: a large and airy, skylit dining room wrapped in a colorful mural of the Tuscan countryside. Here is one gorgeous restaurant, with well-spaced tables dressed in cream-colored cloths and an elegant bar in a comfortable side room. A glass divider and a shelf accented with magnums of wine screen both rooms from each other and from the open kitchen in the back.

Co-owners Raffaele Gallo, the executive chef, and Nino Pisanzio, both from the isle of Capri, offer a high-end dining experience, from the crusty bread that arrives with a saucer of extra virgin olive oil and baby kalamata olives at meal's start to the almond biscotti served gratis at the end.

In between, you're advised to begin with one of the specialty calamari dishes, either grilled in an herb marinade and served with cherry tomatoes and a lemon sauce or lightly fried and served with cherry peppers. Also recommended are the spinach flan with a tangy gorgonzola cream sauce studded with walnuts and the sautéed mussels and clams in a white wine sauce served with crostini. Winning pasta dishes include taglioni with shrimp and asparagus in a lobster bisque sauce and a menu fixture – potato and butternut squash gnocchi, light-as-a-feather dumplings in an ethereal parmesan-almond butter sauce.

A section of the menu is devoted to wild game, a route well taken. You could start with grilled wild boar sausage or venison carpaccio and switch ingredients in the big-hitters: wild boar stew marinated for three days in celery, carrots, onions and chianti wine, served with grilled polenta, or grilled venison loin in a red wine reduction.

Otherwise you'll have a choice among ten entrées, ranging from grilled shrimp on a skewer with mixed bell peppers and onions and a limoncello sauce to grilled kobe steak with a truffle-gorgonzola sauce. The fish of the day might be wrapped with mixed vegetables and olives in parchment paper. The mustard-rubbed roast pork comes with a marsala-pear sauce, while the millefoglie of veal scaloppine is layered with zucchini and eggplant.

Chocolate-almond soufflé cake is the signature dessert. The panna cotta and marsala-laced zabaglione also are recommended.

(203) 894-8995. Entrées, $18.95 to $34.95. Dinner nightly, 5:30 to 10 or 10:30.

Luc's, 3 Big Shop Lane, Ridgefield.

A quintessential French café now occupies this alluring, cave-like hideaway in a former blacksmith shop along Big Shop Lane. The much-loved Le Coq Hardi gave way to Sam's Grill, which gave way to Chez Noüe. Now it's Luc's, named after their infant son by Hervé and Marissa Aussavis, he from Paris and she from Staten Island.

The couple freshened up the T-shaped dining room with mustard yellow walls, gray pillars and dividers, and imported chairs from Paris for the interior as well as the small outdoor dining patio in front.

Their chef executes a classic all-day French menu, from the salade niçoise and croque monsieur preferred for lunch to the crème brûlée and dark chocolate mousse for dessert. The onion soup gratinée is the way it should be, the frisée salad comes with poached egg and bacon, the escargots are cooked in pernod and the charcuterie plate yields pâté and an assortment of cold cuts.

Les plats are predictable as well: steamed mussels with frites, fillet of sole meunière or amandine, cassoulet toulousain, roasted organic chicken, duckling à l'orange, rack of lamb with potato gratin and haricots vert and, of course, that staple of the convivial French café that Luc's seeks to be, le steak-frites.

Desserts range from crème brûlée and chocolate mousse to a plate of assorted homemade cookies. Three varieties of crêpes are house specialties. The all-French wine list is priced from $28 to $62 and consists of the familiar standbys.

With no loftier ambitions than these, Luc's holds to the middle ground of French comfort foods and delivers with care.

(203) 894-8522. Entrées, $17 to $26.50. Open Monday-Friday 11 to 11, Saturday 5 to 11.

La Salière, 3 Big Shop Lane, Ridgefield.

The upper floor above a 19th-century blacksmith shop is home to this lively French brasserie that took the place of Biscotti, a short-lived Italian eatery. In 2004, chef-owner Mario Mollière from Paris opened a seafood-oriented bistro like those along the French Riviera, originally in partnership with the French owner of Luc's café in the former blacksmith shop below. Although the idea of two French restaurants, one above the other, strikes some as odd, each is quite different from the other – in style and ambiance.

An aquarium atop a deli case greets patrons in the cluttered entry near the kitchen of La Salière. Beyond is a busy dining room, which seems even busier with the addition of a massive wooden bar that takes up a third of the space. Beer flags, pennants, mugs and what-not hang from the ceiling and bar. Lineups of tables flank the bar on two sides, and windows look out onto a cheery patio/beer garden in front – authentically furnished with those distinctive brasserie chairs imported from France – and onto Luc's smaller and more sedate dining patio below. Although this is white-tablecloth dining, the ambiance is more that of a brasserie.

Mario offers a colorful menu of traditional French classics that's as large in scope as it is in size. Expect two dozen soups, salads and appetizers and about 30 entrées, plus a dozen shellfish (or raw bar) items. Its original seafood emphasis has been broadened to more meat items, the chatty young waiter advised. You'll find everything from bouillabaisse and coquilles St. Jacques, from steak tartare (as a main course) and coq au vin to filet mignon béarnaise and rack of lamb persillée. There are novel touches. "Organic" steak frites leads the menu. The roast quail comes with a whiskey-grape sauce and the organic duck à l'orange with grand marnier. The fillet of sole is stuffed with crabmeat and shrimp and sauced with champagne. And on it goes, nothing new or exciting but all executed with the deft touch of a French chef.

(203) 438-1976. Entrées, $19.50 to $30. Lunch daily, noon to 4. Dinner, Monday-Saturday 5 to 11. Sunday, brunch 11:30 to 4, dinner 4 to 9:30.

Wild Ginger Café, 461 Main St., Ridgefield.

Overpowering aromas waft outside the door of this Asian restaurant that's wildly popular. They lure such a following that the place expanded in 2005 into an adjacent tuxedo shop, more than doubling in size and allowing a more refined dining experience.

Housed in a strip plaza set back from the street, it's a sibling of Hunan Table in Wilton and Ching's Table in New Canaan, among the smart pan-Asian eateries run by Alan and Jing Lee, who got their start two decades ago in Brooklyn's Park Slope neighborhood. Here, from an open kitchen in the back, their cooks prepare much the same fare as in Wilton and New Canaan. It's served at tables scrunched so close together that you quickly become part of one big happy family beneath a backdrop of modern Asian decor and accents. A dramatic glass divider enhanced with flowers and Asian artifacts separates the cramped original from the new dining room that provides slightly more elbow room between tables, especially the larger tables for four along the divider.

The menu is a short version of dishes from Thailand, Malaysia, Indonesia, Vietnam, Singapore and China. Fifteen of the best are listed under "chef selection." Ginger plays a leading role in several, but none more so than the wok-glazed chicken and shrimp in a bowl lined with slices of sautéed ginger, served with mixed vegetables in a gingery brown sauce. Lemongrass flavors grilled shrimp with steamed watercress. Black bean sauce accents the grilled salmon, steamed with seasonal greens. Spicy curry sauce teams up with turmeric, fennel seeds and basil leaves in a Thai casserole of chicken and shrimp.

The treats begin with an enticing assortment of appetizers, from Thai spring rolls to tempura shrimp, from dim sum to szechuan dumplings. After so many temptations, desserts are limited but refreshing – a choice of vanilla or green tea ice cream.

Arty wall divider separates old and new dining areas at Wild Ginger Café.

(203) 431-4588. Entrées, $9.95 to $15.95. Lunch, Monday-Saturday 11 to 3. Dinner, Monday-Saturday 3 to 10 or 11, Sunday noon to 10.

Southwest Café, 109 Danbury Road, Copps Hill Common, Ridgefield.

A simple café with nine tables and a six-seat bar is where Barbara Nevins dishes up lunch and dinner and lots of takeout orders. Barbara, who used to live in Taos, N.M., returns every summer during hatch chile pepper season to bring back 500 pounds of hand-chosen New Mexican greens to be made into daily specials during the fall and winter.

She's especially known for her green chile sauce. It's the base for a hearty green chile stew of carrots, celery and new potatoes, topped with melted cheese and served with a warm flour tortilla. Barbara also employs the sauce in many of the dinner dishes, such as cheese, chicken, seafood or beef enchiladas (the last layered New Mexican style and topped with a fried egg), chicken or beef chimichangas, chalupas, shrimp tostadas, chicken and mango quesadillas, chorizo-crusted sea scallops, fajitas and huevos rancheros. It's not often you find huevos on both lunch and dinner menus, or Colorado tostadas with chicken or shredded beef and New Mexican red chile sauce, for that matter. New chef Robert Ubaldo added Mexican specialties to the mix from his training in Oaxaca, Mexico.

Variations on the same menu is available at lunch, as are sandwiches and salads, ranging from chicken and artichoke to shrimp and vegetables. Southwest dishes include a bowl of green chili and green chile chicken, vegetable or beef stew. Start with tortilla soup and end with Mexican flan, strawberry cobbler or kahlua-pecan pie. Bossa nova jazz is offered on Thursdays, and there's outdoor dining in season.

(203) 431-3398. Entrées, $14.95 to $18.95. Lunch daily, 11 to 4. Dinner nightly, 4 to 9:30 or 10.

Current and Cool

Upstream Lounge, 426 Main St., Ridgefield.

Hidden in an alley off Main Street, this Manhattan-style restaurant and lounge is mainly bar, the likes of which Ridgefield has never seen – nor ever expected to see. Low curving couches, flat-screen TVs and a mini-waterfall behind the bar contribute to a cool urban vibe for a hip crowd that gathers for drinks, live music and eclectic food.

Chef Mike Galgano, a Culinary Institute of America graduate, serves small and large plates of globally influenced American fare. The small plates are fairly large and you can make a meal by grazing through a couple. Choices include grilled sea scallops with seaweed salad, calamari sautéed with andouille sausage and minced walnuts, pan-seared wild Alaskan salmon. and filet mignon drizzled with gorgonzola butter.

The food, which gets good reviews, takes a back seat to the bar that dominates the room. The drink list (martinis for $11) reads like a dessert menu. Caramel appletini, key lime pietini and cinnamon toast sound like something you'd rather eat than sip. Try them for dessert, if you don't have far to drive.

(203) 438-1456. Small plates, $9 to $15. Large plates, $18 to $31. Dinner, Tuesday-Sunday 5 to 10 or 11, lounge to 1 or 2 a.m. Closed Sunday in winter.

Offbeat Gourmet

Chez Lenard, Main Street, Ridgefield.

We can't give you a proper address for this operation, which he officially calls "Les Delices Culinaires de la Voiture," but it's usually in front of 458 Main St. near the corner of Prospect Street. Anywhere else but in Ridgefield it would be merely a hot dog cart, but this one has chutzpah, or we should say its pusher, young Chad Cohen, who changes his hats with the seasons, has. He and wife Kirsten bought the long-running business in 1999 from founder Michael Soetbeer, who opted for early retirement.

Year-round on even the chilliest days, the "voiture" dispenses le hot dog, le hot dog choucroute alsacienne, le hot dog garniture Suisse (topped with cheese fondue), and le hot dog façon Mexicain, $2.50 to $4.25.

Chad and Kirsten, who also run a catering business, claim "the first gourmet hot dog rolls in the world," made for them at Martin's Bakery with semolina flour and potato water. We thought le hot dog supreme with the works ($3.25) was the best we'd had. Beverages to go with these elegant hot dogs are cold sodas Americaines and San Pellegrino with lime (de rigeur in the area). For dessert, Chad offers candies – "for the kids."

Open year-round, daily 11 to 5 in summer, to 4 in winter and sometimes closed Monday.

Lodging

The Elms, 500 Main St., Ridgefield 06877.

At Ridgefield's oldest operating inn, parts of the original 1760 structure look appropriately ancient, but the inside of the newest in the lineup of gray buildings that make up the Elms complex is as up-to-date as can be.

The former Scala family homestead on the other side of the restaurant from the main inn was converted in 2001 into three spacious suites, one per floor and each with a kitchenette. The ground-floor suite has a kingsize front bedroom, living room, huge bath with clawfoot tub and separate shower, a dining room and traditional furnishings. The second-floor suite is nearly a mirror image, but contains two bedrooms instead of a dining room. The third floor is one vast open room with vaulted ceiling and a brick chimney tilting precariously in the middle. It's a sea of green and white florals, from wallpapers to puffs and shams on the king bed.

Thirteen rooms and three suites are located on three floors in the main inn. They are spacious, carpeted and, like the others, outfitted with television and telephones. Many of the bathrooms have dressing areas. Antique furnishings, a few four-poster beds and striking wallpapers add a feeling of tradition and luxury. Four rooms and suites above the restaurant are redecorated but retain their historic look, even to sloping floors. Two have stenciled bluebirds on the walls.

Innkeeper Viola Scala, having vacated the family homestead, remains on site in a cottage in back. A continental breakfast with croissants is delivered to guests' rooms.

(203) 438-2541. www.elmsinn.com. Thirteen rooms and six suites with private baths. Doubles, $155 to $195. Suites, $215 to $425.

Stonehenge, Route 7, Box 667, Ridgefield 06877.

Instead of a country inn, this is now a fine inn in the country, stresses owner Douglas Seville of the "new" Stonehenge, southwestern Connecticut's grand old inn. He was showing some of the sixteen redecorated guest rooms – six in the inn, six in the Guest Cottage and the rest in a large newer outbuilding called the Guest House, set amid bucolic surroundings within earshot of Route 7.

Fashioned in 1947 from a farmhouse into an English inn by a World War II veteran who had been stationed on the Salisbury Plain near the ancient monument of the same name, Stonehenge has been synonymous with fine food for many years. Since the guest rooms were refurnished and more were added, it has been a place for country getaways as well.

Each room has its own style, from the corner Windsor Room in the inn with a bookcase, antique dresser, wing chairs and ornamental fireplace to the spacious bridal suite with large living room and kitchenette in the Guest House. The two master bedrooms and two suites can sleep four, and are particularly sumptuous and comfortable. All rooms have private baths, air-conditioning, telephones and TV.

Trays containing continental breakfast are delivered to the rooms each morning. In season, guests like to take them to the pond to watch the antics of the geese, ducks and swans. Guests also enjoy a cozy, fireplaced parlor in the main inn.

(203) 438-6511. Fax (203) 438-2478. www.stonehengeinn-ct.com. Fourteen rooms and two suites with private baths. Doubles, $120 to $160. Suites, $200.

West Lane Inn, 22 West Lane, Ridgefield 06877.

Adjacent to Bernard's, the former Inn at Ridgefield restaurant, this quiet B&B is much favored by corporate types moving into the area or visiting on business. Innkeeper Deborah Prieger has decorated the comfortable rooms in the early 1800s home in soft colors. Two have working fireplaces. All have one or two queensize beds, upholstered wing chairs and/or sofas, TVs and telephones.

Fourteen rooms are in the main inn. Six more are out back in a converted garage named "The Cottage on the Hill." Each of the latter has a kitchenette and a private

Wide front porch is feature of early 1900s residence that now houses West Lane Inn.

rear balcony looking onto emerald-green lawns. Three suites have been fashioned from the former home of the innkeeper, hidden behind green plantings and a redwood fence between the inn and the restaurant.

Off the inn's rich, oak-paneled lobby is a cheery breakfast room for a complimentary continental breakfast. A full breakfast is available from a menu. You can choose to have it in summer on the wide front porch with its inviting wicker furniture.

(203) 438-7323. Fax (203) 438-7325. www.westlaneinn.com. Twenty rooms with private baths. Doubles, $145 to $215.

Gourmet Treats

Balducci's/Food Lover's Market, 21 Governor St., Ridgefield. Hidden behind Main Street in the old Grand Central supermarket is this outpost of New York's original food emporium in Greenwich Village. When it opened in 1991 as **Hay Day, The Country Farm Market,** it was the biggest and most diverse of the small Westport-based market chain. The 10,000-square-foot facility became the model for the relocation and expansion of the original Westport store, which began as a farm stand. The Hay Days were taken over by the Sutton Place Gourmet chain in Washington, D.C., which merged with Balducci's and assumed the latter's name in 2004. It's a food lover's paradise of produce, bakery, fish store, butcher shop, gourmet shelf items (complete with a caviar menu) and a deli to end all delis with wonderful prepared foods. Not to mention a coffee-espresso bar, a flower shop, a small pastry café where you can order sandwiches to go and an adjacent wine store. Best of all for noshers: you can sample your way through the store, tasting perhaps a spicy corn chowder and an addictive chunky clam and bacon dip at the deli, exotic cheeses, hot mulled cider and Connecticut macoun apples, and French vanilla coffee at the door. Open Sunday-Thursday 9 to 7, Friday and Saturday 8 to 8.

The Complete Kitchen at 410 Main St. is one of the better kitchen stores in Connecticut. The shop carries all kinds of bakeware, gadgets and hard-to-find tools to help the home cook. Chef-proprietor Paul Robert teaches morning and evening cooking classes in his demonstration kitchen in the back of the store. Some of the area's leading chefs also make guest appearances.

Sweet Pierre's, 3 Danbury Road, is what every chocolate store should look like. The cottage is dressed inside with French toile window treatments and enveloped outside in tiny white lights. For candy lovers, it's like opening Dorothy's door and walking into the Land of Oz. Owner Janice Mazzamaro makes fudge in the rear kitchen and imports European chocolates for her display cases. She named the enterprise for her late brother, who loved to cook. He'd surely love her sweets.

Some think the best ice cream around is served at **Mr. Shane's Homemade Parlour Ice Cream,** 409 Main St. Energetic John Ghitman bought the former branch of Dr. Mike's, a well-known Bethel operation, where he learned how to make ice cream. Now he serves up dozens of flavors, from a rich chocolate ("very powerful," says John) to spiced apple, pumpkin and eggnog. We can vouch for his pralines 'n cream, as well as his caramel swirl ice cream "that's been flying out the door." John also offers frappes (milkshakes, to those not familiar with the Massachusetts variety), brown cows (root beer with two scoops of ice cream) and frozen yogurt he doctors up from Columbo.

New in Copps Hill Common at 103 Danbury Road is **Common Grounds Café,** offering coffee, soups, salads and baked goods to start. Not yet opened at our latest visit, it was planning to reopen the lower-level café that earlier was part of the Ridgefield General Store and later J&J's Gathering Place.

For those too busy to cook, **Parmadeli** at 56 Danbury Road has plenty of answers. Caterers Nicholas and Concetta Simeone of Parma Gourmet & Catering expanded their impressive deli operation to feature countless pastas, cheeses, Italian specialties, hot wraps and paninis, and prepared meals to go. Their latest addition is a bakery.

A Destination for Cooks

The Silo, 44 Upland Road (off Route 202), New Milford.

No report on culinary affairs in this section of Connecticut would be complete without mention of the fabulous cookery shop and cooking classes at Hunt Hill Farm Trust, owned by Ruth Henderson, wife of the late Skitch Henderson, symphony conductor and founder-director of the New York Pops. In former stables and dairy barns are displayed everything from oversize Mexican pottery planters in shapes of rams and hens to a sizable collection of cookbooks interspersed among cooking equipment and jars and bottles of the most wonderful jams, sauces and herbs. The Gallery features changing exhibitions of Connecticut artists and craftsmen. Well-known cooking teachers give classes here; chefs from area restaurants do as well. There are two-week seminars and interesting one-session courses – for example, "One Potato, Two Potato," "An Asian Dinner Party," "Hair of the Dog Do-Ahead Brunch Party," "Fall Tailgate Picnic" and "My First Dinner Party" (ages 8 and up). The 200-acre Hunt Hill Farm, set among rolling hills and flower gardens where kittens tumble around and horses and cows are pastured nearby, is a destination in itself.

(860) 355-0300 or (800) 353-7456. www.hunthillfarmtrust.org. Open Wednesday-Monday, 10 to 5.

Southeastern Connecticut

Down the River and Along the Shore

For reasons not entirely evident, many of Connecticut's better restaurants have clustered through the years along the lower Connecticut River and the shore of Long Island Sound.

Perhaps it is the natural affinity of restaurants for water locations. Perhaps it is the reputation for the good life that accompanies people of affluence with demanding palates and high tastes. Perhaps it is the low-key resort status of the shore, summer home to thousands of inland Connecticut and Massachusetts residents.

Some of Southern New England's top innkeepers and restaurateurs put the area on the dining map in the 1970s. Several fine French restaurants followed, and in recent years, more restaurants and bistros have joined the scene.

Except for Mystic, the Connecticut shore has been discovered relatively lately by most travelers.

The area this chapter covers has no large cities. Rather, it harbors quaint villages like Chester and Stonington, affluent enclaves like Essex and Old Lyme, and resort areas like Mystic and Old Saybrook. It also claims the growing Foxwoods and Mohegan Sun resort casinos, two of the largest and most profitable in the world for the Native American tribes that own them.

Because this is our home territory, we cover our favorites in a broad sweep down the lower Connecticut River and east along the shore of Long Island Sound.

Dining

The Best of the Best

Restaurant du Village, 59 Main St., Chester.

Of all the Southern New England restaurants in which we've dined, we think this is the most like what you would find in a French village. Its blue wood facade – with specially grown ivy geraniums spilling out of window boxes in summer and the bottom half of the large windows curtained in an almost sheer white fabric – is smack on the main street of tiny Chester. One enters by walking up a brick path attractively bordered with potted geraniums to a side door.

Alsatian chef Michel Keller and his Culinary Institute-trained American wife Cynthia run their top-rated establishment very personally. A third-generation pastry chef, Michel spends his time in the kitchen and bakes the breads and desserts. Cynthia does the soups and some of the fish dishes, but is in the front of the house to welcome guests in the evening.

Through the small bar-lounge, decorated with plump piggies (the logo of the restaurant) with a few tables for overflow, you reach the utterly charming dining room. Along one wall, two sets of french doors open onto the brick walk for welcome breezes on warm evenings. A sideboard between the doors contains the night's desserts and a large floral arrangement. A few oil paintings, large copper pans and sconces adorn the stucco-type walls.

The air of elegant simplicity is enhanced at the thirteen tables by white cloths and napkins, vases of colorful flowers, votive candles, open salt and pepper dishes, and blue sprigged service plates.

Tables are set for elegant dining at Restaurant du Village.

What may be the best French bread you will taste in this country is brought to the table with generous cocktails. Crunchy and chewy, made of Hecker's unbleached flour that gives it a darker color, the baguette is cut into thick chunks. Each diner is served an individual crock of sweet butter. If you get near the last piece of bread – and most do – the basket is whisked away and refilled, which could be detrimental to one's dietary health. On one of our visits it came back three times.

Of the appetizers, standouts are the cassoulet, a small copper casserole filled with sautéed shrimp in a light curry sauce; the house-smoked trout with sliced walnut bread and horseradish crème fraîche sauce, and the escargots alsacienne, broiled in a garlic and parsley sauce. We also like the baked French goat cheese on herbed salad greens with garlic croutons. The soup changes daily, but often is a purée of vegetables or, on one summer night we dined, a cold cucumber and dill.

The half-dozen entrées might include peppercorn-crusted Canadian swordfish steak seared with a cognac sauce, monkfish roast with garlic cloves and European bacon with a sherry-wine vinegar and crème fraîche sauce, rabbit flamande (a specialty of Belgium), roast leg of lamb flavored with herbs of Provence, tournedos of beef forestière and Cynthia's specialty, a stew of veal, lamb and pork with leeks and potatoes. These could be accompanied by such treats as a warm salad of tiny Frnch lentils in a sherry wine vinaigrette, dauphinoise potatoes with melted gruyère, and yellow squash and zucchini with a sherry vinegar-shallot flavoring. The salad of exotic greens is tossed with a creamy mustard dressing that packs a wallop.

The well-chosen, mostly French wine list features vintages from Alsace.

Desserts are notable as well. At a recent visit, Michel was preparing an open fruit tart with blueberries and peaches in almond cream, a gratin of passionfruit, and paris-brest, in addition to his usual napoleons and soufflés glacé.

(860) 526-5301. Entrées, $27 to $32. Dinner, Wednesday-Saturday 5 to 9, Sunday 5 to 8:30.

Gabrielle's, 78 Main St., Centerbrook.

This Victorian-era house with a gazebo-like front porch has been a culinary landmark in the area since 1979. New owner Mauricio Salgar of the long-running Black Seal tavern in Essex tore down walls of what had been Steve's Centerbrook Café and created more open dining areas that are suave in ecru with white trim, accented by stunning art works and greenery.

Refurbished dining area at Gabrielle's.

It's a stylish setting for the contemporary and artistic American fare created by talented chef J. Daniel McManamy, veteran of many a leading area restaurant. Here he is at his best, tweaking the menu often and tending to his new showplace garden. "I wanted a little greenhouse for herbs," Dan said, so his boss built behind the kitchen a nursery-size affair in which Dan "learned how to be a farmer," producing fifteen varieties of lettuce, heirloom tomatoes and vines laden with haricots vert.

A perfect lunch here brought the signature mussels and frites, incredibly thin fries that were addictive when paired with the tarragon aioli dip, and cornmeal-crusted fried oysters with chipotle aioli. These and other mainstays on the lunch menu turn up as appetizers and small plates at night. The fairly extensive dinner menu also offers salads, thin-crust pizzas and fifteen entrées from grilled brook trout with shiitake mushrooms in a carrot-ginger sauce to grilled New York sirloin steak with roasted walnut-gorgonzola butter. A dish called lobster in vatapa (simmered with shrimp and scallops and served in a spicy sauce over rice), Thai-spiced breast of duckling with yellow curry and roasted pears, and roast poussin stuffed with a wild mushroom-gorgonzola risotto indicate the kitchen's range. Dan might serve grilled brook trout atop a warm salad of fingerling potatoes, haricots vert, beets and arugula tossed in a citrus vinaigrette. His duet of beef might be braised short rib and tarragon-sauced grilled tenderloin with horseradish-mashed potatoes.

Desserts include profiteroles, vanilla bean crème brûlée, a pinenut-crusted lemon tartlet with raspberry sauce or a chocolate phyllo purse filled with chocolate ganache and pineapple-raspberry compote, served with white chocolate-rum ice cream.

(860) 767-2440. www.gabrielles.net. Entrées, $19 to $27. Lunch, Tuesday-Friday and Sunday 11:30 to 3. Dinner, Tuesday-Sunday from 5 to 9 or 9:30.

Café Routier, 1353 Boston Post Road, Westbrook.

The lovable French restaurant that started in a truck stop has been reborn as a Yankee bistro, relocating in 2002 to the 1872 house that had been renovated for the original Aleia's restaurant. Chef Jeffrey Renkle moved into a stylish space more

No longer a truck stop, Café Routier takes on glamorous ambiance in new quarters.

than double the size of the former Old Saybrook truck stop gone upscale and with more kitchen space for Jeff and the pastry chef to work their magic. He was joined in 2005 by a new team of owners who gave the interior an open, more clubby look with high-back tufted booths along every wall. The new quarters done up in beige and brown seat about 100 at black dining tables, a zinc dining counter and a communal table in back, plus another 30 outside on the patio. There are two bars, a small one tucked neatly behind a new wall along the side of the main dining room and another in a separate lounge.

The first-rate fare continues to be American bistro with a pronounced French accent, although no one involved is French. Jeff attributes it to his training at the Culinary Institute of America, followed by stints at Max on Main in his native Hartford and at Aureole, Union Square Café, Bouley and Les Halles in New York.

Although some people never stray far from the French specialties, others mix and match the seasonal and regional offerings. "Seasonal" could be sautéed "filet mignon" of salmon with balsamic butter sauce and a succotash of corn, chanterelles and scallions, or pan-seared sea scallops with red wine sauce and an autumn ratatouille. "Regional" changes periodically, from Spain to Sicily to French farmhouse. At a recent visit it featured "Friuli-Venezia Giulia, Italy" (prosciutto and fig salad over radicchio, beef and pork "gulasch" over soft polenta, rabbit braised in white wine and drunken prunes, and pan-roasted duck with spiced plum and grappa demi-glace).

Crusty bread, served with flavorful olive oil, staved off hunger before our party dug into the likes of fried oysters with a chipotle-mustard dipping sauce, a zesty Asian duck salad, an endive and arugula salad dressed with a bit too much gorgonzola, and a rather paltry clams and chorizo dish to start. No one could fault the second courses, an Alsatian tart, the signature "camp-style" grilled trout with whole-grain mustard sauce and lyonnaise potatoes, the sautéed calves liver with balsamic jus and sweet roasted onions, and the steak frites, a flavorful strip steak with house-made fries and a wilted watercress salad.

Desserts included crème brûlée enhanced with lavender picked just outside the door, double chocolate torte, profiteroles, and homemade ice creams and sorbets – ginger and lemon-crème fraîche at our visit.

(860) 399-8700. www.caferoutier.com. Entrées, $19 to $26. Dinner nightly, from 5:30.

Semi-open kitchen is on view from rear tables at River Tavern.

River Tavern, 23 Main St., Chester.

Here's a chic city bistro in the country, as fashioned by chef-owner Jonathan Rapp, who made a name with his brother Tom at the restaurant Etats-Unis on New York's Upper East Side.

The minimalist decor is what he calls "comfortable modern." An orangey-yellow wall glows above a wainscoting effect that looks to be abstract brick (but isn't). A bar flanks half the other side of the long and narrow room. Rich wood breakfronts separate the casual section from the rear dining area, white-clothed tables set side by side in the big-city style beside a wall of windows framing bamboo trees in a planter, backlit for all to see. A break in the side wall yields a designer glimpse of the kitchen.

The contemporary American menu, printed daily, also is comfortably modern, offering four to six choices for each course. "Appetizers" are in the Mediterranean tapas style at rather dear prices: hummus, marinated olives, roasted eggplant and walnut tapenade with pitas or antipasti of salamis and roasted vegetables. The real appetizers are called first courses: perhaps oxtail consommé, baked oysters, Thai fish stew or house-cured salmon "bacon" served with an apple-fennel slaw and juniper oil.

Main courses are as complex as mustard-fried grouper with sweet and sour cabbage and apples, served with purple-top turnips, and as straightforward as beef bourguignonne with handmade porcini mushroom pappardelle. How about Chinese barbecued wild king salmon with a pea shoot-ginger-vegetable lo mein and a lemon-miso broth?

Dessert could be baked-to-order date pudding with dark rum caramel or dark chocolate soufflé, warm apple and concord grape crumble or wine-poached pear with toasted pecans and honey-vanilla mascarpone.

More choices are listed on the café menu, which included at one visit a charcuterie plate, a bowl of mussels and a dish called "two eggs baked with smoked bacon, thyme and cream." Aforementioned appetizers and sandwiches served with potato salad have been featured lately.

(860) 526-9417. www.rivertavernchester.com. Entrées, $24 to $26. Lunch daily except Tuesday, 11:30 to 2. Dinner nightly except Tuesday, from 5:30.

Lupo, 189 Middlesex Ave. (Route 156), Chester.

Lupo is an Italian word for wolf, and Shelley DeProto once had a wolf for a pet in Utah. So when she left her Salt Lake City restaurant to return east to her home area, she named her new restaurant for the wolf and gave it a dramatic logo that resembles a wolf's face.

The result is Lupo, a sophisticated yet convivial hangout on the Chester-Haddam Road, where the style is Mediterranean and the menu offers a smorgasbord of "little bites" that draws the locals in droves. Shelley took over the storefront spot vacated by La Vita Gustosa when it moved to larger quarters in East Haddam. She gave the place a new entrance and renovated two simple but stylish rooms. One side is a dining lounge where people sit at the bar and sip wines as they graze through the little bites that make up more than half the menu. Up a few steps is a darkened dining room with close-together tables illuminated by halogen lamps hanging from a vaulted ceiling.

You can make a meal from a list of two dozen little bites and five salads. How about lobster ravioli in a creamy tomato sauce, a wild mushroom and spinach salad or al dente asparagus spears swathed with manchego cheese and toasted pinenuts, sautéed tiger shrimp with garlic and chiles, scallop gratin or Moroccan spiced chicken wings with scallion yogurt?

The list goes on, but consider the "big bites:" the bouillabaisse that's been a hit from the start, horseradish-crusted salmon, sautéed chicken with artichoke hearts and sundried tomatoes, and grilled bistro steak with wild mushrooms in rioja-shallot sauce with garlic-mashed potatoes. Seared sea scallops tossed with white truffle cream and handmade linguini is a sure winner.

The eclectic little wine list is gently priced, with half available by the glass.

(860) 526-4400. Entrées, $17 to $24. Lunch, Tuesday-Friday 11:30 to 2. Dinner, Tuesday-Sunday from 5.

Restaurant Bravo Bravo, 20 East Main St., Mystic.

Contemporary Italian fare is delivered with flair at this 50-seat restaurant with a new martini bar on the main floor of the Whaler's Inn. You can sit at high metallic tables in the sleek martini bar, or at close-together tables in a dining room where small mirrors serve as wall art and large windows look onto the street.

The extensive, seemingly by-the-rote menu overseen by chef-owner Carol Kanabis rarely changes. But a modicum of excitement is found, especially among the specials.

Meals might begin with marinated olives and a white bean-red pepper spread for the warm, course country bread. For dinner, grilled shrimp wrapped in prosciutto with skewered artichokes, seafood sausage stuffed with lobster and scallops, and sirloin carpaccio make good starters. Pastas include fusilli with shrimp in a sundried tomato-vodka sauce and black pepper fettuccine with grilled scallops, roasted tart apples and a gorgonzola alfredo sauce. Typical entrées are crab cakes topped with lobster-chive sauce, a saffron-seasoned seafood stew, osso buco and braised lamb shanks. Grilled local ostrich with a sweet corn sauce was a special at one visit. Another was sautéed tilapia over risotto with haricots vert.

The lengthy dessert roster includes the obligatory tiramisu as well as tartufo, fruit napoleon with mascarpone cheese and ricotta cheesecake with grand marnier sauce.

(860) 536-3228. Entrées, $15.95 to $24.95. Lunch, Tuesday-Saturday 11:30 to 2:30, also Sunday in summer. Dinner, Tuesday-Sunday 5 to 9 or 10.

Water Street Café, 143 Water St., Stonington.

The dining fortunes in the tony borough of Stonington have been elevated by Walter Houlihan, former chef at the UN Plaza Hotel in New York. He and his wife Stephanie, who oversees the front of the house, turned their original café into such a hot spot that it traded spaces with Walter's Market & Deli across the street. The move produced larger quarters in an arty and funky, bright red and black dining area in front of a curving solid mahogany bar on one side and more close-together tables and two long communal tables in a former lunch counter area on the other.

From his somewhat larger new kitchen, Walter fulfills a with-it, contemporary menu, supplemented by specials that change nightly. Typical starters are lobster spring rolls with spiced soy sauce, crab cake with rémoulade sauce, tuna tartare, escargot pot pie, prosciutto quesadilla with jack cheese and sour cream, and a warm duck salad with asparagus and sesame-orange dressing. London broil and sweet and sour spareribs conclude the all-day menu.

Evening yields up to fifteen blackboard specials, usually including seared yellowfin tuna and the specialty duck and scallops with oyster mushrooms. Others could be Caribbean mako shark, pepper-seared halibut with roast corn-shiitake salsa, pan-roasted venison steak with crab cream sauce, grilled hanger steak and rack of lamb with tequila-goat cheese sauce.

Desserts vary from pear-mango bread pudding and coconut-walnut-chocolate cake to crème caramel and poached pears with ginger ice cream.

(860) 535-2122. Entrées, $18 to $26. Breakfast, Friday and Monday 7 to 11:30 and Saturday and Sunday 8 to 2:30. Lunch daily, 11:30 to 2. Dinner nightly, 5 to 10 or 11.

The Up River Café, 37 Main St., Westerly, R.I.

Just across the Pawcatuck River from Connecticut is this stylish bistro in a restored woolen mill, with great food and a terrific waterside setting at the edge of downtown Westerly. Owners Daniel and Jennifer King from California took over the former Three Fish restaurant and added fireplaces in the casual, brick-walled River Pub as well as in a couple of the white-clothed dining rooms with large windows overlooking the water. They also added a large and perfectly idyllic dining patio beside the river on a peninsula with water on two sides.

The regional American menu is so enticing that decisions are difficult. Typical main courses are Atlantic salmon marinated in miso and sake, seared Stonington sea scallops bearing a white truffle sauce on lobster-mushroom risotto, fire-roasted lamb chops with aged goat cheese and medallions of beef tenderloin with green peppercorn sauce. A burger on a baguette with house-made pickles and fries is among the offerings. So are such appetizers as a jonah crabmeat, spinach and artichoke gratin with house-made pita chips; Asian fried calamari with wasabi aioli, duck and wild mushroom crêpes with madeira cream sauce, and a grilled pizza that changes daily.

Dining rooms on two levels look onto riverside patio at Up River Café.

The lobster nachos with spicy homemade guacamole were sensational but more than one of us could finish for lunch. The other reveled in the signature crab cake sandwich with chipotle rémoulade on a house-made burger roll, a hefty, spilling-over-the-sides affair that leaves competitors in the dust.

Neither of us had room for such desserts as guava crêpes with hot passionfruit sauce, warm chocolate and banana bread pudding with Dan's drunken bourbon sauce, the Chickie's root beer float or even the assorted cookie plate.

(401) 348-9700. www.theuprivercafe.net. Entrées, $23 to $32. Lunch daily, 11:30 to 5. Dinner nightly, 5 to 10.

More Dining Choices

Jack's American Bistro and Wine Bar, 286 Main St., Old Saybrook.

"Global comfort food" is featured in this convivial new bistro opened in 2004 by Jack Flaws, former chef at the celebrated Max Downtown restaurant in Hartford. He and his parents transformed a former restaurant space into a rich, sophisticated setting in gold and ruby red, with an L-shaped banquette along two walls at the rear of the dining room. Tables are covered with pale yellow cloths and set with shiny gold service plates and oversize wine glasses. A separate room houses a wine bar.

Typical starters are tuna tartare marinated in ginger and lime and served on toast points with wasabi aioli, beef carpaccio with creamy peppercorn sauce and shaved manchego cheese, southwestern chicken and black bean spring rolls with warm chipotle salsa, and duck confit salad.

Among the dozen entrées are crab-crusted tilapia with bloody mary butter, honey-roasted swordfish with chardonnay-mustard sauce and chipotle-marinated shrimp with roasted corn, avocado and pecans. The cornish game hen is served Peking style, rolled in butternut squash crêpes and served with hoisin pan gravy and crispy onions. Black truffle consommé, tiny root vegetables and foie gras mousse timbale embellish the braised veal osso buco.

Tables are set for fine dining at Jack's American Bistro and Wine Bar.

Desserts are less exotic: carrot cake with maple cream cheese, profiteroles and warm chocolate truffle cake with caramel and chocolate sauces. A griddle in the kitchen might produce beignets with espresso syrup and hot chocolate dipping sauce.

(860) 395-1230. www.jacksamericanbistro.com. Entrées, $22 to $29. Lunch, Tuesday-Friday 11:30 to 4. Dinner, Tuesday-Sunday, 5 to 10 or 11. Sunday brunch, 11:30 to 2.

Sherlock's 221, 9 Halls Road, Old Lyme Marketplace, Hall's Road, Old Lyme. This wine bar and grill in the Old Lyme Marketplace strip plaza took its new name following a contest among customers who linked the name of owner Lynne Sherlock with the address of detective Sherlock Holmes. The snug and dark dining room bears a stylish Mediterranean bistro look in earth colors and is open to a wine bar in back. A few tables are outside for sidewalk dining in season.

The menu offers an eclectic variety of Mediterranean-inspired fare, from caramelized scallops drizzled with white truffle oil on roasted beet risotto to rack of lamb with mango-mint slaw. Herb-crusted tilapia on squash tossed with artichoke, sundried tomato and pancetta in a red onion vinaigrette was a recent autumn hit. So was the roasted duck breast and cranberry and duck crepinette with cider sauce.

Favorite appetizers are the crab cake with rémoulade sauce and grilled corn relish and the lobster and scallop sausage simmered in a lobster sauce. The signature pasta choice is sautéed lobster and crab with shiitake mushrooms and black truffles on fresh rolled fettuccine. Lynne's specialty pizza comes with roasted onions, port-soaked figs, spinach and gorgonzola cheese.

Specialty cakes and desserts like pot de crème come from the grill's bakery adjunct.

(860) 434-9837. www.sherlocks221grille.com. Entrées, $19 to $28. Lunch, Monday-Saturday 11:30 to 2:30. Dinner Monday-Saturday 5 to 9 or 10.

Skipper's Dock, 66 Water St., Stonington.

The folks who made the Harborview one of the great restaurants in the state returned to its last remaining adjunct, the Skipper's Dock on the water at pier's end in Stonington harbor. Ainslie Turner and her late husband Jerry turned the place into a cheery, year-round restaurant and tavern with fireplaces ablaze in cool weather and lots of nautical memorabilia and nostalgia.

The result is a happy cross between the haute Harborview (since destroyed by fire and rebuilt as the Inn at Stonington) and the casual Skipper's Dock of old. The food is more than a mix, with a decided emphasis on the side of the Harborview's creativity. Yes, you can still get a mug of creamy clam chowder and cherrystone clams on the half shell. You also can get stuffed quahogs Portuguese and the specialty oysters Ainslie, toasted with garlic aioli and panko crumbs. And wild mushroom and sausage strudel, baked escargots, and crab cakes rémoulade.

Main dishes include the Harborview's classic Marseilles-style bouillabaisse, fillet of sole français and an old specialty, coquilles St. Jacques. The dessert list might feature the Harborview's signature grasshopper pie, a Vermont maple-pecan pie and crème brûlée with fruit.

The food and service seem to be best at lunch, when some of the same treats are available along with sandwiches and an exotic pan-seared duck breast and warm goat cheese salad. The fried oysters with french fries and slaw and the Grand Central pan roast, a seafood sauté with an addictive sauce, were first-rate treats at our latest lunch.

Much of the fare is offered day and night in the **Harbar,** a high-style Colonial-look pub with framed magazine covers on the walls and boating gear hanging overhead. The best place for all this good eating, of course, is on the expansive deck right out over the water.

(860) 535-0111. www.skippersdock.com. Entrées, $16.95 to $26.95. Lunch daily, 11:30 to 4. Dinner nightly, 4 to 9:30 or 10. Closed Tuesday in winter and month of January.

Noah's, 113 Water St., Stonington.

This endearing restaurant – long known for good food, casual atmosphere and affordable prices – has been gussied up a bit lately. The once-funky double storefront now has fine art on the walls of the main dining room, where cherry booths beneath paddle fans and a tin ceiling draw the locals in for three meals a day. A front room with a handsome horseshoe-shaped mahogany bar offers a bar menu.

Co-owners John Papp and Stanley Schwartz post international specialties nightly to complement traditional dinners on the order of broiled flounder, grilled pork chops and grilled breast of chicken. The night's numerous specials have been upscaled lately and are a tad pricier, as you'd expect for dishes like prosciutto-wrapped monkfish with chianti sauce, spice-rubbed mako shark, spice-rubbed bluefish with mango-lime relish, grilled rare tuna with wasabi and pickled ginger, and lobster and shrimp sauté. Seafood is featured, but you might find grilled brace of quail with chardonnay cream sauce, venison hunter stew with dumplings or veal flank steak with pinot noir sauce.

The fare is mighty interesting, from the house chicken liver pâté seasoned with brandy, sherry and pistachios to the welsh rarebit and the Korean bean and onion pancakes at lunch (many of the same items are offered on the bar menu). A bowl of clam chowder with half a BLT and a bacon-gouda quiche with side salad made a fine lunch for two for about $15.

Save room for the scrumptious homemade desserts, perhaps chocolate-yogurt cake, bourbon bread pudding, or what one local gentleman volunteered was the best dessert he'd ever had: fresh strawberries with Italian cream made from cream cheese, eggs and kirsch.

(860) 535-3925. www.noahsfinefood.com. Entrées, $12.95 to $24.95. Bar menu, $7.25 to $12.95. Breakfast, 7 to 11, Sunday to noon. Lunch, 11:15 to 2:30. Dinner, 6 to 9 or 9:30. Closed Monday.

An Enchanting Culinary Destination

The Golden Lamb Buttery, Hillandale Farm, 499 Wolf Den Road (off Route 169), Brooklyn.

We fell in love with this rural restaurant more than 25 years ago and every time we go back we are smitten again. It's a Constable landscape, a working farm, a hayride, folk music and much more.

It's also the home of Bob and Jimmie (for Virginia) Booth, who set the stage for a magical evening. Bob is the genial host who makes wonderful drinks (the manhattan is garnished with a fresh cherry because the Booths don't like to use preservatives) and oversees the dining rooms. Jimmie does much of the cooking with originality, energy and love – assisted lately by their son Bobby, who joined the operation in 2005 to keep it going year-round.

The evening begins around 7 with cocktails in summer on a deck off the barn overlooking a farm pond or on a wagon drawn by a tractor over fields while you sit – with drink in hand – on bales of hay, perhaps listening to the fresh voice of Susan Smith Lamb, who accompanies herself on the guitar. Before you set off on this adventure, your gingham-clad waitress takes your order from the four or five entrées written on the blackboard.

Dinner ($65, complete) starts with a choice of about four hot or cold soups. We have never tasted one that wasn't wonderful. Using herbs and vegetables from the farm's gardens, Jimmie makes soups like cold lovage bisque, a green vegetable one using "every green vegetable you can name," raspberry pureé, scotch barley, cold cucumber and an unusually good cabbage soup made with duck stock.

Almost always on the menu are duck (a crispy half, done with many different sauces), châteaubriand for one, grilled lamb and fish (perhaps salmon or swordfish), cooked over applewood on the farm's smoker. Lately, Jimmie has added the occasional pasta entrée. Salt is not used, but many herbs, and essences of lemons and limes, are. Crisp and thinly sliced onion bagels are the only starch.

What we always remember best are the vegetables – six to eight an evening brought around in large crocks and wooden bowls and served family style (yes, you can have seconds). They could be almost anything, but always there are marinated mushrooms and nearly always cold minted peas. Tomatoes with basil, braised celery and fennel, carrots with orange rind and raisins, a casserole of zucchini and summer squash with mornay sauce – they depend on the garden and the season.

Desserts like coffee mousse, raspberry cream sherbet, heavy butter cake with fresh berries, pies (made by neighborhood women) and a chocolate roll using Belgian chocolate, topped with chocolate sauce and fruit, are fitting endings.

During all this, you are seated in a dining room in the barn or in the attached building with a loft that once was a studio used by writers. The old wood of the

Owners Jimmie and Bob Booth relax at barn entrance to Golden Lamb Buttery.

walls and raftered ceilings glows with the patina of age, as do the bare dark wood tables in the flickering candlelight. The singer strolls from table to table taking requests.

It's all so subtly theatrical, yet with a feeling of honest simplicity, that you feel part of a midsummer night's dream.

Lunch, with entrées in the $13 to $18 range, might be oyster stew, salmon quiche, seafood crêpes or the delicious Hillandale hash. It may not be as romantic as dinner, but you get to see the surroundings better.

Folks reserve a year in advance for the December madrigal dinners, when a group of renaissance singers strolls through the dining rooms singing carols, and pork tenderloin is the main course.

Although we have had more interesting entrées on our wanderings, we never have had such a satisfying total dining experience. It's not inexpensive, but what price can you put on pure enchantment?

(860) 774-4423. www.thegoldenlamb.com. Prix-fixe, $65. Lunch, noon to 2:30, Tuesday-Saturday April-December, Friday and Saturday January-March. Dinner, Friday and Saturday, one seating from 7, year-round. Dinner reservations required far in advance.

From Snack Bar to Gourmet

The Blue Oar, 16 Snyder Road, Haddam.

Who'd ever think a former snack bar at river's edge overlooking a marina would dispense good, innovative fare?

Third-generation restaurateur Jim Reilly, former owner of the defunct River Walk Cafe in Deep River, saw the possibilities for the one-room shack at the Midway Marina off Route 154 north of Tylerville. He painted picnic tables in rainbow colors on the grounds, installed chairs at a counter running around the perimeter of a wraparound porch, hung blue oars overhead and built a pavilion outside. You bring your own bottle, review the blackboard menu, place your order and find a table.

Jim cooks "whatever's fresh that day" on a six-foot industrial grill on the porch with sauces he prepares ahead. The six-item menu at our September visit listed the likes of grilled salmon with dill-sour cream sauce, grilled rosemary pork loin with maple glaze, and grilled ribeye steak with blue cheese. Starters are generally simple: chowders, potato-cheddar-bacon soup, perhaps crab cakes with red pepper aioli and usually steamers. Desserts are anything but simple. They're displayed in a pastry case at the counter, where no one fails to see them and order. Jim's wife obtains them daily from a lady in Middletown: perhaps key lime mousse, white and dark chocolate mousse tower, turtle cheesecake and strawberry-rhubarb tart.

The snack bar heritage is evident in burgers, deli sandwiches and hot dogs, available day or night.

Dinner is by candlelight, and the setting by the river, though very much weather-dependent, is pleasantly rustic and refreshing. "Good food and good location – that's all you need," says Jim. He offers both.

(860) 345-2994. Entrées, $15.95 to $19.95. Lunch, Tuesday-Sunday 11:30 to 5. Dinner nightly, 5 to 9. Closed Columbus Day to Mother's Day. BYOB. No credit cards.

The Real Thing

Abbott's Lobster in the Rough, 117 Pearl St., Noank.

For more than 50 years, this old lobstering town has been the home of a lobster pound like those you dream of and too seldom find. Gourmet it's not, but people from all over manage to find their way to the hard-to-find spot at the mouth of the Mystic River, partly because of the delectable lobsters and partly because of the setting overlooking Fishers Island and Long Island Sound

You sit outside at gaily colored picnic tables placed on ground strewn with mashed-up clam shells. You order at a counter and get a number – since the wait is often half an hour or more and the portions to come are apt to be small, bring along drinks and appetizers to keep you going. A 1¼-pound lobster comes with coleslaw, a bag of potato chips and a paper bib. Also available are steamers, clam chowder, mussels, shrimp in the rough, lobster or crab rolls and a complete lobster feast. Adjacent shacks dispense desserts and shellfish from a raw bar.

If lobsters aren't your thing, head to **Costello's Clam Shack,** just beyond in the Noank Shipyard, an open-air place beneath a blue and white canopy right over the water. Now owned by Abbott's (they're Abbott's and Costello's, in friendly competition with each other), it's smaller and less crowded. Although you can get a lobster dinner here, it's best for its fried clams and fried scallops.

(860) 536-7719. www.abbotts-lobster.com. Entrées, $15 to $23. Open daily, noon to 9, May to Labor Day; Friday-Sunday noon to 7, Labor Day to Columbus Day. BYOB.

Costello's: (860) 572-2779. www.costellosclamshack.com. Open daily, noon to 9, Memorial Day to Labor Day. BYOB.

Dining and Lodging

Copper Beech Inn, 46 Main Street, Ivoryton 06442.

This imposing mansion, shaded by the oldest copper beech tree in Connecticut, is back on top as one of Connecticut's premier dining spots. Owners Ian and Barbara Phillips undertook extensive refurbishing of the dining facilities, lured a chef team from Nantucket and upgraded some of the accommodations.

Dining of distinction is offered in four elegant rooms, including the chandeliered

Refurbished Ivoryton Room is setting for elegant fare at Copper Beech Inn.

main Ivoryton Room with a warm Victorian motif. The paneled Comstock Room with a beamed ceiling retains the look of the billiards parlor that it once was. Between the two is a pretty garden porch with a handful of romantic tables for two. Windows in the clubby blue Copper Beech Room with its cozy bar afford views of the great tree outside. Tables in each dining room are set with crisp white cloths and dressed with lavish flowers.

This is a place to be pampered. Expect dinner to take a couple of hours, and pick a choice selection from the Wine Spectator award-winning cellar that gets better all the time.

The formal, contemporary French fare has been refreshed by executive chef William Von Ahnen, who moved to the Copper Beach after sixteen years at the famed Chantecleer in Nantucket, where he last served as sous chef. He is joined in the kitchen by his wife Jacqueline, who also worked at the Chantecleer and is the inn's pastry chef.

Written as always in French with English translations, the menu ranges widely from fillet of grey sole stuffed with a scallop mousse and presented in a lobster-ginger sauce to roasted rack of Colorado lamb with a rich red wine sauce. Indeed, all the food tends to be rich here, from the house-made lobster and sole sausage with truffle beurre blanc to the sautéed foie gras with a caramelized blackberry-chardonnay sauce. Thc lobster française, a house specialty deglazed with madeira, brandy and cream and garnished with black truffle risotto, is fabulous. So is the changing assortment of grilled seafood served with a pinot noir sauce and a fricassee of wild mushrooms. The grilled magret and confit of duck with peach chutney and the grilled veal chop with marchand du vin sauce are also first-rate.

Finish with one of Jacqueline's spectacular desserts, perhaps a chocolate ganache cake, chocolate mousse enrobed in a chocolate shell, a creamy mixed-fruit tart and – finally – a light and ethereal tarte tatin with calvados ice cream. An after-dinner sip of single-batch bourbon sent us happily on our way with memories of a superior meal.

Overnight guests enjoy accommodations that have been enhanced by the Thomases, who formerly owned the historic Bradley Inn at Pemaquid Point in Maine. They first renovated the guest quarters upstairs above the restaurant, refurbishing three period rooms and a kingsize suite overlooking the rear gardens. The most deluxe is the sumptuous front master bedroom, big enough to include a kingsize carved mahogany poster bed, a couple of sitting areas and a new gas fireplace. Its redone bath has been tiled in marble and boasts a hydro-massage tub and a heated floor. We still like best the nine rooms in the rear carriage house. Each has a jacuzzi or hydro-massage tub and french doors onto an outdoor deck or balcony overlooking the gardens. Second-floor rooms retain their original vaulted ceilings with exposed beams. Mahogany queensize or kingsize beds, club chairs, TVs and telephones are the norm. Guests relax in a wraparound atrium/solarium in the front of the inn, where windows afford views of the majestic tree outside.

A continental-plus breakfast buffet has been augmented lately with a couple of prepared egg dishes such as quiche or coddled eggs.

(860) 767-0330 or (888) 809-2056. www.copperbeechinn.com. Twelve rooms and one suite with private baths. Doubles, $165 to $350.

Entrées, $26 to $38. Dinner, Tuesday-Sunday 5:30 to 10, Wednesday-Sunday in winter.

Bee and Thistle Inn, 100 Lyme St., Old Lyme 06371.

Stately trees, gardens all around and a flower-bedecked entrance welcome visitors to this cheery yellow inn, set on five acres bordering the Lieutenant River in the historic district of Old Lyme. Built in 1756 with subsequent additions and remodeling, the structure is a charming ramble of parlors and porches, dining rooms and guest rooms.

This inn's restaurant, as overseen by Culinary Institute of America-trained chef-owner Philip Abraham, consistently wins statewide awards for "romantic dining" and "best desserts." Candlelight dinners are served on the enclosed side porches or in a small rear dining room.

Cocktails are offered club-style in the comfortable front living room, where the seamless service begins and continues through after-dinner coffee. The contemporary international dinner menu ranges widely from pesto-grilled salmon with a roasted tomato coulis and sautéed lobster tail and sea scallops in a lime-chipotle cream sauce to rack of lamb with hunter-style demi-glace. You might start with a Maryland crab cake set atop a cornbread crouton with jalapeño sauce, spice-rubbed carpaccio of filet mignon with horseradish-mustard aioli, or a burrito of slow-roasted duck in a habañero plum sauce.

For a celebratory birthday dinner, one of us indulged in a perfectly seared roasted filet mignon sauced with a tomato-oregano vinaigrette, served with a gorgonzola-onion-potato flatbread and garnished with a roasted yellow and red pepper and black olive salad. The other enjoyed the dijon-crusted rack of lamb with house-made tomato-mint chutney and mashed potatoes. Another occasion produced sensational crab cakes with saffron aioli and thin-sliced, rare breast of duck served on a passionfruit puree with a spiced pear beggar's purse.

Sunny dining porch at Bee and Thistle Inn.

Desserts, always the inn's strongest suit, might be frozen key lime mousse with mojito sauce atop mango salsa, warm bittersweet chocolate cake topped with blackberry ice cream or latte cheesecake dusted with cinnamon. Or indulge in the "sweet miniatures," an assortment of bite-sized confections including pecan diamonds, truffles and cookies.

Jazz guitarists entertain on Friday evenings, and harpists play on Saturdays.

The inn offers eleven upstairs guest rooms with period country furnishings. They vary in size from small with double or twin beds to large with queensize canopy beds and loveseats. Four-poster and spool beds are covered with quilts or afghans. The prime accommodation is in a riverside cottage, where a deck off the queensize bedroom wraps around a fireplaced reading room, a TV room and a kitchen.

Breakfast is available for an extra charge on the sunny dining porch, a great place to start the day. The Bee and Thistle popover filled with scrambled eggs, bacon and cheese draws the public as well as overnighters.

(860) 434-1667 or (800) 622-4946. Fax (860) 434-3402. www.beeandthistleinn.com. Eleven rooms and one cottage with private baths. Doubles, $130 to $239 EP.

Entrées, $25 to $39. Breakfast daily, 8 to 10, Sunday to 9:30. Lunch, Saturday 11:30 to 2. Dinner, Wednesday-Sunday from 5:30. Sunday brunch, 11 to 2.

The Inn at Mystic, Route 1, Mystic 06355.

This is the crown jewel of the Mystic Motor Inn, the area's nicest motel and inn complex situated beside Pequotsepos Cove. Above the motor inn (which also boasts deluxe inn-style rooms in its East Wing) is an eight-acre hilltop estate with a white-pillared Colonial revival mansion and gatehouse offering sumptuous bedrooms – spacious, full of antiques, and with whirlpool-soaking tubs and spas in the bathrooms. Lauren Bacall and Humphrey Bogart spent their honeymoon here when this was a friend's private home.

As a guest in one of the five rooms in the mansion, you may feel like a country squire soaking in your private spa, relaxing on a chintz-covered sofa by the fire in the drawing room with its 17th-century pin pine paneling, or rocking on the wicker-filled veranda overlooking manicured gardens, with Long Island Sound in the distance. Behind the inn, the four guest rooms with fireplaces and jacuzzi tubs in the secluded Gatehouse, redone with Ralph Lauren sheets and coverlets, could have come straight out of England.

Sisters Jody Dyer and Nancy Gray, whose father started this as Mystic's first motor inn of size in 1963, revamped the twelve rooms in the motor inn's East Wing, all with Federal-style furniture, queensize canopy beds, wing chairs and fireplaces, plus balconies or patios with views of the water. Six rooms here have huge jacuzzis in the bathrooms with mirrors all around. The 38 rooms in the original two-story motor inn are handsomely furnished as well.

Although breakfast is no longer included in the rates, complimentary tea and pastries are served from 4 to 5 at the **Flood Tide,** the inn's glamorous restaurant, which dishes up some of the area's fanciest meals along with a view of Pequotsepos Cove looking toward Long Island Sound. A new exhibition kitchen with a clay-pit brick oven along one side may take some diners' eyes off the view in the formal dining room, whose refurbished setting is one of updated nautical elegance.

The brick oven is put into play with entrées categorized as wood-fire grilled, brick-oven baked and "from the sauté station." That might translate to grilled tuna steak with papaya and mango salsa and oyster sauce, sautéed Stonington sea scallops with couscous, baby bok choy and Thai red curry, and naturally raised filet mignon with cheesy stacked potatoes and sherried cream demi-glace. Rack of lamb is carved tableside for two, chateaubriand style.

Start with a lobster crêpe with madeira-shallot cream sauce, baked stuffed oysters with prosciutto or one of the Tuscan brick-oven tarts. Extravagant endings are lavender crème brûlée, bananas foster and Belgian chocolate mousse served with strawberries romanoff in an almond-brandysnap basket.

(860) 536-9604 or (800) 237-2415. Fax (860) 572-1635. www.innatmystic.com. Sixty-seven rooms with private baths. Rates, EP. Doubles, $125 to $295 late June through October, $75 to $295 rest of year.

Entrées, $24 to $38. Dinner nightly, 5:30 to 9, to 9:30 or 10 May-November.

Stonecroft, 515 Pumpkin Hill Road, Ledyard 06339.

Ten deluxe guest accommodations and an acclaimed restaurant are the hallmarks of this inn on six rural acres surrounded by 300 acres of Nature Conservancy woodlands and stone walls northwest of Mystic.

The inn began in a handsome yellow 1807 Georgian Colonial residence, converted first into a B&B by Joan Egy and her late husband Lynn. It became an inn upon expanding into a three-story barn showcasing **The Grange** dining room on the ground floor and six large guest rooms upstairs.

From the expansive, granite-walled dining room, floor-to-ceiling, multi-paned windows yield a grand view of a landscaped stone dining terrace, a grapevine-covered pergola and a water garden. The interior is furnished like that of an English country manor, with a lounge area of high-back couches facing a fireplace and well-spaced tables set with cream-colored linens and Villeroy & Boch china

It's a thoroughly delightful setting for outstanding fare that tied for the highest restaurant ratings in Connecticut in the 2005-06 Zagat Survey. As prepared by James Veal, the inn's original sous-chef, dinner begins with an amuse-bouche, usually a couple of morsels – perhaps a spring roll with apricot-fennel filling, a shumai dumpling or a mushroom tart – that hint of treats to come.

We were pleased with a couple of sensational starters, baja-style scallop seviche with cucumber and a grilled tortilla and the trio of exotic shrimp: curry-coconut with

Granite-walled Grange dining room at Stonecroft looks out onto landscaped terrace.

spiced banana chutney, spicy rangoon with ginger-hoisin sauce, and chile-cilantro grilled over cucumber.

Sesame-seared Asian tuna with shrimp and scallop lo mein and rack of lamb with garlic aioli are signature main courses. We liked the paupiette of veal paillard stuffed with artichokes and bel paese cheese and wrapped in prosciutto, and the pan-roasted duck breast and confit with bing cherry glaze and a fabulous brie and wild rice risotto.

The dessert specialty is the night's chocolate trio, at our visit a little pot of intense chocolate mousse, three homemade truffles and a chocolate fudge brownie, plus a bonus, chocolate ice cream with a stick of white chocolate. An equal triumph was the banana and Bailey's Irish cream cheesecake with brûléed bananas and chocolate sauce.

Afterward, we had only to head upstairs to one of the barn rooms and suites, which are larger and more sumptuous than those in the main house. Each has a king or queensize bed, a sitting area, a gas fireplace with a built-in TV overhead, and a large bath with double whirlpool tub and separate shower. They're elegantly furnished in country French or English styles, plus one in Colonial decor for Yankee purists. All open to private or shared wraparound balconies overlooking the rural scene.

Terrycloth robes, bath sheets rather than towels, Crabtree & Evelyn toiletries and soft music throughout the common areas help provide a serene stay.

Breakfast is an event, served in the original B&B's dining room, the restaurant or on the tiered flagstone terrace beneath a venerable maple tree. Baked bananas, pineapples and mangos in a lemon-rum sauce might precede buttermilk waffles with strawberries and whipped cream, herbed scrambled eggs with turkey bacon or a cloud omelet (so-called because it's four inches high) layered with smoked salmon or cheese. The ginger scones and cheese-almond danish are addictive.

(860) 572-0771 or (800) 772-0774. Fax (860) 572-9161. www.stonecroft.com. Eight rooms and two suites with private baths. Doubles, $150 to $300. Off-season, $99 to $200. Entrées, $18 to $30. Dinner by reservation, Tuesday-Sunday 5 to 9.

The Inn & Vineyard at Chester, 318 West Main St., Chester 06412.

The Inn at Chester, a hostelry built in 1983 around the historic 1776 John B. Parmelee House on twenty rural acres west of town, has a new name and a new look. The official name now is amended by a small, would-be vineyard, but the more significant name is that of owner Edward Safdie – as in "Edward Safdie is back." That's how the initial press release announced the reopening of the renovated inn, as if that would tell it all.

It tells a lot. Ed Safdie is the nationally known restaurateur, hotelier, spa innovator and cookbook author who in 1995 sold the nearby Norwich Inn & Spa he had created in the image of his famed Sonoma Mission Inn & Spa in California. A resident of Old Lyme, he came out of retirement in 2003 to purchase the fading Inn at Chester. He closed the inn for three months to refurbish every guest room and renovate every bathroom. His wife Carlene, an Old Lyme antiques dealer, redecorated the guest rooms and suites in a minimalist, country elegant look with mostly queensize pencil-post beds, Eldred Wheeler furniture, French toile and Schumacher fabrics, and Berber carpeting. French doors were added to sixteen rooms on the main floor to open onto private decks and patios. Each room has a flat-screen TV, data port and cordless telephone. Newly tiled baths contain pedestal sinks, massage showerheads and quite an array of spa-quality toiletries.

Ed Safdie, who has run twenty celebrity restaurants from California to Monaco, devoted much of his early effort to expanding and enhancing the restaurant operation.

The 50-seat Bar & Bistro was totally refashioned in a modern, drop-dead red motif, with leather banquettes, windsor chairs and upholstered chairs at a polished wood bar. The main post and beam Vineyard dining room in the 200-year-old barn retains its rough-hewn walls, fieldstone fireplace, wrought-iron chandeliers and soaring windows. Outside beneath a century-old maple tree is a new, three-tiered deck that seats 150 diners, overlooking a pond and a fountain.

Executive chef Kristofer Rowe, a Culinary Institute of America grad who served as executive chef at the Old Inn on the Green in the Berkshires, cures his salmon and pork loin in a smoker outside the kitchen door. He also has the tables set with new Riedel stemware lined up on the diagonal and uses square plates to set off his dramatic presentations.

His cassoulet of lamb shank, duck leg and rabbit sausage and the free-range chicken breast roasted on the rotisserie quickly became signature dinner dishes. Other entrées could be roasted swordfish with corn-shrimp salsa, a napoleon of crispy sweetbreads and grilled quail, and filet mignon with a cabernet glaze.

Starters might be roasted corn and crab chowder, ginger-crusted ahi tuna with seaweed salad, a shrimp martini with chipotle cocktail sauce and jìcama batons or a chopped romaine and house-smoked pork loin salad. Featured dessert at our visit was a fall apple sampler: a mini-apple pie, caramelized apple bread pudding, apple crisp and a dollop of vanilla bean ice cream.

Most of the appetizers plus salads and sandwiches are available in the Bar & Bistro. Both the dining room and tavern menus are available seasonally on the Maple Terrace, which also has a barbecue menu. A spa menu features items from Safdie's books, *Spa Food* and *New Spa Food.*

Overnight guests enjoy continental breakfast in the bistro.

Although the man called the father of the American spa movement didn't want another spa, he planned exercise trails for walking or jogging, a tennis court and wellness treatment rooms for relaxation or deep tissue massage services. And, yes, he planted a small vineyard of vidal blanc grapes – "the first organic vineyard in New England," he said – although stray deer finally got the best of it.

(860) 526-9541. Fax (860) 526-1607. www.innatchester.com. Thirty-nine rooms and five suites with private baths. Doubles, $135 to $295. Suites, $250 to $450.

Vineyard, entrées $21 to $28, dinner Tuesday-Saturday 5:30 to 9. Bar & Bistro, $8 to $13, open Tuesday-Friday 11:30 to 9, Saturday 11:30 to 3, Sunday 11:30 to 7.

Gourmet from the Past

Randall's Ordinary, Route 2, Box 243, North Stonington 06359.

Relive the old days with a hearthside meal in this 1685 farmhouse secluded in the midst of 27 rural acres.

The atmospheric restaurant offers Colonial-style food, cooked as it was 200 years ago and served by waitresses in period garb in three beamed dining rooms. For dinner, up to 75 patrons gather at 7 o'clock in a small taproom where they pick up a drink, hearth-roasted popcorn, crackers and cheese. Then they watch cooks preparing their meals in antique iron pots and reflector ovens in an immense open hearth in the old keeping room. You sit at long tables with hand-loomed placemats, Bennington black and white pottery, flatware with pistol-grip knives and three-tined forks, and such unusual accessories as a pewter salt plate and a sugar scoop. Some of the chairs are so low that we had to switch to reach the table comfortably.

The prix-fixe meal involves a choice of four or five entrées, perhaps roast capon with wild rice stuffing, roast ribeye beef, roast pork loin or hearth-grilled salmon. We tried the succulent Nantucket scallops with scallions and butter – "the best you'll ever eat," advised the innkeeper. He was right. They're lightly breaded and cooked with herbs and paprika in a wok-like skillet.

The meal includes soup (often onion, butternut squash or Shaker herb), anadama or spider cornbread, vegetables like cauliflower duBarry and corn pudding, a conserve of red cabbage and apples, and desserts like apple crisp, Thomas Jefferson's bread pudding or pumpkin cake.

Lunch, with similar food but less fanfare, is à la carte. The restaurant also offers breakfast to the public. Maple toast with fried apples and Shaker apple salad, griddle cakes and breakfast pie might be the fare.

Overnight guests relive the old days in three ancient bedrooms upstairs in the main house. They have ornamental fireplaces and queensize four-poster beds with hand-loomed coverlets, as well as modern baths with whirlpool jets in the tubs.

Twelve newer-feeling rooms and suites are located in the rear barn. Designed in what might be called a rustic contemporary style, they retain their original beams, barn siding and bare floors. Most have queensize canopy beds, baths with whirlpool tubs and heat lamps, TVs and telephones. Four have loft bedrooms with skylights and spiral staircases from the sitting rooms. Formerly rather spartan, the rooms have been refurbished with art works and new period furniture for a warmer ambiance.

"We are what we are, rustic but with modern amenities," said a spokesman for the owners, the Mashantucket Pequots. The tribe, owners of the nearby Foxwoods casino, have maintained the Randall's tradition.

(860) 599-4540 or (877) 599-4540. Fax (860) 599-3308. www.randallsordinary.com. Ten rooms and five suites with private baths. Weekends: doubles $169, suites $195 and $350. Midweek: doubles $149, suites $165 and $300. Closed January-April.

Prix-fixe, $39. Breakfast, Friday-Sunday, 7 to 11. Lunch, Friday-Sunday noon to 2 or 3. Dinner nightly, 5:30 to 9. Closed January-April.

Lodging

Bishopsgate Inn, Goodspeed Landing, Box 290, East Haddam 06423.

Situated in a secluded setting a block from the Goodspeed Opera House, this 1818 Colonial house was built by an Essex shipbuilder and was once occupied by a Goodspeed. Now it's lovingly run by energetic Colin and Jane Kagel and their son Colin, wife Lisa and infant son. "Ours is a real family enterprise," says Jane. And a winning one, at that.

The house is full of books, artworks and family collections. Among them are Jane's silver urns in an open cupboard above the huge fireplace in the living room and Colin's prized canvasback decoys on a shelf in the upstairs sitting room.

The six guest rooms, all with featherbeds and antique furnishings, are decorated with character. Four with queen beds have working fireplaces. The most dramatic is the Director's Suite, with a beamed cathedral ceiling, a kingsize brass and iron bed, its own balcony and a dressing area off a theatrical bathroom with lights around the mirror of the double vanity and its own sauna.

Jane and Lisa cook full breakfasts in the former 1860 kitchen, which has a small fireplace and baking oven. Crustless spinach quiche is a favorite, as are a variety of french toast recipes. Other possibilities include salsa omelets and waffles with hot peaches or blueberry sauce. All are served by candlelight at a long table in a beamed dining room where there's a lot to look at.

(860) 873-1677. Fax (860) 873-3898. www.bishopsgate.com. Six rooms with private baths. Doubles, $115 to $155. Suite, $185.

Riverwind, 209 Main St. (Route 9A), Deep River 06417.

A sense of history pervades this charming, atmospheric B&B, and new owners Elaine and Leo Klevens capitalize on it. The house feels older than its 1850 date because a rear addition was built to look 100 years older than the existing inn. The result is a seamless blend of old and new.

The heart of the house is the beamed keeping room and dining room with a huge fireplace in the new/old section at the rear. Upstairs is another sitting room with a fireplace and herbs hanging from the beams.

Bedrooms on two floors vary in configuration and style. Five have queen beds and three have one or two double beds. All are air-conditioned and appointed with period antiques and stenciling. The blue and white Hearts and Flowers Room comes with flowers on the bedroom wallpaper, hearts on the bathroom wallpaper and a specially made, heart-filled, stained-glass window. Zelda's is a two-room suite that's delightfully Gatsby. Every room is charming, but the ultimate is the rear Champagne and Roses Room with a private balcony, a bathroom with a shower and a Japanese steeping tub, a queensize half tester bed canopied in pink and blue floral fabrics, and a sofa that converts into an extra bed. The new, third-floor Moonlit Suite has a mission-style queen bed (with an extra sleigh bed in an alcove), a brick fireplace, double whirlpool tub and satellite TV.

From a twelve-foot stone cooking fireplace in the keeping room come a variety of breakfast treats. Elaine might offer poached pears and a ham and egg casserole baked in herbed pastry or her specialty, apple-baked french toast. Guests are welcomed with sherry and snacks in the afternoon by the crackling fireplaces.

(860) 526-2014. Fax (860) 526-0875. www.riverwindinn.com. Six rooms and two suites with private baths. Doubles, $120 to $210. Suites, $165 to $225.

Deacon Timothy Pratt House B&B, 325 Main St., Old Saybrook 06475.

Listed on the National Register, this 1746 center-chimney Colonial once was the home of the deacon at the pillared Congregational meetinghouse across the street. It served five generations of Pratts and now houses an expanding B&B. Former electrical engineer Shelley Nobile opened with four guest quarters and added four more rooms in the former James Pharmacy building next door.

Each room has a queensize canopy or poster bed, working fireplace, bath with whirlpool tub, TV, telephone and stereo/CD player. A fishnet canopy bed is angled from the corner in the Sunrise Room, which has two Queen Anne wingback recliners and an oversize jacuzzi. The premier accommodation in the main house is a suite with a carved four-poster rice bed, french doors opening onto a TV room with a day bed and an extra-large bathroom with a double jacuzzi.

A full breakfast is served by candlelight on weekends in a formal dining room with an extra-long table for sixteen. The fare might be bananas foster french toast or pecan-encrusted waffles one day and eggs benedict the next. A continental breakfast buffet is offered on weekdays. A sideboard holds afternoon beverages, cookies and decanters of port.

Next door, Shelley continues to operate the James Gallery & Soda Fountain, a gift shop and an old-fashioned ice cream parlor.

In 2006, she opened **3 Liberty Green,** a deluxe four-room B&B in a restored 1734 Colonial farmhouse in nearby Clinton.

(860) 395-1229 or (800) 640-1190. Fax (860) 395-4748. www.pratthouse.net. Seven rooms and one suite with private baths. July-October: doubles, $190 to $220 weekends, $120 to $150 midweek. Rest of year: doubles, $170 to $200 weekends, $110 to $130 midweek.

Steamboat Inn, 73 Steamboat Wharf, Mystic 06355.

This inn, transformed from a vacant restaurant along the Mystic River, offers ten luxurious guest rooms right beside the water in the heart of downtown Mystic.

Named after ships built in Mystic, all have whirlpool baths and televisions hidden in cupboards or armoires. Six have fireplaced sitting areas facing the river. A local decorator outfitted the rooms in lavish style: mounds of pillows and designer sheets on the queensize canopy or twin beds; loveseats or sofas with a plush armchair in front of the fireplaces. Mantels and cabinetwork make these rooms look right at home.

Our favorites are the second-floor rooms at either end, brighter and more airy with bigger windows onto the water, a couple with half-cathedral ceilings. Rooms in the middle are darker in both decor and daylight. Four rooms on the ground floor are suite-size in proportion and come with double whirlpool tubs and wet bars with microwaves, but are on view to the constant stream of passersby on the wharf. Each room is distinctively different and has its own merits. "One couple stayed here four times in the first month and worked their way around the inn, staying in different rooms," reported co-owner John McGee.

Guests have little reason to leave their rooms, but there's a common room on the second floor. It has all the right magazines as well as glass tables for continental breakfast. Homemade breads and muffins are put out each morning, and tea and sherry in the evening.

(860) 536-8300 or (800) 364-6100. Fax (860) 572-1250. www.steamboatinnmystic.com. Ten rooms with private baths. Doubles, $235 to $300 summer and fall weekends, $200 to $270 summer midweek, $165 to $225 fall midweek. Rest of year: $190 to $260 weekends, $125 to $180 midweek.

The Old Mystic Inn, 52 Main St., Box 733, Old Mystic 06372.

The sweet aroma of apple-cranberry coffeecake baking in the oven greeted our arrival at this historic hostelry near the head of the wide Mystic River.

Innkeeper Michael Cardillo Jr., a Culinary Institute of America-trained former private chef, treats overnight guests to afternoon cakes, brownies and popcorn. They bed down for the night in four antiques-furnished guest rooms in a red and white 1784 Colonial house up against the rural road and four newer rooms in a blue carriage house built out back in 1988. Rooms are named after New England authors (the house at one time was the antiquarian Old Mystic Book Shop). All have queen beds, and three in the main house have working fireplaces. Two larger rooms in the carriage house have gas fireplaces and whirlpool tubs, canopy beds, and a loveseat and two wing chairs in one, a loveseat and a wicker chair in the other.

The main house has pleasant sitting rooms upstairs and down, a front porch and an atmospheric front dining room where four tables are set for breakfast. Michael calls his fare "country gourmet." You might have baked stuffed french toast with maple-walnut syrup, caramel-apple pancakes or herbed scrambled eggs in puff pastry with smoked gouda-mornay sauce and steamed asparagus.

(860) 572-9422. Fax (860) 572-9954. www.oldmysticinn.com. Eight rooms with private baths. Doubles, $145 to $195 May-October, $115 to $155 rest of year.

Antiques & Accommodations, 32 Main St., North Stonington 06359.

Ann and Thomas Gray, who are really into cooking, nearly enrolled in the Johnson & Wales culinary program but decided instead to open a B&B. Their 1861 yellow house with the gingerbread trim of its era became the focal point for a complex that eventually grew to include seven guest rooms, a garden cottage suite, an antiques shop in the barn and extensive gardens before they scaled back in 2005.

Tom puts his cooking skills to the test with an outstanding English breakfast, served by candlelight at 8:30 or 9:30 in the formal dining room, on the flower-bedecked front porch or the stone patio in the garden. It always includes fresh fruit in an antique crystal bowl, perhaps melon with a yogurt, honey and mint sauce or cantaloupe-melon soup. Main courses could be eggs benedict, crab soufflé, a stilton and aquavit omelet with dill sauce, an apple-rum puff garnished with strawberries and a signature sweet bread pudding laced with dried apricots and cream sherry. "Breakfast goes on for hours," says Ann, who was still serving at 11 the December weekday we first called in. These hospitable hosts also have been known to dispense wine late into the evening while everyone lingers on the patio.

Memories of traveling in England inspired the Grays to furnish their home in the Georgian manner with formal antique furniture and accessories, many of which are for sale.

Besides a parlor with TV, the main house offers an elegant downstairs bedroom with yellow painted walls glazed with gold, a queen poster bed, working fireplace and a stereo system. Upstairs are another guest room with canopied bed and a bridal room filled with photographs of honeymooners who have stayed there.

(860) 535-1736 or (800) 554-7829. www.mysticbb.com. Three rooms with private baths. Doubles, $99 to $189. Closed in January and February.

The Inn at Stonington, 60 Water St., Stonington 06378.

The old Harborview Restaurant was destroyed by fire, and from its ashes in 2001 rose this luxury B&B facing the waterfront, the first real place to stay in the borough.

Inn at Stonington fronts on Cannon Square in historic borough.

Owner Bill Griffin spared no expense in producing a handsome gray and white-trimmed, three-story inn up against the sidewalk in front, with docks and water behind.

Four guest rooms on the first floor and eight on the second come with fireplaces and ten have jacuzzi tubs. Beds are queensize except for two kings. English-style fruitwood furniture, rich fabrics, upholstered club chairs and built-in shelves around the fireplaces are the norm. The striking color motifs vary from moss green and taupe to yellow and pale blue.

Six rooms open through French doors onto private balconies overlooking the water. The best view may be from the cheery yellow third-floor sitting room with a common balcony outfitted with Parisian-style bistro chairs.

Six larger rooms with high ceilings are available in a new brick annex next door. All come with jacuzzi tubs and five have kingsize beds and fireplaces.

On the main floor of the main inn are a living room/dining area where a substantial continental breakfast is served. Wine and cheese are complimentary in the afternoon.

(860) 535-2000. Fax (860) 535-8193. www.innatstonington.com. Eighteen rooms with private baths. April-October: doubles, $199 to $440 weekends, $180 to $299 midweek. November-March: doubles, $155 to $395 weekends, $140 to $270 midweek.

Another Second Penny Inn, 870 Pequot Trail, Stonington 06378.

Guests at this atmospheric, 1710 Colonial home on five rural acres enjoy large accommodations with updated amenities, gourmet breakfasts and a distinct feeling of times gone by.

The house had been a tavern at one time and retains a big old kitchen that innkeepers Jim and Sandra Wright use for hearthside cooking as well as an upstairs suite with a swinging partition in the middle that could be raised to make enough space for a dance hall. On one side of the Russell Suite is a queensize poster bed, gas fireplace and a bath with jetted clawfoot tub. On the other is a sitting room with a day bed. Elsewhere on the second floor, the Denison Room has a queensize poster bed, gas fireplace and a bathroom so big it holds not only a jetted clawfoot tub but also a small refrigerator, a dressing table and a yellow slipper chair in the middle. The front Noyes Room comes with two twin beds that can be joined as a king, an electric fireplace and a full bath. All rooms have TV/VCRs and are decorated in Colonial style with oriental rugs and handmade quilts employed as wall hangings.

Guests gather in a cozy front library and in the dining room for a breakfast to remember. The morning of our visit brought vanilla-poached pears, maple-oatmeal-walnut muffins, a garden vegetable quiche and the usual "dessert," a selection of Jim's homemade sorbets, including apple, kiwi, peach and mulled cider. An apple-cranberry compote with yogurt and an omelet of cream cheese, crabmeat and chives was on tap the next day.

As for the B&B's name, it comes from an obscure parable cited by the president of Mills College when colleague Jim had second thoughts about having splurged to buy an old yacht: "If you have two pennies, with the first buy bread for your stomach, and with the second buy hyacinths for your soul." Jim named the boat "Second Penny," and the B&B when he retired became another.

(860) 535-1710. Fax (860) 535-1709. www.secondpenny.com. Two rooms and one suite with private baths. Doubles, $135 to $195 in summer and fall, $99 to $139 rest of year.

Breakfast Gourmet

Kitchen Little, 135 Greenmanville Ave. (Route 27), Mystic.

People line up for breakfast on hottest summer and coldest winter days at this little gem beside the Mystic River. We waited our turn in the January chill for a dynamite breakfast of scrambled eggs with crabmeat and cream cheese, served with raisin toast, and a spicy scrambled egg dish with jalapeño cheese on grilled corned-beef hash, accompanied by toasted dill-rye bread.

The coffee flows endlessly into red mugs, the folks occupying the nine tables and seats at the counter are convivial, and you can eat outside at picnic tables beside the water in season. Florence Klewin's open kitchen certainly is little (she says the entire establishment measures nineteen feet square). But it doesn't prevent her from serving some remarkable omelets and other breakfasts "like Momma didn't used to make" with a creativity and prices that put bigger restaurants to shame.

She also serves more ordinary lunches on weekdays, but it's breakfast where Kitchen Little shines.

(860) 536-2122. Entrées, $3.25 to $11.95. Breakfast and lunch, Monday-Friday 6:30 to 2. Weekends 6:30 to 1, breakfast only.

Gourmet Treats

Chester's Main Street is home to several shops of interest to gourmands. Unusual coffee mugs and pasta bowls are among the hand-painted majolica pottery from the Umbrian and Amalfi regions of Italy featured at **Ceramica.** Colorful pottery from France is on display at **Souleiado en Provence**. **R.J. Vickers Herbery** offers gifts for and from the garden. Beyond the main street, **Wheatmarket** at 4 Water St. is a well-stocked specialty-foods store where you can order a prepared picnic (the Lovers' includes orange-passionfruit sodas, bliss potato salad and chocolate kisses) or eat at one of the small tables in the front. Sandwiches include country pâté with sweet and rough mustard, turkey breast with cranberry conserve and cheddar, and roast beef with garlic and herb cheese. Also on the docket are salads, soups, stews, a handful of hot entrées and deep-dish pizzas (the chicken with artichoke and the eggplant with sundried tomatoes are especially popular). Browse among the racks for Belgian butter-almond cookies, Coryell's Crossing jams, Guiltless Gourmet dips, beluga caviar, saffron and such.

Feast Gourmet Market at 159 Main St., Deep River, took over the space long known as Pasta Unlimited and continues to make the freshest pasta imaginable. Owner Drew McLachlan's pasta machine is in the window, and nothing gets cut until a customer orders it. Available types include spinach, pumpkin, tomato, lemon-dill and a dynamite black-peppercorn pasta that we tried with his good clam sauce. At another visit, we took home pumpkin pasta and topped it with the raphael sauce (artichoke hearts, plum tomatoes and romano cheese) – oh, so good. Recent additions are scallop and lobster raviolis and new kinds of extruded pasta. The little shop also has an espresso bar, as well as gourmet food items. Sandwiches, soups, salads and desserts like key lime zest or black and white espresso cake are available. The new owner, who formerly was executive chef at a pasta restaurant in Portland, Ore., planned on Thursday evenings to offer four-course dinner feasts in the $45 range at a chef's table for twelve in the center of the shop.

More pasta, much of it frozen, is featured at the inviting new retail store of **Pasta Vita** at 225 Elm St., Old Saybrook. Its "gourmet pasta factory" in an industrial park area produces countless pasta treats as well as refrigerated and freezer cases full of ready-to-go Italian-inspired meat, seafood and vegetable dishes, appetizers and desserts – more than 70 kinds of a typical day, generally in portions to feed two or more. The choices are staggering, and hundreds of people seem to visit daily to put together their evening meal. We went home with a walnut and gorgonzola salad, a chicken, spinach and artichoke main course, and cauliflower gratin that made a heat-and-serve dinner as good as it gets, $22 and enough for three.

Fromage at 873 Boston Post Road, Old Saybrook, is an upscale shop where Christine Chesanek purveys wonderful cheeses, fine foods and coffees. She stocks ten kinds of olives, like french black olives in sunflower-seed oil and roasted garlic. Aged chèvre, her own cheese spreads, Harney & Sons teas, pâtés, pastas and more are on the shelves. Christine also has an Italian machine that makes a good cup of latte for $2.50.

Vanderbrooke Bakers and Caterers, 65 Main St., Old Saybrook, produces dynamite breads, pastries, salads, sandwiches and hot entrées, available at the retail shop or from the deli to eat in or take out. The bread repertoire includes country french, flanders (a Belgian white with oats), squaw, mustard-tarragon, sourdough, and gorgonzola and roasted red pepper, about eight changing varieties each day. The pastry case is full of delights. The deli also impresses with sandwiches (roast beef and brie or genoa salami, capicola and roasted peppers), salads (Moroccan chicken, minty barley, ginger coleslaw), soups like shrimp and corn chowder and the day's entrées.

The original clam hash draws food lovers to **Pat's Kountry Kitchen** at 70 Mill Rock Road (Route 154 at the junction of Route 1), Old Saybrook. It's an utterly delicious blend of clams, onions and potatoes, topped with a fried egg and sensational for breakfast or lunch with coleslaw. The hash, for which Pat Brink closely guards the recipe, resulted from an accident (her kids threw out the broth distilled from two bushels of quahogs destined for the day's chowder, and she improvised to use up the dried clams). Pat's serves good, old-fashioned country meals daily except Wednesday from 7 a.m. to 9 p.m.

Mystic Pizza, established in 1973, produces the pizza that made the 1988 hit movie famous, or was it the other way around? The expanded pizzeria at 56 West Main St., Mystic, was the focus and setting for the film. A second Mystic Pizza, which serves a full dinner menu, is located at the Route 2 and Route 184 rotary in North Stonington.

For pizzas with a difference, head to **The Pizza Grille,** Route 27, Mystic, just north of I-95 and the Mystic Carousel & Fun Center. Timothy Doyle from Providence, who says he's the only Irishman offering pizzas in that city's Little Italy called Federal Hill, offers wood-fired grilled pizzas here. This is no ordinary pizza parlor. It's paneled in pine, upholstered in burgundy leather and has a bar. The thin-sliced pizzas come from a wood grill and thicker, traditional pizzas from a traditional oven. The wild mushroom pizza (portobello, crimini and shiitake, with diced tomatoes, grilled onions and two cheeses, $13.50) teamed with a mesclun salad makes a good meal. Open daily, 11 to 10 or 11.

The area's best gourmet marketplace and deli is **Mystic Market East** at 63 Williams Ave. (Route 1), on the eastern outskirts of Mystic. At this branch of the original **Mystic Market** at 375 Noank Road in West Mystic you'll find sleek kitchen-store shelves full of specialty foods as well as a coffee bar and deli and pastry cases laden with treats. Sample a few salads (perhaps saffron-marinated cauliflower, horseradish coleslaw, kamut and currant waldorf) or a sandwich (Connecticut smoked turkey and swiss cheese on a baguette). Save room for one of the delectable desserts – a fruit tart, peach cobbler or lemon bar – beckoning from the counter top. The rear kitchen is on view through windows from the counter area. Tables beside the big front windows look out onto the passing scene along Route 1.

A Jewel of a Winery

Chamard Vineyards, 115 Cow Hill Road, Clinton.

The founder of this money-is-no-object winery was William R. Chaney, chairman and CEO of Tiffany & Co., so you know things are done with class. And classy all the way is Chamard, reached via an unremarkable residential street north of Exit 63 off I-95, not far from the Clinton Crossing factory outlet stores. Overlooking a manmade farm pond, one of the Northeast's best wineries occupies a gray shingled house built in 1988 as "a New England château" near the front entrance to a 40-acre property that is half planted with vines. Wines are tasted with crackers and cheese in a richly furnished tasting room with vaulted ceiling, a fieldstone fireplace and the air of a deluxe hunting lodge.

Larry McCulloch has been the active winemaker since Chamard began in 1985. Bill and Carolyn Chaney were involved on weekends until they sold in 2005 to Dr. Jonathan M. Rothberg. The founder and CEO of the Branford-based CuraGen, a leading genomics-based pharmaceutical company, planned to "push the frontiers of winemaking" here. Eighty per cent of the 6,000-case annual output is white wines, primarily an award-winning chardonnay that sells for $10.99. The cabernet sauvignon and merlot generally sell out as quickly as they are released. Bill Chaney acknowledged that his connections helped place Chamard's chardonnay in some of New York's finest restaurants, but merit keeps them there. Chamard's emerging chardonnay style is more European than Californian, and wine writers have ranked it among the best wines produced in this country.

(860) 664-0299 or (800) 371-1609. www.chamard.com. Tours and tastings, Tuesday-Sunday 11 to 5.

Commodore's Room at the Black Pearl restaurant looks onto Newport waterfront.

Newport, R.I.

In Pursuit of Pleasures

Few cities its size can match in quality or quantity the astonishing variety of restaurants of Newport.

Little wonder. Newport has been a center for the good life since the Victorian era when America's affluent built summer "cottages" that now form the nation's most imposing collection of mansions in one place. Visitors from around the world come to view the mansions as well as the restorations of some of America's oldest buildings. Sailing and tennis have given modern Newport a sporty face, too.

With all the attractions come the trappings. Restaurants, inns, B&Bs and shops are part of a tourist/building boom that has transformed Rhode Island's most visited city in recent years.

It was not until the early 1970s that Newport's restaurants became known for much more than fresh seafood, served to the masses on venerable waterfront wharves. An immensely popular establishment called The Black Pearl changed that. The first of the town's innovative restaurants, it blended elegant cuisine with more casual fare in a mix that triggered a trend.

Now Newport is home to notable French restaurants, the nation's oldest continuously operating tavern, small eateries with pace-setting chefs, contemporary seafood houses, assorted ethnic spots and sidewalk cafés everywhere in a growing smorgasbord of fine and fast food. "The best of the lot here match the best restaurants in Boston," asserted the maître-d' at the Clarke Cooke House, whose owner formerly owned Locke-Ober in Boston.

Summers and weekends in Newport are pricey and crowded; dinner reservations a week in advance are the alternative to two-hour waits. It's best to visit midweek or in the off-season.

The myriad pleasures of this small historic city will surprise you. So will the numbers of people pursuing them. On a sunny day, it may seem as if the whole world has come to Newport and its restaurants.

Dining

The Best of the Best

The Place, 28 Washington Square, Newport.

This wine bar and grill keeps Newport abuzz with its exciting cuisine. An adjunct to Yesterday's Ale House, a pubby downtown institution, it was opened by owners Maria and Richard Korn as a showcase for their longtime chef, Alex Daglis. Alex moved to a separate kitchen, hired a staff and devised a contemporary American menu with a European flair that, Richard says, "expands and challenges your tastes."

Everyone raves about the entrées, which range from pan-seared lobster with plum wine and ginger to grilled beef tenderloin on black bean chili sauce with a corn tamale and cajun onion rings. Sake-glazed wild salmon with pineapple salsa, roasted leg and grilled breast of duck with a sweet and spicy chipotle-cherry sauce, and pecan-crusted rack of lamb with a balsamic glaze also entice.

But we never got beyond the appetizers, which were so tantalizing that we shared and made a meal of five. The Asian lobster and shrimp potstickers, terrific scallops with cranberries and ginger, the gratin of wild mushrooms, and the crab raviolis with goat cheese and ginger were warm-ups for a salad of smoked pheasant with poached pears and hazelnuts that was out of this world. Each was gorgeously presented on black octagonal plates. Strawberry margarita sorbet with fresh fruit and a warm apple crêpe with apple fries and apple sorbet were worthy endings to a fantastic meal.

All this is stylishly served at white-clothed tables on two levels of a long, narrow dining room with brass rails, oil lamps and sconces. A vaudeville curtain from a New Bedford theater, framed and back lit on one wall, dominates the decor.

To accompany, two dozen wines are offered by the glass and 150 by the bottle. "Flights" offer a tasting of four wines for $13.50.

From the adjacent Ale House come not flights but "schooners" featuring 36 microbrews. Four seven-ounce pilsener glasses for $6 arrive in an elaborate homemade wooden schooner. A recent lunch here produced a stellar cheddar and bacon soup, mussels dijonnaise and a pasta special blending a portobello mushroom with olives and asparagus. There were interesting sandwiches and salads but, alas, no appetizers at all, let alone any with the appeal of those available at dinner next door. Yesterday's is deservedly popular, but we'll stick with The Place.

(401) 847-0116. www.yesterdaysandtheplace.com. Entrées, $23.95 to $29.95. Dinner nightly, 5:30 to 10 or 11. Closed Monday and Tuesday, December-March.

Yesterday's, entrées $11.95 to $17.95, open daily 11 to 10, Sunday to 9.

Bouchard Restaurant Inn, 505 Thames St.

After training in France and sixteen years as executive chef at the famed Le Château in New York's Westchester County, Albert J. Bouchard III struck out on his

Sarah and Albert Bouchard in front of display of china cups at Bouchard Restaurant.

own. He, his wife Sarah and their three youngsters moved to Newport because of its water and yachting (they live in the summer on their yacht once owned by Humphrey Bogart). They sought a small establishment where he could exercise "total artistic control," which turned out to be the former tearoom in a 1785 Georgian-style house.

The two-section, 43-seat dining room is a beauty in celadon and cream. Assorted chairs with upholstered celadon or mauve seats are at well-spaced tables dressed in cream-colored, floor-length cloths and topped with Wedgwood china, expensive stemware and tall oil lamps bearing small shades. Four shelves of demitasse cups and saucers, part of his father's collection, separate the front section from the back, and a small bar in the front room looks to be straight out of Provence. A landscaped brick patio in back is pleasant for drinks and hors d'oeuvre in summer.

The food is classic French with contemporary nuances in the style of Albert's former domain. It has received rave reviews and, combined with the elegant sense of comfort and flawless service, contributes to a memorable dining experience.

Entrées at a recent visit ranged from roasted cod with creamy mustard sauce to filet mignon au poivre. Dover sole with sorrel sauce, Atlantic salmon with a spicy Thai crust and lemongrass sauce, crispy veal sweetbreads with a tarragon sauce, and coffee-crusted magret duck breast finished with a brandy-balsamic sauce testify to the small kitchen's scope.

Typical starters are salmon tartare, lobster and asparagus in puff pastry, smoked scallops with horseradish cream sauce, escargots in phyllo with tomato-tarragon sauce, and roquefort and eggplant cheesecake with tomato butter sauce. Warm pear salad with roasted walnuts, blue cheese and greens is a mid-winter refresher.

Albert, with two talented assistants in the kitchen, prepares the crusty sourdough rolls as well as the desserts, which range from a mocha phyllo napoleon to chocolate crêpes and grand marnier soufflés. Some of the wines, which date back to the 1960s, come from his personal cellar.

In 2005, the Bouchards opened the two upper floors as a B&B with five rooms and a two-bedroom suite. Doubles rent for $99 to $205, the suite from $450 to $600.

(401) 846-0123. www.restaurantbouchard.com. Entrées, $24 to $38. Dinner nightly except Tuesday, 6 to 9:30 or 10. Sunday brunch, 11 to 2.

The West Deck, 1 Waite's Wharf.

Exciting bistro cuisine at refreshing prices draws those in the know to this waterside spot beside the harbor, a century-old structure that once served as a garage for an oil company. Here, in an airy, garage-like space that's one-third cooking area, 30 diners can be seated at tables dressed in white and ten more cozy up to an L-shaped eating bar facing the open kitchen to watch chef-owner James Mitchell at work. A long sun porch alongside nearly doubles the capacity, and more can be accommodated seasonally on a super outside patio where there's a wood grill.

The menu is printed nightly, and at our latest visit offered a dozen entrées from almond-crusted mahi mahi with mango-lime sauce to grilled filet mignon with stilton cheese and port wine sauce.

An amusé of pâté on toasted breads preceded a couple of excellent salads, one with goat cheese, sundried tomatoes, roasted beets and a parmesan crisp, and a mesclun salad with maytag blue cheese, apples and cajun pecans. The night's terrine of duck, rabbit, quail and foie gras with hazelnuts and port wine glaze proved fabulous. So was a superior leg of venison with sundried cherry sauce, served with thyme-mashed potatoes, although a couple of elements in the signature mixed grill of petite filet, lamb chop, chicken and andouille sausage proved surprisingly tough. A tasting of several of the rich desserts – grand marnier crème brûlée, peach bread pudding with whiskey-caramel sauce and cappuccino-praline mousse with espresso sauce – compensated.

Many of the well-chosen wines, most refreshingly priced in the twenties and thirties, are available by the glass. A captain's list adds more expensive choices.

In season on the waterfront deck, the outdoor grill furnishes the bulk of the dishes on a simpler, all-day menu that ranges from burgers and a fish sandwich to fried chicken, pork ribs, teriyaki steak and twin lobsters.

(401) 847-3610. Entrées, $22 to $32. Dinner, Wednesday-Sunday from 6. Sunday brunch, noon to 3, October-May. Outside deck open for lunch and dinner daily noon to 9, Memorial Day to Labor Day.

The White Horse Tavern, corner of Marlborough and Farewell Streets.

Claiming to be the oldest operating tavern in the United States, established in 1673, the tavern was restored by the Newport Preservation Society and opened as a restaurant in 1957. It's also known for some of the best – albeit most expensive – food in town.

The White Horse is a deep red Colonial building that imparts an unmistakable feeling of history. It's most appealing for cozy, cold-weather dining, with its dark interior, beamed ceilings, wide-plank floors, huge fireplace and classical music. The

Dining room decor is elegant Colonial in historic White Horse Tavern.

dark rose and white draperies complement the handsome burgundy and off-white china and the winter arrangements of silk flowers and dried berries. Brass candlesticks with Colonial candles inside large clear hurricane chimneys are on each table.

Service by a tuxedo-clad staff is formal and even at lunch, prices start at $9 (for a turkey club sandwich) and top off at $26 for lobster pot pie. On a spring afternoon, we tried the day's soup, an interesting chilled mixture of yogurt, cucumber, dill and walnuts. Baked marinated montrachet with garlic purée and herbed croutons was a delicious appetizer. The fish of the day, halibut in a sauce with grapefruit pieces and a hint of brandy, was excellent. The chicken salad resting in a half avocado was surprisingly bland.

Wines are expensive, as you would imagine, but many are available by the glass. The old bar room in one corner of the building is atmospheric as can be.

The classic continental fare takes on more trendy twists at night. Besides a signature baked escargots en croûte, expect such appetizers as Atlantic salmon carpaccio on a crisp potato cake, peekytoe crab napoleon with house-made tuiles garnished with flying fish roe, and a grilled scallop and endive salad tossed with walnuts, red onions and sweet peppers in a dijon-sage dressing.

Seafood entrées can be complex, as in paupiettes of grey sole stuffed with caramelized onion and fennel mousse and finished with an apple brandy sauce, filet of salmon topped with crabmeat in puff pastry, and shrimp and oyster stew tossed in a champagne-truffle sauce. More traditional are such menu staples as grilled duck breast glazed with port wine, individual beef wellington, and Colorado rack of lamb encrusted with a sage-pecan pesto and served over a raspberry-pommery reduction.

You might finish with a chocolate truffle trio, lavender crème brûlée or triple silk chocolate torte on a bed of raspberry-melba sauce. It's not exactly Colonial fare or prices, but well-heeled folks who appreciate fine food and formal ambiance keep the White Horse busy most of the time.

(401) 849-3600. www.whitehorsetavern.com. Entrées, $30 to $42. Lunch, Wednesday-Saturday 11:30 to 2:30. Dinner nightly, 5:30 to 9:30 or 10; jackets recommended. Sunday brunch, 11 to 2.

The Black Pearl, Bannister's Wharf.

Since this rambling establishment opened in 1972 as the first of Newport's innovative restaurants, it's been one of our favorites, serving a staggering 1,500 meals a day in summer from what owner Tom Cullen calls "the world's smallest kitchen."

Outside under the Cinzano umbrellas on the waterside patio, you can sit and watch the world go by as you enjoy what we think is Newport's best clam chowder – creamy, chock full of clams and laced with dill, served piping hot with a huge soda cracker ($5.75 a bowl, and seemingly better every time we order it). You also can get a Pearlburger with mint salad served in pita bread for $7.25, and a variety of sandwiches or stew of the day.

Inside, the tavern is informal, hectic, noisy and fun, offering much the same fare as the outdoor café plus heartier offerings (baked cod with pepper jack cheese, grilled calves liver, and a shrimp and scallop brochette) that can serve as lunch or dinner. In fact, after a bowl of chowder, the crab benedict with french fries was almost too much to finish. You also can get several desserts – we remember a delectable brandy-cream cake – and espresso as strong as it should be, plus cappuccino Black Pearl, enhanced with courvoisier and kahlua.

The pride of the Pearl is the **Commodore's Room,** pristinely pretty with white linens, dark walls, low ceiling, ladderback chairs and a view of the harbor through small-paned windows.

Longtime chef J. Daniel Knerr, who was named the American Culinary Federation's chef of the year in 2004, rarely tinkers with an extensive menu that some think is dated but seems to work for most. Dinner appetizers range from fried brie and pâté de maison to escargots bourguignonne and Scottish smoked salmon. Start, perhaps, with a shrimp, crab and lobster cocktail with three sauces, "black and blue" tuna with roasted pepper sauce or a salad of exotic lettuces with goat cheese and sundried tomatoes. Typical entrées are salmon fillet with mustard-dill hollandaise, grey sole meunière, grilled swordfish with tomato-basil beurre blanc, medallions of veal with morels and champagne sauce, sliced blackwing ostrich filet with red wine sauce and special, dry-aged sirloin steaks obtained from a New York butcher.

It's an ambitious menu, the more so considering the size of the kitchen. But the Black Pearl can expand or contract its service with the season and the crowds. While many others have come and gone, it's been a pearl on the Newport scene for more than three decades.

(401) 846-5264. www.blackpearlnewport.com. Entrées, $17.50 to $35; tavern, $15.50 to $28. Tavern and outdoor café open daily from 11. Dinner in Commodore's Room, from 6; jackets required. Closed early January to mid-February.

The Clarke Cooke House, Bannister's Wharf.

Dining is on several levels and a breezy yet formal upper deck in this 1790-vintage Colonial house, another venerable Newport establishment nicely located on the waterfront. Two kitchens offer different renditions of contemporary European fare.

Casual fare is served at down-to-earth prices in the ground-level **Candy Store** café, a summer sushi bar and a porch with harbor view. We can vouch for a lunch of eggs benedict, salad vinaigrette and great french fries, and a thick and creamy cup of clam chowder – one of the best we've had lately – with a juicy hamburger on an onion roll, again with those addictive french fries.

Waterfront is on view from glamorous upper Porch at The Clarke Cooke House.

Up one level on the other side of the café is the **Grille,** a middle-of-the-road bistro offering lunch and dinner from the Candy Store menu.

The food gets considerably more expensive, the service more polished and the atmosphere more haute in the upper-level venues. A formal dining room called the **Skybar** is colorful in green and white, with banquettes awash in pillows beneath a beamed ceiling. In summer it opens to a breezy but elegant canopied upper deck called the **Porch** with a great view of the waterfront.

Executive chef Ted Gidley's takes on contemporary French fare range from wood-grilled native swordfish with anchovy vinaigrette and sautéed fillet of halibut embellished with caviar vin blanc and lobster vinaigrette to pan-seared breast of magret duck with seared foie gras and roasted apricots, steak au poivre and roast rack of lamb persillade. Carpaccio of yellowfin tuna, raviolis of lobster and morels with champignon sauce, and pan-seared breast of squab with foie gras au torchon are typical appetizers. A signature lobster salad is served with hazelnuts and haricots vert.

Dessert might be tarte tatin, vanilla crème brûlée, chocolate mousse cake with raspberries and crème anglaise, and a chocolate-studded triumph called "snowball in hell."

(401) 849-2900. www.clarkecooke.com. Entrées, $27 to $39. Dinner nightly in season, 6 to 10 or 10:30, weekends in off-season.

Candy Store and Grille, entrées $17.95 to $32.95. Lunch daily, 11:30 to 4, weekends in winter. Dinner nightly from 5, Wednesday-Sunday in winter.

More Good Dining

Asterisk, 599 Lower Thames St.

One of Newport's more trendy and eclectic restaurants is run by the scion of a family of Danish restaurateurs. John Bach-Sorenson alighted from Copenhagen in Newport – "it reminded me of home" – and looked for a restaurant site. He found it in a working auto-repair garage, now transformed into a airy and colorful space with a partly open rear kitchen and a remarkable handcrafted bar along one side. A romantic, dimly lit salon look is conveyed by shaded gas lamps flickering on close-together white-linened tables beneath a high, industrial-look ceiling. In summer, garage doors open onto an enclosed, canopied sidewalk café out front.

John, his partner-become-wife Tracy Tarigo and an artist friend are responsible for the splashy effects and artworks. The artistry continues in the kitchen, the ever-changing, continental-Asian menu ranging widely from potato-wrapped grouper and a classic sole meunière to pork chops with melted brie and peaches, veal scaloppini and steak au poivre with spinach anglaise and french fries. You might find roasted baby snapper Cantonese style with mandarin soy sauce, crispy salmon with mushroom-asparagus-orzo risotto, kalamata olive-encrusted swordfish with cabernet sauce and free-range chicken Peking style with hoisin vinaigrette. The filet mignon might be à la milanaise (a mouthful of a menu description: tomato espagnole sauce, shredded ham, mushrooms and white truffle oil with roasted pasta). You can opt for mussels marinière with frites or "le petite asterisk:" one-half lobster, ten oysters, four shrimp, and eight clams and mussels ($42).

Appetizers could be escargots bourguignonne, crab cakes rémoulade, a firecracker shrimp spring roll, steak tartare and a crab and shrimp salad with fresh coconut. Frozen tiramisu parfait, raspberry crème brûlée and profiteroles are popular desserts.

The place is named for one of John's favorite French comic-strip characters, known for fighting the bureaucracy, which he had to do to win a wine and beer license. He also runs **Boulangerie,** a bakery and sandwich shop at 382 Spring St., and lately took on **La Petite Auberge,** a classic French restaurant at 19 Charles St.

(401) 841-8833. Entrées, $19 to $32. Dinner nightly, from 5.

Cheeky Monkey Café, 14 Perry Mill Wharf.

The former owner of Providence's acclaimed Gatehouse Restaurant branched out with this small, two-level dining room, bar and an upstairs cigar lounge with a great view of the harbor.

The name refers to the British expression of endearment for a fun-loving, devilish person. Owner Henry Kates chose it to reflect a cheeky point of view on foods and spirits, and provided a dark and vaguely jungle-look decor of black wood tables and faux-leopard skins on the benches and wainscoting. Everything from the leopard print design to the positioning of the comical monkey family portraits is playful yet elegant. Dining is on two levels, facing an open kitchen.

The short, international dinner menu is full of Asian twists. It might start with coconut-red curry mussels, crispy sea scallops with a "cheeky" tartar sauce and a panko-crusted tuna nori roll with a tamari dipping sauce. The lobster bisque might be garnished with "a tarragon black pepper monkey tail cracker."

Main courses range from grilled Moroccan salmon fillet and house-smoked pork tenderloin with banana-plantain gravy to grilled filet mignon topped with lobster-peppercorn butter sauce. Typical are seafood paella, five-spiced seared chicken breast and pork tenderloin crusted in creole mustard and goat cheese.

Dessert could be bananas foster, butterscotch crème brûlée, chocolate truffle cake or assorted sorbets.

Start with a drink in a separate bar across the hallway. Finish with an after-dinner cordial in the upstairs cigar lounge. It has a parlor-like ambiance of sofas, overstuffed chairs, floor lamps and – what every parlor needs – a humidor cabinet.

(401) 845-9494. www.cheekymonkeycafe.com. Entrées, $21.95 to $29.95. Dinner, Tuesday-Saturday from 5:30.

Tucker's Bistro, 150 Broadway.

For romance, there's no more idyllic place in Newport than this newish French bistro in the heart of the off-the-beaten-path restaurant row beloved by locals along Broadway. Co-owners Tucker Harris and Ellen Coleman fashioned a 1920s deco bistro in a double storefront. The bar is in a small room with a library look. Most of the dining takes place in couple of larger rooms with white-clothed tables holding antique shaded lamps amidst red lacquered walls hung with impressionist paintings and a ceiling draped in vine branches, rhinestone strands and twinkling white lights. Tucker likens the decor to a cross between art gallery and bordello.

The fare is primarily Mediterranean. The partners tweak the regular printed menu with a trio of daily specials, including soft-shell crab tempura and baked striped bass fillet with gorgonzola sauce at our visit. Otherwise, expect about a dozen entrées, from lobster and scallop stew or slow-roasted Atlantic salmon with a red wine and leek vinaigrette to seared duck breast and confit with a port-star anise sauce, pork shanks braised in bourbon and molasses, and roasted ribeye steak with brandy and green peppercorn sauce.

Appetizers go international, as in Thai shrimp nachos, escargots crostini, Asian-style calamari sauté, beef tartare and antipasti. Desserts are Tucker's forte. His specialty is a signature banana pudding, but he may offer chocolate cheesecake and a pecan bread pudding with white chocolate and dried cranberries as well.

(401) 846-3449. www.tuckersbistro.com. Entrées, $20.95 to $29.95. Dinner nightly, from 6.

Scales and Shells, 527 Thames St.

Almost as fast as seafood can be unloaded from the docks out back, retired sea captain Andy Ackerman and his staff cook up a storm in an open kitchen near the door of this casual Italian seafood restaurant, a local favorite billed as Newport's singular "only fish" restaurant. Plain and exotic seafood – simply prepared and presented in stylishly simple surroundings – comes in many guises.

The delicious aromas almost overpowered as we read the blackboard menu with an immense range but nary a non-fish item in sight. Start with deep-fried calamari, grilled white clam pizza, Sicilian mussels or mesquite-grilled shrimp from the list of appetizers. From this you could make a meal and, Andy says, many people do, ordering and sharing Chinese style. Monkfish, scallops, shrimp, swordfish, snapper, scrod – you name it, it comes in many variations as a main dish, wood-grilled, broiled or tossed with pasta. Shrimp or clams fra diavolo are served right in their own steaming-hot pans.

Tabasco, red pepper and parmesan cheese are on the tables, which are covered with black and white checked cloths. The floors are bare, and the decor is pretty much nil except for models of fish on the walls. You can pick and choose from the raw bar near the front entrance.

Italian gelatos (apricot and hazelnut are a couple), crème brûlée, tiramisu and tarts comprise the dessert selection. The short list of Italian and California wines is affordably priced.

A second-floor addition called **Upscales,** a smaller and quieter room, is open May through September. It offers a more sophisticated menu ($16.25 to $22.25, for the likes of grilled marinated toro tuna with haricots vert and baby bliss mashed potatoes).

(401) 846-3474. www.scalesandshells.com. Entrées, $10.95 to $21.95. Dinner nightly, 5 to 9 or 10. Closed mid-December to mid-January. No credit cards.

Café Zelda, 528 Thames St.

Newporters consider this old-timer one of their favorite restaurants – a neighborhood kind of place that's comfortable, unpretentious and enjoyable any time of day or night. Its food fortunes rise and fall with the executive chef, but has been on a roll lately under John Philcox, a veteran on the Newport scene.

He offers a reprise of some of the specialties we enjoyed when he owned Le Bistro on Bowen's Wharf, from steak tartare to bouillabaisse. That place hasn't been the same since his departure, but Zelda fans are the richer for it, both in terms of good food and pleasant prices.

His international dinner menu includes comfort foods like the popular Zelda burger with Vermont cheddar and onions, steak frites and herb-roasted chicken breast with Zelda's mac 'n cheese. You'll also find entrées like seared rare ahi tuna, wood-grilled salmon fillet, braised beef shortribs, grilled lamb chops and Portuguese-style pork chops with littleneck clams. Start with mussels Brittany, escargots bourguignonne or smoked chicken spring rolls with sweet chili dipping sauce. Beet and goat cheese "sandwiches" and truffled foie gras "crème brûlée" with walnuts and armagnac prunes were recent winners.

Eggs Copenhagen is a Sunday brunch favorite.

(401) 849-4002. www.cafezelda.com. Entrées, $18.95 to $27.95. Lunch, daily 11:30 to 3, Friday-Sunday in winter. Dinner nightly, 5 to 10 or 10:30. Sunday brunch, 11 to 3.

Mamma Luisa's, 673 Thames St.

Newport has better-known and flashier northern Italian restaurants, but none more authentic nor more endearing than this, a fixture since 1992 in the little Victorian house that formerly was home to the late Frick's restaurant.

The gaudy sign out front, most un-Newport like, hardly does justice to the treasure within. Tables in intimate rooms on different levels on either side of the tight entry foyer are elegantly set in white over patterned cloths, each topped with a Lalique-style lamp. The cheery yellow walls are bedecked with Italian plates, pictures and bric-a-brac.

It's a charming setting for food lovingly prepared by chef-owner Marco Trazzi, his wife Antonietta and chef Alessandro Ancarani and his wife Manuela, all from Bologna. Marco named it for his mother, whose likeness graces not only the big yellow sign outside but a painting in one of the dining rooms. She runs her own restaurant in Bologna and her husband is a professional sommelier. Most of the recipes on the short menu come from their family.

Beef carpaccio, melon with prosciutto, a couple of bruschettas and an antipasti sampler are classic starters. More adventuresome palates are assuaged by the "insalata esotica," a masterful salad of radicchio and arugula accented with dates, goat cheese, walnuts and red grapes bathed in a honey-mustard vinaigrette.

Favorites among pasta dishes are the homemade ricotta and spinach gnocchi with arugula and "our family's marinara sauce" and tagliatelle with sautéed shrimp and sea scallops tossed with garlic and basil.

Main courses range from seared tuna steak puttanesca to grilled veal chop with porcini mushroom sauce. The tender veal scaloppine picatine is sautéed with artichokes, capers, lemon juice and white wine. The sautéed chicken breast might be topped with prosciutto and provolone. The thin-sliced pork loin is rolled around a stuffing of prosciutto and parmesan cheese, baked and served with a delicate mushroom and spinach cream sauce.

Marco, a vegetarian, ensures there are several "vegetariano" dishes on the menu. The dessert tray includes tiramisu and an acclaimed fresh fig tart. The heavily Italian wine list is long on reds and affordably priced.

(401) 848-5257. www.mammaluisa.com. Entrées, $17.95 to $26.50. Dinner nightly, 5 to 10, Memorial Day to Columbus Day. Closed Wednesday rest of year.

Dining and Lodging

Castle Hill Inn & Resort, 590 Ocean Drive, Newport 02840.

There's no more sumptuous setting for dining in Newport than at this upgraded Victorian inn, grandly situated atop a hill out in the Ocean Drive mansion area overlooking Narragansett Bay. The entire inn and its accommodations have been enhanced by the father-and-son ownership team of Tim and Paul O'Reilly of the Newport Harbor Corp.

Especially salubrious for meals is the oval Sunset Room, a large windowed porch just across from the romantic mahogany bar and lounge, jutting out toward the bay. Redecorated with a billowing cream-colored taffeta canopy on the ceiling, this is the setting for Castle Hill's long-popular Sunday brunch – that is, when it's not taken to the accompaniment of live jazz on the inn's lawn sloping toward the sea.

The kitchen is under the tutelage of New Mexican-born chef Casey Riley, who transferred here after opening Agora at the Westin Hotel in Providence and serving as sous-chef at Boston's famed L'Espalier. He says his modern American cuisine is "inspired by world-wide flavors," showcasing local foods with original touches. He's likely to incorporate ten different ingredients into a single dish, but "I'll try to make sure that you can taste each one of them."

Consider his version of fish and chips: pan-fried Georges Bank cod loin with chourico, onion and vinegar-dressed french fries, vegetable slaw and spicy rémoulade. Or his grilled juniper-rubbed Texas antelope with a white sweet potato-sheep cheese tart, crispy enoki mushrooms, micro greens and bitter berry jus. Other recent examples were red snapper with pink grapefruit marmalade, chile-rubbed grilled pork tenderloin with maple-cider glaze and grilled beef fillet wrapped in apple-smoked bacon.

You might start with the foie gras of duck, pan roasted with dried fruit flapjacks, toasted pecans, balsamic syrup, micro greens and Normandy butter. Or how about the autumn squash trio: butternut soup with sage crème fraîche, acorn ravioli with brown sugar butter and spaghetti squash with spiced pecans?

Desserts are equally extravagant. Typical are s'more crème brûlée, a mille-feuille of roasted summer fruits, chèvre cheesecake with black mission figs and ruby port syrup, and a vanilla bean and lime bavarian with carpaccio of melon and lime sorbet.

Adjourn for an after-dinner drink to the bar – long a favorite hangout of Newport's in crowd. Those willing to pay the piper can stay in the inn's upgraded accommodations.

Traditionalists and romantics might opt for the eight Victorian guest rooms and three suites in the main inn or adjacent Swiss-style chalet, the former laboratory of original owner Alexander Agassiz, the Harvard marine biologist. Most have king or queen beds, double whirlpool marble baths, fireplaces and original antiques. The opulent 30-foot-high Turret Suite includes a deep soaking tub beside the window on the main bedroom level, which is joined by a winding mahogany staircase to a loft sitting area with a 360-degree view.

More private are six outlying Harbor House units overlooking the bay from a cliff about 30 feet from the mansion, each with porch, kingsize bed, gas fireplace, whirlpool bath and TV.

Eight enlarged and refurbished Beach House rooms rank with the best beachside cottage accommodations in southern New England. Elegant with vaulted ceilings, gleaming hardwood floors and beachy decor, each has a kingsize bed, TV/VCR, sofabed in the sitting area, fireplace, granite-counter galley kitchen, double whirlpool tub and separate shower, and an outdoor deck facing the ocean. From the whirlpool tub in several, you can look out onto the beach – and be there in no time.

An extravagant breakfast with a choice of juices, fruits and entrées is served to guests in the Sunset Room. The fare includes lobster omelets, eggs benedict, french toast made with raisin challah and smoked salmon with breakfast garnishes.

(401) 849-3800 or (888) 466-1355. Fax (401) 849-3838. www.castlehillinn.com. Fourteen rooms, three suites and eight cottages with private baths. July to mid-September: doubles $409 to $950, suites $989 to $1,459. Rest of year: doubles $229 to $729, suites $399 to $1,029. Cottages, $5,039 to $5,559 weekly in summer.

Entrées, $24 to $42. Lunch, Monday-Saturday 11:30 to 3 in summer, noon to 2 in off-season. Dinner nightly, 6 to 9, to 8 weeknights in off-season; jackets requested. Sunday brunch, 11:30 to 3.

The Chanler at Cliff Walk, 117 Memorial Blvd., Newport 02840.

A boutique hotel and restaurant, the reborn Chanler occupies Newport's most dramatic oceanside location and makes the most of it. The extravagant French Empire-style showplace, enveloped in lush landscaping behind a sweeping stone entry identified only by a plaque, is situated on four acres at the terminus of the Cliff Walk and overlooks Easton's Beach and the open Atlantic.

Built in 1865 as the summer home of Congressman John Winthrop Chanler of New York, it was renovated in 2003 to the tune of $10 million plus by John and Jean E. Shufelt, who undertook a similar renovation earlier at the Mission Point Resort on Michigan's Mackinac Island. Given his wife's associations with Newport and their experience opening the five-room **La Farge Perry House,** a B&B at 24 Kay St. here, he saw an upside potential for the three-story, cream-colored building long known as Cliff Walk Manor.

Twenty sumptuous guest rooms are furnished and decorated to different eras, among them Renaissance, Greek Revival, English Tudor, Louis XIV, Colonial, Federal, French Provincial, Victorian and Mediterranean. All have plump king or queensize beds and jacuzzi baths and all but two have gas fireplaces. Most come with crystal chandeliers, fine paintings, flat-screen TVs, DVD players and wet bars. Best for water views are the largest (Renaissance) with a rooftop deck in the main house and three villas in the east wing with ocean-facing decks with hot tubs and a more casual New England island theme. Three garden villas in front with floral names and themes have both baths with jacuzzis and private garden courtyards with hot tubs under pergolas and two sitting areas to compensate for their smaller size and lack of ocean views.

The Chanler's restored elegance is evident in the mahogany paneled, fireplaced lounge and the luxurious **Spiced Pear Restaurant** overlooking the Atlantic. Spencer Wolff, who spent fifteen years as an architect before attending and instructing students at Le Cordon Bleu's outpost in Chicago and cooking in leading Chicago restaurants, succeeded the founding chef here in 2005. He presides over a custom-designed show kitchen that's partly visible on the left as you enter the dining area

The Chanler's piazza offers romantic dining for Spiced Pear patrons at night.

from the lounge. The serene, 85-seat dining room at the far end yields ocean views from floor-to-ceiling windows on two sides. Adjacent is a covered and heated outdoor terrace that seats another 125 people in season.

The bill of fare is exotic and complex, as in our appetizers of peekytoe crab on green papaya puree and diver scallops with ossetra caviar and champagne. Entrées range from dayboat cod in a potato jacket with saffron brandade and black olive sauce to stuffed saddle of rabbit, coriander-crusted cervena venison and châteaubriand of kobe beef, carved tableside for two. The signature lamb loin with tomato-mint relish proved excellent, but the real hit of our summer meal was the buttery poached lobster paired with "macaroni and cheese," actually a creamy orzo laced with mascarpone cheese and truffle oil. Desserts included a tarte tatin prepared with mango rather than apple and a trio of chocolate, vanilla and hazelnut ice creams.

A bistro menu, with entrées priced at $20, is offered daily from 11:30 to 9:30.

(401) 847-1300. Fax (401) 847-3620. www.thechanler.com. Twenty rooms with private baths. Doubles, $345 to $1,195 in summer, $295 to $1,195 rest of year.

Spiced Pear: (401) 847-2244. www.spicedpear.com. Entrées, $26 to $48. Dinner, Wednesday-Sunday 5:30 to 9:30. Bistro, daily 11:30 to 9:30.

Lodging

Cliffside Inn, 2 Seaview Ave., Newport 02840.

Based in a quirky 1880 summer villa built by a Maryland governor, this Victorian charmer is among the most luxurious and comfortable B&Bs in the land.

As restored by late owner Winthrop Baker, a former broadcast executive, Cliffside's bedrooms became places in which to linger – not from which to escape, as may be the case with museum-piece Victorian inns. Even the smallest of rooms now have been ingeniously expanded to include jacuzzi tubs and sitting areas facing TVs hidden behind mirrors above their new corner fireplaces. Each of the thirteen accommodations in the main house has one or two working fireplaces. Their "bathing salons" – eleven with whirlpool tubs and two with steam baths – are some of America's most glamorous.

The entire lower floor of the six-sided Tower Suite is devoted to a wood-paneled bathroom, including whirlpool tub, marble shower and bidet. Upstairs is a bed-sitting room beneath an octagonal cathedral ceiling, with Eastlake queen bed, fireplace and bay window.

No room in the house has escaped the Baker touch, be it the sumptuous Governor's Suite with its fireplace visible from both the bedroom and the jacuzzi in the bathroom or the enlarged Garden Suite, a great summer space with a bay window off the front porch and a 28-foot-long "habitat bathroom" beneath, so-called "because you can live in it," what with a Victorian book nook at one end and french doors at the other opening onto a courtyard. The inn's many floor-to-ceiling and bay windows bathe the rooms with light, blending rich Victoriana with an airy Laura Ashley freshness.

The newest and most luxurious accommodations are in the Cliffside Cottage, a onetime ranch house near the Cliff Walk at the foot of the property. Each of its three suites comes with three fireplaces and sound-system bathrooms. The Seaview on the lower floor is a stone-walled hideaway with an antique French kingsize bed and wood-burning fireplace. Its plush sitting room shares a see-through gas fireplace with the marble bathroom, which holds the first Allure tub, shower and sound system sold by Jacuzzi. It's quite a sight, with whirlpool tub, hand-held shower, steam bath, TV, CD player and operating gadgets all integrated into one glass enclosure that looks as if it belongs in a hospital. Upstairs are two equally majestic suites, both newly configured as Cliffside repositions to stay in the vanguard. The queensize Atlantic enjoys an ocean view as well as a sitting room with a media center sporting LCD TV, DVD, VCR, CD and multi-room stereo system. The kingsize Cliff has "his and her" sitting rooms, one a living room and the other a study.

Besides offering every amenity one could want, Cliffside pampers guests with exotic tea service in the inn's formal parlor or on the wide front veranda. Classical music or opera plays in the background as Victorian tea is presented with an impressive array of finger sandwiches and sweets in the afternoon. Guests choose from a remarkable collection of one-of-a-kind heirloom, antique and specialty cups. Crab-stuffed mushrooms, spinach and portobello puff pastry squares, cucumber pinwheel sandwiches, meringues, baklava, shortbread, maraschino tea cake, lemon bars – they're offered here, and detailed by popular demand in the *Cliffside Inn Tea and Breakfast Cookbook.*

The cooks work full-time to prepare the tea treats as well as nightly turndown sweets and a lavish breakfast in the morning. Ours began with fresh orange juice, two kinds of muffins and a remarkable (for winter) array of raspberries, blackberries and strawberries to lather upon homemade granola and yogurt. The main event was eggs benedict with a subtle hollandaise sauce.

There's food for thought here, too, in the more than 140 paintings of reclusive artist Beatrice Turner, onetime owner of the house, whose life story and background are full of mystery.

(401) 847-1811 or (800) 845-1811. Fax (401) 848-5850. www.cliffsideinn.com. Eight rooms and eight suites with private baths. Doubles, $175 to $330. Suites, $245 to $580. Add $50 weekends, May-October.

Self-portrait of artist Beatrice Turner overlooks breakfast table at Cliffside Inn.

The Francis Malbone House, 392 Thames St., Newport. 02840.

Elegant guest rooms, commodious common rooms and a large rear courtyard and lawn make this an exceptional B&B choice in downtown Newport.

Owned by five local partners, it opened in 1990 in a former physician's residence, having been converted from a shipping merchant's home. The main house holds eight corner bedrooms on the second and third floors plus a main-floor suite. Six have fireplaces. The four front rooms are bigger and yield harbor views. All are handsomely furnished with antique queen beds covered by duvet comforters monogrammed in white.

The prime accommodation is the sunken Counting House suite (formerly the physician's office) with its private entry, a queensize four-poster bed facing the TV, a sitting area with a sofabed and two chairs, and a two-part bathroom with shower and dressing room/vanity.

A nine-bedroom addition in the rear has larger rooms, all with kingsize poster beds and jacuzzi tubs, writing desks, fireplaces and TVs hidden in recessed bookshelves. Bigger, more private and quiet because they're away from the street traffic, they encompass all the nuances that "we couldn't have in the original house and wanted here," in the words of innkeeper Will Dewey. The four rear rooms in the new wing open into two private garden courtyards with wrought-iron furniture. The courtyard suite adds a wet bar and a sitting area.

The most luxurious are two suites in the 1710 Mason House at the rear of the property. The downstairs holds a living room, dining room, kitchen and sunroom with a courtyard. Upstairs are two spacious bedrooms, each with king bed, fireplace, and double jacuzzi tub and TV in the bathroom.

All guests enjoy the inn's lovely, high-ceilinged front parlors, a library with TV and a small dining room that served as the kitchen when the house was built in 1760.

Breakfast is served beneath domed ceiling in dining room at Francis Malbone House.

Check out the hidden servants' stairway leading to the attic beside the tiled fireplace and the old bread oven in the hearth.

A spectacular dining room goes off a corridor walled with glass and Portuguese tiles leading to the courtyard wing. It's a beauty in pale yellow and gray with a domed ceiling, four round tables and two tall shelves displaying Will's collection of blue and white English china. Will, a culinary graduate of Johnson & Wales University, and his staff prepare a full breakfast. The fare includes fruits, breads, perhaps raspberry croissants or cinnamon-raisin strudels, and a main course ranging from eggs benedict to belgian waffles. Homemade cookies and beverages are offered in the afternoon.

(401) 846-0392 or (800) 846-0392. Fax (401) 848-5956. www.malbone.com. Sixteen rooms and four suites with private baths. Mid-April to mid-November: doubles $245 to $345, suites $395 to $475. Rest of year: doubles $99 to $260, suites $200 to $345.

Abigail Stoneman Inn, 102 Touro St., Newport 02840.

"Menus" for pillows, bathing and tea, and a "water bar." These one-of-a-kind luxury amenities distinguish Newport's most deluxe small B&B, opened by the Cliffside Inn and its expanding Legendary Inns of Newport group. The 1866 Renaissance-style Victorian is notable not so much for the five accommodations, sumptuous as they are, what with its legendary art theme (here 75 artworks of Newport women, in honor of Abigail Stoneman, Newport's first female innkeeper), high-style Victorian antique furnishings, kingsize beds, fireplaces, two-person whirlpool tubs, steam baths and media centers concealed behind mirrors or in armoires. But rather for the complimentary "amenities menus" that elevate personalized room service to the next level.

Even guests who have – and expect – everything probably don't have some of these.

The pillow menu offers guests twenty styles of pillows from a collection worth more than $10,000. There are wool, anti-snoring, maternity, magnetic therapy buckwheat hull and who-knows-what-all pillows. We tried the mediflow water pillow and the head cradle, but quickly reverted to the four perfectly adequate pillows already on the bed.

For bathing in some of the most glamorous whirlpool-tub settings you'll find, the British Penhaligon amenities would suffice anywhere else. Here you can supplement them with a choice of 30 imported soaps, bath salts, foams and oils from halfway around the world. The leftovers go home in a soap "doggy bag."

The inn's J.B. Finch Pub is a water bar, offering 25 of the world's best bottled waters – a selection of which you'll also find in the entry hall and in your room. The inn went through 120 cases of the trendy Voss artesian water from Norway in its first five months. We went home with a couple of the distinctive containers for other uses.

And then there are the teas, an exceptional offering of 40 kinds, available around the clock and sometimes taken in the cozy Tea for Two Room off the entry hall. The tea service was cited as one of the nineteen best in America in the 2002 book, *The Great Tea Rooms of America.* It's served daily at 4:30 in the parlor, accompanied by a changing feast of savories and sweets equal to those of the finest restaurants.

Breakfast is another gourmet event, taken at individual tables in the parlor or, by most, in their rooms. Ours culminated in an asparagus, ham and tomato omelet, expertly prepared and served by the charming William, known across Newport as Billy Rose, an ex-shoeshine boy who danced professionally with Martha Graham and the Alvin Ailey troupe. He "came with the house," having worked at the former James B. Finch House before the B&B ascended to a higher level.

How high? An early entry in the inn's guest book extolled: "Nothing can compare, only dreams."

(401) 847-1811 or (800) 845-1811. www.abigailstonemaninn.com. Two rooms and three suites with private baths. Doubles, $275 to $425. Suites, $335 to $645. Add $50 weekends May-October.

The Old Beach Inn, 19 Old Beach Road, Newport 02840.

Look beyond the ornate Victorian facade, colorful in grayish beige, yellow and green, and you might see an old anchor embedded in the third-story turret of the home built as the Anchorage in 1879. It's one of the surprises that abound in this stellar B&B lovingly run by Luke and Cyndi Murray.

They offer seven guest rooms furnished in English country decor, named after flowers or plants and full of whimsical touches.

In the Rose Room, a white iron canopy bed angles from the corner beneath a black bamboo-beamed ceiling. Done up in black and pink, it has a fireplace and a hand-painted dresser with hand-carved rose drawer pulls, and even the white toilet seat cover is sculpted like a rose.

Hand-painted Victorian cottage furniture, a faux bookcase along one wall and an antique wood-burning fireplace grace the Ivy Room, where a palladian arch leads into the jacuzzi bathroom. Check out the bishop-sleeve draperies with valances and the fireplace in the first-floor Wisteria Room, and the wicker loveseat and chair in the Forget-Me-Not Room.

Two rooms with separate entrances are in a rear 1850s carriage house. These have TVs and a more contemporary air. The Sunflower, lovely in pale yellow and burgundy, contains a wicker queensize sleigh bed, a wicker loveseat and two chairs, and a sunflower motif, from the lamps on the nightstands to a hand-painted shelf.

Guests gather in a small front parlor or a larger Victorian living room where two plush chairs and a couch face a glass cocktail table resting on four bunnies. Here are a pretty tiled fireplace, a rabbit fashioned from moss and a copper bar in the corner. The Murrays serve breakfast at four tables in the dining room or outside on the back porch or a brick patio overlooking a pleasant back yard with a gazebo and fish pond. It usually involves juice, fruit, homemade granola and pastries, plus a main dish such as egg casserole, quiche or, perhaps on Sundays, blueberry-stuffed french toast.

The Murrays also have put together a categorized collection of restaurant menus, drawing on Luke's experience as a restaurant consultant and beverage manager for the Black Pearl.

(401) 849-3479 or (888) 303-5033. Fax (401) 847-1236. www.oldbeachinn.com. Seven rooms with private baths. May-October: doubles, $125 to $300. Rest of year: $85 to $225.

Hydrangea House Inn, 16 Bellevue Ave., Newport 02840.

Fancy breakfasts and a garden retreat in the heart of Newport are among the draws at this Victorian townhouse decorated to the hilt by a pair of antiques dealers. Dennis Blair and Grant Edmondson turned their former antiques shop and art gallery into common rooms and moved some of their antiques and artworks into the guest rooms.

The B&B expanded into an adjacent building and was renovated in 2004 to produce nine reconfigured rooms, some enlarged into split-level affairs and all now with fireplaces and jacuzzi tubs. The ultimate is the 50-foot-long Hydrangea room on the third floor. Furnished with Edwardian antiques, it has a kingsize canopy bed, a fireplace, a skylit double whirlpool tub encased in Italian marble in the room, a steam bath in the bathroom, and a TV/VCR and stereo system.

Four second-floor guest rooms go off a wide hallway with stippled gold walls painted with a pastry brush to look like marble. Each is decorated with splashy draperies and wallpapers that match; the fabrics may be repeated on the bed headboards or, in one case, a valance over the shower.

The rear of the second floor opens onto a remarkable veranda, a 16-by-30-foot deck filled with plants, where afternoon tea is offered. It lends a more residential, verdant feeling than you'd suspect from the building's front and overlooks a showplace garden, complete with a spreading bamboo tree. The third floor opens onto a sundeck formed by the roof for the veranda below.

The main floor holds an elegant living room with fireplace and stenciled moldings, where guests await the opening of the doors to the formal dining room for breakfast. "They meet and talk and by the time they sit down they're all friends," says Dennis. That makes for a convivial breakfast at a mahogany table set for fourteen, with a fireplace and tapestry wall hangings beside and a crystal chandelier overhead. It's an elegant backdrop for the morning repasts cooked up by Grant. He offers fresh orange juice, granola, homemade breads and perhaps raspberry pancakes or seasoned scrambled eggs in puff pastry. In summer, the garden veranda serves as the breakfast venue.

(401) 846-4435 or (800) 945-4667. Fax (401) 846-6602. www.hydrangeahouse.com. Nine rooms with private baths. Doubles, $265 to $475 May-October, $250 to $425 rest of year.

Formal dining room is set for breakfast at Hydrangea House Inn.

Architects Inn, 31 Old Beach Road, Newport 02840.

The 1873 Woodbine Cottage in which local architect George Champlin Mason resided has been turned into one of Newport's nicest B&Bs. Harlan and Sheila Tyler chucked their corporate careers locally and spent a year renovating the house a few blocks from where Sheila was raised. Beige with white gingerbread trim, the vaguely Swiss-style house was perfect for their B&B purpose. It had been custom-made by the town's leading architect, who designed some of Newport's finest homes in the late 19th century.

The Tylers offer three spacious guest rooms, each with queensize bed, working fireplace, sitting area and TV/VCR. The most popular is the Redwood Room with majestic canopy bed and a clawfoot soaking tub. Two suites with king or queensize beds have sitting rooms with new fireplaces. The premier Perry Suite also has a jacuzzi tub.

Guests enjoy the large main-floor living room and library, each with fireplace and eleven-foot-high ceiling. A fireplace also enhances the dining room, where breakfast begins with a buffet of cereal, muffins, yogurt, fresh fruit and juices. A plated seasonal fruit, perhaps warm apple compote or bananas foster, follows. The main event could be eggs benedict, breakfast casserole or french toast made with Portuguese sweet bread. Harlan does the baking, Sheila the cooking and both serve. The side porch is employed for breakfast and afternoon refreshments in season.

(401) 847-7081 or (888) 834-7081. Fax (401) 847-5545. www.architectsinn.com. Three rooms and two suites with private baths. Doubles, $199 to $285 May-October, $125 to $175 rest of year.

Admiral Fitzroy Inn, 398 Thames St., Newport 02840.

The interior of this plain, shingled box-like structure masks its not-so-distant status as the St. Mary's Church convent.

Newly billed as "a European-style hotel in the heart of Newport" by the Newport Harbor Corp., also owner of the posh Castle Hill Inn & Resort, the seventeen-room B&B is quite appealing inside, especially the striking hand-painted decorative touches everywhere. Done for the former innkeeper by a young artist, they vary from borders to murals and entire walls and are worthy of a gallery. One guest room's large mural of an apricot tree in a clay pot is so realistic it even shows bugs and a butterfly.

An elevator serves rooms on three floors, most of them quite spacious by Newport standards and artfully furnished with antique queensize or king beds, white duvet comforters, and upholstered or wicker loveseats and chairs. All have TVs and small refrigerators, some hidden in hand-stenciled armoires.

A European-style continental breakfast is taken at individual tables in the cheery main-floor dining room, its walls highlighted by hand-painted garlands of flowers.

(401) 848-8000 or (866) 848-8780. Fax (401) 848-8006. www.admiralfitzroy.com. Sixteen rooms and one suite with private baths. Doubles, $175 to $325 late June through mid-September, $85 to $295 rest of year.

Gourmet Treats

With everything from delis to food boutiques, the Newport area is a paradise for the palate of the wandering gourmet. Among the possibilities:

Newport Mansions. On most visitors' must-see lists, several of Newport's principal tourist attractions also hold special culinary appeal. The dining rooms in all are on display, and at the Marble House is a gold ballroom in which the owner once gave a ten-course dinner for 100 dogs in full party dress. At the fabulous Breakers, you get to see a number of kitchens and butler's pantries, an area larger than most houses. The dining room at Kingscote, an oft-overlooked Greek Revival cottage, is one of the nicest rooms in all the mansions – decorated with Tiffany glass tiles and stained-glass panels of dahlias.

The Market on the Boulevard, 43 Memorial Blvd., is a large, upscale grocery store with a market café and espresso bar, a bakery, deli and "gourmet to go." And what wonderful things do go – in our case, a dish of oriental beef with a vegetable medley for supper at home, plus a ginger-pear tart and lemon-raspberry roulade for dessert. There are wonderful breads, choice meats, exotic produce, select condiments, fresh pastas – you name it, Newport's beautiful (and ordinary) people come here to buy it. From salads to pastries to sandwiches (the last delightfully named for behind-the-scenes workers at the mansions), all the makings for a gourmet picnic, lunch or dinner are here.

Boulangerie Obelix, 382 Spring St., is the place where restaurateur John Bach-Sorenson and crew bake and sell their marvelous breads and pastries. Besides an ample supply to go, there are novel sandwiches to try here. One mouthful – in more ways than one – is composed of roasted eggplant, zucchini, peppers, green onions, spinach, tomatoes, Vermont goat cheese, extra virgin olive oil and balsamic vinegar. Another combines prosciutto and asiago, with arugula and artichoke tapenade. You can order soups, a ham and swiss quiche, scones, a peach tart and danish pastries. Open daily, 7 to 7 (to 5 winter weekdays).

For casual dining, the recently relocated and enlarged **Cappuccino's Bakery & Café,** run by chefs Paul and Cindy Donnelly, is an exceptional breakfast and lunch spot on the outskirts of town at 890 West Main Road (Route 114) in Middletown. The salads are great, the chicken-onion-bacon quiche was hearty and we drooled over the white-chocolate and strawberry bars. **Ocean Breeze Café** at 580 Thames St. stocks breakfast pastries, baked goods and an array of sandwiches and salads along with gourmet coffees and teas. **The Wharf Pub & Restaurant** on Bowen's Wharf offers build-your-own sandwiches and 36 microbrews, best taken on an outdoor deck. Nearby, the aromas drifting through the door may draw you into the **Cookie Jar** for chocolate chip, gingersnap or oatmeal-raisin cookies. The new **Panera Bread Bakery** at 49 Long Wharf Mall draws the faithful for the usual suspects.

Coffee and espresso are the rage in this seaport town, as elsewhere. **Starbucks** is at a prime corner at Thames and Church, beside the Trinity Church green. **Ocean Coffee Roasters** occupies a key location at 22 Washington Square and **Coffee Grinder** holds a strategic position on Bannister's Wharf. Out Lower Thames are **Espresso Yourself** and the excellent **Steaming Bean Expresso Café,** where old magazines displayed in the windows draw browsers inside for pastries, sandwiches and desserts, and **Espressibles of Newport,** which advertises collectibles, gifts and antiques but seemed to be mainly coffee. **Higher Grounds** serves the upper crust along Bellevue Avenue.

Fragrant dried flowers hang from the ceiling and jars of loose teas, herbs and teapots line the shelves at **Tea & Herb Essence,** 475 Thames St. Proprietor Laureen Grenus offers everything from passionfruit to hibiscus heaven teas to herbal remedies and health-care products, handmade soaps, gifts and more. Some of the herbs and flowers come from her gardens out front.

Lower Thames Street harbors not one but two gourmet pet stores, **Salty Dog** ("gifts for dogs and cats and the people who love them") and **The Gourmet Dog,** with a fire hydrant at the entrance and a "dog bakery" dispensing all-natural premium dog biscuits.

A most colorful kitchen shop is **Runcible Spoon** (the title taken from "The Owl and the Pussycat") at 180 Bellevue Ave. Amid the garlic salsa and the lobster platters, we were taken with a line of Portuguese pottery with tiny vegetables like radishes and scallions depicted thereon. Another good shop is **Kitchen Pot Pourri** at 42 West Main Road, Middletown, a house full of kitchen gadgets and accessories, baking items, pots and pans, placemats, cookbooks and the like.

Nearby, the growing **Newport Vineyards & Winery** at 909 East Main Road (Route 138), Middletown, has raised its profile under the ownership of John and Paul Nunes. The brothers bought the vineyard in 1995 and expanded plantings to 50 acres, much of it on land their great-grandfather had acquired in 1917. They produce quite a variety of European-style reds and whites, most in the $12.99 to $19.99 range. Their most popular is the Great White wine ($9.99), a gold medal winner at the International Eastern Wine Competition. Their white port wine is one of the few released along the East Coast, as is their new vidal icewine. The winery is open for tours and tastings daily 10 to 5 (Sunday noon to 5). The complex includes a restaurant, bakery and deli, gift shop, art gallery and farmer's market.

Also of interest in Middletown is **Coddington Brewing Co.,** Newport County's first brew pub and restaurant, open daily from 11 o'clock at 210 Coddington Hwy.

Gourmet Side Trips

Take a side trip down pastoral Route 77 along the picturesque East Bay. At 2753 Main Road in Tiverton, stop at **Here & Now Tea Room** with a wall-size mural of an English garden, a water view and a deck for afternoon tea (Tuesday-Sunday from 11:30, $10). In the quaint hamlet of Tiverton Four Corners is **Provender,** a specialty-foods store and upscale sandwich shop, where you can obtain lunch to eat in or take out. Across the intersection is **Gray's Ice Cream,** a favorite of Rhode Islanders since 1923. It offers 32 flavors from coffee to ginger, plus eleven varieties of sherbet and frozen yogurt. Try a cabinet, the local version of a milk shake. Farther along are **Walker's Roadside Stand,** where the folks from suave Little Compton shop in summer for produce and preserves, and **Olga's Cup & Saucer,** a seasonal place next door, where you can stop for coffee, biscotti or pizzas.

Sakonnet Vineyards, the largest and oldest continuously producing winery in New England, is three miles south at 162 West Main Road in Little Compton. Owners Earl and Susan Samson are known for some of the East's better wines. Among their annual output of up to 50,000 cases are a distinguished reserve chardonnay and a pinot noir, retailing for $24.95 and $15.95 respectively. Since 1999 Sakonnet has produced a world-class sparkling wine, made in the traditional methode champenoise ($29.95). Its latest gold-medal award winner is an estate gewürztraminer that won "best of show" among all white wines at the Monterey International Wine Competition. You can sample the offerings in a large tasting room with oriental rugs on the floors, daily 10 to 6 Memorial Day through September (11 to 5 rest of year). The winery hosts numerous special events of culinary interest, including a winter Master Chef Series of cooking classes ending in dinner. **The Roost,** the original farmhouse on the property, offers three bedrooms with private baths and breakfast for overnight guests (doubles, $125).

To the northwest of Newport across Narragansett Bay is the historic village of Wickford, one of New England's most picturesque. For gourmands, the highlight among many fine shops and historic structures is **Wickford Gourmet Foods** at 21 West Main St. Here are two floors chock full of great specialty foods, condiments, cookbooks, a coffee bar, Rhode Island's largest selection of cheeses and pâtés, chocolates and superior takeout foods to go. Or you can choose from **The Café at Wickford Gourmet** menu of salads, sandwiches and specialty plates in the $7 to $9 range and eat upstairs or outside on a patio. And on Thursday and Friday evenings, you can enjoy more substantial café dinners ($16.50 to $21.50) prepared by acclaimed French chef Pascal Leffray, whose oft-changing repertoire recalls favorites from his former Chez Pascal restaurants in Providence and Narragansett. In an historic barn behind is **Wickford Gourmet's Kitchen & Table Store.** This expanding enterprise offers everything from cooking classes to gift baskets. Gourmet Retailer magazine ranks it among the top twelve retailers in the country.

Crowds enjoy food and festivities in Waterplace Park in downtown Providence.

Providence, R.I.

Cinderella of Cuisine

Not all that long ago, Rhode Island's capital city was known for its colleges, its historic architecture and its earthy Little Italy. If you had to find a place to eat here, your choices were pretty well limited to the downtown MacDonald's, student haunts on College Hill and the dated, gaudy shrines to spaghetti along Federal Hill.

In terms of culinary excitement, however, Providence has gone from rags to riches. This Cinderella of cuisine has vaulted into the national food limelight. Thousands of restaurant seats have been added in a city whose population has remained roughly stable at 160,000. More than one-third of the city's 565 restaurants opened in four years between 1996 and 1999. A Providence entry was ranked among the year's best new restaurants nationally by Esquire magazine almost every year since 1994. Budding chefs and restaurateurs have been drawn to Providence. And successful Providence restaurateurs have branched out – in Boston, Miami and Los Angeles.

Some credit former mayor Vincent A. (Buddy) Cianci Jr. for the city's heightened culinary awareness. A food lover as well as civic booster, he initiated a revolving loan fund for new restaurant start-ups and helped cut through the red tape for liquor licenses. He also marketed his own brand of marinara sauce and followed with the Mayor's Own Coffee and the Mayor's Own Olive Oil.

Others credit the expansion of Johnson & Wales University, whose College of Culinary Arts students and graduates provide a steady stream of well-trained kitchen, dining room and management staff.

Still others credit George Germon and Johanne Killeen, who opened Al Forno in 1980 and turned it into one of the top-rated restaurants in the country. Not only have they trained many a leading chef (a dozen played starring roles in a 1999 alumni dinner they hosted in Boston). They also have helped several open their first restaurants.

Providence's culinary revival has gone hand in hand with the restoration of the city's downtown riverfront, which underwent a $1.5 billion facelift as part of the most ambitious renewal project in America. The Providence River, for years obscured by the world's widest bridge, has been uncovered and flows like a canal beneath graceful new Venetian-style spans connecting downtown with College Hill and the historic East Side. Cobblestone riverwalks, an amphitheater and food vendors enhance Waterplace Park with its celebrated WaterFire "singing bonfires" blazing in the middle of the river on summer nights. The emerging "Downcity" arts and entertainment district and the huge new Providence Place shopping mall draw people downtown day and night.

Providence offers countless riches for the gourmand. They go beyond the indigenous jonnycakes and quahogs to the homegrown Italian markets of Federal Hill and the fresh seafood catch from the Rhode Island shore. Nowhere are the riches more evident than in its restaurants. They helped spark this Cinderella city's rejuvenation, and now share in its success.

Dining

The Best of the Best

Al Forno, 577 South Main St.

Food at its gutsiest is served at this widely honored restaurant, a bustling yet comfortable establishment that generates national publicity and turn-away crowds.

Rhode Island School of Design graduates Johanne Killeen and George Germon applied their artistic talents to northern Italian cooking and developed a cult following for Al Forno, which literally means "from the oven."

Their followers love the grilled pizzas done over the open fire with ever-changing toppings, they love the salads dressed with extra-virgin olive oil and balsamic vinegar, they love the oven-baked pastas bearing such goodies as grilled squid and spicy scotch bonnet peppers, they love the grilled items done on the wood grill using fruitwoods and even grapevines from nearby Sakonnet Vineyards, and they love the fabulous desserts cooked to order. And they don't seem to mind the often long waits for a table.

The husband-and-wife team, then in their twenties, started modestly enough in 1980 in pintsize quarters on Steeple Street at the foot of College Hill after working in Italy. They had no room for a wood-fired pizza oven so cooked thin pizza dough over a wood grill. Their grilled pizzas caught on, and the couple expanded beyond northern Italian confines to offer cuisines from other regions of Italy and its Mediterranean neighbors.

Even with a relocation to a much larger, 19th-century brick building near the waterfront, there still are usually lines at the door when the restaurant opens for dinner, since the demand exceeds the supply and no reservations are taken.

Al Forno occupies two floors of a building that once served as the municipal stables for Providence. Dining is at close-together tables seating a total of 140, casual in a downstairs room and a bit more formal upstairs. The rest of the space seems to be half kitchen, one for each floor with ten cooks in each. The fare is deceptively simple. Al Forno's magic is in transforming the simplest, most seasonal ingredients into something intensely flavorful.

On the clamorous main floor we enjoyed one of our more memorable meals. Grilled pizza has always been Al Forno's signature dish. With a crackly thin crust and different toppings every day (ours had onion, gorgonzola, chicken, tarragon and tomato coulis), it is sensational. We also loved a starter of cool vermicelli with five little salads (cucumber, jìcama, carrot, red pepper and Egyptian beans).

Johanne Killeeen and George Germon at Al Forno.

The menu changes daily, but you might find a spicy clam roast with hot sausage and native corn in a tomato broth, roasted haddock on a bed of roasted vegetable stew, pepper-grilled chicken paillard agro dolce with arugula and parmigiano-reggiano on a bed of balsamic onions, confit of duck legs with a trio of homemade chutneys, grilled rabbit and veal sausages over roasted carrots, and grilled veal tenderloin with roasted crimini and portobello mushrooms on grilled polenta. Lasagna, made with light sheets of pasta folded over freestyle, might contain sliced grilled chicken breast with fresh tomato salad or turkey, béchamel sauce and diced vegetables. Our choucroute garni included three of the fattest sausages we ever saw topping mild sauerkraut, accompanied by wide noodles sparked with fresh coriander. The skirt steak, seared right on the coals, came with wilted watercress and a green chile sauce. Portions are huge and we saw many others leave, as we did, with doggy bags.

The wine list, featuring Italian vintages, starts reasonably and goes sky high.

Dessert, which must be ordered with the main course, is the icing on the cake. We'd try any of Johanne's special tarts for two; the lemon soufflé version is ethereal. Another masterpiece is a sourdough waffle with caramel-walnut ice cream and chocolate. The "grand cookie finale" for two has been widely imitated. Here a large tray on a pedestal holds two kinds of chocolate cookies, ricotta fritters, pinwheels, ginger molasses cookies and chocolate truffles – a mix and match play on textures and flavors that's heaven for cookie lovers.

Al Forno's decor is secondary to the food. Short fabric curtains hang from the high beams, tables are covered with sheets of paper, the wine is poured into stemless glasses like those used for vin ordinaire in France, and the atmosphere is jolly and just right. George designed the upstairs room in a sophisticated European style, using lots of dark slate and bluestone marble to go with brick and stone walls. The couple turned to Italy for many of their accessories, including cutlery from Florence in the trattoria style, with long-tined pasta forks and pasta spoons. They are artists and restaurant designers as well as highly inventive cooks who wrote the cookbook, *Cucina Simpatica.*

The accolades continue to flow freely to the unassuming, down-to-earth couple, who travel widely to teach cooking and share their secrets. The James Beard Foundation has named them the best chefs in the Northeast and cited them in 1999 for having the best restaurant.

(401) 273-9760. www.alforno.com. Entrées, $23.95 to $32.95. Dinner, Tuesday-Friday 5 to 10, Saturday 4 to 10.

New Rivers, 7 Steeple St.

The intimate space where Al Forno got its start is now the setting for nationally honored chef Bruce Tillinghast, a former art teacher who trained with Madeleine Kamman in Boston. He cooked in executive dining rooms before returning to his hometown to open his own operation, happily unpretentious and lacking in attitude. Nice things happen to nice people, and it wasn't long before he was a finalist for the annual James Beard Award, "Best Chef of the Northeast."

Dining area near front entrance at New Rivers.

New Rivers tucks tables for 40 and a small bar into a pair of rooms in 1870 twin storefronts in the front of a 1793 warehouse built for iron merchants at the base of College Hill, near the confluence of the two recently uncovered rivers for which the restaurant is named. A striking still life of six red pears glistening against a stone wall sets the theme in the main dining room, a beauty in persimmon red with hunter green trim, where tables are dressed with pale yellow cloths and fresh flowers. The smaller side dining room has more pale yellow, from cloths to walls, and a yellow-tiled bar at which some folks like to perch and eat. A shelf above the bar displays an assortment of pears – gifts to the chef inspired by the painting in the main room.

Bruce and his chef de cuisine make a point of supporting sustainable agriculture and favor organic products. They change their creative, contemporary fare frequently, borrowing from Tuscan, Thai, Portuguese, Middle Eastern and Caribbean cuisines. The menu is nicely categorized by nibbles, starters and salads, small meals and pasta, and main dishes from the grill and oven. Three-course bistro meals for $22, available Monday-Thursday, are the best deals in town.

Nime chow spring rolls combining lobster meat, julienned vegetables, sprouts and pungent basil rolled in cool Thai rice wrappers, served with a gingery dipping sauce, are the specialty appetizer. You also could start with sesame-ginger crêpes with Maine crabmeat, radish slaw and hoisin-lime vinaigrette or baked oysters with pickled onion and tasso ham stuffing and horseradish aioli.

Move on to one of the small meals or pastas, as basic as a half-pound burger on a Portuguese sweet roll or as exotic as sundried tomato and artichoke tortellini with Tuscan sausage, roasted fennel, olives and mint. The polenta with wild mushrooms is like eating a cloud. These plus a dessert of fresh fruit and cookies will satisfy most diners.

Heartier appetites are well served by items from the grill and oven: perhaps native striped bass on sweet corn polenta with tomatillo and cubanelle pepper relish, sage-rubbed pork tenderloin on white beans with grilled radicchio and braised onion jus, and grilled ribeye steak with caramelized shallot butter, asparagus and frites.

A made-to-order lemon tartlet, garnished with seasonal fruit, is the specialty dessert. Other standouts are warm apple crostada with pumpkin ice cream, homemade ice creams like huckleberry or rum-spiked praline, and a cookie plate bearing eight New Rivers favorites.

The extensive, reasonably priced wine list has been honored by Wine Spectator.

(401) 751-0350. www.newriversrestaurant.com. Entrées, $25 to $35. Dinner, Monday-Saturday, 5:30 to 10.

Mill's Tavern, 101 North Main St.

A four-foot-long silver fork placed horizontally on the wall above the stone-framed kitchen sets the culinary motif at this updated, 21st-century tavern specializing in wood-fired, modern American cooking.

Considerable hype was accorded the restaurant's rich but subtle interior as fashioned by chef-owner Jaime D'Oliveira's wife Kim , a partner in her father's Morris Nathanson Design firm and also the daughter of Roxy Nathanson, who ran our favorite Arboretum restaurant in East Providence a couple of decades back.

Little remains of the converted 1850s mill for which the place is named. Instead, picture a blend of timeless Manhattan steakhouse and modern New England tavern: high ceilings, wrought-iron candle chandeliers, planked oak floors, wood paneling and white-clothed tables flanked by leather banquettes or dark wood chairs upholstered in black and cream.

The modern menu reflects the evolution of chef Jaime, ranked by Food & Wine magazine as one of the country's ten best new chefs when he was at his former Angels restaurant a few doors away. He went on to become executive chef and director of kitchen operations for the Providence-based Ned Grace restaurant group. He opened ten Capital Grilles across the country and drew heavily on his steakhouse background as well as his earlier work at Al Forno for this, the first venture of his new Providence Hospitality Group.

The rotisserie, wood oven and grill impart a smoky, outdoorsy flavor to meats such as beef tenderloin steak with a velvety mushroom glace de viande and a veal porterhouse with grilled peach and opal basil "relish."

A tart tomato-citrus jam serves as a counterpoint for crispy sweet salmon, a signature item pan-seared and served with a mound of French lentils. Grilled swordfish is sauced with capers and mustard, and roasted Carolina trout with heirloom tomatoes and cucumber vinaigrette. Two of the more intriguing offerings are roasted "osso buco" of monkfish in a spicy crab broth and roasted saddle and leg of rabbit with dry vermouth and black mission figs.

Communal table fronts kitchen at Mill's Tavern.

The raw bar here, good as it is, is upstaged by the "salad bar," a bar in name only. It might yield a grilled salad of octopus, sunflower sprouts, olives and black mission fig and a shaved fennel and pear salad with mache, walnuts, cabrales and hazelnut dressing. "From the pantry" come such appetizers as braised littlenecks and grilled chorizo in a spicy tomato and Sagres beer broth, open-face rabbit ravioli with mascarpone and truffled corn jus, and the signature "Mill's sandwich:" a fluffy buttermilk biscuit studded with black currants and filled with duck confit, topped with rich seared foie gras and balanced with sweet, tea-braised figs.

An artisan cheese plate is a fitting ending to such a procession of taste treats. So are desserts like warm pumpkin spice cake with maple-cream cheese ice cream and candied pumpkin seeds, roquefort cheesecake with pear confit and port-thyme elixir, and the Mill's sundae with ginger ice cream, roasted pears, butterscotch and spiced pecans.

(401) 272-3331. Entrées, $17.50 to $31. Dinner nightly, 5 to 10 or 11.

Café Nuovo, One Citizens Plaza.

The owners of Capriccio, a glamorous Italian restaurant of the old school in the city's financial district, branched out with this dramatic spot along the revived downtown riverfront. The views of water and skyline are sensational from the soaring windows that make up one side of the angular dining room off the lobby rotunda of the Citizens Bank tower. The best riverfront tables in town are those for 60 diners on the outdoor terrace beside the Providence River.

The large and airy interior seating 130 is spectacular in gray, white and red. Sleek red lacquered chairs and banquettes flank well-spaced tables set with white cloths, votive candles, fresh flowers, and clear glass salt and pepper shakers. A partly open kitchen plays a starring role at one end. The sedate bar area wraps around the curve of the rotunda near the other end. A few abstract artworks provide color.

The setting matches the trendy food that's architectural as well as unusual. Chef Timothy Kelly, formerly in Manhattan, has been with owner Dimitri Kriticos since

Patrons enjoy Cafe Nuovo's outdoor tables for dinner beside downtown riverfront.

Café Nuovo opened in 1994. He calls the cuisine fusion, although his classic French training is evident in his terrific sauces.

His wide repertoire certainly is appealing. As we dipped excellent rustic breads into a saucer of olive oil garnished with roasted red peppers, one of us said she could happily eat everything on the lunch menu, which is seldom the case. She settled for a couple of stellar appetizers, the nime chow shrimp rolls with cellophane noodles, tiny vegetables and a lemongrass dipping sauce, and a chopped salad of cucumbers, tomatoes, asparagus, snap peas and more, standing tall in a radicchio cup. Both were as exciting to taste as to look at. Against these high-rise theatrics the low-rise smoked salmon club sandwich with side potato and tossed salads looked somewhat mundane, though it proved to be good and filling.

The pastry chef's desserts are the talk of the town. The pot o' mousse yields dark and chocolate mousses in a chocolate pot with chocolate, mango and raspberry sauces and cappuccino ice cream. The strawberry baba with grand marnier foam and mascarpone ice cream is another knockout. We enjoyed the "crystal bowl" filled with a selection of fruit sorbets and ice creams, studded with a candy stick.

At night, the chef traverses the world for appetizers like escargots bourguignonne, beef carpaccio, lobster and avocado sushi maki, and a treat called beef papasan – spicy tenderloin with crisp salsify sticks, ginger-grilled shiitake mushrooms and lemon-tamari lacquer. The arugula salad with warm pecan-coated Vermont goat cheese, baby pear tomatoes and lemon-thyme triangular tuiles is a work of art.

Nuovo's innovative pasta and risotto dishes give new meaning to the genre: perhaps a risotto of creamy carnaroli rice with sea scallops and a halo of pinot noir syrup, penne tossed with tomatoes and basil and topped with chicken and artichoke hearts, and lobster-stuffed raviolis with half a lobster tail over Narragansett succotash. One of the main courses could be rainbow trout wrapped in crisp potato strands, stuffed with mustard greens and portobello mushrooms and served around an arugula salad with raspberries and frizzled leeks. Others could be Hudson Valley duck breast and confit with salmi sauce and "lamb two ways:" Moroccan lamb tagine and rack of lamb crusted with goat cheese and almonds. An addition to the menu details seven meat and fish dishes in the steakhouse style.

The wine list covers a wide range from the high twenties to $375. Waiters take orders without notes and seem to get everything right.

(401) 421-2525. www.cafenuovo.com. Entrées, $21.95 to $31.95. Lunch, Monday-Friday 11:30 to 3. Dinner, Monday-Saturday 5 to 10:30 or 11.

Neath's, 262 South Water St.

West meets East in Cambodian chef-owner Neath Pal's stylish New American bistro. Neath (pronounced Nee-it) immigrated to Providence with his family in 1975 and worked summers in Newport restaurants before going off to study at LaVarenne in Paris. He returned for a job at Al Forno, "the best restaurant in my home city." In the kitchen there he met his Irish-Italian wife Beth Toolan, now a physician. He moved on to help start L'Epicureo and Grappa before opening his own place in 1998 in a former industrial-look restaurant in a restored warehouse along the river.

He kept the angular main-floor bar but warmed and softened the upstairs space with bold yellow and red walls beneath a high wood ceiling. White cloths, votive candles and small vases with fresh flowers top the widely spaced tables seating 75, some next to big windows overlooking the developing parkland along the river. The whole family pitched in, from his sister, a restaurant designer in California, to his mother-in-law, who made aprons for the wait staff. Neath paused to reflect beside a montage of photos of family and staff along the stairway that tells the story.

Although he table-hops nightly and his wife hostesses weekends, there's nothing he'd rather do than "be back behind the line cooking." His is the vision that fuses New England ingredients with French and Asian preparations for a highly personalized cooking style. It showed up in appetizers of shrimp and shiitake-mushroom dumplings, steamed and then grilled and served with a shoyu dipping sauce, and wood-grilled baguette slices lathered with a coconut and scallion sauce and a bowl of extra dipping sauce for good measure. The star of the evening was a special salad of chilled Maine crab with diced cucumbers and tomatoes and delicate potato gaufrettes, the crabmeat stunningly pure and the wafers so thin and intricately latticed as not to be believed.

Signature main dishes are lobster with snow peas and shiitake mushrooms, simmered in coconut milk with red curry and served over garlicky chow foon noodles; grilled pork loin chop with stir-fried Asian broccoli and sweet potato gratin, and pan-roasted Hudson Valley duck breast and confit with a subtle ginger glaze over sweet potato gratin and wilted spinach. We were well pleased with the oven-roasted Chilean sea bass, succulent and of the melt-in-the-mouth variety, teamed with jasmine rice and a cool cucumber salad. The chicken breast rubbed with lemongrass was wood-grilled and served with a Thai basil salad, but we couldn't find the green papaya that the menu promised. The lapse was redeemed by extra ginger ice cream on the signature dessert of crunchy fried wontons filled with molten chocolate, which everyone raves about but must be an acquired taste. Passionfruit crème brûlée served in an almond lace cookie is another favorite.

Pleasantly priced, the primarily American wine list included a Bonny Doon Pacific Rim riesling that was quite appropriate for the fare. Flawless service was provided by a waitress who not only recited the complicated specials but also took the orders without notes. As darkness fell, the interior walls glowed and the lights of the city

Chef-owner Neath Pal relaxes in upstairs dining room at Neath's.

gleamed across the river shimmering outside the window – a fitting backdrop for some mighty interesting food.

(401 751-3700. www.neaths.com. Entrées, $21 to $28. Dinner, Tuesday-Sunday 5:30 to 10 or 10:30.

XO Steakhouse, 125 North Main St.

"Life is uncertain, order dessert first," begins the menu at this unconventional restaurant. It then proceeds to list the sweets, prior to the caesar "the way it should be" salad and the tuna seviche cones, the tempura-grilled Maine lobster and the slow-cooked shortribs with Korean slaw. John Elkhay, executive chef and co-owner, wants you to save room for the grand finale.

Peripatetic John, whom we first met years ago at the late Café in the Barn in nearby Seekonk, Mass., has always been in the vanguard – at In-Prov, Angels, Atomic Grill and now here, in the space once occupied by Angels and a succession of short-lived restaurants. He and co-owners Rick and Cheryl Bready doubled the size, expanding into an adjacent storefront to produce the XO Café – lately renamed XO Steakhouse – with an open wood-oven kitchen and the most offbeat, eclectic decor in town.

It's an avant-garde fantasy in ivory, gold and black, augmented by pop art and mirrors. A banquette along one wall serves close-together tables topped with black lamps trimmed in gold roping. The opposite wall is home to two sensuous black-mesh nude sculptures and four art panels endearingly pairing artists with chefs and inscribed in gold: Picasso-Pepin, Warhol-Bocuse, Schnabel-Child and Manet-Elkhay. Engraved inscriptions identify seats of regulars in the convivial, cigar-friendly bar in the original dining room. Exotic martinis are served in what the barmaid calls the fanciest stemware in Rhode Island.

The food measures up in the Elkhay tradition of on-the-edge style, innovation and presentation – no longer fusion to the max, but rather cutting-edge steakhouse. Still the favorite starter is the bento box sampler, a shiny black Japanese box yielding four of the best: crunchy, rice flour-battered calamari rings with smoked jalapeño mayonnaise and chopped hot peppers, lobster wontons, tempura mushroom fries and teriyaki beef on a stick.

Yucca-crusted Norwegian salmon, hoisin-roasted duck and braised lamb shanks are listed among house specialties. The rest of the menu is comprised mainly of prime steaks and chops with a choice of sauces, culminating in the XO filet topped with sliced seared scallops and macadamia nut butter on a bed of roasted asparagus. Lobster-mashed potatoes, red pepper- parmesan spaetzle and truffle fries are among the sides.

The crème brûlée tray is a selection of three tiny pots of caramelized custards whose flavors could be banana, ginger, mango, coconut, maple, clove or rosewater. The pineapple upside-down cake with guava sorbet appealed at an autumn visit.

The place is named for a zesty Asian sauce, but also plays on the word extraordinary. That's just how Elkhay fans describe it.

(401) 273-9090. www.xocafe.com. Entrées, $18 to $35. Dinner nightly, 5 to 10 or 11.

L'Epicureo, 311 Westminster St.

From a humble start in her late father's butcher shop, Rozann and Tom Buckner built a hugely successful Federal Hill bistro that moved in 2005 into showy quarters in the Hotel Providence. The move was not only a feather in the new hotel's cap but provided a larger kitchen and a wider arena for Tom Buckner's much-acclaimed cooking skills.

Beyond a posh lounge and piano bar called Brio is a 120-seat, Renaissance-style dining room with floors of slate, a trickling fountain in the center and three massive crystal chandeliers overhead. Huge gilt-framed paintings by the Old Masters enrich one burgundy wall of the main dining room, while vintage wine bottles are on display in a wall of glass and stainless steel. A smaller, less opulent dining room handles overflow or private parties, and a courtyard terrace is used for dining in season.

The food measures up to the surroundings, thanks to Tom's twenty-year association in the meat market with his late father-in-law, Joseph DiGiglio. "He was known for the best meat market in the country," says Tom. "And we're trying to be the best restaurant." As his mentor taught him, Tom ages the restaurant's beef for six weeks, smokes his own salmon on a state-of-the-art wood grill, cuts his own halibut, stuffs his calamari ("nobody does that any more"), bakes all the rosemary-perfumed focaccia and makes his own ice creams. When his wife utters the usual buzzwords that "everything is made from scratch," you know that's the case here.

The Buckners' newly broadened menu ranges widely from the modern (broiled swordfish with citrus butter, mango chutney and sweet potato fries) to the classic (veal osso buco, presented not sliced but on the bone, shank upright, garnished with a parsley-garlic gremolata and encircled by risotto milanese). Surprises include an open-face Maine lobster pot pie with truffle sauce, the lobster's head and tail positioned so the dish looks like a lobster. Another is a Tuscan-style slow-braised pork belly, full of flavor after having been marinated for two days in a blend of thirteen herbs, then brined for two days and finally poached in its liquid to cook for twelve hours. Still another flavorful dish is handmade lobster ravioli, enhanced by caramelized sea scallops in a cognac cream sauce. Ditto for the English pea risotto with chicken livers and apple-smoked bacon.

A crab, artichoke and potato napoleon, shrimp and spinach crespelle with

Chandeliers and gilt-framed paintings convey Renaissance-era theme at L'Epicureo.

gorgonzola cream, lobster fritters with spicy salsa and an asparagus and artichoke salad with goat cheese dressing are among the starters, but knowing regulars go for the chef's antipasto sampler for the table to share. And everyone goes for Tom's exemplary desserts, be they the special tiramisu over espresso crème anglaise, the rustic apple crostada or the trio of exotic ice creams with a shortbread cookie.

Although the size and grandeur of the new L'Epicureo dwarf the understated and intimate original, the Buckners' sophisticated style and polished service continue.

(401) 521-3333. Entrées, $20 to $39. Dinner, Monday-Saturday 5 to 10 or 11, Sunday noon to 9.

10 Steak and Sushi, 55 Pine St.

Call it exotic, funky, sexy, sophisticated, as the ads and reviewers do. Cutting-edge chef John Elkhay calls it "the next evolution in food," as served at another of his new Providence restaurants.

Always at the cutting edge, in this one he joined the most unlikely of dining trends – healthful, low-fat cuisine and prime red meat – in one improbable combination and pulled it off. Designed with a capital D, the high-ceilinged interior is a palette of blues on blue, from the menu to the cobalt blue bottoms of the water glasses to the lights behind the stainless-steel bar. It's also sinewy and curvy, from the outlines on the windows and a pair of nudes on the walls to the prime tables positioned around a circular banquette in the front window and the curving sushi bar in back. A partition of undulating ironwork – complete with hanging bud vases holding exotic flowers that are changed weekly – separates the main bar from the long and deep dining area where close-together tables are dressed with white linens and tiny lamps. Pulsating Latin music plays in the background to complement the sensuousness of the ambiance as well as the menu terminology ("fore play" and "entrées we love.")

The left side of the oversize menu lists nigiri and sashimi, sushi rolls "for beginners," "designer rolls" and large samplers called "love boats for party animals." There are also seviche and items from a raw bar, as well as a handful of appetizers and "green things." The menu's right-hand side details a few fish and other entrées, such as mahogany-glazed salmon, seared ahi tuna over sesame spinach and grilled meatloaf. The heart of the menu is titled the 1010° Fahrenheit Grill. It includes the signature aged prime steaks as well as rack of lamb and veal chop Tuscan style. Three sauces are available, as are ten sides.

Prime window tables at 10 Steak and Sushi.

Those who order – and finish – the specialty 40-ounce prime porterhouse steak have their names engraved on the Club 10 plaque in the foyer.

For lunch, we were well satisfied with the bento box, bearing a panoply of treats from sushi rolls to tempura shrimp, and a perfect cobb salad, properly arranged in rows over a creamy avocado dressing.

The dessert menu is presented with three-D glasses for greater impact. Up pop the goodies, ranging from the specialty chocolate soufflé, pre-ordered with the meal in the local tradition, to mango-papaya carpaccio with coconut sorbet and a trio of chocolate mousses.

Martinis, margaritas and mojitos are featured in the lively bar.

(401) 453-2333. www.tenprimesteak.com. Entrées, $19.95 to $36.95. Lunch, Tuesday-Friday 11:30 to 5. Dinner, Monday-Saturday 5 to 10 or 11.

Gracie's, 194 Washington St.

It wears a low profile, but this relocated restaurant is considered locally among the best in town. Owner Ellen Gracyalny closed the original Federal Hill spot to move to larger quarters in the arts and entertainment district downtown. Renovations transformed the former Players Corner Pub into a picture of elegant yellows and browns: a high-ceilinged dining room with soaring windows, well spaced tables and rich wood columns and dividers between dining area and bar. Splashes of stars are the decorative theme, representing "a dream come true" for the Gracie team and cut into everything from sculptures to desserts.

Executive chef Christopher Carno, a Johnson & Wales grad like most of the cooking staff, offers an appealing menu that aspires to the heights. Made for grazing is a series of salads and appetizers, perhaps a smoked salmon and corn salad, braised frog's legs, foie gras au torchon or crispy veal sweetbreads with curried chanterelles and sea urchin roe cream. Best choice may be the signature cheese

Accents of stars on walls and divider set decorative theme at Gracie's.

tasting "with treats and surprises" – a white plate studded with wedges of three cheeses adorned with a dab of tomato concasse, a diced brunoise of sweet figs or half a kumquat sweetened in a sugar syrup for a mesmerizing combination of tart and sweet.

The treats continue with main courses like pan-roasted halibut with an arugula pesto, grilled beef tenderloin with bordelaise sauce or, novelty, a vegetable tasting. The trio of pork – grilled maple-glazed pork tenderloin with warm peaches, smoked pork shoulder with white beans and a barbecued pork belly with potato salad – illustrates the style. A house favorite departing from the contemporary American fare is rigatoni campanaro, a Gracyalny family recipe that mixes sweet and spicy sausage with plum tomatoes and sprigs of parsley.

Dessert could be vanilla crème brûlée, bittersweet chocolate mousse with a caramel center or a seasonal fruit puff pastry tart with ricotta, berry coulis and orange marmalade glaze.

(401) 272-7811. www.graciesprov.com. Entrées, $20 to $35. Lunch, Tuesday-Friday 11:30 to 3. Dinner, Tuesday-Saturday from 5, Sunday from 4.

Other Top Choices

Raphael Bar Risto, 1 Union Station, Providence.

Cranston native Raphael Conte's "progressive Italian" cuisine has impressed Rhode Islanders in five distinct incarnations since 1981. The latest is this sleek place on the ground level of the old Union Station. As designed by wife Elise, the restaurant's streamlined, retro-modern look features, blond maple, travertine marble, big windows and white walls with deco curves and dramatic art. There's an armless and headless Venus de Milo backed by a crackled glass wall with cascading water at the entry. Ahead lie the Tunnel Bar and two dining rooms that could be a modern art museum: an eclectic mix of original pop art, a trio of Warholesque portraits of Marilyn Monroe and a 24-foot-long mural. Photos of Elizabeth Taylor and Humphrey Bogart designate the appropriate rest rooms.

Chef Conte, who never rests on his reputation, recently revamped his menu as well as his philosophy about food. He also discontinued lunch service to concentrate on dinner. He says he's simplifying, backing away from the dozen-ingredients-per-entrée trend for a less complicated (but no less adventurous) menu. Look for such offerings as potato-encrusted Chilean sea bass with pancetta and artichokes, red snapper puttanesca, crispy duck with port wine-plum sauce and grilled veal rib chop with porcini sauce. They join the restaurant's signature lobster fra diavolo and grilled beef tenderloin with crimini demi-glace.

A fisherman, Ralph (short for Raphael) Conte often adds his morning catch to that supplied by his purveyors. Blue crab cakes with lobster scallion salad and cornmeal-fried calamari with cherry pepper aioli are some of his appetizers. A wood grill in the open kitchen produces a with-it roster of pizzas.

The chef imparts an innovative, sometimes flamboyant spin on traditional pastas such as black ravioli stuffed with crabmeat and vodka-flashed shrimp, and tagliatelle with sea scallops, smoked salmon, roasted bell peppers and provolone in a light oregano cream.

Desserts include an acclaimed tiramisu with espresso bean sauce, banana rum baba flambé, cappuccino semifreddo and a refreshing lemon napoleon – lemony cream custard layered with lemon shortbread and lemon anglaise.

(401) 421-4646. Entrées, $19 to $32. Dinner, Monday-Saturday from 5.

Providence Oyster Bar, 283 Atwells Ave.

A strictly seafood house in Federal Hill? That was the niche targeted by Michael Degnan and Frank DiBiase when they opened this bistro-style venture in 2000 in the old Roma Market. The market's pressed-tin ceiling, hardwood floors and brick walls made a stylish backdrop for a raw bar in front, a bar along one side, and a sleek and dark dining room with booths and tables beside a semi-open kitchen.

Seafood in general and oysters in particular get top billing. The raw bar is apt to offer at least a dozen varieties of oysters, about half from Rhode Island and the rest mainly from the Canadian Maritimes. There are fried oysters, oysters rockefeller and a baked oyster trio among such starters as cajun crab cakes, tuna tartare, coconut-crusted shrimp, lobster wontons and steamed littlenecks.

For lunch, we enjoyed a novel salad comprised of sea scallops wrapped with apple-smoked bacon served over field greens with goat cheese and topped with a poached egg. The salad was fabulous. So were the seven-grain and rustic white breads that accompanied, dipped in an unusual (and spicy) reddish oil flavored with five peppers, including habanero and jalapeño, which gave it quite a kick and showed that this is one serious kitchen. Also excellent was the oyster po-boy, a knife-and-fork affair laden with succulent oysters and flanked by fries and coleslaw – an unusually generous platter for $7.95.

Entrées are all seafood, except for blackened chicken pappardelle and filet mignon. Typical are bacon-wrapped monkfish, parmesan-crusted tilapia, blackened tuna with wasabi mayonnaise, grilled swordfish with lemon-herb butter and lobster bouillabaisse.

Desserts include lemon xango (a deep-fried cheesecake), seven-layer cake, white chocolate mousse and key lime tart.

Lately, the owners took over a vacant storefront next door to open **Providence Prime,** a steakhouse. Another first for Federal Hill, it turned out to be as good for prime beef as the Oyster Bar is for seafood.

(401) 272-8866. Entrées, $16.99 to $34.99. Lunch, Tuesday-Friday 11:30 to 4:30. Dinner, Monday-Saturday 5 to 10 or 11.

Moda, 525 South Water St.

The view of the Providence River is terrific and so is the food at this chic, ultra-modern bistro living up to its Spanish-Portuguese name for "style." A lively younger crowd gathers around a back-lit bar in the clubby main-floor lounge with a mirrored ceiling, mostly black quilted walls, a cool tile floor and windows onto the water. Upstairs is quieter and favored for fine dining with a backdrop of city lights reflected in floor-to-ceiling windows and mirrors. Banquette seating flanks black tables beside black walls beneath a hot pink ceiling.

The lounge is the priority of young owner Dino Passaretta, a Rhode Island native who returned after managing lounges in Boston. To oversee the kitchen he lured hotshot local chef Jules Ramos, whom he met when both worked at Café Nuovo a decade earlier.

The chef's credo is progressive American food with Asian and Latin overtones. He offers a fresh take on such appetizers as blue crab rangoon with mango-lime sweet and sour sauce, prime sirloin steak tartare, a duck confit spring roll with spicy szechuan dipping sauce and a signature treat called "hazelnut duck french toast" starring sliced rare duck on a tiny piece of french toast, topped with foie gras mousse and surrounded by grape preserves. Entrées are equally "progressive," from cajun Block Island swordfish with mango salsa and pan-roasted halibut alantejana with chourico sausage and littleneck clams to five-spice pork tenderloin and hazelnut-crusted rack of lamb with goat cheese. Braised rabbit stew over truffled pappardelle is a robust winter dish. Potatoes and vegetables are available as sides.

Warm chocolate valrhona cake with green tea ice cream, Portuguese bread pudding with dried currants and coconut dulce de leche, and lemon-vanilla bean cheesecake with crème fraîche and blueberry confiture are stellar desserts.

(401) 331-2288. www.modarestaurant.com. Entrées, $17 to $34. Dinner, Monday-Saturday 5 to 10 or 11.

Siena, 38 Atwells Ave.

Here is the worthy successor to L'Epicureo, which vacated its intimate quarters in 2005 for a larger location downtown. Into its space moved chef Anthony Tarro and his brother Christopher, the manager, whose family has deep roots in Federal Hill. They undertook a rehab, reconfigured the Italian marble bar to face the open kitchen, warmed up the interior with Tuscan colors and artworks, and added a serene dining room in back. Such a class act is not what you would traditionally expect to find in Providence's Federal Hill section, long a tight little enclave of ethnic eateries, most of them southern Italian.

The promised "Tuscan soul food, Siena style" here is a cut above. Patrons say the tagliatelle alla bolognese is out of this world, thanks to its masterful sauce of prosciutto, pork, pancetta, sirloin, diced vegetables, tomatoes and a touch of cream. They also rave about the branzino, a pan-seared Chilean sea bass fillet finished

Patrons enjoy late Sunday afternoon dinner on sidewalk outside Siena on Federal Hill.

with sea scallops and a creamy scallion sauce, the classic veal dishes and the charcoal-grilled sirloin strip steak drizzled with Tuscan olive oil and served with roasted garlic and a side of warm gorgonzola cream sauce.

To start, there are wood-grilled pizzas, a trio of Tuscan crostini, two superior fried calamari dishes and an assorted antipasti plate. The chocolate torte with raspberry-chocolate sauce and warm pear tart are favorite desserts. The international wine list is affordably priced.

(401) 521-3311. www.sienaprovidence.com. Entrées, $14 to $29. Dinner, Monday-Saturday from 5, Sunday from 3.

Pot au Feu, 44 Custom House St.

The first of Providence's fine downtown restaurants, this split-level establishment (a charming bistro in the basement; a glamorous French salon upstairs) has been one of our favorites since its founding in 1972. Lovingly tended by Bob and Ann Burke, it helped inspire the city's initial culinary renaissance, but like many old-timers clings to a comforting niche.

No less an authority than Julia Child was partial to its food, which received the first five-star rating granted by Rhode Island Monthly magazine reviewers on the occasion of its twentieth anniversary in 1992. Wine Spectator honors its wine list, and Bob Burke was one of the first in New England to be inducted into Moet's Club des Sabreurs for those who pop champagne corks with sabers.

In the **Bistro,** with its zinc bar, ancient stone and brick walls, and tiny lights illuminating a brick shelf lined with empty wine bottles, you order typical French provincial bistro food – omelets, onion soup, pâtés (one of duck foie gras), crêpes, salmon gravlax, quiche and salade au chèvre, all at reasonable prices. The vanilla mousse with praline sauce is not to be missed. The twenty or so dinner entrées might include salmon citron topped with mandarin oranges, roasted chicken with a pecan and maple syrup glaze, veal grenobloise, tournedos béarnaise or bordelaise and the namesake pot au feu, the traditional French "pot on fire" of braised beef, chicken and vegetables.

Upstairs in the **Salon,** amid crisp white linens, lacquered black chairs and wall panels painted black with gold, the haute menu is traditional, except perhaps for a recent offering of grilled medallions of ostrich with a caramelized onion and madeira sauce. You can order à la carte, but the three-course table-d'hôte dinners represent good value for an extra $10.

On the winter night we dined we were celebrating a double birthday. Fond memories of escargots bourguignonne and clams épinard dance in our heads, as do thoughts of the mushroom soup, the salad with fresh mushrooms and cherry tomatoes, the French bread served from a huge basket with sweet butter, the pink roast lamb, the tournedos with blue cheese, the crisp vegetables, the crème brûlée, the mousse au citron, the espresso. Memories are a bit blurred by a couple of the best martinis we've had and a bottle of La Cour Pavillon Medoc – well, it was a birthday! We hope to return before too many more roll around.

(401) 273-8953. www.potaufeuri.com. Salon: Entrées, $24 to $34. Dinner, Thursday-Saturday 6 to 9 or 9:30.

Bistro: Entrées, $13.95 to $23.95. Lunch, Monday-Friday 11:30 to 2. Dinner, Monday-Saturday 5:30 to 9 or 10.

Rue de L'Espoir, 99 Hope St.

Originally a Left Bank-type bistro, this favorite of the College Hill crowd has evolved over 30 years into a contemporary American bistro and now is French more in name than in fact.

Its loyal following continues to cherish the ambiance of a café that could have been lifted from the streets of Paris. The Rue's recently refurbished look features lots of wood and decorative panels sponged in cranberry and peach colors around an interior dining room on several levels. Seating is in cozy booths and at unusual tables made of quarry tile that dress up with white linens at night.

Owner Deb Norman and her longtime chef, Michael Koussa, offer a with-it dinner menu featuring such entrées as lobster macaroni and cheese, roasted salmon with pistachio-orange crust, a "duet" of duck breast and monkfish served with two sauces, and wood-grilled filet mignon dusted with espresso, cinnamon and coriander and served with a shallot-madeira demi-glace. Mix and match some of the small plates: perhaps a lobster and mushroom madeira crêpe, Thai crab cakes, skewered lemongrass scallops or cognac-laced chicken liver pâté served on a cheese board with toasts of Portuguese sweet bread. Some of the specialty salads, among them niçoise, roasted salmon or duck, and caesar with grilled chicken or shrimp, are meals in themselves. For lunch, the grilled scallops and tomatoes on a bed of greens has a nippy citrus-thyme vinaigrette, pan-sautéed mussels are served with a champagne sauce on a bed of wilted greens, and from the dessert tray we recall a memorable charlotte malakoff (lady fingers, whipped cream, nuts, kirsch and strawberry preserves). A large selection of beers is available, as are interesting and affordable wines.

This remains a great place for breakfast. Although famous for its honey oat bread french toast with yogurt and fruit, we could only manage the $4.95 special: two eggs, coffee, corn muffin and crispy home fries. The fries were so addictive that most were snitched by the person who only came in for orange juice and caffe au lait.

In 2005, the Rue launched a return to its roots as a quiche and crêpe bistro. The new **Rue Bis** at 16 Bassett St. in the Jewelry District serves breakfast and lunch, Monday-Friday 7:30 to 3:30.

(401) 751-8890. www.therue.com. Entrées, $19.95 to $27.95. Breakfast, Monday-Friday 7:30 to 11, weekends 8:30 to 2:30. Lunch, Monday-Friday 11:30 to 5. Dinner nightly, 5 to 9, weekends to 10:30.

Red Stripe, 465 Angell St.

Just as his Mill's Tavern redefined the modern American tavern concept locally, so his new bistro in the heart of the tony East Side commercial district called Wayland Square redefines the American brasserie.

Jaime D'Oliveira and his interior-designer wife Kim transformed the former Newport Creamery in 2005 into a large and ever-so-French-looking bistro with an open kitchen along one side, close-together bistro tables and a handful of wrought-iron tables on the sidewalk out front. The trademark fork sculpture/logo above the entry marks the spot.

If the place looks continental, the menu follows suit – to a point. You can order the classic steak frites, nine versions of mussels and frites, an omelet with fine herbs, three ziti pasta dishes, stout-battered fish and chips, Indonesian-style roasted whole fish and Portuguese fisherman's stew. But you also can get prosciutto-wrapped cod loin roasted on a cedar plank, braised lamb shoulder, grilled tea-smoked tofu steak with a bag of roasted veggies or the red plate special, a different American bistro classic every day. The "everything but the kitchen sink chopped salad" proved an early favorite, as did the charcuterie and Moroccan antipasto platters.

Traverse the globe with such starters as a New England cod cake over baked beans, escargots bordelaise, grilled margarita pizza, sweet potato latke and crispy duck roulade. Or settle for a grilled cheese sandwich with oven-roasted tomato soup or frites.

(401) 437-6950. Entrées, $12 to $18. Lunch daily, 11 to 5. Dinner nightly, 5 to 11.

Quite the Scene

CAV, 14 Imperial Place.

What to make of a place whose name is an acronym for Coffee, Antiques and Victuals, and also alludes to a French wine cellar (cave, pronounced *cahv*)? Gourmet, you ask? Very much so, avows owner Sylvia Moubayed from Alexandria, Egypt, citing endorsements by Bon Appetit magazine and the New York Times. The former executive director of the Providence Atheneum library opened this coffeehouse cum restaurant cum antiques shop in 1989. "My taste for decor was more expensive than my pocketbook," she said, so selling the decor helps pay the bills.

The former factory space with fourteen-foot-high ceiling is rather dizzying and overwhelming, what with chairs and rugs hanging from the rafters, dining tables tucked between glass cases of art objects and displays of Asian bronzes and carved wooden masks, a staff of young women in black, and people emerging here, there and everywhere. The tables are set with kilim rugs, a couple of booths are

Kilim rugs cover tables and wooden sleigh hangs from ceiling in dining room at CAV.

topped with hoods and the enormous menu comes in an album. It runs to at least eight typewritten pages, not counting specials of the day and night.

This is much more than an ambient pause for coffee or tea and pastries. It's a lunch stop for ladies who shop, a celebratory venue for a special-occasion dinner, and a jazz club with live music on weekends. The eclectic, international menu covers all the bases – small plates, pastas and entrées, from sesame-encrusted tuna with wasabi aioli to rack of lamb in a rosemary and green peppercorn jus – and all price ranges. The food, though upstaged by the ambiance, is quite good. Sit back, watch the scene and enjoy.

(401) 751-9164. www.cavrestaurant.com. Entrées, $21.95 to $28.95. Lunch daily, 11:30 to 4. Dinner nightly, 4 to 10 or 11.

Coffee and Breads, Country Style

Olga's Cup and Saucer, 103 Point St.

Coffee with the best artisan breads and pastries in town is the hallmark of this small café with a bakery of great note. It's the offspring of the much-loved Olga's Cup and Saucer in Little Compton, which baker Olga Bravo runs with Rebecca Wagner, an Al Forno alumnus who's known for her soups.

When they added a year-round bakery in a charming English-style cottage in the India Point section just south of downtown Providence, their summer following wanted lunches as well as breads, so the partners obliged. The thin-crust corn and tomato pizzas, sandwiches, pastas, tempting entrées and delicious desserts pack in the noonday crowds. Morning coffee, enormous muffins, scones and breads for toasting are so popular that you can barely get in the door.

There's a handful of tiled tables made by the owners, who also are artists. Most choice are those outside beneath apricot trees beside a showplace little English garden, full of raised and potted beds bursting with flowers, vines and herbs. It's a touch of country in the midst of the city.

(401) 831-6666. Entrées, $6 to $9. Open Monday-Friday, 7 to 6, Saturday 8 to 5. Lunch, 11 to 3.

Lodging

The Westin Providence, 1 West Exchange Street, Providence 02903.

Built and owned by the state as part of the new Rhode Island Convention Center complex, this is New England's fanciest hotel outside Boston. From the striking, 25-story-high gabled roof that denotes its Neoclassic presence on the Providence skyline to the majestic four-story lobby rotunda with its marble floor and columns, the Westin exudes class.

Each of the 364 handsomely appointed rooms and suites comes with kingsize or two double beds, at least one easy chair with ottoman, a spacious writing desk, a TV hidden in an armoire, two telephones, a mini-bar and a coffeemaker stocked with Starbucks coffee. Our quiet cocoon of a room came with a triple-sheeted kingsize bed topped with six big pillows, two upholstered chairs and large windows that opened. A deluxe corner room on the nineteenth floor, it was bright and cheery by day and yielded a knockout view of the city lights at night. The contemporary European decor in champagne tones supposedly reflected the interior of a Newport mansion. The more memorable Newport touch was the immense bathroom, where for some reason the rack with hand towels was clear across the room from the washstand. Chocolates and a weather forecast arrived at nightly turndown, and the day's newspaper was at the door the next morning.

Guests enjoy the hotel's fitness center with indoor pool beneath the dome atop the rotunda building. The Library Bar & Lounge off the lobby rotunda is the ultimate in plush surroundings and a refuge for creative appetizers, single-malt scotches and cigars. Take the long escalator up to the second-floor lounges, which include a sports bar serving light lunch and dinner fare. The elegant **Agora** restaurant was an early favorite of the national food media, but a change in chefs coincided with a switch to a new look and an expensive steakhouse menu ($20 to $35). **CitiPerk** offers less lofty fare for breakfast and lunch.

(401) 598-8000. Fax (401) 598-8200. Three hundred sixty rooms and four suites. Doubles, $189 to $419. Suites, $474 to $1,700.

Providence Biltmore, 11 Dorrance St., Providence 02903.

An early feather in Providence's cap, this historic downtown hotel appears a bit dowdy lately in comparison with its all-new neighbor across the plaza and gets mixed reviews, except for rooms on its concierge floors.

The brick dowager opened in 1922 to a special trainload from New York, a 50-piece band and a sea of roses as it recreated the high standards of living enjoyed at the Vanderbilt Biltmore Estate in North Carolina. After falling on hard times and closing in 1973, it reopened following a $15 million renovation in 1979. It later was taken over by the Omni chain and since has become a Grand Heritage hotel. At the top of the three-story lobby is a wonderfully ornate, original gilt ceiling, and the crystal chandelier and palm trees remind some of the Plaza in New York. A glass elevator shoots from the lobby up the side of the seventeen-story building.

The original 500 bedrooms have been converted into 291 larger accommodations, done in soft and soothing colors. Most have kingsize or two double beds, plus armchairs and sofas in elegant sitting areas, with TVs concealed in armoires. Some suites have kitchenettes. Amenities include a new fitness center and a Paul Mitchell Salon and Spa.

The hotel claims the largest and most stylish **Starbucks** in America, one with a salon setting of leather lounges and club chairs beneath a gilt tin ceiling. Fine dining is offered in the hotel's new **McCormick & Schmick's** seafood restaurant.

(401) 421-0700 or (800) 294-7709. Fax (401) 455-3050. www.providencebiltmore.com. Two hundred fifty-eight rooms and 33 suites. Doubles, $239 to $319. Suites, $250 to $750.

The Hotel Providence, 311 Westminster St., Providence 02903.

Providence's first European-style boutique hotel opened in 2005 in the heart of the suddenly chic Downcity arts and entertainment district. Providence real estate developer Stanley Weiss joined two late 19th-century brick buildings with a newer structure to provide 61 rooms and nineteen suites, plus a first-rate restaurant and piano bar.

Sumptuous fabrics and antiques from the owner's personal collection convey a turn-of-the-last-century flavor. All rooms have pillow-top king or queensize beds with down comforters, armoires of tiger maple wood, two upholstered armchairs, oversize desks with ergonomic chairs and large-screen TVs. Bathrooms have pedestal sinks, gold-framed mirrors, rain-head showers and marble floors. Junior suites add a separate living room with a sofabed. Four deluxe king suites come with original oil paintings, granite wet bars and whirlpool tubs.

The Dunfey Hotel Group is managing the hotel. Weiss persuaded friends Tom and Rozann Buckner to relocate their acclaimed **L'Epicureo** restaurant from Federal Hill to larger quarters on the hotel's main floor.

(401) 861-8000 or (800) 861-8990. Fax (401) 861-8002. www.thehotelprovidence.com. Sixty-one rooms and nineteen suites. Doubles, $239 to $279. Suites, $319 to $800.

The Old Court, 144 Benefit St., Providence 02903.

You can stay on historic Benefit Street and relive the Providence of yesteryear, thanks to the conversion of an 1863 Episcopal church rectory into a fine B&B. Owners Jon and Carol Rosenblatt, who also own a series of small East Side restaurants, spared no expense in the restoration. Italianate in design, the Old Court has ornate mantelpieces, plaster moldings and twelve-foot-high ceilings.

Each of the ten guest rooms is decorated differently, if rather sparely. Some have brass beds, some four-poster, and most have exotic wallpapers. All beds are queen or kingsize except for one with two doubles and another with twins. The large Eastlake Room is done with Eastlake furniture and offers a sofa and wet bar. Lace curtains and old clocks convey a feeling of the past. Air-conditioning, telephones and televisions are concessions to the present.

Because there is no common room, the Old Court seems like a small hotel. A full breakfast is served in a pink breakfast room, graced with an oriental rug and fresh flowers. The specialty is crêpes, but the day's menu might dictate eggs, pancakes or french toast.

(401) 751-2002. Fax (401) 282-4830. www.oldcourt.com. Ten rooms with private baths. Mid-March to mid-November: doubles, $135 to $175 weekends, $115 to $145 midweek. Rest of year: doubles $115 to $145 weekends, $95 to $115 midweek.

State House Inns, 43 Jewett St., Providence 02908.

What began as a modest ten-room B&B has become two B&B inns and a B&B hotel in the Smith Hill residential neighborhood overlooking the State Capitol across Interstate 95. All go under the umbrella name of the original. Two are one house apart from each other and about a block from the Shaker-style State House Inn opened in 1990 by Monica and Frank Hopton. They added two larger properties in 2003 in partnership with her parents, former Nantucket innkeepers Kenneth and Phyllis Parker.

The Christopher Dodge House at 11 West Park St., a majestic three-story 1858 Italianate brick mansion that had been converted into an apartment house, is the largest and most deluxe of the three. Now restored as "a B&B hotel," it has fifteen elegant, high-ceilinged bedrooms with ornate plaster moldings, tin ceilings, polished wide-board pine floors and white or light-colored painted walls. Crisply appointed in Shaker, Colonial or Mission style, a typical room has a king or queen bed, a TV concealed in an armoire, a gas fireplace beneath a marble mantel, a comfortable armchair, a desk and a view of the State House dome through the rippled panes of the inn's tall antique windows. Guests meet for breakfast near the fireplace in a brick-walled dining room, where the sideboard holds a continental buffet that's mere preliminary to a main course of perhaps baked apple french toast, quiche or eggs benedict – the same kind of fare served at the related B&Bs. Doubles here range from $149 to $159.

Newest is the thirteen-room **Mowry-Nicholson House** at 57 Brownell St., an 1865 Victorian converted into a B&B from a condemned boarding house. Its eight rooms and five family suites are furnished in simpler early American style that complements its wide wraparound front porch. Doubles here are $129 to $139 and suites, $139 to $149.

The original **State House Inn,** a bit farther removed from the interstate highway, has a loyal following who like its nicely furnished rooms, each with king or queensize bed topped with quilt or comforter, TV, telephone and an overstuffed chair. Two rooms have fireplaces. Hooked rugs or carpets cover the maple floors that are original to the house. The main floor harbors a small guest parlor and a bigger, fireplaced dining room where breakfast is served. Doubles here are $99 to $149.

(401) 351-6111. Fax (401) 351-4261. www.providence-inn.com. Thirty-three rooms and five suites with private baths. Doubles, $99 to $159.

The Cady House. 127 Power St., Providence 02906.

The owner's eclectic collections of folk art are everywhere evident in this imposing 1839 residence with pillared entrance on College Hill.

Their offspring gone, Anna Colaiace and her husband Bill, a radiologist, offer three much-decorated Victorian guest quarters with queen beds and private baths. A side suite contains a daybed with trundle bed in the living room and a sturdy armoire and dresser in the bedroom. A rear bedroom has a luxurious settee in a windowed alcove and a giant bathroom with clawfoot tub, separate shower and a circular stand holding a multitude of plants. Guests enter a front bedroom through the bathroom to find a spacious room with sofa and tiled fireplace. The wild wallpapers throughout "are my interpretation of Victorian," says Anna, who did the decorating herself.

A former caterer who used to make desserts for CAV, she serves an ample breakfast of eggs, frittata or french toast on the weekends (continental during the week) in a formal dining room opening onto a delightful screened porch. The porch overlooks a curved terrace and showy gardens on a triple lot. Folk art and sculptures continue in the lower garden.

"We just got a little crazier," Anna said at a recent visit, noting her husband's display of African masks all over the living room. "He went crazy on eBay for two months after a trip."

Along with their growing collections, the couple's two dogs are much in evidence.

(401) 273-5398. www.cadyhouse.com. Two rooms and one suite with private baths. Doubles, $120.

Hotel Dolce Villa, 63 DePasquale Plaza, Providence 02903.

This new all-suite boutique hotel is as European-looking as anything else in Providence's ethnic Federal Hill section. Gianfranco Marrocco, an Italian-born barber turned Federal Hill restaurateur, added a third floor to a one-time chicken factory in 2005 to produce nine one-bedroom and five two-bedroom suites, each with full kitchen, state-of-the-art entertainment center and bath with whirlpool tub. Two-bedroom suites have gas fireplaces.

He based the hotel's lemon-yellow Mediterranean facade on the architecture of Positano, Italy, but credited the ultra-modern look of Miami's South Beach for the nearly blinding white-on-white interior. Except for the black and steel of the appliances in the kitchen, everything is white – leather sofas and chairs, marble floor tiles, cabinets, bedspreads, curtains and flat-screen televisions perched high on the walls.

From a pair of two-bedroom suites on the third floor, guests can sit on their balconies and watch the passing parade on the plaza for live entertainment.

Privacy and quiet are afforded behind the building in the hotel's vine-covered Tuscan villa, converted by a previous owner from a stable into a residence. Its two floors are the reverse of a normal house, with a jacuzzi in the downstairs bedroom and the living quarters upstairs. Its brick walls, wood floors, mosaic-tiled baths and two stone courtyard patios stand in charming contrast to the hotel's modern interior.

(401) 0383-7031. Fax (401) 383-7041. www.dolcevillari.com. Fourteen suites and one villa with private baths. Doubles, $179 one-bedroom, $209 to $259 two-bedroom. Villa, $349.

Gourmet Treats

Providence Place, a huge and appealing downtown mall, bills itself as New England's premier shopping and dining destination. For shopping, you have not only Filene's, Lord & Taylor and Nordstrom but **Crate & Barrel,** the **Pottery Barn, Williams-Sonoma, Lindt Chocolates** and **Godiva Chocolatier**. There's a food court as well as free-standing restaurants like **Fire & Ice, The Cheesecake Factory** and the **Napa Valley Grille.** Our favorite here is **Café Nordstrom,** a dark and elegant corner space hidden away on the third floor of the Seattle-based Nordstrom. The caféteria-style food offerings are far more innovative than the norm – and rationally priced.

The **Union Station Brewery,** 36 Exchange Ter., produces specialty ales, lagers and stout in a section of the old Union Station, along with some snacks and light fare to go with. Award-winning beers also emanate from **Trinity Brewhouse**, across from the Providence Civic Center at 186 Fountain St.

L'Elizabeth, 285 South Main St., is a romantic spot for a tête-à-tête coffee or drink. Tended since 1973 by Elizabeth Mahoney, it has a true European feeling, with the look of a salon where there are different groupings of sofas and chairs, and is very dimly lit at night. No meals are served, but L'Elizabeth's torte cake with raspberry, apricot and chocolate, and perhaps chocolate mousse pie are offered with tea or coffee. Espresso, cappuccino, international coffees, hot toddies and a large selection of single-malt scotches and liqueurs are available. It's open daily from 3 to midnight, weekends to 1 a.m.

Two new shops are of interest at Wayland Square. Artisan cheeses and "unique edibles" from vinegars to preserves are featured at **Farmstead Inc.,** 186 Wayland Ave. Farmstead carries more than 100 "cutting edge" cheeses, many from small-batch New England cheese makers. Owners Matt Jennings and Patrick Flynn give classes and lead cheese excursions around town and as far away as Vermont. Fabulous tableware is displayed across the street at **Runcible Spoon,** offshoot of a Newport kitchen shop.

Culinary Treasures

Culinary Archives & Museum, 315 Harborside Blvd.

The 1989 gifts of Chef Louis Szathmary of Chicago's famed Bakery restaurant launched this little-known museum in a vast, unlikely-looking warehouse on an outlying campus of Johnson & Wales University. They were the nucleus of holdings that have quickly yet quietly grown into the largest archive of cookbooks and food-related objects in the world. Students lead hour-long tours that show a portion of the more than 500,000 items billed as "the Smithsonian of the food service industry." Our guide pointed out highlights: an exhibit of "stoves and ranges: from open hearth to microwave," another tracing the history of cooking schools back to the 15th century, an early Michelin guide, a history of chef's uniforms, publisher Earle MacAusland's collection of Gourmet magazines and a letter from Escoffier planning a dinner for Gilbert and Sullivan. You might see a circular sofa from Boston's Copley Plaza Hotel, an 1860 collapsible Russian cook's bed, a Victorian grape slicer and a 5,000-year-old flint kitchen knife from Egypt. A presidential collection traces "The History of the First Stomach."

(401) 598-2805. www.culinary.org. Open Tuesday-Sunday 10 to 5. Adults, $7.

A Touch of Italy, Plus

An entire book could be written on Federal Hill, Providence's enclave of ethnic eateries, bakeries, markets and pasta stores. Lately, the pasta and red sauce stalwarts have been joined by the likes of **Mediterraneo, Pane e Vine, Renaissance, Zooma** and **Costantino's Ristorante.** Not to mention the sleek **Aquaviva Eurobistro, Opa, Mia Sushi Bar & Grill, Don Jose Tequila's** and the **Bombay Club.** Traditionalists still dote on the long-running **Blue Grotto, Cassarino's** and **Camille's.** Visitors mix with regulars at old kitchen tables in **Angelo's Civita Farnese,** an unlikely-looking spot where you roll up your sleeves for family-style food like Mama really did make.

The heart of the area is DePasquale Plaza, a charming cobblestone plaza with a fountain, pots of flowers, tiny white lights in the trees, outdoor tables and benches, and Italian music playing. Here you can lunch on an Italian tuna sandwich or one of prosciutto, fresh mozzarella and tomatoes followed by an imported dessert at **Caffe Dolce Vita.** You can sup on a "legendary grilled pizza" from Geppetto's Pizzeria. You

Diners flock to tahles outside Costantino's and other restaurants around DePasquale Plaza.

can also "see your chicken alive," according to the sign in the window of **Antonelli's Poultry.**

Around the corner at 92 Spruce St. is **Pastiche,** a bakery and gourmet dessertery par excellence. Partake of an exotic homemade dessert (perhaps toffee-walnut torte or a fabulous looking fruit tart ($5 a slice) with cappuccino or café au lait in stylish digs beside the fireplace.

Relocated and vastly expanded across the plaza from its original space is glamorous **Venda Ravioli** at 265 Atwells, an Italian gourmet food emporium featuring 150 varieties of handmade pastas and sauces (the cheese ravioli with wild mushroom sauce is heavenly). The long, central deli display case is a wonderland of tempting salads, meats, cheeses and prepared meals. We've rarely seen such a fabulous display, and took home some chicken saltimbocca, roasted sweet potatoes and tomatoes stuffed with goat cheese for a dinner that tasted as good as it looked. Owner Alan Costantino stocks many exclusive imported food items, kitchenware and cookware. He offers an espresso bar, gelatos and sit-down lunches at tables placed around the perimeter. Across the plaza is **Costantino's Ristorante and Caffe.**

Pick out panini sandwiches or dinner to go from another remarkable selection at **Tony's Colonial Food Store** at 311 Atwells Ave. One of the early Italian merchants on the avenue, Anthonio DiCicco bought an original Greek grocery and kept the Colonial name. He cut back on groceries in favor of gourmet items, mostly Italian, but still has a grand assortment of cheeses and deli meats. There's an amazing selection of olive oils, vinegars and pastas, plus colorful ceramic pasta dishes and spoon rests at the entry. We enjoyed Tony's chicken cutlets, broccoli rabe and garlic breadsticks at home after one long day in Providence. The newer **Roma Gourmet** across the street is equally fun to browse in. It has a butcher and a small café and bakery at the side. **Scialo Brothers Bakery** at 257 Atwells, a fixture since 1916, offers terrific muffins, breads and pastries.

The natives are right when they say they have a touch of Europe here.

Cape Cod

New Capers on the Old Cape

The time was not all that long ago when dining on Cape Cod meant, for many, the three C's: Chillingsworth, the Christopher Ryder House and clam shacks.

When you thought of places to stay, you hoped to luck into a friend's summer house or you rented a cottage, preferably somewhere near the beach. The few inns tended to be large and posh and were far outnumbered by all those funny-looking motels with glassed-in swimming pools near Hyannis.

Well, Chillingsworth is still there, as good as ever. The Christopher Ryder House has been converted into condominiums, and the clam shacks are overshadowed by a burst of serious restaurants.

There are more summer houses, cottages, deluxe inns and funny-looking motels than ever, of course. But there's also a new breed of country inns – not full-service like their predecessors, but more than bed-and-breakfast houses.

In spring, the season starts gearing up, yet crowds and prices are less than at summer's height. Then comes the July and August crush, and the high season ends abruptly after Labor Day.

Knowledgeable visitors have long preferred the Cape in the off-season. They avoid the tourist trappings of busy Hyannis, whose restaurants this chapter purposely omits. For the Cape is a place for escape, for relative solitude, for respite in a sandy, seaside setting unsurpassed in New England.

Note: Although the Cape's season is lengthening every year and more places remain open year-round, the owners' plans often change. Restaurant hours vary widely. Reservations may be required far ahead for peak periods. Minimum stays for lodging are not unusual. Planning, flexibility and/or luck overcome such caveats.

People who haven't been to the Cape lately – or who haven't ventured far from the beach if they have – might be surprised by the "new" Cape that co-exists with the old.

Dining

The Best of the Best

Chillingsworth, 2449 Main St. (Route 6A), Brewster.

The revitalized dowager of Cape Cod restaurants offers what some reviewers call the best serious resort-area dining in New England. For two years it outranked all 500 Boston restaurants in the Zagat survey. Another year, chef-owner Robert (Nitzi) Rabin won Gourmet magazine's Great American Chef award. In an era of shortcuts and cost-shaving, he is one of the last of a breed maintaining a tradition of impeccable haute cuisine.

For most, this is a special destination – so special, in fact, that we stopped by to reserve a table six weeks in advance for a mid-October Saturday. As it turned out, we didn't get the specific time or the table we had picked out, but that was our only complaint from a memorable dinner that lasted past midnight.

The restored 1689 house is named for Chillingsworth Foster, son of its builder. Its quaint and unassuming Cape Cod exterior gives little clue to the treasures inside – room after room full of priceless furnishings, antiques and museum pieces. The

Chef-owner Robert (Nitzi) Rabin oversees Chillingsworth restaurant and bistro in this rambling Cape Cod house.

large Terrace Room in which we ended up dining is not, to our mind, as special as one of the smaller rooms like the Empire, where we had booked, or the table for four in an alcove off the living room, which one innkeeper of our acquaintance thinks is the most exquisite around.

Limoges china, a hurricane oil lamp and a vase of flowers graced our heavily linened table. A harpist was playing in the background as the waiter asked if we had questions about the menu, which is typewritten daily. The meal consists of seven courses at a fixed price of $62.50 to $70, depending upon choice of entrée. Although locally considered pricey, Chillingsworth offers better value than do its peers elsewhere – far better in that you get seven exotic courses. And the bistro menu is a relative steal.

We chose a French vouvray to accompany our appetizers, grilled duck and pepper quesadilla with coriander and tomatillo salsa and a feuilleté of oysters with spinach and lemon-butter sauce with roe. A dozen appetizers are offered, from crab cakes with cucumber julienne and golden caviar to carpaccio of beef tenderloin with truffle vinaigrette, parmesan and baby greens.

The cream of mussel soup that followed was superb, as was the consommé of mushrooms. A second helping of the night's squash bread – after all, we weren't seated until 9:30 – was followed by a salad of four baby leaf lettuces, arugula, radicchio and sorrel, enriched with a crouton of warm chèvre and dressed with a zesty vinaigrette. A grapefruit sorbet with a sprig of mint, served in a crystal sherry glass, cleared the palate.

All that was literally prelude to the main event – stunning entrées, beautifully presented. Chillingsworth teamed grilled rare tuna loin with wasabi butter sauce long before it became the rage. Now it offers rare seared tuna tournedos with foie gras, roasted halibut with a roasted tomato and arugula chiffonade and truffle vinaigrette, and roasted beef tenderloin with truffle sauce and a potato, fennel, leek and artichoke "ragoût." Our breast of duck was garnished with citrus rind and fanned in slices around the plate, interspersed with kiwi and papaya slices. A side plate contained julienned carrots and a spinach soufflé with nutmeg and wild rice. Our other entrée was an equally imaginative treatment of lamb with veal kidneys, grilled with herbs from Chillingsworth's garden. With these we had a Rodney Strong cabernet, among the least expensive California vintages on a choice wine list priced well into the hundreds.

Desserts here are anything but an anti-climax. One of us chose a raspberry tulipe, an intriguing presentation atop a speckled-striped pattern of napoleon. The other enjoyed a hazelnut dacquoise with coffee butter cream. Before these came the "amusements" – a plate of gingerbread men, rolled cookies around citrus and macaroons. The finale was a serving of chocolate truffles, intense to the max.

Nitzi Rabin made the rounds of diners as they lingered over coffee. He and wife Pat work fourteen-hour days overseeing the expanding operation they purchased in 1975. Both had worked summers at Chillingsworth, he advancing from busboy to captain to manager and picking up an MBA at the Tuck School at Dartmouth. The Rabins winter in Colorado ski country and travel to France or California to continue to enhance their highly creative American version of modern French cuisine.

Lunch and dinner are available in a contemporary bistro and greenhouse lounge area with skylights, walls of glass and plants, and outdoor seating. The lunch menu embraces some of the dinner items as well as other creative fare at more down-to-earth prices (entrées, $12.50 to $17). A broader bistro menu at night offers exotic appetizers in the $8 to $12.50 range and main courses from $17 for roasted chicken to $36.50 for grilled veal chop with wild mushrooms. This is the place for those who want to sense the Chillingsworth flair but feel the main dining room serves more than they can eat, or who don't like precise seatings at perhaps awkward hours.

Lately, the former gift shop space was converted into a cocktail lounge with a bar and fireplace, where the bistro menu also is available. The shop, which offers many Chillingsworth specialties for sale, relocated to an outbuilding. Nitzi calls it "a nice catering business without the delivery problems." Upstairs, the Rabins offer three elegant guest rooms for overnight stays. Rates are $110 to $150, B&B.

(508) 896-3640 or (800) 430-3640. www.chillingsworth.com. Prix-fixe, $62.50 to $70. Lunch in summer, Tuesday-Sunday 11:30 to 2:30. Dinner by reservation, Tuesday-Sunday, seatings at 6 and 9; weekends only in spring and fall. Closed after Thanksgiving to mid-May.

The Regatta of Cotuit, 4631 Falmouth Road (Route 28), Cotuit.

This elegant restaurant in a handsome 1790 Federal-style house has been lovingly run since 1987 by Wendy and Brantz Bryan, whose landmark Regatta in Falmouth was the highlight of our Cape Cod summer adventures for more than three decades until it closed in 2001.

While the Falmouth restaurant was summery, New Yorkish and on the waterfront, the Cotuit venture serves up terrific seafood, regional dishes and New England Americana year-round. The Bryans advertise their fare as "contemporary American with a focus on French and Asian."

Eight intimate dining rooms, one with only two tables, are beautifully appointed in shades of pink and green, with authentic print wallpapers, needlepoint rugs and

Wendy and Brantz Bryan welcome diners at entrance to The Regatta at Cotuit.

furnishings of the period. Tables are set with pink and white Limoges china, crystal glassware and fine silver.

Executive chef Heather Allen has helped the Regatta earn a reputation for fine dining every bit as stellar as that of Chillingsworth, which is more widely known.

Appetizers are oriented toward the sea: from housemade ravioli with lobster and scallops to a signature sautéed crab cake with diablo sauce, corn salsa and local baby pea tendrils. The seafood trilogy is a winner: one spring night produced firecracker shrimp with a "sweet, sour and sassy" hoisin sauce, blackened tuna sashimi and grilled scallops. We gobbled up a rich chilled lobster and sole terrine, served with a saffron sauce garnished with truffles, and loved the broiled Wellfleet oysters with black American caviar.

A complimentary sorbet follows the appetizer course. Our dinner could have ended happily there, but on came the entrées. The seafood fettuccine contained more shrimp, scallops, lobster and artichoke hearts than it did spinach pasta, and the pan-seared fillet of halibut came with a key lime beurre blanc, lobster-mashed potatoes, haricots vert and sea bean salad. At a later visit we enjoyed the palette of fresh fish, each with its own sauce (yellowfin tuna with pinot noir sauce and roasted shallots, and swordfish with caramelized-lemon and white-butter sauce), and the grilled breast of pheasant. Next time we must sample the signature buffalo tenderloin, the presentation varying each evening. Brantz says the Regatta sells more tenderloin of buffalo and elk than any restaurant on the East Coast.

Desserts are high points. The chocolate seduction on a lovely patterned raspberry sauce and the grand marnier crème brûlée garnished with red and gold raspberries and blackberries are among the best we've tasted. Best bet is a tasting trilogy of three favorites ($15.50 for two). Ours brought a chocolate truffle cake, almond torte with framboise sauce and hand-dipped chocolate strawberries. The wine list, which emphasizes good reds, is priced from the twenties.

The Regatta's decor is a wonderful sight, matched by the colorful trousers of Brantz Bryan, who explains that he wears them in summer "to make people laugh and feel at ease." He and Wendy were the first high-end restaurateurs on our travels to anticipate the change in eating habits in the early 1990s and offer alternatives. They added three-course early dinners, as well as a bar menu offering most of the evening's appetizers. Perhaps such flexibility is why the Bryans have been so successful for more than three decades.

(508) 428-5715. www.regattaofcotuit.com. Entrées, $23 to $35. Dinner nightly, 5 to 10; closed Monday in winter.

The Red Pheasant Inn, 905 Main St. (Route 6A), Dennis.

The exterior is strictly old New England – a rambling, red, 200-year-old saltbox house and barn. Inside are a new wine and martini bar with a fireplace and a bistro menu, a couple of dining rooms and an enclosed porch with a wall mural bearing flowers matching those in the garden outside. It's a comfortable mix of upholstered chairs and white linens, barnwood walls and flickering oil lamps. Tables are well spaced, background music is at the right level, and the service is deft and unobtrusive.

The food is on the cutting edge, with inspired touches of regional New England cuisine and fusion accents. The creative hand in the kitchen belongs to chef Bill Atwood Jr., son of the founder. Bill's wife Denise oversees the front of the house and is responsible for the beautiful side gardens.

Bill, elected to the Master Chefs of America, says his efforts have evolved over the years into a Cape Cod cuisine with "a truly local flavor." He smokes his own bluefish, cod cakes and venison sausage, mixes local cod and calamari in new presentations, and stuffs quails with duck sausage. He also experiments with Asian and Mediterranean fare, "which keeps me fresh."

For starters, we were impressed with a caesar salad as good as we can make at home and the fried goat-cheese raviolis on a lovely tomato coulis, with asparagus spears and frizzles of leek radiating out. Recent choices included light spinach gnocchi with shaved manchego cheese and roasted tomato sauce, lobster salad on a bed of baby arugula and toasted brioche, house-cured duck prosciutto salad and a trio of house-cured seafood (monkfish pâté, salmon gravlax and scallop seviche).

Main courses range from porcini-crusted salmon with sauce duglère to grilled veal sirloin with madeira sauce. The pan-roast organic chicken breast might be accented with preserved lemon and fresh thyme. The native bouillabaisse, in a tomato-saffron broth, is served in custom-designed bowls from the nearby Scargo Pottery. Our choices could not have been better: roast boneless Long Island duckling served with a rhubarb, dried cherry and caramelized ginger sauce, and grilled pavé of beef with fried oysters, wrapped in leeks with bordelaise sauce. We were too full to sample the desserts, which for a warm summer night seemed rather heavy. Later choices were crème brûlée, strawberry charlotte, profiteroles, strawberry-rhubarb tart on lemon curd and chocolate flourless cake with crème anglaise.

Open to the dining porch, the new lounge holds a handful of tables and a stunning bar, all made of the South American hardwood angelique used in ships, an appropriate choice for the one-time ship's chandlery. A bistro menu is offered here for $15 to $17. The distinguished wine list, 300 choices strong, has been cited by Wine Spectator.

(508) 385-2133 or (800) 480-2133. www.redpheasantinn.com. Entrées, $19 to $32. Dinner nightly, 5 to 8:30 or 9. Reduced schedule in January.

Floral mural on wall reflects gardens outside porch windows at The Red Pheasant Inn.

Inaho Japanese Restaurant, 157 Main St. (Route 6A), Yarmouth Port.

The little white house that long harbored La Cipollina restaurant is the home of a Japanese eatery that relocated from Hyannis and joined the ranks of top-rated restaurants on Cape Cod. Ugi Wantanabe, who had worked as a sushi chef in New York and Newport, and his Portuguese-American wife Alda live upstairs, in the European fashion, and travel every other day to Boston for fresh fish and provisions.

A long sushi bar where singles can be comfortable faces one wall of the rear dining room; Japanese-looking booths flank the other. The far end is all windows gazing onto a courtyard garden, where spotlights focus on a few Japanese plantings. There are two front dining rooms as well. The bare wood tables topped only with chopsticks and napkins hint that here you'll find the real thing.

An order of gyoza dumplings staved off hunger as we nursed a bottle of Chalk Hill sauvignon blanc from a small but well-chosen wine list. One of us sampled the nine-piece sushi plate; the sushi was fresh and delicious. The other was pleased with the bento box yielding salad, a skewer of chicken teriyaki, tempura and a California roll. Sashimi, teriyaki, tempura and katsu items completed the menu, although specials such as grilled tuna steak were offered at our latest visit. Also available are shabu shabu and sushi special dinners, $42 for two.

Among desserts are bananas tempura, a poached pear on ice cream with ginger sauce and a frozen chocolate cake as thick as fudge, served with vanilla ice cream. But we could not be dissuaded from our favorite ginger ice cream, rendered here to perfection.

(508) 362-5522. Entrées, $14.50 to $27. Dinner, Tuesday-Sunday from 5.

Abbicci, 43 Main St. (Route 6A), Yarmouth Port.

Veteran restaurateur Marietta Hickey was among the first to bring northern Italian cooking to Cape Cod at the former La Cipollina nearby. She continues to be in the vanguard at this with-it establishment, offering a variety of dining options in a charming Cape-style house painted butterscotch yellow with the date 1755 engraved on the chimney. Locals crowd into the 75 seats in four dining areas and a reception area with mod seats at a black slate bar and tables against the windows for food rated up there with the Cape's best.

The kitchen executes an ambitious menu created by Marietta, who changed the format in 2005 to add a lengthy repertoire of tapas and make most entrées available in small and large portions. The tapas, antipasti and homemade pastas are first-rate, among them the beef carpaccio with shaved parmesan, the prawns sautéed with garlic and chiles, the crispy fried calamari with lemon vinaigrette and the tomato tagliatelle with smoked salmon, English peas and fennel in grappa-sage cream sauce.

Entrées range from breast and confit of poussin roasted with prosciutto and rosemary to grilled beef tenderloin with cabernet demi-glace. Typical options include almond-crusted wild Alaska king salmon with a fig and balsamic glaze, pan-roasted diver sea scallops with white truffle cream sauce and sautéed veal rib chop milanese.

Desserts are to die for, especially the raspberry-peach mousse torte, the vanilla bean panna cotta with mixed berry compote and the banana fritters with vanilla ice cream and rum-caramel sauce. Finish with the seductive Abbicci cappuccino, a heavily liqueured concoction that might just finish you off. The extensive wine list is mostly Italian, well chosen in a broad price range.

We returned lately for a lunch that got off to a shaky start with too-loud jazz playing in the background and niggardly glasses of white wine. Things improved with crumbly, piping-hot rolls and our main choices: a kicky steak sandwich with arugula and gorgonzola, served on grilled country bread, and an assertive linguini and shellfish, with all kinds of vegetables from squash and peppers to tomatoes and asparagus. Warm raisin gingerbread with lemon mousse and applejack brandy sauce was a memorable dessert.

The decor is crisp and contemporary in white and black. Bottles of San Pellegrino water and olive oil act as centerpieces on the white-clothed tables. The subdued maps of ancient Italy on the yellow or royal blue walls were hand-drawn by Marietta's son, a San Francisco architect who oversaw Abbicci's redesign.

(508) 362-3501. www.abbicci.com. Entrées, $26 to $34. Lunch, Monday-Saturday 11:30 to 2:30. Tapas daily, 2:30 to 9:30. Dinner nightly, from 5. Sunday brunch, 11:30 to 2:30.

Abba Café, 89 Old Colony Way, Orleans.

Mediterranean-Thai cuisine is the unusual pairing at this chic charmer that began as a takeout shop. French-trained chef-owner Erez Pinhas and his wife Christina Bratberg, a New Yorker whose family had summered on the Cape, fashioned a sophisticated, 40-seat restaurant from the old Brown Bag Restaurant in back, a famous spot for breakfast in years past. Old-timers would never recognize its transformation into a contemporary showplace in pale gray and off-salmon colors, with white-clothed tables and artworks on loan from the Blue Heron Gallery.

From their basement kitchen, Erez and sous chef Pry Grasint, a cook from Thailand with whom he had worked for five years at top restaurants in his native Israel, send forth a delectable array of uncommon-for-the-area fare. Thai steamed mussels in coconut milk and pineapple, shrimp noodle salad, Wellfleet oysters on the-half shell with Thai-lemon sauce, and Moroccan "cigars" with hummus and turkish salad quickly became signature appetizers.

House favorites among main courses include a terrific scallop and shrimp pad thai, duck breast with gnocchi and broccolini in a satay sauce, and spice-rubbed

Owners Christina Bratberg and chef Erez Pinhas take a break at Abba Café.

grilled rack of lamb. Exotic flavors enhance such options as Cape Cod sea bass in a sweet and spicy tamarind sauce and grilled filet mignon with green coconut-curry pasta and grilled eggplant.

The taste treats culminate in memorable desserts. Among them are caramel cheesecake with poached pears, lemongrass crème brûlée, rhubarb napoleon with strawberry sorbet, and warm walnut-date pudding cake with toffee sauce and ginger ice cream.

The wine list, from boutique wineries around the world, is as unusual as the rest of the fare.

(508) 255-8144. www.abbarestaurant.com. Entrées, $25 to $34. Dinner, Tuesday-Sunday from 5.

902 Main, 902 Main St. (Route 28), South Yarmouth.

A romantic glow is cast by candles and tiny white lights flickering everywhere – behind the bar, above the mantel, inside the fireplace, reflected in gilt-framed mirrors – in this 45-seat restaurant hidden inside a former pizza parlor. Even the funky restrooms sparkle, from a chandelier overhead and faux gems embedded in the sinks.

Gilbert and Kolleen Pepin, Maine natives who trained at the Regatta in Cotuit, returned from Florida in 2003 to open their own stylish restaurant to unusually quick and high acclaim, he in the kitchen and she out front. Within two years, the Zagat Survey propelled it into one of the its top-rated Cape restaurants and Boston magazine named it the Cape's best in 2005.

The unassuming roadhouse exterior and the plain-jane name mask an enterprise of uncommon appeal, from superior food to charming ambiance to flawless service. At a spring dinner, two unexpected amusés – a smoked salmon canapé and mozzarella with tapenade – hinted at the treats to follow. Homemade bread arrived fresh from the oven in a tin basket and a Crosspoint chardonnay from California was served in a silver bucket engraved with wine appellations.

Champagne sorbet topped with lemon zest in a liqueur glass cleared the palate for our entrées, sautéed soft-shell crabs in a winning lemon, caper and brown butter sauce and fabulous sautéed lobster and shrimp, served with white wine-butter sauce, oyster mushrooms, sugar snap peas and lemon fettuccine. Other choices that night ranged from bouillabaisse and roasted duck breast and leg with port wine and cranberry sauce to grilled buffalo sirloin sauced with cabernet-horseradish cream and grilled veal tenderloin with morel cream sauce.

Starters included smooth lobster bisque with aioli toast, a smoked salmon palette (smoked, tartare and cured), homemade game sausage and sautéed foie gras with morels and sauternes sauce. Desserts were a raspberry napoleon, chocolate trilogy, grand marnier crème brûlée and homemade mango sorbet.

The mix of booths and well spaced tables, elegant yet homey, made for a comfortable dining experience.

(508) 398-9902. www.902main.com. Entrées, $25 to $33. Dinner, Tuesday-Sunday from 5:30.

The Eldredge Room, 70 Queen Anne Road, Chatham.

Ever since it was rescued from near ruin in 1978 by Austrian Guenther Weinkopf, the 30-room Queen Anne Inn and its small dining room have had their ups and downs. That was particularly true of the roller-coaster restaurant, depending on the succession of chefs who came and left in efforts to make it work.

Toby Hill's Eldredge Room appears to have succeeded. The Johnson & Wales culinary graduate settled into the Queen Anne kitchen in 2005 with considerable fanfare after stints at Spire and The Federalist in Boston and at Chillingsworth and the Chatham Bars Inn on the Cape. It marked a homecoming of sorts for the young chef, whose mother's maiden name was Eldredge and whose ancestors settled in Chatham in the 1600s.

The intimate, 40-seat dining room at the back of the inn looks out onto gardens and Oyster Bay Pond in the distance. It's an antiquey, European-style and unlikely setting for a culinary pioneer to use unexpected combinations of ingredients to create a truly original cuisine. He calls it "American Experience Cuisine" and focuses on local growers and vintners.

Dinner is available à la carte or in tasting formats of six or eleven courses ($65 and $100 respectively).

The menu begins with seven kinds of caviar and serious stuff like pickled beet and feta salad, Chatham fluke tartare and walnut-crusted foie gras with all the fads and flourishes of contemporary cuisine. Perhaps typical is the appetizer listed as Broken Arrow Ranch venison lollipops, with "Knob Creek 9-yr. Straight Bourbon Whiskey vinaigrette, Renwood Old Vine Zinfandel gastrique and whole-grain mustard and honey sauce."

For main courses, the chef might wrap Chatham monkfish in Smithfield ham and serve it with a carrot consommé, potato puree, and caramelized brussels sprouts and shallots. The grilled Wolfe's Neck farm sirloin on a fall menu is served with peanut "chili," herb-roasted hedgehog mushrooms and mushroom-infused beef sauce. The Grimaud Farms muscovy duck comes with a duck heart confit, grape and shallot compote, pickled shallot puree, mustard greens and seared foie gras. Even the fish and chips is elevated here to truffle-crusted Chatham cod with frites, offered with truffle tartar sauce and a malt vinaigrette.

Desserts are equally exotic. The chef made his own root beer for a summer root-beer float laden with sweet cream ice cream and topped with foamy vanilla cream. In the fall that became a caramel-apple soda float with caramel soda, mulled apple cider ice cream and Granny Smith apple foam. The springtime strawberry composition included a milkshake, a panna cotta topped with strawberries, a strawberry compote flavored with basil and balsamic vinegar, and a tiny strawberry soufflé. A Hawaiian chocolate soufflé served with peanut butter ice cream was a hit all season long.

Some diners opt for the American cheese selection displayed in the restaurant's foyer. Up to eight choices are offered with a selection of house-made sourdough crackers, nuts, jams and fruits.

The meal is heightened by a high-end American wine repertoire of sixteen wines by the glass that you can order in two- or four-ounce increments, plus a remarkable selection of whole and half bottles of New England's and the West Coast's best.

(508) 945-2990. www.eldredgeroom.com. Entrées, $25 to $37. Dinner, 6 to 10, nightly in July and August, nightly except Tuesday in May-June and September-October, Wednesday-Sunday in April and Thursday-Sunday in November and December. Closed January-March.

L'Alouette Bistro, 787 Main St. (Route 28), Harwich Port.

Modern French cuisine is served up with style at this old-timer under new ownership.

Proprietors Alan and Gretchen Champney took over the shingled Cape Cod house with blue-gray shutters and awnings and dormer windows upstairs from French owners in 2004. They freshened up the decor in a series of three dining rooms, open one to the next. White-clothed tables are well spaced and illuminated by track lighting.

Executive chef Steven Graves accompanied the couple from the Nauset Beach Club and Abbicci, where the men had worked together for eleven years. They rewrote the French menu in simplified style in keeping with their dramatic new logo.

The chef is known for spectacular sauces, as in a lime, coriander and cumin beurre blanc for the seared diver scallops and a basil oil and saffron red pepper vinaigrette for the tapenade-crusted salmon. A ginger-mustard sauternes sauce dresses the roast chicken, and a Bordeaux lamb sauce enhances the Colorado lamb loin crusted in walnuts and basil. The Kobe rib steak is prepared with garlic-parsley butter and served with an heirloom tomato and mozzarella salad and frites.

Typical starters range widely from a chilled summer gazpacho with poached shrimp to a foie gras torchon with pear chutney on toasted brioche. You might also find a gratin of native mussels, warm oysters with a light fennel curry and salmon caviar, escargots in puff pastry and a pepper-seared tuna napoleon with miso vinaigrette.

The pastry chef's desserts run from tarte tatin to crème brûlée to a trio of chocolate mousses – chocolate grand marnier, white chocolate with pistachio and bittersweet with raspberry sauce and crème anglaise.

The well-chosen wine list is categorized by French regions and "new world." Fine estate-bottled wines, poured in Riedel stemware, are featured at good values from the high twenties.

(508) 439-0405. www.lalouettebistro.com. Entrées, $22 to $34. Dinner nightly, from 5.

Provincetown Prizes

Some of the best eating on the Cape takes place in far-out Provincetown. "We're more progressive up here," one restaurateur said in explaining both the quality and quantity of culinary creativity. An entire chapter could be devoted to Provincetown, but space limitations preclude more than a sampling of the very best:

Chester, 404 Commercial St., Provincetown.

Poised in a pillared Greek Revival sea captain's house, this stylish restaurant garnered rave reviews shortly after opening – one calling it the town's best and probably the hottest restaurant on the entire Cape.

Owners John Guerra and Jay Coburn, who know their food and wine, named it for their pet airedale terrier. Jay oversees the kitchen staff of seven, while John, a former diplomat with the U.S. Foreign Service, manages the front of the house.

The dining room with butter yellow walls and white trim is pristine and serene. A few artworks provide color. Rows of tables are lined up ever-so-perfectly facing banquettes along walls on two sides. The demeanor is proper to the point of being uptight – some find it a bit austere.

Understated, beautifully presented food is the hallmark of the kitchen staff, who procure local seafood and pick produce from a garden behind the restaurant. The menu is short and focused, listing all the ingredients, as in roasted Atlantic salmon with carrots and harissa, carrot puree, garden-grown mint pesto and sugar snap peas. Other main courses in the seasonal repertoire might be butter-poached lobster with orzo and mascarpone, roast free-range chicken with sage cream and brussels sprout-bacon-apple hash, and grilled lamb sirloin with parsnip-celery root puree and maple-glazed cranberries. Chester's autumn surf and turf yielded Chinese five-spice-crusted diver scallops and seared free-range duck breast à l'orange.

Starters included cod cakes with celery root rémoulade, an item called "quack, quack: confit of duck with polenta and house-smoked duck breast with micro greens salad" and a trio of beets: red and golden beet napoleon with chèvre, roasted beet tartare and truffled beet micro greens.

Dessert could be peach tarte tatin with basil ice cream, molten bittersweet chocolate cake with raspberry sorbet and chocolate tuile, individual goat-cheese cheesecakes with poached figs and pistachio praline, homemade ice creams and sorbets, or a selection of artisanal camembert cheeses with muscat-poached apricots. Chester's award-winning wine list features more than 160 vintages from small producers around the world, most priced between $30 and $100 and not commonly seen elsewhere in the area.

(508) 487-8200. www.chesterrestaurant.com. Entrées, $27 to $39. Dinner nightly in season, from 6; fewer nights off-season. Closed January-March.

The Mews Restaurant & Café, 429 Commercial St., Provincetown.

Innovative fare is offered here in a dynamite waterfront setting – a romantic downstairs dining room that looks like an extension of the beach just outside its walls of glass. The designer even took samples of sand to Boston to match with the paint on the terra cotta walls, which are hung with changing abstract art. Floodlights illuminate the beach, and from virtually every white-clothed table you have the illusion of eating outside.

Owner Ron Robin and executive chef Laurence de Freitas feature American fusion

Window tables are right beside the beach at The Mews Restaurant.

cuisine. A basket of breads arrived as we were seated for dinner. Among appetizers, we liked the oysters with crabmeat béchamel and pancetta, albeit a precious little serving that we had planned to share, and a classic caesar salad. Garlicky shrimp with a chile pepper sauce, panko-crusted calamari with a szechuan cilantro-lime sauce and tempura-fried tuna maki rolls with a spicy mayo are among the fiery possibilities.

Main courses range from hoisin-brushed, sesame-crusted Atlantic salmon with sweet chili sauce to Mediterranean spice-rubbed rack of lamb. Our smoked pork tenderloin with apricot-serrano chile sauce was served with sweet potato polenta, while the shrimp curry came in a puff pastry with black mission figs.

Creamy key lime pie was a hit from the dessert tray, as was the ginger-chocolate pot de crème. Service was polished and the food preparation satisfying, but the romantic beachside setting – illuminated as darkness fell – is what remains etched in our memories.

The upstairs bar area called **Café Mews** offers a casual American bistro menu of appetizers, sandwiches, pastas and light entrées. Here you'll also find a vodka bar, billed as New England's largest, with more than 175 brands from 27 countries.

(508) 487-1500. www.mews.com. Entrées, $23 to $32; café, $9.95 to $21.95. Dinner nightly, from 6. Sunday brunch, 11 to 2:30 late May-September.

Front Street Restaurant, 230 Commercial St., Provincetown.

Chef-owner Donna Aliperti has endowed this perennial local favorite with her special creative touch nurtured by Julia Child. Growing up in a restaurant family in New Jersey, she worked in the kitchen with her father before summering in Provincetown and taking over Front Street in 1986. Confessing that she was a self-taught chef, Julia Child advised, "Donna, you must say you learn day by day." She now says every day has become a learning experience, and she's had a lot of them.

Gourmet magazine requested Donna's recipe for corn and crab chowder, while Bon Appétit inquired about her coffee-toffee pie. She and Kathy Cotter, sous chef and pastry chef, offer two menus: an Italian featuring authentic recipes and a continental menu that changes every Friday. Potato-crusted salmon with raspberry butter and thyme, tea-smoked duck, herb-crusted rack of lamb and grilled angus ribeye with white truffle cream sauce are perennial favorites. Good starters are the duck and mango spring roll, tuna carpaccio, smoked salmon chowder, grilled quail framboise and the mozzarella antipasto, made daily on the premises. The raspberry-chocolate tiramisu, the nectarine tarte tatin with bourbon-pecan ice cream, and the pistachio and warm chocolate ganache cake with crème anglaise are to groan over. If they don't finish you off, the homemade ice creams and sorbets will.

The dining room with brick walls in the cellar of a Victorian house is dark, intimate and very bistro-ish. Striking tables made by a local artist are topped with tiny pieces of cut-up wood under a layer of polyurethane. Wines are showcased in backlit storage shelves along one wall.

(508) 487-9715. www.frontstreetrestaurant.com. Entrées, $19.95 to $26.95. Dinner nightly in summer, 6 to 10; Wednesday-Sunday in off-season. Closed January-April.

L'Uva Restaurant, 133 Bradford St., Provincetown.

The entry to this white shingled house with red trim, born about 1840 as the Sidehall Cottage, is now identified by a cluster of grapes to go with its new name. Chef Christopher Covelli, a graduate of the French Culinary Institute in New York and senior instructor at the Toscana Saporita Cooking School in Italy, was pastry chef at Chester and the Martin House in Provincetown before opening his own 107-seat restaurant with co-owner Peter Garza.

L'Uva retains the aura of a private residence with its warren of small, candlelit dining rooms where white-clothed tables are set against a backdrop of pale sunset hues. Greenery strung with white lights envelops the garden terrace in season.

The chef divides the main part of his menu into French, Italian, Spanish and "haute American" categories relating to his background. His Abbruzzi heritage is reflected in such pastas as pappardelle with bacon, tomatoes and shrimp, and ravioli stuffed with crabmeat and lobster. Duck à l'orange and pernod seafood stew testify to his French training. His Spanish offering might be oven-roasted cod with piquillo peppers and spinach. Pork tenderloin Rio Grande style and filet mignon with a tamarind-chipotle demi-glace are representative American choices.

Typical starters are tortilla soup, puff pastry with three cheeses, a dim sum plate and escargots. Desserts include lavender crème brûlée, panna cotta with grilled pineapple and berries, and a pastry crisp filled with white pistachio ice cream and blueberries.

The wine list carries a Wine Spectator award. Adjourn to the upstairs bar – arguably the most atmospheric in town – for an after-dinner grappa.

(508) 487-2010. www.luvarestaurant.com. Entrées, $18 to $27. Dinner nightly in summer, from 6; Thursday-Sunday in off-season.

The Red Inn, 15 Commercial St., Provincetown.

Three waterfront dining areas are strung out along the rear of this recently renovated 1805 sea captain's house, an old-timer painted bright red with white trim in the residential West End. Under new ownership, the 54-seat restaurant sports a polished, more contemporary look than its wide-board hardwood floors and beamed ceilings would indicate.

Executive chef Phillip Mossy from Louisiana, one of the inn's four owners, presents new American cuisine equal to the waterside setting. Repeat diners tend to go for

Red Inn dining room looks out onto gardens on the left and ocean on the right.

the raw-bar selections as preliminaries to the inn's "big 22-ounce porterhouse steak" or pepper-crusted filet mignon with Jack Daniels sauce. Others like to start with the spicy lobster corn chowder and perhaps a bacon-wrapped oyster brochette or lobster and artichoke fondue in a warm sourdough bread bowl.

Chef Mossy imparts Louisiana accents to such main courses as shrimp and crawfish sautéed with mushrooms in a sherry-creole tomato cream sauce over pasta, and creole-seasoned duck breast grilled with a passionfruit-maple glaze. His pan-roasted local cod might be served on a bed of rosemary potatoes and applewood bacon with a lemon-garlic confit.

The Red Inn also offers four beachfront guest rooms, two suites and two cottage-style residences renting for $220 to $445 a night.

(508) 487-7334 or (866) 473-3466. www.theredinn.com. Entrées, $23 to $42. Dinner nightly, 5:30 to 10, May-October; Thursday-Sunday in off-season. Brunch, Thursday-Sunday 10 to 2:30 in summer, weekends in late spring and early fall. Closed January to mid-April.

Ross' Grill, 237 Commercial St., Provincetown.

Some of the most interesting food in town is served at this urbane and hip café and raw bar. The place is right above the beach, on the second level at the far end of a shopping arcade called Whaler's Wharf.

The pity is it's so small and, for the not so hip, rather uncomfortable. Beneath a high jet-black ceiling stand eight bleached-pine tables, half of them of the high bar variety flanked by bar-stool perches. Thirteen more seats for dining line the central bar.

From a tiny open kitchen beside the entry, chef-owner Ken Ross prepares the likes of crispy Tuscan cod, shellfish risotto, crab cakes with spicy rémoulade sauce, steak frites and rack of New Zealand lamb. Start with his escargots in puff pastry, chicken liver and pistachio pâté or even a basket of hand-cut french fries. Finish with a dessert from the pastry case beside the door – the crème brûlée is highly recommended. Cobb salad and oyster po-boys star on the lunch menu.

(508) 487-8878. Entrées, $16 to $30. Lunch, Wednesday-Monday 11:30 to 4. Dinner, Wednesday-Monday 5:30 to 9:30. Closed in February.

More Good Dining

The Barnstable Restaurant and Tavern, 3176 Main St. (Route 6A), Barnstable Village.

This Barnstable landmark moved up a notch in Cape culinary circles with its acquisition in 2005 by chef Bob Calderone and his wife Susan Finegold, former proprietors of Anago restaurant in Cambridge and later in Boston. In a reversal of the usual movement of chefs from the hinterlands into the city, the Calderones tired of the reverse commute from Boston to their weekend home on Cape Cod. After a few years at a Mashpee Commons catering establishment, they wanted to get back into the restaurant business and this "fell into our laps," according to Susan.

The restaurant, built new to look old in the 1980s, never lived up to its potential under previous owners. The Calderones dressed up the 90-seat dining room with four stunning paintings of vegetables from their Cambridge restaurant, retained the atmospheric tavern and put to good use the lovely courtyard dining patio out front. They expanded the menu in an effort to make the fare "more accessible" to Cape Cod wallets and palates, lowering the price point and supplementing some Anago-like favorites with a wide-ranging repertoire of Italian specialties, tavern sandwiches and – talk about down-scaling – fried seafood.

The last lures the multitudes necessary to make a go of so large a year-round venture, they say. Purists are well satisfied by such Calderone signature dishes as lobster ravioli with shrimp, scallops and mussels in saffron cream, sole piccata and roast duck with orange liqueur, cranberries and ginger. Appetizers range from two presentations of steamed mussels to fried calamari with caper berries, hot peppers and tartar sauce. Desserts could be crème caramel, tiramisu or Susan's cheesecake with lemon cream.

(508) 362-2355. www.barnstablerestaurant.com. Entrées, $13.75 to $24.50. Lunch daily, 11:30 to 4. Dinner nightly, 4 to 9.

The Brewster Fish House Restaurant, 2208 Main St. (Route 6A), Brewster.

Vernon Smith and his brother David took over what had been a retail fish market and converted it into one of the Cape's best seafood restaurants. Now run by Vernon and his wife Melissa, it's a simple but stylish little café where the self-taught chef mans the kitchen and produces a satisfying array of creative treats incorporating the freshest fish available.

Small and personal, this is a pure place – nothing like the take-a-number-and-hope-for-the-best of the ubiquitous fried-fish ilk. The only meat on the printed menu involves free-range chicken and braised beef shortribs. Otherwise it's all seafood, from crispy whole fish with soy-lime dipping sauce to a butter-poached lobster tart with fava beans, carrots, pearl onions and preserved lemon in puff pastry. In between are treats like herb-roasted saddle of monkfish with pancetta emulsion, sautéed local cod with pesto sauce, and pan-seared dayboat sea scallops with basil oil. The mixed grill might combine swordfish, shrimp, scallops and andouille sausage with a creole dipping sauce.

All the appetizers save one – a salad of baby lettuces, roasted beets and gorgonzola – involve seafood. Bigeye tuna tartare, steamed littlenecks and mussels in a saffron broth and sautéed Maine jonah crab cake with preserved lemon butter are typical. Or you might start with fish chowder or lobster bisque.

The day's desserts could be crème brûlée, flourless chocolate torte with raspberry sauce and roasted hazelnut cheesecake. The wine list is as well chosen as the rest of the menu. Many wines are available by the glass.

Dining is at white-clothed tables topped with candles and flowers. Classical music or soft jazz plays in the background.

(508) 896-7867. Entrées, $18 to $29. Lunch daily, 11:30 to 3. Dinner, 5 to 9:30 or 10. Closed Monday in off-season. Closed late December to April.

Nauset Beach Club, 222 Main St., East Orleans.

On the way to the beach, this summery little white Cape-style house with red awnings is a landmark for casual, contemporary Italian cuisine. New owner Art Duquette oversees the intimate restaurant seating about 55 in the main dining room and a smaller room with a fireplace on the upper level.

His chefs make good use of a wood-fired oven for the signature sliced grilled prime sirloin alla griglia, enhanced with shaved pecorino-romano and truffle oil. Among other entrées, consider the sundried tomato-crusted halibut with lobster essence reduction and the grilled pork chop with caramelized peaches and shallots. The sautéed veal sirloin cutlet milanese is topped with a salad of roasted tomato, basil, aged balsamic vinegar, virgin olive oil and shaved parmigiano-reggiano. The pistachio-crusted roast rack of lamb comes with a balsamic demi-glace, caramelized fennel and piccoline olive polenta.

Start with smoked salmon crostini, roasted oysters or shiitake mushroom-stuffed quail. Homemade pasta dishes such as fettuccine with lobster and asparagus tips and ravioli stuffed with ricotta cheese and swiss chard are available as appetizers or main courses.

Instead of the usual Italian suspects for dessert, look for the likes of cappuccino mousse torte, orange shortbread and blackberry napoleon with orange-blossom honey crème fraîche, amaretti-crusted mascarpone cheesecake with mountain blackberries, and dark coffee gelato with homemade caramel and biscotti. An assortment of artisan cheeses also is available.

The international wine list, starting in the low thirties, has an interesting selection of Italian reds.

(508) 255-8547. www.nausetbeachclub.com. Entrées, $22 to $34. Dinner nightly, from 5.

Pisces, 2653 Main St. (Route 28), South Chatham.

"Coastal cooking" is the theme of this summery, low-profile charmer, ensconced in a sweet yellow house up against the road. Chef-owner Susan L. Connors named it for a favorite Barbados eatery on the water, adding it's "a good name for a mostly seafood restaurant."

Sue, who became executive chef at the Inn at Harvard in Cambridge at age 25, is a veteran of top Boston area restaurants. For her solo venture, she gutted the former Andiamo restaurant and created a stylish 48-seater that's nicely nautical in white and royal blue. Booths and white-clothed tables are set against a backdrop of white walls hung with seashore artworks. A couple of brass fish sculptures are focal points.

The menu is rolled up in a blue ribbon. Untie it to reveal a panoply of culinary treats. Look for appetizers such as seared rare tuna drizzled with wasabi-lime mustard and soy glaze, served with a gingered vegetable salad, and crab and lobster cakes with mango salsa and sweet and spicy dipping sauce. Sue's risotto of the day is always a good choice, as are her pasta dishes, perhaps lobster ravioli with sautéed mushrooms, butter beans and parmesan-prosciutto cream.

Typical main courses are a Mediterranean-style fisherman's stew in a saffron-lobster broth, grilled salmon fillet with dill-butter sauce and roasted local cod brushed with lemon-thyme oil. Meat-eaters are well served by the likes of a veal T-bone chop with portobello mushroom and balsamic demi-glace and grilled garlic-rubbed ribeye steak topped with creamy gorgonzola butter.

Sweet endings could be a signature oreo cookie cheesecake, bananas foster and chocolate-walnut tart. The Godiva chocolate martini is recommended for an unusual "dessert in a glass."

(508) 432-4600. www.piscesofchatham.com. Entrées, $20 to $27. Dinner nightly in summer, from 5; Wednesday-Sunday in off-season. Closed December-March.

The Cape Sea Grille, 31 Sea St., Harwich Port.

A few tables on the sun porch in this former sea captain's house offer a view of the ocean down the street. The scene inside the pale yellow and green main dining room is handsome as well with white linens and Lalique-style lamps atop nicely spaced tables. It's a serene setting for some highly regarded food offered by a succession of owners.

The latest, Douglas and Jennifer Ramler from Boston, offer a menu they tout as "creative American cuisine." Doug, a veteran of Boston area restaurants including Hamersley's Bistro, is in the kitchen and his wife runs the front of the house.

The emphasis is on seafood: perhaps seared sea scallops with a grilled andouille pan sauce, coriander-encrusted tuna with a ginger-lime beurre blanc, and pan-seared lobster with pancetta and a calvados-saffron reduction. Orange- and soy-roasted chicken with orange-honey butter sauce and chile oil, filet mignon au poivre, and herb-crusted rack of lamb with minted jus and roasted garlic custard are other entrée possibilities.

The chefs get creative with such starters as asparagus bisque with crème fraîche and smoked salmon, crispy oysters with green goddess dressing and avocado, and beef carpaccio with herbed goat cheese and radish slaw. A cheese plate is available before or after dinner. Other options to finish with are a hazelnut fig tart with cinnamon-mascarpone ice cream, cherry spice crème brûlée, and assorted ice creams and sorbets.

On busy nights, the rear garden room that used to be a country lounge is opened for overflow. It's a delightful space with a remarkable, full-length mural of a Cape Cod scene on the far wall.

(508) 432-4745. www.capeseagrille.com. Entrées, $25 to $33. Dinner nightly, 5 to 10. Closed mid-November to April.

Bleu, 10 Market Square, Mashpee Commons, Mashpee.

The menu arrives in two slabs of wood tied together at this with-it new bistro in the up-and-coming Mashpee Commons lifestyle center. The interior of the restaurant is cool in shades of blue with rust accents and white paper globe lights hanging from the ceiling. A sleek aquarium occupies a central position in the front bar.

Executive chef Frederic Feufeu, a native of Brittany, offers some of the Cape's more arresting contemporary fare. Seated for lunch on the sidewalk patio, we enjoyed the grilled ahi tuna niçoise salad – not composed as usual but rather a slab of tuna grilled medium rare on a bed of mesclun – and a good but gloppy sandwich of grilled lamb loin kabob in pita bread with goat cheese, sliced cucumber and tabbouleh.

At night, regulars go for the bistro specialties, ranging from salmon baked on an oak wood plank to braised rabbit casserole with smoked bacon and wild mushrooms in sparkling cider. Other entrées vary from potato-crusted halibut with miso-mustard hollandaise to roasted rack of lamb with a pecan and goat cheese crust. Starters might be "Fred's bacalao" codfish chowder, scallop seviche over daikon radish and cucumber, poached foie gras au torchon, or the night's "trio for two," at our visit salmon tartare with fennel cream and fried shrimp tempura, assorted tomato tartare with basil oil and reggiano toast, and duck terrine with wild mushrooms and cranberries and garlic sausage.

Typical desserts are caramelized apple tarte tatin with crème fraîche, hot chocolate truffle cake with vanilla bean ice cream and raspberry crème brûlée.

(508) 539-7907. www.bleurestaurant.com. Entrées, $18 to $29. Lunch, Monday-Saturday 11:30 to 4. Dinner nightly, 5 to 10. Sunday jazz brunch, 11:30 to 3:30.

Chapoquoit Grill, 410 West Falmouth Hwy. (Route 28A), West Falmouth.

People wait up to two hours on busy nights for one of the 95 seats in this trendy but affordable grill. They come for wood-fired pizzas from a huge brick oven that occupies an open room off the entry, "big-flavored" appetizers and entrées, specials that are truly special and a wine list with many choices priced under $20.

Unassuming on the outside, "Chappy's" is much bigger than it looks with a bar and waiting area and a large rear dining room. The last has a vaguely tropical theme: splashy patterned cloths on the widely spaced tables, colorful sea prints on the salmon-colored walls and the odd fish silhouette hanging from a trellis screening the two-story-high ceiling.

The printed menu offers appetizers like littleneck clams steamed Portuguese style, deep-fried calamari, and the chef's antipasti. Entrées range from penne alla vodka and wild mushroom ravioli to cioppino. Specialty pizzas are available in small and large sizes. They include margarita, shrimp diavolo, southwestern and chef Carl Bonnert's favorite – grilled chicken with broccoli, mushrooms and provolone.

The specials board generates the most excitement. Consider one night's selections: snapper marinated in tequila and ginger and served with coconut-mango relish, cumin-rubbed swordfish with roasted jalapeño butter, roasted coffee-encrusted pork tenderloin with raspberry and hoisin sauce, and grilled sirloin marinated in tequila and cilantro with a chipotle demi-glace.

Desserts follow suit: a classic tiramisu, mango cheesecake with macadamia nut crust, exotic gelatos and sorbets made by a neighbor down the road.

"We keep things changing so people will come back," says the chef. People certainly do.

(508) 540-7794. Entrées, $11.50 to $25.95. Dinner nightly, 5 to 10.

Dining and Lodging

The Bramble Inn & Restaurant, 2019 Main St. (Route 6A), Brewster 01631.

White linens, pretty floral china in the Victoria pattern from Czechoslovakia, candles in hurricane lamps and assorted flowers in vases grace the five small dining rooms seating a total of 60 at this inn renowned for its restaurant. Ruth and Cliff Manchester, who got their start at his parents' Old Manse Inn nearby, have continued the tradition here – lately augmented by their daughters and sons-in-law, all talented chefs in their own right.

Star chef Ruth, an inventive cook, is still the inspiration and guiding light for the family-run endeavor. Joining her in the kitchen are her sons-in-law, David Plum, formerly of the famed Ryland Inn in New Jersey, and Paris-born Jim Alarie, lately the executive chef of the Marco Island Radisson Resort in Florida. Jim's wife Elise is the Bramble's pastry chef. Ruth's other daughter, Andrea, fills in as assistant pastry chef and helps Cliff manage the dining room.

The four-course, prix-fixe dinners ($44 to $68, depending on choice of entrée) draw rave press reviews and a devoted following. The soups are triumphs: perhaps Bermuda fish chowder, chilled cherry with port and crème fraîche, four-onion soup with brie croutons or a lettuce and scallion bisque. Ruth has fun with the appetizers, among them a roasted Tuscan vegetable "caviar" bruschetta, clam and black bean hush puppies with chipotle pepper-tartar sauce or an "SLT," a Scottish smoked salmon rillette in a tomato flute. We were mighty impressed with the New England seafood chili: cod, clams and tuna in a spicy tomato sauce with black beans, jack cheese and sour cream.

A salad or sorbet precedes the main course, the choices ranging from flat fish ka'anapali (boneless stacked fillets of local catch with banana stuffing, pickled ginger-melon salsa and citrus beurre blanc) to pinenut-crusted rack of lamb with a gingered carrot and crème fraîche puree. Ruth's version of surf and turf is parchment-roasted chicken with lazy lobster in a champagne sauce. We loved her signature dish – assorted seafood curry – combining lobster, cod, scallops and shrimp in a light curry sauce accompanied by banana, coconut, almonds and chutney.

Desserts are inventive: white-chocolate coeur à la crème (a recipe requested by Bon Appétit magazine), a strawberry mousse and angel cake tower layered with vanilla crème fraîche, and a treat called lemon jewel tarte, a toasted pistachio butter pastry lined with blueberries and topped with a baked lemon filling, brandied whipped cream and blueberry-maple nectar.

The small, paneled Hunt Room houses a service bar. The limited but serviceable wine list offers good values.

Upstairs in the 1861 house are five guest rooms with sloping floors, furnished with queen beds and TVs in a comfortable country style. One in the rear has a new balcony. Guests enjoy a full breakfast on the cheery dining porch of the main inn.

(508) 896-7644. www.brambleinn.com. Five rooms with private baths. Doubles, $138 to $168.

Prix-fixe, $44 to $68. Dinner by reservation, nightly except Monday in summer, 6 to 9; Thursday-Sunday in spring and fall. Closed January to early May.

Wequassett Inn, Pleasant Bay, Chatham 02633.

Cape Cod has perhaps no more majestic water view amid more elegant surroundings than from the restored, 18th-century "square top" sea captain's mansion that houses the dining room at this venerable inn, resort and golf club.

After a $2 million renovation, the dining facility reopened under a new name, **Twenty-Eight Atlantic.** Floor-to-ceiling windows on three sides yield bay views in a large room that became more stunning with rich wood paneling, subtle maritime paintings, stylish upholstered chairs and candles in huge glass hurricane lamp

Twenty-Eight Atlantic dining room offers panoramic view of Pleasant Bay.

chandeliers. A two-tiered garden terrace off the lounge overlooking Pleasant Bay is an enjoyable place for cocktails. Behind the dining room is **Thoreau's,** a club-like bar with leather and suede furnishings, fireplace and mahogany bar. Also new is the beachy **Outer Bar & Grille.** Beside the bay with a canopied deck above the water and large tropical-style rattan chairs at glass tables, it offers lunch and dinner daily in summer.

These are the varied settings for superior food created by executive chef Bill Brodsky, most recently from the Charleston Grill in the Charleston Place hotel in South Carolina, who brought his culinary team with him.

Menus come in weighty double covers that contain gel resembling sea water, sand and shells. The food descriptions cannot do justice to the complexities of the innovative combinations of ingredients nor their architectural presentations.

Dinner might start with a trio of tartare – spicy yellowfin tuna, gingered hamachi and truffled salmon – or a trio of tomato and goat cheese – chilled soup, parfait and sandwich. The wait staff has a bit of explaining to do when it comes to the duo of foie gras (one seared with coffee and fig french toast and the other a torchon with eos jelly), the composed salad of baby lola rossa and tango with candied pecans, and the lobster egg foo young with Thai basil puree and lemon-soy butter.

More exotica is imparted in such entrées as shallow poached dayboat haddock with trout roe sauce, crispy trout with caviar butter and ratatouille moderne, and roasted lamb with yellow pepper-black bean romesco. The strip steak comes with a trio of sauces, and the beef tenderloin may be enhanced with seared foie gras.

Desserts could include crème brûlée, cranberry mousse in an almond tuile with a red and white sauce underneath looking as lacy as a doily, and a frozen chambord mousse in a parfait glass. With candles lit and reflecting in the windows, it's a romantic atmosphere in which to linger over cappuccino and cordials.

We had only to amble off to our room, one of several in duplex cottages right by the bay, with a deck almost over the water. The 104 handsomely furnished rooms with all the amenities are in eighteen Cape-style cottages, motel buildings and condo-type facilities. They range from water-view suites to villas with cathedral ceilings and private balconies overlooking the woods and tennis courts.

(508) 432-5400 or (800) 225-7125. Fax (508) 432-5032. www.wequassett.com. Ninety-three rooms and eleven suites with private baths. Rates, EP. Doubles. $415 to $1,240 mid June to Labor Day, $310 to $825 in early June and September, $155 to $750 off-season. Closed December-March.

Entrées, $24 to $42. Lunch daily, 11:30 to 2. Dinner nightly, 6 to 10.

Crowne Pointe Historic Inn & Spa, 82 Bradford St., Provincetown 02657.

A multi-million renovation and plenty of extras helped this inn earn a four-diamond rating shortly after opening, and the addition of a bistro in 2005 cemented the deal.

David Sanford and Tom Walter from New Jersey restored a sea captain's mansion and various carriage houses that made up portions of two old inns to create a showy early-Victorian-era compound crowning a bluff in the center of town.

Common rooms and some of the 40 guest quarters are graced with period antiques, moldings, wainscoting and hardwood floors. All accommodations include a queensize bed dressed in 250-thread-count cotton linens, TV/VCR, aromatherapy bath amenities, chairs with reading lamps, a coffeemaker and refrigerator, as well as access from the main house to a two-story wraparound porch. Deluxe accommodations add "an expanded amenity," such as a kingsize bed, outdoor deck, fireplace or a whirlpool tub, and a few have two. Some open onto private porches or a spacious sundeck.

The property includes a nicely landscaped garden courtyard with a heated pool and a couple of ten-person whirlpool spas. A new Shui Spa, accessed via a bridge across a koi pond, offers full-service treatment rooms with licensed therapists.

Guests are welcomed at a complimentary wine, beer and cheese reception in the afternoon. An elaborate hot buffet breakfast – augmented by scrambled eggs and sausage or caramelized banana pancakes at our visit –is offered in the morning in the dining room or on the patio.

Beyond the foyer and Library Lounge, **The Bistro at Crowne Pointe** is set up at night in the dining room and an enclosed side porch. Executive chef Amy Howell's menu offers soups, salads and four appetizers (vegetable spring rolls and sesame-crusted tuna sashimi are a couple) and light fare (angus or turkey burgers, salade niçoise).

Her short list of main dishes ranges from steamed salmon served atop an herbed vegetable slaw to spice-crusted grilled lamb steak with apricot-almond-mustard chutney. Each lists a recommended pairing of both white or red wine (a French pouilly fuissé or cabernet sauvignon with the grilled filet mignon; a New Zealand pinot noir or a sauvignon blanc with the steamed seafood catch of the day). Other main-course selections at our visit included curried chicken breast, peking duck braised in a grand marnier reduction and grilled rack of lamb with a pomegranate-hoisin glaze.

Spa lunches are served at the Shui Spa.

(508) 487-6767 or (877) 276-9631. Fax (508) 487-5554. www.crownepointe.com. Thirty-six rooms and four suites with private baths. Doubles, $239 to $499 in summer, $119 to $479 rest of year.

Entrées, $21 to $32. Dinner, 6 to 8:30 nightly in summer, Thursday-Sunday in winter.

Breakfast on the rear deck is an extravagant event at High Pointe Inn.

Lodging

Among the many places to stay on the Cape, here are some with special appeal for vacationing gourmands.

High Pointe Inn, 70 High St., West Barnstable 02668.

Country breakfasts by candlelight are one of the hallmarks of this posh new B&B with a view overlooking Cape Cod Bay. Rich and Debbie Howard downsized in 2004 from the eleven-room Cabernet Inn they ran with great hospitality and flair in North Conway, N.H. Here, where they are closer to their offspring and grandchildren, they offer three deluxe guest rooms in a beautifully landscaped Cape-style house of 1989 vintage in a residential area of substantial homes.

The guest rooms are extra large and all yield views across the second-largest salt marsh on the East coast, with the dunes of the Sandy Neck barrier beach and Cape Cod Bay in the distance. Each has a queensize pencil-post or canopy bed dressed in 300-count linens and a modern bath outfitted with Gilchrist & Soames toiletries. The summery, cream-colored Sand Dollar Room on the main floor has a rattan chaise lounge beside a wood-burning fireplace and french doors onto a private deck. Picture windows in two colorful upstairs rooms frame panoramic bird's-eye views of the dunes and bay. Each has a cozy reading nook with a pair of swivel rockers or reclining wing chairs for taking in the view across the Great Salt Marsh..

On the main floor, pocket doors separate a cozy living room with a small bar and a games table from an airy great room with fireplace and a TV/DVD entertainment center with a growing library of movies. Bottled water and after-dinner cordials from the help-yourself bar are complimentary. You also can watch TV as you work out in the lower-level exercise room.

A raised deck stretches for 75 feet across the back of the house above gardens, plants and flowering trees that attract an array of native birds. It has lounge chairs for sunning and tables for al fresco breakfasts or cocktails.

Guests gather for breakfast on the deck or at a long farm-style table beneath a wrought-iron chandelier in the wainscoted dining room. A choice of five hot dishes is offered the night before by Rich, a former travel agency manager who honed his skills taking weekend courses at the Culinary Institute of America. The choice might involve his specialty, a German omelet made with sautéed apples, cranberry sauce and sausages. People travel from afar for his crispy french toast, a secret recipe flavored with spiced rum and vanilla imported from Tahiti. Other favorites are eggs benedict, an Italian omelet, pumpkin pancakes, belgian waffles and a northern Mexican egg dish called migas. Debbie bakes the muffins or coffeecakes that accompany.

(508) 362-4441 or (888) 362-4441. Fax (508) 362-4401. www.hpinn.com. Three rooms with private baths. Doubles, $185 to $195 in summer, $125 to $150 off-season.

Ashley Manor, 3660 Olde Kings Highway (Route 6A), Box 856, Barnstable 02630.

One of the more gracious houses on the north shore is a serene B&B hidden behind huge privet hedges. Notable breakfasts are served by innkeepers Vince Toreno and Patricia Martin, who moved here in 2004 from the Boston area.

In summer, the extravaganza is served on a delightful terrace in back of the house, with a fountain garden, a tennis court, gazebo and spacious lawns beyond. In other seasons, guests breakfast by the fire in the original keeping room that the couple redecorated in a warm Colonial style in a section of the house built in 1699.

Birds flitted in and out of a remarkable birdhouse as we breakfasted on fresh orange juice, followed by goodies like cranberry pie, banana crumble and mini-croissants stuffed with cream cheese and raspberry preserve. Vince, who calls himself a frustrated chef, succeeds with such main courses as apricot and sausage quiche, crunchy applesauce pancakes, eggs southwest, and stuffed crêpes with farmer's cheese, strawberry sauce and sour cream.

In the evening, cordials are set out for guests by the fireplace in the library and in a well-furnished living room, where the massive open hearth has a beehive oven.

The spacious Queen Charlotte's Suite in which we stayed on the main floor has a lace queen canopy bed and a sitting area with matching wing chairs. By the fireplace in the bedroom is a secret stairway to the second-floor suite and attic above – said to be where Tories were hidden during the Revolutionary War. The bathroom contains a large double whirlpool tub and a second bath area has a walk-in shower. Similar attributes are featured in the Ashley Suite, entered through french doors off the rear patio. It has an entertainment center with TV and mini-refrigerator.

Upstairs are two rooms and two suites, all but one with working fireplaces. Each is welcoming, but we especially like the end King George's Suite with a kingsize canopy bed, a double jacuzzi in an old closet, and two velvet wing chairs facing the fireplace. The Canterbury Suite has a queen poster bed, fireplace, ivory wing chairs and armoire with TV/VCR and jacuzzi tub, plus an adjacent sitting room with a twin poster bed and reclining chair with ottoman. The Terrace Room with queensize antique iron bed and Nantucket speckled floor has a balcony. All rooms have magazines, bedside chocolates, and luxurious towels of 100 percent Egyptian cotton.

(508) 362-8044 or (888) 535-2246. Fax (508) 362-9927. www.ashleymanor.net. Two rooms and four suites with private baths. Mid-May through October: doubles $155, suites $215. Rest of year: doubles $120, suites $165.

The Whalewalk Inn & Spa, 220 Bridge Road, Eastham 02642.

Sophisticated country charm and a new spa and wellness center are offered in this delightful, six-building compound headquartered in an 1830s sea captain's house on three-plus rural acres of lawns and gardens.

Twelve of the sixteen accommodations come with fireplaces and eight have private balconies or patios. They're decorated with English country antiques in a light and airy style that's more often associated with California than New England. Expect plump chairs and down comforters, interesting art, fresh flowers, dhurrie rugs and whimsical accents – a floral wallpaper border in place of a chair rail here, a lush potted geranium in a bathroom window there.

Traditional favorites are a deluxe room with kingsize four-poster bed off the patio, a honeymoon suite in the secluded Salt Box cottage, and four ample suites with living/dining rooms and wet bars in the attached barn or the outlying Guest House.

A Carriage House addition off the Guest House offers four luxury queensize guest rooms on the first floor and two larger accommodations with sitting areas upstairs. Each has a gas fireplace and a private patio or balcony overlooking a wildflower meadow. Three have whirlpool tubs. The upstairs rooms add king beds, phones, TV/VCRs in cabinets, and extra-large bathrooms containing wet bars and small refrigerators.

The ultimate lodging is in the new penthouse suite above the spa – a 1,000-square-foot area with a great room, dining area, french doors onto a private deck, a cathedral-ceilinged bedroom with a remarkably high antique kingsize bed, fireplace and a luxurious bath with double whirlpool tub and glass block shower.

Accommodations vary in size, but guests have plenty of space in which to spread out. The main inn harbors a handsome living room, a cozy den with windows onto a large and colorful courtyard terrace (a festive setting for breakfast in summer), a sun porch where breakfast is served at a long antique table for ten in the off-season and a butler's pantry with a guest bar. Breakfast is a series of culinary treats, as are the assorted hors d'oeuvre during BYOB cocktail hour with innkeepers Elaine and Kevin Conlin.

Elaine prepares breakfast dishes like the Whalewalk eggs benedict (with prosciutto rather than Canadian bacon), frittata primavera, Cape Cod pancakes mixing cranberries and blueberries, granola breakfast pizza topped with berries and sour cream, and croissant french toast drizzled with chocolate, mandarin oranges and raspberries.

Work off any calories in the inn's spa and wellness center, opened in 2005 in a separate building toward the rear of the property. The main floor includes a carpeted fitness facility, an indoor resistance pool, Swedish sauna and a hot tub. Massage therapy treatments are available.

(508) 255-0617 or (800) 440-1281. Fax (508) 240-0017. www.whalewalkinn.com. Eleven rooms and six suites with private baths. Memorial Day to Columbus Day: doubles $205 to $340, suites $290 to $450. Rest of year: doubles $175 to $285, suites $215 to $395. Closed January to mid-March.

The Nauset House Inn, 143 Beach Road, Box 774, East Orleans 02643.

Here's a B&B with exceptional personality and character, reflecting the taste and energy of its owners, Diane Johnson and her daughter and son-in-law, Cindy and John Vessella. It's also a B&B of great value, given all the food, comfort and charm.

Well-known for her stained-glass objects, Diane has refurbished the inn with many of her works, and has painted artistic touches here and there, starting with cats on the gate posts at the driveway entrance. She and Cindy stenciled most of the sweet bedrooms where quilts, crewel work and afghans abound. Named for

Lush plants surround sitting area in inviting conservatory at The Nauset House Inn.

native wildflowers, eight of the fourteen rooms in the main inn and a couple of outlying buildings have private bathrooms with showers. Diane painted a trompe-l'oeil cabinet on the wall of the Sea Oats Room to make it appear bigger. She painted a curtain for the bathroom window of the pale yellow Rosebud, which comes with a queen bed, rattan loveseat and two chairs plus a rear balcony enhanced by flowers in window boxes. We were happily ensconced in the Beach Plum, largest of four rooms in the Carriage House, where a wall of windows stretches toward the top of the cathedral ceiling. It has a kingsize bed and a sitting area with couch and side chairs around a coffee table. The most coveted accommodation may be the Outermost Cottage, where the bed is situated beneath a stained-glass window and a sunken bathroom awaits beneath a faux painted sky.

Breakfast is served in the beamed, brick-floored dining room with its huge open hearth, looking for all the world like a British pub. Guests have so enjoyed Diane's treats (homemade granola, strawberry frosty, ginger pancakes and Southern-style french toast) that she has published the recipes in a small cookbook. We can attest to her veggie frittatas and raspberry pancakes.

The dining room separates the plush and comfortable living room, where guests congregate around the fire and play board games, from the fabulous Victorian glass conservatory, filled with wicker furniture and plants centered by a weeping cherry tree. The rhododendron and clematis were in bloom at one visit; at another, grapes from the vines garnished the breakfast plates. Folks hang out in the spacious conservatory in the off-season and feel is if they've been transported to a tropical island.

Every afternoon around 5:30, Diane and her daughter set out hors d'oeuvre like guacamole, an olive-nut spread, or a cream-cheese and chutney spread with crackers to accompany complimentary wine or cranberry juice. Guests debate the spirited reviews of their predecessors in a guest book called "Where Did You Eat and How Did You Like It?"

The inn is so comfy and the grounds so pretty that you might not want to leave, but Nauset Beach is nearby. Don't miss the shop out back where Diane sells her stained glass, painted furniture, picture frames, little boxes and other handicrafts.

(508) 255-2195 or (800) 771-5508. Fax (508) 240-6276. www.nausethouseinn.com. Eight rooms with private baths and six rooms with shared bath. Doubles, $100 to $175 private, $75 to $85 shared. Closed November-March.

Penny House Inn & Spa, 4885 County Road (Route 6), Eastham 02642.

Hidden behind a thick hedge along busy Route 6 is this sprawling Colonial inn and day spa, vastly upgraded by Australian innkeeper Margaret Keith, her late husband and their daughter Rebecca. The bow-roofed 1690 saltbox farmhouse in which guests are served a sumptuous breakfast has grown like topsy into old and new wings to incorporate guest rooms (most with fireplaces and double whirlpool tubs), a day spa and, outside, a swimming pool, landscaped terraces and gardens.

All the spacious guest rooms but the Captain's Quarters have penny in their name: Pretty Penny, Penny for Your Thoughts, Pennies from Heaven and the like. They reflect the era of the buildings in which they are housed. Two rooms up steep stairs in the original house have been created from four smaller rooms that had shared baths in the early lodging house taken over in 1988 by the Keiths, who started with thirteen rooms and five baths. Seven more deluxe rooms are in sections they call the old barn, carriage house and breezeway. Three spiffy suites with balconies overlooking the pool or gardens are in the latest wing added in 2002. Most rooms have kingsize beds and all have TV/VCRs hidden in armoires, sitting areas with wing chairs and updated baths. Outside at the side are a saltwater pool shaped like a lagoon and in the rear, a large garden patio.

Breakfast is served at individual tables for two in a country-charming dining room. It might involve a choice among three juices, three or four fruits, peach muffins and perhaps eggs benedict, ginger pancakes with mandarin oranges or croissant french toast with chicken-sundried tomato sausages.

The spa offers massages, facials and body treatments in a spa room or the Penny Earned Couple's Room, a large main-floor room with a hydrotub that doubles as a guest room.

(508) 255-6632 or (800) 554-1751. Fax (508) 255-4893. www.pennyhouseinn.com. Nine rooms and three suites with private baths. Summer, doubles $195 to $350, suites $395. Rest of year: doubles $175 to $325, suites $325.

The Captain's House Inn of Chatham, 369-377 Old Harbor Road, Chatham 02633.

There's more than a touch of Britain amid all the Americana at this supremely elegant inn that originated in Captain Hiram Harding's restored 1839 Greek Revival home, set on shaded lawns screened by high hedges in a sedate residential section north of the village.

Their predecessors built this into one of the first small AAA four-diamond inns in New England. Through attention to detail and an uncanny knack for knowing what the luxury market wants, Jan and David McMaster have taken it to a higher level. They expanded and beautified the dining porch, added a few whirlpool tubs and built four deluxe rooms with fireplaces. They also developed new English perennial gardens with a three-tiered fountain pond in a rear corner of the two-acre property. "That manicured lawn was made for croquet," said Dave, a former California computer company CEO.

And proper British accents are heard often as the McMasters continue the tradition of staffing their inn with English students from the University of Bournemouth, which happens to be Jan's home town.

The heart of the main house is the dining porch, a beauty in white and dusky rose. An addition projects eight feet out into the gardens with floor-to-ceiling windows. The floor is tiled and trailing wisteria is stenciled on the walls. Two fancy serving areas along the sides simplify breakfast service at individual linen-covered tables set with sterling silver and fine china.

Here is where Jan McMaster and chef Jo Del Negro offer a true English tea (cream tea is complimentary, afternoon tea costs $10 a couple and $15 per person for outside guests). The chef has expanded the breakfast offerings to include both a savory and a sweet entrée to supplement the traditional fresh fruit, breads and muffins. Favorites are smoked salmon corncakes with broiled tomatoes and cheese, waffles with strawberries or blueberries, quiches and apple crêpes. Sandwich lunches are available for $10 at the pool.

The sitting room with a fireplace and the adjacent library contain decanters of sherry and port, and Poland Spring water is in each guest room. Evening snacks are put out in the kitchen area.

Thirteen of the sixteen guest accommodations have fireplaces and five have TV/VCRs, refrigerators and coffeemakers. All are furnished with antiques, comfortable chairs for reading, pretty sheets, thick towels and French toiletries.

The original nine bedrooms in the main Greek Revival house have been reconfigured lately into three rooms and two suites.

Rooms with beamed and peaked ceilings are among the more deluxe in a rear carriage house. Also coveted is the Captain's Cottage, where the sumptuous Hiram Harding suite looks like a library with dark walnut paneling and beamed ceiling, fine oriental rugs on the wide-plank floor, large fireplace, plush sofa and side chairs, and lace-canopied kingsize four-poster bed. A jacuzzi tub has been added here, as well as in the newly enlarged Lady Mariah Room adjacent. In the latter, an old kitchen was converted into what Jan calls a "fantasy bathroom," a smashing space with a double whirlpool flanked by four pillars and two wicker chairs facing a corner fireplace. The fireplace is also on view from the extra-high, step-up kingsize bed.

Top of the line are three jacuzzi accommodations in the Stables, a new building behind the cottage. The upstairs suite has fireplaces in both living room and bedroom, a kingsize bed and french doors leading to a full-length balcony. Each of the two downstairs rooms has a queen canopy bed, fireplace and a private deck, plus a TV/VCR hidden in an 1875 chest or the armoire.

Always improving, the McMasters recently added a heated outdoor swimming pool with an impressive fitness facility beside.

(508) 945-0127 or (800) 315-0728. Fax (508) 945-0866. www.captainshouseinn.com. Twelve rooms and four suites with private baths. Mid-May to late October: doubles $250 to $350, suites $250 to $450. Rest of year: doubles $185 to $250, suites $225 to $295.

Carriage House Inn, 407 Old Harbor Road, Chatham 02633.

High-school sweethearts Jill and James Meyer from New Jersey fell in love with Cape Cod during family vacations. They finally settled here in 2003, taking over a six-room B&B where he put into practice his degree in hospitality management from Boston University and his training at the Boston Harbor Hotel.

The enthusiastic couple, both in their late twenties, have been gradually refurbishing and expanding the accommodations in their Cape Cod-style house and carriage house at the corner of Old Harbor and Shore roads. They redecorated the guest living room in crisp yellows, blues and greens, with exposed hardwood floors and "less is more" window treatments for a brighter, more contemporary look. They added a computer with high-speed internet access and installed TVs and DVD players in the guest quarters, which, as one older guest was quick to point out to James, "really shows your age." And when the couple moved into a house nearby in 2005, they turned the main-floor owners' quarters into a guest suite with a kingsize bedroom and a fireplaced living room with a sofabed and a private deck.

All the other guest rooms – three of which are upstairs in the main house – have oversize showers in the updated bathrooms and queensize beds, dressed in chintz and floral fabrics. The choicest accommodations are in the renovated rear carriage house, away from the road. Each has an arched window beneath a vaulted ceiling, a corner fireplace and, a boon in summer, a flower-bedecked sitting area outside.

Guests gather by the fireplace in the main living room, which has a games table. The guest refrigerator is stocked with cold beverages, the cookie jar holds homemade goodies and a fruit bowl is filled with the season's bounty.

Breakfast is served at a table for six in the chandeliered dining room, or at tables for two on an adjacent sun porch. James is the chef, cooking up such treats as apple-cinnamon pancakes, sweet bread french toast and banana-sour cream waffles. Among savory items are seafood strata, baked eggs florentine and a sausage, egg and cheese casserole.

Jill was compiling the recipes along with their innkeeping stories into a cookbook with an intriguing title: *James Cooks While Jill Spills the Beans.*

(508) 945-4688 or (800) 355-8868. Fax (508) 945-8909. www.thecarriagehouseinn.com. Six rooms and one suite with private baths. Late June to Labor Day: doubles $175 to $205, suite $240. Rest of year: doubles $95 to $165, suite $160 to $195.

The Simmons Homestead Inn, 288 Scudder Ave., Hyannis Port 02647.

"I can't abide empty spaces," says Bill Putman, who has filled every available space, and then some, at this eclectic B&B full of personality.

Part of the personality comes from Bill, an outgoing, marketing type who proudly displays his varied collections throughout the former sea captain's house. But most comes from the inn and its furnishings. Start with the 32-foot-long living room, comfortable as can be and now a jungle of hanging plants because, Bill says, "the only empty spaces left are on the ceiling." The room is notable for brass birds on the mantel and inanimate wildlife everywhere, a remarkable tapestry of animals done by his late wife and large parrots from Pavo Real.

Parrots, a theme repeated in many rooms, adorn the chandeliers in the 20-by-40-foot dining room, which has a fantastic collection of mugs depicting different fruits to coordinate with the fruit du jour china. Here guests gather at communal tables for a full breakfast with perhaps cheese omelets or blueberry pancakes. Bill does the cooking – "I learned quickly," says he, although he did defer once to a skeptical guest, Dinah Shore.

The theme is elephants in Room 3 with a queensize poster bed and working fireplace – they turn up inside the shutters, on the windows, on the mantel. Room 6 is the rabbit room, with a kingsize bed and bunnies all around. Room 8 is simply wild: beneath the cathedral ceiling is a loft that's a jungle of plants and animals, including a purple rhinoceros. Animals are appliquéd all over the walls, the queensize bed is purple, the floor is painted green, and somehow it all works. Birds and butterflies hang from the vaulted ceiling in Room 10, the largest and brightest, which has its own little patio bedecked with spirea.

The largest accommodations are in the old Barn Annex, which Bill rebuilt as his house but now shares with guests in a large bedroom and a two-room family suite. The open main floor holds a guest living room with the inn's only TV, the innkeeper's bedroom that's home for a dozen cats he calls "the children" (except when he vacates it for guests), and his office named Hyannis Port. The open kitchen is stocked with 465 different single-malt scotches – more than we've seen in any one place in Scotland, and he professes never even to have been to Scotland. Weeknight guests in winter are invited to sample a few.

Otherwise, Bill serves complimentary wine in front of the roaring fireplace in winter and on the breezy porches in summer beside an outdoor hot tub. The wine hour is "from 5:30 to 7:30 or whenever – that's p.m., but we are flexible," he stresses.

Bill, a former race-car driver, displays the hoods of his race car and Paul Newman's on the upstairs landing in the main house and racing photos in a long upstairs hallway. That's mere prelude to the collection of five dozen bright red sports cars in a garage area he calls Toad Hall and parked outside, including a restored 1967 right-hand drive Bentley that he uses to shuttle guests.

"I wanted to create a place where you feel at home," Bill says. Although it's not like any home we know, we'd feel quite at home as guests.

(508) 778-4999 or (800) 637-1649. www.simmonshomesteadinn.com. Ten rooms and two suites with private baths. Mid-June to late September: doubles $180 to $250, suites $250 to $300. Off-season: doubles $110 to $200; suites $200 to $250.

Gourmet Treats

The Cape is full of kitchen and specialty-food shops, along with every other type of shop imaginable. Among our favorites:

Green Briar Jam Kitchen, 6 Discovery Hill Road, East Sandwich.

Your first stop on the Cape might be this charmingly low-key place, where four paid cooks and many Thornton W. Burgess Society volunteers employ turn-of-the-last-century methods to produce jams, continuing a tradition begun in 1903. You get to see the old wood stove that founder Ida Putnam started with, as well as probably the oldest solar-cooking operation in the country – the hot-house windows in which ingenious racks slide in and out to make the prized sun-cooked strawberries with vodka, as well as blueberries with kirsch. Of course, you get to watch – and smell – some of the 20,000 bottles of jams, chutneys and relishes as they are lovingly prepared for sale in the gift shop. You also see Thornton Burgess's framed, handwritten description of the Jam Kitchen in 1939: "It is a wonderful thing to sweeten the world which is in a jam and needs preserving." Adjacent to the kitchen is the Green Briar Nature Center, including the Old Briar Patch conservation area, home of Brer Rabbit and his animal friends.

(508) 888-6870. www.thorntonburgess.org. Kitchen open Monday-Saturday 10 to 4, Sunday 1 to 4, April-December; Tuesday-Saturday 10 to 4 rest of year. Donation.

The **Lemon Tree Village** complex at 1091 Route 6A in Brewster is worth a visit. The **Lemon Tree Pottery** is full of interesting pottery and other crafts. **The Cook Shop** offers specialty foods and kitchen essentials while its large offshoot across the way, **The Tabletop Shop,** is a terrific, two-story kaleidoscope of hard-to-find fine china, flatware, glassware, table linens and cookbooks to please the most discriminating of hostesses. **Brewster Sweets** offers fine chocolates and confections. **Café Alfresco,** with tables inside and out, is a great place for an interesting meal at refreshing prices. We enjoyed a smoked salmon sandwich with avocado and sprouts and a lobster club with pancetta and the works. A raspberry square was a tasty dessert. Pick up a homemade pastry from the deli case, or order a dinner special from the blackboard. Open daily, 9 to 8:30 in summer, shorter hours in winter.

The open-air showroom of **Scargo Stoneware Pottery** at 30 Dr. Lord's Road South is quite a sight in the woods beside Scargo Lake off Route 6A in Dennis. Harry Holl and his family have been producing the stunning stoneware for decorative and kitchen purposes since 1952. Harry, whose majestic bird feeders grace the back yards of some of our favorite B&Bs in the area, turned to painting lately. His daughters and a son-in-law continue at the potter's kiln.

The Chocolate Sparrow at 4205 Route 6 in North Eastham is where dietitian Marjorie Sparrow produces her luscious chocolates, chocolate-covered cranberry cordials, English toffee crunch, assorted nut barks and more. Its offshoot is **Hot Chocolate Sparrow,** the quintessential coffee and dessert bar at Lowell Square, 85 Route 6A, Orleans. We stopped at the espresso bar here for fat-free cranberry muffins and a latte and watched touring families devouring the candies and terrific ice-cream concoctions, among them a raspberry-sorbet lime rickey and a frozen espresso shake. More exotic coffees and ice creams are served up across the street at **Emack & Bolio's,** a branch of a Boston outfit.

Hatch's Fish Market at 310 Main St., Wellfleet, has fresh herbs, homemade pesto, baby vegetables, fruit popsicles and smoked mussel pâté as well as every kind of fish imaginable, including a tray of sushi. The all-day **Wicked Oyster** at 50 Main St., Wellfleet, is touted by locals for innovative fare. That may be the case for dinner, but our breakfast of huevos rancheros ($8.50) and eggs benedict ($9) turned out so pedestrian that we did not investigate further.

The place for gourmet specialties in Provincetown is **Angel Foods** at 467 Commercial St., which stocks all the right items from cheeses and pastas to baked goods and deli sandwiches.

Fancy's Farm Stand, 199 Main St., East Orleans, is the Cape's ultimate produce stand. Recently sold by founders Art and Meredith Fancy to Brian Smith, the indoor/outdoor market also purveys potpourris and wreaths (we coveted a huge one with all kinds of geese for $100), fancy cheeses and local jellies, baked goods and soups. You can make up a meal to go with, perhaps, kale and corn chowder, the offerings from an extensive salad bar, a deli, prepared foods from turkey pie to chicken noodle casserole, roll-ups, a pastry or a piece of pie.

A favorite stop almost across the street in East Orleans is **Sundae School Ice Cream,** which dispenses homemade ice creams and frozen yogurts in flavors from crème de menthe to kahlua chip. We thought a small cone of ginger ice cream tasted like ginger ale, only to be told no one had ever said that before. Those with heartier appetites can splurge for a hot fudge sundae or a giant banana split.

The **Cornfield Market** complex at 1291 Main St. in West Chatham is a gourmet haven. The former Fancy's Farm Market here was acquired in 2002 by Kathy and Michael Dougert and renamed the **Pampered Palate Market.** The couple, whose love for food is obvious throughout, are proudest of their meat department, which includes dry-aged beef, specialty game and – we were delighted to find – frozen sweetbreads that went home for a subsequent dinner. It also offers the most extensive cheese selection on the Cape. For prepared foods, mosey over to **The Pampered Palate,** an excellent deli and gourmet foods shop that's part of the complex. Pick up a lobster salad sandwich on a croissant or a smoked salmon sandwich on a french roll with cucumber and wasabi mayo for a super picnic. It offers all kinds of salads, prepared foods and desserts to go. Supplement this with the market's produce or the extensive selection at **Chatham Fish and Lobster** next door and you have the makings for a great party.

Everything is made from scratch at **Marion's Pie Shop,** 2022 Main St., Chatham. Attached to a small Cape house, the landmark pie shop bearing its founder's name was sold by her daughter in 2002. The new owners still bake 200 to 300 pies a day, including a blackberry pie ($12) that's even better than the ones we make at home. Clam and seafood pies were available at our latest visit.

The Casual Gourmet, a catering service run by Olive and David Chase in the Bell Tower Mall at 1600 Falmouth Road, Centerville, has a large deli section dispensing salads, sandwiches, baked goods and prepared foods. Try the egg, bacon and cheddar calzone for breakfast or a hefty tarragon chicken salad sandwich for lunch.

In Falmouth, **Bean & Cod** at 140 Main St. is a paradise of New England specialty foods and gourmet gift items, from cookbooks to napkins to dishes. The store's name derives from the melding of the co-owners' background – Janet Bain lives in the Boston (Beantown) area and Carol Mara in Falmouth. The selection of crackers, cheeses, vinegars, pâtés, preserves and candies is exceptional, and surprises unfold on shelf after shelf. The expanded store has its own kitchen, providing take-out sandwiches, soups, and salads. The blackboard might list prepared foods and breads, from crab cakes and lobster ravioli to dessert squares.

One of our favorite shops for browsing at the Cape is **Tree's Place,** Route 6A at 28, Orleans. An exceptional art gallery, a tilery (the largest selection of designer tiles in the country, they say) and a gift shop occupy several rooms filled with such diverse items as Russian lacquer boxes, jewelry, Swiss musical paper weights, Hadley stoneware, hand-blown glass, pottery, carved birds – even tartan ties. We love the biscuit baskets of glazed stoneware made by Eucalyptus Pottery in California. You can choose any of the tiles to be framed for use as a trivet. One of us could spend hours mooching around here, but the other always says that it's time to be moving on.

Gourmet Chips

Do you think, as we do, that Cape Cod potato chips are absolutely the best? Then stop in Hyannis at their place of origin, **The Cape Cod Potato Chip Co.,** 100 Breed's Hill Road, in an industrial park area off Route 132. There's an informative, self-guided tour of the plant, which evolved from Steve and Lynn Bernard's storefront kitchen that started in 1980 producing 200 bags of Cape Cod Potato Chips a day. Still hand-cooking chips in kettles one batch at a time, the plant in Hyannis produces 150,000 bags daily and goes through more than 40 million pounds of potatoes a year. The company also makes a full line of tortilla chips, popcorn and pretzels. This is big business, and we were surprised by the number of people touring on a summer weekday. You can pick up samples as well as buy more in the gift shop at tour's end.

(508) 775-3358. www.capecodchips.com. Tours, Monday-Friday 9 to 5.

Table set for dinner on porch at Straight Wharf Restaurant overlooks Nantucket harbor.

Nantucket

The Ultimate Indulgence for Gourmets

For an offshore island with a year-round population of 10,000 (augmented by up to 40,000 high-livers and free-spenders in the summer), Nantucket has an uncommon concentration of good restaurants.

Ever since French chef Jean-Charles Berruet took over the rose-covered Chanticleer Inn in the hamlet of Siasconset in 1969, knowledgeable diners have been flocking to Nantucket in droves. Other restaurateurs and culinary businesses have followed.

"I don't know of another resort area that can beat Nantucket for good restaurants per square mile," says Neal Grennan, chef-owner of Le Languedoc.

With an increasingly sophisticated local population supplemented by jet-setting vacationers, the island's food situation has changed dramatically. The island now has a dozen superior restaurants, another dozen good ones, and countless more of the ordinary variety. At one of our visits, two cookbooks by Nantucket chefs had just been published and another was in the works. The 21 Federal restaurant opened a "branch" in Washington, D.C., and local chef Peter Wallace ran a second restaurant in New York. Latest with a branch was Sfoglia, which opened a Tuscan outpost in Manhattan's Upper East Side.

What other seaside resort dines so fashionably late? Many restaurants don't open for dinner until 6:30 or 7 – the 4:30 early-bird specials of Cape Cod don't play here. Dining is an event and a pricey one, given local chefs' preoccupation with fresh and exotic ingredients, their island location and a captive, affluent audience.

Lately, prices have raised a few eyebrows. That you might expect when menus list baked codfish at $24 for lunch at Brant Point Grill, a plate of sorbets for dessert went for $18 at the Chanticleer before it closed in 2005 and some restaurants specify hefty per-person food minimums and shared-plate surcharges. Such prices are "insulting," according to local chefs like Michael Geller. The explanation is not the island's remoteness, adds innkeeper Bob Taylor, a former restaurateur. Rather it's a perception that "if you don't charge enough, you're no good. So people charge what the traffic will bear."

We know people who vacation at Nantucket for a month every summer, eating out almost every night, and relishing every minute as the ultimate gustatory experience. Book a room, reserve the ferry or an airplane seat, raise your credit-card limit and indulge in the gourmet splendors of Nantucket yourself.

Dining

The Best of the Best

21 Federal, 21 Federal St., Nantucket.

One of Nantucket's larger and higher-profile restaurants, 21 Federal occupies a handsome sand-colored house with white trim, designated by a brass plaque and elegantly decorated in the Williamsburg style. It is the icon where founding chef Robert Kinkead got his start before being dispatched to open a second 21 Federal in 1987 in Washington, D.C. That consistently won high ratings until it closed in 1993 and relocated to rave reviews as Kinkead's at 2000 Pennsylvania Ave.

With executive chef Russell Jaehnig at the helm since his graduation from the Culinary Institute of America, 21 Federal continues to be known for new American grill cuisine. The 1847 Greek Revival structure offers six intimate dining rooms – some with their white-linened tables rather close together – on two floors of museum-quality, Federal period decor.

In summer, lunch is served on a nifty outdoor courtyard ringed with impatiens, where the white linens on the tables are topped by herbs in clay pots and classical music wafts across the scene. Our latest produced a smashing pasta – spaghettini with two sauces, one thyme-saffron and one smoked tomato, topped with crabmeat-stuffed shrimp – and a grilled shrimp salad with Greek olives, feta cheese, pinenuts and spinach. Calvados ice cream and an intense pineapple-mint sorbet served with wonderful small coconut and lemon squares topped off a flavorful meal.

The short dinner menu changes weekly. You might start with lobster and corn bisque bearing a toasted brioche and ossetra caviar, seared sea scallops and foie gras with a sage-grape chutney, beef tartare with roasted vegetables and tarragon aioli, or a tuna, crab and avocado napoleon with cilantro vinaigrette.

Entrées could be sautéed halibut with foie gras butter and lobster risotto cakes, chipotle-glazed yellowfin tuna with a sweet potato-goat cheese gratin and anaheim chile pepper ragoût, roast pork loin with smoked fig jam and, from the grill, aged sirloin steak or veal loin chop with potato-leek gratin. The 21 Federal version of surf and turf might yield half a grilled lobster and braised beef shortrib, served with succotash and fontina and white truffle polenta.

Dessert could be warm chocolate lava cake with kahlua caramel, blueberry-montrachet tart with whipped cream or one of the great homemade ice creams and sorbets with fresh berries.

This is Nantucket dining at its best, not as pretentious or as pricey as some and more exciting than some of the others.

(508) 228-2121. www.21federal.net. Entrées, $23 to $38. Lunch, Monday-Saturday in summer, 11:30 to 2:30. Dinner, Monday-Saturday 6 to 9:30. Closed mid-December to mid-May.

Settings are historic yet elegant in dining rooms at 21 Federal.

The Boarding House and The Pearl, 12 Federal St., Nantucket.

When it opened in 1973, the Boarding House was the summer's success story and provided our first great meal on Nantucket. It since has moved around the corner to considerably larger quarters, and several owners and chefs have come and gone. It's better than ever, having been taken over by Seth and Angela Raynor, he a former sous chef at 21 Federal and both having worked at the late Chanticleer. In 1999, they expanded upstairs with their crowning fillip, a showy, aquatic-look, designer restaurant called **The Pearl,** specializing in high-style coastal cuisine. Billed as a separate restaurant for more leisurely dining, "it's like two siblings in a family," said Angela.

The original Boarding House is a beauty, its cathedral-ceilinged Victorian lounge with small faux-marble tables on a flagstone floor opening into a sunken "Wine Cellar Dining Room." The latter is striking in rich cream and pink, with a curved banquette at the far end in front of a mural of Vernazzia, a destination featured in Gourmet magazine the month after the mural went up. The Raynors own the originals but sell lithographs of the exclusive Nantucket series "Streets of Paris," which hang on the walls. Villeroy & Boch china of the Florida pattern graces the nicely spaced tables, which allow for one of Nantucket's more pleasant dining situations.

Upstairs, The Pearl is ever so cool in white and blue, with an aquarium at the entrance and a scrim curtain giving the illusion of floating at sea. Indeed, facing the leather-like banquette against the fish tank, you might feel as if you're diving beneath the sea. An onyx bar lit from beneath contributes to a surreal look that catches the eye of restaurant design magazine editors. Off a custom-designed kitchen is a chef's table for eight on an outside deck overlooking fountains and gardens.

Equal to the dramatic settings is the cooking of Seth, who was one of 30 chefs chosen to appear on the "Great Chefs of the East" public television series only nine months after taking over the Boarding House. We certainly liked our dinner here. Starters were mellow sautéed crab cakes with scallion crème fraîche and crispy fried oysters with rémoulade sauce. Main dishes were pan-roasted salmon with Thai

Murals evoke Mediterranean feeling in wine cellar dining room at Boarding House.

curried cream and crispy rice noodles, and a spicy Asian seafood stew with lobster, shrimp and scallops. Accompanying was a powerful Caymus sauvignon blanc from a well-chosen wine selection with less than the normal Nantucket price markup. Coffee ice cream with chocolate sauce and a dense chocolate-kahlua terrine were worthy endings.

With the opening of The Pearl, the Boarding House is billed more as a bistro with a cocktail bar and a covered outdoor terrace that appeals for a bistro lunch and drinks. We've also found it a felicitous setting for an after-dinner liqueur while watching the late-night parade pass by.

While chef de cuisine Erin Zircher oversees the Boarding House, Seth directs the larger Pearl. Typical of starters here is an island-style seafood platter bearing Nantucket oysters, sashimi of striped bass, a martini of yellowfin tuna and steamed ginger shrimp dumplings.

For a main course, Seth might dish up wok-seared lobster with Thai curry, coconut and cilantro or grill angus tenderloin with seared foie gras and caramelized cippolini onions. Dessert could be lemongrass-infused crème brûlée or yuzu cheesecake with red wine-cherry sauce.

The chef's Zen-like garden tasting table provides gourmands with both a multi-course culinary adventure and a bird's-eye view into the state-of-the-art kitchen.

Boarding House, (508) 228-9622. www.boardinghouse-pearl.com. Entrées $26 to $34. Patio lunch in summer, Wednesday-Sunday noon to 2. Dinner nightly, 6 to 10, fewer nights in winter.

The Pearl, (508) 228-9701. Entrées, $35 to $44. Dinner nightly, 6 to 11. Closed January-March.

Oran Mor, 2 South Beach St., Nantucket.

Former Wauwinet executive chef Peter Wallace took over the old Second Story restaurant space and renamed it for a Gaelic phrase meaning "Great Song."

A copper and wood staircase rises from the ground-level entrance to a reception podium in the front room on the second story with windows onto the harbor. There you find a couple of booths and a neat small, semi-circular bar fashioned from the portico of the local electric company, which was rescued on its way to the dump. The intimate bar area hews to a maritime theme in its use of vintage ship masts as glass racks and a dory hull standing tall to serve as a wine rack.

Three small, off-white dining areas with seafoam green trim are dressed with paintings by local artists. Peter considers them a soothing backdrop for international cuisine that is at the cutting edge. He's back in the kitchen after opening a restaurant called Laight Street in New York's trendy TriBeCa section and consulting as executive chef at the historic Old Drover's Inn in the Hudson Valley.

For starters, we liked his champagne risotto with sweetbreads and wild mushrooms, and his Asian fried quail with sticky rice. Expect other choices like tuna tartare with horseradish crème fraîche, a Thai littleneck clam hot pot with somen noodles, grilled Hudson Valley foie gras with rhubarb popover and banyuls sauce, and a salad of soft-shell crab over field greens.

Main courses vary from grilled squab paella with shrimp and spicy chorizo sausage to organic ribeye steak diane and sautéed veal medallions with artichoke and Meyer lemon. We enjoyed the seared tuna with shallot jus and spinach, and grilled swordfish with orange and black sesame seed butter.

Wife Kathleen's desserts include fruit croustade in a tulipe, quenelles of chocolate mousse topped with pralines, and molten chocolate cake with a trio of ice creams.

(508) 228-8655. Entrées, $26 to $34. Dinner nightly in season, 6 to 10. Closed Wednesday in off-season and Sunday-Wednesday in winter.

American Seasons, 80 Centre St., Nantucket.

This innovative, off-the-beaten-path establishment is a find for those who want distinguished, ever-changing cuisine defined by season and region. Chef Michael La Scola, who started working in the restaurant as a teenager and now is the owner, retained the concept and decor launched by the restaurant's founders.

Whimsical decor characterizes the square 50-seat dining room in which high-backed banquettes serve as room dividers. A local artist hand-painted the table tops to resemble game boards and added a stunning wall mural of a vine-covered Willamette Valley hillside in Oregon. A couple of dim wall sconces and candlelight provide illumination. Outside is a pleasant patio for dinner in summer.

As our meal unfolded, we discovered why people had said that the presentations were so striking and that every plate was different. It turned out it wasn't the plates (most are white) but the decorative garnishes on the rims that made them look different.

Interestingly, the menu is categorized by regions – Pacific Coast, Wild West, New England and Down South – each with two or three appetizers and entrées. You're supposed to mix and match, pairing, say, Florida rock shrimp gumbo with andouille sausage, okra and biscuits with a lobster and corn enchilada in a blue cornmeal crêpe. Those and a lentil salad with goat cheese, frisée and grilled leeks made a memorable meal. Or you could start with a Pacific smoked salmon and goat cheese roulade with horseradish vinaigrette and golden caviar and enjoy a main dish of cumin-dusted yellowfin tuna with red jalapeño and curried shrimp sauce from the Wild West. A New England "soup and sandwich" – English pea soup with truffled cream and a lobster panini – and a Southern molasses-glazed pork chop with cheddar-corn bread pudding and collard greens in a shallot-bourbon gravy make another interesting pairing.

We shared a dessert of raspberry-mango shortcake with raspberry coulis, presented artistically with fresh fruit on a square plate decorated with squiggles of chocolate and crème anglaise. Other choices might be ginger crème brûlée, banana and spiced rum cake with coconut ice cream, blackberry and anise bombe, and a "chocolate lover's sampler" yielding white chocolate sorbet, mint truffles, and a hazelnut and chocolate pyramid.

The all-American wine list has been honored by Wine Spectator.

(508) 228-7111. www.americanseasons.com. Entrées, $26 to $34. Dinner nightly in summer, 6 to 10, fewer nights in off-season. Closed January to April.

Straight Wharf Restaurant, Straight Wharf, Nantucket.

Chef Marian Morash of television and cookbook fame put this summery restaurant on the culinary map, and Steve and Kate Cavagnaro have kept it there. The Cavagnaros, owners of the much-acclaimed Cavey's restaurant in Manchester, Conn., spend the summer in Nantucket, he in the kitchen and she out front.

The interior is a pristine palette of shiny floors and soaring, shingled walls topped by billowing banners and hung with striking paintings by an island artist. There's also a wildly popular bar/grill, which is Nantucket's nightly gathering spot for the under-40 crowd, all of whom seem to know each other and who usually spill outside onto a terrace in front. The dining and bar areas are well separated, so one does not interfere with the other. The same kitchen serves both, with a sophisticated seafood menu in the dining room and more rustic, casual grill fare that locals consider some of the island's best in the bar.

Starters are standouts, among them the signature smoked bluefish pâté with focaccia melba toasts, a rich lobster bisque heavily laced with sherry, seared beef carpaccio with shards of parmigiano-reggiano, white truffle oil and mesclun, and local black bass with a vegetable mignonette.

A sauté of halibut with lobster and morels and grilled rare tuna with white beans, escarole and roasted garlic were excellent main courses. Choices range from butter-poached Nantucket lobster with green tomato chutney to rosemary-grilled rack of lamb with olive tapenade and tabouleh.

The dessert specialty is warm valrhona chocolate tart with orange cardamom gelato, but we usually go for the trio of refreshing fruit sorbets.

(508) 228-4499. Entrées, $34 to $39. Dinner by reservation, Tuesday-Sunday 6 to 10:30. Open Memorial Day to late September. Grill, $16 to $22, no reservations.

Cinco, 5 Amelia Drive, Nantucket.

A two-ton bronze sculpture of a horse outside the entrance sets the stage for things to come in this new Latin-Spanish restaurant and bar on the outskirts of town. So do the splashy artworks – a flamenco dance in bold reds and yellows, surreal fish paintings and Picasso-like abstracts – hung on the walls variously painted mango, pistachio and chocolate inside.

It's an arty backdrop for one of the hottest culinary scenes on the island, as rendered by proprietor Michael Sturgis, who after 24 years as Nantucket's celebrity bartender decided the time was ripe to open his own restaurant. "My job was always to host the best cocktail party, and now I want to run the best dinner party."

And so he does, with a considerable assist from his executive chef, Jason Carroll.

Their menu reflects the creative and fun spirit of the decor. Though Cinco offers a handful of compelling entrées, it is the three dozen or so tidbits and tapas that are the focus – any assortment of which would make a memorable meal.

Start with assorted canapés – perhaps the house-marinated olives, fish tacos with tomatillo sauce and lettuce chiffonade or poached shrimp with Thai peanut sauce – as you peruse the menu. How about a bowl of lobster gazpacho or black bean soup with roasted poblano crème fraîche followed by citrusy shrimp seviche with habañero sauce and spice-rubbed pork tenderloin with cilantro pesto and caramelized fuji apple? These are "small plates" mind you (and priced mostly in the $7 to $12 range), so order a few more to share: perhaps salt cod fritters with romesco sauce, seared native black bass with corn puree and achiote butter, and marinated beef shoulder with brandy sauce. Cauliflower gratin, caramelized brussels sprouts with holland peppers and fruitwood-smoked bacon, and chile relleno tart with smoked tomato vinaigrette are enticing side dishes.

Cinco's paella – loaded with chicken, chorizo, calamari, mussels, shrimp and lobster on saffron bomba rice – is a must-have among large plates (two-person minimum, $26 each). But you might also go for the seared native fluke, the quail stuffed with spinach, raisins, pinenuts and chayote, or the grilled lamb chops with oregano, garlic and lime mojo.

A pitcher of first-rate sangria – made with red wine, citrus juices, brandy and cava, the sparkling wine of Spain – is a sweet accompaniment to dinner. Most of the other choices are from Spain, Portugal or South America.

Desserts are equally enticing, among them the signature Mexican chocolate silk torte with kahlua-caramel sauce, pumpkin-ginger flan with caramel sauce, and grilled pineapple with coconut-rum sauce and coconut sorbet.

(508) 325-5151. www.cinco5.com. Entrées, $17 to $32. Dinner nightly, 6 to 10:30.

Le Languedoc, 24 Broad St., Nantucket.

Longtime chef-owner Neil Grennan oversees the kitchen at this family-owned restaurant, where he keeps tight rein on what he admits are Nantucket's steep prices and where he produced one of our best meals in Nantucket a few years back. A local institution for three decades, Le Languedoc continues to please an expanding clientele.

Downstairs is an intimate bistro with checkered cloths, where you can dine casually and quite well (an abbreviated bistro menu is also served on the canopied side terrace). Upstairs are four small dining rooms elegant in peach and white, with windsor chairs at nicely spaced tables, each bearing a candle in a hurricane chimney and a vase containing one lovely salmon-hued rose.

Lately, the fare has been expanded from its base of classic French fare to include more contemporary cuisine. The menu varies seasonally from poached turbot with black trumpet mushrooms and star anise vinaigrette to seared Colorado lamb with rosemary brûlée. Steak frites with truffled watercress is a dinner staple. The appetizer selection is exotic, treats like warm veal salad with poached quail eggs and haricots vert, lobster soufflé with tomalley emulsion and ragoût of oxtails with a savory tuile and mustard sorbet.

Our autumn dinner began with an appetizer of smoked Nantucket pheasant with cranberry relish, very good and very colorful with red cabbage and slices of apples and oranges on a bed of lettuce. For the main course, one of us tried the noisettes of lamb with artichokes in a rosemary sauce and the other enjoyed sautéed sweetbreads and lobster in puff pastry. Nicely presented on piping-hot white oval plates, they were accompanied by snow peas, broccoli, puréed turnips, yellow peppers, sweet potatoes and peach slices. Desserts were blueberry and apricot napoleon with white peach puree and a dense chocolate-hazelnut torte spiked with grand marnier.

Lunch in the garden yields a panoply of French bistro treats from salade niçoise to a lobster and black truffle beignet.

(508) 228-2552. www.lelanguedoc.com. Entrées, $22 to $39. Lunch seasonally, Tuesday-Saturday noon to 2. Dinner nightly, 6 to 9:30. Sunday brunch, 11 to 2. Closed January to mid-April.

Company of the Cauldron, 7 India St., Nantucket.

In a dark red Colonial house with ivy-covered windows, this tiny restaurant is full of charm and romance.

An antique wrought-iron baker's rack is laden with flowers at the entry, and copper pots, cauldrons and ship's models hang from the stucco walls. A mix of orange and purple floral cloths covers the old wood tables, which are lit only by candles. It's all very dark and intimate for a dining experience likened to being a guest at a dinner party with a private chef.

Owner Allen Kovalencik, a Hungarian from New Jersey who bought the place after serving as its chef since 1987, and his wife Andrea post the night's prix-fixe, no-choice menu a week in advance. You reserve (early) for the evening's meal you want and take what's served, which is produced and served with great finesse.

For two decades, "All" has been the only chef, cooking in a kitchen visible from the dining room. He often serves one or more courses of the meal himself so he can chat with diners.

A harpist plays as a typical dinner evolves, yielding perhaps a trio of lobster, crab and smoked salmon cakes with individual sauces, an arugula and watercress salad, beef wellington and bourbon pecan pie with vanilla ice cream. Another night you might be served a classic pappardelle bolognese, a mixed green salad, Atlantic sole and lobster in parchment with champagne beurre blanc, and chocolate soufflé cake with raspberry sauce.

Every once in a while you might get the signature vinewood-roasted salmon, the grilled Atlantic halibut tandoori, wood-grilled châteaubriand over roasted wild mushrooms or the ginger-crusted rack of lamb with sweet plum sauce.

(508) 228-4016. www.companyofthecauldron.com. Prix-fixe, $50 to $55. Dinner nightly, seatings at 6:45 (also at 8:45 on busy nights). Closed Columbus Day to mid-April.

Fifty-Six Union, 56 Union St., Nantucket.

Light, healthful global fare is served up by chef-owner Peter Jannelle and his wife Wendy in this casually elegant eatery located in a former diner called the Elegant Dump on the outskirts of downtown. The couple seat about 100 in a pair of dining rooms set with nicely spaced white-clothed tables flanked by black windsor chairs. The pale yellow walls are hung with framed black and white pictures of local children by Nantucket photographer Lucy Bixby. A bar at the side has counter seats for nine, and a canopied garden patio sparkling with lights in back offers outdoor dining in season. Peter also offers a multi-course tasting menu for six to twelve people at a private chef's table in the garden.

Tourists rarely find this lovable place, but the residents – year-round and summer

Front dining room at Fifty-Six Union is stylish in yellow and black.

people who try to keep it to themselves – go for such starters as curried mussels in a Thai yellow curry broth over scallion and ginger rice, grilled shrimp with lemongrass and ginger, and sweetbread strudel with walnuts, chèvre and prosciutto in a brandy-walnut demi-glace.

Everyone raves about the Javanese spicy fried rice, a year-round menu mainstay in which shrimp and chicken are tossed with sambal, ginger and Asian vegetables. Be advised: it's an overpowering portion for one and best shared for two. Other favorite main dishes include almond-crusted halibut with a roasted beet coulis, pan-seared ahi tuna rubbed in Japanese seven-spice powder and served with sesame-garlic vinaigrette, grilled Jamaican jerked chicken with spicy Caribbean fruit salsa and jìcama slaw, and a surf-and-turf duo of grilled sea scallops and shortribs braised in a cider-ancho demi-glace, served with black-eyed peas and broccolini. The mixed grill might combine lamb, smoked lemon-chicken sausage and pork tenderloin with creamy mascarpone polenta.

Dessert choices include berry shortcake, toffee sundae and vanilla crème brûlée. The most extravagant is the chocolate mousse tower bearing chocolate-rum mousse, hazelnut-praline ganache and a chocolate shortbread crust. For an after-dinner jolt, try the espresso martini.

(508) 228-6135. www.fiftysixunion.com. Entrées, $24 to $31. Dinner nightly in summer, 6 to 10, Wednesday-Sunday 6 to 9 in off-season. Sunday brunch, 10 to 1.

The Club Car, 1 Main St., Nantucket.

Chef-owner Michael Shannon is a local icon, as is his sumptuous establishment. You enter through a red train car used as a lounge (open from 11 o'clock and lately the scene of chowder and sandwich lunches in season) and a lively piano bar famed for singalongs. The lounge represents a bit of history: it is the last remaining club car from the old Nantucket Railroad Co., which operated from here out to 'Sconset. Beyond the lounge is an expansive dining room of white-over-red-linened tables topped by enormous wine globes, upholstered cane-back chairs, an array of large artworks and a colorful shelf of copper pans.

The continental menu, which varies only modestly from year to year, has traditionally ranked as the town's priciest. Appetizers start at $14 for broiled sesame eel and go to $100 for beluga caviar on warm toast points with Stolichnaya vodka. Crab cake with mustard sauce, cold Nantucket lobster salad with citrus and avocado and "Octopus in the Style of Bangkok" are among the possibilities.

Typical main courses are roasted almond and walnut-crusted swordfish, calamari steak provençal, Norwegian salmon with truffle vinaigrette, veal sweetbreads grenobloise, roasted poussin stuffed with goose liver pâté, and roast rack of lamb glazed with honey mustard and served with minted madeira sauce.

Finish with one of a dozen desserts, perhaps chocolate mousse cake with crème anglaise and fresh berries in devonshire cream.

(508) 228-1101. Entrées, $30 to $45. www.theclubcar.com. Dinner nightly, 6 to 10. Closed Monday-Wednesday in off-season and after Christmas Stroll to Memorial Day.

Tuscan Treat, Tried and True

Sfoglia, 130 Pleasant St., Nantucket.

You have to know about this intimate and true trattoria, hidden in a former fish market across from the Stop & Shop supermarket. But ignore the disarming area and facade and enter for a meal like grandmother used to make – if that grandmother happened to be from rural Italy.

A pair of young Culinary Institute of America grads who cooked in cutting-edge Boston and New York restaurants serendipitously chose Nantucket to spawn their solo venture, which would "blow away the competition were it in Boston," according to a Boston Herald reviewer. Chef Ron Suhanosky named the place for his favorite sheet of uncut pasta. He does the cooking and his wife Colleen bakes focaccia that's sold across the island and dessert pastries that are to die for.

Like their grandmothers' kitchens, the enamel-topped tables are mismatched and apt to be shared, the all-Italian boutique wines are poured in squat glasses and dining is convivial by candlelight. The meal progresses through simple antipasti, handmade pastas like potato gnocchi with chicken livers and fennel cream, pappardelle alla bolognese and linguini with littlenecks, sausage and chopped rabe. Secondi could be Sicilian orata baked under a soufflé of egg whites and sea salt, chicken crisped under a brick, roasted pork ribs or veal scaloppine.

Desserts range from brandied bread pudding with currant-caramel sauce to baba al rhum with clementines and spiced cream, plus biscotti and gelati.

Prompted by their success in Nantucket, in 2006 the owners opened a second restaurant of the same name offering lunch and dinner at 1402 Lexington Ave. on Manhattan's Upper East Side.

(508) 325-4500. www.sfogliarestaurant.com. Entrees, $21 to $26. Dinner, Monday-Saturday 6 to 9. No credit cards.

Casual Dining Choices

Even the most determined Nantucket gourmand may tire of fancy, high-priced meals. Luckily, the island has other possibilities, among them:

Black-Eyed Susan's, 10 India St., Nantucket.

This quirky place where you may sit on a picnic bench in a back alley while awaiting a table is a local favorite. It's a small storefront run by partners Susan Handy and chef Jeff Worster, both with long backgrounds in local restaurants, the most recent being the Summer House. The space was formerly a breakfast bar, said Susan, and "all we had to do was clean it up." They still serve breakfast, probably a bit more fancy than before, with the likes of sourdough french toast with orange Jack Daniels butter and pecans and a spicy Thai curry scramble with broccoli and new potatoes. Most dishes come with a choice of hash browns or black-eyed peas, and you can add garlic, cilantro and/or salsa to your omelet for 25 cents each.

From his open kitchen behind the counter, Jeff, a chef-taught chef with experience in Los Angeles, where he got many of his cross-cultural culinary ideas, offers eclectic dinner fare – a mix of salads, pastas, seafood, poultry and lamb items. One spring night's menu yielded things like Tunisian chickpea soup, Brazilian hearts of palm salad, lime-marinated red snapper, a ragoût of penne with New Zealand lamb and crimini mushrooms, and barbecued pork with szechuan pineapple-fried rice and rapini. Grilled halibut with salsa verde, oyster gumbo and Moroccan lamb stew on minted couscous were a few of the intriguing dishes on the fall dinner menu. The one dessert a night might be a cobbler or bread pudding.

There's a social, European café atmosphere, and singles like to eat at the long bar. The owners only recently got a telephone, to take reservations for the 6 p.m. seating. Otherwise, summer diners face waits of more than an hour. Says Susan: "you can put your name in and then go off and have a cocktail somewhere." She added that the idea was to be here for the local population more than for the tourists, but the word got out.

(508) 325-0308. Entrées, $15 to $26. Breakfast daily, 7 to 1. Dinner, Tuesday-Saturday 6 to 9. BYOB. No credit cards. Closed November-March.

Sconset Café, Post Office Square, Siasconset.

The founder of the famed Morning Glory Cafe, Pam McKinstry, moved on to the Sconset Café before giving it up to lead treks to Africa. Now it's run by Rolf and Cindy Nelson, who met working here in 1983 and who continue to pack in habitués at eight tables for three meals a day amid a casual green and white decor, track lighting and arty accents. We enjoyed a delicious lunch of croque monsieur and boboli, a pizza-like creation with pesto and artichoke hearts. Finishing touches were homemade rum-walnut ice cream with chocolate sauce and a slice of frozen key lime pie, both heavenly.

Dinner dishes could be Thai seafood pasta, Star of India halibut, lamb dijon or veal osso buco. Start with the specialty crab cakes rémoulade, pot stickers or the café ravioli with artichokes and cheese. Save room for desserts like fresh peach pie, bête noir and bread pudding flavored with grand marnier. Some of the recipes are detailed in the café's three cookbooks.

(508) 257-4008. www.sconsetcafe.com. Entrées, $19 to $28. Breakfast daily, 8:30 to 11. Lunch, 11:30 to 3. Dinner, from 6. Open mid-May to mid-October. BYOB. No credit cards.

Centre Street Bistro, 29 Centre St., Nantucket.

Another of Nantucket's ubiquitous cafés, this small place gets high marks under chef-owners Ruth and Tim Pitts, who cooked earlier at the Summer House in 'Sconset and before that at DeMarco.

They offer creative breakfasts in the $6.50 to $8 range – perhaps scrambled eggs with sliced tomato and herbed goat cheese toast, a breakfast burrito with black beans and salsa or huevos rancheros. The kitchen and the counter are bigger than the six-table bistro, which is augmented by a sidewalk café in the summer.

The bistro branches out at night with elegant dinners of what Ruth calls "Nantucket comfort cuisine." You might start with a warm goat cheese tart or a layered version of the morning's potato pancake with smoked salmon. Typical among the half-dozen entrées are seared salmon with citrus-soy and spice glaze, sautéed shrimp with chanterelles and linguini, and seared tenderloin of beef with syrah sauce and roquefort cheese. The bistro pad thai is a tangle of red curry rice noodles with sesame-crusted shrimp, mango, lime and cilantro. One innkeeper reported that two of her guests ate there several times and pronounced it better than anything in New York.

(508) 228-8470. www.nantucketbistro.com. Entrées, $20 to $24. Breakfast on weekends, 8 to 1. Lunch, Wednesday-Friday 11:30 to 2. Dinner, Wednesday-Sunday 6 to 9:30. No credit cards.

Sushi by Yoshi, 2 East Chestnut St., Nantucket.

This is the latest takeout endeavor associated with the folks at 21 Federal. Actually, they lease the space to Tokyo-born Yoshi Mabuchi, whom we remember from his partnership with Donald Noyes in the halcyon days of Hatsune in New Haven, Conn. Here he seats up to eighteen people at three tables and a small sushi bar, and offers his sensational sushi to go.

Besides more kinds of sushi than you probably thought existed in so small a place, Yoshi offers other Japanese appetizers and entrées at moderate prices, here or to take out. Look for classic dishes ranging from gyoza (fried pork dumplings) to udon noodles and chicken teriyaki. Dessert could be green tea ice cream, coconut cake or banana tempura.

By reservation, Yoshi has been known to offer a seven-course Japanese dinner.

(508) 228-1801. Entrées. $10.50 to $15.20. Open daily, 11:30 to 2:30 and 4:30 to 10. Mid-October to April: lunch, Thursday-Saturday, dinner nightly.

Natural Gourmet

Something Natural, 50 Cliff Road, Nantucket.

Gourmet magazine requested the recipes for the carrot cake and the herb bread made at this rustic cottage at the edge of town. There are old school desks on the deck and picnic tables on the grounds for enjoying one of the nineteen sandwiches available on the wonderful whole wheat, oatmeal, rye, pumpernickel, herb, six-grain and Portuguese breads baked here and served at many a restaurant in town. We found half a sandwich of smoked turkey with tomato and swiss cheese plenty for a late lunch. You also can get salads, Nantucket Nectars and, for breakfast, muffins and raisin rolls. Owner Matthew Fee has branched out with the **Nantucket Bagel Company**, across town at 5 West Creek Road.

(508) 228-0504. Open daily, 7 to 5:30. Closed mid-October to mid-April.

Dining and Lodging

The Wauwinet, Box 2580, Wauwinet Road, Nantucket 02554.

Gloriously situated on a strip of land between Nantucket Bay and the Atlantic, the Wauwinet House had seen better days before it was acquired by Boston

Topper's is luxurious dining room at The Wauwinet.

developer Stephen Karp and his wife Jill, island vacationers who restored the place into a Relais & Châteaux member property to the tune of many millions of dollars.

The secluded location next to the Great Point Wildlife Sanctuary is unsurpassed – a parkland/residential area on a spit of land with the Atlantic surf beyond the dunes and an endless beach across the road in front, the waters at the head of Nantucket Harbor lapping at the lawns in back.

Our bayview room, one of 25 in the inn, was snug but nicely located on a third-floor corner facing the harbor, the better to watch spectacular sunsets at night. It had a queensize bed with lace-trimmed pillows, wicker and upholstered armchairs, and a painted armoire topped with a wooden swan and two hat boxes (one of the inn's decorating signatures). Deluxe rooms with kingsize or two queen beds include bigger sitting areas, but many did not seem to be as well located as ours. Every room holds a TV/VCR, tapes for which may be ordered from a library of 500, along with a bowl of gourmet popcorn.

Courtyard cottages across the road contain five more guest accommodations. One is a four-bedroom cottage with a kitchenette and fireplace.

The inn's main floor harbors a lovely living room and library done in floral chintz, a back veranda full of wicker that you sink into, an award-winning restaurant and a small, classy lounge. Outside, chairs are lined up strategically on the back lawn, a croquet game is set up, drinks and snacks are available at a small beachside grill, and two tennis courts are tucked away in the woods.

A full breakfast is included in the room rate. Guests order from a menu spanning a spectrum from strawberry and rhubarb pancakes to egg-white omelets with spa cheese and fresh vegetables.

Topper's at the Wauwinet, named for the owners' dog, is an elegant but summery setting for some of the island's best food. Two side-by-side dining rooms harbor masses of flowers and well-spaced tables with upholstered chairs in blue and white. The outdoor terrace overlooking lawn and bay is favored for lunch and drinks.

Executive chef Christopher Freeman is known for refined regional cuisine. Meals lately have been prix-fixe, $23 to $33 for lunch (three to five selections) and $83 for dinner (three courses). Among appetizers, we were impressed with the signature lobster and crab cakes with smoked corn, jalapeño olives and a divine mustard sauce, and the coriander-seared yellowfin tuna sashimi with soba noodles and pickled vegetables, served on handmade sushi boards of purple heart wood.

Every main course we've had here has been superior. Among them were roast rack of lamb with potato-fennel brandade and grilled veal chop with wild grape compote, both accompanied by baby vegetables (tiny pattypan squash and carrots about a big as a fingernail) and a wedge of potatoes. The Nantucket lobster stew incorporates abundant lobster, salsify, leeks, island tomatoes and tomalley croutons.

Desserts include a signature chocolate marquise with raspberries and grand marnier and an "ABC tart" comprised of almonds, rum-soaked bananas and chocolate that's to die for.

The wine list, featuring more than 800 vintages and 18,000 bottles, is a consistent winner of the Wine Spectator Grand Award. Service is friendly, the water comes with a lemon slice, the bread is crusty, and everything's just right.

An pleasant perk for people staying in town is boat service aboard the Wauwinet Lady, which shuttles diners out to Topper's for lunch or dinner.

(508) 228-0145 or (800) 426-8718. Fax (508) 228-6712. www.wauwinet.com. Thirty-three rooms and five cottage suites with private baths. Mid-June to mid-September: doubles $460 to $1,060, cottage suites $620 to $1,950. Off-season, doubles $360 to $850, cottage suites $610 to $1,495. Closed November to early May.

Dinner, prix-fixe $83. Lunch, Monday-Saturday noon to 2. Dinner nightly, 6 to 9:30. Sunday brunch, 10:30 to 2. Closed November to early May.

The White Elephant, 50 Easton St., Nantucket 02554.

The White Elephant is no longer the "white elephant" of Nantucket, especially following its upgrade by the owners of the Wauwinet.

Its in-town harborfront location comes with lush lawns, fancy walkways lined with hedges, and plantings that focus on a white elephant statue in the middle. There are two nine-hole putting greens and a pleasant pool to the side of the outdoor terrace and restaurant. The hotel includes a new fitness center and offers spa treatments.

The newest lodgings in the renovated hotel have kingsize beds, many with working fireplaces and some with harbor views. We're partial to the corner rooms with windows onto Children's Beach, although others might find them too public and cherish the privacy of the interior.

Seclusion is an asset in the eleven rose-covered garden cottages scattered about the property. They offer one to three bedrooms and the living rooms of some have bay windows overlooking the water. Some have fireplaces and a few have kitchenettes. The Breakers annex, located on the White Elephant's grounds, is like a small inn. It offers 25 spacious guest rooms, many with harbor views and all with private patios or balconies. Breakfast may be enjoyed there or in the new harborside lounge. All guests enjoy a glass of port or sherry or lemonade with cheese and crackers in the hotel's Library.

The **Brant Point Grill** is billed as Nantucket's premier steak and seafood house, featuring native lobster, prime aged beef and gourmet chops. The casually elegant dining room occupies several levels, some with water views through a gently curved

Summery dining room looks out toward ocean at Summer House in Siasconset.

wall of large windows. You might start with lobster and crab cakes with red pepper aioli, beef tartare or lime-marinated tuna atop a wakame-sesame seaweed salad. Expect main courses like grilled tuna with avocado cream and wasabi-mascarpone, pan-seared duck breast with a cranberry-black currant demi-glace, double pork chop with roasted peach butter and maple-balsamic syrup, and roasted rack of New Zealand lamb with pecan-mint pesto. The cedar-planked salmon is broiled on an outdoor FireCone grill. Desserts vary from a chocolate turtle cake on caramel-pecan sauce to cranberry bread pudding with citrus curd. The changing trio of sorbets is served in an edible cookie cup.

A large harborfront terrace beside the pool makes the restaurant a favorite for lunch. A light menu is available day and night, and a raw bar is featured in late afternoon on the terrace.

Hotel: (508) 228-2500 or (800) 475-6574. Fax (508) 325-1195. www.whiteelephanthotel.com. Twenty-two rooms, 31 suites and eleven cottages with private baths. July to September: doubles $435 to $600, suites $535 to $930, cottages $535 to $1,605. Off-season: doubles $235 to $635, suites $315 to $900, cottages $315 to $1,505. Closed late October to late May.

Grill: (508) 325-1320. www.brantpointgrill.com. Entrées, $25 to $35. Lunch daily, noon to 2:30. Dinner nightly, from 6. Closed mid-December to early May.

The Summer House, 17 Ocean Ave., Box 880, Siasconset 02564.

A more romantic setting could scarcely be imagined than the veranda or the summery interior dining room of this rose-covered inn with a Bermuda-style setting overlooking the ocean. It's a dream-like mix of white chairs and painted floors, good 'Sconset oils and watercolors on the whitewashed walls, and fresh flowers and plants everywhere.

Michael Farrell, the restaurant's chef-proprietor, has elevated the contemporary fare back into the island's top echelons.

Typical appetizers might be a smoked salmon, lobster and scallop sausage with black caviar, and a spring roll of goat cheese, citrus, mint and snap peas with fennel and watercress. Assertive, complex flavors continue in such entrées as tuna nori and szechuan-seared tuna with tempura lobster tail, tangerine-soy emulsion and grapefruit-braised greens; amandine roast trout and littlenecks with asparagus and truffle risotto, and grilled beef tenderloin with a jonah crab cake, marrow-crusted potato roësti and elephant garlic crème fraîche.

A brandy tart with dollops of whipped cream, blueberries and slices of kiwi proved a memorable choice for dessert. Our meal was enlivened by the piano music that makes you want to linger over one of the island's largest selections of single malts, cognacs and ports. We were content to toddle off to our room in one of eight Bermuda-like cottages strung in a horseshoe pattern around a garden between restaurant and sea.

Beneath a canopy of trees and ivy with bridal veil spilling over the roofs, the charming, rose-covered cottages have been redecorated with antiques, eyelet-embroidered pillows and lace-edged duvets on the beds, lace curtains, and painted floors and chests. A New York artist hand-painted floral borders along the tops of the walls for the finishing touch. Interesting roof lines, stained glass, leaded windows, and little nooks and crannies contribute to the charm. Modern amenities include telephones and renovated marble bathrooms, each with a jacuzzi.

Jimmy Cagney cherished the privacy of the cottage-suite named in his honor. Although each has its own or a shared small terrace, we felt on display reading on ours as arriving diners passed at cocktail hour. There are no real sitting areas, public or private, inside the cottages or main building.

An elaborate continental breakfast buffet – juices, fresh fruit, granola, bran cereal and baked goods – is offered in the morning on the sun-drenched veranda, where you can savor the sun rising over the open expanse of azure-blue ocean. It's a magical setting, like none other we know of on the Northeast Coast.

Summer House principals Peter Karlson and his wife, Danielle DeBenedictis, expanded the traditional poolside café into the full-blown **Summer House Beachside Bistro.** It's another glamorous setting beside the ocean for lunch and dinner.

Sequestered halfway down the bluff in the dunes above the beach, the spacious, umbrella-topped patio is decked out in white, enhanced by potted plants and surrounded by pink roses, climbing vines and the chef's garden. A long bar under a white awning adds an almost tropical touch.

Former Summer House chef Charles Salliou returned in 2005 after a decade in Florida to prepare an ambitious-for-the-site menu. His contemporary French/American fare – from lobster bisque and lump crab cakes to sirloin steak rossini and apple-cranberry strudel – was well received.

(508) 257-4577. Fax (508) 257-4590. www.thesummerhouse.com. Seven cottage rooms and suites and three two-bedroom cottages with private baths. Cottages, $575 to $675 June to mid-September; $225 to $425 rest of season. Closed early December to mid-April.

Restaurant: (508) 257-9976. www.the-summer-house.com. Entrées, $32 to $48. Dinner nightly, 6 to 10. Closed Monday and Tuesday in off-season and mid-October to mid-May.

Beachside Bistro: (508) 257-4542. Entrées, $24 to $42. Lunch in summer, 11:30 to 5. Dinner, 5:30 to 8. Open mid-June to mid-September.

Cliffside Beach Club, Jefferson Avenue, Box 449, Nantucket 02554.

The Cliffside Beach Club, situated for more than 80 years on the marvelous open

Canopied outdoor deck offers seaside dining at Galley Beach.

beach on the north shore, has been owned since 1954 by the Currie family, whose offspring now run a deluxe small inn/hotel and a beguiling oceanfront restaurant.

Club members coveted the same umbrella and assortment of chairs and used to wait years to reserve one of the more prestigious spots on the west beach, according to general manager Robert F. Currie. Now guests don't have to wait – they simply walk out of their rooms onto the beach. Some of the old bathhouses have been converted into fourteen contemporary bedrooms with cathedral ceilings and modern baths. All the beds, doors, tables, vanities and even the pegs for the beach towels were fashioned by Nantucket craftsmen. Angled wainscoting serves as the headboards for the built-in queensize beds. Prints by local artists and oriental rugs on the dark green carpets set off the old wood walls. Wicker furniture, antique wooden toys and black leather couches are among the appointments.

Nine air-conditioned beachfront studio apartments, each with a private deck and the phones and TVs characteristic of all the rooms, and several suites are of newer vintage. A health club is said to be one of the busiest spots in town.

A continental breakfast is served in the club's spectacular high-ceilinged lobby that Monique Currie decorated in South of France style. It has quilts on the ceiling and is full of smart wicker furniture and potted flowers, so prolific and splashy that tending them has become "my fulltime job," says Monique.

Lunch and dinner are available to guests and the public at **Galley Beach,** situated between the club and the studio apartments, with an L-shaped, canopied deck on the beach facing the ocean. Here you sit at tables with white over striped cloths, backing up to planters filled with petunias and geraniums with hanging pink paper globes overhead. It's enchanting by day or night.

We thoroughly enjoyed a couple of the best bloody marys ever before a lunch of salade niçoise and chicken salad Hawaiian. Service is by waiters who spend their winters working at a club in Palm Beach, which helps explain the level of professionalism here.

A jazz pianist plays at night, when the place conveys a clubby air. Executive chef Scott Osif's seafood-oriented dinner menu ranges from flounder meunière with orange-chardonnay beurre blanc and seared sea scallops in a creamy muscat-sea urchin sauce to curried pork tenderloin on a black and orange lentil ragoût with wilted arugula. Start with the signature New England clam chowder with smoked bacon, pernod-scented escargots served on a bed of buttery leeks, a lobster spring roll or shrimp tempura with Asian slaw. Finish with a lemon-lime tart on blueberry coulis, chocolate soufflé cake or homemade cognac ice cream.

Retired owner Jane Currie Silva's sons David, who used to be sous chef, and Geoffrey, the maître-d, oversee the front of the house. Many of the Galley's paintings and the menu cover are by Belgian artist Lucien van Vyve, the first chef at the old Opera House here, whom Jane considered her mentor.

Lodging: (508) 228-0618. Fax (508) 325-4735. www.cliffsidebeach.com. Thirty-one rooms and suites with private baths. Mid-June to Labor Day: doubles $395 to $625, suites $755 to $1,535. Off-season: doubles $255 to $445, suites $450 to $1,115. Closed Columbus Day to Memorial Day.

Restaurant: (508) 228-9641. Entrées, $29 to $45. Lunch daily in summer, 11:30 to 2. Dinner nightly, 6 to 10, late May to late September.

Ships Inn, 13 Fair St., Nantucket 02554.

Built in 1831 by whaling captain Obed Starbuck, this has been nicely restored by chef-owner Mark Gottwald and his wife Ellie. It now claims some of Nantucket's most comfortable inn accommodations as well as a highly regarded restaurant.

The guest rooms, named after ships that Starbuck commanded, contain many of original furnishings and retain the look of the period. They have been refurbished with new wallpapers and tiled baths and come with interesting window treatments, down comforters, Neutrogena toiletries and mini-refrigerators in cabinets beneath the TV sets. Most have reading chairs and half have desks. All but two tiny single rooms are more spacious than most bedrooms in Nantucket inns.

Guests enjoy afternoon tea with coffeecake and cookies. A continental breakfast of fruit, cereal, homemade granola, scones and muffins is set out in the morning.

Meals here have received considerable notice since the Gottwalds took over. Chef Mark, who trained at Le Cirque in New York and at Spago in Los Angeles, calls the style California-French.

Among entrées, you might find grilled yellowtail flounder with lemon-thyme beurre blanc, braised local cod with kaffir lime and coconut-curry cream, grilled duck breast with sweet pea raviolis and vidalia duck demi-glace, and roquefort-crusted filet mignon. Or consider a pasta, perhaps rigatoni with duck bolognese and ricotta salata. Finish with raspberry sorbet or chocolate soufflé cake.

Start with cold poached salmon with sorrel puree, grilled sea scallops with black truffle hollandaise, a cold terrine of foie gras or a lobster and white asparagus salad with a roasted beet vinaigrette. Finish with a tangerine napoleon cake sauced with grand marnier, chocolate soufflé cake or raspberry sorbet.

The dining room is attractive with apricot walls over white wainscoting, exposed beams, a white fireplace in the center of the room, candles in the many-paned windows, and white-linened tables dressed with candles and fresh flowers. There also are tables for eating in the adjacent Dory Bar.

(508) 228-0040 or (888) 872-4052. www.shipsinnnantucket.com. Ten rooms with private baths. Doubles, $195 to $250. Closed Columbus Day to Mother's Day.

Entrées, $22 to $34. Dinner. Thursday-Monday 5:30 to 9:30. Closed Columbus Day to Mother's Day.

Dining area is set for breakfast at The Pineapple Inn.

Lodging

The Pineapple Inn, 10 Hussey St., Nantucket 02554.

Breakfast is a high point of a stay at this deluxe B&B. That's no surprise to anyone familiar with the innkeepers, Caroline and Bob Taylor. They were known for their breakfasts during the fifteen years they owned and operated the Quaker House Inn and Restaurant here before they turned their attention to the Pineapple in 1997.

More than half the comments in the inn's guest book relate to the food. "We like different things," says Bob, who rises early every day to bake the pastries and prepare the entrée. "You won't get muffins here." What you will get, perhaps, are scones with flavored creams or blueberry-coffee crumb cake. Or clafouti, the recipe for which was requested by Gourmet magazine. Or, in our case, a savory tart of spinach, cheese, basil and sundried tomatoes, teamed with a slice of the day's nectarine and blueberry tart, a delicious and custardy affair. These followed a choice of cereals: berndt muesli or dry mix with granola. Fresh orange juice, a fruit cocktail and an endless reservoir of café latte came with. "The only holdovers here from our restaurant are the espresso and juicing machines," Bob advised. He puts both to good use.

The leisurely repast takes place between 8 and 10 at a table for ten in an elegant, chandeliered dining area on the inn's lower level. In good weather, it's served outside at umbrella-covered tables beside a fountain on a large, plant-bedecked rear terrace. Roses were bursting into bloom there at our June visit.

The Taylors are among the few Nantucket innkeepers who live on the premises and attend to their guests personally. They spent nearly $1 million to transform an 1838 Greek Revival ship captain's house into one of the town's more comfortable B&Bs. "We wanted to bring our accommodations to the highest standard possible on the island," says Bob.

The house is conveniently situated along a quiet, one-way residential street at the edge of downtown. The building had to be gutted to install private baths, all finished in white marble. The twelve air-conditioned guest quarters, named for whaling ship captains whose biographies are in the appropriate room's welcome book, are spread over four floors. Each features a handmade Eldred Wheeler four-poster canopy bed of tiger maple, king or queen size, covered by a Ralph Lauren duvet in a Williamsburg pattern. Sitting areas have wing chairs or small sofas. Amenities include TVs hidden in highboys, telephones, handmade oriental carpets, and 19th-century antiques and artworks. Three rooms have ornamental fireplaces. The Captain Pollard on the lower level adds a private patio.

In cool weather, guests gather on tapestry sofas in front of the fireplace in the side parlor in this B&B that lives up to its name, the Colonial symbol for hospitality. The Taylors do it up right.

(508) 228-9992. www.pineappleinn.com. Twelve rooms with private baths. Mid-June to late September and special events and weekends: doubles $195 to $325. Off-season, $110 to $250. Closed late October to late April.

Union Street Inn, 7 Union St., Nantucket 02554.

A former hotel manager from Connecticut and his wife, Ken and Deborah Withrow, run this luxury B&B in a restored 1770 house, converted from a guest house by previous owners. They offer twelve spacious accommodations with air conditioning, designer wallpapers, Frette bedding, antique furnishings and cable TV. Scatter rugs dot the original wide-plank pine floors. Six rooms have working fireplaces, including a suite with queen canopy bed, mini-fridge and sitting room with VCR and telephone. Another premier room has a king poster bed and fireplace. Others have king or queensize beds, including a small room with a queen bed and a hall bath.

Because of its location (and zoning), the Union Street can offer more than Nantucket's highly regulated continental breakfasts. The Withrows serve things like scrambled eggs and bacon, blueberry pancakes, challah bread french toast and, every fourth day, eggs benedict. These are in addition to a cold buffet that includes a fresh fruit platter, cereals and muffins. The repast is taken in a large dining room or at three handsome garden tables on the side patio beneath an ivy-covered hillside.

"Debbie cooks and I'm the bus boy," quips Ken, who had been manager of the Hyatt UN Plaza Hotel in New York and the Ambassador East Hotel in Chicago. They wanted their own business and a family life for their son, and found both here.

(508) 228-9222 or (800) 225-5116. Fax (508) 325-0848. www.union-street-inn.com. Eleven rooms and one suite with private baths. Mid-June through mid-September: doubles $215 to $435, suite $465. Spring and fall: doubles $120 to $230, suite $255. Closed December-March.

The Sherburne Inn, 10 Gay St., Nantucket 02554.

Built in 1835 as headquarters for the Atlantic Silk Company, this house in a residential area has been a lodging establishment since 1872. When Pennsylvanians Dale Hamilton III and Susan Gasparich purchased The House at 10 Gay, they changed its name and continued renovating and redecorating it into a first-class B&B.

The pair offer eight guest rooms, now all with private baths. Two have king beds and six are queensize. Four are on the main floor and four on the second; a beautiful winding staircase connects the two. The bedrooms, bright and cheery, are decorated to the Federal period. They contain canopy and poster beds, oriental rugs and fine artworks as well as TV/DVDs and high-speed internet access. We liked No. 8 upstairs in the rear with a king bed, clawfoot tub with shower and a private balcony overlooking the side and rear yards. Another room holds a small library and a mini-refrigerator.

Susan bakes blueberry or rhubarb muffins to supplement the natural breads, bagels and English muffins served for continental breakfast. Fresh fruit and juice accompany. The meal is taken in the main-floor parlor, on a deck on one side of the house or in the yard surrounded by gardens and a privet hedge. Tea and cookies or wine and cheese may be served in the afternoon.

(508) 228-4425 or (888) 557-4425. Fax (508) 228-8114. www.sherburneinn.com. Eight rooms with private baths. Doubles, $195 to $325 Memorial Day to mid-October, $95 to $150 rest of season. Closed January-March.

Anchor Inn, 66 Centre St., Box 387, Nantucket 02554.

Charles and Ann Balas, who used to own the Nantucket Fine Chocolates store, are still hands-on innkeepers at this venerable B&B. They feel their in-residence position helps set the Anchor apart. Built by a whaling ship captain in 1806, this was the home in the 1950s of the Gilbreths of "Cheaper by the Dozen" fame, who wrote of their experience in the book *Innside Nantucket.*

Ten guest rooms, named after whaling ships, have queen beds and period furnishings amid the original random-width floorboards and antique paneling. An eleventh room on the third floor has twin beds. Most bathrooms have showers only, but are equipped with hair dryers.

Guests help themselves to continental breakfast on an enclosed wraparound side/rear porch with individual tables and café curtains. Charles's homemade muffins are served to the accompaniment of classical music.

The Balases, who by nature and avocation know all the food goings-on around the island, share their insights with guests on the patio in the side pocket garden or in the front parlor, where the fireplace is lit in cool weather.

The couple, who now stay open even in mid-winter, also offer four larger rooms and a suite three doors away at the 72 Centre Street Inn.

(508) 228-0072. www.anchor-inn.net. Eleven rooms with private baths. Doubles, $185 to $225, June to mid-September and most weekends; rest of year, $85 to $145.

Truly a 'Boutique Hotel'

Vanessa Noel Hotel, 5 Chestnut St., Nantucket.

Couture designer Vanessa Noel, who has been selling sophisticated shoes to a cult following since 1987, is a Nantucketer at heart. She first opened a seasonal shoe boutique on the wharf not far from her family's summer home. Then she bought the old Quaker House Inn & Restaurant in the center of town and converted it into a boutique hotel that, for once, lives up to the name.

The hotel – dubbed VNH, for short – is disguised behind a gray weathered-shingled house built in 1847. Enter the high-chic lobby with its original wide-plank floor illuminated by a 1930s Baccarat crystal chandelier. To the left of the lobby is Vanessa's namesake store stocked with more than 100 styles of women's shoes. To the right is the Vanno Bar, a 27-seat lounge serving caviar and gravlax from Manhattan's Caviarteria. Here, guests sip champagne or whatever on leopard-print banquettes and – for the romantics who buy Vanno's line that "I always wanted to create a place to sit and eat *sexy* food on the island" – two whimsical indoor swings suspended from the ceiling between walls lined with faux privet hedges.

Leopard-trimmed carpeting leads guests up the Colonial staircase to eight bedrooms where chic meets beach. Each has a sky-blue ceiling, woven sisal carpet and hand-sewn Italian silk-taffeta shades atop the windows. Frameless soft feather beds are dressed in 300-count Frette sheets and duvets and topped with nine pillows. Bathrooms incorporate Italian honey-colored marble, designer fixtures, Bulgari toiletries, Frette robes and bath sheets. The stocked minibar contains Vanessa Noel Water. A fifteen-inch flat screen plasma television set offers diversion.

At the end of its first season, Departures magazine crowed that VNH brought "a dash of city style to beautiful but staid Nantucket." Gushed the writer: "Move over blue whales, creaky floorboards, and gloppy lobster rolls. Here is 100 percent over-the-top indulgence."

As if. Nantucket barely noticed.

(508) 228-5300. www.vanno.com. Eight rooms with private baths. Doubles, $340 to $480.

Gourmet Treats

Rarely have we encountered a small area so chock full of gourmet shops, specialty-food takeouts, caterers and other services pertaining to matters culinary.

Many cheeses, gazpacho, Thai noodle and curried couscous salads, muffulettas, apple-peach muffins and sandwiches in the $6 to $8 range are available from **Provisions** at 3 Harbor Square, behind the bandstand on Straight Wharf. Also part of the food complex here is the **Straight Wharf Fish Store,** where soft-shell crab and swordfish steak sandwiches were going for $8.95 last we knew. The store carries some specialty foods along with fresh fish.

For our money, the best homemade ice creams and yogurts in town are served at **The Juice Bar,** a pastry and ice cream shop at 12 Broad St. across from the Whaling Museum. We enjoyed an oversize cup of different fruit sorbets after one dessert-less dinner.

Satisfy your sweet tooth at **Sweet Inspirations** at 26 Centre St. You can indulge in handmade chocolates, pecan and caramel tuckernucks, award-winning cranberry truffles, chocolate-almond buttercrunch, and an exclusive line of Nantucket fruit preserves and chutneys. A recent favorite is cranberry bark, available in dark, milk or white chocolate, each studded with bright red dried cranberries. The confections are made here daily the old-fashioned way, smoothed and cut by hand.

The Complete Kitchen at 25 Centre St. offers Nantucket jams, jellies and ketchup made just for the store, caviars, crème fraîche and California tortas with fresh basil, garlic and pinenuts or smoked salmon, mustard and dill. All those items the beautiful people need for their cocktail parties are here, as are a good selection of cookbooks and cookware. Around the corner at 4 India St. is the **Nantucket Gourmet,** with more specialty foods, a deli case for salads and sandwiches, and a lot of high-tech kettles, toasters and such, as well as a practical oyster opener for $13.95.

If you're interested in pepper grinders, check out the Peppergun, invented and made on the island. Ads headlining it as "Nantucket Native" tout the fast-grinding one-hander as the world's most efficient peppermill. It's on sale at local stores.

The Lion's Paw at the foot of Main Street carries wonderful hand-painted pottery, including great fish plates. We think it's the nicest of several gift shops of interest to gourmands.

Majolica at 1 Old North Wharf specializes in hand-painted, one-of-a-kind pieces of the imported Italian pottery and ceramics. The colorful store displays teapots, trays, vases, salad bowls, demitasse cups and the trademark rooster pitchers in several sizes. You can even buy a set of hand-painted animal plates from Tuscany.

Only in Nantucket would you not be surprised to come across **Cold Noses,** a small gourmet shop for cats and dogs near Straight Wharf. As well as gourmet natural dog cookies, you'll find "doggie duds," cat beds, pearls pour le pouch and perfect purrls for cats, and even cologne from Paris for Fluffy or Spot.

The choicest prepared foods, cheeses and wines in town come from **Fahey & Fromagerie,** 49A Pleasant St. Michael Fahey gives a sample of brin d'amour from Corsica to go with a taste of a fine bordeaux while French chef Jean Dion works in the kitchen. Their specialty is fine foods to go, as in a deli case brimming with the likes of salmon mousse, spinach and roquefort pâté, salads, stuffed zucchini boats, roasted free-range chicken and sliced beef tenderloin.

Although its wines don't seem to turn up in many off-island restaurants, **Nantucket Vineyard** produces 3,500 cases a year. Vintners Dean and Melissa Long started as an offshoot of **Bartlett's Ocean View Farm** out Hummock Pond Road, where everybody on the island seems to go for fresh produce (if they don't get to the morning selection at the sidewalk stand at Main and Federal streets in town). The Longs gave up efforts to grow vinifera grapes in favor of importing from Washington and California. On sale at the winery at the side of their home at 3 Bartlett Farm Road are their latest bottlings of chardonnay, riesling, pinot gris, merlot and zinfandel. Tastings are offered daily, 11 to 6. The Longs also distill orange-flavored vodka at their **Triple Eight Distillery** and are developing new liquors, including gin, rum and "notch – not scotch"), a single-malt whisky released in 2005. Next door at 5 Bartlett Farm Road – and also inspired by Bartlett's and the vineyard, according to partner Jay Harmon – is **Cisco Brewers,** Nantucket's first microbrewery, best known for its Whale's Tale Pale Ale and 120-calorie Sankaty Light beer. The brewery, winery and distillery are open Monday-Saturday 10 to 6, and the winery also is open Sunday noon to 5. Products of all three are available at their new downtown store, **Isle Drink, Ltd.**, in Courtyard No. 5 near the gazebo on lower Straight Wharf.

They're Juice Guys

Nantucket Nectars, juices that turn up everywhere, got their start in Nantucket. Tom First and Tom Scott, fresh out of Brown University in 1988, started Allserve, a floating convenience store, to serve boats in Nantucket Harbor. During the off-season, they repeated for island friends the taste of a peach nectar that Tom First had enjoyed in Spain. They began making it in blenders and selling it in cups off the stern of the Allserve boat in 1990. Starting with three flavors, the pair known as "Tom and Tom – we're juice guys" expanded to the point where they were the fastest-growing New Age beverage company in the country. Thirty varieties of all-natural fruit juices are sold through their own distribution network in more than 40 states. They come with distinctive purple caps and colorful labels that depict fond memories of days spent in the Allserve General Store still operating behind the Hy-Line terminal at 44 Straight Wharf. The bottle caps contain nuggets of Nantucket lore, and it's the in thing locally to rate mention on a cap. Now based in Cambridge, Nantucket Nectars is backed by the resources of Cadbury Schweppes, its new parent. But its advertising continues to promote the good life on Nantucket, featuring not only the company's founders but people they call "local Nantucket legends." The juice bar operates seasonally at 4 Easy St.

Boston, Mass.

Baked Beans to New Cuisine

If California is America's last culinary frontier, as one food magazine has suggested, Boston is our first. This city situated not far from where the Pilgrims landed has had more than 350 years to refine and redefine itself, to become civilized in cuisine as well as in culture.

No American city has given its name to, nor been associated with, more indigenous foods. Boston baked beans, Boston scrod, Boston lettuce, Indian pudding, Boston brown bread and Parker House rolls got their start here. The nation's first French restaurant dates back to 1793 in Boston. The Parker House opened in 1854 as New England's first leading hotel and dining room. The famed Durgin-Park can safely proclaim it was "established before you were born." Locke-Ober still serves lobster savannah as it did when one of us first had it there as a teenager more decades ago than she cares to remember. Julia Child launched her national reputation in Boston and for most of her life called it home.

Boston's food scene has perhaps changed more in the last 25 years than in its first 350, however. Some of the staples remain, but the new regional cuisine is everywhere – reigning a tad preciously in some of the East's great restaurants (most of them creations of the 1980s and '90s), simply evolving or being accommodated in more traditional places. Boston was among the first to take to bistro cooking, as the economy softened in the early 1990s. And Boston restaurants were among the first to upscale again in the new millennium.

Boston is at the heart of an emerging New England cuisine, with chefs developing original recipes employing regional ingredients. Nearly a dozen have been ranked among the country's best. Several of the city's hotels are in the forefront of Boston's growing culinary reputation, and the chefs they import tend to stay to open their own restaurants.

The leading chefs in America's largest small town consider themselves a family, it seems. They've reached the big time here, and have little inclination to move on.

Dining

More than ever, Boston offers a roster of "hot," high-profile restaurants, whose members come and go. While they receive a lot of the media buzz, others of earlier consequence continue to appeal.

The Best of the Best

L'Espalier, 30 Gloucester St.

The first – and, most agree, still the best – of Boston's great restaurants, L'Espalier offers cuisine, setting and style for a special occasion. It makes such demands upon your palate that we cannot imagine dining here every week, as habitués are known to do. Nor could we often sample the chef's tasting menu, so extravagant that even those of us who were taught to eat every last morsel simply couldn't. It was too much of a great thing.

L'Espalier opened in 1978 under the auspices of Tunisian-born French chef Moncef Meddeb, who sold it a decade later to his sous chef, Frank McClelland. Frank and

Chef-owner Frank McClelland in dining room at L'Espalier.

his wife Catherine devote full-time-plus to the effort. "We're putting lots of energy into upgrading every aspect of the cuisine, service and decor so that we have something very special here," says Frank. Their energy and expertise pay off as L'Espalier keeps raising the bar for perfection (it received the current Boston Globe food critic's first four-star rating, Boston's highest rating for food and decor from Zagat and, since 2000, five-diamond ratings from AAA). Frank's evolving new French-American cuisine keeps getting better and better.

L'Espalier has a totally prix-fixe menu, charging $75 for three courses of multiple choices. A seven-course dégustation menu for $94 offers smaller portions with extra courses of the regular menu plus add-ons. Since we wanted to taste as much as possible, our party of four put ourselves in the chef's hands – which is a princely way to go. About half the 120 diners here each night do likewise.

An amuse-bouche of a fall vegetable tart with smoked pork on toasted brioche and a sampling of five exotic breads got our meal off to a tasty start. First courses included warm Wellfleet oysters in a champagne, leek and pumpkin nage with blinis, herb salad and caviar; a terrine of smoked salmon with leeks, watercress and potato and, for good measure, an incredible dish of roasted foie gras with a savory prune, dried cherry and oatmeal crisp. We'll never forget the cappuccino of chanterelles and white truffles, a vegetarian broth with a foamy topping of essence of mushrooms and truffles steamed in the manner of cappuccino, enhanced with oysters baked with cider and cracked white pepper glaze.

Main courses were melt-in-the-mouth poached halibut with black truffles and crabmeat gratin; roasted apple-smoked chicken in a mille-feuille of sweet potato, apple and turnip; braised stuffed Vermont veal shoulder, served under a dome, and roasted Vermont pheasant with foie gras croutons and côtes du rhône plum sauce. Honestly, it was the exotic accompaniments – doled out family style for sampling on plate after plate – that finished us off. Not to mention the grand assortment of cheeses, a tray of eleven of the best from Massachusetts to Tuscany. We picked out three and the waiter returned with five each.

Desserts, to which we could no longer do justice, were a roasted banana soufflé with toasted coconut crème anglaise, a molten-centered chocolate fondant cake with grand marnier sabayon, a refreshing passionfruit sorbet and raspberry frozen yogurt with a meringue swirl, and – the ultimate – "L'Espalier's study of pears." The last was an artistic rendering of a pear stuffed with ice cream, a grilled pear and a puff-pastry tart called pithiviers. The work was colorfully outlined with chocolate, raspberry and kiwi sauces around the edge of the plate.

More than most, the straightforward menu descriptions belie the complexity of flavors and tastes. Frank cooks in an intellectual style, working daily in a test kitchen on taste and composition so that the diner senses the essence of the food. He also has a passion for vegetables. His was the first mainstream restaurant we encountered to offer a dégustation vegetarian menu ($75 for seven courses, $110 if paired with autumn juices).

The venison, lamb, rabbit and produce – most grown organically – come from L'Espalier's own purveyors. Frank personally buys the selections for the thirteen-page wine list, which is especially strong on Bordeaux and wines from Alsace and Rhône, well aged in three cellars. Although he has a chef de cuisine among a dozen professional cooks in the kitchen, he works a station and personally oversees every dish that goes out. You also can be assured that he's on the scene – when he goes to France for his annual busman's holiday to study with three-star chefs, he closes the restaurant.

His renovated Back Bay Victorian townhouse is a supremely elegant atmosphere in which to dine. After buzzing a doorbell to gain entry, diners proceed to the second floor, which has two high-ceilinged dining rooms in shades of taupe and cream, or to the third floor, where the dining-room walls are a warm lacquered and stenciled terra cotta and the kitchen is next door. There are marble fireplaces, carved moldings, beautiful flower arrangements in niches, pin spotlights on well-spaced tables set with damask linens and fresh flowers, and luxurious yet comfortable lacquered chairs with curved arms.

Frank, besides keeping on top of everything in the kitchen, pops out to greet customers in his dining rooms as well. L'Espalier was not only full of what he termed "discerning diners" but was catering to two private functions the most recent night we were there. It turned out that the obviously discerning party of ten at the corner table by the window across the way from ours was hosted by the Baroness Nadine Rothschild, in town to promote her Lafite and Mouton wines. The sommelier treated us to a rather nice taste of one of their leftovers.

(617) 262-3023. www.lespalier.com. Prix-fixe, $75. Dinner by reservation, Monday-Saturday 5:30 to 10.

Radius, 8 High St.

This super-chic, contemporary French restaurant is one of Boston's few frontrunners without a home-grown chef-owner. Ex-New Yorker Michael Schlow, who gave up a baseball scholarship to pursue cooking, left the tiny Café Louis in a tony Back Bay clothing store for a big ticket at the edge of the Financial District.

Radius features imaginative cuisine in designer-modern dining room.

Radius takes its straightforward geometric name from a large, circular dining room that once housed a bank. This is one restaurant that's designed rather than decorated. "We tried to create Boston's first fully conceptualized modern restaurant," said co-owner/manager Christopher Myers. That translates, apparently, to a lack of signage on the exterior and a stark, minimalist interior of curves within curves in shades of charcoal gray and poppy red. Precise rectangular cuts of dentil molding ornament the lofty white ceiling. Comfortable upholstered chairs and banquettes seat 90 at nicely spaced tables dressed with double sets of thick white linens and topped at our autumn visit with bud vases holding rare Chinese orchids. Eighteen solo diners can join a raised communal table for an overview of the setting, or look out across the bar for a glimpse of South Station.

Expert service is provided by an army of staff in loose-fitting gray designer suits with white T-shirts that look like something your mod kids might wear.

Good, crusty rolls were doled out one at a time during a long, leisurely meal that proved this to be a midday destination rather than a mere lunch break. (How could it be otherwise when the tab for two soared to $75 before tax, tip and parking?)

True, we splurged on the most expensive of appetizers: halibut tartare and fingerling potato tart with ossetra caviar and "three-minute egg sauce." Very unusual, it was an exquisite blend of tastes and textures for a cool $18. Main courses, priced at similar levels, were a superior spice-crusted tender duck confit with tarbias bean cassoulet, carrots and red wine sauce, and a great-sounding Australian farm-raised loin of lamb salad with mesclun, goat cheese and baby beets. The sliced lamb was perfect, though not as abundant as the mesclun. We filled up on rolls and a shared dessert of lemon chamomile cake, served with blueberries, crème fraîche ice cream and honey-thyme syrup.

At night, the noise level rises with the prices. Serious diners join the beautiful people in partaking of an extravagant repertoire at the cusp of pretense. The appetizers give a hint: ahi tuna with breakfast radish salad, yuzu and spicy mustard vinaigrette; spicy shrimp salad with pea tendrils, shaved almonds, lotus root and ponzu sauce; crispy sweetbreads with apples, lentils, smoked bacon and horseradish.

Main courses sound simpler but turn out sublime: perhaps black cod with bacon and carrot-curry vinaigrette, Scottish salmon with caviar sauce, herb-basted chicken with green garlic and foie gras sauce, or a duo of Colorado lamb with cumin jus.

The pastry chef's signature Tahitian vanilla crème brûlée might be upstaged by more recent offerings, perhaps a goat cheese and huckleberry cheesecake with huckleberry ice cream, an olive oil and citrus cake with ruby red grapefruit and pistachio ice cream, or coconut panna cotta with mango gelee and white chocolate praline.

Radius also offers a four-course vegetable tasting for $60, a four-course market tasting menu for $75 and a seven-course deluxe chef's tasting menu for $105. Wine tastings, matched with each course, add $40 and $75 respectively. The prices of the 200-plus wines, incidentally, are tilted toward those who are inclined to spend more for beverage than food.

But it is the masterful food that propelled Radius into a place in Gourmet magazine's annual ranking of America's 50 best restaurants.

The partners have since opened Via Matta, an Italian restaurant, and the Great Bay seafood restaurant in Boston's Back Bay neighborhood.

(617) 426-1234. www.radiusrestaurant.com. Entrées, $34 to $43. Lunch, Monday-Friday 11:30 to 2:30. Dinner, Monday-Saturday 5:30 to 10 or 11.

No. 9 Park, 9 Park St.

A distinguished looking gentleman was polishing the silver door pull shaped in the form of a nine at the front entry as we arrived for lunch. He turned out to be the husband of the chef, Barbara Lynch. Although he has his own business, he shows up at mealtime to keep things polished in one of Boston's most au courant restaurants.

His wife, who grew up in South Boston, is happiest in the kitchen, which is hidden out of sight in an era when many are open to the dining area. Cooking her way through the top restaurants in Boston and Cambridge, she emerged as one of Food & Wine magazine's top new chefs while executive chef at Galleria Italiana. In 1998, she moved a few blocks up Tremont Street to a Beacon Hill brownstone, designed by Charles Bulfinch and facing the Boston Common across from the State House. She was one of the first to name a restaurant for its address.

A quick winner of Best of Boston honors, this evokes a high-end European bistro atmosphere. It's unexpectedly small, with a 30-seat café around the bar and two intimate dining rooms seating a total of 65. The main room in the rear, an austere affair with mahogany wainscoting and a montage of black and white photos of the Boston Common, is notable for its lack of windows – in contrast to the side dining room in front with big wraparound windows onto the Common. Actually, you don't notice the muted taupe decor. It blends into the background as the food eases into the foreground.

Named the Northeast's best chef in 2003 by the James Beard Foundation, Barbara is known for robust yet refined country European fare. She delivered it at our autumn lunch, which began with an amusé, a demitasse cup of the day's chestnut bisque – delicate, studded with wild mushrooms and surprisingly tasty. One of us sampled the three-course, prix-fixe meal for $26. It yielded a perfect bibb salad, a plate of lamb ravioli with an ethereal white bean ragoût and a rich chocolate-hazelnut terrine with espresso anglaise. The other ordered the chilled lobster salad, which arrived squashed in a cylinder shape in the center of a large plate. What appeared to be red caviar atop layers of lobster, mache, watercress and golden potato brunoise turned out to be the tiniest bits of red tomato. The layered effect was deceptive, the salad proving to be far larger than it looked. After espresso, the bill came with a china box holding macaroons.

Chef-owner Barbara Lynch at No. 9 Park.

The chef's signature dishes are available at night. Don't miss her crispy duck, served any number of ways but at a recent visit with a cider reduction, parsnips and a quince confit. Or sample her lacquered sturgeon in ginger broth, bacon-wrapped monkfish, hazelnut-crusted squab or a "duet" of beef sirloin and short-rib. We've heard raves for the rabbit three ways – seared loin, baked rack and braised leg, each with its own accompaniment of parsnip-potato purée, porcini flan and lentils.

Starters might be a lobster napoleon, rock shrimp lasagna, belon oysters au gratin with ossetra caviar, and prune-stuffed gnocchi with seared foie gras.

The pastry chef is known for her bread pudding served with brandied figs and caramel sauce. Or you might try the "local apple" tarte tatin, a fruit vacheron, black pepper cheesecake or the medley of homemade ice creams and sorbets.

The wine list here is extraordinary, which is predictable given its creation by wine expert Cat Silirie, a friend who was rated Boston's top sommelier in a male-dominated profession. She and Barbara collaborated with a Santa Barbara County winery to create their own house wines labeled No. 9.

The chef offers tasting menus of seven courses for $85 and nine courses for $110.

The café menu, served in the convivial bar area, offers bistro fare at its best.

(617) 742-9991. www.no9park.com. Entrées, $29 to $40; café, $18 to $25. Lunch, Monday-Friday 11:30 to 2:30. Dinner, Monday-Saturday 5:30 to 10.

Hamersley's Bistro, 553 Tremont St.

Anticipating a trend to downscaled food and prices, this bistro was the first to open in 1987 in the South End. An instant hit, it paved the way for countless others and relocated to larger quarters across the street, upscaling the food and prices along the way. It remains a big player on the Boston dining scene, without so much as a press agent or a media kit. Instead, it offers a welcoming and chatty website appealing directly to the customer.

The amiable, with-it, 120-seat place is run very personally by two redheads, Gordon Hamersley, once apprentice to Wolfgang Puck in Los Angeles, and his English-born wife Fiona, former New England director of the American Institute of Wine and Food.

Beamed ceilng imparts rustic look to long dining room at Hamersley's Bistro.

The Hamersleys envisioned theirs as an elegant Boston translation of the homey, family-run country bistros of France. Rough wooden ceiling beams salvaged from a Connecticut barn are counterpoints to French floral tapestries in the long, buttercup yellow dining room. In typical bistro style, large squares of white paper are clipped over the tablecloths, the silverware is rolled inside white napkins, bottles of S. Pellegrino water serve as centerpieces, track lights provide illumination and the noise level is high enough that you can't really overhear the couple at the next table. Fiona presides at the bar, which is part of a café that offers both a bistro and the full menu. Outdoor dining is available on a section of the brick patio beside the Boston Center for the Arts.

"We serve high-quality food stripped down to the basics," Gordon says. "Rustic, peasant food" is what he calls it. We call it gutsy.

Our dinner began memorably with the signature grilled mushroom and garlic "sandwich" on country bread, not really a sandwich but two toasted bread slices flanking an abundance of mushrooms and watercress. Also tasty but messy was a whole braised artichoke stuffed with olives and mint.

Among main courses, we loved the duckling with turnips, endive and apple slices – an enormous portion, including an entire leg and crisp slices of breast grilled and blackened at the edges like a good sirloin steak – and a Moroccan lamb stew with couscous and harissa that everybody raves about. The basic roast chicken with garlic, lemon and parsley is a menu fixture. But that's for the timid. More exciting are the New England fish stew of monkfish, calamari and clams with pumpkin, chickpeas and raisins; the wild Alaskan salmon with lentils, bacon and red wine sauce; the slow-roasted and grilled organic Vermont pig with onions, apples, red cabbage and calvados; and the fall game bird mixed grill of quail, grouse and duck with a crêpe filled with wild rice, walnuts and quince. Those aren't concoctions you readily prepare at home, unless, perhaps, you have a copy of Gordon's new cookbook, *Bistro Cooking at Home.*

Ever experimenting at the edge, Gordon offered a three-course autumn mushroom tasting menu ($49) at a recent visit. An appetizer of braised wild mushrooms with polenta and asiago cheese was followed by a cream of black trumpet soup with white truffle oil. The main dish was a complex salmi of guinea hen with golden chanterelles and foie gras sauce.

The wine list, like the menu, changes with the seasons. Fiona seeks out the unique among wines from around the world and there was scarcely a vintner we recognized. Symbols distinguish the type of grape for the uninitiated.

Typical desserts are the signature souffléd lemon custard, apple tarte tatin with thyme-infused buttermilk ice cream, and a sticky date and toffee cake with toasted pecans and caramel. We remember fondly the trilogy of sorbets – brandied pear, green melon and concord grape – served with biscotti, a refreshing end to a terrific meal.

(617) 423-2700. www.hamersleysbistro.com. Entrées, $25 to $36. Dinner, Monday-Friday 6 to 10, Saturday 5:30 to 10:30, Sunday 5:30 to 9:30.

Mistral, 223 Columbus Ave.

Named for the winds that sweep through the South of France, this is the high-profile venture of chef Jamie Mammano, who elevated Aujourd'hui at the Four Seasons Hotel to five-diamond status. Here he's backed by nightclub impresario Seth Greenberg and developer Paul Roiff, who spared no expense in providing cutting-edge cachet.

Chef Jamie Mammano relaxes in dining room at Mistral.

The facade of the restored black building looming above the Mass Turnpike is unobtrusive, marked only by its name spelled out in wrought iron in the window above the door. Inside is a drop-dead beautiful, tasteful space sectioned into lounge, bar, bistro and dining area seating 200. The decor is Beaux Arts elegant rather than Provençal cute. Twelve-foot-high arched windows on three sides shed light on sandstone walls and slate floors. Shaded curling wrought-iron chandeliers are suspended from sixteen-foot-high ceilings. Green rattan chairs are at angled tables in the front section of the room accented with pillars and plants. Yellow-print fabric banquettes flank the perimeter. Intriguing details everywhere catch the eye, not the least of which is a broad lineup of sawed-off branches inexplicably standing upright above the stone-topped bar.

While his partners provided wall-to-wall buzz, chef Jamie simplified and made accessible his French-Mediterranean fare that commanded top dollar at Aujourd'hui. The menu is short and spans a broad price range.

Two signature starters at either end of the spectrum illustrate. The "cheapie" is the portobello mushroom "carpaccio." Roasted red peppers, baby arugula and marinated raisins frame thin slices of grilled portobello drizzled with balsamic vinaigrette, a counterpoint of tastes from tart to sour to sweet. The splurge is for foie gras, a substantial slice of goose liver served atop a hollowed-out brioche filled with warm confit of duck, complemented by a tart sauce of dried cherries. Other recommended starters are tuna tartare with crispy wontons and ginger, Maine crab ravioli and any of the grilled thin-crust pizzas. With a side salad, these can make a satisfying meal for the price-conscious.

Main courses range from pan-roasted halibut with poached jumbo lump crab to rack of Colorado lamb presented as a small sculpture, four ample chops soaring skyward beside a gratin of celery root and sides of chantenay carrots and haricots vert. Portions are substantial and the accompaniments enticing. Straightforward braised beef shortribs might come with roasted garlic mash and sweet vidalia crisps, and whole roasted duck with wild mushroom risotto and dried cranberry gastrique.

The primarily French and American wine offerings are as extensive as they are expensive. The reserve list raises the bar from the high double digits well into three and four figures.

Desserts present a difficult choice, from a warm chocolate torte with sauce anglaise to almond-pear cake with cranberry compote and ginger ice cream. The "mini dessert assiette" for two simplifies the problem. It yields a themed sampling of the night's offerings in small clay pots perfect for passing.

(617) 867-9300. www.mistralbistro.com. Entrées, $24 to $44. Dinner nightly, 5:30 to 10:45, later in bistro and bar.

Olives, 10 City Square, Charlestown.

Starting with a tiny but trendy and wildly popular café, celebrated local chef Todd English has built a small culinary empire that's gone national. Todd's eighteen restaurants have turned up in New York, Washington, Aspen, Las Vegas, Seattle and Tokyo, aboard the Queen Mary 2 and who knows where next.

The flagship Olives remains at the foot of America's oldest main street in Charlestown, just across the Charles River from downtown Boston. It is upscale in price and setting, and until lately when some of its luster waned, it was so busy it didn't take reservations.

The relocated Olives – much larger than the original up the street – is an unexpectedly contemporary mix of plush and rustic. The high-ceilinged space has walls of brick and tall windows on two sides. Upholstered banquettes and booths are situated side-by-side with bentwood chairs at bare wood tables. A divider with arched windows separates the main dining room from the noisy bar. At the end is a large open kitchen with brick oven, wood grill and rotisserie.

With his mentor on the move, Todd Winer, a nine-year veteran of the Olives Group, has taken over as executive chef here.

Diners munch on marinated olives and crusty focaccia as they await such starters as yellowfin tuna tartare served over a spun cucumber salad with crispy rock shrimp and whitefish caviar, a wood-oven fired porcini tart with seared foie gras and toasted fennel cream, and a spring artichoke waffle with crispy artichoke ragoût, whipped goat cheese and shaved black truffles. Hand-crafted pastas come in such unusual combinations as apple and taleggio raviolis with shaved truffles, kobe beef stroganoff over egg noodles, and bucatini with sea urchins and lobster tossed with hot cherry peppers.

Entrées replicate the robust flavors of Italy, where Todd English did most of his training. Wild salmon is wood grilled and served with corned beef hash, shaved fall squashes, steel-cut oatmeal and pear-currant marmalade. Golden trout might be layered with prosciutto and sage on charred asparagus and fingerling potatoes and called trout saltimbocca. The spit-roasted ribeye of pork rests on a "pot roast" of black beans with chorizo, creamy honeyed semolina polenta and mustard-almond romesco. The veal steak is braised in morel cream and served over a "moppin' cake" stuffed with peas, fava beans and pea tendrils.

Desserts are a high point: perhaps pumpkin-brioche pudding with pumpkin anglaise and poached cranberries, tiramisu crêpe soufflé with rum-raisin sauce and espresso glaze, and fried banana ravioli with banana flan gâteau. This is not leisurely or intimate dining (the lights are bright and the music loud). But there's no denying the food, which is still the rage in Boston.

(617) 242-1999. www.toddenglish.com. Entrées, $24 to $33. Dinner, Monday-Friday 5:30 to 9:30 or 10, Saturday 5 to 10:30, Sunday 5 to 9.

Locke-Ober Café, 3 Winter Place.

Boston's grand dame of fine dining has take on a new life. The male-based institution that dates to 1875 is now run by Lydia Shire, the nationally known chef from Biba (which has closed and morphed into Excelsior), and co-owner Paul Licari.

Lending a woman's touch to both a setting and a kitchen that had frayed, Lydia polished the original walls and adorned them with tapestries, restored the gold flecking and removed seven layers of covering to expose the hand-cut marble floor around the room-length mirrored bar, a treasury of hand-carved mahogany. She kept the famous painting of the nude Mademoiselle Yvonne in what had been the Men's Bar & Café, now the opulent main dining room (the upstairs dining rooms are usually reserved for functions).

Lydia is in the kitchen these days with chef Mario Capone, who cooked for her at Biba and later was a chef in Las Vegas. She abbreviated the extravagant continental menu to reasonable size, but elevated the prices to astonishing levels – hors d'oeuvre, soups and salads priced in the teens, and entrées rising to $62 for the baked lobster savannah that one of us enjoyed here with her father at the impressionable age of 18.

Classics from the old menu are resurrected – jumbo shrimp cocktail, broiled Boston scrod with hot crab, calves liver with smoked bacon, dover sole meunière, sirloin steak au poivre and carved rack of veal. But the evolving cuisine, while hardly in the over-the-top style of Biba, is more daring than anything the old Locke ever offered. Now you might find red snapper on "pool of white polenta" with mustard fruits and crisped sage or charcoaled duck breast with "bloc of foie gras, crush of concord grapes and anise."

Instead of the old lobster and finnan haddie chowder, the menu offers "our version of hot miso soup." The classic caesar salad is apt to be upstaged by one of pear, perppercress and celeriac with a sweet mascarpone-gorgonzola fritter. The escargots bourguignonne are "potted," the onion soup gratinée is offered with or without oxtail, the creamed spinach bears curry croutons, and the lamb sirloin arrives – in Shire speak – with a whip of tender fava beans.

Desserts like the warm Indian pudding, caramel pots de crème and baked alaska are still without peer.

Despite the Lydia touch, the place retains a buttoned-down male air, from the staff to the clientele – most of whom devoutly wish for it ever to remain so.

(617) 542-1340. www.locke-ober.com. Entrées, $28 to $62. Lunch, Monday-Friday 11:30 to 2:30. Dinner, Monday-Saturday 5:30 to 10 or 11.

Icarus, 3 Appleton St.

A statue of the mythological Icarus, poised for flight, looms above tree branches lit with tiny white lights high on the rear wall of this beloved restaurant, a pioneer in regional cuisine since its opening in 1978. It oversees a sunken, split-level room full of rich dark wood and a mix of booths and round mission oak tables. The tables are left bare except for dusky pink napkins folded sideways between fluted silverware. Recessed aqua lighting outlines the perimeter of the ceiling.

It's an altogether comfortable, clubby backdrop for the fare of longtime chef and co-owner Chris Douglass, whose low public profile masks his standing as one of the best in town. His menu, brief and unpretentious, is the equal of any in the city. It also has held the line on the price inflation that has afflicted many of its peers, although that effort is more obvious at his new, downscaled **Ashmont Grill** on lower Dorchester Avenue.

Seasonal New England ingredients take precedence here in such autumn entrées as pan-roasted lobster with pumpkin, chestnuts and bourbon, and grilled pork chop with sweet potato soufflé and maple-bourbon butter. Other possibilities could be skate wing with lobster hash and peppercress, seared duck breast and roasted leg with cider and bourbon, and pancetta-stuffed Vermont rabbit with picholine olives, fennel, roasted tomato and lemon risotto.

Appetizers span the globe: grilled shrimp with mango and jalapeño sorbet, peekytoe crab cake rémoulade with house-made pickles, and pizzetta with pancetta, caramelized onions, arugula, pears and blue cheese. The soup could be Jerusalem artichoke with duck confit, sweet potato, pecan and garlic, and the salad warm spinach with veal sweetbreads and smoked bacon with pickled red onions and port glaze.

Chocolate molten soufflé cake for two with vanilla bean ice cream and raspberry sauce is the signature dessert. Others could be pumpkin crème brûlée with pecan cookies and a triple chocolate brownie with valrhona chocolate ice cream.

(617) 426-1790. www.icarusrestaurant.com. Entrées, $28 to $36.50. Dinner, Monday-Friday 6 to 10, Saturday 5:30 to 10:30, Sunday 5:30 to 9:30.

Hotel Dining

More than in most cities, some of Boston's best eating takes place in its hotels. And many local chefs have launched or fine-tuned careers there before striking out on their own.

Aujourd'hui, Four Seasons Hotel, 200 Boylston St.

A window table at Aujourd'hui is a prospect on the finer things in Boston life, among them the cooking of world-class chefs and a view of the swan boats plying the pond of the Public Garden.

The newly renovated second-floor restaurant's setting is sumptuous. Beyond an

Renovated room provides sumptuous setting for dining at Aujourd'hui.

enlarged salon-style lounge with a mahogany bar, the light and airy, 124-seat dining room is enveloped in provençal teal, the rich wood paneling and walls hung with watercolors and historical New England portraits. Dark wood chairs are upholstered in subdued yellow and blue floral fabrics. The nicely spaced tables are set with Rivolta linens and Bernaudeau china.

Jérôme Legras, a 30-year-old chef from France's Loire Valley who became chef de cuisine in 2004, employs New England ingredients to create modern French cuisine. Our dinner began with an amusé of salmon mousse with black pepper vodka and crème fraîche, and a bowl of six exotic breads (the most distinctive a profiterole filled with cheese). The six-course "ultimate" tasting menu ($98) produced a parade of appetizers: caramelized diver scallops with calypso bean-lobster ragoût, hamachi with spicy tuna tartare and oven-roasted beets, and an unforgettable, thick slice of seared foie gras with a duck confit spring roll and sour cherry compote. Fish courses were succulent baked arctic char with vegetable relish and seared ahi tuna with pickled eggplant, their multiple accompaniments creating bursts of flavors. One main course was perfectly roasted aged beef sirloin with peppercorn sauce, ragoût of chanterelles, a potato nest, leeks and pearl onions. The other was tender lamb noisettes with black olives, preserved lemon and Moroccan spices, haricots vert and baby garbanzo beans.

A trio of cheeses paved the way for dessert. One was vanilla bean crème brûlée, fancifully decorated with spun sugar. The other was a platter of tea-scented panna cotta, lemon tart and warm chocolate cake with liquid milk chocolate truffle. A tray of "les mignardises" ended a meal that lingers in the memory as one of the best ever.

The regular menu also is enticing – how about lobster navarin with citrus jus, guinea hen with morels and raisin-pear chutney, or roasted loin of venison with huckleberry jus? A four-course tasting menu is available for $76 and a four-course vegetarian tasting menu is $52.

The wine list, one of Boston's best, includes a page of wines by the glass and two pages of California cabernets. We've found a couple of good, better than usual low-end sauvignon blancs, a merlot and a pinot noir in the $40 to $50 range.

(617) 338-4400. www.fourseasons.com/boston. Entrées, $35 to $47. Dinner nightly, 5:30 to 10, Sunday 6 to 10. Sunday brunch, 11 to 2.

Meritage, Boston Harbor Hotel, 70 Rowes Wharf.

Since 1990, the Boston Harbor Hotel has garnered national attention for its annual Boston Wine Festival, fifteen weeks of wine tastings, dinners, seminars and other events involving many of the world's leading winemakers. A principal reason is the distinguished food offered by executive chef Daniel Bruce, Boston's longest-lasting celebrity hotel chef.

Dan, a northern New England native, headed the hotel's Rowes Wharf Restaurant for fifteen years after serving as the youngest executive chef ever at New York's famed 21 Club. All the while he never abandoned his goal of a small dining room where he would have free reign to pursue his passion for pairing food and wine.

His dream came true when the hotel closed its traditional restaurant and relocated the dining room to a smaller space named Meritage. It opened with a bold new dining concept that reverses the traditional pairings of food with wine in favor of coordinating their flavors. Diners must think wine first and then pick the food that's supposed to best heighten the wine experience. Small and large plates ($15 and $29) are available at a fixed price for each of six flavor categories, from sparklers to full-bodied whites to robust reds. The idea is to experience a variety of pairings in one meal.

Because it's new and novel, the menu is disconcerting for some. There are four choices for each category, a total of 24 in all. So what might be an appetizer (sturgeon caviar over melted leeks and frothed crème fraîche) could be ordered as a large plate as well. The menu also produces some non-traditional pairings, especially in terms of seafood with red wines, among them plum-basted wild king salmon, black pepper-crusted seared rare yellowfin tuna and sautéed red snapper. For example, "light whites" might be paired with sautéed Block Island swordfish, pan-seared diver scallops, roasted dayboat cod or steamed Maine lobster. "Fruity reds" go with plum-glazed New Brunswick salmon, sautéed New York foie gras, and a duet of squab and braised beef shortribs.

In addition, the menu mentions only six broad wine categories. For specifics, diners are given a daunting, 42-page wine list categorized by traditional grape varietals and with nearly half priced in the triple digits (a few in the $30s can be found by those who persevere). About three dozen are available by the glass, and a few by the half bottle or magnum.

All is sleek and contemporary in bar and dining room at Meritage.

The taste treats continue to the "finishes" – three cheese options and five categories of sweets. The latter are presented in a tasting format, with plates of three desserts in each category, as in citrus (moro orange buttermilk panna cotta, lemon meringue tart and lime pudding cake), chocolate (bitter, dark and light) and nut (hazelnut cake with banana caramel, pecan-pumpkin parfait and toasted walnut baklava). The tasting plate for two combines sweets from different categories.

With the move, the clubby confines of the old Rowes Wharf gave way to a minimalist, ultra-contemporary space with Asian overtones and soaring windows onto the harbor.

Floor-to-ceiling wine cases at the entry indicate the primary focus. Beyond a small bar, the spacious room holds 88 seats at black granite tables beside the windows, in the middle and facing a room-length silvery metallic leather banquette in back. Framed luminescent artworks accent shiny glass-look beige walls. Amazing corkscrew-inspired chrome lighting fixtures dangling from the ceiling provide sparkling accents that are as novel as the rest of Meritage.

(617) 439-3995. www.meritagetherestaurant.com. Small plates $15; large plates $29. Dinner nightly, 5:30 to 10.

Clío, 370A Commonwealth Ave.

For food-lovers who don't cringe at the portions and prices, this may be the hottest ticket in town. Chef-owner Kenneth Oringer is at Boston's epicenter for personalized, trend-conscious haute cuisine.

The dining room in the upscaled Eliot Hotel turns into what he likens to a Parisian supper club. Floor lamps convey the look of a living-room salon, serene in taupe and white.

The 60-seat main dining room is a comfortable setting for serious eating in the contemporary French-American idiom. The chef started cooking for his family in Paramus, N.J., making stocks and sauces from scratch at age 10. Voted most likely to succeed in his class at the Culinary Institute of America, he worked first at Brooklyn's River Café and then at Al Forno in Providence, where he became known for his pastries. Culinary stints in Connecticut, San Francisco and the Boston suburb of

Hingham prepared him for his own venture, which opened in 1997 to national acclaim. Gourmet magazine's restaurant issue ranked it among the top 50 in America.

The chef is known for exotic starters, among them a cocktail of pico rocco, lobster and calamari with ginger and green sauce (for a cool $35), a seviche of Japanese octopus, a cassoulet of Maine lobster with sea urchins, and lacquered foie gras with sweet and sour lemon and bee pollen.

Main courses vary from sake- and miso-glazed black cod with celery root mousseline, jìcama and pea shoots to grilled Kobe flatiron steak with tuna tempura, matsutake mushrooms and pickled watermelon.

Desserts are generally light and refreshing: frozen lemon verbena soufflé with hot chocolate mousse, chilled concord grape soup with vanilla bean ice cream and ginger lace tuile, a duck egg crème caramel with mandarin orange sorbet and cassis, and a chocolate tart with whole milk ice cream, banana puree and licorice caramel.

The former lounge is now **Uni,** a sashimi bar that offers raw delicacies one morsel at a time. The chef works at a brown marble sushi counter with exotica he imports from the far corners of the world.

In late 2005, Ken Oringer branched out, opening **Toro,** a Spanish tapas bar in a converted meat market at 1704 Washington St. in Boston's South End. Installed as chef de cuisine there was John Critchley, who had run Uni.

(617) 536-7200. Entrées, $32 to $48. Dinner nightly, 5:30 to 10 or 10:30.

Julien, Hotel Langham, 250 Franklin St.

The former Le Meridien Hotel had a distinct culinary theme with a French accent, centered around its flagship Julien restaurant. With its sale to the London-based Langham international hotel group, the theme is not so pronounced, but the restaurant remains in the vanguard under Mark Sapienza, who became the Meridien's first American chef in 1998 and still oversees a busy schedule of cooking classes and wine dinners.

The setting is historic: the former Members Court of the stately Federal Reserve Building built in 1922, across from the site of Boston's first French restaurant, opened in 1793 by French émigré Jean-Baptiste Julien.

Some of Boston's most distinguished food is served in this palatial room with towering gilded ceiling, five crystal chandeliers and lattice work on the walls with lights behind. Mushroom velour banquettes or Queen Anne wing chairs flank tables set with heavy silverware, monogrammed china, tiny shaded brass lamps and Peruvian lilies.

Dinner begins with a complimentary hors d'oeuvre – a small vegetable quiche at our visit. If you're not up to an appetizer like seared lamb carpaccio or spiced Sonoma foie gras with peppered brioche, try one of the masterful soups, perhaps jonah crab with green onion beignets.

Typical entrées are crisp-skin Mediterranean sea bass, yellowfin tuna meunière, sautéed loin of venison with pomegranate, and peppered ribeye steak with a zinfandel-braised oyster mushroom cap. We'll never forget our lobster ravioli, the lobster reconstructed from its head and tail, the body made from ravioli filled with lobster mousse, the legs and feelers represented by green beans and asparagus or snow peas, and the whole topped with tomatoes and truffles – presentation personified.

Among desserts are a caramelized cinnamon apple tower with caramel ice cream, banana crème brûlée flambéed with rum, and a chocolate trilogy of white chocolate ice cream, milk chocolate mousse and dark chocolate cherry cake. The bill is sweetened with a plate of homemade candies and cookies.

Although offering an impressive variety of French wines that helped win Wine Spectator's Best of Award of Excellence, the sommelier also recommends a number of Californias.

The formal atmosphere and service are lightened by piano music in the adjacent Julien bar, the bank's former counting room, where two original N.C. Wyeth murals embellish the paneled walls.

(617) 451-1900. Entrées, $30 to $40. Dinner, Tuesday-Saturday 6 to 10.

Azure, Lenox Hotel, 61 Exeter St.

Among Boston's top hotel restaurants, Azure is innovative as well as comfortable and affordable. It is serene and deluxe in white and pale yellow. Striking iron chandeliers splayed with tangerine-look lights hang from the high dark blue ceiling, white draperies frame the tall windows and azure blue upholstered chairs are at tables dressed in cream-colored cloths. Front and center as you enter is a showy, glowing glass-topped bar backlit in blue against the rear wall. Screened from view at the far end is a partially open kitchen with a custom-built wood-burning oven, wood grill and rotisserie.

Peripatetic chef Robert Fathman touts the cuisine as "contemporary American with subtle French, Asian, Latin and Mediterranean influences and an emphasis on seafood." Call it global, and occasionally obscure. The menu is at once playful and dead serious and difficult to decipher, as in starters of "pure Nubian goat cheese fritter salad" and "oysters in bondage – smoked salmon, potato-encrusted oyster, crème fraiche & caviar." And "really good lobster soup" with lustau amontillado, corn and parsley pudding. You may take their word for it, or experiment with the "blue hubbard squash soup" with pear and golden raisin-mascarpone rangoon. The steamed mussels with smoked tomato broth, garlicky swiss chard and grilled ciabatta might spark a hint of recognition.

Less obscure were such entrées as peekytoe-stuffed grey sole with grapefruit beurre blanc, sautéed striped bass with apple-smoked bacon and steamed cockles, and spiced cashew-crusted chicken with a cranberry-ginger reduction. The ancho- and coffee-rubbed hanger steak with puréed sweet potatoes, garlicky spinach and oaxacan-style mole make the grilled sirloin with pureed potatoes, onion rings, watercress and blue cheese mousse sound comforting.

Dessert could be a milk chocolate torte with dulce de leche ice cream or oatmeal-cashew cake with spiced zucchini and fig ice cream.

(617) 933-4800. www.azureboston.com. Entrées, $19 to $30. Dinner, Monday-Saturday 5:30 to 10 or 11, Sunday to 9.

More Good Dining

Pigalle, 75 Charles St.

The front awning bears the address "75, Rue Charles Sud" and the interior is dark and cozy in the image of an early 20th-century French jazz club, perhaps. This is the small and stylish restaurant opened by chef Mark Orfaly, formerly of Olives, and his wife Kerri Foley, who manages the front of the house. The dominant motif of chocolate brown is leavened by a beige ceiling supported by thick pillars and white-clothed tables flanked by leather chairs or booths.

The contemporary French menu is short and enticing, and there's an equally interesting bar menu at half the price. The signature tuna martini isn't so much sipped as spooned, a cocktail with a kick of raw yellowfin tuna, seaweed salad and spicy crème fraîche. Other appetizers include steak tartare with gaufrette potato chips and toasted brioche, hazelnut-crusted goat cheese cake with frisée and bacon lardons, and seared foie gras served with "papaya three ways." The asparagus soup with crabmeat and shiitake mushrooms appealed at our latest visit.

Main courses vary from spice-crusted black bass with harissa couscous to beef bourguignonne and steak frites. The signature cassoulet might yield braised lamb shanks, confit of duck, pork sausage and white beans. The menu heads eastward with such dishes as lobster à la Thai with julienned vegetables and coconut jasmine rice, and crispy half duck with a fricassee of mushrooms, water chestnuts and lychees.

The fare is so rich and full of flavor that you may not have room for dessert. Succumb, however, to an apricot tart with basil ice cream, homemade sorbets or profiteroles with praline ice cream and bittersweet chocolate sauce.

Following the lead of his colleagues, chef Marc opened a second restaurant in 2005. **Marco** at 253 Hanover St. in Boston's North End endows Italian food and down-to-earth ambiance with the culinary flair and refinements that francophiles expect from Pigalle.

(617) 423-4944. www.pigalleboston.com. Entrées, $25 to $39. Dinner, Tuesday-Saturday from 5:30, Sunday from 5.

Troquet, 140 Boylston St.

A funny thing happened to Troquet on the way from concept to reality. Planned as a wine bar, it turned into a contemporary French/New American restaurant of note, so successfully that owners Chris and Diane Campbell lately expanded onto the second floor to better serve their dinner patrons. It now bills itself, quite rightly, as a food and wine boutique.

The main-floor wine bar and lounge offers more than 40 wines by the glass, specialty cocktails and an exotic bar menu (think yellowfin tuna seviche and English pea soup with peekytoe crab and tarragon crème fraîche).

Upstairs is a white-linened dining room with tall windows onto Boston Common and the State House. The short menu mates food to wine, not vice-versa. The middle section of the menu lists fairly priced wines by two-ounce and four-ounce pours. On either side are matching appetizers and entrées.

In the mood for a chardonnay? Try the Maine lobster poached with saffron, vanilla and marcona almonds for an appetizer and the roasted organic chicken with orzo, corn and chanterelles for a main course. Feel more like cabernet? Go for the crispy duck confit with flageolet beans and black mission figs or the pan-roasted rib steak with root vegetables, glazed onions and potato puree. Ports are recommended for the cheese plates, a choice of three or six, for those looking to keep the wine flowing. The owner personally shows the night's selections and he knows his fromage.

The setting is sleek but stark in grays and blacks, with mirrors and French posters for decorative accents. Chocolate truffles and almond slices arrive with the bill.

(617) 695-9463. www.troquetboston.com. Entrées, $26 to $38; bar menu, $9 to $22. Dinner, Tuesday-Sunday 5 to midnight.

Sel de la Terre, 255 State St.

This "salt of the earth" brasserie is the kid brother of L'Espalier, Boston's temple to haute French cuisine. Co-owners Frank McClelland and Geoff Gardner, former sous chef at L'Espalier, created a more accessible café, bar and take-out boulangerie in the busy downtown area between Faneuil Hall and the harbor. Elegant yet earthy in beige and gray tones, the 160-seat eatery debuted before its time at the height of the Big Dig mess. It matured as the highway construction neared completion and now is a culinary beacon along the revitalized waterfront.

His travels to Provence and his training at L'Espalier paid off for chef Gardner, who imparts a touch of class to the rustic country fare of southern France. What one national food writer called "bourgeois cooking at its best" shows up in such classics as terrines, salade niçoise, bouillabaisse, country roasts and breads.

Start with the fabulous breads, which our waiter claimed turn up on half the tables in the city. An ample assortment arrives here in a metal-wire basket with a round of French butter. You can sample them straight, or embellish with one of the day's "petits goûters," perhaps an eggplant-goat cheese purée with toasted walnuts or a roasted shallot and garlic confit, either one to be spread liberally on slices of bread. Ditto for the charcuterie plate that makes a fine first course, teamed with toasted brioche. The duck liver terrine with port aspic is as smooth and rich as they come. The coarse pork tenderloin pâté and house-smoked ham are more rustic.

The charcuterie plate and an arugula and goat cheese salad, which turn up on the dinner menu as well, made a fine lunch for one of us. The other sampled the day's prix-fixe lunch ($19), which offered a couple of choices for each of three courses. He didn't know what to make of the artichoke soup with tempura-fried pearl onions and pickled vegetables. More like a broth, it arrived in a bowl on a hot plate, upon which the accompaniments stood as if on standby, their utilization unclear. More effective was the tasty main course of sautéed pollock atop braised endive, squash, pinenuts and black currants. Dessert was an almond-chocolate tart – a rich slice of fudge leavened with chantilly cream sauce.

The dinner menu conveys many of the lunchtime choices, minus the sandwiches and with heartier main courses. Prices are the same for all appetizers ($10) and mains ($26). The latter range from cider-poached halibut with red rice, applewood-smoked bacon and littleneck clams to hazelnut-crusted rack of lamb with swiss chard, carrots, chickpea fries and bordeaux jus. Dessert could be crème fraîche apple tart with vanilla bean ice cream or chocolate sourdough bread pudding with brûléed figs and fig ice cream.

The small boulangerie in the restaurant's entryway offers breads, pastries, terrines, salads, sandwiches and other kitchen specialties for takeout. It was doing a land-office business the day we were there.

(617) 720-1300. www.seldelaterre.com. Entrées, $26. Lunch, Monday-Friday 11:30 to 2:30. Brunch, Saturday and Sunday 11 to 2:30. Dinner nightly, 5 to 10; late-night menu, Wednesday-Saturday 10 to 12:30 a.m.

Lala Rokh, 97 Mt. Vernon St.

Home-style Persian cuisine is offered up by Azita Bina-Seibel and her brother Babak Bina at the only eastern Mediterranean restaurant of its kind in New England. The pair earlier ran Azita, a Tuscan charmer at 560 Tremont St. in the South End, where we had a memorable lunch a few years back. They left that space because

Azita felt more at home with the food of her native Azerbaijan, which she considers every bit as sophisticated as that of Tuscany.

Two dining rooms in the Beacon Hill townhouse that formerly housed Odette Bery's famed Another Season are done country style in mustard yellow and burgundy. The family's notable collection of early Persian memorabilia – framed photographs, antique maps and calligraphy dating to the ninth century – adorn the walls. Classical Persian music plays in the background.

It's a subdued setting for food that is anything but subdued. Although unfamiliar in terminology and combinations of ingredients, it's aromatic, heavily spiced and ever so good.

The wait staff can steer you to a succession of mix-and-match appetizers, entrées and side dishes that make for novel taste sensations. The breadth of the offerings defies description. Eggplant, a staple of the cuisine, appears in several appetizers, one of the best being kashk-e-bademjan, a warm dip of roasted eggplant, caramelized onions and goat's milk yogurt, to stand alone or to be spread on the complimentary sesame-topped bread.

Main courses are categorized by cooking style and yield flavorful combinations mainly of chicken, beef, lamb and veal with basmati rice. Diners are encouraged to complement them with mazze (side dishes) and torshi (pickled chutneys and relishes). Particularly good are abgusht (lamb shank in spiced broth with string beans, chickpeas, okra and eggplant) and joojeh (a kabob of grilled chicken breast marinated in saffron, lemon and onions and served with saffron-perfumed basmati rice). A short, wide-ranging wine list is modestly priced.

Desserts are as exotic as the rest of the fare. You might try ranghinak, squares of layered dates stuffed with walnuts and dusted with pistachio, or Persian ice cream scented with saffron and rose water and studded with chunks of frozen cream.

Lala Rokh (pronounced la-la-roke) is the name of a fictional Persian princess seduced by a storytelling suitor in the epic poem of the same name by 19th-century Irish poet Thomas Moore (a slightly faded copy of the work is displayed near the entrance). The spell of the food and the ambiance here will likely seduce you, too.

(617) 720-5511. www.lalarokh.com. Entrées, $14 to $19. Lunch, Monday-Friday noon to 3. Dinner nightly, 5:30 to 10.

Sibling Rivalry, 525 Tremont St.

The name does not do justice to this with-it new restaurant, strategically located on the ground floor of a condominium building where the downtown Theater District gives way to the ultra-hot South End.

The setting does. Here is a designer restaurant designed with the customer in mind: a sinewy layout in three dining rooms and a lounge, full of curves and nooks and dividers that give many diners a sense of privacy. Yet they are still part of the bigger picture – a 150-seat expanse, some of which focuses on an exhibition kitchen with a dining bar for chef's tastings. Depending upon where you sit, the noise level is not outrageous and you don't feel on top of everyone else.

Things otherwise might get competitive at this modern American restaurant whose logo and animated website feature two proud roosters facing off. Brothers Robert and David Kinkead strut their stuff in a dueling menu format in which any winner depends on the preferences of the diners involved. Bob Kinkead was founding chef at 21 Federal in Nantucket and his namesake restaurant in Washington, D.C., is nationally known. Younger brother David also got his start at 21 Federal and teamed

Cooks in semi-open kitchen implement 'dueling' menu at Sibling Rivalry.

up with hometown friend Todd English to open seafood restaurants around the country and eventually became executive chef for the Olives Group.

Here, David is in the bright and busy exhibition kitchen nightly with a crew that helps render the brothers' menu, which proves intriguing if confusing. Two side-by-side columns, one for chef David and one for chef Bob, are categorized by ingredient – shellfish, chiles and tomatillos, arugula, pears, beef, bacon, finfish and the like. Each offers a different approach to a common ingredient, which may be an appetizer (printed in red) or a main course (in black type). Although some choices are forced in concept, the proof is in the delivery. The restaurant scores, because what comes out of the kitchen does.

Chiles and tomatillos might be featured in Bob's spicy steak tartare appetizer or David's grilled salmon fillet. Bacon turns up as pancetta in Bob's pumpkin ravioli and David's bacon-wrapped loin of rabbit and rabbit pot pie. The lobster contest pits David's lobster steak "tournedo" with cucumber salad against Bob's herb-crusted cod with lobster-savory cream and a lobster and macaroni gratin. Pork takes center stage in David's grilled chipotle-orange glazed pork chop and shows up as supporting staff in Bob's signature appetizer of seared sea scallops wrapped in Smithfield ham. And so it goes, through a dozen categories with competing choices for each, Bob's creations a bit more restrained than those of his exuberant brother.

The dueling format ends after lamb, poultry, ginger and lobster. There's no contest among dessert choices, which are enticing in themselves: perhaps a chocolate dacquoise with espresso crème anglaise and gold-leaf top that's as pretty as it is rich, a warm chocolate cake with peaches and Bellini peach sorbet, or a "tropical trio" of chilled mango semifreddo, passionfruit mousse and warm pineapple tartlet. Here and in sorbets and ice creams you need not make choices. You get samplings of three.

(617) 338-5338. www.siblingrivalryboston.com. Entrées, $26 to $34. Lunch, Saturday and Sunday 11:30 to 2:30. Dinner nightly, 5:30 to 10 or 11.

South End Hot Spots

Not every good eating spot in Boston caters to high rollers and beautiful people. Hamersley's Bistro blazed the trail into Boston's close-in South End, ever since then the foodies' hot spot. Others have followed, half a dozen in 2005 alone. Most offer good vibes and quality meals that won't set you back a day's pay or more. Indeed, these are where hip young Bostonians like to eat – and do, regularly.

The Nightingale, 578 Tremont St.

Excellent food, convivial atmosphere and refreshing prices pack customers into the bistro in which Hamersley's got its start. Only the second restaurant to follow the pace-setting Hamersley's in the space, the Nightingale operates in much the same manner as its illustrious predecessor – same configuration, same style of modern yet robust comfort food. That's not surprising, given that chef-partner Michael Burgess served as Gordon Hamersley's sous chef for seven years here and in his larger quarters across the street.

Fifty-four diners can be seated on brick-red chairs at tables covered in white butcher paper over white cloths. Most are in the main dining room with chartreuse green walls and an open kitchen at the back. An adjacent bar with a small dining area is apt to be quieter.

The prices for dinner are more like those for lunch in Boston's best restaurants. And the lunch prices here are considerably lower, too.

The native Vermont chef excels with appetizers, starting with a signature timbale of chicken livers and foie gras, served with onion marmalade and triangles of brioche. Other favorites are an autumn chestnut and leek soup, a pâté of wild boar with pear rémoulade, grilled quail with prosciutto and sundried tomatoes, and a warm spinach and smoked trout salad with fingerling potatoes and pinenuts.

The main course includes vegetable and starch, instead of the extra "sides" currently in vogue elsewhere. Typical are Atlantic salmon counterpointed with lentils and a lemon-green peppercorn vinaigrette, roasted halibut with orange-fennel broth and rock shrimp, grilled pork ribeye brined in cider and paired with camembert and a roasted apple, and grilled venison loin with braised celery root and cranberries. The ubiquitous roasted chicken here is enlivened with green olives.

Desserts follow the seasons. Cranberry bread pudding with cider-maple glaze, cinnamon panna cotta with autumn fruit chutney, and a bosc pear and almond tart with burnt caramel sauce were highlights at our visit.

The name was taken from a favorite vintage song, we were told. Long may this Nightingale sing.

(617) 236-5658. Entrées, $19 to $28. Lunch, Monday-Friday 11:30 to 2:30. Dinner nightly, 5:30 to 10 or 10:30. Weekend brunch, Saturday and Sunday 10 to 2:30.

Aquitaine, 569 Tremont St., Boston.

After launching Metropolis Café in a former ice-cream parlor next to the first home of Hamersley's Bistro, chef Seth Woods also joined the big time, following Gordon and Fiona Hamersley across the street. He created an authentic Parisian neighborhood bistro and wine bar in the old Botolph's on Tremont restaurant space and lately has taken to calling it Aquitaine-Bar á Vin Bistrot.

Tall plate-glass windows, cast-iron columns and exposed ducts beneath a gray, fifteen-foot-high ceiling create a European industrial look, softened by chocolate

High-ceilinged dining area at Aquitaine conveys Parisian bistro look.

brown cushioned booths on one side. A long, leather-look banquette faces white-clothed tables and beige walls with linear mirrors at eye level. Wine bottles climb to the ceiling above the zinc-lined bar at the entrance.

The blackboard menu transports the visitor to France. The plat du jour changes daily (coq au vin on Tuesday, cassoulet Toulousian on Thursday). Look for such entrées as lemon sole meunière, seared sea scallops with a caviar beurre blanc, crisp roasted chicken breast and confit leg with sage jus, châteaubriand of pork with dried cherry demi-glace, steak frites and filet au poivre.

Frisée and lardons salad with aged chèvre and a poached egg, mussels with Sancerre, duck liver pâté and escargots bourguignonne are among the starters. A selection of artisan cheeses is offered with fruit and country bread to start or to finish. Desserts are extravagant and priced accordingly. Typical are caramel bread pudding with caramelized bananas and toasted hazelnuts, vanilla bean crème brûlée and maple-toasted pumpkin soufflé with lavender crème anglaise.

The markup on wines is one of the lowest in Boston, with plenty of good choices in the mid-twenties to mid-thirties.

The owner has since opened an offshoot, **Aquitaine Bis** in Chestnut Hill, and has taken over the restaurant operation at **Armani Café** on Newbury Street, where he served as executive chef shortly after arriving in Boston.

(617) 424-8577. Entrées, $19 to $29. www.aquitaineboston.com. Dinner nightly, 5:30 to 10 or 11. Saturday and Sunday brunch, 10 to 3

Perdix, 560 Tremont St.

Relocating into the lower-level space known earlier as Truc and Azita, chef Tim Partridge re-created – albeit on a larger scale – the convivial neighborhood haunt that he launched in the outlying Jamaica Plain neighborhood. His original twenty-seat bistro was so serious and so successful that it made Bon Appétit magazine's list of best new restaurants in 2001. Here he warmed up the long, narrow room with caramel-colored paint and framed black and white photographs and spruced up the cheery solarium at the rear, where a handful of tables overlook a garden.

No longer does the former geologist-turned-chef cook in an open kitchen that's part of the dining room, lending a convivial home dinner-party atmosphere. Here he is hidden in a narrow side kitchen, sending forth gutsy bistro fare that's just the ticket for the young, professional city-dwellers who like to squeeze together elbow-to-elbow as they fuel the South End's restaurant boom.

Home cooking is elevated to the highest levels in appetizers of seared sea scallops with English pea puree and crispy bacon, a ricotta and thyme tart with sorrel sauce, and an asparagus terrine with crabmeat, cherry tomato salad and buttermilk dressing. The chef's penchant for seafood is evident in main dishes like poached halibut with a cracked olive vinaigrette, homemade lobster sausage with whole Georgia shrimp, farm-raised salmon flavored with tarragon and tomato jam, and roasted striped bass with yellow tomato soup, Israeli couscous and barbecued bacon. The last entrée item is always "today's steak, with whatever Tim wants" – an exceptional carpetbagger steak topped with fried oysters, the night we were there.

Desserts might be warm gingered almond cake with roasted plum puree and vanilla cream, crème brûlée with madeleines, and banana crêpes with grand marnier sauce.

(617) 3388-6070. www.perdixrestaurant.com. Entrées, $22 to $24. Dinner, Tuesday-Saturday 5:30 to 10 or 10:30. Sunday brunch, 11 to 3.

Union Bar & Grille, 1357 Washington St.

When it opened, the Aquitaine Group's latest hot spot marked the coming of age of SoWa (South Washington) neighborhood bistros. "Union is the most grown up, the most fully realized, both broad in its menu and sophisticated in its service," hailed the Boston Globe reviewer. "It's the Hamersley's Bistro of Washington Street."

High praise, that. While Hamersley's started two decades ago as a neighborhood bistro before expanding into a destination restaurant, Union co-owner and executive chef Seth Woods did it all at once. His 125-seat restaurant and separate lounge in a renovated warehouse is big and unexpectedly clubby, a designer expanse of black and white. Padded black leather banquettes flank white-clothed tables around the perimeter and in the middle. Two striking square wrought-iron chandeliers with multi white-shaded lamps hang overhead, and tall windows look onto the wide street.

Union lives up to its dictionary definition as a gathering place. Its aim is to please a range of diners, rather than becoming a shrine for foodies. Union, according to its principals, is "what going out to dinner used to be – not a culinary education, just good food that you want to eat."

The concise menu, as executed by chef de cuisine Stephen Sherman, manages to touch all the bases. You'll find a beef and andouille sausage burger and a grilled reuben sandwich listed after grilled beef tenderloin and rack of lamb. Folks happily make a meal of a couple of appetizers, perhaps mussels steamed with garlic and chiles over spaghettini or barbecued beef shortrib with celery root gnocchi. Or they can feast on bacon-wrapped Idaho trout, sizzled soft-shell crabs with crisp pancetta and watermelon vinaigrette, seared tuna with a roasted tomato vinaigrette. roasted chicken with a cornbread and chorizo stuffing or chipotle-glazed smoked pork tenderloin with mango-cilantro slaw.

Dessert specialties are updates of old standbys: banana cream pie with valrhona chocolate and a vanilla wafer, an upside-down brown sugar cheesecake with a peach confit, carrot cake with ginger ice cream, even an ice-cream sandwich and a chocolate malted milkshake. The chef's tasting for two offers four desserts "fit for every indulgence."

(617) 423-0555. www.unionrestaurant.com. Entrées, $23 to $39. Dinner nightly, 5:30 to 11 or midnight. Sunday brunch, 10 to 3.

Caffè Umbra, 1395 Washington St.

The restaurant is in the shadow of the Cathedral of the Holy Cross and its chef-owner had been working in the shadows of some of Boston's best-known chefs for 25 years. So when Laura Brennan opened her own restaurant, the Latin word for shadow was appropriate. The illuminated cathedral across the way shines in the front picture windows at night. That's about all the "decor" needed in a 90-seat dining room that's warm and welcoming with walls of exposed brick along the sides. Two still lifes of fruits accent a blue wall in back. Bare pine tables at banquettes around the perimeter cast a rustic backdrop for Laura's country French and Italian fare.

Her opening menu was dedicated to ex-Newton culinary expert Madeleine Kamman (her first cooking teacher and "mentor of things French and delicious") and started with "MMK's cream of lettuce soup with lobster butter." Later menus evolved to pumpkin leek soup with sherry and smoked shrimp butter, camembert fritters with baby spinach and hazelnuts, and chicken liver mousse with pickled walnuts and blue cheese toasts. An appetizer called "sticky fingers" yielded slow-braised lamb riblets with ginger, orange, sherry, soy and thin scallion pancakes.

Chicken under a brick is the signature main course. Others range from pan-seared sea scallops with oyster mushrooms and port jus to grilled skirt steak with gorgonzola.

Desserts include an apple-pecan torta rustica and sticky toffee pudding with vanilla bean ice cream. Most share the assorted ice cream and sorbet sampler with a choice of five.

(617) 867-0707. www.caffeumbra.com. Entrées, $22 to $24. Dinner, Tuesday-Sunday from 5:30.

B&G Oysters Ltd., 550 Tremont St.

Where fellow celebrity chef Jasper White's version of a seafood shanty became the huge Summer Shack in Cambridge (and more recently in Boston's Back Bay), Barbara Lynch opted for diminutive. For her second act, she and partner-manager Garrett Harker turned a former crêperie into a neighborhood oyster bar for the young and hip. They dubbed it B&G for their initials and decked it out in marble and mosaic tiles in oceanic colors of cobalt and gray to suggest a Mediterranean cottage, which is about the size of it. There are a complement of small tables along one wall, a few seats at the bar facing an open kitchen, and a gravel patio outside. It's basically a stand-up place and quite the night-time scene as folks nosh on a dozen varieties of succulent oysters from around North America ($2.25 each, and the bill mounts fast).

Half the menu is devoted to "originals" of the clam-shack and raw-bar variety, from fried Ipswich clams and New England clam chowder to a knockout lobster BLT for a cool $21 and a lobster roll with fries for $24. The rest of the menu involves changing seasonal New England fare: perhaps tuna salad niçoise, spicy clam stew with chorizo, dayboat cod with golden chanterelles and scallops with toasted sage, red kuri squash and chestnuts. Finish with a butterscotch sundae or vanilla bread pudding with spiced figs.

Across the street is Barbara's latest hot spot, **The Butcher Shop,** a French-inspired boucherie. Here she offers a small wine bar serving antipasti, steak tartare, a charcuterie plate and a bistro dish like gnocchi with spicy sausage ragu. In back, glass cases display homemade terrines, ready-to-eat treats such as braised shortribs and the finest naturally raised organic meats that money can buy ($30 for a small rack of lamb chops that caught our eye). Mexican chef David Reynoso's large butcher-block workstation holds changing items like house-pickled vegetables, homemade chutneys, breads, and artisanal vinegar and oils.

(617) 423-0550. www.bandgoysters.com. Entrées, $18 to $24. Open Monday-Friday 11:30 to 11, weekends noon to 11. Butcher Shop open Monday-Saturday 11 to 8, Sunday 11 to 5; wine bar daily, 11 to 11 or midnight.

North End Star

Sage, 69 Prince St., Boston.

Boston's storied Italian North End has undergone quite a transformation lately, with old-line places that doled out traditional spaghetti and red sauce giving way to upscale restaurants dispensing creative fare. The change is exemplified by this 28-seat charmer lovingly run by young chef-owner Anthony Susi, a native North Ender who got his start filling orders for nearby restaurants at his father's butcher shop. He helped open Sage in the mid-1990s, left to broaden his horizons in San Francisco kitchens, and returned worldlier to purchase Sage and realize a dream as "chef-owner."

From a closet-size kitchen he and his sous chef dispense highly regarded regional Italian and new American cuisine. They'll stun you with starters like salt cod brandade on saffron toast or a trio of scallops: tartare with truffles, seared with sea beans, and phyllo wrapped with celery root puree. The light-as-a-feather, hand-rolled potato gnocchi with sausage and corn is one of the to-die-for pasta offerings.

For main courses, you might find seared tuna with baby bok choy and sea urchin risotto, rabbit milanese with caponata salad, and braised shortrib with slow-cooked swiss chard.

"Happy endings" include rum cake with peach puree and pistachio ice cream, house-made sorbets and a chocolate plate: cake, cookie, foam and truffle.

The food takes precedence over the decor, which is nonetheless cheery with Italian posters on burnt orange walls and white-clothed tables in rather tight quarters.

(617) 248-8814. www.sageboston.com. Entrées, $20 to $29. Dinner, Monday-Saturday 5:30 to 10:30.

Offbeat Gourmet

Sonsie, 327 Newbury St.

What's this? A "kitchen/bar/bakery" on Newbury Street? Opened by Boston's leading nightclub entrepreneur? Overseen by one of the city's top chefs? With healthful foods?

The name provides a clue – a Celtic word for relaxed and comfortable. A front wall of french doors opens onto Newbury Street. An air-curtain allows patrons to sip cappuccino at little marble tables just inside as they "watch the world go by right out front, even in the dead of winter," in the words of co-owner Patrick Lyons, the local nightclub czar. Inside is a corner salon harboring a clutch of antique stuffed leather club chairs for lounging. A multi-colored curtain parts to yield a vista of bar and dining room beneath a high pressed-tin ceiling. The vision is one of close-together tables, terra cotta colors, wainscoted walls, red swagged draperies and Moroccan hand-blown glass chandeliers.

This is like nothing Boston had seen before, and its consistently hot scene has helped it survive. Chef-partner Bill Poirier, formerly at Seasons at the Bostonian Hotel, directs a cast of dozens – big enough to staff an entire hotel without the rooms, says Lyons, who obviously put his money where his mouth is.

Poirier's wide-ranging international menu covers all the bases, from spiced onion and ale soup with homemade pretzels and inside-out tuna sashimi rolls with ocean salad through assertive pastas, brick-oven pizzas and main dishes to decadent desserts. A note on the menu says the dishes are designed to keep fat and cholesterol levels low; "we use little or no dairy products and lean meats whenever possible." The trendoids who populate the place appreciate entrées like grilled swordfish with roasted shrimp and lemon gremolata, dilled salmon with fried oysters and horseradish crème fraîche, grilled pork tenderloin with cider-apple coulis, and charcoal-grilled duck breast and roasted leg with quinoa grains and pickled grapes. Those into starches can order the five-potato sampler; one each of five offered as sides.

Indulge in dessert, perhaps layered lemon soufflé pudding with mango and coconut meringues or Sonsie's award-winning chocolate bread pudding with chocolate drizzle.

There's lot to look at: a cache of newspapers from across the world, a 1902 hand-carved oak mantel behind the bar from a Commonwealth Avenue mansion, a waterfall of colored water droplets on the way to the downstairs bakery, a ladies' room papered with racy tabloid covers and polyurethaned toilet seats embedded with coins or, ouch, barbed wire. "We wanted to inject a little theater," deadpans Patrick.

(617) 351-2500. www.sonsieboston.com. Entrées, $16.50 to $29.50. Open daily from 7 a.m. Lunch, 11:30 to 2:30, weekends to 3. Dinner, 6 to 11 or midnight.

Gourmet's Digest

Parish Café, 361 Boylston St.

Sandwiches created by some of the area's best-known chefs – many of them mentioned in this chapter – are featured at this funky establishment.

Given their pedigrees, most of the two dozen choices are first-rate. We liked the Lydia – lobster salad with lemon, parsley, celery leaves and balsamic mayo on Lydia Shire's peppercorn brioche. The Via Matta combines slow-roasted pork loin with pancetta, caramelized onions and baby arugula on a ciabatta roll. Parish's own chefs have added appetizers, salads and entrées like fishcakes, BLT pasta and grilled half duck.

There's an impressive list of wines and ales to go with, as well as martinis created by local bartenders to precede. The prominent bar plays a major role, and a rear mural portraying laid-back diners on an outdoor patio sets the theme. The large terrace on the broad Boylston Street sidewalk is pleasant on a nice day.

(617) 247-4777. www.parishcafé.com. Entrées, $8.95 to $12.25. Open daily, 11:30 to 1 a.m., Sunday from noon.

Superior desserts are served in a plush, colorful setting at Finale.

Grand Finale

Finale, 1 Columbus Ave.

In a sweet variation on the eat-dessert-first credo, this large desserterie/bistro/bakery/bar in the Theater District inspires you to eat nothing but. You can get salads and appetizers, but they're mere "preludes" to executive pastry chef Nicole Coady's priorities: perhaps the signature molten chocolate cake, vanilla crème brûlée garnished with orange butter cookies and fresh fruits, an Italian "teaser" or a profiterole "party." Chocaholics find bliss in the chocolate euphoria for two ($26.95). It features a black forest torte with sweet cherries, warm molten chocolate cake and a white chocolate dome with a strawberry liquid center, along with banana gelato, milk chocolate florentines and four handmade chocolates. Each of the dozen or so dessert choices may be paired with a wine recommendation. Cordials, teas, espresso and international coffees also are available.

All this indulgent eating and drinking takes place at lipstick-red velvet and chocolate brown banquettes and booths amid mustard yellow walls and plate-glass windows onto the street.

Overhead mirrors above the dessert station let you watch the treats being assembled in this, the first establishment of its kind in the country. It's the brainchild of Kim Moore and Paul Conforti, who designed it as a prototype for a Harvard Business School project. They found a sweet niche and opened a second in Cambridge.

(617) 423-3184. www.finaledesserts.com. Desserts, $7.95 to $16.95. Open Monday-Friday 11:30 to 11 or midnight, Saturday 5 to midnight, Sunday 4 to 11.

Lodging

Four Seasons Hotel, 200 Boylston St., Boston 02116.

Boston has no more posh, elegant hotel than this, the only AAA five-diamond and Mobil five-star hotel in New England.

Serene and grand, the top-of-the-line luxury hotel has 272 guest rooms and suites reflecting the understated style of a traditional Beacon Hill home. Renovated in

2005-06, they have oversize beds, cherry furniture, plush fabrics in bright citron tones, writing tables, 54-inch LCD TVs, two or three telephones, hair dryers, terrycloth robes and such, plus bay windows that open – a rare blessing for those who cherish fresh air. The 68 executive suites add alcove seating areas. The most desirable rooms overlook the Boston Public Garden.

In the hotel's luxurious eighth-floor health spa, Caribbean-style patio furniture surrounds the swimming pool and whirlpool, from which you can look out over the Public Garden and, at night, the lights of Boston. "Very romantic while relaxing in the jacuzzi," our host advised.

Public rooms are quietly decorated with antiques and fine art. A five-foot crystal chandelier lights the grand stairway to the elegant, second-floor **Aujourd'hui** restaurant, one of the city's best. The airy, main-floor **Bristol Lounge** serves three meals a day. It also offers Viennese dessert buffets (a dozen fabulous concoctions, $24) on weekends from 9 to midnight. Afternoon tea is served by the fireplace here daily from 3 to 4:15. An elegant Sunday breakfast buffet is considered one of the best in the city. Speaking of breakfast, among the room-service options is a Japanese breakfast, from grilled salmon and nori to miso soup, for $18.50.

(617) 338-4400 or (800) 332-3442. Fax (617) 423-0154. www.fourseasons.com/boston. One hundred eighty-seven rooms and 85 suites. Doubles, $475 to $795. Suites, $1,600 to $3,000.

Boston Harbor Hotel, 70 Rowes Wharf, Boston 02110.

A more sumptuous hotel could scarcely be imagined. The floors are marble, the sides of the elevators are brocade, and the walls of the public spaces are hung with fine art and antique nautical prints. Redwood furniture surrounds the 60-foot lap pool. A large lounge at the rear of the main floor has huge sofas in plums, golds and teals for relaxing as you enjoy live piano music and absorb the view of boats and airplanes around the harbor.

Luxury and care extend to the 230 rooms and suites on Floors 8 through 16 (the lower floors are offices). Our oversize room had a kingsize bed, a sofa and an upholstered chair with good reading lamps in a sitting area, an expansive work desk, lovely reproduction antiques, and an enormous marble bathroom full of amenities from fine soaps to terrycloth robes. Breakfronts concealed the TV and a minibar, atop which were three kinds of glasses – highball, lowball and wine. Self-illuminating closets, removable hangers, soundproof windows that open, bottles of spring water and enormous towels are other assets. Doorways are recessed well back from the corridor.

Meals are served in the **Intrigue Café,** which has outdoor seating beneath a lineup of umbrellas along the wharf promenade, and dinner in **Meritage.** Afternoon tea and drinks are offered in a handsome Harborview Lounge on the main floor, and private parties and special events take place in the two-story Rotunda, a copper-domed observatory with views of harbor and city. Guests enjoy the health club and spa, which besides the lap pool has steam rooms and saunas, a hydrotherapy tub and an exercise room with the most up-to-date equipment available.

The hotel is "elaborate, dramatic, even operatic," gushed the Boston Globe's architectural critic shortly after its 1987 opening. It is "an expression of the new wealth of Boston." Stay here, indulge, and you'll surely feel part of it.

(617) 439-7000 or (800) 752-7077. Fax (617) 330-9450. www.bhh.com. Two hundred five rooms and 25 suites. Doubles, $185 to $575. Suites, $565 to $3,000.

The Ritz-Carlton, Boston, 15 Arlington St., Boston 02117.

The oldest Ritz in the United States is not just a hotel. It's an institution – *the* place where proper Bostonians put up visitors or go themselves for lunch in the café, tea in the lounge, or drinks in the Ritz Bar.

Following a top-to-bottom makeover in 2002, the white-gloved bellhops are about the only holdover from the grande-dame Ritz that was Boston's bastion of Brahmin elegance. Automatic elevators now whisk guests up to the 273 rooms, perhaps one of the 45 suites with wood-burning fireplaces billed for romance. They now offer a "fireplace butler," who gives guests their choice of wood from aromatic to crackling. The refurbished rooms are sumptuous, with lounge chairs covered in Belgian velvet, king or queen beds dressed in Italian fabrics and feather duvets, French provincial furnishings and three layers of room-darkening tapestry draperies shielding windows that open. Baths have been modernized and marbleized, and come with a single rose in a bud vase as well as a "bath butler."

The martinis in the Ritz Bar are legendary, as is English tea in the Lounge (light tea, $20; full tea, $28; tea royale with a glass of champagne, $40). The elegant Dining Room closed in 2005, leaving the Café to serve three meals a day.

All the amenities of a four-diamond hotel are here, even if some think they'd seen better days. The "some" included the Millennium Partners of New York, who bought the Ritz and undertook all the renovations after opening a new Ritz across the Boston Common along Tremont Street. Now there are two Ritzes, one classic and one contemporary. Cesar Ritz would be proud.

(617) 536-5700 or (800) 241-3333. Fax (617) 536-1335. www.ritz-carlton.com. Two hundred twenty-eight rooms and 45 suites. Doubles, $325 to $695. Suites, $695 to $4,000.

The Ritz-Carlton, Boston Common, 10 Avery St., Boston 02111.

If the original Ritz-Carlton defines hotel elegance in the Boston of tradition, the new Ritz across the Common sets a benchmark for hotel luxury in the 21st century.

And that benchmark certainly is un-Ritz-like. Traditionalists find the essence of ritz missing from the modernist gray hotel beneath a pair of crystalline towers along the east side of the common. The rooms are larger, the furnishings strikingly contemporary and the atmosphere "charged with congenial energy," according to the hotel literature. Some of the energy resides, no doubt, in the adjacent Sports Club/LA, where guests have complimentary access to the ultimate in fitness, athletic and spa options, and the nineteen-screen Loews Cineplex theaters, the largest in Boston.

Public spaces are at street level, while guest rooms occupy the top four floors of the twelve-story building. "This is all more contemporary, to appeal to a younger crowd," our guide said as he showed a variety of guest rooms notable for kingsize feather beds outfitted with Frette linens and feather duvets, large marble baths with separate showers, modern furnishings and state-of-the-art technology for the wired traveler.

The color scheme is the new Boston taupe in a variety of earth tones. Teak is everywhere – in the rooms, on the doors, in the corridors and lobby, and in the hotel's dot.com-styled restaurant, **Jer·ne,** pronounced journey. The contemporary street-level dining room is as unconventional (for the Ritz) as the hotel itself. So is chef Scott Gambone's contemporary fare, which includes "common dishes" for sharing. The lounge in the sleek, mod lobby offers afternoon tea presented tableside in the Ritz tradition. Breakfast selections include a "juice flight," an eye-opening display of five shot glasses holding fruit and vegetable juices, plus a bircher muesli cocktail and hot oatmeal with banana brûlée.

Thus comes the new, high-energy Ritz prototype for the new generation.

(617) 574-7100 or (800) 241-3333. Fax (617) 574-7200. One hundred fifty rooms and 43 suites. Doubles, $295 to $650. Suites, $395 to $4,000.

Fifteen Beacon, 15 Beacon St., Boston 02108.

The intimate, dark wood lobby looks a bit like a library and the original glass-enclosed birdcage elevators seem incongruous in this newish 61-room high-tech boutique hotel (you can see the cables rising and falling before you board and then glimpse each floor as you ascend). They reflect the historic, residential look sought by developer Paul Roiff, who transformed a ten-story Beaux Arts office building into a playground and workstation for the rich and trendy.

Owner Roiff, who has an abiding interest in food and wine, went for the ultimate. His designer was Celeste Cooper, who previously designed Mistral, the restaurant of which he is part-owner, as well as L'Espalier. Decorated in elegant modernist style, rooms and suites on nine floors blend state-of-the-art conveniences with the intimate touches of a private residence, though no residence in our experience is so overwhelmingly decked out in chocolate brown. They are stylish and decidedly masculine in shades of espresso, taupe and cream with built-in solid mahogany wall units, plump club chairs and chaise lounges, oversize writing desks and gleaming white bathroom fixtures, including a few jetted tubs and glass enclosures with plate-size overhead showers. About the only "color" is provided by fresh flowers and a bowl of tangerines or the shiny red apples in glass vases in each entry; the fruits are changed every other day to keep them edible. The queensize beds (some of them draped in dark canopies) are dressed in Italian 350-thread-count linens.

A bedside keypad activates the TV, a surround-sound stereo system and a gas fireplace enclosed in a shimmering stainless-steel chimney surround. Each room has a business center with three phones (one cordless), a combination fax and color printer, and direct Internet access. Among amenities are a four-inch LCD TV and heated towel racks in the bathrooms (outfitted with luxury Kiehl's toiletries), imported Italian fabric robes, and in-room bars stocked with the finest liquors and half bottles of Chateau Lafite Rothschild, Opus One and Krug champagne.

The hotel's eleventh floor contains an exercise room opening onto a pair of rooftop sundecks with a whirlpool tub and an outdoor bar. The main-floor **Federalist** restaurant serves three meals a day. It claims Boston's finest wine cellar and loftiest prices.

(617) 670-1500 or (877) 982-3226. www.xvbeacon.com. Fifty-seven rooms and three suites. Doubles, $295 to $695. Suites, $995 to $1,900.

Nine Zero Hotel, 90 Tremont St., Boston 02108.

Confidently named for its address (or at least a portion thereof), this ultra-modern boutique hotel was built from the ground up in 2002 to provide 190 guest accommodations and a stylish restaurant.

The nineteen-story hotel has roughly twelve rooms on each upper floor with king or queensize beds (some have two queens). Most quite spacious, they are smartly furnished in contemporary style in pale yellow and black. Frette linens and goose down comforters, striped in yellow and black, dress the beds, which are distinctive for their tall leather headboards whose curves resemble those of the two upholstered

'Tower of power' entertainment center at left is feature of guest room at Nine Zero.

reddish wing chairs beside windows that open. Next to an oversize work desk, fully equipped for the business traveler to whom the hotel caters, is what the staff dubbed "a tower of power." It's a black cylindrical entertainment center and refreshment area with rotating TV, video collection, coffeemaker with the local Karma coffee and such. Marble vanities and tubs enhance the baths, some with whirlpools, although smaller queensize rooms have glass showers in lieu of tubs. Local Mario Russo toiletries are among the amenities. The entire top floor is given over to the Cloud Nine Suite, which claims a panoramic view.

Three meals a day are available in **Spire,** the modernist, 72-seat dining room named for the steeple of the historic Park Street Church on view through floor-to-ceiling windows along with the park-like ancient burial ground. Chef Gabriel Frasca prepares contemporary American fare with a European accent in a semi-open kitchen screened by one of the metallic curtains that also drape the windows and turn up as design elements in surprising places throughout the hotel.

(617) 772-5800 or (866) 646-3937. Fax (617) 772-5810. www.ninezero.com. One hundred eighty-five rooms and five suites. Doubles, $299 to $450. Suites, $700 to $3,000.

Hotel Commonwealth, 500 Commonwealth Ave., Boston 02215.

This five-story newcomer in the rejuvenated Kenmore Square area offers 150 boutique hotel-style guest rooms above a retail corridor, a couple of celebrity restaurants and the T-station, with a direct link to the subway below. Within grand-slam distance of Fenway Park, it quickly became popular with Boston Red Sox fans and the media types who cover the team. It also is convenient for museum-goers, orchestra-goers and visitors to nearby Boston University, which partnered in building it from the ground up on the site of the infamous Rathskeller bar once popular with B.U. students.

The elegant upper lobby with its dark wood furnishings, brocades and divans covered with tapestries and fringes is designed to make visitors feel as if they've stepped into a stately Back Bay residence. Guest rooms on the four floors above balance European charm with contemporary convenience, from pillow-top king or queen beds dressed with Frette linens and down comforters to marble bathrooms with L'Occitane toiletries. Stately oversize writing desks and DVD/TVs are standard. Decor is cheerful in shades of red, beige and brown.

Off the lobby is **Great Bay,** a bold new seafood eatery named Esquire magazine's best new restaurant of 2003, ostensibly because of its owners, previous award-winners Christopher Myers and Michael Schlow of Radius and Via Matta. Downstairs is the classy **Foundation Lounge,** offering a Japanese snack menu of Zensai nightly and live music occasionally. On the west side of the hotel is the hotel's new full-service restaurant, **Eastern Standard.** Run by No.9 Park co-owner Garrett Harker, it serves three meals a day.

(617) 933-5000 or (866) 784-4000. Fax (617) 266-6888. www.hotelcommonwealth.com. One hundred fifty rooms. Doubles, $229 to $389.

The Lenox Hotel, 710 Boylston St., Boston 02116.

Built in 1900 as Boston's answer to the Waldorf-Astoria, this totally renovated, family-owned hotel is on the rise after a period of being overshadowed by the large chain hotels. Personally run by the Saunders family, it is billed as their intimate, boutique property, and the welcome does seem personal and genuine here.

High ceilings, glittering chandeliers, armoires, marble baths, walk-in closets, windows that open and nightly turndown service imbue the hotel with a charm that earned it a surprising place in Norman Simpson's old *Country Inns and Back Roads* guide. A top-to-bottom renovation, which elevated the hotel to AAA four-diamond status, shows off the 216 accommodations to best advantage. The corner room in which we stayed was large and unusually quiet, and contained one of the hotel's fourteen wood-burning fireplaces. Most rooms are furnished in Drexel Colonial reproduction style, although some are done in French provincial.

Chef Robert Fathman's **Azure** restaurant on the main floor ranks among the city's best. **Sola's Irish Pub** features casual food and drink

(617) 536-5300 or (800) 225-7676. Fax (617) 267-1237. www.lenoxhotel.com. One hundred ninety-six rooms and sixteen suites. Doubles, $325. Suites, $695.

B&B in a Beacon Hill Brownstone

The Charles Street Inn, 94 Charles St., Boston 021114.

A four-story brownstone built in 1860 as a model home to showcase Second Empire Victorian architectural styles for potential Back Bay homeowners serves well for 21st-century visitors seeking residential luxury.

Innkeepers Sally Deane and Louise Venden reconfigured rooms, installed deluxe spa-quality bathrooms and added an elevator to cosset guests in nine sumptuous rooms named and themed for famous Beacon Hill residents of the period. The five largest rooms with kingsize beds (one with two doubles) overlook Mount Vernon Square at the back of the house. Four queensize rooms in front face gas-lit Charles Street. Furnished to the Victorian hilt with fine antiques and creature comforts, each has a working marble fireplace, TV/VCR hidden in an armoire, Bose radio, Frette linens, Turkish rugs, mini-refrigerator and a lavish bath with air-jet whirlpool spa tub. Romantic reds envelop the Italian armoire, fainting couch and brass rococo chandelier in the Isabella Stewart Gardiner Room in a style its namesake would have enjoyed. Antique landscape etchings and lithographs embellish the dark and masculine Frederick Law Olmsted Room.

Guests are welcomed with sweets, fruit and snacks in the lobby. Breakfast is delivered to the guest rooms. It involves so many choices it's billed as "deluxe continental."

(617) 314-8900 or (877) 772-8900. Fax (617) 371-0009. www.charlesstreetinn.com. Nine rooms with private baths. Doubles, $225 to $375.

Gourmet Treats

Faneuil Hall Marketplace, the East's busiest tourist destination after Disney World, is a festival arena for foodies, from the great **Crate & Barrel** store to the approximately twenty restaurants and thirty snackeries, salad bars and food stalls in Quincy Market. It wasn't always thus, but now, wouldn't you know, **Starbucks** is first as you enter from the west. As you stroll through, pick up a chowder or pot pie from **Boston Chowda,** a non-alcoholic banana daiquiri from the **Monkey Bar,** tacos or burritos from **Baja Fresh Mexican Grill,** a spanakopita from **Steve's Greek Cuisine,** a swordfish kabob from **Boston & Maine Fish Co.,** a fajita salad at **El Paso Enchiladas** or sausages or a hot dog from **The Dog House.** Finish with a cookie from **Boston Chipyard.** There aren't many foods you can think of that you can't find here, and prices are reasonable. The larger restaurants, though frequented by tourists, are nothing to write home about, with the possible exceptions of Todd English's **Kingfish Hall,** historic **Durgin-Park, McCormick & Schmick's,** the trendy Tex-Mex **Zuma** and the new **Plaza III Kansas City Steakhouse.**

One of the better places in the waterfront area to pick up lunch or a snack is **Rudi's Café Bistro** at 30 Rowes Wharf, near the Boston Harbor Hotel. Billed as a boulangerie, pâtisserie and croissanterie, the upscale spot offers delectable salads, prepared foods and colorful pastries in a curved display case, along with gourmet foods and books. You can eat in a pleasant dining area at the side or take out to the waterfront.

The 100 block of increasingly fashionable Newbury Street holds special interest for food lovers. **Kitchen Arts** at 161 is chock-full of neat gadgets, including a good little hand-held knife sharpener ($8.95) that went home in our shopping bag. Vermont's **Simon Pearce** glass has a branch at 115 Newbury, next door to **Pierre Deux. Teuscher** at 230 Newbury airlifts its chocolates weekly from Zurich.

The old Coffee Connection (at 165 Newbury St. and countless other locations around town) has been absorbed by **Starbucks,** which helps account for the latter's omnipresence across Boston. More coffee is available, along with tea, chocolates and Italian sodas, on a little sunken patio in front of **Espresso Royale Caffe,** 286 Newbury. Adjacent is **Emack & Bolio's,** one of a small local chain offering ice cream, yogurt and a juice bar offering "Boston's best smoothie." The day's special at our visit was a "thick as a brick oreo frappe."

The finest in pots and pans, plus table linens and some cookbooks, are featured at **Seasonings,** a good cookware and accessory store at 113 Charles St. True to its name, it also carries a selection of seasonings and spices.

Savenor's at 160 Charles St. is considered Boston's best gourmet market. It made its name as a butcher (everything from farm-raised lamb to lion meat). Choosy cooks head here for choice groceries, specialty foods, sauces, oils and breads, including imported loaves from Poilane, the legendary all-organic baker in Paris.

Former Mistral pastry chef Joanne Chang has won all kinds of awards for **Flour,** the bakery and café she launched in 2000 at 1595 Washington St., which helped start the South End street's rejuvenation. The breads and dessert pastries are out of this world, and the café offers breakfast pastries, coffees and sandwiches for lunch.

Fresh bread in front window of Lindbergh's Crossing lures passersby along harborfront.

Portsmouth, N.H.

Tastes of the Seacoast

Settled in 1623, Portsmouth is the third-oldest city in the United States and wears the mantle proudly. So it has had plenty of time to spawn restaurants old and new, to the point where there are more than 50 in the compact downtown area alone, an extraordinary number for a small city of 25,000. So it can claim, belatedly if not presumptuously, the title "restaurant capital of New England."

Only recently has it been thus. Sure, noted chef James Haller opened the Blue Strawbery in a former ship's chandlery across from the waterfront in 1970, putting Portsmouth on the map as a culinary destination ahead of the Northeast's dining transformation. The Blue Strawbery became known far and wide, although better regarded nationally than locally. Other restaurateurs of the time catered to the tried and true in this small, self-centered city that likes to eat. Several survive to this day but never really became major players. Others tested the waters in the 1980s and '90s and failed.

The 21st century marked a turning point for a city that had been known more for the number of restaurants than their quality. A young waiter from Connecticut with a business plan opened Jumpin' Jay's Fish Café, the first in a local restaurant empire of five and counting. Entrepreneurs and chefs arrived from Boston, Colorado, California and beyond to launch restaurants of distinction. Suddenly, there was top quality as well as quantity on the local culinary scene.

And that scene spread – geographically across the harbor and the Maine state line into Kittery, and categorically into the broader specialty food trade. Two young men who met as waiters in Portsmouth restaurants started selling homemade jams and vinegars at the Portsmouth farmer's market. That was the start of Stonewall Kitchen, a producer of regional specialty food products selling across the country and headquartered just up I-95 at the gateway to Maine.

"Taste of the Seacoast," a quarterly magazine as slick as they come, emerged in 2003 to cover the area's food and wine trends. Newspapers in Boston and Portland routinely reviewed Portsmouth's restaurants along with their own.

Stonewall Kitchen founders Jonathan King and Jim Stott credit Portsmouth and its culinary excitement for stimulating their start. So too do many of the smaller producers and specialty restaurants that are popping up seemingly every year.

Dining

The Best of the Best

Lindbergh's Crossing, 29 Ceres St., Portsmouth.

The 200-year-old brick and beam building that one was a ship's chandlery is where Portsmouth's gourmet restaurant boom originated. Now a bistro and wine bar with obscure references to Charles Lindbergh, it is across the street from the harbor in a space long occupied by the Blue Strawbery restaurant that Buddy Haller made famous. Although it does not attract the national recognition of its predecessor, the local consensus is that this is less flashy and better.

Scott O'Connor and Tom Fielding are the remaining partners from the group of five who bought the place from the last owner of the Blue Strawbery in 1995. Its new name was admittedly circuitous, in Scott's words. It seems two of the original five traveled the world "picking up stuff." One had an interest in aeronautics and the other had ties with France. Lindbergh's Crossing was the result, and a representation of Lindbergh's flight across the Atlantic flanks the stairway from the ground-level dining room and kitchen to the upstairs wine bar.

Otherwise the Lindbergh theme is not evident. The emphasis instead is on a convivial ambiance, exceptional food and fine wines.

A warm welcome is provided by the co-owners, outgoing hosts who chat with diners in the dark and intimate main dining room and in the wine bar, where a handful of tables look out onto the waterfront and are available on a first-come, first-served basis. The food is the domain of chef Evan Mallett, a former Boston advertising copywriter who joined Lindbergh's as a line cook in 1999. After taking two years off to run a restaurant and gourmet food shop with his wife in San Miguel de Allende, a mountain village and artists' community in Central Mexico, he returned in 2003 to succeed Lindbergh's founding chef Jeff Tenner.

Here he has led the kitchen's migration into the flavors of Iberia, North Africa and the Southern Mediterranean, while adhering to the country French style that made Lindbergh's a local favorite in the past.

His menu is straightforward and blessedly easy to comprehend. It begins with four tapas, small tastes perhaps of sautéed garlic shrimp or whipped foie gras in a brioche. First courses the autumn night we were there ranged from pepper-crusted rare tuna with fried shelling beans, escarole and smoky tomato coulis to Long Island duck breast over cherry couscous with a quince-vinegar drizzle. The signature escargots arrives in a sherry butter sauce and is finished with raclette. Lindbergh's mussels with hand-cut fries and garlic aioli are to die for.

Dining room at Lindbergh's Crossing retains original brick walls and beamed ceiling.

For main courses, Evan might braise monkfish with root vegetables, dates and rainbow chard or stuff pork roulade with roasted figs and scallions and serve it with cider-glazed yams. The seafood paella, stewed with spicy linguica, is mixed with saffron rice. A brandy cream reduction enhances the Canadian beef tenderloin au poivre.

Like the rest of the menu, desserts change with the seasons. At our autumn visit they included a honeycrisp apple tarte tatin, a fig and pistachio tart with cocoa butter crust and vanilla crème fraîche, and three chocolate ganaches with different toppings: berry with saffron, orange with green tea and coffee with ginger. They reflected the work of an ambitious kitchen at its prime.

Scott O'Connor serves as sommelier. His wine list starts around $30 and is worthy of the finest wine bars.

The kitchen bakes its breads daily and showcases them in a display in the front window that catches the eye and interest of passersby.

(603) 431-0887. www.lindberghscrossing.com. Entrées, $21 to $29.50. Dinner nightly, from 5:30.

The Dunaway Restaurant, 66 Marcy St., Portsmouth.

Rustic American cuisine at once returns to its roots and reaches its zenith here, thanks to a partnership between a local restaurateur and the historic Strawbery Banke museum. For Jay McSharry, the Dunaway is the "icing on the cake" of his restaurant ventures. He transformed two levels of a former barn that housed the museum's Dunaway Store into an elegant restaurant with a refined Colonial look suitable to Strawbery Banke, the building's owner.

The old store's entrance reveals a rich, two-story space of posts and beams. Beyond a small bar and lounge in front are a partly open kitchen at one side and airy, white-linened dining areas on the other side and in back. More dining tables get a bird's-eye view of the scene from a loft overhead.

Richly appointed dining area in The Dunaway Restaurant conveys sense of history.

Executive chef Mary Dumont's fare is as rich and historic as the setting. After a decade of cooking in California restaurants, she returned to the New Hampshire Seacoast, where she grew up in the restaurant business and three of her four siblings are in the hospitality trade (her brother Daniel is executive chef at the restored Wentworth by the Sea resort in nearby New Castle). Her timing coincided with the planning for the venture in 2005. "When I walked into the Dunaway with Jay McSharry for the first time," she said, "I felt immediately at home." In the spirit of traditional cooking appropriate for the setting, she adds creative elements to basic fare from land and sea. Her cuisine focuses on seafood fresh off the commercial fishing boats in the harbor and local produce, including historic and rare herbs, fruits and vegetables grown in Strawbery Banke's working kitchen gardens.

Dining is by candlelight, so dim that small flashlights may be offered to illuminate the menu. Our dinner began with a couple of the six "tastes" that head the menu: an excellent tuna tartine with avocado and breakfast radish and a complex, rich lobster hash that arrived on two spoons. A couple of appetizers demonstrated the chef's deft touch with seafood. The first was king salmon carpaccio served with golden and chioggia beets and lemon crème fraîche. The other was a salt cod brandade gratin with arugula, roasted tomatoes, niçoise olives and toasted crostini. Also fine was a main course of pan-seared wild daurade, served with saffron, rouille and crisp serrano ham in a bouillabaisse broth with fingerling potatoes. Other entrées included a roasted breast and confit leg of chicken with a smoky bacon jus, braised roulade of beef shortribs and grilled bavette of beef with perigord sauce.

Desserts like coconut-tapioca napoleon and cider doughnuts with hot mulled cider sounded strange but historic. We succumbed to an almond butter cake embellished with poached seckel pears and fig brandy sauce and a dish of concord grape sorbet that tasted as if it had been picked right off the vine outside.

Others like to finish with the changing array of artisinal cheeses, taking advantage of the chef's experience at San Francisco's Campton Place and at Sonoma Saveurs in California wine country. Her carefully selected wine list, which features some not often seen in the area, is priced mostly in the $40 to $50 range.

(603) 373-6112. www.dunawayrestaurant.com. Entrées, $21 to $25. Lunch seasonally, Monday-Friday 11 to 2:30 May-October. Dinner year-round, Monday-Thursday 5:30 to 9:30, Friday and Saturday 5 to 10..

Pesce Blue, 103 Congress St., Portsmouth.

This contemporary seafood grill has a decided Italian accent, thanks to owner Joachim Sandbichler, an Austrian who spent many years in Italy. While managing restaurants in California, he vacationed in the area and found a potential restaurant site in the former Little Professor bookstore. He turned it into an Italian seafood grill – so successfully that shortly after their 2002 opening, he and his chef were invited to prepare dinner at the James Beard House in New York.

Pesce Blue's dining room is stylish and dramatic.

Pesce Blue's 70-seat space is ultra-dramatic: long, narrow and mod, a palette of blacks, taupes and beiges. Falling curtains partially screen cinder-block walls. Orchids brighten an arty lineup of vases at the entry and show up on each table. Varied lamp spheres dangle from the high ceiling.

It's a contemporary look that "puts the emphasis on the food," says executive chef Paul Arias. And the food draws accolades from Boston reviewers, one of whom declared it to be "the best reason to drive 65 miles for a plate of fish."

Make that perhaps ten plates of fish, the choices varying daily. You might find sautéed Icelandic char with lemon-caper emulsion, sautéed New Bedford skate with orange-ginger sauce or grilled yellowfin tuna with green peppercorn sauce. Some go for the house specialty, mixed grill – an assortment of five of the day's freshest with marinated grilled vegetables. Others go for "the whole thing" – another specialty of grilled sea bream, perhaps, or Mediterranean branzino (sea bass), baked in a salt crust, grilled or oven roasted.

We went for the linguini and diver scallops with saffron, prosciutto and romano beans, a tasty mélange offered both for lunch and dinner. The roasted tomato soup with Tuscan cheddar cheese arrived in a bowl so large and deep that one had to hold onto the spoon to keep it from slipping into the soup. A mixed green salad with roasted pear, dried figs, fennel and camembert accompanied, as did crusty Italian bread to dip into a saucer splashed with olive oil and balsamic vinegar.

Day or night, the treats begin with such appetizers as yellowfin tuna tartare, swordfish carpaccio, fried calamari with three dipping sauces or grilled Portuguese sardines with potatoes, caramelized onions, frisée and warm pancetta vinaigrette. Six seafood pastas and risottos are available as small plates or large.

The night's menu holds only two items called "landfood," usually pan-roasted "flattened" chicken and grilled ribeye steak with a red wine sauce.

Desserts include a selection of sorbets, Italian crêpes, crème brûlée and panna cotta served with local blueberries.

(603) 430-7766. www.pesceblue.com. Entrées, $18.75 to $27.50. Lunch, Monday-Friday 11:45 to 2. Dinner nightly, 5 to 9:30 or 10.

Jumpin' Jay's Fish Café, 150 Congress St., Portsmouth.

Fresh seafood from around the country is featured at this mod place that started small in 2000 and quickly quadrupled in size. It also launched Jay McSharry on the fast track to building the area's largest restaurant empire.

The 30-something restaurateur, who began his career at age 14 as a busboy in his native Connecticut, worked as a waiter at Anthony Alberto's here as he developed his business plan for his first Portsmouth restaurant. He named it to convey a lively and unpretentious atmosphere and "never expected" the expansion that ensued.

Owner Jay McSharry at Jumpin' Jay's Fish Café.

"Fish with an attitude" is how Jay describes the fare at the restaurant ranked No. 1 for "best place for dinner" in the Portsmouth Herald's Best of Portsmouth survey. One day's catch included yellowfin tuna from Baha, halibut from Washington, sable fish from Alaska, grouper from Costa Rica and wahoo from Florida. Each came with a choice of sauces, among them mandarin-sesame, lobster velouté, Mexican mole and mango-ginger-jalapeño. Lobster risotto is a signature dish. Others are haddock piccata and fishermen's stew. Linguini can be ordered provençal style with choice of mussels, scallops, shrimp or chicken – the last, the only non-seafood item when we were there.

Changing appetizers run a wide range from ahi tuna tossed in a hot and sour dressing over Asian slaw to a Maine crab cake topped with chipotle aioli and served with grilled pineapple and black bean salsa. Salads could be sashimi tuna with avocado and caesar with grilled fish. Dessert choices are limited: homemade cheesecake, key lime pie, crème brûlée and hot fudge sundae.

Well-spaced white tables with black chairs are situated beneath string lights in a mod red and white, high-tech setting with several dining areas on different levels. A circular, stainless steel bar is in the center.

Dining areas wrap around martini bar at The Green Monkey.

Since opening his seafood place, Jay has opened four more downtown restaurants, each with a working chef as partner and serving different audiences: Radicci, an Italian bistro almost next door; the Dunaway for fine dining, Dos Amigos for burritos and the Red Door martini bar.

(603) 766-3474. www.jumpinjays.com. Entrées, $18 to $24. Dinner, Monday-Thursday 5:30 to 9 (to 9:30 in summer), Friday and Saturday 5 to 10, Sunday 5 to 9.

The Green Monkey, 86 Pleasant St., Portsmouth.

There are some who tout this newcomer as the best restaurant in a city of many. Ebullient hostess Deb Weeks embraces her clientele in a genuine warmth and her co-owner and chef, Colorado native Phelps Dieck, sends forth from a kitchen hidden in back a level of food that her customers call amazing.

A noisy, fun vibe pervades the place, from the popular martini bar on one side to the nicely spaced dining tables placed around the perimeter. Framed art tapestries and a surfboard provide decorative accents for a place that doesn't really need them, for it's colorful in olive green and burgundy from the floor up the walls to the high ceiling. White butcher paper tops the white-linened tables, each dignified by a tiny shaded gas lamp.

Phelps calls her cuisine "new American with a flair." Make that a global flair. For appetizers, she might steam Prince Edward Island mussels in a green curry-coconut-lemongrass broth and enliven scallop and lobster spring rolls with a hoisin-lime dipping sauce. Cilantro, coconut milk and ginger flavor her spicy lobster bisque. A sauté of wild mushrooms and fire-roasted tomatoes arrives in a nutty amontillado sherry cream sauce on a grilled baguette.

Main courses are similarly assertive. Red snapper is encrusted in ginger and scallions and served with shiitake mushrooms, edamame soy beans and corn in a miso beurre blanc. Hawaiian sea salt and peppercorn-seared tuna is served rare over an Asian slaw and mashed potatoes with citrus butter. The Argentinian grilled flank steak is covered in a chimichuri sauce and served with a crispy potato galette. The roasted free-range chicken breast is stuffed with goat cheese and andouille sausage, and the rack of lamb roasted with a smoky maple-chipotle glaze.

The martini bar concocts some wild specialty drinks and offers specialty beers and wines from around the world.

(603) 427-1010. www.thegreenmonkey.net. Entrees, $20 to $28. Dinner, Tuesday-Sunday from 5.

Anthony Alberto's, 59 Penhallow St., Portsmouth.

A local institution hidden in the 1813 Custom House Cellar, this was generally considered the city's finest restaurant in the 1990s following the decline of the Blue Strawbery. Only recently has it been upstaged by an influx of newcomers, although its haute Italian dining style retains a loyal following.

Tod Alberto and Massimo Morgia, who had been associated with the late Ponte Vecchio across from the old Wentworth By the Sea resort in nearby New Castle, renovated the old Anthony's Al Dente space and named it after Tod's father.

It's romantic, dark and grotto-like with stone and brick walls, arches, exposed wooden beams on the ceiling and oriental rugs on the slate floors. Upholstered chairs, fanned napkins and beige tablecloths add an elegant Mediterranean look.

Executive chef Jethro Loichle's menu is high Italian, as in lobster poached in sauternes and herbed butter and served with handmade lemon-pepper fettuccine, grilled veal ribeye chop topped with a lardon-morel cream sauce, and pan-roasted rack of wild Italian boar with a roasted pepper manicotti. Pan-seared red snapper might be served with a fire-roasted red pepper coulis on a nest of lemon-herb orzo. Or the chef might offer a trio of mallard duck – pan-seared breast, confit and a foie gras potato galette, finished with a port wine glaze.

The house antipasto might be a combination of house-cured duck, smoked rabbit loin and pheasant liver pâté, served with assorted compotes and artisan cheeses. Other typical starters are lasagna layered with rock shrimp and farm cheeses, finished with a leek and whole-grain mustard fondue, house-made herbed potato gnocchi sautéed with assorted mushrooms, wilted arugula and a wild mushroom jus, and pan-fried oysters with a frisée, bacon and potato confit salad, herbed crème fraîche and bowfin caviar.

Desserts include bananas flambé, fruit tarts, tiramisu and crème caramel. The expensive Wine Spectator award-winning wine list is strong on Italian vintages.

(603) 436-4000. www.anthonyalbertos.com. Entrées, $18.95 to $29.95. Dinner, Monday-Saturday 5 to 9:30 or 10:30.

Victory 96 State Street, 96 State St., Portsmouth.

Situated near the Strawbery Banke museum complex, an aura of history surrounds this three-story brick Federal townhouse that served for more than 50 years as the home of the Victory Spa Diner and later Victory Antiques.

Chef-owner Duncan Boyd worked with celebrity chefs Jasper White in Boston and Bob Kinkead and Nora Pouillon in Washington, D.C., before his wife's connections lured him to Portsmouth in 2003 to open his own restaurant.

He retained part of the name a Greek immigrant had given the diner in the waning days of World War II to support his new American countrymen. The name was a natural for the chef to reflect New England seasonal cuisine, some of it influenced by immigrant groups that settled in the area.

Second-floor dining room at Victory 96 State Street is elegant and serene.

His new restaurant on two floors is a beauty, with brick walls and tables spaced well apart from which to enjoy the glow from six fireplaces. There's a casual dining area near the expanded bar and front lounge on the main floor and a more formal setting upstairs. The pine tabletops on the main floor were made with planks from the wide-board floors found in the building's attic during the restoration. The second-floor dining room is hushed and refined, its tables dressed in white linens and its brick walls above mahogany wainscoting hung with nautical prints.

The chef grows herbs in a small garden on the kitchen roof to enhance his seasonal, market-based cuisine. His New England seafood-oriented menu ranges from cedar-planked Maine salmon and roasted monkfish wrapped in cob bacon to pan-roasted duck breast with black mission fig sauce, hunter-style rabbit and grilled beef loin with bordelaise sauce. The "Victory mac n' cheese" teams lobster with Vermont cheddar, aged gruyère, crimini mushrooms and roasted red peppers.

Typical starters include seared foie gras with brandied peaches, steamed mussels with chorizo sausage and sweet peppers, a golden fried tomato stuffed with lobster salad and avocado, and a salad of smoked trout and frisée with potato croutons and a poached egg. Dessert could be a selection of cheeses, peach upside-down cake with buttermilk ice cream or warm chocolate soufflé cake with caramel anglaise.

The full dinner menu is served upstairs and down. A new bar menu, exclusive to the main floor, offers "lite bites and things to share," plus a few entrées like hunter-style chicken with house-made noodles and grilled flatiron steak.

(603) 766-0960. www.96statestreet.com. Entrées, $18 to $27. Dinner, Tuesday-Sunday 5:30 to 9:30.

43° North, 75 Pleasant St., Portsmouth.

A former chef from Anthony Alberto's opened his own restaurant in the space known earlier as The Grotto. No more grotto, this. Geno Gulotta christened it a kitchen and wine bar, hung its aqua brick walls with fine paintings and furnished it with Hungarian antique sideboards, imparting an elegant continental look to one of the best-looking dining rooms in town.

Fine paintings enhance handsome dining room at 43° North.

The wide-ranging contemporary international menu is one of the town's most inspired, too. So we were surprised to find the restaurant virtually empty at 6:30 on a weeknight when the hotshot newcomer across the street was bursting at the seams. It seems the owner wasn't on hand that night, but when he's in the kitchen the architectural presentations are unsurpassed.

The menu is categorized by small plates and bowls, greens, and large plates and bowls. Among the former are wonderful Maine mussels steamed in chardonnay, garlic, fennel and tomato and served with grilled olive focaccia. The crisp duck spring rolls with ginger-jalapeño dipping sauce and a pan-seared Maine crab cake with slivered endive and watercress salad come highly recommended.

For "large plates," consider the baked halibut en papillote, wrapped in savoy cabbage and served with mascarpone cream and a warm shell bean and red grape ragu, or porcini-dusted john dory with oven-dried tomato vinaigrette. Other choices might be seared yellowfin tuna with coconut-wasabi sauce and plum wine ponzu, roasted breast and confit of duck with pomegranate jus, and bacon-wrapped filet mignon with creamy gorgonzola sauce. A mixed grill might pair a juniper-scented ostrich filet and a bourbon-molasses rubbed elk chop with dried blueberry jam.

Dessert could be crème brûlée, hazelnut bread pudding with apricot puree or chocolate-hazelnut ganache.

The changing four-course tasting menus paired with wines on weekends are well received – as you'd expect, given the $45 tab that includes four glasses of wine.

(603) 430-0225. www.fortythreenorth.com. Entrées, $19 to $28. Dinner nightly, from 5.

The Wellington Room, 67 Bow St., Portsmouth.

A waterside setting is enjoyed by diners in this small restaurant backing up to the Piscataqua River.

New Zealand-born chef-owner David Robinson apprenticed in restaurants in

Australia, Europe, Cincinnati and Boston before taking over the intimate space formerly occupied by the Italian-themed Porto Bello in 2002. Its 38-seat dining room, hidden from view above and behind a downtown storefront, is the right size for his one-man show.

The chef's global travels impart Asian, Italian and French accents to his creative American cuisine. Given the restaurant's small size and kitchen, the menu is surprisingly large. It might open with a mushroom and cheese crêpe, Caribbean grilled shrimp and szechuan peppercorn-crusted tuna with a sesame-seaweed salad, and pan-seared duck foie gras served over roasted sweet beets and caramelized shallots.

For seafood dishes, the chef might offer pan-seared sea scallops in a delicate lemon beurre blanc laced with tobiko caviar, deliver oven-roasted haddock with chardonnay-tomato broth and set grilled jumbo shrimp over a spicy tomato arrabiatta sauce on saffron-scented fettuccine tossed with exotic mushrooms and baby spinach. Other entrées include roasted duck breast with a watercress and Australian shiraz reduction, filet mignon tournedos layered with a portobello mushroom and smoked mozzarella duxelle and, of course, New Zealand rack of lamb, with minted blackberry-honey drizzle.

(603) 431-2989. www.thewellingtonroom.com. Entrées, $20 to $31. Dinner, Wednesday-Saturday 5 to 9, Sunday 4 to 9.

Other Choices

The Metro, 20 High St., Portsmouth.

Very popular locally is Sam Jarvis's long-running art nouveau bar and bistro. It's pleasantly decked out with brass rails, stained glass, old gas lights, mirrors, dark wood and nifty Vanity Fair posters. Live jazz is offered weekends in the lounge.

Part of its popularity is attributed to its owner, whose family's lunch spot evolved in 1980 into an urbane bistro named for the Paris subway system. And part is due to the food, which remains familiar to an older clientele attached to the place and the visiting tourists who find it along a downtown side street.

Sam, the ever-present host who has seen more changes in the Portsmouth culinary scene than any other restaurateur in the area, manages to uphold tradition and yet keep up with the times. The menu is at once classic, but contemporary. The old haddock casino has given way to the likes of pan-seared diver scallops and littleneck clams in champagne-tarragon sauce over lemon linguini. The traditional half broiled spring chicken has been replaced by Statler chicken breast with seared foie gras and a port wine glaze. The steak diane has been succeeded by steak frites and a grilled beef tenderloin with a pancetta and horseradish crust. And so the refreshed menu goes, from a layer cake of red snapper, mussels and leeks in a spiced crab broth to rack of lamb with Moroccan couscous.

The Metro's award-winning clam chowder, which took top honors in an all-New England competition at Newport, remains a popular starter. Others have been updated from their early continental bent to include lobster spring rolls with Asian apricot mustard, grilled chicken satay with Thai peanut sauce and pan-fried Maine crab cakes with wasabi aioli. Desserts, attractively displayed on a fancy old baker's rack, include triple chocolate terrine, key lime pie and a classic crème brûlée.

(603) 436-0521. www.themetrorestaurant.com. Entrées, $21 to $29. Lunch, Monday-Saturday 11:30 to 2:30. Dinner, Monday-Thursday 5:30 to 9:30, Friday-Saturday 5 to 10.

The Dolphin Striker, 15 Bow St.

Forever popular with tourists, this long-running riverfront landmark regained some of its glory under new owner Peter DiZiglio, who rescued it from foreclosure. With a new chef and staff having proven their mettle, the three upstairs dining areas with beamed ceilings and bare wood floors were given a more modern look in 2005. The walls were painted in warm earth tones and hung with changing local artworks. A sleek wine bar was added, and wines were stored in display shelves and dividers to create a more open concept for dining.

Chef Gary Caron refreshed the New American menu to highlight organic and local ingredients for an increasingly food-savvy clientele. Look for appetizers such as an herbed crab cake presented on a roasted pepper coulis with fresh basil oil and a slivered radish or slow-cooked duck confit served warm with goat cheese, figs, and a sweet and sour rhubarb gastrique. Lobster shows up in a pasta dish, tossed with oyster mushrooms and sweet peas, and diced in a salad with summer melon, cucumber and tarragon leaves. For main courses the chef serves locally harvested cod, tuna and shellfish as well as naturally raised poultry, pork, beef and lamb. His roasted cod fillet might be glazed with miso and topped with a tangy lemon and parsley salsa verde. The grilled duck breast is sliced over faro risotto with pomegranate molasses and a dried fruit compote. The "duet of beef" might be a grilled hanger steak and wine-braised shortribs served on potato puree with herb-roasted carrots and truffle butter.

Artisan cheeses could be the final course. Or you could finish with cardamom-scented crème caramel, a lemon curd and raspberry tart or chocolate-ginger cake with crème anglaise.

A light menu and live music are offered downstairs in the cozy, stone-walled **Spring Hill Tavern,** which retains its historic ambiance.

(603) 431-5222. www.dolphinstriker.com. Entrées, $20 to $34. Lunch, Friday-Sunday 11:30 to 2. Dinner, Tuesday-Sunday 5 to 9:30.

Anneke Jans, 60 Wallingford Square, Kittery, Me.

The Portsmouth area's restaurant vibrancy spilled across the Piscataqua River into an out-of-the-way commercial block in Kittery with the 2005 opening of this chic bistro that created quite a buzz in the region. Although many of Portsmouth's chefs and innkeepers praise it highly, unsuspecting visitors are generally surprised by what they find.

A sandwich board on the sidewalk beckons passersby into the gleaming, 48-seat bistro in the corner of a four-story building that would be right at home in Boston's Back Bay or South End. Who'd expect such a sleek setting in what had been an antiques shop converted from a post office? Tall windows envelop two sides in glass. Black walls and chairs are backdrops for tables set with cream-colored cloths on one side, a wraparound bar in the other and a semi-open kitchen in back.

Owner Andy Livingston, a founder and executive vice president of Portsmouth-based Environmental Power Corp., partnered here with manager Julie Dunfey, a caterer who was associated with the late Dunfey's Aboard the John Wanamaker floating restaurant in Portsmouth. He named it for his mother, Anneke, and the original Anneke Jans, an early Lower Manhattan landowner whose descendants challenged Trinity Church's acquisition of their land and became embroiled in one the country's longest-running lawsuits.

The menu, encased in a corkboard menu accented with small sea stones, is

Onetime post office is now sleek setting for Anneke Jans bistro.

thoroughly up-to-date in the clipped contemporary idiom. Main courses are listed with their ingredients spaced in stream-of-consciousness style, but minus the usual withs and punctuation, as in "halibut polenta native corn applewood smoked bacon potatoes corn sauce lobster meat." That is one of the signature dishes, as are the mussels "steamed in cream bacon shallots white wine," available alone as an appetizer and served with pommes frites as an entrée. You won't go wrong whatever the presentation of calves liver, the pork chop with apple-cider glaze, the cassoulet of duck confit, garlic sausage and pork shoulder or the straightforward angus sirloin strip with frites.

Start with the tuna tartare with vodka vinaigrette and caviar cream or the crab cake with celery root slaw. Dessert might be a blueberry crumble or a bananas foster upside-down cake. With a bottle of wine in the $25 range from a list of 55 "world wines," you'll likely have a fine meal that won't break the bank.

(207) 439-0001 or (888) 988-0001. www.annekejans.net. Entrées, $14 to $26. Dinner, Tuesday-Saturday 5 to 10.

A Storied Resort Reborn

Wentworth by the Sea, 588 Wentworth Road, New Castle 03854.

Perhaps no grand oceanfront hotel in northern New England was better known than the storied Wentworth, poised on a rise at the tip of the island of New Castle and host to the rich and famous for more than a century. Closed in 1982, it was saved from the wreckers' ball after becoming the first hotel to be placed on the National Trust for Historical Preservation's list of America's Eleven Most Endangered Places.

The rebuilt Wentworth reopened in 2003 as a Marriott hotel and spa, bearing the

Wentworth's exterior look and heritage but with an interior reflecting Marriott motifs and amenities. The sparkling-white hotel with red roof appears squeezed between new front and back access roads and residential development where open expanses of lawns had been.

The elongated, four-story hotel contains 143 guest rooms, some with french doors onto Juliet balconies facing the harbor and ocean in front and the meandering Piscataqua River in back – those on the third floor are most in demand. Rooms generally are on the small side, but are equipped with marble baths and the usual Marriott attributes. The best rooms (and views) are in eighteen bi-level suites at water's edge in the Little Harbor Marina. Formerly called the "Ship Building" for its vague resemblance to early ocean liners, the four-story building is a short hike downhill from the hotel. Its suites have one or two bedrooms, full kitchens, sitting/dining areas and private balconies.

Resort activities include a full-service spa, tennis and guest access to the Wentworth by the Sea Country Club and Marina.

Three meals a day are served in two side-by-side hotel dining rooms, one with pillars and a frescoed domed ceiling. Executive chef Daniel Dumont's contemporary American fare is as complex as it is sophisticated. His appetizers could be a truffled goat cheese and golden beet terrine, a tasting of wild salmon or peppered yellowfin tuna carpaccio with a dropped quail egg niçoise salad. Entrées range from tournedos of yellowfin tuna and smoky bacon-crusted "filet mignon" of lobster to a pot au feu of pheasant with toasted barley truffle flan and herb-crusted loin of lamb. The "variety of Long Island duck" might be a crispy corned leg and a peppered rare breast with a black mission fig-vinegar reduction.

Across the street in the marina, **Latitudes** offers informal dining seasonally inside beside floor-to-ceiling windows or near the fireplace in the bar, and outside on a teak deck overlooking the waterfront. The bistro-style menu is a with-it compendium of appetizers, sandwiches, salads and entrées. At night, you could start with charred ginger rare beef with ponzu sauce, a "tower" of crab and yellowfin tuna or selections from the raw bar for two. Entrées range from fish and chips and wood-grilled salmon with tropical fruit salsa to grilled chicken paillard with lemon-caper vinaigrette and ribeye cowboy steak with house-made tamarind sauce. Finish with berry shortcake, a delectable tropical coconut banana split or a tasting of three versions of crème brûlée.

(603) 422-7322 or (866) 240-6313. Fax (603) 422-7329. www.wentworth.com. One hundred forty-three rooms and eighteen suites. Doubles, $279 to $459. Suites, $369 to $519.

Dining room, entrées, $26 to $36. Lunch daily, 11 to 2:30. Dinner nightly, 5 to 10:30. Latitudes, entrées $21 to $32. Serving daily in season, 11 to 10.

Lodging

Martin Hill Inn, 404 Islington St., Portsmouth 03801.

The first B&B in Portsmouth and still the pace-setter, this has been cosseting guests since 1978, lately under the caring eye of Margot Doering. Leaving a career in corporate lending, she purchased the inn from founders Jane and Paul Harnden in 2004 to fulfill her love of cooking and meeting people.

Her guests enjoy the fruits of her cooking at breakfast around the gleaming mahogany table in the antiques-filled dining room, whose walls display coordinated

Wentworth by the Sea hotel looms behind Little Harbor Marina at water's edge.

English wallpapers and paints. Orange juice and a fruit course like baked pears topped with honey-vanilla cream cheese are preliminaries. Margot alternates sweet and savory dishes each morning, so ginger pancakes with homemade applesauce might be followed by a southwest omelet with biscuits accented with cayenne pepper. The coffee flows as guests discuss culinary topics and trade restaurant suggestions with Margot, who knows her stuff.

Her hospitality is apparent in the rooms and suites, which are spread across the handsome yellow main house dating to 1815 and in an adjacent guest house of 1850 vintage to the side and rear. To encourage guests to mingle, she converted the downstairs front room to mixed use: a guest room in summer and a parlor with game tables in winter. She continued to shun television anywhere in the B&B, seeking instead to create a quiet spot for "relaxation and old-fashioned inter-action."

Although the inn lacks a common room in summer, guests have plenty of room to spread out in three spacious guest rooms in the main house, plus a room and three suites in the adjacent guest house. Besides the Library/Parlor on the main floor, the upstairs Master Bedroom is formal in white and wedgwood blue, with a plush curtained and canopied queensize poster bed, a large English mahogany armoire, and oriental rugs on the wide-board floors.

The Greenhouse Suite in the spiffy side guest house contains a small solarium furnished in wicker looking onto the outdoor courtyard, rattan furniture in an inside sitting room and a queensize bedroom with full bath. Balloon curtains frame the windows in the second-floor Green Room, which has a small sitting room, an antique tub with a hand-held shower, and a queensize iron and brass bed. All rooms have modern baths, loveseats or comfortable chairs, good reading lamps, writing desks, armoires, and nice touches like assorted hard candies in china teacups and the inn's own wildflower glycerin soaps.

Guests find a shady oasis for relaxation in the deep back yard, where 400 plants thrive and a water garden with a gurgling fountain is illuminated at night. The yard, surrounded by cedar fencing, was featured one year on the Unitarian Church's annual pocket garden tour.

(603) 436-2287. www.martinhillinn.com. Four rooms and three suites with private baths. Doubles, $130 to $200 mid-June through October, $105 to $145 rest of year.

Stately white Georgian Colonial is now The Governor's House B&B.

The Governor's House, 32 Miller Ave., Portsmouth 0380l.

Artistry and amenities blend nicely in this stately 1917 white Georgian Colonial that was the former home of a governor and reopened as a B&B in 2002 under owners Bob Chaffee and Barbara Trimble.

The artistry is evident in the framed doilies made years ago by Barbara's grandmother in Czechoslovakia and displayed suavely on the living room walls. It continues in the "carpet" hand-painted on the floor of the side sun porch, and especially in the murals hand-painted on the tiles of the guest bathrooms.

The amenities include Bose radios and TV/DVD players in the guest rooms, luxurious bedding, evening wine and cheese, personalized breakfasts and an outdoor hot tub. There's even a backyard tennis court that's lighted for play at night. The Prescott is the largest and fanciest of the spacious second-floor guest rooms, each with an antique queensize bed dressed in Frette linens and down comforter. A life-size mermaid on the shower wall carries out the nautical theme in the Captain's Room. Around the double whirlpool tub in the Prescott Room are lovebirds with phrases for affection written in French. A butler painted on the wall of the shower in the Governor's Room is "at the governor's service."

A fifth guest room with a king bed and a trundle bed was created in 2005 when the innkeepers moved from the attic into a new carriage house in the rear.

Breakfast is delivered at the time and place of the guests' choosing from a check-off menu placed in each guest room. It offers a selection of fruit, homemade yogurt, muffins or croissants, cereal, and perhaps a four-cheese or spinach quiche.

In season, the breakfast setting of choice is the leafy patio, enveloped by rhododendrons overlooking the tennis court in the hidden back yard.

(603) 431-6546 or (866) 427-5140. Fax (603) 427-5145. www.governors-house.com. Five rooms with private baths. Doubles, $195 to $245 May-October, $165 to $215 rest of year.

Sise Inn, 40 Court St., Portsmouth 03801.

The Queen Anne mansion built in 1881 for ship merchant John E. Sise has been remodeled with great taste and expanded with a large rear addition that blends in very well. Enter the front door past the stained-glass windows on either side, gaze at the rich and abundant butternut and oak throughout, marvel at the graceful staircase and three-story-high foyer, peek into the sumptuous living room and you're apt to say, as its marketing director did upon first seeing it, "this is the real Portsmouth" – albeit Victorian, rather than the Colonial period one usually associates with the town.

Originally opened by a Canadian-based hotel group called Someplace(s) Different Ltd., it has been run lately by owners Diane and David Hodun. Rooms and suites on three floors and in a carriage house vary in bed configuration, size and decor. All are elegantly furnished in antiques and period reproductions with striking window treatments and vivid wallpapers. Geared to the business traveler, they have queen or twin beds, vanities outside the bathrooms (the larger of which contain whirlpool baths), writing desks, clock radios, telephones, and remote-control television and VCRs, often hidden in armoires. Some have sitting areas. Businessmen must like to watch TV in bed, for in many of the rooms we saw the TV wasn't visible from the chairs or, as is so often the case, the single chair. Windows that open, English herbal toiletries and mints on the pillow may compensate for the occasional lack of places to sit.

Or you can sit in the stylish main-floor living room, very much like an English library with several conversation areas and fresh flowers all around.

A help-yourself breakfast of fruits, juices, yogurt, cheese, cereals, granola, bagels, toasting breads and all kinds of preserves and honey is available amidst much ornate wood in the dining room. Cookies and beverages are offered in the afternoon.

(603) 433-1200. Fax (603) 431-0200. www.siseinn.com. Twenty-three rooms and eleven suites with private baths. Mid-May through October: doubles $189, suites $229 to $269. Rest of year: doubles $129, suites $159 to $199.

Portsmouth Harbor Inn & Spa, 6 Water St., Kittery, Me. 03904.

Just across the Piscataqua River in Kittery is this small establishment with a glimpse of the downtown Portsmouth waterfront, which is within walking distance across the Memorial Bridge.

The 1889 Italianate New England structure has been gradually transformed from a two-family house. Nat Bowditch, who served seventeen years as deputy director of the Maine office of tourism, and his wife Lynn took over the B&B section earlier known as the Gundalow Inn and the day spa added by their predecessors in the attached barn in 2004.

The Bowditchs continue to offer numerous spa services and packages as in the recent past, but their priorities lie with the B&B. "We're both foodies and are into good, healthful eating," says Lynn. "And Nat is a fabulous cook."

Guests enjoy tollhouse cookies fresh from the oven with lemonade or cider in the afternoon, and sip complimentary port and sherry in the evening. Lynn says they go well with "the world's best chocolates" she recommends that guests pick up from the Cacao Chocolates shop across the green.

Dreams are sweet in the five upstairs guest rooms, four of which yield glimpses of the waterfront. All are named after gundalows (a corruption of the word gondolas), the 250-year-old flat-bottom boats with sails that plied the Piscataqua and are believed to have transported the bricks for the house downriver from Dover.

Ten-foot-high ceilings and Victorian period antiques are the rule in the second-floor rooms, one of which has a kingsize bed and windows on three sides. A curved stairway leads past a plant-filled shelf beneath a skylight to the third floor, where two guest rooms with deep clawfoot soaking tubs afford good views of the river and of Portsmouth. We're partial to the Royal George, which has a kingsize sleigh bed, two wicker chairs and a table beneath a skylight, an armoire, gray carpeting and cheery yellow walls. Room amenities include TV/VCRs, hair dryers and bottled water.

Breakfast is served at a table for ten in a large, comfortable parlor. It begins with a New England fruit course, prepared like everything else to enhance flavors and textures. The main course could be what Nat calls "vacation eggs," baked in muffin cups with "a little of this and a little of that" and strips of bacon peeking out. His specialty is blueberry-pecan french toast with pecans he toasts himself.

Nat works off the calories during his morning run with the dog. Guests relax on a small front porch furnished in wicker or on a courtyard terrace with a gurgling fountain between the B&B and the spa building.

(207) 439-4040. Fax (207) 438-9286. www.innatportsmouth.com. Five rooms with private baths. Doubles, $145 to $210 May-October, $110 to $145 rest of year.

Gourmet Treats

Portsmouth's historic downtown continues to thrive, increasingly so with the profusion of upscale shops, art galleries, crafts shops and restaurants.

People with an interest in things culinary are drawn to **Attrezzi** at 78 Market St., two-story emporium of fine kitchen accessories and dishware. Upstairs you'll find a good selection of Italian specialty foods, wines and cheeses. An in-house chef offers cooking classes and food tastings in its state-of-the-art demonstration kitchen.

Wearing a T-shirt urging "squeeze me, crush me, make me wine," jovial proprietor David Campbell brings a sense of fun along with expertise to his wines, specialty foods and gift baskets at the **Ceres Street Wine Merchants.** His is the oldest and largest private wine store in a state defined by state-run liquor stores. Eldon Collymore features artisan cheeses along with wines at **Corks & Curds,** his new shop at 13 Commercial Alley.

The **Stonewall Kitchen** company store at 10 Pleasant St. sells the nationally recognized line of specialty foods that got their start in Portsmouth.

Breaking New Grounds features an enormous variety of coffees and teas, here or to blend at home, in its prime location at 14 Market Square. You can get pastries to go with, but no longer the fabulous café fare of Café Brioche that occupied the space for so many years. For more substantial fare, check out **Currents Mediterranean Bistro** at 23 Market St. and **Isis on Penhallow,** 106 Penhallow St. The latter's specialty is brunch, served daily from 8:30 to 2:30. The owner also runs **The Stockpot** at 53 Bow St., where the specialty soups are augmented by lunch and dinner fare with a harbor view.

Across the river in Kittery Foreside is a must-stop for chocolate lovers. Former lawyer Susan Tuveson opened **Cacao Chocolates** in a little house at 64 Government St. and lured a receptive clientele who dote on her truffles and caramels. In a couple of small kitchens she and sidekick Greta Evans make chocolate delicacies in 70 flavors – always something new and usually in unlikely combinations. They include teas, chiles, cheeses – "anything that catches our imagination," says Susan, who offers samples that ensure sales. Her snug salesroom is simple and unprepossessing. The truffles we tried (the szechuan black pepper and the chèvre with cognac) were first-rate. The shop is open Tuesday-Friday noon to 5 and Saturday 10 to 4.

Tables are set for gourmet breakfast on riverside porch at Bufflehead Cove Inn.

Southern Maine

Sophistication by the Sea

It wasn't so long ago that proper Bostonians thought fine dining ended at Portsmouth and the New Hampshire-Maine state line.

The Southern Maine coast was known for lobster shacks and seafood roadhouses. About the only restaurant of note was the Whistling Oyster in Ogunquit.

How times have changed. Such popular and sophisticated summer resort areas as Ogunquit and Kennebunkport have spawned countless new restaurants and inns. Most of the better establishments today did not even exist two decades ago. A restaurant supplier said that in one boom year in the late 20th century, twelve major restaurants had popped up along the Maine coast since the previous summer.

The region's focus of culinary interest is Portland (see next chapter), which offers more quality and variety in dining and food attractions than cities many times its size.

But the treats begin almost at the Maine border, where the headquarters and company store of the rapidly expanding Stonewall Kitchen specialty-foods business greets visitors at a prime location next to the York information center just off the exit ramp from the Maine Turnpike.

The other centers of culinary interest are in York-Ogunquit and Kennebunkport, two of the better-known summer colonies along the coast south of Portland. Ogunquit's famed Whistling Oyster closed, but worthy successors have emerged. And former President George H.W. Bush and his summer neighbors in Kennebunkport no longer have to go to Ogunquit for a fine meal – they have plenty of good restaurants of their own.

Dining

The Best of the Best

Arrows, Berwick Road, Ogunquit.

Two chefs who apprenticed with Jeremiah Tower at Stars in San Francisco came east to take over this restaurant in a rural area just west of the Maine Turnpike. With great attention to detail, Clark Frasier and Mark Gaier painstakingly crafted a chic and uniquely personal destination restaurant that offers some of the most exciting food in Maine.

Their setting is hard to beat: a 1765 Colonial farmhouse that imparts a vision of pastoral paradise. Through leaded panes reminiscent of the Mission style, patrons in the spacious rear dining room look out onto fabulous gardens. On the entry table, flowers and branches of berries rise to the ceiling from a bowl flanked by produce spilling out of baskets. The dark wood ceiling, wide-plank floors, handsome service plates, crisp white linens, fresh flowers, and cherry and walnut chairs with upholstered seats are as pretty as a picture.

The affable owners' insistence on purity and perfection goes to extremes (which warranted their nomination by the James Beard Foundation as best chefs of the Northeast in 2005). Their full-time staff of 35 includes two gardeners who tend a showplace acre of vegetables and herbs, presenting a detailed list of what exotica is available each day to the chef. Raised beds and cold-frame covers allow them to produce lettuces for salads from April to early December, and their garden-to-table freshness is manifest in every delicious bite – especially on the nightly six-course tasting menu ($95) called "a dinner from the garden." The owners replaced every piece of glassware with fine crystal, the better for connoisseurs to enjoy the most extensive wine cellar in Maine, which includes twenty by the glass, many by the half bottle and an impressive selection of rare Bordeaux from the 1960s.

Surrounded by fields and flowers (spotlit from above and below) as well as trees and bushes bedecked in lights, up to 70 diners a night feast on the view of jaunty black-eyed susans and a sea of zinnias as well as some of Maine's most sophisticated fare. Formally clad waiters in black and white take orders without making notes, quite a feat since the contemporary American menu with Pacific Rim overtones changes nightly.

For starters, how about the three types of oysters in three different presentations, two with a mini-bloody mary, two with horseradish fondant and two with champagne mignonette? Roasted giant bacon lardons might come with a gratin of jumbo sea scallops, spring peas with tarragon and a red wine mousseline sauce. Or a roulade of foie gras might be teamed with poached pears and a vidalia onion confit. We liked the tea-smoked quail with a garlic-ginger vinaigrette and red chile mayonnaise (the description cannot do justice to its complexity) and one of the evening's three salads, a trio of Japanese delicacies: zucchini with soy, carrot with sweet peanut dressing and mushroom with green onion. Each was a visual as well as a gustatory work of art, as was each dish to come.

Among the six entrée choices, you might find sautéed Maine cod with white truffle pasta, a spinach-crème fraîche sauce and foie gras mousse, or a duo of grilled Maine lobster tail on a lemongrass skewer with crispy shallots, lime leaf-cilantro vinaigrette and coconut "jello", and lobster in lemon-curry beurre blanc with house-

Garrett Scholes Photo

Clark Frasier and Mark Gaier gather bounty for 'dinner from the garden' at Arrows.

made rice noodles, roasted yams, basil and mint. The tea-smoked duck breast and ginger confit duck leg with garlic greens, jasmine rice and a scallion and Chinese black bean sauce was a masterpiece. The only dish we weren't wild about was the grilled tenderloin of beef, which we thought had too intense a smoky taste. The accompaniment of fire-roasted red onion, grilled radicchio, green and yellow beans, tarragon mayonnaise and the best thread-thin crispy french fries ever more than compensated.

A dessert of pineapple, peach-plum and mango sorbets, each atop a meringue and each with its own distinctive sauce, was a triumph. But we'd return anytime for any of the pastry chef's offerings, say the citrus panna cotta with berries and cinnamon shortbread, the lemon curd tart with mango, rhubarb gelato and strawberry "jerky," and the amaretto and sour cherry semifreddo with chocolate genoise, orange syrup and chocolate sauce.

At meal's end, chef-owners Clark and Mark like to table-hop and chat about food with their customers. Clark, who studied cooking in China, hails from California. Mark trained with Madeleine Kamman and was executive chef at the late Whistling Oyster in Perkins Cove. Mark is usually in the kitchen here or at their new MC Perkins Cove bistro (see below) and Clark is out front, although they sometimes trade places so each can keep tabs on what's going on. And they take advantage of their winter break to travel, research food ideas and rejuvenate. "Instead of burning ourselves out," says Clark, "we come back re-energized and ready to go again. After twenty years, we're still excited." So are their fans.

(207) 361-1100. www.arrowsrestaurant.com. Entrées, $39.95 to $44.95. Dinner, Tuesday-Sunday 6 to 10 in July and August, Wednesday-Sunday in June and September to mid-October, Friday-Sunday in April, May and mid-October to early December. Closed Dec. 8 to April.

98 Provence, 262 Shore Road, Ogunquit.

Team a local restaurateur and his French-Canadian wife with her talented brother as chef. The result is this winner, a true place seemingly transplanted from the countryside of France to the hubbub of Ogunquit.

Country-French dining room at 98 Provence.

Johanna Gignach had run a small French restaurant in Old Montreal during the Olympics before being wooed to Ogunquit to marry Paul Haseltine, known to everyone at Barnacle Billy's Etc. restaurant as "Hez." It seems her brother, Pierre Gignach, was too young then to be a chef, but after training at Chez la Mère Michel, one of our favorite Montreal restaurants, and working in Winnipeg, he was ready. The Haseltines fashioned a country-pretty dining room and living room/lounge from the old 98 Shore Road breakfast eatery, added a new kitchen and bar, and awaited the arrival of Pierre with his visa.

Chef and visa arrived in the nick of time for the 1996 summer season, and they've been going strong ever since.

Pierre excels with the classic dishes of Provence, perhaps roasted black sea bass with potato and fennel gratin, roasted monkfish on ratatouille or filet of beef au poivre with Corsican cheese and caramelized fennel. One night's menu ran the gamut from pan-seared St. Peter fish with a pistachio-butter sauce to roasted veal rib chop with a chanterelle fricassee in juniper cream sauce. He might offer a Toulousian cassoulet with duck confit, lamb, bacon and apple-pork sausage and serve a venison stew with chestnuts and quinces on swiss chard gnocchis.

Francophiles are in heaven with the starters, perhaps lobster and celery bisque, a rillette of rock crab with parmesan wafers, frog's legs meunière, fricassee of escargots, and boneless quail with black figs on a potato nest. Desserts are prepared in the French style. Savor fondant au chocolat, profiteroles, strawberry bavarois or a pear and prune crisp with mascarpone ice cream.

Ocean is on view from refurbished dining rooms at MC Perkins Cove.

A three-course table d'hôte menu with several choices for each course represents good value for $46.

The dining room with its café curtains, barnwood walls decked out with plates, and its colorful floral tablecloths and service plates will charm you into thinking you're in the South of France. The food will convince you.

(207) 646-9898. www.98provence.com. Entrées, $24 to $32. Dinner nightly except Tuesday, 5:30 to 9. Closed Monday-Wednesday in off-season and December-March.

MC Perkins Cove, Oarwood Lane, Perkins Cove, Ogunquit.

Seventeen years after vaulting their rural Arrows into the rarefied realm of top 50 American restaurants, Mark Gaier and Clark Frasier moved into the thick of the Ogunquit scene. Taking over the building formerly housing Hurricane, they built an addition and added an upstairs bar/lounge beside the ocean in 2005. Their American bistro "has taken the simple to the sublime," gushed Bon Appétit magazine.

The two-story restaurant is a beauty of black chairs, faux copper tables and polished wood floors. Soaring windows onto the ocean provide the "decor." Mark Gaier generally is on hand to oversee the kitchen, which focuses on seafood and a handful of steaks. Sample the shellfish tower or the peekytoe crab parfait from the oyster bar. Or start with gingered cockles steamed in beer, deep-fried local oysters in beer batter, an artichoke stuffed with house-cured prosciutto, a pizza with chorizo and three cheeses, Clark's Beijing pork jaozi or one of the four hefty garden salads.

"Maines" range from deep-fried "drunken chicken" marinated with orange, ginger and star anise to hanger steak. Grilled yellowfin tuna, sesame-crusted rainbow trout and plank-roasted salmon are typical. Your choice of sauces and "evil carbos" such as Mark's Mom's corn custard come with. "Virtuous vegetables" like creamed spinach or roasted red beets are extra.

Most of the appetizers, additional salads and burgers, a lobster roll and a Maine cod sandwich are offered at lunch. The dessert repertoire includes a banana split, a cookie sundae, strawberry-blueberry shortcake and vanilla bean crème brûlée.

(207) 646-6263. www.mcperkinscove.com. Entrées, $21 to $29. Lunch daily, 11 to 2. Dinner nightly, 5 to 11.

Joshua's, 1637 Post Road (U.S. Route 1), Wells.

This acclaimed newcomer is a dream come true for Joshua Mather. He grew up on the family's organic farm, learned to cook at his mother's side and before his first job at a deli/restaurant in Wells, he drew a picture of the restaurant he someday wanted to own. That day came in 2004 when, after wowing patrons at the trendy Five-O in Ogunquit, at the tender age of 29 he turned a 1774 house sidling up to U.S. Route 1 into a big-hit restaurant.

It's also a dream come true for area residents. They turn out en masse to Joshua's comfortable fine-dining restaurant that features farm-fresh organic food made from scratch. Most know the Mather family – his mother Barbara, who manages the three small dining rooms with brick fireplaces and a cozy bar, and his father Mort, the restaurant's farmer, who helps out at night after tending the gardens from which they made a living selling vegetables, organic meats and baked goods to restaurants from Ogunquit to Portland.

The locals like that the self-taught chef cooks in the down-home style, without pretense or architectural presentation. He bakes his own breads, simmers the stocks and soup bases, makes the desserts and ice cream and, of course, uses the ingredients with which he is familiar. "We're farmers," Josh says. "Food should speak for itself, which is why I pay so much attention to purveyors, because I don't want to have to do a lot to what comes through the door. And when it's from our farm, I never have to worry."

His fare is never boring. Dinner might start with "sliders," a trio of small tastes served on a bird's-eye maple cutting board. The slider can be anything from crostini to an endive leaf to a homemade potato chip, topped with a bit of grilled lamb with chutney, an oyster or thin-sliced scallop, or a small brochette of beef or fish.

For appetizers, he might sauté tiger shrimp with tomato, roasted jalapeño and garlic or brush chunks of lamb with mustard and coriander on a skewer of rosemary stems that infuse them with flavor on the grill. The most exotic item is likely to be his foie gras torchon, served with truffle beet salad, wheat toasts and mustard mousse.

Among the eight entrées (always including a vegetarian choice) are two stalwarts. His most popular dish is Atlantic haddock in a caramelized onion crust accented with chive oil, served with a wild mushroom risotto. The other is filet mignon, sauced with a burgundy reduction and served with mashed potatoes. Others could be grilled duck breast and leg with port wine sauce, roast pork tenderloin with sherry mushroom ragoût and rack of lamb marinated in roasted garlic.

Portions are ample and include fresh bread and vegetable of the day. Few can resist the Mather family's renowned desserts, among them fudge pie with vanilla ice cream, maple-walnut pie with maple ice cream, fruit cobbler or – one of more recent vintage – vanilla crème brûlée.

All convey Joshua's motto, "fresh food, simply prepared." And wicked good, too.

(207) 646-3355. www.joshuas.biz. Entrées, $19 to $28. Dinner, Monday-Saturday 5 to 10.

Grissini Italian Bistro, 27 Western Ave., Kennebunkport.

Spirited Tuscan cooking with a New England accent emanates from this casual

Beamed ceiling and fieldstone fireplace contribute to Adirondack lodge look at Grissini.

but elegant bistro owned by Laurie Bongiorno of the high-end White Barn Inn. It's a stunning space, with vaulted beamed ceilings three stories high and a tall fieldstone fireplace – looking straight out of the Maine woods – that fits right in. Sponged pale yellow walls, large tables spaced well apart, comfortable lacquered wicker armchairs, and fancy bottles and sculptures backlit in the windows create a thoroughly sophisticated feeling. On warm nights, crowds spill onto a tiered outdoor courtyard that rather resembles a grotto.

Opera music played in the background as a plate of tasty little crostini, some with pesto and black olives and some with gorgonzola cheese and tomato, arrived to start our dinner. We liked the bread, prepared in the in-house bakery and served in slabs unexpectedly plunked – in most un-White Barn-like fashion – smack onto the table, with the server pouring an exorbitant amount of olive oil into a bowl for dipping. Everything else came on enormous white plates, except for the wine (in beautiful stemmed glasses) and the ice water (in pilsener glasses).

Among antipasti, we loved the wood-grilled local venison sausage on a warm caramelized onion salad and the house-cured Maine salmon carpaccio with olive oil, herbs and lemon juice and topped with pasta salad. Secondi range from pan-seared lobster tail with olive oil, smashed potato and herbs to osso buco. The wood-grilled leg of lamb steak with Tuscan white beans, pancetta, garlic and rosemary was sensational. A sampler plate of tiramisu, a chocolate delicacy and strawberries in balsamic vinegar with mascarpone cheese wound up a memorable dinner.

(207) 967-2211. www.restaurantgrissini.com. Entrées, $20.95 to $26.95. Dinner nightly, 5:30 to 9 or 9:30.

Pier 77, 77 Pier Road, Cape Porpoise, Kennebunkport.

This is the trendy successor to our favorite Seascapes restaurant, the latest incarnation of a landmark building that's been a restaurant at the edge of Cape Porpoise Harbor for more than 70 years.

Chef-owner Peter Morency renovated the place to reflect his New England roots and wife Kate's sense of San Francisco laid-back flair. "Contemporary American fine dining without attitude" is their hallmark. That and an unbeatable view of the harbor through floor-to-ceiling windows on two sides, with a stylish, less-is-more decor that capitalizes on the outdoor scene. The harbor waters lap at the door of the walkout lower-level **Ramp Bar & Grill,** where you can drink at outdoor tables or order from an appealing grill menu amid sports memorabilia inside.

We sampled the creative kitchen's fare at an autumn lunch. The clam chowder, though tasty, contained far more potatoes than clams. The roasted chicken taquito with guacamole and salsa fresca was delicious, and the star of the show was succulent fish and chips, paired with superior coleslaw. Desserts were pumpkin cheesecake with caramel sauce and warm banana cake with milk chocolate ganache.

At night, the chef shines with the likes of seafood stew, roasted halibut with orange-mussel butter, smoked pork tenderloin with sundried cherry and port wine reduction, seafood mixed grill, and sirloin steak with red wine demi-glace and maytag blue cheese. We'd gladly make a meal of the hangtown fry: pan-fried oysters, pancetta and a boiled egg over mixed greens.

Downstairs, the Ramp offers a predictable mix of clam chowder, crab cakes, fish and chips, fish tacos, fried clams and lobster roll along with the unexpected, North Carolina-style pulled pig barbecue sandwich with tidewater slaw.

(207)967-8500. www.pier77restaurant.com. Entrées, $19 to $30. Lunch daily June-September, 11:30 to 2:30. Dinner nightly, 5 to 10. Ramp menu, $6 to $14, open 11:30 to 10. Both closed Tuesday in off-season and January-February.

Hurricane Restaurant, 29 Dock Square, Kennebunkport.

The old family-style seafood restaurant that inspired owner Brooks MacDonald to think about the restaurant business is now Hurricane, offshoot of the Ogunquit trend-setter that closed in 2004 after fourteen years. In place of the soda fountain where he hung out as a teenager is a hand-crafted mahogany bar serving 60 wines by the glass in a Colonial-look tavern area. Beyond is a 90-seat dining room set on pilings over the Kennebunk River. Windows on two sides yield water views beneath a wraparound mural of billowy white clouds and blue sky to brighten any otherwise gloomy day.

The contemporary American menu is categorized by soups and salads and small plates that change seasonally, and lunch and dinner entrées posted daily. You could make a good lunch or supper of lobster gazpacho ("so hot it's cool") or lobster chowder (the house specialty), caesar salad with lobster, the Maine lobster cobb salad, or the lobster and shrimp tempura with raspberry-ginger sauce.

We liked the gloppy five-onion soup crusted with gruyère cheese and the Thai beef salad with greens, soba noodles and a peanut sauce so spicy it brought tears to the eyes. At the other end of the taste spectrum was a soothing sandwich of surprisingly delicate grilled crabmeat and havarti cheese on butter-grilled sourdough bread. Big eaters at the next table praised desserts of apple-walnut-cinnamon bread pudding and lemon-blackberry purse with ginger anglaise.

Come back at night to try the lobster cioppino or perhaps rare tuna with sweet chili-ginger sauce, roasted halibut with a rum-caramelized beet puree, arctic char with almond brown butter or the grilled veal chop with wild mushrooms. A bento box of shrimp, scallop and salmon lumpia, Maine lobster rangoon, vegetable nori rolls and marinated beef with a wakame salad is a specialty appetizer to be shared. The pastry chef's desserts could be chocolate-grand marnier crème brûlée or a liquid-center chocolate cake with homemade coffee ice cream and Bailey's anglaise.

(207) 967-9111. www.hurricanerestaurant.com. Entrées, $19 to $39. Lunch daily, 11:30 to 3. Dinner nightly, 5:30 to 10:30 in summer, to 9:30 rest of year. Closed January to mid-February.

On the Marsh, 46 Western Ave. (Route 9), Lower Village, Kennebunk.

The soaring, barn-like interior of the former Salt Marsh Tavern is chicly elegant, thanks to owner Denise Rubin, an interior designer who bought the converted barn and farmhouse restaurant and set about redecorating the place.

Now she offers diners "a feast for the eyes as well as the palate," changing the decor with the seasons. Tables on two floors are flanked by fancy padded chairs that the owner designed and are draped to the floor in white over raspberry cloths – officially "raspberry sorbet," her favorite color. All the artworks on the walls, most of the antiques adorning the lofts, and even the chairs and the silverware are for sale. Large rear windows look onto a salt marsh stretching toward Kennebunk Beach.

With an eye for the dramatic, the owner and her chefs categorize their menu by "prologue" and "performance." Warm up with crunchy tiger shrimp and leeks with a sundried tomato-saffron aioli, a foie gras torchon with dried cherries, or lobster ravioli with leeks and peas. Typical main courses are grilled swordfish with fennel and orange relish, oven-roasted halibut with herb butter, muscovy duck breast and confit, and seared filet mignon with béarnaise sauce.

Desserts might be a trio of crème brûlées, dark chocolate pâté with rum crème anglaise and, the owner's favorite, blueberry-raspberry sorbet with Belgian chocolate spears.

For a different experience, you might gather at the owner's table to sample executive chef Peter Dwyer's tasting menu. There's also a chef's table for two to four in the kitchen, where guests get an inside look at the culinary goings-on.

(207) 967-2299. www.onthemarsh.com. Entrées, $24.95 to $31.50. Dinner nightly, from 5:30. Closed Monday and Tuesday in off-season and month of January.

Stripers, 127 Ocean Ave., Kennebunkport.

This stylish newcomer began life as Stripers Fish Shack and dropped the "fish shack" from its name when it relocated in 2004 from an outbuilding behind the former Schooners Inn to the main waterfront dining room of the Breakwater Inn. It's now Stripers, "a waterfront restaurant and raw bar."

And how. Here is ubiquitous White Barn Inn owner Laurence Bongiorno's shrine to seafood, still something of a "fish shack" in terms of food concept but as stylish as all get-out in its new digs at the rear of the inn. Call it a fish shack nonpareil, this stunning place seating 110 diners in well-spaced comfort amid floor-to-ceiling windows onto the water and blue chairs slip-covered to the floor in Ritz-like fashion. A mini-aquarium harboring a tropical fish inside is atop each table, mirroring the giant aquarium at the entry. So is a stash of appropriate sauces for what amounts to the original fish shack fare.

The menu is short and deceptively straightforward, given the kitchen's creativity, and eons removed in delivery from the clam shack and fish fry idiom. Look for the day's catch (swordfish, Atlantic salmon, halibut, shrimp), available chargrilled, broiled or pan seared and served – as are most entrées – with rice pilaf or fries and what the menu calls "mushy" peas, a mix of crushed and whole peas in a rich buttery and creamy mash. Also look for lobster, bouillabaisse and blackboard specials, perhaps pan-seared scallops with lobster-cognac sauce or yellowfin tuna with provençal sauce.

Perhaps the best fish and chips you ever ate comes in the form of ale-battered haddock with fries, garnished with wedges of lemon and lime. Other favorites are the seafood platter – an array of oysters, shrimp, clams, mussels and cracked lobster – and the occasional bento box. One night's box yielded seared scallops, gravlax, shrimp and panko-fried oysters with seaweed salad. Seafood-oriented soups, stews, salads and appetizers are offered to begin. The only "fishless options" are grilled chicken, filet mignon and rack of lamb. Desserts include peanut butter pie, apple crumble and vanilla bean crème brûlée.

Just off the porch is a spacious raw bar with seating for dining and cocktails.

(207) 967-3625. Entrées, $18.95 to $32.50. Dinner nightly, 5 to 9:30. Sunday brunch, 10:30 to 2. Closed late October to May.

Bandaloop, 2 Dock Square, Kennebunkport.

This lively new restaurant overlooking Dock Square is a favorite with the late-night crowd, but it also earns plaudits for its assertive contemporary cuisine at down-to-earth prices.

Chef-owner Scott Lee, who came to town to open On the Marsh, moved on to his own place in 2004. He named it for the fictional tribe that claimed to know the secret to eternal life, which he celebrates here with good food and wine – make that healthful food, for he serves organic, natural and local products whenever possible. You don't often see tofu skewers or three-grain organic tempeh on a menu hereabouts. He offers those and more, pairing half a dozen entrée selections with an equal number of sauces, all vegan or vegetarian.

You could order pan-seared haddock, pork medallions or grilled ribeye steak and pair them with miso-lime-tamari broth, ginger-blood orange glaze or blackberry-merlot sauce – whatever turns you on. If those don't appeal, try the night's specials, perhaps pan-blackened escolar with red pepper coulis, grilled yellowfin tuna with sweet mango-Chinese mustard glaze or free-range Australian lamb loin medallions with an ouzo and roasted garlic sauce.

Start with a Vermont cheddar quesadilla, an avocado timbale, steamed mussels or egg rolls. Finish with the signature deep-dish brownie or the blueberry and apple crisp, flourless and vegan "unless we add vanilla ice cream."

The bar swings with live music some evenings.

(207) 967-4994. www.bandaloop.biz. Entrées, $18 to $23. Dinner nightly from 5:30. Closed Tuesday in off-season.

Dining and Lodging

White Barn Inn, Beach Street, Box 560C, Kennebunkport 04046.

Long known for its restaurant, the White Barn has been vastly upgraded in terms of accommodations as well. Such has been the infusion of money and T.L.C. by the hands-on Australian-born owner, personable Laurie Bongiorno, that the inn was

Floral backdrop outside window changes seasonally in dining room at White Barn Inn.

only the second in New England to be accepted into the prestigious Relais & Châteaux, the world-wide association of deluxe owner-operated hotels.

Its restaurant was the first to be accorded five stars for all three categories of food, service and atmosphere by the Maine Sunday Telegram. In 1993, the restaurant earned the AAA's first five-diamond dining rating in New England outside Boston. In 1999, the restaurant won the highest ranking of any resort restaurant worldwide in the annual Condé Nast Traveler Best of the Best awards. In 2002, Travel & Leisure weighed in, ranking the White Barn among the top five hotel restaurants in North America. In 2006, the late-coming Mobil Guide came aboard, awarding a fifth star to make it one of its top 15 restaurants in the United States.

And yes, it's really *that* good.

Dinner is served in a three-story barn attached to the inn, where you can look out through soaring windows onto an incredible backdrop that changes with the seasons – lush impatiens in summer, assorted mums in fall, and spruce trees dressed with velvet bows and tiny white lights for Christmas. Up to 120 diners can be seated at tables spaced blessedly well apart in the main barn and in an adjoining barn. They're filled with understated antiques and oil paintings dating to the 18th century, and the loft holds quite a collection of wildlife wood carvings. The tables are set with silver, Schottowelzel crystal and Villeroy & Boch china, white linens and white tapers in crystal candlesticks. A pianist plays most evenings in the entry near the gleaming copper-topped bar.

The food is in the vanguard of contemporary New England cuisine with a European flair. Dinner is prix-fixe ($89 for four courses), with at least half a dozen choices for most courses. The complex menu changes weekly. It's executed by a kitchen staff of sixteen and served with precision by a young waitstaff who meet with executive chef Jonathan Cartwright beforehand for 45 minutes each night. Guests at each table are served simultaneously, one waiter per plate.

Our latest dinner began with a glass of Perrier-Jouët extra brut (complimentary for house guests) and the chef's "welcome amenity," an herbed goat cheese rosette, an onion tart and a tapenade of eggplant and kalamata olives. Interesting olive bread and plain white and poppyseed rolls followed. We'd gladly have tried any of the appetizers, but settled on a lobster spring roll with daikon radish and snow peas in a Thai-inspired spicy sweet sauce, and the seared Hudson Valley foie gras on an apple and celeriac tart with a calvados sauce. Both were exceptional.

Champagne sorbet in a pool of Piper Heidsieck extra-dry cleared the palate with a flourish for the main courses, of which a recent entry – "grilled cutlet of lamb and medallion of farm-raised veal filet on oregano-scented garden tomatoes with a parcel of forest mushroom risotto and chardonnay jus" – might be considered typical.

One of us settled for a duo of Maine rabbit, a grilled loin with roasted rosemary and pommery mustard and a braised leg in cabernet sauvignon, accompanied by wild mushrooms and pesto-accented risotto. The other chose pan-seared tenderloin of beef topped with a horseradish gratin and port-glazed shallots on a pool of potato and Vermont cheddar cheese, with a side of asparagus. A bottle of Firestone cabernet accompanied from an excellent wine list especially strong on American chardonnays and cabernets.

Dessert was anything but anti-climactic: a classic coeur à la crème with tropical fruits and sugared shortbread and a trio of pear, raspberry and mango sorbets, served artistically on a black plate with colored swirls matching the sorbets. A tray of petits fours came with the bill. Following an after-dinner brandy in the inn's living room, the little raisin cookies we found on the bed back in our room were – almost – superfluous.

The 29 guest accommodations in the main inn, outbuildings and cottages vary considerably, as their range in prices indicates. A renovated cottage beside the elegant pool area is the ultimate in plush privacy with a living room, porch, kingsize bedroom, double-sided fireplace and double jacuzzi. Almost its equal is a loft suite, adjacent to the main inn with king bed, fireplace and oversize marble bath with whirlpool and separate steam shower. A private deck overlooks the inn's grounds.

The six fireplaced suites in the refurbished May's Annex also are the height of luxury. Each has a library-style sitting area with chintz-covered furniture, wood-burning fireplace, dressing room, spacious bathroom with a marble jacuzzi and separate shower, Queen Anne kingsize four-poster bed, secretary desk and a flat-screen TV. We felt quite pampered in the Green Room here, thanks to a personal note of welcome from the innkeeper, fresh fruit, Poland Spring water, terry robes and Gilchrist & Soames toiletries. Four large renovated rooms in the Garden House also claim fireplaces and jacuzzis, as well as cathedral ceilings, queensize sleigh beds and sitting areas with wing chairs.

Rooms upstairs in the inn, although nicely furnished and cheerfully decorated with whimsical hand-painted furniture and trompe-l'oeil accents, could not possibly be as spacious or sumptuous. Except, that is, for a junior suite, which incorporated two older rooms. It's appointed in rich damask fabrics and boasts an elaborate marble bath with whirlpool, separate steam shower and matching Victorian-style porcelain sinks with hand-painted cabinets.

The newest accommodations are four cottage units fashioned from fish shanties beside the Kennebunk River. They are furnished more like cabins in Arts & Crafts style, each with a snug queen bedroom, kitchenette, living room with fireplace and TV/VCR.

A lavish continental breakfast is served in the elegant Colonial dining room. Fresh orange juice and slices of cut-up fruits are brought to your table by a tuxedoed waiter. You help yourself to assorted cereals, yogurts and an array of muffins and pastries the likes of which we've seldom seen before – including a sensational strawberry-bran muffin with a top the size of a grapefruit and a cool crème d'amandes with a sliced peach inside. Hot entrées are available for a surcharge.

Lunch is available for house guests daily in summer, served al fresco beside the pool.

In the last few years, owner Bongiorno has acquired four nearby waterfront properties and turned them into acclaimed lodges and inns: The Yachtsman Lodge & Marina, The Beach House Inn, the Breakwater Inn and the Schooners Inn, now called the Breakwater Hotel.

(207) 967-2321. Fax (207) 967-1100. www.whitebarninn.com. Sixteen rooms, eight suites and five cottages with private baths. Doubles, $290 to $565. Suites and cottages, $580 to $820.

Prix-fixe, $89. Dinner by reservation, Monday-Thursday 6 to 9:30, Friday-Sunday 5:30 to 9:30. Closed two weeks in mid-January. Jackets required.

Cape Arundel Inn, Ocean Avenue, Kennebunkport 04046.

A choice location facing the open ocean and an excellent dining room commend this Shingle-style inn that represents the essence of Maine.

Veteran restaurateur Jack Nahil, who formerly owned the White Barn Inn and later the Salt Marsh Tavern, now devotes his artistic and culinary talents to his latest acquisition, the Cape Arundel. He added larger beds and in-room telephones in the seven upstairs rooms, created more windows for what he rightly bills as "bold ocean views" and completely refurnished the 1950s motel units to convey a country inn motif. He also refurbished the inn's living room, through which diners pass to get to the restaurant. An artist and avid gardener, he has maintained the appropriately simple grandeur without adding the glitz so common today.

Dining here is better than ever, thanks to the assured Nahil touch. Executive chef Rich Lemoine, who has been with him since White Barn days, presents exotic contemporary fare. Add the romance of dining at a window table, watching wispy clouds turn to mauve and violet as the sun sets, followed by a full golden moon rising over the darkened ocean. For gourmands who like their food with a view, it's a dream come true.

The 60-seat, two-level dining room itself is a study in white and cobalt blue. An arty display of cobalt glass is on a shelf above a painting of cobalt glass.

Our latest dinner began with remarkably good crusty basil-parmesan-rosemary bread. Appetizers were a composed spinach salad with prosciutto and oyster

Lobster sculpture is arty centerpiece for table at Cape Arundel Inn.

mushrooms and an exemplary chilled sampler of ginger-poached shrimp, a Maine crab-filled spring roll and tea-smoked sirloin with wasabi-citrus rémoulade, each artfully presented and interspersed with colorful slaw.

Oversize dinner plates speckled with herbs yielded a superior sliced leg of lamb teamed with cavatelli pasta and wilted arugula, and a mixed grill of duck sausage, veal london broil and loin lamb chop. Other choices ranged from macadamia nut-crusted halibut over rainbow chard with cabernet aioli to a duo of duck: grilled breast marinated in grand marnier and confit with raspberry-orange demi-glace.

The dessert of cinnamon ice cream with strawberries over ladyfingers was enough for two to share. A Blackstone merlot from California accompanied from a small but unusually interesting wine list.

Happily, we had only to adjourn to our room in Rockbound, the former motel section. Each room here has a full bath and TV, plus a small balcony with a front-on view of the ocean beyond the wild roses. Our end room was spiffily furnished in florals and reproduction furniture. A queen bed with a sturdy white wood headboard crafted by a local artisan was angled from the corner.

At an earlier visit, we enjoyed Room 4 on the far-front corner of the main inn, where white organdy curtains fluttered in the breeze. From two chairs in the corner we could take in the bird's-eye panorama of the ocean and the George Bush family compound at Walker Point.

A rear carriage house has a second-floor suite called Ocean Bluff, with a queen bed, a gas fireplace and panoramic views.

The inn's spacious front porch is a super place to curl up with a good book or the morning newspaper before breakfast. Breakfast is a hearty continental buffet. Ours began with fresh orange juice, cereal, muesli, fruit and yogurt, and superior scones and croissants. The highlight was the day's extra: toasted basil-parmesan bread and a small spanakopita, prepared by the chef's wife and "presented" in the dinner style on an oversize plate.

(207) 967-2125. Fax (207) 967-1199. www.capearundelinn.com. Thirteen rooms and one suite with private baths. Doubles, $285 to $365 mid-June to mid-October, $125 to $345 rest of year. Closed January and February.

Entrées, $25 to $36. Dinner, Monday-Saturday 5:30 to 8:30 or 9. Closed January to mid-April.

Lodging

Hartwell House, 312 Shore Road, Box 1937, Ogunquit 03907.

The British flag flies alongside the American in front of this sophisticated B&B on the main road between the center of Ogunquit and Perkins Cove. Owners Jim and Trisha Hartwell have an English background, which explains their extensive use of English antiques in the thirteen guest rooms and three suites, and the lush lawns and sculpted gardens out back, which provide the profusion of flowers inside.

The enclosed front porch is a lovely space with arched windows, colorful French chintz on the loungers and wicker chairs, and an array of plants and flowers. Here is where guests gather for an afternoon pick-me-up of iced tea, poured from a glass pitcher topped with strawberries and orange slices on a silver tray. Everything except the wood floor in the stunning living room is white.

The formal dining room has one long table, willowware china and a silver service on the sideboard. Hooked rugs dot the wide-board floors.

A full breakfast of fresh fruit and a hot dish, perhaps stuffed crêpes, frittatas, baked chicken in puff pastry or belgian waffles, is served here or on the enclosed porch.

Most of the nine rooms in the main house have french doors onto terraces or private balconies looking over the rear yard. Across the street in an addition to the house where the innkeepers reside are seven more luxurious rooms and suites. The latter include a living room, dining area, kitchen with refrigerator and wet bar and a balcony or terrace. Trisha's favorite is the James Monroe Suite, a two-level affair all in white.

In 2005, the inn assumed ownership of a coffeehouse/café in the Thompson Green Plaza across the street. Renamed the **S.W. Swan Bistro** and under separate management, the stylish 36-seat American bistro is open daily for breakfast and nightly except Wednesday for dinner.

(207) 646-7210 or (800) 235-8883. Fax (207) 646-6032. www.hartwellhouseinn.com. Eleven rooms, three suites and two studio apartments with private baths. Doubles, $160 to $245 in summer, $140 to $195 in spring and fall, $120 to $175 November-April.

Bufflehead Cove Inn, Gornitz Lane, Box 499, Kennebunkport 04046.

Past a lily pond at the end of a long dirt road is this hidden treasure: a gray shingled, Dutch Colonial manse right beside a scenic bend of the Kennebunk River. Owners Harriet and Jim Gott have turned their family home since 1973 into a stunning B&B – the kind of waterfront home we've always dreamed of.

The public rooms, the setting and the warmth of the welcome are special here. A wide porch faces the tidal river and downtown Kennbunkport in the distance; there are porches along the side and a huge wraparound deck in back. A large and comfy living room contains window seats with views of the water. The dining room, which is shaped like the back of a ship, has a dark beamed ceiling, paneling, stenciling and a carpet painted on the floor. There are a dock with boats, and five acres of tranquility with which to surround oneself.

All bedrooms are bright and cheerful. The spacious Balcony Room is perhaps the most compelling of those in the main house. It offers a wicker-filled screened balcony overlooking the river, a kingsize bed dressed with a plump floral comforter, a fireplace, a window seat and a chaise lounge. Its large bathroom has a shower, refrigerator/wet bar and, most spectacular, a corner jacuzzi for two, positioned dramatically beneath hand-painted pots of apple blossoms stretching overhead.

Reflections of sun on the river shimmer on the ceiling of the River Room, which has a queen bed and a balcony. The walls and ceilings are hand-painted with vines in the Cove Suite, two rooms with lots of wicker and a gas fireplace.

Although it lacks a river view, the Garden Room in back is ever-so-engaging with its own entrance and patio, a wicker sitting area, gas fireplace, a handcrafted queensize bed and grapevine stenciling that echoes the real vines outside the entry.

We enjoyed the secluded Hideaway, fashioned from the Gotts' former quarters in the adjacent cottage. Mostly windows, it holds a kingsize bed, a tiled fireplace open to both the bedroom and the living room, rattan chairs, and an enormous bathroom with a double jacuzzi surrounded by a tiled border of fish. Pears seem to be a decorative theme, showing up on the fireplace tiles and at the base of a huge twig wreath over the mantel. Outside is a private deck where early-morning coffee was provided and we would gladly have spent the day, had we not been working.

The latest treat is the deluxe River Cottage with cathedral-ceilinged living room/bedroom, fireplace, small kitchen, a loft with a library and entertainment center, and a soaring palladian window onto the water.

Breakfast at 8:30 on the inn's front porch brought fresh orange juice and an elaborate dish of melon bearing mixed fruit and homemade pineapple sorbet. The main event was a delicious zucchini crescent pie, teamed with an English muffin topped with cheddar, tomato and bacon, and roasted potatoes with onions and salsa. Lobster quiche, soufflés, asparagus strata, green apple-stuffed french toast, waffles and popovers are other specialties. Jim often cooks breakfast when he's not out on his rounds as a lobster fisherman.

Wine and cheese are served in the early evening. Decanters of sherry and bottles of sparkling water are in each room.

(207) 967-3879. www.buffleheadcove.com. Three rooms, one suite and two cottages with private baths. June-October: doubles $175 to $315, suite and cottages $210 to $375. Off-season: doubles $115 to $245, suites $175 to $325. Closed December-April.

The Captain Lord Mansion, Pleasant Street, Box 800, Kennebunkport 04046.

This beautifully restored 1812 mansion – one of the finest examples of Federal architecture in the country – boasts an octagonal cupola, a suspended elliptical staircase, blown-glass windows, trompe-l'oeil hand-painted doors, an eighteen-foot bay window and a hand-pulled working elevator. Not to mention park-like grounds that create a bucolic oasis in the heart of Kennebunkport, or a gas fireplace in every guest room – a feature for which the pace-setting B&B is widely known.

Chocolates are placed every evening in the bedrooms, which are elegantly furnished in antiques, most with four-poster or canopied beds. Six have new

Fireplace warms Lincoln Bedroom at Captain Lord Mansion.

whirlpool tubs, and two more have deep clawfoot soaking tubs. A number have minibars.

The prime quarters seem to change with every upgrade, of which peerless innkeepers Rick Litchfield and his wife Bev Davis never seem to tire. Lately they redid all four guest rooms in their annex called Phoebe's Fantasy, installing a whirlpool tub in a main-floor suite and endowing the rest with the latest bells and whistles. Guests here take breakfast at a seven-foot harvest table in a gathering room with a chintz sofa, fireplace and television.

Earlier, they made remarkable enhancements in the main building, particularly in terms of bath facilities. The first-floor Merchant Room was expanded into a deluxe suite with king canopy bed, two fireplaces, and a bathroom with heated marble floor, a ten-jet hydro-massage waterfall shower, double jacuzzi, bidet and three vanities. The Dana, Mary Lord and Excelsior rooms on the second floor gained renovated baths with heated Italian tiled floors and double whirlpool tubs. The Champion added a mini-bar and a large bath with twin vanities and double whirlpool tub. The Lincoln gained a king bed and a bath with heated marble floor, marble shower and oversize antique vanity. The third-floor Mousam became a two-room suite with queen canopy bed and a new bath with a heated black granite floor and double-headed shower for two.

The corner rooms are especially spacious and airy. All rooms have period reproduction wallpaper and nice touches like sewing kits, Poland Spring water, and a tray with wine glasses and a corkscrew.

Guests gather beneath crystal chandeliers in the richly furnished parlor for herbal tea or Swedish glögg, or beside the fire in the Gathering/Dining Room. Downstairs in what was once the mansion's summer kitchen is another common room with a fireplace.

A three-course breakfast for guests in the main inn is served family-style at large tables in the big, cheery kitchen. The meal begins with fresh fruit, French vanilla yogurt and whole-grain muesli cereal. Next come a variety of homemade muffins. The main course could be baked egg casserole, vegetable quiche, cheese strata, cinnamon french toast or belgian waffles. Bev's zucchini bread is renowned, as are some of the hors d'oeuvre she prepares for wine gatherings for guests during holiday celebrations.

(207) 967-3141 or (800) 522-3141. Fax (207) 967-3172. www.captainlord.com. Eighteen rooms and two suites with private baths. June-October and weekends through December: doubles $248 to $389, suites $259 to $499. Rest of year: doubles $133 to $339, suites $133 to $389.

Old Fort Inn, Old Fort Avenue, Box M, Kennebunkport 04046

This well-established B&B with an inviting swimming pool and a tennis court is a quiet retreat on fifteen acres of immaculately maintained grounds and woodlands, away from the tourist hubbub, but within walking distance of the ocean. At night, the silence is deafening, says David Aldrich, innkeeper with his wife Sheila.

The couple cosset guests in fourteen large and luxurious rooms in a stone and brick carriage house, plus two suites upstairs in the main lodge. They are furnished with style and such nice touches as velvet wing chairs, stenciling on the walls and handmade wreaths over the beds. "My wife agonizes over every intricate detail," says David. "I call her Ms. Mix and Match." Her decorating flair shows; even the towels are color-coordinated. In the hall, her framed shadow boxes containing Victorian outfits are conversation pieces.

Each air-conditioned room has a phone, TV and deluxe wet bar with microwave, since this is a place where people tend to stay for some time. In the most deluxe rooms, of which there seem to be more at every visit, the TV may be hidden in a handsome chest of drawers, the kingsize four-poster beds are topped with fishnet canopies, and the baths are outfitted with jacuzzis, Neutrogena amenities and heated tile floors.

Besides the pool, the gathering spot of choice is the main lodge in a converted barn. At the entry is the reception area and Sheila's antiques shop. Beyond is a large rustic room with enormous beams, weathered pine walls and a massive brick fireplace, the perfect setting for some of her antiques.

It's also where the Aldriches set out their buffet breakfast. Guests pick up wicker trays with calico linings, help themselves to bowls of gorgeous fresh fruits and platters of pastries, and sit around the lodge or outside on the sun-dappled deck beside the pool. Sheila bakes the sweet breads (blueberry, zucchini, banana, oatmeal and pumpkin are some). The croissants are David's forte and there are sticky buns on Sundays. The Aldriches added granola and yogurt to the spread, and quickly found they were going through twenty pounds of granola a week. Quiche or waffles are the latest additions to the daily fare.

A plate of chocolate chip cookies greets guests at check-in. Chocolates are at bedside at night.

(207) 967-5353 or (800) 828-3678. Fax (207) 967-4547. www.oldfortinn.com. Fourteen rooms and two suites with private baths. Doubles, $160 to $375 mid-June to late October, $99 to $295 rest of year. Closed mid-December to mid-April.

The Inn at Harbor Head, 41 Pier Road, Kennebunkport 04046.

The tranquil setting of this rambling shingled home on a rocky knoll right above the picturesque Cape Porpoise harbor is an attraction at this small B&B.

Another is the artistry inside the house. The four guest quarters, each with king or queensize canopy bed, are decorated with hand-painted murals. The entrance to the main-floor Garden Room is paved with stones and a little fountain, and original drawings of peach and plum blossoms float on the wall. The Greenery in which we stayed has a mural of fir trees by the shore, a bathroom with hand-painted tiles and jacuzzi tub, and a view of the front gardens. Painted clouds drift across the ceiling of the Summer Suite, which offers the best view of the harbor from its balcony. It also has a gas fireplace and a cathedral-ceilinged bathroom with skylight, bidet and jacuzzi tub.

Breakfast is another attraction. From the country kitchen of innkeepers Eve and Dick Roesler come such dishes as bananas foster, pears poached with lemon and vanilla and topped with raspberry sauce, or broiled grapefruit with kirsch and brown sugar. The "Maine" course could be zucchini frittata, honey-pecan french toast, crabmeat and bacon quiche, or wild Maine blueberry pancakes with warm maple syrup. Homemade lemon-poppyseed or cranberry muffins might accompany. The meal is served at 9 a.m. in the dining room at a long table where there is much camaraderie.

Afterward, you may have neither the energy nor the will to leave the premises. Enjoy the colorful gardens beyond the rear terrace or relax on the lawn sloping to the shore, where you can swim from the floats or loll in an oversize rope hammock, watching the lobster boats go by.

(207) 967-5564. Fax (207) 967-1294. www.harborhead.com. Three rooms and one suite with private baths. Mid-June to mid-October: doubles $195 to $270, suite $325. Rest of year: doubles $160 to $245, suite $245 to $275. Closed November-April.

The Captain Fairfield Inn, 8 Pleasant St., Kennebunkport 04046.

This circa-1813 Federal sea captain's mansion, listed on the National Register and overlooking the River Green, has been nicely enhanced by recent owners. The latest are Leigh and Rob Blood, who learned the trade by managing the Sherburne Inn in Nantucket before buying this and becoming resident innkeepers. They come by their roles naturally, both having taught, coached and lived in student residences at a New England preparatory school.

Here, their maturing B&B's nine air-conditioned guest quarters have new full baths, mostly queensize beds dressed with designer linens and lots of pillows, and comfortable sitting areas furnished to the period . Six have fireplaces. The Bloods added flat-panel TV/DVDs and portable CD players along with wireless Internet access to the guest rooms.

The prized main-floor Library room has a fishnet canopy queen bed, a bath with double whirlpool tub and separate shower, a gas fireplace and its own porch with two rocking chairs. A first-floor corner room has become the Polly Lord Suite with a step-up kingsize poster bed and a small sitting room in what had been a little-used dressing area. The Bloods added oriental rugs and hung artworks in the public areas, already notable for beautiful woodwork and molding and fresh flowers. The formal living room is elegant yet comfortable. Tea and cookies are offered here in the afternoon.

Breakfast, a highlight here, is served in a cheerful dining room. The four-course repast might begin with a fruit smoothie, poached pears or apple "soup," and blueberry muffins, cranberry-orange scones or cream cheese biscuits. The main course at our autumn visit was a choice of a tomato and chive omelet or cinnamon french toast with maple-pecan glaze. Planned the next day were apple-cinnamon pancakes and the Fairfield omelet incorporating spinach, cheddar cheese and sweet Italian sausage. Rob and Leigh alternate cooking and serving duties, but no matter who is in the kitchen, Sunday always yields a choice of eggs benedict and wild blueberry crêpes.

Some guests say they don't need to eat again until dinner.

(207) 967-4454 or (800) 322-1928. Fax (207) 967-8537. www.captainfairfieldinn.com. Eight rooms and one suite with private baths. Doubles, $150 to $325 late June to late October, $120 to $250 rest of year.

Gourmet Treats

Their Wooden Goose Inn was one of the fanciest, most gourmet-oriented B&Bs ever. But owners Tony Sienicki and Jerry Rippetoe traded innkeeping life for retail, running **TJ's at the Sign of the Goose,** 1287 Route 1, Cape Neddick. Former guests will immediately detect their sense of style in furnishings and accessories for home and garden. Like their B&B, it's the kind of stuff of which design-magazine editors' dreams are made; not the least of which are the magnificent crystal candelabra collected over the years by Jerry and the incredible decorative birdhouses (some resembling high-rise hotels) made by Tony and scattered about the gardens.

In Ogunquit, several places of culinary interest distract passersby from the traffic travails at the life-threatening main intersection in the center of town. No doubt contributing at least to the pedestrian traffic are the side-by-side **Latest Scoop** for ice cream, **Native Grounds** for coffee, **Fancy That** for baked goods and sandwiches, and the **Village Market.** Across the intersection is the **Flaming Gourmet,** offering specialty foods for the gourmet cook. **Amoré Breakfast** is just the ticket for those into exotic coffees and creative food, so good that owner Leanne Cusimano could sustain a breakfast-only operation and gave up lunch service when she moved to 178 Shore Road. There are thirteen kinds of omelets and seven benedicts, including lobster. Bananas foster french toast is the house specialty. For provisions, head for **Perkins & Perkins,** purveyors of fine foods, wines and gifts at 478 Route 1 north. Its outdoor **Vine Café** offers cheese plates, appetizers and light entrées starting at 4 p.m. daily in season.

A must stop for baked goods is **Borealis Breads,** supplier to many a restaurant, with a retail outlet and bakery at 1165 Route 1 in Wells. More than twenty varieties of crusty artisan loaves are baked daily, including French peasant, cranberry-apple (with which we make fabulous french toast) and savory herb. Scones and sandwiches also are available.

In Kennebunkport, **Keys to the Kitchen** out Port Road (Route 35) in the Lower Village is well worth a visit. Owner Dodie Phillips has an unusual flair for displays. The cookbook area is distinctive, and upstairs around an open atrium we found some pretty and summery placemats that now grace our patio table at home. At **Stonehouse Port & Cheese,** Shawn O'Neil stocks wines, cheeses, pâtés and hard-to-find sauces and condiments.

Incredibly gourmet is the **Market Day,** just beyond at 135 Port Road (Route 35).

Racks of olive oils, specialty foods, cookbooks, wines, cheeses and fresh produce vie for attention. Among the takeout food offerings are sandwiches in the $6 range.

Out of town in Cape Porpoise, the market of choice is **Bradbury Brothers,** with the usual, plus essentials for summer residents like bread from When Pigs Fly in York, Greek olive pesto and local jams.

The high-end, dark beers are particularly good, we're told, at the **Kennebunkport Brewing Co.** at the Shipyard Shops, 8 Western Ave., facing the river in the Lower Village. You can tour the main-floor brewery and sample the beers upstairs at its **Federal Jack's Brew Pub,** where lunch and dinner are available daily at sturdy wood communal tables in a big room beside the water. On the ground floor is **KBC Coffee & Gift Shop,** billed as a European-style coffee shop with a section selling gourmet foods.

Gourmet Success

Stonewall Kitchen Company Store, Stonewall Lane, York, Me.

The jams and condiments in the elegant jars taking over specialty-food stores across the nation are made and sold here in a sparkling new facility off Route 1, conveniently located at the end of the York exit ramp from I-95, adjacent to the York visitor center. Jonathan King and Jim Stott, who met as waiters at leading restaurants in Portsmouth, N.H., started selling homemade jams and vinegars at the Portsmouth farmers' market in 1991 for extra spending money. One customer bought out their entire inventory for her store, and therein began a phenomenon that quickly projected them into Dean & DeLuca, Williams-Sonoma and 6,000 stores nationwide. Now with several hundred products and nearly as many employees, they are the talk of the gourmet food industry. They became the first company to win the Outstanding Product Line award at the International Fancy Food and Confection Show in Philadelphia two years in a row. Their ginger-peach tea jam was named the outstanding new product of the year, followed a year later by a maple-chipotle grill sauce and lately the roasted garlic and onion jam. "We love to create new products," says Jonathan, who loves to cook and first gave his jams to his family as Christmas presents. "Some people think in words or in pictures, but I think in terms of tastes." Those tastes have led to all kinds of jams (how about lemon-pear marmalade?), oils, vinegars, mustards, coffees, crackers, dessert toppings, relishes, salsas and more. They sell here for $3 to $20 – with countless samples available for tasting – and appeal to the high-end market. A new line, inspired by their children, is called "Kids Like Good Food, Too." Stonewall Kitchen has since opened company stores in Portsmouth, Portland, Camden, North Conway, Newton, Mass., and Avon and South Windsor, Conn. *The Stonewall Kitchen Cookbook* was published in 2001, and another book was on the way.

The latest additions to the York Company Store are a large home, garden and bath shop and the suave **Stonewall Kitchen Café** with indoor and outdoor terrace seating. Enjoying coffee from the espresso bar and a quick take-out lunch from the display cases, we viewed the inspired menu overseen by executive chef Sara Littlefield and vowed to return for a proper sit-down lunch in the bistro.

(207) 351-2712 or (800) 207-5267. www.stonewallkitchen.com. Store open Monday-Saturday 8 to 7, Sunday 9 to 6. 10 to 5 or 6.

Café, (207) 351-2719. Lunch Monday-Saturday 11 to 3, Sunday brunch 10 to 3. Takeout, Monday-Saturday 8 to 6, Sunday 9 to 6.

Portland, Me.

Bounty by the Bay

Perhaps no other Northeastern state has such close associations with indigenous foods as Maine. Think Maine lobsters. Maine crabs. Maine blueberries. Think fiddlehead ferns. Smoked mussels. Smoked salmon.

As a coastal area where such bounty is found in abundance, it's no surprise that Maine inspired good restaurants earlier and in greater numbers than other northern New England states. And, when some found they couldn't survive year-round in the seasonal tourist areas, their owners converged on Portland, the state's largest and most sophisticated city and a seaport facing Casco Bay.

"There's no other place in Maine with a year-round food audience," says top chef Sam Hayward, who opened one of Maine's first great restaurants in Brunswick in 1981. It lasted ten years, as did David Grant's pioneering Aubergine, Maine's first nouvelle cuisine restaurant launched in Camden in 1979. But after a decade, both knew they had to move to Portland for economic reasons. This is where the customers are, they explained.

Other top chefs gravitated from outlying areas to the city, and lately chefs have arrived from out-of-state food centers. Now Portland claims the nation's densest concentration of restaurants per capita after San Francisco. It ranks third in per-capita restaurant spending after New York and San Francisco. Its food scene has garnered national attention in the New York Times, Bon Appétit and Travel & Leisure.

Although Commercial and Congress streets boast more enduring restaurants (Boone's dates to 1898 and The Roma Café to 1924), the heart of the food area is the restored Old Port area between downtown and the waterfront. A single block of quaint Wharf Street harbors nearly a dozen restaurants. Not one but two restaurant rows have blossomed at either end of Middle Street.

Not only does Portland (population, 65,000) have more good and more varied restaurants than cities several times its size, it also has "strong regionalists" as proclaimed by Rob Evans of Hugo's. He eschews the ubiquitous Chilean sea bass, for instance, in favor of Casco Bay cod or diver scallops from local purveyors, all of whom he credits on the menu. Other chefs do likewise, helping support what may be the largest and most varied food-producing industry in New England.

Nowhere is the import of food in Portland more evident than in the privately funded Portland Public Market, a model of its genre. Two dozen purveyors of Maine-raised meats and produce as well as regional fishmongers and bakers meet a receptive clientele in the block-long downtown food hall.

Portland also is home to specialty food stores, kitchen shops and wine stores that rank with the best anywhere.

The culinary treats are affordable, approachable and seemingly endless here.

Dining

The Best of the Best

Fore Street, 288 Fore St., Portland.

Two of Maine's best-known restaurateurs, Sam Hayward and Dana Street, joined to open this hot-ticket establishment that gained well-deserved recognition when it

Cooks prep for dinner in open kitchen facing tables on two sides at Fore Street.

was ranked sixteenth – tops in New England – in Gourmet magazine's list of the nation's best restaurants.

The restaurant is as low profile as the name. And the menu is understated, too, but be assured, there's more here than meets the eye.

Start with the exterior, a garage-like brick low-rise at the edge of the historic Old Port area. It still looks like the tank storage warehouse it served as during World War II. Inside is a soaring space with brick walls, tall windows, and assorted booths and tables on two levels, all overlooking a big and busy open kitchen. Indeed, this kitchen is so open that it forms a large portion of the restaurant. With tables set around the perimeter, the dozen cooks manning the applewood-fired grill, rotisserie and oven are actors nightly for dinner theater-in-the-round. There's a small cocktail lounge with a waiting area in front.

"Refined peasant food" is how Sam, the operative chef, describes the fare. We first sampled his product at the late 22 Lincoln, his early Brunswick restaurant, which was ahead of the times. He then took a prime post as executive chef at the Harraseeket Inn in Freeport. He moved here for a simpler operation, one that he could call partly his own. The emphasis, as at his former venues, is on Maine ingredients and produce. The exotica and complexities of his past performances are understated here, as they always have been at his partner's Street and Co. seafood restaurant in the Old Port (see below).

The menu, printed nightly, offers about a dozen main courses at prices that make penny-pinching Bostonians swoon. They're categorized as pan seared (marinated Cape Cod bluefish, Atlantic skatewing fillet). Or turnspit roasted (dry-rubbed natural Quebec pork loin or farm-raised rabbit). Or applewood grilled (dayboat Grand Banks swordfish loin, breast of Quebec duckling, natural angus hanger steak). Or wood-oven roasted and simmered (Maine lobster or wild coho salmon fillet, whole Casco Bay mackerel, fishermen's stew). That's it – no highfalutin language, just a few surprises like an autumn mixed grill of lamb sirloin, game sausage, duck confit and farm-raised elk liver, teamed with a chestnut-garlic mash and wild Maine chanterelles.

We could make a meal of appetizers: perhaps a platter of seasonal salads that resembles an antipasto plate, roasted jumbo oyster mushrooms, wood oven-roasted raft-cultured Bang's Island mussels in garlic-almond butter, grilled Vermont quail, or Quebec duck foie gras with Maine elderberries and toasted brioche. Plus perhaps a wood-oven pizza of roasted eggplant and oven-dried tomatoes, an oven-roasted tomato tart with herbed goat cheese mousse, or Fore Street's ultimate "BLT" layering lobster, apple-smoked bacon, sliced tomato, bibb lettuce and basil aioli on toasted country bread.

No wonder the place is so popular that we couldn't get a reservation on a Thursday night. Fellow inn guests who did snag a table, both high-living Californians, were mighty impressed with the gutsy food and style. So are innkeeper friends who trek often from Connecticut to Portland, mainly to eat at Fore Street, and have never been disappointed.

We'll try again, if only for the desserts, no fewer than fourteen to-die-for choices like pear pain perdu, white chocolate-espresso napoleon, wild huckleberry tart, and a trio of passionfruit, blackberry and peach sorbets. How about a selection of cheeses? Or perhaps an assortment of handmade chocolates for two?

The wine list is short but select, and reflects Sam's award-winning expertise.

Although some find Fore Street rushed and noisy, no one doubts the success of its kitchen theatrics. Simple is best, they say. Reserve a ringside seat and enjoy the show.

(207) 775-2717. Entrées, $17 to $30. Dinner nightly, from 5:30.

Hugo's, 88 Middle St., Portland.

New owners took over Hugo's Portland Bistro, shortened the name, upgraded the decor and refined the menu. Another destination restaurant was the happy result for Rob Evans, who was cited among Food & Wine magazine's best new chefs of 2004, and his partner, Nancy Pugh.

A self-taught chef, the Massachusetts native had been chef for five years at Goose Cove Lodge in Down East Maine before leaving to perfect his trade in two of the nation's best-known kitchens, the Inn at Little Washington in Virginia and the French Laundry in California's Napa Valley. He returned east, met up with the former owner of Hugo's, and found the place serendipitous for a restaurant of his own.

Nicely spaced tables dressed with white linens are the setting for some of the best – and certainly the most complex – food in town. The dinner menu is basically prix-fixe, $60, with four choices for each of four courses. "We believe that several smaller courses, offering many flavors, are essential for a complete dining experience," the menu says. A set seven-course tasting menu for $85 is available for the entire table. Or you can choose your own tastes from eight to ten of the night's treats on an à-la-carte bar menu for $9 to $12.

The chef, who produces original, cutting-edge cuisine in a small kitchen with only four cooks, is known for his wizardry with Maine-grown potatoes – in fact, one of his monthly nine-course wine dinners was called, "Rob's Potato Dégustation." A sample turned up as a first course on one autumn menu, Maine corolla potato blinis with citrus-cured salmon and tarragon crème fraîche. Others ranged from shaved corned beef tongue salad with a quail egg and mustard mousse to chilled lobster cannelloni with saffron emulsion.

Stylish dining room is setting for innovative fare at Hugo's.

Second-course options might be Atlantic fluke en croûte, honey mead-glazed pork belly, pan-fried veal sweetbreads and ravioli, and a Scottish salmon taster combining a flash-fried cake, rare seared belly and smoked roe with fingerling potatoes and shaved fennel salad.

The progression gets more exotic and difficult to pronounce. His third course might offer a New England "seafood platter:" parchment-baked hake, lobster pierogi, peekytoe crab and littleneck clams, served with savoy cabbage, fried fingerling potatoes and deconstructed tartar sauce.

Another choice could be potato-wrapped beef ribeye steak with tomato-tripe crépinette, oxtail marmalade and "multiple onion preparations." Or "duck three times" – sous vide breast, braised leg and stuffed cabbage – served with a balsamic poached pear, rutabaga, salted pumpkin seed brittle and long pepper jus.

Desserts follow suit. One could be "just peachy" (roasted, fresh, compote and sorbet, with three sauces). Others include salt-cured foie gras brûlée with figs and buttermilk bread pudding, Spanish mita cana cheesecake with Maine blueberries, and El Rey dark chocolate and tonka bean fondant with salted peanut ice cream, caramelized banana and sweet soy.

Tall bistro tables in front near the bar are nifty perches for sampling treats from the bar menu, which also is available throughout the restaurant.

The chef's tasting menu of thirteen courses, booked ahead for $120, is the ultimate adventure in dining here.

(207) 774-8538. www.hugos.net. Prix-fixe, $60. Dinner, Tuesday-Saturday 5:30 to 9 or 9:30.

Back Bay Grill, 65 Portland St., Portland.

A twenty-foot-long mural along one wall attests that this grill has nothing to do with the Back Bay in Boston. Done by local artist Ed Manning Jr., the life-like rendering depicting the restaurant's early days spreads out above the plush leather wall banquettes, documenting its history and characters as a tapestry might in a continental setting and making the intimate 34-seat room appear bigger.

The mural is a focal point of the highly regarded and urbane establishment,

Artist's mural of local scenes and characters enlivens dining room at Back Bay Bistro.

"dean" of Portland's gourmet restaurants at the ripe young age of fifteen or so. The chic interior has high ceilings, track lighting, antique mirrors, modern upholstered chairs and mahogany tables rather close together. Roses and candles are atop the tables in the dining room. On the other side of the restaurant, a new lounge offers a bar menu to appeal to a younger crowd.

The bar area was refurbished after Larry Mathews Jr., who became the executive chef in 1997 when he was 24, purchased the restaurant from founding owner Joel Freund in 2002. Larry, who trained at the White Barn Inn in Kennebunkport and at the Inn at Little Washington in Virginia, now oversees the front of the house as well as the kitchen, where he and his chefs tinker with the menu seasonally.

Start perhaps with chilled cantaloupe soup in summer; parsnip and pancetta soup in winter. Appetizers might be house-cured gravlax, tuna tartare, a Maine crab cake with lime-curry aioli, crisp fried veal sweetbreads with smoked bacon, or endive and mussel salad with curry crème fraîche.

Entrées range from swordfish with sundried tomato-basil vinaigrette and line-caught halibut with chorizo-saffron sauce to grilled free-range chicken with cilantro-sour cream sauce and rack of lamb with foie gras and lingonberry sauce. The duck might be served two ways – a lavender-marinated breast and a confit leg – with Israeli couscous, pesto and leeks.

Typical desserts are an acclaimed crème brûlée, chocolate-banana mousse, and pecan-bourbon tart with caramel ice cream. Rhubarb shortcake with candied rhubarb and rhubarb sorbet in a warm vanilla crème fraîche sauce was a springtime hit.

The award-winning wine list is reasonably priced. Many are available by the glass. Also available are samplers giving a choice of three from the list of single-malt scotches and small-batch bourbons. A short bar menu is offered in the revamped lounge.

(207) 772-8833. www.backbaygrill.com. Entrées, $22 to $33. Dinner, Monday-Saturday 5:30 to 9:30 or 10, also Sunday 5 to 9 in July and August.

Five Fifty-Five, 555 Congress St., Portland.

Some of the most exciting fare in the city is served up by Steve and Michelle

Corey, who returned to New England from California wine country with a couple of stops in top Maine coastal restaurants before taking over the downtown space formerly occupied by the French bistro Aubergine.

Chef Steve calls his fare new American in the California style and adapts it to New England tastes and ingredients. His food concept is innovative, divided into five "plate" subsections, some with whimsical names and offbeat pairings but all tasty and well received.

Dining situation is private on loft at Five Fifty-Five.

Small plates include a dynamite lobster risotto that's sometimes offered as a main course, a carpaccio and reggiano-parmigiano treat called "steak and cheese," and grilled flatbread bearing house-smoked duck confit, Vermont aged cheddar, heirloom apples and organic onions. "Green plates" are salads, among them an enhanced spinach salad named "bacon and egg."

"Savory plates" are main dishes ranging from truffled macaroni and cheese to garlic-marinated hanger steak topped with black pepper and maytag blue cheese butter. The chef might grill organic Irish salmon with watermelon-sweet pepper syrup, pan sear peppercorn-crusted diver scallops and offer pork "every which way" – a star-anise crispy pork belly and pan-seared tenderloin with soft whole-grain mustard dumplings, braised rainbow chard and date-fennel compote. A mixed grill "paella" yields organic chicken, spicy house pork sausage, Bang's Island mussels and smoked paprika-spiked baby octopus with creamy saffron arborio rice.

Ten exotic cheese plates were part of a recent menu. You also could finish with the pastry chef's "sweet plate," perhaps a goat cheese beignet with house-churned sugar plum ice cream or a truffle martini of chocolate-infused vodka.

All this good eating takes place in a converted firehouse that's really quite stunning, with a hip main-floor dining area augmented by loft seating on a wraparound mezzanine. White linens dress the tables, and the brick and taupe walls are hung with mirrored artworks. A copper roof tops the partly open kitchen.

The wine list, categorized by new world and old world, carries a Wine Spectator award.

(207) 761-0555. www.fivefifty-five.com. Entrées, $17.95 to $27.95. Dinner nightly except Tuesday, 5 to 10. Sunday brunch, 10:30 to 2:30.

Street and Co., 33 Wharf St., Portland.

Pure, pure, pure is the feeling of the small, Mediterranean-style "eating establishment" run by Dana Street in the heart of the Old Port. You enter past an open grill/kitchen and face a blackboard menu, both good indicators. Ahead is a small room with bare pegged floors and 40 seats, where strands of herbs and garlic ng on a brick wall. An adjacent space has added twenty more seats as well as a ine bar that doubles as a waiting area. Outside are about two dozen more seats along Wharf Street for summer dining. The tables might turn four times on a busy night, which seems to be the norm.

The freshest of seafood and a purist philosophy draw a steady clientele. Self-taught chef Abbie Harman, who apprenticed under Dana, offers half a dozen varieties of fish that could be grilled, blackened or broiled. Mussels marinara, clams, shrimp and garlic are available over linguini. Other possibilities are scallops in pernod and cream, sole française, grilled lobster with butter and garlic over linguini, and lobster fra diavolo ($34.95 for two). That was it – at our first visit, and at every subsequent visit. Nothing outré or adjectival here. There may be a "whole fish" offering, and a pasta alfredo and primavera. Nary a meat item or even free-range chicken is in sight. Meals come with French bread and fresh vegetables (asparagus, zucchini and red bell peppers at one visit) sautéed in butter and white wine.

Equally straightforward are the appetizers: mussels provençal, steamers, calamari and seasonal salad.

The wine list is affordable, and there are great homemade desserts.

The formula works, so why change?

(207) 775-0887. Entrées, $16.95 to $20.95. Dinner nightly, 5:30 to 9:30 or 10.

Bibo's Madd Apple Café, 23 Forest Ave., Portland.

Some of the best cooking and best values among serious restaurants in town are found at this old favorite. Bill Boutwell, a talented chef whom we first met at Seascapes in Kennebunkport, later put Café Stroudwater at Embassy Suites on Portland's culinary map. From that unlikely location he ventured out on his own with partner Andrea Raymond, turning up at the Madd Apple, where we'd enjoyed many a delectable treat under previous owners.

Here he quickly stamped his imprint on an intimate café that we always felt was under-rated. He added a quirky appellation derived from the opening letters of his first and last names and tweaked the curtain and floral treatments in the prominent front windows, but otherwise retained the colorful, arty surroundings complete with kiva stove, garden fountain and potted plants. He embellished the menu with the latest accents.

Situated next to the Portland Performing Arts Center, the café finds its business driven by the theater, which may explain why we were the only customers for a late lunch one September weekday. It won't be our last, however, given the caliber of the food and the reasonable prices. A shrimp and avocado sandwich on toasted rye bread and a juicy lamb burger arrived on oversize plates. Both knife-and-fork affairs, they were flanked by abundant mesclun salad, roasted potatoes or hand-cut fries and garnishes of what the menu calls garlic-marinated cucumbers and we call pickles. A trio of the day's sorbets – raspberry, apple and orange-cranberry – was served atop squiggles of matching coulis. With tax and tip, the tab came to less than $20.

Although the focus is on straightforward salads and sandwiches at midday, the menu becomes more complex at night. Expect entrées like soy-marinated salmon over sesame-whipped potatoes with seared Chinese cabbage and Thai sweet chili sauce, pork medallions topped with apples and aged cheddar over polenta, braised leg of rabbit with a juniper-infused red wine reduction, and roasted loin of lamb dusted with cornmeal spices and served with a sweet corn broth.

Starters could be grilled coconut-curry sea scallops over a watermelon-tomato kimchee, Maine crab and lobster cakes with tomato-ginger coulis or a rose of smoked salmon stuffed with goat cheese and drizzled with raspberry-horseradish crème fraîche. Desserts follow suit, among them chocolate-macadamia stout pâté ("a.k.a. fudge with an attitude") and chocolate-banana-coconut dumplings with coconut and chocolate sauces. One delight is called "Bibo's crackerjacks" – peanut butter mousse atop a bed of old-fashioned caramel corn garnished with bittersweet chocolate sauce.

Amidst all the fun and culinary sizzle is a choice wine list, almost every bottle pleasantly priced in the teens and twenties.

(207) 774-9698. Entrées, $15.95 to $18.95. Lunch, Wednesday-Friday 11:30 to 2. Dinner, Wednesday-Saturday from 5:30. Sunday, brunch 11 to 3, dinner from 4.

More Dining Choices

Uffa! 190 State St., Portland.

This storefront eatery facing Longfellow Square has been known for creative, healthful fare. It gained inordinate fame when featured in Bon Appétit magazine's 1999 spread on Portland. The Louisiana writer – taken, no doubt, by its rustic wood tables, bare wood floor, funky art and high ceiling – likened it to being transported to New York's East Village.

Window tables in front alcove at Uffa!

It was portrayed as primarily vegetarian, although in the year's interim between research and publication the restaurant had changed hands and the new owners favored California cuisine more than vegetarian. Another owner has since taken over, and enhanced both the cooking style and decor to create what reviewers call one of Portland's premier dining establishments.

Owner-investors Todd and Laura Wauters, who view Uffa! as the flagship of five planned restaurants in the Portland area, partnered here with young chef James Tranchemontagne, a native Mainer who mixes classical French technique with his love for New England/French Canadian comfort food. The former sous chef at Back Bay Grill makes a point of using local organic products.

The new team updated the formerly rather funky decor for what it calls "city dining." Fresh flowers are in the tall front windows and the wainscoted walls are hung with local artworks that appear dwarfed beneath an extra-high ceiling. Windsor-style or slat-back chairs are at bare wood tables with basic place settings.

From a rear kitchen visible up a half flight of stairs comes cuisine that is a mix of haute and simple. The menu changes monthly. Entrées tend toward the high end:

when we were there, grilled swordfish with tangerine glaze, seared Maine trout with a lobster-drambuie cream sauce, pork tenderloin in a garlic demi-glace and petite filet mignon with béarnaise sauce. The night's specials were what the chef considers comfort food: a seafood crêpe, turkey pot pie and duck leg cassoulet, plus a traditional bouillabaisse.

Dinner might start with a pâté or cheese plate, a signature arugula and tomato salad tossed with croutons and garlic dressing or grilled dayboat scallops with a fingerling potato cake and horseradish cream sauce. Finish with desserts prepared by one of a dying breed of all-around chefs, perhaps a moist chocolate gâteau with vanilla mocha ice cream, profiteroles, a classic crème brûlée or homemade ice cream topped with caramelized bananas or grand marnier.

(207) 775-3380. www.uffarestaurant.com. Entrées, $12 to $27. Dinner, Wednesday-Sunday 5 to 9 or 9:30. Sunday brunch, 9 to 1.

Cinque Terre, 36 Wharf St, Portland.

This former ship chandlery was converted into a restaurant by an Italian restaurateur who named it for his family's home region of the Cinque Terre, five remote fishing villages that dot the rocky Ligurian coast along the Italian Riviera. It's a dramatic, 80-seat dining room on two levels with brick walls, high skylit ceilings and a cheery decor of celadon green and sunflower yellow. A grand staircase leads to a mezzanine bordered by a wrought-iron railing, from which diners get a bird's-eye view of the open kitchen.

Head chef Lee Skawinski, former executive chef at the Harraseeket Inn in Freeport, cooked an Italian coastal seafood dinner in 2005 for the James Beard Foundation in New York. He favors refined Italian country fare with local ingredients, including seafood off the boats and produce from new owner Dan Kary's organic farm.

Besides offering an authentic Northern Italian menu, Cinque Terre tries to replicate a truly Italian dining experience. Diners are encouraged to share four or five courses in leisurely fashion, and half portions are available. You might start with beef carpaccio, bruschetta with lobster and tomato or a dish called asparago – roasted asparagus, pancetta and a sunny-side-up egg with shaved parmigiano.

Consider some of the homemade pastas, perhaps crespella alla pansotti, a Ligurian specialty with walnut and sage sauce, or the gnocchi with Ligurian pesto and beans.

Save room to sample main courses such as grilled swordfish with artichokes, roasted cherry tomatoes and arugula; roasted halibut with basil-olive crust and pea shoot salad, and crispy semolina scallops with sautéed local greens. Meat-eaters go for the grilled veal T-bone with truffled cannellini beans and vin cotto and the locally ubiquitous Wolfe's Neck Farm hanger steak with roasted peppernata.

Finish with a typical Italian dessert, such as strawberry and lemon panna cotta with campari sorbetto, ricotta-orange tart with maple-ginger gelato, a biscotti plate or a sampling of four chocolates.

The all-Italian wine list, categorized by region, has been honored by Wine Spectator.

(207) 347-6154. www.cinqueterremaine.com. Entrées, $15 to $24. Dinner nightly, 5:30 to 9:30 or 10.

Natasha's, 82 Exchange St., Portland.

This restaurant started small at the edge of downtown before moving into the thick of the action in 2001 in the heart of the Old Port. Its new home is stylish, from

Eclectic dining room is ready for lunch patrons at Natasha's.

a loft-like dining room off the entry with an exposed brick wall, beamed ceiling and a collection of modern light fixtures and sconces to a main dining room with a blond wood bench wrapping around one wall, facing linoleum-look table tops and tall chairs draped in long brown velvet. In summer, patrons spill out from the bar onto sidewalk tables beside a pocket park.

As orchestrated by Natasha and Steve Durham, it's a sleek and urbane setting – "quite eclectic," volunteered a manager, "just like her food." The food proves equally elusive to categorization. It's a fusion of Asian, American and Italian traditions, here amalgamated as "new world cuisine."

Chef Natasha's menu is full of assertive flavors and pleasant surprises. She gives international twists to local favorites, as in appetizers of Casco Bay mussels roasted in chipotle adobe broth, Maine lump crabmeat with pancetta and a calamari martini with peppered balsamic. Or you might start with the dim sum for two, which changes nightly, vegetable dumplings with ginger-tamari sauce, or tuna carpaccio with fennel and a sieved egg.

The dozen main courses range from grilled organic salmon with riesling emulsion and a shrimp and leek cabbage roll to filet mignon with prosciutto-wrapped scallops, stilton, poached artichoke, whipped potato and morel oil. In between are the likes of shellfish stew, a Peking duck noodle bowl and a very mixed grill – hanger steak or duck breast or organic chicken with a choice of shrimp, crab cake, prosciutto-wrapped scallops or fried oysters.

Desserts include white chocolate-raspberry cheesecake, crème brûlée and double chocolate cake with hazelnut ganache.

In 2004, the Durhams branched out, opening **Mims Brasserie,** a chic French-style bistro serving three meals a day to mixed reviews in the former Portland Bakehouse quarters at 205 Commercial St.

(207) 541-3663. Entrées, $18.50 to $28. Lunch, Tuesday-Saturday 11:30 to 3. Dinner, Tuesday-Saturday 5 to 10.

Walter's Café, 15 Exchange St., Portland.

Noisy and intimate, this "now" kind of place has been packed to the rafters since it was opened by Walter Loeman and Mark Loring. The two have since parted, selling to chef Jeff Buerhaus and his wife Cheryl in 2004. The emphasis on spirited, global-accented food at pleasant prices continues here.

We faced a twenty-minute wait for a weekday lunch in July, but were glad we stayed. A BOLT – bacon, lettuce, tomato and red onion sandwich with sweet cajun mayonnaise – arrived in a pita, served with a pickle and "gnarly" fries. The "chilling pasta salad" yielded a zesty plateful tossed with chicken, avocado and red peppers.

From our table alongside a brick wall in the long and narrow, high-ceilinged room we could see the cooks splashing liberal amounts of wine into the dishes they were preparing in the open kitchen. Green plants backlit on a shelf above the kitchen area provided accents amid the prevailing brick. More seating is available upstairs.

The dinner menu is equally eclectic within the prevailing Italian and Asian theme. Typical starters are a mussel pan roast, lavasch crab rolls, cracklin' calamari, and crispy Asian raviolis stuffed with chicken and lemongrass.

Expect entrées like bacon-wrapped scallops with "dueling sauces" of red chiles and green tomatillos, "griddled haddock" in a dill-horseradish cream sauce, linguini milano with chicken or shrimp, crispy soy-lacquered duck breast and hoisin-marinated skirt steak. The "mixed lobster grille" yields a roasted lobster tail, shrimp and scallops with edamame blini, tempura asparagus and a spiced mango-tamari sauce.

Irish cream cheesecake, orange mousse with wild blueberries, and varied chocolate creations typify the dessert list.

(207) 871-9258. www.walterscafe.com. Entrées, $17 to $24. Lunch, Monday-Saturday 11 to 3. Dinner nightly, 5 to 10.

Ribollita, 41 Middle St., Portland.

Here's a trustworthy small restaurant in the Tuscan style where the menu rarely changes and neither do the prices. Occupying the space of a former Mediterranean restaurant called Luna D'Oro, Ribollita is convivial, warm and intimate. It seats a mere 35 people inside and a few more outside in season.

Chef-owner Kevin Quiet makes his own pastas for such treats as shrimp carbonara with pancetta and artichokes, pan-seared gnocchi with prosciutto and peas, and roast chicken puttanesca with pappardelle.

Those are meals in themselves, especially when preceded by the hearty Tuscan vegetable and bread soup from which the restaurant takes its name. Or perhaps by a caramelized onion tart with black olives and goat cheese, or polenta-crusted calamari with roasted peppers.

Secondi await those who prefer. Consider tuna steak niçoise, radicchio-wrapped salmon with pesto and roasted pepper sauce, chicken breast saltimbocca, and osso buco with creamy polenta. A specialty is market risotto, changing nightly depending on what's at the market – mussels, saffron and spinach, when we were there.

Dessert could be vanilla bean flan, apple croustade with cinnamon ice cream, and chocolate torte. The wine list is all-Italian.

(207) 774-2972. Entrées, $13.50 to $17.95. Dinner, Tuesday-Saturday from 5.

Joe's Boathouse, 1 Spring Point Drive, South Portland.

This is one of those rarities where the food is equal to the view. The view is of boats bobbing in the marina where Portland Harbor opens into Casco Bay and, beyond, the enchanting islands out in the bay itself. The food is sophisticated and first-rate.

Joe Loring, a former bricklayer whose construction skills helped transform a small hamburger shack into a 45-seat restaurant at Spring Point Marina, partners with chef Nate Chalaby to draw city slickers as well as the yachting set. They come as much for the fare as the watery ambiance. There's an eat-at bar popular with single diners just inside the main entrance. Beyond are a couple of simple, low-slung dining rooms, the main one with a fireplace and large windows. The tables of choice in summer are outside on a patio beside the harbor, where torches are lit at night.

Lunch was a festive treat as 1950s music played in the background. Word of the portobello and asiago club sandwich preceded our arrival. It turned out to be a knife-and-fork whopper, paired with homemade chips and served on the restaurant's colorful Fiestaware. Another treat was the orange-ginger crispy salmon salad – a plateful of greens, rice noodles, bamboo shoots, red peppers and scallions, with a spicy-sauced salmon fillet on top and many contrasting tastes in competition with each other. It took desserts of chocolate-kahlua mousse and homemade sorbets to clear the palate.

Aforementioned spicy orange-ginger sauce often shows up for dinner on stir-fried sea scallops with vegetables, pineapple and cashews over Asian rice noodles, topped with crispy wontons. Other possibilities are lobster fettuccine, seafood gumbo, hickory-smoked pork ribs with a blueberry barbecue sauce and grilled filet mignon with a shallot-port wine sauce. Best of the starters are cajun chicken and corn egg rolls with a honey-mustard dipping sauce, and crab cakes drizzled with rémoulade over crisp fried potatoes and greens.

Folks from the nearby Casco Bay islands like to sail over here for Sunday brunch. There's a dock for mooring, of course.

(207) 741-2780. www.joesboathouse.com. Entrées, $14.95 to $22.95. Lunch, Monday-Saturday 11 to 3. Dinner nightly, 5 to 9:30. Sunday brunch, 9 to 3.

Restaurant Oolong, 100 Commercial St., Portland.

"Where Far East Meets Northeast" is the billing for this 130-seat upscale Asian eatery in two improbably deep dining rooms with brick and painted walls, high beamed ceilings and a mix of booths and tables, a few with a glimpse of the harbor from an upper level in back.

We snagged one of the latter for lunch and quickly recognized the Far East part of the equation. The Northeast part was more obscure. Could it have shown up in the hoisin chicken wings listed on the menu under "pan-Asian snacks, street food and dim sum?" Or in the braised beef shortribs with daikon and cabbage slaw under "inspiration from Mainland China?" Or the ginger crème brûlée for dessert?

Who could tell from the day's "spicy hot and sour soup" whose spicy-ness turned up AWOL or the kung pao chicken that had to be enlivened by ample pours from the jars of Vietnamese sambal and Chinese chile pepper oil and a pitcher of soy sauce on each table? The Cantonese roast chicken and watercress salad – like most menu items, prepared mild for the western palate – was the best of the lot.

Although chef Adam White gives mainland Chinese cuisine top billing, the menu at Oolong is pan-Asian. Mango chicken with cashews and shaking beef sirloin are entrées from Vietnam. A sauté of scallops, mussels, clams and whitefish with coconut milk, curry, kaffir lime leaf and lemongrass emanates from Laos.

The snack and street food items that make up nearly half the menu find a receptive audience. Folks also like the Asian cocktails, the varietal teas and, for dessert, the banana spring roll and the trio of coconut, ginger and pistachio-tea ice creams topped with a chocolate-dipped fortune tuile.

(207) 775-6569. Entrées, $16 to $20. Open daily, 11:30 to 10 or 11.

Blue-Plate Special

Blue Spoon, 89 Congress St., Portland.

You'd have to know about this tiny gem of a neighborhood café to find it, hidden up Munjoy Hill in the East End. But locals adore the place and keep its 25 seats filled. They liken it to eating in someone's dining room, which is the way owner David Iovino, a New Jersey native who trained at the French Culinary Institute in New York, wanted it.

The sign outside announces "food from friends, family and travels," featuring American, European, Mediterranean and Latin cuisines. But the sign doesn't prepare you for food that is both first-rate and reasonably priced, let alone the choice beers and wines served in burgundy stemware and the polished but friendly service.

Half of the changing menu is devoted to small plates and salads, perfect for a grazing dinner. Typical starters are steamed mussels, wild mushroom salad drizzled with black truffle oil, an Italian fritto misto of vegetables, prosciutto-wrapped sea scallops or a goat cheese gratin. Two people could sample the mezzi plate, an antipasti platter bearing the likes of peppered sausage, olives, roasted red peppers, a fish roe spread, fresh mozzarella and flatbread wedges. Main courses might be a saffron-scented seafood stew, trout stuffed with Tuscan greens over a bed of brown rice, chicken roasted under a brick or skirt steak with a smoked paprika aioli, plus vegetarian and vegan options.

A slice of apple and pear pie, cheesecake or chocolate cake might finish a meal that won't begin to break the bank.

(207) 773-1116. Entrées, $10 to $15. Lunch and dinner, Tuesday-Saturday noon to 9 or 9:30. Sunday brunch, 9:30 to 2.

A Maine Original

Duckfat, 43 Middle St., Portland.

Who'd ever think to open a high-end "sandwich and soda shop" with a name like Duckfat and quirky as all get-out? Rob Evans and Nancy Pugh came up with a true original as different as the food served in their fancy Hugo's restaurant down the street. "We wanted a casual neighborhood place serving European-style street food made from scratch," Nancy said. They named it Duckfat for the fat in which their signature Belgian fries are fried for extraordinary flavor.

Duckfat's classic fun-food themes differ from Hugo's dinners of creative abandon, but both places manifest their owners' passion for employing the finest ingredients, most of them local, to create the best possible product.

Here is a true original, like much of Hugo's cooking. The fries are served in tall paper cones ($3.50 or $4.50) with a choice of five homemade sauces for dipping. They stand on their own or accompany the soups, salads or crispy panini pressed sandwiches. Or they make way for the homemade all-natural sodas like sassafras root beer and ginger brew (with free refills), espresso or mocha milkshakes so thick the straws not only stand straight but cannot be functional. Or they precede beignets dusted with cinnamon sugar or drizzled with chocolate sauce, or sweet panini (grilled brioche) with sour cherry butter or fig and port jam.

The fries, shakes and sweets are addictive adjuncts to the heartier fare, available here or to go. The panini come in eight flavors, from Maine meatloaf to Italian to roasted turkey to your basic ham and cheese, dressed here with a red wine-shallot marmalade.

We tried the Long Island duck confit panini, laden with peppered cream cheese and black currant chutney and served on a bamboo cutting board covered with butcher paper. Our duck confit salad had lots of frisée and tomato but only three visible pieces of duck.

These treats and more – cheese plates, gelato, wine and beer, French-press coffee – are taken on high bar stools at a few tables and at a side counter facing a wall of magnetic letters used by customers to make up sayings or poems. Said counter is decorated with river stones in glasses and roses in Coke bottles. Several tall tables on the sidewalk out front attract passersby.

Duckfat is "more than simply a place to eat," said Nancy. "We want to make eating fun again."

(207) 774-8080. www.duckfat.com. Panini, $6.95 to $10.95. Open daily from 11, Monday-Thursday to 8, weekends to 9, Sunday to 7.

For a Seafood Fix

Scales, 25 Preble St., Portland.

On a scale of one to ten, this urban seafood shack in the Portland Public Market rates at least a nine.

The city's leading restaurateurs, Sam Hayward and Dana Street of Fore Street et al, took over the corner space in which a number of predecessors had come and gone. The pair upheld the market's elegant rusticity and kept things pure, white and minimalist. You place your order at the counter and find a table on an upper level.

For a quick lunch, we sat on stools at the raw bar and watched the crew shucking oysters (succulent Damariscottas), $1.75 each or $17.50 a dozen. After sampling a few, one of us enjoyed a fried oyster sandwich and the other had mussels in a spicy tomato sauce – both with fries that arrived in a paper cone as in Europe. The blackboard listed some interesting wines by the glass ($5).

The changing menu ranges from a hot dog to a shore dinner. Interesting blue-plate specials ($7.95 to $13.95) included fried calamari with spicy red sauce and chipotle aioli, homemade fish cakes with black beans and coleslaw, and pan-seared swordfish or marinated bluefish with rice and sautéed fiddleheads. All are every bit as tasty as at the owners' home restaurants.

(207) 228-2008. Entrées, $7.95 to $24.95. Open Monday-Saturday 11 to 8, Sunday 11 to 5.

Dining and Lodging

Portland Harbor Hotel, 468 Fore St., Portland 04101.

The brick facade and residential-style lobby spell elegance at this new boutique hotel at the edge of the Old Port district. From Fore Street, you'd never guess that it was built atop an existing three-level parking garage – a creative use of otherwise wasted space. From the entry, an elevator and stairs rise to the second-floor lobby, where the day's newspapers await guests in comfortable sitting areas and the unobtrusive Lobby Bar.

Beside the lobby is **Eve's at the Garden,** an elegant but casual-looking cross between coffee salon and dining room. It opens through big windows and french doors to a large courtyard garden terrace, where umbrellaed tables are set for al fresco dining. The menu is a cut above your average city hotel fare. The contemporary continental menu offers the likes of Atlantic halibut meunière, lobster thermidor, veal saltimbocca and grilled filet mignon oscar.

Courtyard garden is on view from window table at Eve's.

The four-story hotel offers 100 accommodations with views of the city, Casco Bay or the rooftop garden. Cheery in pale yellows and blue-grays, rooms have king or queen beds dressed with 250-thread count linens, duvet coverlets and down feather pillows. Custom-made furnishings include armoires with his and her sections. Granite surrounds enhance soaking tubs and enclosed showers, and jacuzzis are available in a few suites. A chocolate treat accompanies evening turndown service.

(207) 775-9090 or (888) 798-9090. Fax (207) 775-9990. www.theportlandharborhotel.com. Ninety-seven rooms and three suites. Doubles, $259 to $399 May to mid-October, $179 to $289 rest of year.

Eve's: (207) 523-2045. Entrées, $24 to $38. Lunch, Monday-Friday 11 to 2, weekends noon to 2. Dinner nightly, 5:30 to 9 or 10.

Portland Regency Hotel, 20 Milk St., Portland 04101.

This downtown hotel is superbly located in the heart of the Old Port. The fact that it's in the restored 1895 armory, providing some unusual architectural treatments, is a bonus. It wears its designation as a member of the Historic Hotels of America proudly.

Most of the 95 guest rooms and suites go off a three-story atrium above the dining room. Rooms are plush, many with kingsize four-poster beds and minibars. Corner rooms come with gas fireplaces, sitting areas and recently added whirlpool tubs.

There's nightly turndown service. Complimentary coffee and newspapers are placed at the door in the morning. The health club is up-to-date, and the Armory

Lounge offers complimentary hors d'oeuvre with cocktails and nightly entertainment in a warren of downstairs rooms.

The downstairs Armory restaurant was closed in 2005 in favor of a new main-floor restaurant serving three meals a day. **Twenty Milk Street** is a luxurious, salon-style dining room in beige and brown, with a glowing fireplace and cushy upholstered armchairs at well-spaced tables. Prime steaks are featured, although the menu offers considerable variety from pecan-crusted yellowfin tuna to pan-seared moulard duck breast.

(207) 774-4200 or (800) 727-3436. Fax (207) 775-2150. www.theregency.com. Ninety-five rooms and suites with private baths. Doubles, $229 to $329 July-October, $159 to $239 rest of year.

Entrées, $22.95 to $37.95. Lunch daily, 11:30 to 2. Dinner nightly, 5:30 to 9:30.

The Inn by the Sea, 40 Bowery Beach Road (off Route 77), Cape Elizabeth 04107.

Big bucks went into this luxury resort on the site of the former Crescent Beach Inn in the Portland suburb of Cape Elizabeth. And it looks it, from the marble-tiled lobby and the twelve John James Audubon hand-colored engravings gracing the inn's walls to the luxury suites with two TVs (the one in the sitting room hidden in the armoire) and no fewer than three telephones. There's an ocean view from every room's patio or balcony.

Handsomely designed in the Maine shingle style, the resort has 25 one-bedroom suites in the angular main building and eighteen condo-style units of one or two bedrooms in four attached cottages. All have living rooms with reproduction Chippendale furniture, TVs hidden in armoires, kitchenettes, and balconies or patios looking onto manicured lawns, a pleasant pool and the ocean beyond. We liked our initial stay in a garden suite facing the lawn and ocean on the first floor, its living room opening through sliding doors onto an outside patio. Its small bedroom with a four-poster queen bed was quite adequate, though the windows opened onto the parking lot. Next time we reveled in the extra space of one of the loft suites on the second floor, which offered a better water view from its balcony and a three-section bathroom even bigger than the kingsize bedroom. Furnishings are most comfortable and the decor understated in a Maine woods theme.

Owner Maureen McQuade, a Maine native who had managed large properties, lucked into buying this inn in foreclosure. A hands-on innkeeper, she's very much at home here and her enthusiasm shows. The friendly young staff is dressed in khakis and bids everyone "a nice Maine day."

Families are in evidence, at least in summer. So are pets. The four-diamond, four-star inn not only accepts but encourages travelers' pets, pampering them almost as much as guests of the human persuasion.

Pets or not, you can swim in a pleasant pool or saunter down a boardwalk to a private entrance to the beach at Crescent Beach State Park. The tea garden with rose bushes and fish in a fountain pool is a quiet retreat.

Breakfast and dinner are served in the Audubon Room, a harmonious space striking in white, with comfortable chairs and an enclosed porch around two sides. Tables are topped with white linens, English bone china and fresh flowers. The dinner fare has been elevated in recent years. We hear the rack of lamb is to die for, but were quite content at one visit with a couple of salads (spinach with grilled portobello mushrooms and caramelized walnuts, and fanned breast of duck on baby spinach and arugula) and main dishes of medallions of jerk-spiced pork on a

Afternoon goodies await guests in penthouse common room at The Inn by the Sea.

papaya and sundried-cherry relish, and local haddock encrusted in wasabi and macadamia nuts and sauced with a lemongrass-sake reduction.

Another occasion produced a fabulous seafood fettuccine, loaded with lobster, diver scallops and tiger shrimp in an ethereal seaweed and saffron cream sauce, and a rich seafood strudel. Though there were no chilled desserts on the menu, the kitchen managed to turn up a dish of chocolate ice cream garnished with blueberries.

Breakfast (not included) is a feast as well. You can order a lobster and cheese omelet, amaretto or grand marnier french toast, or eggs benedict with lobster. Portions are abundant, and the lady at the next table exclaimed that her pancakes and blueberries were the biggest she ever saw.

They do things up big here. Even the bill comes on an oversize computer printout.

(207) 799-3134 or (800) 888-4287. Fax (207) 799-4779. www.innbythesea.com. Forty-three one and two-bedroom suites with private baths. Rates, EP. Doubles, $369 to $679 late spring to early fall, $169 to $319 rest of year.

Audubon Room: (207) 767-0888. Entrées, $24 to $29. Lunch daily, noon to 2, to 4 in summer. Dinner nightly, 6 to 9, to 10 in summer.

Lodging

Pomegranate Inn, 49 Neal St., Portland 04102.

Two exotic plant sculptures (often holding live plants, no less) welcome guests at the entrance to this exceptional in-town B&B, one worthy of its designation as "queen of the B&Bs" by the New York Times.

The art theme continues inside the handsome 19th-century house in Portland's residential West End. The antiques collections and contemporary artworks of owner Isabel Smiles make it a cross between a museum and a gallery. The seven bedrooms on the second and third floors, all with modern tiled baths, televisions and telephones, are a kaleidoscope of design.

Each is unique, blending antique rugs, colorful fabrics, antique and contemporary furnishings, charming eccentricities and prized artworks. Four have gas fireplaces. A deluxe, two-room suite has been added upstairs in the renovated carriage house across a terrace beside the main inn. We happily splurged for the downstairs garden room in the carriage house. It had two plush chairs and a puffy duvet on the bed, a marble bathroom and walls painted with riotous flowers. It opened onto a secret courtyard, so quiet and secluded it was hard to imagine we were in the midst of a city.

Walls in guest rooms, hand-painted by Portland artist Heidi Gerquest Harbert, are themselves works of art. Most striking is a robin's-egg-blue wall with a swirl design taken from a pattern on a Japanese kimono. Paisley, birds and flowers are painted in other rooms, and the hallways are sponged a golden color. Isabel's daughter, Amy Russack, painted faux finishes on moldings, fireplace mantels and columns. The downstairs parlors are almost a gallery of marble columns, Greek statuary, contemporary artworks and, near the long hand-painted Italianate dining table, three huge papier-mâché vegetables, each perched atop a small clay pot on a shelf in the front window. At check-in, Irish tea or a glass of wine are offered by the fire in one of the sitting rooms or in the garden.

Breakfast is served between 8 and 9:30 at the aforementioned communal table, or at a couple of small tables for those who prefer. Poached eggs with capers, creamy quiches and pancakes with sautéed pears turn the meal into another show of artistry. Our tasty waffles with bananas and raspberries were preceded by a dish of dainty nectarines with tiny blueberries and vanilla yogurt and a glass of mystery juice, whose contents no one at the table could fathom. "Just orange and cranberry," Isabel said breezily. "I should tell everybody it's pomegranate juice."

(207) 772-1006 or (800) 356-0408. Fax (207) 733-4426. www.pomegranateinn.com. Seven rooms and one suite with private baths. Doubles, $175 to $265 Memorial Day through October, $95 to $165 rest of year.

The Danforth, 163 Danforth St., Portland 04102.

The landmark 1821 Georgian brick mansion that was the rectory for the Roman Catholic Archdiocese of Portland is now an urbane B&B. Energetic owner Barbara Hathaway offers nine deluxe guest rooms and a number of intriguing common areas, more than most inns twice its size.

The nine accommodations (one a two-bedroom suite) on the second and third floors are spacious, light and airy with tall windows and thick off-white carpeting. They're outfitted with updated baths, queensize beds bearing pillow-top mattresses, television, telephones, loveseats or wing chairs, antique armoires, writing desks with data-port terminals and all the accoutrements of the good B&B life. Indian shutters cover the windows and Baccarat crystal knobs open the doors. All the tiled fireplaces are working and wood-burning. The only shortcoming in some is the lack of good lights where one might like to read.

The main floor holds a double parlor, the front portion of which is a plush living room and the rear is a dining room, with a sun porch alongside. On the other side of the wide entry hall are a function room and a garden solarium that serves as the reception area. To the rear is a cozy library with a wet bar in an old vault and one of the mansion's thirteen fireplaces. The day's newspapers are set out here with morning coffee. Late afternoon brings cookies and lemonade or tea and, in cool weather, hot soups with rustic breads. Decanters of port, brandy and sherry await in the evening.

Downstairs is the original billiards room, paneled and looking much as it did a century ago. Way upstairs on the rooftop is the enclosed widow's walk – occasionally used for sunrise breakfasts – with a wraparound view of the city. There's more. A vacant third-floor room was converted into a garden "conservatory" because the owner believes guests on every floor should enjoy a common area. Occupants of the six second-floor rooms have a parlor opening onto a deck overlooking the colorful side garden.

Breakfast is continental plus, with seasonal fruit, pastries, cereals, homemade granola and hard-boiled eggs. On weekends, the foregoing is supplemented by a hot dish – the menu posted at our visit listed baked apple and scrambled eggs in puff pastry.

As we paused to take everything in atop the widow's walk, Barbara acknowledged she "saw the building, fell in love with it and turning it into an inn was the only way for me to have it." Her guests are lucky to share it.

(207) 879-8755 or (800) 991-6557. Fax (207) 879-8754. www.danforthmaine.com. Eight rooms and one suite with private baths. Doubles, $139 to $329 mid-May through October, $119 to $249 rest of year.

Gourmet Treats

The Portland Public Market and the burgeoning Theater Arts District have shifted some of the visitor focus away from the Old Port area to another part of downtown. Otherwise, the restored Old Port area remains the center of shops appealing to those interested in food.

Portland Public Market, Preble Street and Cumberland Avenue, Portland.

New England's biggest farm market was built from scratch at the edge of downtown in 1998 by Maine philanthropist Elizabeth Noyce, who was on a personal campaign to revitalize downtown Portland when her advisor happened across Seattle's famed Pike Place Market. That inspired her privately funded, $9 million beauty built on land that had been awaiting a higher use than a parking lot. A block long and half as wide, the L-shaped structure is an architectural marvel of timbered beams, walls of windows and soaring ceilings. A granite central fireplace is flanked by stone benches, where you can rest your weary bones after navigating the aisles.

Although the market has not achieved the artisanal-food dreams of its founder, the oft-changing food growers and vendors purvey everything from elk to eels and soups to spices. We often stop here to pick up an interesting cheese or two, plus some of the locally acclaimed Big Sky peasant breads (the cinnamon-walnut-raisin bread is great for french toast). A couple of butcher shops sell exotic meats raised on nearby farms. Besides all the market stalls, there's a state-of-the-art demonstration kitchen where cooking classes are conducted seasonally. At the far ends of the market are a family steakhouse restaurant called **Maverick's** and the casual **Scales** seafood shack.

On the mezzanine stands a tribute to Mrs. Noyce, who died shortly before her dream was realized. It's a small sculpture of a woman pushing a cart laden with vegetables and feeding corn to a crow. Her lawyer called it "Betty Sharing the Bounty."

(207) 228-2000. www.portlandmarket.com. Open Monday-Saturday 9 to 7, Sunday 10 to 5.

Diners enjoy lofty seating while shoppers buy Maine foods in Portland Public Market.

Le Roux Kitchen – an off-shoot of a Martha's Vineyard shop – is the better-than-ever successor to the beloved Whip and Spoon, a store for serious cooks at 161 Commercial St. Owners Michael Levandowski and April Krajeski recently expanded onto a second floor, freeing up retail space on the formerly overstuffed main floor and adding a demonstration kitchen for cooking classes on the second. Stocking more than 8,000 individual products for the kitchen, it is now the most complete store for all things culinary in New England. From lobster picks to chopping blocks to food processors, you can find everything – including magazines for cooks, a great collection of Maine-made foods, chocolates, wines and things you never thought you'd need or find. You could spend hours here, browsing and buying.

Modeled after a European coffee bar, the **Portland Coffee Roasting Co.** at 111 Commercial St. draws locals as well as tourists for a coffee fix or the "eggspresso" breakfast (scrambled eggs, bagel and coffee). Small sandwiches, pastries like sticky buns and almond crescents and delicious Samantha juices (made in nearby Scarborough – we loved the strawberry-orange) are also on the board. Tall windows reveal the passing scene as you sip cappuccino or café au lait at modern little tables beneath a high pressed-tin ceiling. Owner Gerrie Brooke offers a traditional cream tea, with scones and double devon cream. As we nursed a latte and caffe mocha outdoors on a ledge with a view of the waterfront and the sounds of the seagulls, we could picture ourselves in Seattle, the latte capital of the world.

Fit to Eat is a new "healthy deli" at 65 Market St. Straw parasols hang from the ceiling against a tropical peach and chartreuse backdrop and New Age music for a quick-order repertoire of wraps and paninis (each with nutritional profile), soups, 40-item salad bar, pizza pies, fruit smoothies and a coffee station. Order at a bamboo counter and take to a seat by the front window.

Black Tie Bistro at 184 Middle St. is part of a side-by-side gourmet lineup that includes Starbuck's, Cold Stone Creamery and Stonewall Kitchen. Primarily a catering operation, it moonlights by day as a multi-faceted lunch and takeout spot. Creative, reasonably priced soups, sandwiches and wraps are offered in the rear Pantry and heartier fare (crab cakes, meatloaf, turkey pot pie, \$7.95 to \$10.95) in the Courtyard Café in the garden in back.

For interesting pottery and dishware, check out **Maxwell's Pottery Outlet** at 384 Fore St. (we liked the blue and white pottery bearing sailing ships) and, across the street, **Maine Potters,** a co-op, where we admired dishes for dips depicting different shellfish.

Restaurateurs and locals in the know get their breads and pastries from executive baker Alison Pray at Dana Street's **Standard Baking Co.,** located at 75 Commercial St., behind and beneath the Fore Street restaurant. Country boules, baguettes, rosemary focaccia, black olive rolls, morning buns, cranberry-walnut scones, fruit tarts, almond biscotti – you name it and this sparkling place probably has it.

Seafood Showplace

Browne Trading Market, 262 Commercial St., Portland.

The top gourmet seafood supplier in the United States caters to big names like Wolfgang Puck, Daniel Boulud and Alain Ducasse, who savor its variety, freshness and consistency. Now owner Rod Browne Mitchell and his wife Cynde cater to mere mortals at their gourmet market on Merrill's Wharf.

Here is one amazing place for the connoisseur, an absolutely gorgeous – and delicious – showplace, offering everything from the Browne company's long-famed caviars to the most comprehensive wine selection north of Boston. Few will ever see such an array of exotic fish, from loup de mer to John Dory to daurade royale to arctic char to dover sole. Not to mention Browne's smoked products, food specialties like Japanese crab butter and foie gras de mer, sea salts from France, cheeses, balsamic vinegars and fancy chocolates.

The choices are mind-boggling.

(207) 775-7560 or (800) 944-7848. www.browne-trading.com. Open Monday-Saturday, 10 to 6:30.

Tastes of Tuscany

The Clown, 123 Middle St., Portland.

This stylish establishment in the Old Port area is an antiques, arts and wine shop par excellence. Taking over the old Carbur's restaurant property, Kyle A. Wolfe and Martin Kolk opened a considerably larger and year-round offshoot of the seasonal shop they'd run since 1996 in rural Stonington. Here they stock the main floor with European antiques and accessories, among them stunning ceramics, plus paintings and sculpture by contemporary artists, most with a European focus.

The downstairs seemingly was made for Maine's largest wine cellar. Among the more than 1,100 labels are two excellent chiantis – one a reserve classico and one a table wine – from the 350 cases produced annually at the couple's Tramonti vineyard in Tuscany. The owners doubled the size of their Tuscan farm to add more grapes as well as olive trees, the fruits of which turn up in some mighty fine olive oils for sale along with balsamic vinegars and specialty food products from Piedmont. Wine tastings are scheduled here monthly as part of what the couple call "the art of considered living."

(207) 756-7399. www.the-clown.com. Open daily, 10 to 6 or 7, Sunday noon to 5.

Everyone likes to eat lobster beside the ocean, as here at Two Lights Lobster Shack.

Lobster by the Ocean

Two Lights Lobster Shack, 225 Two Lights Road, Cape Elizabeth.

Near Two Lights State Park and almost in the shadow of the two lighthouses south of Portland, this is located on a bluff overlooking nothing but rocks and open ocean. You can eat inside, but we prefer to sip a drink outside at a picnic table (BYOB) as we await our order. This is a great place to bring youngsters because they can clamber around on the rocks while waiting for dinner and because the Lobster Shack offers hot dogs, hamburgers, fried chicken and clam cakes as well as boiled lobsters, fried seafood, chowder and steamers.

(207) 799-1677. www.lobstershack-twolights.com. Entrées, $7.95 to $19.95. Open daily from 11 to 8, April to mid-October, to 8:30 in July and August.

Ultimate Gourmet

Aurora Provisions, 64 Pine St., Portland.

"Beautiful food for busy people" is the apt credo for this upscale market and café in Portland's West End. Owner Marika Green and head chef Jill Smith draw the cognoscenti to the very visible adjunct to their catering business. The shelves are stocked with the finest specialty foods, wines and kitchen gadgets, but the focal points of the establishment are the espresso bar and the central deli and pastry cases, dispensing more – and more innovative – treats than you might think existed. Stop here for a breakfast burrito, a cranberry scone or café au lait. Lunchtime brings sensational soups, salads and sandwiches, including an avocado wrap, Asian beef wrapped in flatbread and a changing selection of panini. Or how about a slice of the terrific smoked seafood quiche? Later in the day, the possibilities for takeout dinners are endless. There are tables inside and out upon which to partake. We seldom can pass through Portland without indulging in something extravagant from Aurora.

(207) 871-9060. www.auroraprovisions.com. Open Monday-Saturday 8 to 6:30.

Mid-Coast Maine

Where the Real Maine Starts

The sandy beaches of southern Maine yield to Maine's more typical rockbound coast north of Portland. There are those who say that this is where the real Maine starts.

The coastline becomes more jagged, its fingers protruding like tentacles toward the sea between inlets, rivers and bays. Poke down remote byways to Bailey Island, Popham Beach, Westport, Christmas Cove and Pemaquid Point. You'll find life quieter here and the distances between points long and roundabout. One look at the map as you eye the shore across the inlet and you'll understand why the natives say "you can't get theah from heah" – except by boat.

Here also are two of Maine's leading tourist destinations – busy Boothbay Harbor, a commercial fishing village surrounded by a choice and remote shoreline beyond and on either side, and upscale Camden, where the mountains meet the sea and the windjammer fleet sets sail from the colorful harbor.

These two resort areas have long been favored by visitors, whose arrival has fueled the inevitable influx of souvenir shops and golden arches nearby. But the Mid-coast's increasing gentrification also has attracted new and better restaurants, inns and B&Bs, and – a surprise at a recent visit – a little drive-through called Java Express serving espresso on the Route 1 Bypass near Damariscotta.

Side by side with touristy Boothbay and Camden are postcard fishing hamlets like Ocean Point and Port Clyde. The busy towns of Brunswick, Bath, Rockland and Belfast co-exist with salt-washed villages like Rockport and South Harpswell.

Before you head Down East, tarry along Maine's mid-coast. Here, as elsewhere in Maine, entries are generally presented geographically, from southwest to northeast.

Dining

The Robinhood Free Meetinghouse, Robinhood Road, off Route 127, Georgetown.

Yes, this place with the odd name really was a church until 1989. It was transformed in 1996 into a restaurant-cum-gallery by chef-owner Michael Gagné, who moved up the road after putting the Osprey restaurant at Robinhood Marine Center on the culinary map.

Well known in the area for his catering and cooking classes, he oversees an ambitious, contemporary fusion menu that has gone beyond its original New American base to embrace continental and oriental cuisines (some dishes are marked "very peppery" and "spicy hot"). He and his staff make their own breads, pastas, sausages and ice creams. From their dream of a kitchen, they turn out up to three dozen different entrées a night, not to mention three soups, six salads, twelve appetizers, four pastas and a staggering fourteen desserts. Skeptics call it overkill, but they recognize Michael as one of Maine's best chefs.

Although he gave up a waterfront location, he gained a better arena in which to show his stuff. The lower floor of the meeting house bears a clean, stark New England look. It's pristine in white and cream, with oriental runners on the wide-board floors and Shaker-style chairs at tables clad in white. Arty sculptures dress a window ledge, and the upstairs chapel has been turned into a gallery.

Michael invites customers to "mix and match appetizers, pastas and salads to

Chef-owner Michael Gagne in dining room of The Robinhood Free Meetinghouse.

make up a meal that fits your appetite." You'll be tempted by the likes of a goat cheese quesadilla, grilled shrimp adobo on homemade tortillas with banana salsa, and avocado and crab "sushi" in rice paper with soy-ginger dipping sauce. The smoked seafood sampler served with a baguette and horseradish-mustard mousseline proved sensational, as did the corn-fried oysters with fresh salsa and chipotle cream. A tart cherry-lemon sorbet cleared the palate for our entrées. The gutsy scallops niçoise in puff pastry with saffron rice and the grilled chicken with sundried tomatoes over fettuccine were both so ample as to require doggy bags, since we wanted to save room for the trio of ice creams – ginger, raspberry swirl and childhood orange. The signature "obsession in three chocolates" – white, dark and milk, all flavored with different liqueurs – is as good as it gets. No wonder the Maine Sunday Telegram reviewer awarded the ultimate five stars in a recent review.

Quite a selection of wines is available by the glass. The wine list is priced mostly in the teens and twenties, with less than the usual markup. The dessert list has been known to offer a flight of six ports, as if anyone could manage.

"Theme nights" offer foods from around the world, four prix-fixe courses at $28 a person, Thursday nights from mid-October to mid-May.

Michael's signature 72-layer hand-cut cream cheese biscuits made in the restaurant are available fresh or frozen to go. They're also sold by mail-order and in gourmet shops along the coast.

(207) 371-2188. www.robinhood-meetinghouse.com. Entrées, $24 to $28. Dinner nightly, 5:30 to 9 mid-May to mid-October, Thursday-Saturday to 8 rest of year.

Star Fish Grill, 100 Pleasant St., Brunswick.

A former New York attorney and a free-standing storefront location overshadowed by a video store are an unlikely combination for a with-it seafood restaurant. Alyson Cummings moved to Portland, where she practiced law by day and apprenticed nights in the kitchen at the acclaimed Street & Company seafood restaurant. In 1998, she and a friend, Tom Cary, took over a former pizza establishment and opened the Star Fish to four-star reviews and a lengthy feature by Down East magazine in 1999 about "what might be Maine's best new restaurant."

The name originated in a brainstorming session among friends, Alyson recounts. They settled on starfish, "because they're mollusk eaters, like our customers. They love feeding on them." They decorated the place in "peaceful blues" – navy on the ceiling, aqua on the walls and vividly bright on the tiled floor – with hundreds of tiny starfish stenciled on the front windows. It gives some diners the illusion of being underwater, a feeling enhanced by pinpoint "star lights" on the ceiling and wavy illumination from scallop-shaped sconces on the walls. The butcher-block tables are dressed with fresh flowers and votive candles, but no tablecloths. "We wanted this to be accessible for the locals, who might otherwise think it was too fancy and just for visitors," Alyson advised.

Given her legal training, everything was carefully calculated, from the straight-ahead presentation of the freshest of fish to the credo that here was a place to have fun (she was singing and joking with staff in the prep kitchen, her hands covered with pastry dough, when we stopped by one mid-afternoon). She even was thinking about somehow reconfiguring the restaurant to take advantage of the rushing Androscoggin River in back rather than busy Route 1 out front.

Meanwhile, from the open kitchen in the center of the esablishment comes an assortment of grilled fish and seafood, each basted with the house citrus oil – a blend of extra virgin olive oil and lemon and lime juices.

Also available are more complex choices: seafood cassoulet, sea scallops flamed in brandy, grilled tuna niçoise, organic salmon tagine with North African spices, coconut-crusted curried shrimp with green onion chutney and a duo of pan-seared escolar and rock shrimp piccata style.

About the only non-seafood entrées are a summer duck salad, Mediterranean chicken, skewers of Greek lamb and grilled organic Maine sirloin steak with a bourbon barbecue sauce.

But almost everyone here, at one time or another, orders the signature lobster paella for two, an extravagant takeoff on the Spanish classic. It features a sizable split lobster, loads of mussels, calamari, chorizo, chicken morsels and Mediterranean vegetables served on a bed of tomato-saffron rice in the traditional pan, redolent of sea flavors and so ample that some of it usually goes home for another meal.

Typical starters are salmon and pistachio pâté, Pacific Rim shrimp with spicy peanut sauce, crab cakes with horseradish-caper rémoulade and half an avocado stuffed with rock shrimp. Caesar salad may be paired with shrimp, scallops, chicken or tuna.

Desserts could be the cheesecake of the evening, caramelized lemon tart, bananas foster, or a tangy pink grapefruit sorbet spiked with campari and paired with homemade cookies

(207) 725-7828. www.starfishgrill.com. Entrées, $18 to $25. Dinner, Tuesday-Sunday 5 to 9. Wednesday-Sunday in winter..

Amalfi, 421 Main St., Rockland.

When a Maine coast restaurant is launched in the dead of winter and acquires a wide reputation before summer arrives, you know it's worth seeking out.

That was the happy circumstance for this intimate Mediterranean eatery near the famed Farnsworth Art Museum and the Wyeth Center in Rockland. Chef-owner David Cooke from Chicago converted a downtown storefront into a colorful space

Chef Melissa Kelly and baker Price Kushner cater event as owners of Primo.

with purple runners and pink napkins on the tables and a mural of a Tuscan vineyard painted on the wall by a friend from Kennebunkport.

A Culinary Institute of America grad, chef David turns out dinner dishes such as roasted haddock fillet, fish stew, duck risotto, Moroccan chicken kabob, braised lamb shanks and grilled strip steak. His signature Spanish paella comes in three varieties – vegetable, seafood and house (shrimp, mussels, chicken and chorizo).

Tempting starters are the nightly trio of tapas, kefta (Moroccan meatballs with pistachios and cumin), Pemaquid oysters roasted with shallots and asiago cheese, a caramelized onion and goat cheese tart, and steamed mussels in two versions (standard and augmented with cilantro and marinara sauce to become "hot, hot, hot"). A pan-seared haddock salad with greens, vegetables and caper aioli was featured at a recent visit.

Dessert could be a signature chocolate soup with berries, lemon tart, crème brûlée, or homemade ice cream or sorbet.

The Mediterranean-inspired wine list is priced mainly in the teens and twenties.

With tasty food at modest prices, it's little wonder that Amalfi's 35-seat dining room fills quickly – often, David says, two or three times a night. Lately, a new dining area in the basement has taken up the overflow.

(207) 596-0012. www.amalfi-tonight.com. Entrées, $13.95 to $20.95. Dinner, Tuesday-Saturday 5 to 9, Sunday 5 to 8.

Primo, 2 South Main St. (Route 73), Rockland.

Foodies from across the country flock to Rockland to try celebrity chef Melissa Kelly's sparkling restaurant.

Cited by the James Beard Foundation as the best chef in the Northeast in 1999 when she was cooking in New York's Hudson Valley, she teamed here with Price Kushner, her fiancé and a baker and pastry chef of note. Named for her Italian grandfather, Primo Magnani, the chic hot spot occupies the late 19th-century Victorian residence that formerly housed Jessica's European Bistro restaurant.

The fare reflects the award-winning cuisine and baked goods for which the couple was known at the famed Old Chatham Sheepherding Company Inn in Old Chatham,

N.Y., which closed suddenly in 1999 following the departure of Melissa, its founding chef.

"This is the fifth restaurant I've opened but the first for myself," she said. "We're here for the long-term." Both were looking for a place to settle down and chose the Maine coast for its access to "great fish and farms." Her family from Long Island used to have a home in Maine. Price went to summer camp there and his family has built a summer house there.

The pair renovated the existing kitchen to serve their purposes and installed a wood-fired brick oven. They imparted a cozy, elegant country look to five small, white-tablecloth dining rooms with deep mustard-colored walls and a large, more casual upstairs bar area where a bar menu, pizzas and paninis are available.

Melissa's flavorful, relaxed cooking style draws its roots from the Mediterranean and its indigenous ingredients from Maine, some from the elaborate herb and vegetable gardens the pair planted outside.

A complimentary amuse-bouche of smooth duck liver mousse on brioche followed by crusty, rustic sourdough breads with choice of olive oil or butter got our dinners off to an auspicious start. Scallops with risotto and hand-rolled ravioli filled with Maine lobster in a celeriac sauce were tasty appetizers.

Main courses range from cedar-planked ivory white king salmon with salsa verde to grilled leg of lamb served with eggplant caponata, stuffed summer squash, tapenade-filled tomato and crisp fried baby artichokes. Ours were pork saltimbocca, served on garlic mashed potatoes and spinach, and venison fanned around cabbage and wild rice studded with huckleberries.

Desserts were assorted homemade ice creams and a stellar pear tarte tatin with ginger-almond ice cream. Les mignardises came with the bill.

The owners spend part of the off-season at their new Primo, the signature restaurant in the J.W. Marriott Grande Lakes Hotel in Orlando, Fla. In 2005, they opened a third Primo at the J.W. Marriott Starr Pass in Tucson, Ariz.

(207) 596-0770. www.primorestaurant.com. Entrées, $22 to $36. Dinner nightly except Tuesday, 5:30 to 9:30, Thursday-Sunday in off-season. Closed early January to mid-April.

Natalie's at the Mill, 43 Mechanic St., Camden.

A contemporary residential setting, from the landscaped facade to the sofas in the airy lounge, is conveyed by this chic new restaurant overlooking a millpond and perched above a waterfall.

Owner Abby Alden, former manager of the Lord Camden Inn, produced two serene dining rooms and a wraparound porch in a section of the old Knox Mill building that formerly housed the MBNA credit card company.

The atmospheric place seats 80 at well-spaced tables in a main dining room with windows on three sides and a smaller room on the far side of a partially open kitchen. Showy flower arrangements, splashy artworks and exquisite table settings enhance the residential look.

The splashy falls of the Megunticook River outside the soaring windows adds to the effect. Facing the millpond is a large wraparound dining porch, a portion of it perched right beside the waterfall.

Although considered pricey, Chef Brendan Suhesky's highly rated fare makes the most of exotic ingredients. A typical dinner might start with a roasted spaghetti squash bisque flavored with black truffles and ginger, a terrine of foie gras with figs, fuji apple and pistachios, or a pan-roasted crab cake with a celeriac grain mustard

Main dining room opens onto salon-style lounge at Natalie's at the Mill.

salad. A 50-year-old sherry vinegar might dress the salad of young greens with niçoise olive tapenade and Maine feta cheese.

Among entrées, vanilla-poached lobster might be served with chanterelles, leeks and a foie gras beurre blanc. Caramelized diver sea scallops in orange brown butter come with a lemon corn cake and crisp pancetta. Truffled squash ragoût accompanies the madeira-sauced grilled beef tenderloin. Desserts are similarly extravagant: ginger tea crème brûlée paired with ginger shortbread, chocolate passionfruit terrine with coconut crème anglaise and hazelnut nougatine, and a port wine-poached pear with saffron candied fennel and vanilla bean ice cream.

(207) 236-7008. Entrées, $28 to $34. Dinner, Tuesday-Saturday 5:30 to 9.

Atlantica, One Bayview Landing, Camden.

Local art is served up alongside Atlantic cuisine at this self-styled "Gallery & Grille" on the Camden waterfront. The place is both highly rated and wildly popular, so much so that the first time we tried to eat here we couldn't endure the lengthy wait for a table. When we tried to case out the art, so many people were milling about that we could barely get the picture.

We did get the picture at a subsequent visit in the off-season, when we managed to snag a table on the second floor near a window, although the night was so foggy we were unable to see much of anything. The picture doesn't really matter here. The food is assertive and consistently top-notch, the surroundings convivial and the contemporary nautical ambiance pleasing.

Dining is on two floors seating 35 each, including a much-coveted upstairs turret with a single table for five. Fifty more can be accommodated outdoors in season on an upper deck and on a covered terrace beneath.

Chef-owner Ken Paquin's seafood-oriented menu might feature pan-seared ahi tuna with lemon-cumin beurre blanc, roasted Atlantic halibut with ginger-lemongrass emulsion, and sautéed scallops with ginger-orange moscato sauce. One of us made

Dining areas yield harbor views at Atlantica.

a most satisfying dinner of two appetizers: spicy Maine mahogany clams steamed with oriental black beans and cilantro, and crispy spring rolls filled with Maine shrimp and served with a zippy sweet Thai chili dipping sauce. The other enjoyed the caesar salad that came with the seafood pasta entrée. One of the best we've had, the pasta was brimming with lobster, scallops, whitefish and shrimp in a pineapple-ginger sauce with basil and roasted macadamia nuts. Unusually good hot rolls and a Gieson sauvignon blanc from New Zealand accompanied.

Typical desserts are orange crème brûlée, chocolate cake with a center filled with ganache and our choices, ginger ice cream and red raspberry sorbet.

(207) 236-6011 or (888) 507-8514. www.atlanticarestaurant.com. Entrées, $19 to $28. Lunch seasonally, Tuesday-Sunday 11:30 to 2:30. Dinner, Tuesday-Sunday 5:30 to 9:30, Wednesday-Saturday in off-season. Closed in winter.

More Dining Choices

The Thistle Inn, 55 Oak St., Boothbay Harbor.

With the demise in 2004 of the acclaimed Christopher's Boathouse restaurant on the waterfront, this restaurant in a restored 1861 barn and stable took top honors for in-town dining in Boothbay Harbor. The place seats 60 in three nautical-themed dining rooms and outside on an expanded deck.

New owners Mark Osborn and Steve Bouffard from Boston and their chef offer an innovative menu. They feature "some exotic items that other restaurateurs don't do around here," Steve said, citing ostrich, crawfish and grouper as examples. Typical entrées run from bouillabaisse, seared diver scallops served on a bed of mascarpone-lobster risotto and seared ahi tuna with a soy and ginger dipping sauce to chicken madeira, pan-seared duck breast and confit with cherry brandy demi-glace and herb-crusted rack of lamb with a rosemary-red wine demi-glace.

Appetizers could be crab cakes rémoulade atop a black bean sauce, ahi tuna tartare with crispy wontons and grilled foie gras atop a grilled crouton, plus several exotic salads. Dessert could be pineapple upside-down cake with ginger ice cream, strawberry-mascarpone trifle with riesling syrup or a trio of sorbets served in a pizzelle cup.

Lighter fare is served in the atmospheric **Dory Pub,** home to an eighteen-foot dory that sailed the waters of Boothbay long ago.

The inn also rents six renovated rooms with private baths for $100 to $120 a night.

(207) 633-3341 or (877) 633-3541. www.thethistleinn.com. Entrées, $16 to $29. Dinner in summer, nightly from 5. Rest of year, open Tuesday-Saturday, lunch 11:30 to 2 and dinner from 5.

Café Miranda, 15 Oak St., Rockland.

The beige and green colors of the exterior are repeated inside this trendy, family-run café at the edge of downtown Rockland. Operated by chef Kerry Altiero and his wife, Evelyn Donnelly, a craftswoman by day, the café draws throngs for its laid-back atmosphere and the gutsy cooking emanating from the wood-fired brick oven in the open kitchen.

The ambitious menu denotes small plates and "big, bigger, biggest" plates, ranging from appetizers for one to dinner for one or appetizers for two. Kerry cooks almost everything in the brick oven, even the fish of the day, going through a cord of wood a month.

His offerings range widely, from pasta with sundried tomatoes, ricotta and artichoke hearts to pierogies, chicken mole, lamb steaks and braised rabbit. North African and Thai influences show up in such dishes as grilled salmon with mandarin oranges and cilantro, served with couscous, and pork with gorgonzola, polenta and three chiles with avocado salsa. Expect such innovations as Armenian peppers stuffed with lamb, chargrilled pork and shrimp cakes with peanuts, and stir-fried salmon strips tossed with Thai chiles, lime, mint and greens.

We would gladly make a meal of small plates like fried oysters over arugula or shrimp tossed with avocado-corn salsa on roasted romano grits.

Evelyn's talents are evident in the desserts, perhaps chocolate-kahlua torte, homemade ice creams, blueberry crisp or frozen lemon mousse pie.

Rainbow-colored cloth napkins and candles grace the blond wood tables, which are flanked by distinctive chrome-backed chairs. Single diners enjoy gathering at one of the three counters – two smack in the middle of the room and one facing Kerry in the kitchen. Outside is a side patio with a billowing sail for a canopy.

There's a select and varied, reasonably priced wine list. One of the folksy descriptions touts an unfamiliar California boutique white as "rich, powerful, spicy – the way we like 'um." The same can be said for Kerry's food.

(207) 594-2034. www.cafemiranda.com. Entrées, $17.50 to $22. Dinner nightly, from 5:30. Closed Monday in off-season.

The Gallery Café, 297 Commercial St. (Route 1), Rockport.

"Art of food" is the theme of this café at the new Prism Glass Studio & Gallery. Patrons enjoy watching resident glass blower/owner Patti Kissinger at work in the adjacent barn studio before dining in the house containing the café and Lisa Sojka's Glass Gallery shop.

Sip a glass of wine as you view the work of more than 100 glass artists. Then settle down for a meal in a 40-seat dining room, where the resident glass blower's work is evident in the vases on the tables and the sconces on the walls. Umbrellaed tables on a shady rear patio are popular in season.

Chef Tim Pierre Labonte's dinner menu might start with lobster velouté topped with crème fraîche, five-spiced quail with lemon-dressed orzo or a dish called "3X Duck," chilled roulade of mallard duck breast stuffed with duck confit and foie gras.

"Maine courses" range from grilled swordfish over a four-farm garden vegetable succotash (the farms all credited on the menu) and grilled free-range chicken over serrano ham fondue to molasses-grilled pork tenderloin with chipotle-rouille sticky rice. "Black and blue lamb" pairs one portion with a black mission fig demi-glace and another with melted saga blue cheese.

Sweet endings include frozen lemon parfait, macadamia-key lime pie and vanilla malt crème brûlée.

A smoked turkey noodle wrap and a mango reuben typify the innovative lunch menu. Sunday brunch yields a signature duck croque madame and a fascinating dish called lamb and eggs – lamb bolognese served over arugula with poached eggs, herbed gnocchi and parmesan cheese. Now that's novel.

(207) 230-0061. www.prismglassgallery.com. Entrées, $20 to $35. Lunch, Wednesday-Saturday 11 to 3. Dinner, Wednesday-Saturday 5 to 9. Sunday brunch, 10 to 3. Closed in winter.

The Waterfront Restaurant, Harborside Square off Bay View Street, Camden.

This popular old-timer is notable for its expansive outdoor deck shaded by a striking white canopy resembling a boat's sails, right beside the windjammers on picturesque Camden Harbor, and for its affordable international menu.

The Waterfront is a great spot for lunch, when seven good salads in glass bowls are offered with outstanding dressings. Dinner options turn eclectic, although chef Charles Butler – named Maine lobster chef of the year – offers four lobster entrées.

Among appetizers are calamari and shrimp, mussels marinière and soups, perhaps an award-winning clam chowder or chilled raspberry accented with grand marnier. The superlative smoked seafood sampler was our choice for sharing. For main courses, we've been well satisfied by Maine crab cakes with creamy mustard sauce, an assertive linguini with salmon and sundried tomatoes, shrimp with oriental black beans over angel-hair pasta, and grilled chicken with lime, cilantro and olives. Mint chocolate-chip pie with hot fudge sauce and whipped cream proved to be the ultimate dessert.

All sorts of shellfish and light fare from burgers to lobster rolls are available at the oyster bar and outdoor grill.

(207) 236-3747. www.waterfrontcamden.com. Entrées, $14.95 to $21.95. Lunch daily, 11:30 to 2:30. Dinner, 5 to 10. Raw bar, 2 to 11.

Francine Bistro, 55 Chestnut St., Camden.

Hidden on a side street, this newcomer serves some of the most innovative food in town, although the choices are severely limited, changing nightly, and the setting is funky, to say the least. Chef Brian Hill of New York took over in 2004 from the original owners, also from New York. They had converted a former bicycle shop into a casual, L-shaped, European-style bistro that's deliberately shabby chic with church pews for benches, chocolate brown walls and a linoleum floor, four stools at the bar and a covered sidewalk patio.

Church pews serve as benches in shabby chic dining room at Francine Bistro.

At lunch, they had run out of many of the offerings, so we settled for an oyster po-boy sandwich and a goat cheese salad with fried almonds and pears. Great warm French bread with sweet butter preceded and was reordered because of desultory service and small portions, said salad amounting to little more than a mound of goat cheese, four almonds and about a quarter of a pear.

Locals advise the dining experience is best at night, which may explain why lunch service has been discontinued. The evening menu might offer spinach soup with foraged mushrooms, a crispy duck confit salad with pistachio vinaigrette, and a "BLT" of heirloom tomatoes, prosciutto, olives and shallot marmalade.

A new chef who worked with Todd English in Boston offers a handful of changing entrées. The four choices for main dishes at our latest visit were seared sea scallops with bordelaise sauce, grilled swordfish with corn relish, wood-roasted chicken with a chèvre fondue and that bistro staple, steak with provençal herb frites.

The bistro has a beer and wine license, but has shed its status as a daytime hangout for coffee and espresso.

(207) 230-0083. Entrées, $20 to $26. Dinner, Monday-Saturday 5:30 to 10. Closed mid-February through March.

Bouchée Bistro, 31 Elm St., Camden.

The setting is understated and the food highly regarded at this bistro that opened in 2005 in snug quarters formerly occupied by the Frogwater Café. Chef-owner Robert Taylor moved in 2005 from the Canoe Club in Hanover, N.H., to renovate the place with his partner, Ami Moore, the hostess. Bouchée translates in French roughly to mouthful, the chef says. He features seasonal New England ingredients, most of them organic or free-range, with a hint of a French influence.

Salads are featured on the appetizer menu, from "greens, greens and more greens" and a roasted heirloom beet salad with Vermont chèvre to a duck confit salad. The house salad contains baby spinach, apples, cranberries, candied pecans and blue cheese, dressed with a cider vinaigrette. A mushroom tart and steamed mussels were the only non-salad starters at our visit, the latter served with a pile of garlicky fries in such demand they can be ordered as a stand-alone appetizer.

Main courses range from wild king salmon with herbed crème fraîche to free-range sirloin with a marchand de vin butter. The crispy Long Island duck breast might be sauced with port wine and cherries. Pomegranate molasses flavors the grilled natural pork chop.

Desserts are where the chef really concocts a few surprises. You can't go wrong with his vanilla bean crème brûlée or his individual German chocolate cake. The golden pineapple and raspberry red wine sorbets are hailed; the Thai basil sorbet was rather odd.

The unusual wine list is full of unfamiliar names. It's priced from $18 to $40.

(207) 236-8998. www.boucheebistro.com. Entrées, $20 to $26. Dinner nightly except Tuesday, 5:30 to 9 or 10.

A 'Secret' Lobster Find

Waterman's Beach Lobster, 343 Waterman Beach Road, South Thomaston.

Rockland may be the lobster capital of the world, but the best place to eat lobster hereabouts is about five miles south at this off-the-beaten-path seasonal lobster shack that won a James Beard award in 2001 as an American classic – "just a regional award, not fancy gourmet or anything," owners Anne and Lorri Cousens assured. Order a lobster roll ($9.95), steamed clams or a one-pound lobster dinner ($11.95), or splurge for the lobster and steamed clam combo ($21.95). Sides of corn on the cob and coleslaw are 95 cents each. The only non-seafood item is a hot dog and chips for $1.75. The owners also bake superior rhubarb, lemon sponge and blueberry pies. Take your meal to one of the cloth-covered picnic tables on an open deck overlooking a jetty and watch lobster being unloaded from lobster traps or arriving from the Spruce Head lobster pound a mile away. No buildings are in sight to mar the view or tranquil setting.

(207) 596-7819 or (207) 594-7518. Lobster dinners, $11.95 to $35.95 depending on size. Open mid-June to Labor Day, Thursday-Sunday 11 to 7. BYOB.

A Jolly Cantina

Dos Amigos, 144 Bayside Road, Northport.

Adobe-colored with aqua trim, the jolly exterior of this unlikely-looking Mexican cantina alongside Route 1 deceives. It appears small, but inside is a colorful space with quite a collection of sombreros on the walls and seating for 125. A newly enlarged outside deck is colorful as well.

The food as orchestrated by owners Don and Tarijita Warner is authentic and packs a wallop. Chips and excellent salsa laced with cilantro get meals off to a good start, along with, perhaps, a zinger of a "cadillac" margarita incorporating cointreau and grand marnier. For a summer lunch, the chorizo and corn chowder was excellent, and the fire-roasted chicken fajita salad assertive. So was the open-faced steak fajita sandwich, accompanied by spicy island fries. Our mouths were left tingling, even after sharing the margarita cheesecake for dessert.

Umbrella-covered tables on expanded outdoor deck flank entrance to Dos Amigos.

The interesting menu covers all the usual bases and then some: scallops acapulco, spicy crab cakes with smoky chipotle cream sauce, cancun soft lobster tacos, lobster and brie chile rellenos, blue crab enchiladas, and roasted red chile pork over rice. All dishes are considered mild to mildly spicy, but can be made hotter and spicier on request. Ask for the red-hot firecracker salsa if you like really hot. The jalapeño corn fritters, the crab empanadas, and the smoked duck and jalapeño jack flautas are recommended starters. Kahlua mousse and the chambord torte are refreshing endings.

(207) 338-5775. Entrées, $9 to $15. Lunch from noon, daily in summer, Friday-Sunday in late spring and early fall. Dinner nightly, from 5. Closed January and February.

Dining and Lodging

Harraseeket Inn, 162 Main St., Freeport 04032.

In Freeport, where the supply of rooms can hardly keep up with the onslaught of shoppers, sisters Nancy Gray and Jody Dyer of Connecticut's Inn at Mystic got their foot in the door in 1984 with an elegant, five-room B&B in an 1850 Greek Revival farmhouse. A few years and many millions of dollars later, they added a three-story, 49-room inn and 85-seat restaurant and followed that with an expanded tavern, an enclosed swimming pool and 30 more guest rooms.

Standard rooms contain two double beds or one queensize with blue and white fabric half-canopies and a single wing chair. Our deluxe third-floor room offered a kingsize bed with a partial-canopy headboard and botanical prints, a sofa and wing chair beneath a palladian window, a working fireplace, a wet bar and a small refrigerator, a TV hidden in an armoire, and an enormous bath with a jacuzzi. Turndown service produced chocolates at night. The newest wing holds 30 more rooms, a mix of luxury units with fireplaces and jacuzzis and others with two double beds for traveling families. All told, the inn offers 41 accommodations with whirlpool tubs, 23 of those with fireplaces.

Excellent meals are available in two venues. The stylish **Maine Dining Room,** divided into three sections and warmed by two fireplaces, is pretty as a picture. Black windsor chairs and a few banquettes flank tables set formally with white linens, heavy silver, silver service plates and pink stemware. From a state-of-the-art kitchen comes some highly rated new American fare. The stress is on products from area farmers and growers, all of whom are nicely credited on a page at the back of the menu. Main courses range from organic chicken stuffed with mushrooms and spinach to "tableside classics" for two – tamarind-glazed rack of lamb and all-natural châteaubriand. Recent choices included onion-seed-crusted halibut with a brunoise of provençal vegetables and locally raised beef tenderloin with a smoked peppercorn gastrique. Lobster turns up in such starters as sherried lobster stew, chilled lobster cannelloni, lobster risotto and lobster bruschetta or in a main course of lobster fricassee. Finish with a flourish: rum-flamed Jamaican bananas, chocolate overdose flamed with grand marnier, a choice of crêpes, the evening's soufflé or one of the exotic homemade ice creams and sorbets.

The relocated **Broad Arrow Tavern** now fronting on Main Street is a beauty in hunter green, with seating for 100 plus a pleasant outdoor patio that catches passersby. The tavern is outfitted with old snowshoes, paddles, fly rods and a moosehead. "It's my life in review," said Nancy Gray, recalling her upbringing in a Maine sporting camp. The extensive tavern menu features hot-rock cooking, as well as grilled items from a wood-fired oven and grill in an open kitchen.

A full breakfast buffet, from fresh fruit and biscuits to scrambled eggs and french toast, is included for overnight guests. Guests also enjoy afternoon tea with quite a spread of pastries and sandwiches, served in a large and sumptuous, mahogany-paneled drawing room.

(207) 865-9377 or (800) 342-6423. Fax (207) 865-1684. www.stayfreeport.com. Eighty-two rooms and two suites with private baths. July-October: doubles $189 to $299, suites $295 to $305. Rest of year: doubles $125 to $252, suites $230 to $260.

Entrées, $21 to $35. Lunch daily, 11:30 to 2:30. Dinner nightly, 5:30 to 9 or 9:30. Sunday brunch. Tavern, daily from 11:30; entrées, $8.95 to $34.95.

The Lawnmere Inn and Restaurant, Route 27, Box 505, West Boothbay Harbor 04575.

Virtually every table has a water view in the wide dining room of this Southport Island inn's restaurant that's stylish in white by day and romantic by candlelight at night.

Chef Bill Edgerton supplements the regular menu with a page of daily specials – things like garlicky linguini tossed with smoked salmon and peas alfredo as an appetizer and a trio of fish (swordfish with pesto, tuna with soy and garlic, and sole with crabmeat and tomato) as an entrée, both of which proved exceptional. When one of us chose the fish trio over the lobster Johnny Walker but wanted to sample the sauce, the chef obliged with a taste on the side.

We also can vouch for the shrimp in parchment with julienned vegetables, new potatoes and crisp yellow squash and zucchini, and the poached salmon with dill-hollandaise sauce. Other main dishes could be Maine lobster risotto, chicken paprikash, peppercorn-rubbed filet mignon with cognac demi-glace, and grilled london broil of venison with oyster mushrooms and bordelaise sauce.

Enclosed porch is pleasant setting for breakfast or dinner at Hartstone Inn.

Vermont maple crème brûlée, blueberry bread pudding with crème anglaise, grand marnier mousse and key lime pie are among the delightful desserts.

New owners Scott and Corinne Larson of the Newagen Seaside Inn, who took over the old Lawmeer in 2004 and restored its original spelling, reconfigured and refurbished the lobby, front desk and common areas to take better advantage of the waterside location. They also renovated the inn's second and third floors to produce seven rooms and four suites, most with water views. Updated with a light 21st-century look, rooms are painted in Victorian Painted Lady colors and furnished with stunning original artworks. Twenty more rooms, some with king beds or queen four-posters, are in two annex buildings on either side. There's a charming cottage for two with a kingsize bed and a sun deck at water's edge.

Drinks are available in the Wobbly Lobster bar, painted a stunning poppy red.

Breakfast, included in the rates and available to the public, is served in the sunny dining room flanked by a spacious new deck. Ours produced a superior tomato and herb omelet with whole-wheat toast and roast beef hash topped with two poached eggs.

(207) 633-2544 or (800) 633-7645. www.lawnmereinn.com. Twenty-seven rooms, four suites and one cottage with private baths. Doubles, $155 to $189 late June to Labor Day, $89 to $165 rest of season. Closed mid-October to late May.

Entrées, $15.50 to $29. Dinner 6 to 9, nightly mid-June to Labor Day, Tuesday-Sunday to Columbus Day, Thursday-Sunday in spring. Sunday brunch, 8 to 11.

Hartstone Inn, 41 Elm St., Camden 04843.

Their work in gourmet restaurants for Hyatt and Sonesta hotels inspired Michael and Mary Jo Salmon to take over the small Hartstone Inn in 1998. They prettied up the dining room in beige and white, added an enclosed porch along the side and now seat twenty people for dinners of distinction.

Michael, named the Caribbean's top chef in 1996 when he was at a Sonesta Beach resort on Aruba, buys his food fresh daily for his changing five-course menus and teaches occasional cooking classes at the inn in winter. In 2005 he published favorite recipes in a 248-page cookbook, *Hartstone Inn, Signature Recipes from an Elegant Maine Inn.*

His cuisine is contemporary and his presentations artistic. One night's dinner began with Maine crab and shrimp cakes with sweet corn relish and Caribbean rémoulade and a salad of baby greens with snow peas, crisp rice noodles and ginger dressing. Blueberry sorbet prepared the palate for pistachio-crusted rack of lamb with anna potatoes. Dessert was grand marnier soufflé with an orange crème anglaise.

Typical main courses are Maine lobster with angel-hair pasta and asparagus, veal saltimbocca with mushroom-thyme couscous, and potato-crusted filet mignon with portobello-merlot butter and herbed potatoes. Individual warm soufflés are usually the dessert, variously featuring blueberry-hazelnut, chocolate, chambord and macadamia nut flavors.

The feast can be accompanied by a selection from Michael's choice and growing wine cellar.

In the main inn the Salmons offer eight guest rooms, two with fireplaces and all with queen beds covered with feather duvets. They perked up the decor, shunning the former country style for a more traditionally elegant look. All rooms have CD players, tiled-floor baths and triple-paned windows to muffle street noise. On the main floor, a formal parlor harbors a fireplace and a rear library is furnished in leather. A restored carriage house in the rear offers two bi-level suites done in contemporary barn style, with kingsize beds, fireplaced living rooms, TVs hidden in armoires and private entrances overlooking the gardens in which the Salmons grow herbs and vegetables for their restaurant.

Tucked away in a flower garden are two new suites with sitting rooms created when the Salmons vacated their quarters and moved to an adjoining property they now call the Manor House on Free Street. The Cottage Suite has a queen poster bed, fireplace and bath with whirlpool tub. The Manor House contains two more large guest rooms, one the summery, cathedral-ceilinged Arbor with kingsize mahogany sleigh bed, gas fireplace and TV/VCR.

An extravagant breakfast is served in the dining room or the adjacent enclosed porch. The morning of our visit began with a poached pear and pound cake with blueberry-walnut sauce. A baked egg with prosciutto and spinach tortilla followed. Michael's recipe for lobster and asparagus quiche was requested by Gourmet magazine.

(207) 236-4259 or (800) 788-4823. Fax (207) 236-9575. www.hartstoneinn.com. Ten rooms and four suites with private baths. Late June through October: doubles $125 to $250, suites $245 to $250. Rest of year: doubles $100 to $185, suites $175 to $195.

Prix-fixe, $45. Dinner by reservation, Wednesday-Sunday at 7, June-October; Thursday-Sunday rest of year.

Inn at Ocean's Edge, U.S. Route 1, Lincolnville (Box 704, Camden 04843).

Secluded at the foot of a seven-acre slope just 150 feet from the ocean, this new and expanding inn has all the bells and whistles required for a four-diamond AAA rating as well as the dramatic facilities that make for a show-stopper along the Maine coast.

Cool blue room at The Edge opens onto wood-fired bar area and windows onto water.

What began in 1998 as a fifteen-room inn, an outgrowth of a modest B&B, evolved in 2005 into a four-building complex – literally at ocean's edge – with 27 rooms and suites, a spa with a spectacular "horizon-edge" swimming pool, and an over-the-top restaurant. The latter upgrades are the work of new owners Tim and Joan Porta, who run Migas Lodge in the Sebago Lake region, and their partner-in-residence, Jesse Henry.

All but one of the guest rooms in the original buildings face the ocean (the exception is an enormous handicapped-accessible suite that's twice the size of the rest). The others are no slouches at 400 square feet each. They are virtually the same, but with different wallpapers and linens. Each has a kingsize four-poster bed, wing chairs facing a corner fireplace, a TV/VCR, an oversize jacuzzi flanked by pillars and open to the bedroom, and a separate bathroom with the inn's own toiletries. The twelve newest in the Hilltop Building come with private balconies that take advantage of the ocean view.

Breakfast for inn guests is served in the main inn's soaring Great Room with vaulted ceiling and two levels of windows onto the oceanfront. There's another Great Room in a new building that looks like someone's house, between the inn and the restaurant. Here spa treatments are available, and two new guest rooms overlook a heated outdoor swimming pool, which gives the illusion that you could swim off the edge right into the ocean.

The crowning glory is the new two-story restaurant and lounge, which opened in stages in 2005 and 2006. First came **The Edge,** a 40-seat restaurant on the main floor. It's edgy in cool blue and beige, with upholstered-seat chairs and leather banquettes at modern wood laminated tables facing floor-to-ceiling windows onto a deck with a view of the ocean beyond. Nine more seats are set around what the staff calls a wood-fired bar for its cooking oven. Downstairs is the plush Tantalus Bar with a stone fireplace, plus a wine room for private parties. A grand, stone-rimmed flagstone terrace beside the water is used for drinks and appetizers, but meals were to be served here with the opening in 2006 of an addition with another 30-seat dining room, bar and deck.

Executive chef Bryan Dame, a New England Culinary Institute alumnus who has cooked in restaurants from Philadelphia to Deer Isle, oversees some serious culinary endeavors. Notable for their succinct, straightforward terminology, his short opening menus featured the likes of mustard-glazed salmon, crispy seared halibut, salt-roasted lobster and pan-roasted filet mignon.

Typical starters were port-glazed veal sweetbreads with sweet potato ravioli and a brick-oven roasted crab cake with malt vinegar aioli. Sweet endings included a three-mousse "martini," warm apple pie with Katahdin cheddar, and a selection of cheeses "from Maine and Away."

Although the restaurant is within leisurely walking distance of the main inn, it is a longer walk from the public parking area. Diners are shuttled to and fro in golf carts.

(207) 236-0945. Fax (207) 236-0609. www.innatoceansedge.com. Twenty-six rooms and one suite with private baths. Doubles, $239 to $295 early June through mid-October, $159 rest of year.

The Edge, (207) 236-4430. Entrées, $28 to $34. Dinner nightly from 5:30, July-October, Thursday-Sunday in off-season. Closed January-March.

Lodging

Log Cabin – An Island Inn, Route 24, Box 410, Bailey Island 04003.

This started as a restaurant in a log cabin, but you'd never know it following its recent upgrade. Downsizing and ultimately closing (to the public) their popular restaurant to add lodging, Sue and Neal Favreau offer nine comfortable accommodations, each with its own deck upon which to savor the water views.

The bright and airy second-floor York Room has a queen bed, TV and telephone, kitchenette, jacuzzi tub and separate shower. The Mount Washington suite atop a former garage comes with a full kitchen, separate kingsize bedroom, two TVs, stereo and a deck with a private hot tub, from which on a clear day you can see New England's tallest peak 90 miles away. The new Harpswell suite also has an upstairs kingsize bedroom with private balcony and bath with jacuzzi tub, living room with gas stove, kitchen and private hot tub on the lower-level deck. Along with the TV/VCRs standard in all rooms, the Sunset and Westview rooms offer gas fireplaces as well as jacuzzi tubs and queensize beds.

With the switch in emphasis from restaurant to lodging, the Log Cabin added a great new swimming pool.

Dinner is available for inn guests in a cozy, lodge-like room with a moosehead above the fireplace, in an intimate front bar and on enclosed porches with water views. Sue, who has been in the restaurant business since she was 13 and originally ran the late Rock Ovens nearby, oversees the kitchen. A typical menu includes lobster, filet mignon, a chicken dish and two or three special entrées as well as appetizers and desserts.

Guests enjoy a complimentary breakfast of eggs or french toast with meats and home fries.

(207) 833-5546. Fax (207) 833-7858. www.logcabin-maine.com. Nine rooms with private baths. Doubles, $159 to $309 in summer, $99 to $209 in spring, $139 to $259 in fall. Closed November-March.

Coveside Bed & Breakfast, 5 Gott's Cove Lane, Georgetown 04548.

Memorable breakfasts are among the treats at this stylish B&B, vastly upgraded by new owners Tom and Carolyn Church. But for the forested five-acre setting beside the water, former guests – we among them – barely recognize the place, such is the extent of renovations inside and out, plus the addition of a new guest cottage on the site of the former carriage house. The changes were impressive enough that Coveside served as a background in 2001 for the Coldwater Creek catalog.

The Churches have furnished the parlor and bedrooms smartly in updated summer-cottage style reminiscent of the early 1900s. Four guest rooms in the main house and three in the cottage yield water views down the lawn or through the trees to Gott's Cove and Sheepscot Bay.

Prime quarters are upstairs in the cottage, which offers a common lounge with fireplace and wet bar and a screened porch overlooking the water. Rooms here have kingsize beds and sitting areas in front of a fireplace. The two upstairs have cathedral ceilings and private decks. Rooms in the main house come with queensize beds topped with handsome quilts. One room has a private porch and another a fireplace with sitting area and a whirlpool tub.

Breakfasts are prepared by Carolyn, a former pastry chef, and served in an atrium or on the back deck. Expect such treats as sourdough blueberry pancakes, orange-date french toast, cheese blintzes with blueberry sauce and even crab cakes with oven-roasted potatoes.

Outside, flower beds surround an expansive patio with several sitting areas from which to take in the watery scene.

(207) 371-2807 or (800) 232-5490. www.covesidebandb.com. Seven rooms with private baths. Doubles, $115 to $189. Closed mid-October to Memorial Day.

Five Gables Inn, Murray Hill Road, Box 335, East Boothbay 04544.

Perched on a hillside overlooking Linekin Bay, this five-gabled establishment dates back more than 110 years and was the last remaining summer hotel in the area. It was love at first sight for Mike and De Kennedy, who had just concluded a "mid-life break" in which they crewed on a yacht in French Polynesia and backpacked for six months from Bali to Nepal.

Previous owners had renovated the old Forest House into their dream B&B by the water. The Kennedys had only to add their personal touches and experiences, which they have in abundance. Mike, a graduate of the Culinary Institute of America when it was in New Haven, has worked his way around much of the world. He and De moved to Maine from Atlanta, where he renovated old homes, performed in TV commercials and gave historic tours. De, an artist, comes from an old Southern family and prepped for innkeeping by organizing house parties at her family's ante-bellum retreat in the Georgia hills.

Here they entertain guests in sixteen rooms on three floors, all with a water view. All have modern baths and queensize beds (one kingsize), and five have working fireplaces. Lace curtains and quilts color-coordinated to De's artistic accents and the pictures on the walls enhance the decor, all of which is light, airy and new. De crocheted the afghans that grace many of the rooms.

Mike puts his cooking background to the test at multi-course breakfasts, served in a spacious common room appointed with wing chairs and bouquets of fresh flowers. His repertoire lasts for two weeks, a daily procession of, say, zucchini-walnut pancakes, quiche lorraine, blueberry french toast or basil-tomato frittata.

Potatoes anna, fried tomatoes, blueberry crisp and pear in puff pastry might accompany, along with fresh-ground Columbian coffee.

De offers afternoon tea in the English manner, served with chocolate chip cookies and poppyseed or banana bread and taken in the airy living room or on the wraparound veranda, where a hammock and abundant sitting areas take in the view of the bay. Port, sherry and madeira are put out on the sideboard in the evening.

(207) 633-4551 or (800) 451-5048. www.fivegablesinn.com. Sixteen rooms with private baths. Doubles, $140 to $210. Closed November to mid-May.

Welch House Inn, 56 McKown St., Boothbay Harbor 04538.

Gourmet breakfasts are the forte at this B&B, housed in a 19th-century sea captain's home atop McKown Hill in the center of Boothbay Harbor and enjoying some of the best views in town.

The panorama captivated Susan Hodder and Michael Feldman, a Massachusetts couple who gave up high-tech careers for innkeeping. They offer fourteen guest rooms with remodeled bathrooms, two with new whirlpool tubs. Many have gas fireplaces. Beds are king or queensize except for a couple with two double beds. Rooms in the Victorian-style main inn have TV/VCRs and telephones. Art by local artisans adorns the walls, and decor is a mix of old and new. Five more nautical rooms are in the adjacent Sail Loft.

A recent addition, all glassed in to take advantage of the harbor view, houses a large living room with fireplace and a huge room for breakfast. The best views are from the enlarged main-floor deck and the rooftop sundeck, now big enough to accommodate all guests at once – and then some.

Susan prepares a gourmet breakfast, perhaps poached eggs florentine one day and strawberry-cream cheese stuffed french toast the next. She figures most people who come to Maine ought to have lobster for breakfast, so she obliges on weekends with a lobster soufflé or a lobster and crabmeat omelet.

(207) 633-3431 or (800) 279-7313. Fax (207) 633-3752. www.welchhouseinn.com. Fourteen rooms with private baths. Doubles, $135 to $195, Memorial Day to Columbus Day, $85 to $145 rest of year.

The Harbor View Inn at Newcastle, 34 Main St., Box 791, Newcastle 04553.

On a hillside just off Coastal Route 1, this newish B&B offers gourmet breakfasts, comfortable accommodations and water views.

The breakfasts are the labor of love of owner Joe McEntee, who left the corporate world to enroll in culinary school. After working as a chef and manager at leading Philadelphia restaurants, he bought this house in 1996 to begin a new career as a bed and breakfast host. From his gorgeous kitchen open to the dining room, he serves a multi-course repast at an oval table for six beside a brick fireplace or outside on a deck looking onto the harbor. The main course might be a fancy egg dish or french toast garnished with fresh fruit. Joe's lemon-raspberry muffins are a favorite of guests.

The common facilities are distinctive here, especially the extra-large living room with big windows and several conversation areas, and the expansive side deck. There's also a reading area in the second-floor hallway.

Guest rooms are large and airy with tiled baths, sitting areas, TVs and telephones. The two upstairs rooms also have fireplaces and private decks. The largest is the Damariscotta with a kingsize sleigh bed and a loveseat beneath an unusual beamed and pitched ceiling notable for interesting angles. Decor is crisp and stylish throughout.

(207) 563-2900. www.theharborview.com. Three rooms with private baths. Doubles, $135 to $195 July-October, $115 to $160 rest of year.

The Berry Manor Inn, 81 Talbot Ave., Rockland 04841.

This handsome B&B is painted berry red with mustard yellow trim to honor the memory of merchant Charles Berry, who built the house in 1898. Original signed wallpaper and a water downspout are encased in glass to indicate the meticulous restoration of one of Rockland's larger houses, located in a quiet residential section.

Michael LaPosta and his wife, Cheryl Michaelsen, installed seven gas fireplaces, five jacuzzi tubs and several hundred rolls of wallpaper to turn it into Mid-coast Maine's first AAA four-diamond B&B. They offer eight spacious corner bedrooms on the second and third floors. Each comes with king or queensize bed, comfortable sitting area, telephone and full closet with built-in chest of drawers. All enveloped in luxury, some are feminine and manifestly Victorian. Others are masculine and quite un-Victorian.

Three high-end rooms and a suite, all with fireplaces and three with jacuzzi tubs, were added lately in the side carriage house.

The inn's entire main floor is turned over to guests: a formal sitting room, a more casual living room with big-screen TV, a dining room with individual tables and a guest pantry stocked with everything from cookies or cakes and raspberry pies baked by Mike's mother to soft drinks and beer.

Cheryl's multi-course breakfasts are big deals and feature blueberries in some form every day. The meal when we were there began with juices and warm fruit compote over homemade granola. Baked eggs with tomato and basil were accompanied by new red potatoes with dill. Blueberry buckle followed. Other main-course favorites are lemon-blueberry pancakes, blueberry-stuffed french toast, eggs florentine and shirred eggs with havarti cheese.

(207) 596-7696 or (800) 774-5692. Fax (207) 596-9958. www.berrymanorinn.com. Eleven rooms and one suite with private baths. Mid-June to mid-October: doubles $145 to $235, suite $340. Rest of year: doubles $105 to $165, suite $220.

The Hawthorn, 9 High St., Camden 04843.

Elegance and comfort are the hallmarks of this 1894 Queen Anne-style beauty, one of the few B&Bs in town with glimpses of the Camden harbor. Well-traveled owner Maryanne Shanahan offers ten guest quarters and a nicely landscaped back yard sloping down toward the harbor and a gate opening onto the town amphitheater.

Six guest quarters are in the main inn and four in the rear carriage house, painted in barn red with a pale yellow trim that matches the house. Most have queensize beds.

Appointed in upscale cabin style, the new Cloud Nine Suite covers much of the third floor. It has a sitting room with day bed and a gas log fireplace, and a bath with slipper soaking tub and separate shower. The large kingsize bedroom, decorated in gray and mauve, has a TV/VCR and a cozy table for two in the turret.

The other four prime accommodations, three with double jacuzzis and three with gas fireplaces, are in the carriage house. All have private rear decks or patios, aqua blue upholstered rocker or swivel chairs, and TV/VCRs. Maryanne renovated the downstairs Watney into "a sensuous and serene retreat," installing a double jacuzzi and two-person shower in its large bath. A collection of birdhouses is hung as art on the walls of the Cabriolet, prized for its garden patio. The best view is from the upstairs Norfolk, a huge room with kingsize bed, extra day bed, gas stove and private deck overlooking a meditation garden, a shady lawn and the harbor. The adjacent Broughman Room offers a mahogany poster bed, stenciling around the jacuzzi and another great water view.

Back in the main house is a double parlor with not one but two turrets. Healthful breakfasts featuring locally grown and organic products are served at individual tables in a formal dining room or on a spacious rear deck extending nearly the width of the house. The fare the day we visited included a fresh fruit plate, Maryanne's secret hazelnut granola (so good she packages it for sale at the request of guests) and individual cheddar soufflés with homemade tomato salsa and mixed organic greens in a lemon-champagne vinaigrette. Other favorites are raspberry-pecan belgian waffles with sour cream, crêpes incorporating five types of organic mushrooms and dry vermouth, and peach-pecan pancakes with blueberry-peach topping. In lieu of breakfast meats she might serve fish, smoked and otherwise. Guests tell Maryanne she serves the best breakfasts they ever had.

Limeade and iced tea are offered summer afternoons on the deck.

(207) 236-8842 or (866) 381-3647. Fax (207) 236-6181. www.camdenhawthorn.com. Eight rooms and two suites with private baths. Doubles, $129 to $289 May to mid-November, $99 to $199 rest of year.

Camden Maine Stay, 22 High St., Camden 04843.

Started rather simply by doting innkeepers whose skills were the envy of their colleagues, the Maine Stay expanded, upgraded and lured a repeat clientele to the point where it was the one B&B in Camden that always seemed to be fully booked when others hung out "vacancy" signs.

Retired business executive Bob Topper and his Austrian-born wife Juanita inherited a going concern when they took over the rambling 1802 farmhouse that started with nine bedrooms sharing three baths. The Maine Stay now has eight bedrooms and suites, all with updated baths (some with Corian tiled showers), and some with gas fireplaces or wood stoves. All are comfortably furnished and decorated with style.

The former Room 3, upstairs front, is typical of the accommodations as they have evolved. Formerly two small rooms with a shared bath, it is now the Christina Topper Suite with a sofabed and gas fireplace in the front sitting room, a queen brass bed in back and a private deck. The attached carriage house harbors a delightful downstairs room, cheery in white with blue trim and yellow accents, with queen bed, gas stove and private stone patio – who would guess it was once a root cellar with no windows and a dirt floor? Another favorite is the Common Ground Room decorated with agricultural fair posters. It has a vaulted ceiling, tall windows, queen bed, Maine cottage furniture and a Vermont Castings stove, plus an outside deck.

Guests are welcome to light the fireplaces in two parlors and a library/TV room, enjoy the rear sun porch or seats in the two-acre back yard, or come into the expansive country kitchen for cookies and cheer.

Breakfast is a convivial gathering, served amidst fine Aynsley china and Simon Pearce crystal at a harvest table in the dining room or at tables for two on the sun porch overlooking the garden. Juanita, who does the cooking, prepared quiche the morning of our latest visit and was planning peach french toast the next day.

(207) 236-9636. Fax (207) 236-0621. www.camdenmainestay.com. Six rooms and two suites with private baths. Doubles, $135 to $250 June-October, $110 to $175 rest of year.

Trellis and turret enhance Victorian B&B known as A Little Dream.

A Little Dream, 66 High St., Camden 04843.

Piles of thank-you notes on the table at the entry, books of love letters and poems, an abundance of lace and a welcoming lemonade, served in a tall glass with a sprig of mint plus blueberries and strawberries, signify that this charming place is special. It's a little dream for Joanne Fontana and her husband, Billy, a sculptor and handyman-remodeler, who have decorated their turreted Victorian house with great flair.

From the pretty wicker and chintz furnished parlor to the elaborately decorated dining room to the conservatory they added off the dining room, everything is accessorized to perfection. Lace pillows on a chaise, tea sets, old playing cards, tiny sentimental books tucked here and there – you know that Joanne, who says "I have the nicest guests in the whole world," loves to pamper them.

Three spacious bedrooms and a suite in the house are decorated to the hilt with Victorian clothing, lace, ribbons and at least eight pillows on each bed. Every room has TV and telephone, designer linens and down duvets, spa-style robes, a basket of hand towels, Crabtree & Evelyn amenities and imported chocolates.

Three deluxe accommodations in the carriage house offer seclusion and Penobscot Bay views.

The Isle Watch here is a huge room with kingsize iron canopy bed, a chintz sofa and wing chair, and a window seat looking onto a glorious private porch. The porch, furnished with wicker rockers and a hanging glider/swing, yields a great view of Penobscot Bay, Curtis Island and the lights of passing boats at night. The bath contains a double soaking tub and separate shower. There's also a hidden TV, its whereabouts a pleasant surprise – one of several "surprises" with which Joanne entices her guests.

The top level of the carriage house holds a Loft room and Treetops, a suite with living room, queen bedroom and a front balcony with an island view.

Breakfasts, served on lace-clothed tables topped with floral mats and heavy silver, are gala here. Guests choose from a fancy menu placed in their rooms the night before.

The choice might involve lemon-ricotta soufflé pancakes with fresh raspberry sauce, banana-pecan waffles with maple country sausage, or three kinds of omelets: smoked salmon, apple-cheddar and ham-swiss. The coffee is breakfast blend or chocolate-raspberry or hazelnut. Orange or cranberry juice, fresh fruit and muffin of the day come with.

At check-in, the Fontanas serve the aforementioned lemonade or strawberry or peach herbal iced tea, with fresh mint from the garden. Cocktail time may bring a tray of pâtés, including smoked trout, and olives.

(207) 236-8742 or (800) 217-0109. www.littledream.com. Five rooms and two suites with private baths. Mid-May through October: doubles $159 to $225, suites $215 to $295. Rest of year: doubles $115 to $135, suites $125 to $195.

The Inn at Sunrise Point, U.S. Route 1, Lincolnville (Box 1344, Camden 04843).

Here is the inn of an inn reviewer's dreams. After critiquing others across the country, California-based travel writer Jerry Levitin opened his own B&B on four forested acres at the foot of a private lane descending from Route 1 to Penobscot Bay. "I built what I'd like to stay at," said Jerry, who eventually tired of innkeeping and sold to Stephen Tallon from Ireland and his wife Deanna from Australia.

They converted the seasonal operation into a year-round endeavor, offering three rooms in the shingle-style main house plus four cottages and two suites.

A new suite, just twenty feet from water's edge, is the former owner's quarters with queen bedroom, living/dining room, kitchen and deck. The Tallons named the suite for Jerry Levitin and decorated it in a travel theme.

The Winslow Homer Cottage that we occupied right beside the water contains a kingsize bed, a fireplace, TV/VCR, wet bar and an enormous bathroom with a jacuzzi for two and a separate shower.

Also close to the water and with the same attributes is the Fitz Hugh Lane Cottage.

Two smaller cottages possess queen beds as do three smaller rooms upstairs in the main inn. Each has a fireplace, music system, built-in desk, double whirlpool tub, armoire holding TV and VCR, and a private balcony overlooking the water. The new Loft Suite has a king bed, polished hardwood floors, clawfoot soaking tub and a steam shower.

Guests are welcomed in the main inn with afternoon beverages. The Tallons have a full liquor license – one of the "plush upgrades" they added to the inn.

The main floor harbors a wonderful living/dining room that's mostly windows onto the water, an English hunting-style library with a fireplace and a small conservatory for tête-à-tête breakfasts. Deanna serves treats like grand marnier-french toast, stratas, scrambles and Irish soda bread. We feasted here on fruit, pecan coffeecake, a terrific frittata with basil, bay shrimp and jack cheese, potatoes dusted with cayenne, crisp bacon and hazelnut coffee.

Upon departure, we found a card under our windshield: "Our porter has cleaned your windscreen to allow you to get a clear picture of our Penobscot Bay."

(207) 236-7716. Fax (207) 236-0820. www.sunrisepoint.com. Three rooms, two suites and four cottages with private baths. Doubles, $310 to $330. Suites and cottages, $350 to $495. Off-season: doubles $225 to $245, suites and cottages $250 to $300.

Breakfast is served in formal dining room at Norumbega.

A Regal Experience

Norumbega, 61 High St., Camden 04843.

Ensconced in one of the finest "castles" along the Maine coast is this elegant B&B with great style and a combination lock on the front door to deter curious passersby.

The cobblestone and slate-roofed mansion, built in 1886 for the inventor of the duplex system of telegraphy, was for a few years the summer home of journalist Hodding Carter. The exterior is said to be Maine's most photographed piece of real estate.

Inside are endlessly fascinating public rooms (the woodwork alone is priceless), eleven bedrooms and two suites, all with sitting areas and telephones, and some with TVs. The ones in back have breathtaking views of Penobscot Bay. Most have fireplaces and canopy beds, all kingsize except for a queen in the smallest garden-level room. The ultimate is the penthouse suite, a bit of a climb up a spiral staircase from the third floor. It offers a kingsize bed, a regal bath with pillows around a circular ebony tub big enough for two, a wet bar, a sitting room in pink and green, and a see-through, three-sided fireplace, plus a little porch with two deck chairs and a fabulous water view.

Guests have the run of the common areas and a small library, an intimate retreat for two beside a fireplace on the landing of the ornate staircase, and flower-laden rear porches and balconies on all three floors overlooking expansive lawns and the bay.

Breakfast is a highlight. Served at a long table in the formal dining room or at a round glass table beside a telescope in the conservatory, it is a feast of juices and fruits, all kinds of breads and muffins, and, when we stayed, the best french toast ever, topped with a dollop of sherbet and sliced oranges. Eggs florentine or benedict, vegetable omelets, crêpes with an almond filling and peach topping, and ginger-apple pancakes are other favorites.

(207) 236-4646 or (877) 363-4646. Fax (207) 236-0824. www.norumbegainn.com. Eleven rooms and two suites with private baths. July to mid-October: doubles $160 to $340, suites $365 to $475. Rest of year: doubles $95 to $225, suites $250 to $375.

Gourmet Treats

The treats in this area begin at **Clayton's,** 106 Main St., Yarmouth, a must stop right off Route 1. Starting as a gourmet market affiliated with Treats in Wiscasset (see below), Martha and David Clayton made good use of their space in the old Masonic Hall, adding a coffee bar in the center and a café for lunch on the stage. The latter serves good sandwiches, salads and vegetarian items in the $5 range. We also like Clayton's for all its copper pots, cheeses, specialty foods, baked goods and even a canoe stocked with bargain wines.

In Freeport, home of outlets to serve almost every interest, a large **Ben & Jerry's Ice Cream** stand is set up right beside L.L. Bean. All the flavors of one of Vermont's best-known exporters are available, but not exactly at outlet prices. And you thought **L.L. Bean Co.** was just for great sportswear and equipment. This ever-changing and expanding emporium has a gourmet food shop with Maine-made and New England mail-order products, including its own line of raspberry jams, bittersweet fudge sauce, maple syrup and the like. From saltwater taffy and dandelion greens to Bean's-blend coffee beans, this place has it – or will soon.

If you tire of the Freeport outlet scene, head for South Freeport Harbor wharf and the **Harraseeket Lunch & Lobster Co.** This is what coastal Maine is supposed to look like, a lobster pound by a working dock. While it used to be little known, at recent visits there was no place to park and the lineup stretched a long way from the outside service window, where we like to pick up our food and then eat at a picnic table on the dock (there's a small dining room as well). The owners are noted for their basket dinners, varying from clam cakes to scallops to shrimp to "just fish," and combinations thereof. Other favorites are a fishwich, clamburger royale and lobster roll. Lobsters can be packed for travel.

Gourmet-oriented places seem to come and go in Brunswick. Lately, the action has been at **The Humble Gourmet,** 103 Pleasant St. Talented chef Chris Toole left the Harraseeket Inn to open this bakery and gourmet takeout place in a strip plaza along Route 1. Although the stress is on catering, the place offers lunchtime sandwiches and wraps, prepared foods (from pork tenderloin to shepherd's pie) and great baked goods. The intense lemon bars are to die for. In downtown Brunswick, **Scarlet Begonias** at 212B Maine St. draws locals and students from nearby Bowdoin College to a plant-filled haunt for interesting sandwiches, pastas and pizzas, worthy of either lunch or dinner. **Provisions** at 148 Maine St. is known for its wines and cheeses, but also offers specialty foods, breads and a café dispensing blackboard specials like Mediterranean fish stew and roasted vegetable lasagna.

In Wiscasset, English cheeses from a Covent Garden firm are one of the strengths of **Treats,** a special store on a prime corner of Main Street. Owner Paul Mrozinski offered a taste of cashel blue and we had to buy some, it was so buttery and delicious. We also had to buy one of the great breads from area bakeries, a crusty olive loaf (one of the others was rosemary and hazelnut), although we managed to resist the luscious-looking peach-raspberry pie. Paul describes the flavors of his farm cheeses much the way he distinguishes among his fine wines. Lately he has added to his selection of fine New England cheeses. In his expanded coffee bar and café, he also offers muffins and scones, sandwiches and salads for picnics, and dinner entrées to go. Across the street at the **Marston House,** Paul and his wife Sharon rent two B&B rooms with private baths in the carriage house behind their home, which is also an antiques shop. The $90 tab gets you a queensize bed, fireplace, private entrance and a hearty breakfast.

Native produce, specialty foods, wine, candies, pâtés, smoked salmon and croissants abound at **Weatherbird,** a gourmet food store and gift shop in a sprawl of a building called Northey Square off Main Street in Damariscotta.

You'll find at least 52 flavors at **Round Top Ice Cream,** 526 Main St., Damariscotta. This is the original home of the ice cream favored by restaurants throughout the region, an unpretentious spot on the farm where it began in 1924. The choices range from cappuccino to watermelon, from ginger to raspberry. Cones come in three sizes. You also can get a banana split.

"Color is our passion," say Chris and Richard Hilton of **Edgecomb Potters,** Route 27, Edgecomb. And colorful is their extraordinary glazed porcelain in various hues, shown inside and out at this must-stop place on the road into Boothbay Harbor. They have all kinds of pottery for kitchen and dining room, from garlic cellars and pâté dishes to snack trays and soup tureens, as well as decorative accessories.

Specialty foods, cookware, kitchen gadgets and fine pottery are among the wares at the rambling **Village Store,** part of the suave House of Logan enterprise in Boothbay Harbor.

Heading toward Rockland along Route 1, look for **The Well Tempered Kitchen**, in the stable of a 19th-century farm at 122 Atlantic Highway, Waldoboro. It holds quite an array of cookware, linens, Maine foods and more of interest to those "who love the process of cooking."

The Brown Bag at 606 Main St., Rockland, is a casual spot for breakfast, lunch or a snack. Four sisters started with a bakery and deli in the middle and expanded into a restaurant on one side and a gourmet food shop on the other. The extensive menu lists healthful selections at prices from yesteryear. Stop here for an oversize blueberry muffin, a lentil burger on a whole-wheat roll, a crab and cheddar melt, a loaf of basil bread or a slice of apple-raspberry pie.

A striking, plum-colored building with lavender trim houses **Miss Plum's Parlour** along Route 1 in Rockport. It's famous for ice creams and yogurts, served at a takeout window and available in changing flavors from red raspberry chip to toffee bar crunch. Sundaes, frappes, root-beer floats, lime rickeys, banana splits and more may be taken to lavender-colored picnic tables at the side. A stylish little restaurant offers a clever menu for inside dining. Come for a heart-healthy breakfast, a midday plum dog (frankfurter with chili, cheese, onion, salsa and sour cream) or a crabmeat cobb salad, fried clams, or meatloaf and gravy for a light dinner anytime. Open daily 7 a.m. to 10 p.m. in summer and fall.

Rockport folks favor **The Market Basket** at the junction of Routes 1 and 90, a specialty-food and wine store where you'll find everything from zucchini-feta casserole and Madagascar potato salad to Shaker cheddar soup and peach or strawberry pie. The frozen lemon mousse pie is one of the best desserts ever.

Our favorite shop among many in Camden is **Lily, Lupine & Fern,** 43 Main St. Owners Gary and Bunni Anderson have augmented its traditional flowers with cheeses, gourmet foods and a selection of wines and microbrewery beers.

Down East Maine

Lobster, Plus

We know, we know.

You're going Down East on vacation and you can't wait to clamp your teeth around a shiny red lobster. In fact, you can hardly think of anything else. Oh, maybe some fried clams or a bucket of steamers, but lobster is what you're really after.

So you'll stand in line to get into some dive for the $9.95 lobster special. You'll suck out the feelers and wrestle with the claws of your one-and-one-quarter-pound (if you're lucky) crustacean. You'll end up with about three ounces of lobster meat, debris all over your clothes and hands that reek for two days.

And you'll probably gush, "That was the *best* lobster I've ever had!"

Well, friends, we're here to tell you that there is life after lobster in Maine. A lot of fine, creative cooking is going on in the Pine Tree State, and in the last two decades a number of excellent restaurants have emerged Down East along the coast, many of them with young and innovative chefs.

Also available are suave inns and bed-and-breakfast establishments, which are giving visitors an alternative to the traditional cabins, campgrounds and motels that abound along the coast of Maine.

And, sign of the times, the coffee craze has infiltrated Maine. On a recent trip we were surprised by the Coffee Express Drive-Thru at the Maine Coast Mall in Ellsworth.

In this final chapter, we meander our way along the coast, peninsulas and islands, hitting the high spots from the Blue Hill Peninsula and Deer Isle to Bar Harbor, Acadia National Park and the Schoodic Peninsula – the epitome of Down East Maine.

Dining

The Best of the Best

Arborvine, Main Street, Blue Hill.

The chef who spearheaded the changes in Down East dining tastes a generation ago is back for an encore.

John Hidake, who launched Blue Hill's acclaimed Fire Pond restaurant in 1977 and led it through its glory years, and his wife Beth converted a rambling, 200-year-old Maine farmhouse on Tenney Hill into a fine-dining restaurant and headquarters for their Moveable Feasts catering service. Lately, they added the Vinery, a piano bar and bistro, open for light fare in what had been a deli/takeout shop at the rear of the property.

John had sold Fire Pond in 1987 because "we had achieved what we had set out to do" and he wanted to spend more time with his young family. "But I really missed the creativity of a restaurant kitchen, which you can't do in the catering business." He also missed his regular patrons, who had become close friends. His wide following missed him, too – in its earlier days, a trip to the Penobscot Bay area without a dinner at Fire Pond was unthinkable. All these factors conspired to prompt his return.

The new restaurant seats about 50 in two small front dining rooms and a larger, L-shaped room that doubles as a reception area and bar. Mismatched tables and

Original posts and beams are incorporated into dining room at Arborvine.

chairs in the Shaker, Heppelwhite and Windsor styles are set with antique linens, flowers and votive candles. Oriental rugs dot the floors. Each dining area has a fireplace and is furnished with antiques. John made some of the furniture himself.

The dinner menu features local seafood as well as heartier fare like tournedos bordelaise and rack of lamb with wild mushroom sauce. Seasonal dishes include broiled halibut with mushrooms and scallions in green curry sauce, grilled yellowfin ahi tuna with ginger-soy aioli, amaretto-glazed duckling with apple-ginger chutney, medallions of pork with apples and calvados-maple glaze, and grilled sirloin steak with a five-spice rub and cardamom-scented maitre d' butter. The night's specials might add treats like galettes of Maine crabmeat and shrimp with a light dijon sauce on a bed of herbed bulgur and grilled magret of moulard duck with plum-mint salsa.

Typical appetizers are a medley of smoked salmon, trout and mussels with horseradish cream, brie in puff pastry with figs and toasted almonds, and a salad of baby beets, leeks and pears with gorgonzola. Specials could be a soup of chilled avocado with crème fraîche and a salad of strawberries, mango and melon with toasted pistachios and a prickly pear vinaigrette.

Dessert favorites include grand marnier chocolate mousse, white chocolate cheesecake with berries and lemon curd tartlets.

The **Vinery,** a brick-floored conservatory, offers pastas and light fare in the $9 to $14 range. It's now run by the Hikades' son Andrew, who cooks in a separate kitchen. Son Tim serves as sous chef in his father's kitchen.

(207) 374-2119. www.arborvine.com. Entrées, $22 to $29. Dinner, Tuesday-Sunday 5 to 9:30, Friday-Sunday in winter. Vinery in season, Wednesday-Sunday 5 to 9.

The Wescott Forge, 66 Main St., Blue Hill.

Also back for an encore is our beloved Fire Pond – this time, after several reincarnations under different owners, with a new name, a new look and an acknowledged nod to the Fire Pond tradition.

After Frenchman Jean-Paul Lecomte closed his nighttime Jean-Paul at the Fire

Pond and his daytime Jean-Paul Bistro across the street, the Fire Pond building beside the millstream lay dormant until its rescue by Blue Hill resident Johnny Bravo and folks formerly associated with the late Thrumcap café and wine bar in Bar Harbor. Anneliese Riggall and chef Daniel Sweimler opened the Wescott Forge in 2005, with backing from Thrumcap's owner, Tom Marinke.

Dining porch overlooks millstream at Wescott Forge.

A substantial renovation on two floors of the old mill building created an elegant open dining area on the lower level seating 50 beside a gas fireplace. The tables of choice continue to be on a delightful enclosed porch beside the millstream, which is illuminated at night. Well-spaced tables dressed in white with beige overlays downstairs and an upstairs lounge with a bar and couches help create an easy elegance to the historic building, renamed for one of the last blacksmiths to occupy the structure. Touches of the old forge show up in the wrought-iron stair railing and light fixtures.

"We wanted to bring back what Blue Hill had lost," Anneliese said of the move to Blue Hill, which coincided with the closing of Thrumcap. With her came New York-trained chef Dan, whom Tom Marinke described as "the best chef we ever had" at Thrumcap and its predecessor, the Porcupine Grill.

Dan designed the Forge's fare to be "progressive new French with Asian and Italian influences," reflecting his New York background and local ingredients. He pledged to "keep it fresh – for myself, as well as for everybody else."

His opening menu was short but sweet, the kind upon which almost everything appeals. It featured such entrées as poached halibut with salsa verde, seared seaweed-crusted ahi tuna with wasabi-pea coulis, pork tenderloin with a plum glaze and grilled sirloin with a burgundy reduction. Starters included house-smoked mussels with jícama and mango curry, tuna tartare, a roasted beet and asparagus tart with goat cheese, a crisp spring roll with jonah crab and shiitake mushrooms, and lobster salad with nectarines, watercress and pomegranate syrup. Desserts were Schokinag chocolate soufflé with bourbon cream, strawberry-rhubarb shortcake with fromage blanc ice cream and Earl Grey crème brûlée. Also offered was a cheese plate with fruits and quince paste.

A rustic bar menu with smoked fish, terrines and charcuteries is offered in the main-floor lounge. The short wine list is priced mainly in the high twenties and thirties.

(207) 374-9909. www.thewescottforge.com. Entrées, $17 to $23. Lunch, Monday-Saturday 11:30 to 3, Thursday-Saturday noon to 3 in winter. Dinner, Monday-Saturday 5:30 to 9:30, Wednesday-Saturday 4 to 9 in winter.

Interior dining room is among settings for gourmet seafood at The Burning Tree.

The Burning Tree, Route 3, Otter Creek.

Tops on almost everyone's list of culinary havens on Mount Desert Island is this pure restaurant in a rural location south of Bar Harbor. There are tables on the long front porch, one section of which is a waiting area. Beyond are two small dining rooms, cheerfully outfitted in pinks and blues, their linened tables topped with tall, blue-edged water glasses. Local art and colorful paintings adorn the walls.

Such is the summer-cottage setting for what chef-owners Allison Martin and Elmer Beal Jr. call "gourmet seafood" with a vegetarian sideline. The only other dishes are a couple of versions of chicken: roasted free-range breast or a pan roast with sausage, clams, fennel, potatoes and a tangy shellfish broth. But it's seafood that most customers are after – basic like oven-poached codfish in a seafood-wine broth and lofty as in pan-seared yellowfin tuna over lemony blue cheese croustades. Vegetarians relish such treats as a cashew, brown rice and gruyère terrine and pan-fried polenta with pigeon peas, hominy, ceci beans, sweet peppers and a tomato-ginger sauce.

"We're the only restaurant that buys right off the boat," advises Allison. "Elmer knows three fishermen who supply him with grey sole, monkfish, flounder and cod." He gets his crabmeat from his cousin in Bass Harbor and his chicken from a farm on Deer Isle.

Our party was impressed with starters of mussels with mustard sauce, grilled scallops and an excellent vegetarian sushi. The cioppino came so highly recommended that two of us ordered it. The others chose baked monkfish with clams and artichokes on saffron orzo and the cajun crab and lobster au gratin, a fixture on the menu. The garden out back provides vegetables and herbs, and the owners use organically grown produce whenever possible.

Desserts are to groan over: perhaps nectarine mousse cake, Ukranian poppyseed cake or strawberry pie. A good wine list, chosen with as much care as the menu, is affordably priced.

(207) 288-9331. Entrées, $19.50 to $25. Dinner nightly except Tuesday, 5 to 10, mid-June to mid-October.

Mandarin red walls of Havana dining room radiate a glow at night.

Havana, 318 Main St., Bar Harbor.

The name and the phone number (288-CUBA) hint that here is one cosmopolitan restaurant, widely considered the best in town. Local restaurateur Michael Boland and his wife, Deirdre Swords, offer innovative, Latin-inspired fare served in stylish surroundings. The walls, painted mandarin red, radiate a glow at nightfall in a bar and adjacent dining room with votive candles and fresh flowers on white-clothed tables spaced well apart.

Chef Jesse Souza varies the menu frequently. Typical appetizers are crab cakes with shaved cucumber and cilantro rémoulade, carnitas of duck with a green chile sauce and crispy mushroom spring rolls with a truffled corn sauce. For a different take on lobster, consider the langosta flojita – sautéed lobster and Spanish chorizo with black olives, toasted garlic, cilantro and lime.

Main dishes could be coriander-dusted Alaskan king salmon with sour orange aioli, achiote-dusted scallops with a brown butter-soy vinaigrette, grilled pork chop with a mustard and scallion chimichurri and grilled filet mignon rubbed with garlic and pepper adobo and served with a smoky tamarind barbecue sauce. Lobster plays a starring role in Havana's paella.

Typical desserts are guava mousse in a chocolate-dipped waffle cone and a mango and tuaca chocolate truffle torte.

Havana is one of only two Maine restaurants whose eclectic wine lists won Wine Spectator's best of award of excellence in 2004.

(207) 288-2822. www.havanamaine.com. Entrées, $24 to $33. Dinner nightly, from 5.

Red Sky, 14 Clark Point Road, Southwest Harbor.

Red sky at night, sailor's delight. Red sky in morning…"we don't serve breakfast."

So says James Lindquist, owner of this new restaurant that shines at night. He summered as a child at nearby Seal Harbor and returned after working for restaurants in Mystic, New York City and Aspen to help open the Havana restaurant in Bar Harbor. In 2003, he took over the former Preble Grill with his wife Elizabeth and niece as partners. They gutted the interior to produce a warm dining room in yellow and deep burgundy. The handsome bar of white pine and mahogany was made by his brother-in-law from a tree in Camden. The bar is as deep as a table so it serves as a supper bar as well.

Folks sit at the bar or at white-clothed tables to enjoy a panoply of changing contemporary treats. You might start with an appetizer like Maine shrimp dumplings with tamari-ginger sauce, roasted quail stuffed with quinoa and almonds, or house-made duck and pork sausage with cranberry-pear relish. Salads take equal billing, among them one of crabmeat with a light citrus-riesling dressing atop bibb lettuce and another of spinach with feta cheese and toasted pinenuts, served in a crispy phyllo bowl.

Typical main courses run from panko-crusted halibut and grilled scallops with a chile-molasses glaze to pan-roasted duck breast with plum wine demi-glace and plum salsa or grilled New York strip steak topped with blue cheese and served over red wine-caramelized onions. Lobster risotto with asparagus and wild mushrooms is a menu fixture.

Finish with a cheese course, four types served with fruit. Or sample innovative desserts such as Belgian bittersweet chocolate pudding, sour lemon tart with strawberry sauce and raspberries, or the Red Sky's ice cream sandwich with Belgian chocolate and Madagascar vanilla bean ice cream.

(207) 244-0476. www.redskyrestaurant.com. Entrées, $21 to $30. Dinner, Monday-Saturday 5:30 to 10, Wednesday-Saturday 5:30 to 9 in off-season. Closed January to mid-February.

More Dining Choices

The Maritime Café, 27 Main St., Stonington.

The harbor views outside the wraparound windows are a major attraction at this with-it establishment, run by an Austrian by way of Colorado.

Rudi Newmayr, a contractor who built many a restaurant but said this is the first he ever owned, took over the old Atlantic Café space in 2004 and added some interesting twists. He dispenses typical Maine fare, of course, but with a sophisticated flair. He also has an espresso and crêpe bar geared to the after-theater crowd from the Stonington Opera House and a barbecue grill outside serving up spicy German sausages.

For lunch, we sampled a spicy organic Colorado sausage sandwich after savoring a bowl of fishermen's chowder in a fragrant saffron lobster broth. The oversize broiled haddock sandwich on a toasted bun also proved succulent.

The dinner menu ranges widely from roasted halibut with watermelon syrup and wasabi oil and sugar cane-skewered tiger shrimp with pineapple salsa to herb-roasted chicken breast with truffle poultry jus and pistachio-crusted rack of lamb. Grilled duck breast with sweet potato hash and cranberry-fig relish and grilled venison chop with roasted plum barbecue sauce and Asian slaw were hits on the autumn menu.

You might start with steamed mussels with fennel, tomatoes and garlic in a white wine broth or seared quail in a lavender-honey glaze. Lobster might show up in a "B.L.T" – lobster layered between buffalo mozzarella and tomatoes. Finish with one of the specialty dessert crêpes.

With windows onto the water, the 28-seat dining room is simple but stylish with white paneling, wide-board flooring and benches imported from Colorado. The rope-wrapped wall sconces help convey a maritime look.

An outdoor deck with umbrellaed tables beside the harbor is put into service at lunchtime. It proves an idyllic setting for the evening lobster bakes on summer weekends. A 1¼-pound lobster with mussels, corn on the cob and coleslaw was going for $19.95 at our latest visit.

(207) 367-2600. www.maritimecafe.com. Entrées, $18 to $24. Lunch daily, 11:30 to 2:30. Dinner, 5:30 to 8:30. BYOB. Closed November-April.

Cleonice, 112 Main St., Ellsworth.

Imagine: a restaurant of this caliber, a wide-ranging menu upon which everything appeals, and down-to-earth prices – all off the tourists' path.

Richard Hanson, chef for seven years at the acclaimed Jonathan's restaurant in Blue Hill, imagined such a place. When Jonathan's closed abruptly in 2002, he took over a vacant restaurant space in downtown Ellsworth, renamed it for his mother and turned it into an appealing Mediterranean bistro.

Built by immigrants in 1938 to resemble a village restaurant in their Italian homeland, the building had housed a succession of eight nondescript restaurants since 1980. Now nicely restored, it's a beauty with an authentic European neo-classical look and intimate booths, tall columns and hand-carved olive leaves in the rich cherry and mahogany woodwork. A bar running along one side is perfect for sampling the tapas and small plates featured as appetizers and light meals.

The ever-changing tapas menu is authentic: perhaps artichoke-pesto bruschetta, escalavida (a Spanish roasted vegetable salad), Sardinian mullet roe with lemon on flatbread, loukanika (Greek sausage with orange and cinnamon), Rich's signature calamari salad, grilled octopus with piri piri sauce, or hummus and tzatziki with pita crisps. A chilled glass of dry wine, Manzanilla sherry or the sweeter Amontillado are recommended to go with.

The tapas, available at the bar or at the table, are supplemented by up to a dozen dinner entrées, perhaps a Turkish vegetarian kofte, lobster fra diavolo tossed with linguini or a special of grilled tuna kabob with tomato-feta vinaigrette. The choices range widely from a classic paella and steak frites to grilled lamb casablanca. The native rabbit baked with lemon, garlic and feta and the zarzuela of mixed seafood with sofrito, romesca sauce and roasted potatoes sounded mighty tempting.

Desserts are in the Mediterranean style as well.

The lunch fare was not as interesting as the dinner menu posted the day we were there, perhaps because the place was catering to the workday crowd. The noise level rose to a jarring clatter as we lunched on a bowl of crab, chicken and sausage gumbo, a spiced lamb burger and a grilled portobello mushroom and chèvre sandwich on focaccia. The smart ones chose to sit at one of the handful of tables on the sidewalk out front and listen to the passing traffic.

(207) 664-7554. www.cleonice.com. Entrées, $19 to $21. Lunch, Monday-Saturday 11:30 to 2:30. Tapas and dessert fare, Monday-Saturday 2:30 to 5. Dinner nightly, from 5.

Café This Way, 14½ Mount Desert St., Bar Harbor.

The food is first-rate and the interior somewhat theatrical at this pleasant café down a side street with a sign pointing the way. Chefs Julie Harris and Julie Berberian, both from Bar Harbor's former Fin Back restaurant, and partner Susanne Hathaway turned the old Unusual Cabaret dinner theater space into a casual mélange of tables and bookcases surrounding a circle of sofas in the center. But for the theater lights overhead, the dining area looks like a large living room.

The contemporary menu features seafood, as in entrées of a Thai seafood pot simmered in coconut-curry broth, grilled salmon with a gingery maple glaze, grilled tuna with sautéed apples and smoked shrimp, and crab cakes with tequila-lime sauce. Or you might try bibimap, a Korean dish of stirfried vegetables, a fried egg and spicy pepper sauce served over rice in a hot stone bowl. Several main dishes also are available as appetizers on this mix-and-match menu. Otherwise the stars are homemade tuna and salmon sausage crusted with sesame seeds, Maine seafood spring rolls, and mussels steamed in cider with garlic, chipotles and bourbon chicken sausage.

Folks rave about the salads, perhaps lobster caesar, watercress with grated asiago cheese and prosciutto, or warmed endive with grilled shrimp over greens with citrus vinaigrette.

Chocolate turns up in most of the desserts. Typical are chocolate-amaretto mousse, raspberry-chocolate truffle cake, and peanut butter and chocolate fudge cake.

Five versions of eggs benedict are featured on the breakfast menu, which offers some of the most creative and affordable fare in town.

(207) 288-4483. www.cafethisway.com. Entrées, $16 to $22. Breakfast, Monday-Saturday 7 to 11, Sunday 8 to 1 Dinner nightly, 5:30 to 9. Closed November-March.

McKay's Public House, 231 Main St., Bar Harbor.

A lovely gravel patio and front porch draw diners to this homey new restaurant in a house moved from the site of the new Bar Harbor Grand Hotel and bearing quite a history. Ask your server to tell you some of its past as you consider whether to have pub fare or go full bore, knowing that the prices won't break the bank.

The pub menu yields things like chicken pot pie, fish and chips, shepherd's pie and a lamb burger.

Local savants praise the dinner fare as first-rate. The menu typically offers lobster with champagne-vanilla sauce, porcini-encrusted halibut, pecan-encrusted pork loin finished with bourbon barbecue jus, crispy duck breast with champagne-curry sauce, grilled filet mignon with green peppercorn-brandy sauce and the signature rack of lamb. The seafood risotto – local scallops and shrimp over a lemon-truffle risotto tossed with peas and cherry tomatoes – comes highly recommended.

Rope-cultured mussels steamed in Irish ale, sesame-crusted rare tuna with seaweed salad and wasabi cream, and citrus-cured lobster-scallop seviche with watermelon and greens make good starters. So do the sherried lobster stew and the salad of almond-crusted goat cheese, roasted red beets and mango slices over field greens.

(207) 288-2002. www.mckayspublichouse.com. Entrées, $15.95 to $24.95. Lunch in summer, 11:30 to 3. Dinner nightly, 5 to 10.

Fiddlers' Green, 411 Main St., Southwest Harbor.

Chef Derek Wilbur, son of a local boat builder, and his wife Sarah gutted an aging family eatery to create a stylish restaurant with windows onto the harbor and a side deck. They offer three simple but sophisticated dining areas – one, all in yellow, has views of the ocean. Another is smaller with rag-rolled walls of burnt orange. A

Main dining room at Fiddlers' Green overlooks side deck and harbor.

statue of Neptune and a fountain are situated beside the hostess station. A downstairs wine vault holds more than 160 labels, including rare vintages.

The menu itemizes changing choices in the modern international idiom. From the raw bar come such delicacies as lobster timbale with sake-infused melon, seaweed and tobiko roe and a sashimi martini with smoked mussels, scallop seviche, raw tuna and pear-tahini cream. Other appetizers could be a spicy scallop and shrimp skewer with black bean and ginger salsa, pan-fried crab cakes with a three-chile honey-mango sauce, mesquite-smoked duck with apricot-cherry chutney, and a perennial favorite, mussels steamed in Guinness with shallots and garlic.

Main courses range from coq au vin to grilled beef tenderloin with a brandy-shiitake demi-glace and roasted garlic. The chef serves his wok-fried spiced salmon and crab in a nori roll with citrus-peanut sauce and miso rice, teams his lamb loin with mint chutney and potato latkes, and offers slow-cooked pork with mild ancho chile and garlic. Venison chops might arrive with a port-black cherry sauce atop sautéed red, green and napa cabbage.

Typical desserts are vanilla bean crème brûlée, lemon mousse napoleon, cream puffs and chocolate truffle torte.

(207) 244-9416. www.fiddlersgreenrestaurant.com. Entrées, $18 to $26. Dinner from 5:30, Tuesday-Sunday in July and August, Thursday-Sunday in off-season. Closed November-April.

Garden of Eden

Eden Vegetarian Café, 78 West St., Bar Harbor.

At age 19, Mark Rampacek was the youngest person to graduate from the Culinary Institute of America. He went on to cook at the Four Seasons Hotel in Boston and at the former Porcupine Grill and George's in Bar Harbor. It was there that he met up with Lynn Ambielli and they decided to open their own place – an all-vegetarian restaurant, a challenge to make a go of even in the largest markets. Not only did they make a success of a totally meatless menu in resorty Bar Harbor, in 2005 they eliminated use of dairy products. "We're vegan now, but we don't say so," advised Lynn.

They discovered a receptive following for their inspired vegetarian fare, employing mostly organic ingredients from the area's farms and small growers. "People find it different and don't even miss not having animal products," said Mark, who takes his inspiration from the recipes of mainstream restaurants and re-creates their dishes in vegan form. "He's amazing," says Lynn. "He can smell a shrimp dish cooking in the kitchen of another restaurant and two weeks later his version will show up on our menu." Volunteers a fellow restaurateur: "Mark's food is so good you don't even realize you're not having meat, and I love meat."

At least go and try a couple of his appetizers, she suggests. You'll likely be impressed with his Chesapeake-style vegetable cakes with sweet and sour slaw and spicy cherry pepper rémoulade, the roasted mushroom and asparagus bruschetta with truffled onion marmalade and balsamic syrup or the summer nori roll of crisp vegetables, coconut noodles and Thai chili dipping sauce. The warm spinach salad with tamari sunflower seeds, garlic croutons and smoked dulse vinaigrette is another winner.

You might well stay for a main course. Among the choices at our visit: A bento box bearing grilled tofu, local pac choi, seasoned edamame beans, wakame seaweed salad, a mango inside-out roll and wasabi ponzu. Pan-fried seitan cutlets with sage-mashed potatoes, sautéed greens and Mediterranean eggplant-caper relish. Chinese five-spice roasted tempeh with vegetable-fried jasmine rice, pac choi and Chinese hot mustard sauce. Fusilli pasta with arugula-walnut pesto, sundried tomatoes and local beet greens.

Dessert could be butternut crunch mousse cake, chocolate baklava with vanilla silken cream, and banana "ice cream" with coconut butterscotch and cashews.

Beverages include an acclaimed and all-organic selection of loose teas, cocktails (the Eden martini is made with organic vodka and organic garlic-stuffed olives), wines, and beers and ales.

Lynn, an artist, created the intricate, diamond-shaped stained-glass still lifes, landscapes and seascapes that decorate the pale green walls of the pristine storefront restaurant.

(207) 288-4422. www.barharborvegetarian.com. Entrées. $13.50 to $16.50. Dinner nightly, 5 to 9. Closed November-March.

Ethnic Gourmet

XYZ Restaurant, end of Bennett Lane off 80 Seawall Road, Manset.

The letters stand for Xalapa, Yucatan and Zacatecas, and the food represents the Mexican interior and coastal Maine. Owner Janet Strong first opened the restaurant in a gallery-motel along the shore here and in 2004 moved into the island interior. Beside their house hidden down a dirt lane off the Seawall Road, she built a new restaurant "from scratch – just like our food," in the words of cook Robert Hoyt.

A trip for dinner here is not unlike visiting a ranch in Mexico, such are the rural surroundings and the exterior of the low-slung house with a wide front veranda.

Inside, all is colorful and cheery. And the cooking aromas are seductive, thanks to Robert, who's traveled in Mexico for years and describes himself as "a nut for the food there for a long, long time."

We could easily become nuts for his food, too, after a couple of dinners here. Everything, as Robert says, is "real," from the smoked jalapeño and tomatillo sauces served with the opening tortillas to the fine tequila he offered with dessert as a digestive.

Busy hostess Janet recommended we try her partner's sampler plate ($21 each): two chiles rellenos and a chicken dish with mashed potato and pickled cucumber. Thoroughly smitten, we returned another time to enjoy the pollo deshebrada (shredded chicken in a rustic sauce of chiles with cilantro and onions) and tatemado (pork loin baked in a sauce of guajillo and ancho chiles). The menu changes weekly, so you might find camarones ajo (tiger shrimp with garlic, ancho and poblano chiles) or lengua Mexicana (native beef tongue stewed in a mild broth of tomato and herbs), a house specialty.

Desserts range from flan, Mexico's version of crème caramel, to the sensational XYZ pie, layers of coffee and buttercrunch ice cream divided by a ridge of solid chocolate and covered in warm kahlua-chocolate sauce.

(207) 244-5221. Entrées, $21. Dinner, Monday-Saturday from 5:30. Open mid-May through September.

Tea on the Lawn

Jordan Pond House, Park Loop Road, Acadia National Park.

Tea on the lawn, with an incomparable setting in the national park, is a Bar Harbor tradition. Green lawns sloping down to Jordan Pond and the Bubbles mountains in the background are the backdrop for a steady stream of visitors drawn by the unexpected novelty of day-long tea (two popovers with butter and strawberry preserves, $8.25) and, lately, cappuccino or Oregon chai and popovers ($9.50).

We're drawn more often for lunch to this storied landmark, which was rebuilt in contemporary style after fire destroyed the original. The tables of choice are outside on the "porch," which is more like a covered terrace. The last time we enjoyed a fine seafood pasta and a curried chicken salad, garnished with red grapes and orange slices, and shared a popover – good but a bit steep at $3.50, given that it was mostly air.

The dinner menu is fairly standard, with the predictable grilled salmon, baked haddock, sautéed Maine crab cakes with a green onion sauce, prime rib and steamed lobster. If you're hungry, start with lobster stew and popovers. Finish with homemade ice cream, cappuccino flan or – if you're not popovered out – popover à la mode. Flickering candles, fresh flowers and the sunset over pond and mountains create an unforgettable setting.

There's a full bar, and the large gift shop (one of several Acadia Shops on the island) is fun to browse in.

(207) 276-3316. www.jordanpond.com. Entrées, $14 to $20. Lunch, 11:30 to 2:30. Tea on the lawn, 11:30 to 5:30. Dinner, 5:30 to 8 or 9. Open mid-May to late October.

Lobster Pounds

Okay, okay, we can hear some of you thinking.

"Beef tongue, for heaven's sake," you sneer. "Wakame seaweed salad, what kind of garbage is that? Snap peas, schnapp peas. We want *lobster.*"

We confess. Once each Maine trip we want lobster, too. But not a one-pound weakling. What we do is go to a lobster pound, order steamers and maybe onion rings and a couple of two-pound lobsters. We sit at picnic tables beside the water and watch the boats, and we pig out, just like everyone else.

In this area, our favorites:

Thurston's Lobster Pound, Steamboat Wharf Road, Bernard.

From the jaunty upstairs deck here you can look below and see where the lobstermen keep their traps. This is a real working lobster wharf. And if you couldn't tell from all the pickup trucks parked along the road, one taste of the lobster will convince you.

We enjoyed ours ($9.75 to $10.75 a pound, plus $4.75 for the extras, from corn to blueberry cake). Together we also sampled the lobster stew (bearing tons of lobster), a really good potato salad, steamers and two pounds of mussels (about one pound too much). Oh well, this *was* our first lobster feast of the summer. You wait in line for one of the square tables for four on the covered deck or on the deck below, place your order at the counter and select from a choice beer and wine list (imagine, a lobster pound offering a Kendall-Jackson reserve chardonnay). They provide the candles, and a small wash basin outside the kitchen so customers can wash the lobster debris off their hands.

This is a true place, run by Michael Radcliffe, great-grandson of the lobster wharf's founder, and his wife Libby. A local couple, whose license plate said "Pies," was delivering the apple and rhubarb pies for the day one time we stopped by.

(207) 244-7600. Entrées, $8.50 to $16. Open daily, 11 to 8:30, Memorial Day through September.

Tidal Falls Lobster, Tidal Falls Road, Hancock.

There's perhaps no more picturesque and verdant setting for a lobster dinner than this, beside a wide river and one of the most spectacular reversing falls in New England. That the food is so inspired is a bonus.

The Hodgkins family served lobster in a rustic pound here for nearly half a century, but it was left to the Frenchman Bay Conservancy to acquire the property, upgrade the kitchen, expand and reopen the restaurant, and open the preserve as a public park in 2001.

Now, under the aegis of energetic manager Karin Wilkes, who knows her food, the fare is equal to the surroundings. The hallmark is steamed lobster, $13.95 a pound at our latest visit, also available in a roll or salad. But the surprise is the new additions to a place that formerly offered only hot dogs and lobster: steamed mussels, mesclun salad, potato salad, a chicken wrap and such specials as charbroiled New York sirloin steak. The hot crab dip with crackers is an addictive starter.

The drink of choice is fresh lemonade (they squeeze cases of lemons every day) garnished with mint and lemon zest. If you bring your own wine, they'll serve it in real wine glasses etched with the establishment's logo.

There's interior seating, but most prefer to eat outside at tables scattered around the shady lawns beside the water. Or go around back and upstairs to the Captain's Deck, where the waterside view is like that from a ship.

(207) 422-6457. Entrées, $9 to $16.95. Open Monday-Friday 5 to 9, Saturday and Sunday noon to 9, June 21 through Labor Day. BYOB.

Abel's Lobster Pound, Route 103, Mount Desert.

This widely promoted icon is favored by old-timers (and reviewers) who remember it as a simple, outdoors-oriented place in the evergreens beside Somes Sound. Something was lost when it enlarged the indoor dining facility, added a bar and waitress service, catered to the hordes and lost the rustic outdoorsy feeling – the waterfront views marred by industrial-looking boatyard ventures beside. Lobster-lovers still recommend it, though some consider it pricey. Six versions of lobster dinner, served with rolls and baked potato or french fries, range from $22 for a one-pounder to $37 for a biggie with steamed clams. Blueberry pie is the favored dessert.

(207) 276-5827. Entrées, $18 to $27. Lunch daily, noon to 4. Dinner, noon to 9. Open mid-June to Labor Day.

Dining and Lodging

Pentagoet Inn, Main Street, Box 4, Castine 04421.

Here's a switch. The latest owners of this turreted inn built in 1894 are refurbishing to the period instead of adding the updated amenities such as fireplaces and whirlpools tubs offered by many of their peers.

"Rather than modernizing," said Jack Burke, owner with his wife, Julie Van de Graaf, "we're going back to our roots as a steamboat inn." The couple redid the coveted Turret Room in which we once stayed with a marble-top vanity in the bath and an Eastlake headboard for the kingsize bed. They scoured the countryside to find antique headboards for the beds and steamboat-era prints and lithographs for the walls.

The eleven guest rooms in the main inn and five in the adjacent 200-year-old cottage (called 10 Perkins Street) have antique furnishings, a historically authentic feeling and international accents from Jack's twenty years' service with the United Nations in Africa.

He turned the inn's former Victorian library into Passports Pub, a playful hodgepodge of vintage photos and foreign memorabilia that's appropriate for an international town that has flown the flags of four countries. Besides the atmospheric pub, guests relax in a parlor area with a nifty turret window seat looking toward the harbor, on shaded verandas made for rocking and on a showy garden patio off the dining room.

Julie's background as owner of a pastry shop in Philadelphia is evident at breakfast, which might feature featherbed eggs or baked-apple french toast, muffins and scones.

Dinner is served at widely spaced tables in two elegant dining rooms and outside on the wraparound veranda. Chef Mark Swartzbaugh's menu features such starters as sorrel soup garnished with gougère, a "big ol' bowl of local mussels" in white wine broth, crab cakes with mustard aioli and a choice of five salads, one of them eggs à la russe. Entrées range from the signature lobster bouillabaisse in a rich saffron broth to pappadum-coated rack of lamb with rhubarb chutney. The pistachio-dusted diver scallops might come with a sweet curry-carrot butter and asparagus risotto, while the seared duck breast might wear a sour cherry-pinot noir sauce.

Desserts could be a pear-franzipane tart, plum crisp with vanilla ice cream and double chocolate torte with espresso cream.

Guests linger over after-dinner drinks in the old-world pub, where the remarkable collection of oversize photos of personalities from Grace Kelly to Mahatma Gandhi are subjects for lively conversation.

(207) 326-8616 or (800) 845-1701. Fax (207) 326-9382. www.pentagoet.com. Sixteen rooms with private baths. Doubles, $95 to $225. Closed November-April.

Entrées, $21 to $27. Dinner, Monday-Saturday 5:30 to 8; off-season, Tuesday-Saturday 6 to 8. Closed November-April.

New tavern dining room expands casual options at Pilgrim's Inn.

Pilgrim's Inn, 20 Main St., Deer Isle 04267.

An expanded restaurant and tavern plus updated accommodations have enhanced this Colonial-style inn, based in a dark red house dating to 1793 and listed on the National Register of Historic Places. Nicely located on a spit of land with a harbor in front and a mill pond in back, the inn has long been a favorite of sophisticated diners – and promised to remain so with its acquisition in late 2005 by Tina Oddleifson, an innkeeper in Brookline, Mass., and her husband Tony Lawless, a chef for 25 years, who taught lately at the Cambridge School of Culinary Arts.

In an effort to broaden its appeal to locals, the ground-floor restaurant was expanded in 2005 and renamed the **Whale's Rib Tavern.** The attached former goat barn in which it was based was upscaled and refurbished to resemble a 1793 tavern, with windsor chairs at white-clothed tables and multiple windows onto the outdoors. The rest of the ground floor was reconfigured to add a new bar and separate lounge, plus a more casual tavern dining room adjacent. And a landscaped terrace was added in back for outdoor dining with a partial water view.

A much-expanded, something-for-everyone menu with up to 40 entrées lures the locals as well as inn guests. The tavern portion includes the likes of burgers, fish and chips, seafood pot pie, chicken nachos, pot roast and shepherds pie. The traditional menu might start with crab-stuffed mushroom caps, crispy artichoke hearts, seven salads and shellfish from "ye olde steam pot." Entrées range from seafood au gratin and mandarin halibut to chicken kabobs, baby back ribs, "smothered" london broil and veal marsala.

Upstairs, the guest rooms have been freshly redecorated in what might be called contemporary period style. All but one now have king or queensize beds topped with down pillows and duvet comforters. Each has a wood stove and some of the updated baths have vanities topped with Deer Isle granite.

A vintage house next door contains two efficiency suites with TVs and gas stoves, sharing a large deck overlooking the water. The deluxe Rugosa Rose cottage is a two-level affair with kitchenette, dining/sitting area and water-view deck on the main floor and a queen bedroom with gas fireplace on the upper level.

Breakfast involves a choice between an egg dish as and a sweet like brioche french toast with fruit compote. Homemade granola, muffins and Maine-roasted Carpe Diem coffee accompany.

(207) 348-6615 or (888) 778-7505. www.pilgrimsinn.com. Twelve rooms and three efficiency suites with private baths. July-September: doubles $135 to $235, suites $255 to $265. Off-season: doubles $105 to $205, suites $195 to $245. Closed late October to early May.

Entrées, $9.95 to $23. Dinner nightly, 4:30 to 9:30. Closed January-March.

Goose Cove Lodge, Deer Isle, Box 40, Sunset 04683.

Some of the most inspired meals in Maine are served at this food-oriented, family-style lodge on 70 acres along the remote shores of Deer Isle. The only problem (?) is that you may have to stay for a week in season to partake or manage to slip in for dinner as a transient via a one-and-one-half-mile-long dirt road through the evergreens, starting in the middle of nowhere and terminating at the open ocean at the End of Beyond.

Joanne Parisi, a former Massachusetts caterer and now innkeeper with her husband Dom, oversees the kitchen end of things. She and her chefs present healthful, new American fare for lodge guests and outside diners by reservation. Sturdy, shiny pine tables are set in summery pink in the handsome **Point Dining Room** wrapping around the ocean end of the main lodge, with an expansive seaside deck for outdoor dining.

Guests gather for cocktails and complimentary hors d'oeuvre in the bar or on the deck before dinner. The imaginative, much-acclaimed dinner fare changes weekly. At a recent visit the entrées included pan-roasted halibut with a lemon-herb compound butter, Mediterranean seafood stew, pan-seared duck breast with raspberry demi-glace and grilled butterflied lamb with rosemary demi-glace. The vegetarian entrée showed the kitchen's reach: seared tofu with quinoa, grilled butternut disk and wilted greens served with a roasted portobello mushroom and vegan pesto.

Among starters were peekytoe crab cakes with honeydew-cucumber salsa, tuna tartare with wasabi cream and duck confit served on stilton polenta with a wild blueberry-bordelaise sauce. Typical desserts are peach bread pudding on caramel sauce, chocolate decadence with raspberry sauce and poached pear on a flourless chocolate pâté with vanilla crème anglaise.

The Monday night lobster feast on the beach is a highlight of the week for the long-termers, who tend to be repeat guests year after year. Counselors entertain and supervise children during the adult dinner hour. String quartets, folk singers, a lobster fisherman or a local writer may entertain after dinner.

Breakfast is a buffet, included in the rates.

Besides the dining area, the epitome of a Maine lodge includes a lobby with an enormous fieldstone fireplace and stylish sofas, chairs, benches and bookcases. Up to 80 guests are accommodated in twenty cabins, rooms and suites. Seven rooms and suites are in the East and North annexes near the main lodge. Most in demand are the nine secluded cottages and four duplex cabins, each with ocean

Seaside deck is salubrious setting for dining at Goose Cove Lodge.

view, sun deck, kitchenette or refrigerator and fireplace. Some of the larger require payment for a three-person minimum.

The lodge property – marked by five trails, sandy beaches and tree-lined shores – is a paradise for nature lovers. At low tide, you can walk across a sand bar to Barred Island, a nature conservancy full of birds and wildlife.

(207) 348-2508 or (800) 728-1963. Fax (207) 348-2624. www.goosecovelodge.com. Twenty rooms, suites, cottages and cabins with private baths. July and August: doubles, $270 to $650 MAP. Off-season: doubles, $120 to $295 B&B. Cottages rented weekly in summer; other rooms, two-night minimum. Closed late-October to mid-May.

Entrées, $15 to $27. Dinner by reservation, Tuesday-Sunday 5:30 to 8:30. Closed Columbus Day to mid-June.

Le Domaine, 1515 U.S. Route 1 (Box 519), Hancock 04640.

Here is a perfect getaway for gourmets: a country auberge with a handful of elegant upstairs guest rooms, some with private decks overlooking the rear gardens, and a main-floor restaurant and lounge purveying superior French cuisine and wines.

The unassuming, red frame building semi-hidden behind huge evergreens seems as if it were lifted from provincial France and plunked down in rural Hancock, which is even down east from down east Bar Harbor. Inside is an extraordinarily appealing place in which to stay and dine.

Founded in 1945 by a Frenchwoman, Marianne Purslow-Dumas, Le Domaine was run with equal competence until 2005 by her daughter, Nicole Purslow, a graduate of the Cordon Bleu School and an advocate of country-French haute cuisine. She sold it "as is" to a longtime customer, Eugene Dixon of Philadelphia and Winter Harbor, who retained the cook and wait staff. Nicole has continued to live on the property and concentrates on Mano, her new gourmet food shop next door.

A side entrance serving both diners and overnight guests opens into a reception area and delightful wicker sun porch. Dining is in two long and narrow rooms, one dominated by a huge stone fireplace framed by copper cooking utensils. Walls are decorated with maps of France and pictures of folks in provincial costumes. Tables

Provincial decor makes for charming dining room at Le Domaine.

are set elegantly in the country French manner with green linen cloths embossed with the fleur de lis over bright yellow undercloths. Hardwood floors are polished to a sheen.

The menu changes frequently and features local produce from nearby gardens and herbs that grow by the kitchen door. Four or five entrées are offered each night. They could include a medley of vegetables wrapped in fillet of sole, grilled halibut with roasted tomatoes and basil chiffonade, veal with wild mushrooms in a rich cream sauce and filet mignon bordelaise garnished with roquefort butter. We'd return any time for the sensational sweetbreads with lemon and capers, the grilled salmon with fennel, lamb chops dusted with rosemary and thyme, and a house specialty, rabbit with prunes marinated in brandy.

The French bread is toasted in chunks and the rolls are marvelous. For starters on various occasions, we've tried malpeque oysters with a shallot-sherry vinegar dipping sauce, coquilles St. Jacques in a heavenly wine sauce, smoked trout, and a salad of impeccable greens tossed with goat cheese and walnuts.

The cheesecake on raspberry sauce is ethereal, as is the frozen coffee mousse. Another visit produced a raspberry tart and frozen raspberry mousse with a meringue, plus perfect French-roast coffee. The wine list (mostly French, of course) is expensive, but some bargains are to be found.

Relaxing after dinner on the wicker sun porch with snifters of heady eau de vie, we almost didn't care about the cost. We toddled upstairs to our overnight home in one of the inn's attractive, country-fresh guest accommodations with balconies and porches in back.

Lately enlarged and redecorated, rooms are lavishly outfitted in provincial fabrics and chintz. The amenities you'd expect are here, including antiques, clock radios, books, French magazines, bedside reading lamps, Egyptian cotton bedding, goose down pillows, French soaps and bath oils (and a night light in the shape of a shell), plus complimentary Perrier water. Behind a studied simplicity are many artistic touches. On our balcony, for instance, a spotlight shone on a tree growing through it and a piece of driftwood was placed perfectly on the stairs.

The next morning, we admired a circular garden surrounded by large rocks in back, looking casual but probably taking hours to plot. A number of trails had been cleared through a forest of pine trees on 100 acres. We took a long walk to a pond, picking blueberries for sustenance along the way.

Later, a copious breakfast tray was delivered to our balcony, bearing bowls of peaches and raspberries, granola, crème fraîche, hot milk in a jug, homemade blueberry preserves, three of the flakiest croissants ever and a pot of fragrant coffee, all on floral china with linen napkins. Sheer enchantment!

(207) 422-3395 or (800) 544-8498. www.ledomaine.com. Three rooms and two suites with private baths. Doubles, $200. Suites, $285. Closed mid-October to June.

Entrées, $29.50 to $31.50. Dinner, Tuesday-Sunday 6 to 9. Closed mid-October to June.

High Style in Bar Harbor

Harborside Hotel & Marina, 55 West St., Bar Harbor 04605.

The legendary Bar Harbor Club has been incorporated into this showy new hotel and resort complex at water's edge in downtown Bar Harbor. Tom Walsh, who numbers the Bar Harbor Regency among his growing empire, spent many millions converting the aging Golden Anchor Motel complex into an urbane oceanfront resort worthy of the site. It now stretches along the waterfront from the Pier Restaurant to the spa, fitness facility and restaurant in the old Bar Harbor Club.

The half-timbered Tudor look of the historic club and casino is reflected in the architecturally interesting, three-story hotel, which sprawls in long corridors opening from a mahogany paneled lobby with a marble floor. All 187 hotel-style rooms and suites have full or partial water views, best enjoyed from good-looking balconies or patios laden with colorful plantings. Suites come with fireplaces, kitchens and whirlpool tubs. A heated pool and hot tub are stunningly located in a courtyard area between the hotel and the casual **Pier Restaurant,** overlooking the marina.

A fine-dining restaurant, variously called the **Bar Harbor Club** and the **Club Dining Room,** and the **Vanderbilt Lounge** opened at the rear of the former Bar Harbor Club building in 2005. The hotel-style dining room has an elliptical section with windows onto the harbor.

Executive chef Ryan Phillips's menu aimed for the heights with such entrées as braised halibut with Wellfleet clams, garlic-studded breast of chicken with sauce soubise and beef two ways, grilled filet mignon and braised shortribs. Pan-roasted foie gras seasoned with smoky sea salt and vanilla bean-stewed rhubarb and seared dayboat scallops with summer corn and black truffle risotto typified the appetizers. Desserts varied from a molten chocolate popover to a trio of crème brûlées. Another option was a tasting of New England artisan cheeses.

(207) 288-5033 or (800) 328-5033. Fax (207) 288-3089. www.theharborsidehotel.com. One hundred eighty-seven rooms. Doubles, $209 to $469 in summer, $119 to $369 off-season. Closed November to early May.

Bar Harbor Club, entrées, $26 to $32. Dinner nightly, 5 to 10. Closed November to early May.

Bar Harbor Inn, Newport Drive, Bar Harbor 04609.

The prime downtown location in Bar Harbor is occupied by this large and totally renovated complex that began as a hotel and motor inn. Now it better reflects owner

David Witham's vision for luxurious accommodations on eight landscaped acres with the sea on two sides.

Rebuilt in 2000, the main inn features a wing with 43 deluxe jacuzzi rooms, all with king or queen beds and most with fireplaces and bayfront balconies. We're partial to the 64-room oceanfront lodge, closest to the shore and constructed on the site of the original motel. It offers rooms with kingsize or two queen beds, sitting areas and private balconies with stunning views of rocks, water and islands. There's a large heated pool, as well as a small public beach adjacent. A complimentary continental breakfast is served in the lobby of the oceanfront lodge.

The inn's circular, many-windowed restaurant called the **Reading Room** claims the finest ocean panorama in town. Harp or piano music plays as you consider a roster of lobster specialties. Other entrées range from grilled Atlantic salmon napped with a roasted red pepper and basil rémoulade to chicken oscar and dijon-crusted rack of lamb with rosemary jus. Start with smoked salmon carpaccio or a lobster and mango timbale. Finish with bananas foster bread pudding or a triple chocolate dessert called chocolate trillium.

The Terrace Grille, situated at harbor's edge with yellow umbrella-covered tables, is lovely for waterside meals. It's known for a Down East lobster bake ($32.95), and serves light fare, lunch ($12.95 to $20.95) and selections from the Reading Room menu.

(207) 288-3351 or (800) 248-3351. www.barharborinn.com. One hundred forty-two rooms and eleven suites with private baths. Doubles, $199 to $369 late June to Labor Day, $79 to $329 rest of year. Closed Thanksgiving to late March.

Entrées, $21 to $34. Dinner nightly, 5:30 to 9:30. Sunday brunch, 11:30 to 2:30. Grille open Monday-Saturday, 11:30 to 9:30. Closed mid-November to mid-April.

Lodging

Blue Hill Inn, Union Street, Box 403, Blue Hill 04614.

This trim white Colonial inn with dark green shutters has been a landmark in the heart of Blue Hill for nearly 170 years. Innkeepers Mary and Don Hartley have enhanced the twelve guest accommodations with plush carpeting, new wallpaper and modernized bathrooms. Some have sitting areas converted from small bedrooms, and four have fireplaces.

Our rear bedroom – occupied the previous night by Peter of Peter, Paul and Mary fame following a concert for Paul Stryker's hometown fans at the Blue Hill Fair Grounds – was comfortable with a kingsize bed, two wing chairs, colorful bed linens, plump towels and windows on three sides to circulate cool air, which was welcome after a heat wave. The other rooms we saw also were nicely furnished with 19th-century antiques and traditional pieces.

Next door is a luxurious efficiency suite. The cathedral-ceilinged Cape House offers a kingsize canopy bed, a fireplace, living room with telephone and TV, kitchen and a rear deck for enjoying the back yard.

Back in the main inn, a small library-game room is furnished in antiques. The larger main parlor, where classical music plays in the background, has a fireplace and a ten-candle Persian chandelier. This is where the Hartleys serve hors d'oeuvre (perhaps smoked bluefish or local goat cheese) during a nightly reception for guests.

Breakfast is a culinary event. Ours started with the usual juices, a plate of cut-up fresh fruit and a wedge of apple-custard pie that one of us thought was dessert. The main course involved a choice of eggs scrambled with garden chives in puff pastry, an omelet with chèvre or brie and Canadian bacon, waffles with fresh strawberries or blueberry pancakes. Excellent french roast coffee accompanied.

(207) 374-2844 or (800) 826-7415. Fax (207) 374-2829. www.bluehillinn.com. Ten rooms and two suites with private baths. Mid-June through early October: doubles $158 to $195; suites, $205 and $285. Off-season: doubles $138 to $175, suites $165 and $235. Closed November to mid-May.

Castine Inn, Main Street, Box 41, Castine 04421.

Food has long been foremost here – that is, until gung-ho celebrity chef-owner Tom Gutow had a premature midlife crisis in 2005 and closed the inn's 60-seat dining room that had been its principal raison d'être. "I did it for a lifestyle change," he said. "I turned 35, had two young daughters and wanted to spend time with my family."

So the century-old Castine Inn – which had been one of Maine's leading restaurants during his eight-year tenure and that of his predecessor – became essentially a large B&B. Tom said he would devote more effort to the breakfast end of the equation and offered private dinners for two to 50 by advance reservation – "kind of like dining at a chef's table in my dining room."

Tom and his wife Amy are gradually upgrading the accommodations, which open hotel-style off long, wide corridors on the second and third floors. All rooms are carpeted and comfortable with queensize or twin beds. Half yield distant water views. The Gutows turned two small rear rooms into a large room with a queen poster bed, two club chairs and a large bath with an antique tub sunk into a black and white tiled top, separate shower and a vanity in an alcove. Decor is modest yet stylish, with understated floral fabrics and window treatments.

Guests enjoy chef Tom's creations at breakfast. The menu generally offers three entrées: perhaps an omelet with goat cheese and herbs, corned beef hash topped by a poached egg and homemade apple-bread french toast with Maine maple syrup.

A fireplace wards off any chill in the guest parlor, which is hung with local artworks. Across the spacious front hall is hidden a dark and cozy pub with hand-painted tables and a fireplace. A wraparound porch and a side deck yield views of spectacular gardens and the harbor beyond.

(207) 326-4365. Fax (207) 326-4570. www.castineinn.com. Nineteen rooms with private baths. Doubles, $90 to $225. Closed Dec. 20 through April.

The Inn at Bay Ledge, 1385 Sand Point Road, Bar Harbor 04609.

Reindeer fashioned from vines stand sentry at the entrance to this clifftop retreat overlooking Frenchman Bay. They reflect the "upscale country ambiance" that Jack and Jeani Ochtera have imparted since our first stay in this early 1900s house that has been "added to a million times," in Jeani's words.

King or queen canopied and four-poster beds plump with feather mattresses and countless pillows, Ralph Lauren towels and linens, and colorful quilts with matching window treatments are the rule in seven guest rooms, three with jacuzzi tubs. All have picture windows or french doors and balconies affording splendid water vistas. A paneled upstairs sitting room harbors a hidden TV/VCR amidst a decorative scheme of old family fishing gear, hand-carved birds and Jeani's handmade samplers. Jeani painted a colorful faux window and flower box to dress up a blank yellow wall in Room 10. She collected her favorite Claire Murray rugs with Nantucket scenes for the deluxe new Summer Cottage – complete with stone fireplace, whirlpool tub, wet bar, TV with surround sound, deck and kingsize featherbed in the second-level master suite – vacated by the couple when they moved into a house next door.

Rolling lawns and gardens lead to a sheer cliff, where a steep staircase descends 80 feet to the stony beach and a cave along the bay. An expansive, tiered deck stretches along the back of the inn. Here are umbrellaed tables and twig chairs where you may read and relax at this truly relaxing place. A small heated swimming pool is on a lower level of the deck, and tall pine trees all around make the salt air even more refreshing. Roses brighten the expanded gardens.

The inn's first floor contains a sauna and steam shower, as well as a sunroom where Jeani offers an ample breakfast of fresh fruit, cereal, granola, breads, flaky croissants with Nervous Nellie's preserves and perhaps three-cheese and bacon quiche, blueberry buckle or cheese strata. We took ours out to the deck and watched cheeky chipmunks race around, vying for crumbs.

The inn also offers three other cottages, one with kingsize bed and fieldstone fireplace, hidden in the trees across the road.

(207) 288-4204. (Winter: 207-875-3262). www.innatbayledge.com. Seven rooms and four cottages with private baths. Doubles, $150 to $375. Cottages, $175 to $475. Closed mid-October through April.

Ullikana Bed & Breakfast, 16 The Field, Bar Harbor 04609.

Hospitable owner-innkeepers, creative breakfasts, a quiet in-town location near the water and a guest book full of grateful raves. These are among the attributes of this summery but substantial, Tudor-style cottage built in 1885, tucked away in the trees between the Bar Harbor Inn and "The Field," a meadow of wildflowers.

Transplanted New Yorkers Roy Kasindorf and his Quebec City-born wife, Hélène Harton, bought it from a woman who had turned it into a B&B at the age of 86. They retained many of the furnishings, adding some of their own as well as artworks from artist-friends in New York. Later, they added six more guest rooms across the street in the summery Yellow House, recently fronted by a sculpture garden.

Ten bedrooms in the main house hold lots of chintz, wicker and antiques. Some come with balconies, fireplaces or both. One dubbed Audrey's Room (for Roy's daughter) on the third floor contains two antique beds joined together as a kingsize and a clawfoot tub with its original fixtures, from which the bather can look out the low window onto Frenchman Bay. We were happily ensconced in the second-floor Room 5, a majestic space outfitted in country French provincial fabrics with king bed, two wing chairs in front of the fireplace and a water-view balcony upon which to relax and enjoy the passing parade.

The main floor harbors a wicker-furnished parlor with lots to look at, from collections (including two intricate puppets beside the fireplace) to reading materials. It's the site for a convivial wine and cheese hour in the late afternoon. Beyond a dining room with shelves full of colorful Italian breakfast china is the kitchen from which Hélène produces the dishes that make breakfasts here such an event. In summer, they're served outside at tables for two or four on a pleasant terrace with glimpses of the water. Roy is the waiter and raconteur, doling out – in our case – cantaloupe with mint sauce, superior cinnamon-raisin muffins with orange glaze, and puff pancakes yielding blueberries and raspberries. Your feast might start with Hélène's grilled fruit brochettes bearing peaches, strawberries and kiwi with a ricotta-cheese sauce or grapefruit segments in cinnamon syrup, followed by an Italian omelet with homemade tomato sauce and mozzarella cheese or crêpes with frozen

Wraparound sun porch is setting for extravagant breakfast at The Bass Cottage Inn.

yogurt or a rum-cream sauce. All this is served on matching dishes and placemats – a rainbow of pastels, as cheery as the setting.

(207) 288-9552. Fax (207) 288-3682. www.ullikana.com. Sixteen rooms with private baths. Doubles, $170 to $320, off-season $125 to $250. Closed November-April.

The Bass Cottage Inn, 14 The Field, Box 242, Bar Harbor 04609.

Stylish accommodations and gourmet breakfasts are the hallmarks of this deluxe B&B, grandly reborn in 2004 after a year's renovations.

Teri and Jeffrey Anderholm offer an uncommon amount of common space and ten spacious guest rooms, all suavely decorated by Teri in her vision of "grand cottage style." Antiques and 19th-century architectural elements blend comfortably with light colors, stunning art and contemporary amenities for a refined 21st-century look. Rooms on four floors vary from a queen bedroom with a fireplace on the main floor to a skylit "penthouse retreat" in the old attic with a kingsize bed, whirlpool tub and separate shower. The largest is a second-floor corner room with kingsize poster bed, a white chaise lounge beside the fireplace and a whirlpool tub for two.

All rooms have TV/DVDs, telephones, Poland Spring bottled water and abundant toiletries, and five yield water views. The main-floor common areas include a rattan-furnished front atrium/sun porch, a large parlor that doubles as a library and music room with a baby grand piano, a clubby lounge with a fireplace and a well-stocked guest pantry off the professional kitchen.

Teri, who trained as a chef and helped open Yanks restaurant near their former home on Boston's North Shore, handles the kitchen duties. Complimentary wine and hors d'oeuvre are offered in the afternoon. Chocolates are put out at turndown.

The dining room section of the wraparound sun porch is dressed like a restaurant with ten tables set with white linens. It is the setting for a breakfast to remember. Cappuccino muffins and lobster quiche with a side of roasted tomatoes were featured at our latest visit. Egg and crab strata with blueberry scones and spicy pecan waffles with chicken-bourbon sausage are other guest favorites.

(207) 288-4234 or (866) 782-9224. www.basscottage.com. Ten rooms with private baths. Doubles, $195 to $350, off-season $175 to $275. Closed late October to mid-May.

Lindenwood Inn, 118 Clark Point Road, Box 1328, Southwest Harbor 04679

Towering linden trees shade this turn-of-the-century sea captain's home, grandly refurbished by Australian owner Jim King. After opening the Kingsleigh Inn here, he took over the Lindenwood and imbued the house with his eclectic decorating touch, setting palm trees on the wraparound porch, splashing vivid colors on the walls and spattering collections of shells and stones in the bedrooms. "We don't have New England decor here," he asserts, "and people love it."

The two parlors are contemporary, accented with green and white striped upholstered chairs. Potted plants throughout the main floor bring the outdoors inside. The eight guest accommodations, all with TV and several with fireplaces, vary in size. Check out Room 6 with its six-foot-long clawfoot tub. It's one of six rooms with private decks or balconies affording views of the harbor. The ultimate is the queen-bedded penthouse suite with a curved sofa and gas fireplace, opening onto an enormous rooftop deck holding an oversize spa.

Outside at the side, screened by a trellis from the street, is a heated gunite pool and a separate spa topped by a sculptured mask spraying a stream of water. We basked in the lap of luxury in the pool-side cottage with a gas fireplace in the cathedral-ceilinged living room, an efficiency kitchen and a queensize bedroom.

For breakfast in one of the dining rooms, we helped ourselves to fresh fruit and raspberry-banana muffins from the buffet and were served a main dish of fruit crêpes. Other days might produce stratas, herbed omelets or stuffed french toast.

(207) 244-5335 or (800) 307-5335. www.lindenwoodinn.com. Four rooms, three suites and one cottage with private baths. July to Labor Day: doubles $125 to $195, suites $275 to $295, cottage $225. Off-season: doubles $95 to $155, suites $195 to $225, cottage $165. Closed November-April.

The Kingsleigh Inn, 373 Main St., Box 1426, Southwest Harbor 04679.

A wraparound porch full of wicker and colorful pillows embellishes this B&B where breakfasts are a highlight of the day.

Taking over the B&B in which Lindenwood Inn owner Jim King got his start (and left his name), Dana and Greg Moos redecorated the common rooms with an eclectic mix of antiques and contemporary furnishings. More antiques and artworks enhance the eight bedrooms, many with harbor views. One has a balcony with chairs overlooking the water, and another a deck. The Turret Suite on the third floor offers a kingsize poster bed, fireplace, television and a great view from a telescope on a tripod between two wicker chairs. Port wine and homemade truffles are in each room.

Afternoon tea and homemade cookies are served on the porch or in cool weather by the fireplace. A three-course breakfast by candlelight, considered by Dana "a special occasion," is taken at tables for two in the dining room. The meal might start with juices, homemade granola and muffins, scones or popovers. The fruit course could be blueberry and lemon ricotta parfait or rum-raisin pears with rum-infused mascarpone cheese. The main event could be a goat cheese, roasted red pepper and crab strata or her signature chocolate-banana stuffed french toast with banana puree and raspberry coulis. Her wide repertoire includes individual egg soufflés with roasted red pepper sauce, baked eggs in ham crisps, and crêpes filled with pears, fig preserves and brie, served with a warm pear coulis and toasted hazelnuts.

(207) 244-5302. Fax (207) 244-0349. www.kingsleighinn.com. Seven rooms and one suite with private baths. Mid-June to mid-October: doubles $135 to $165, suite $260. Rest of year: doubles $110 to $130, suite $175.

Ann's Point Inn & Spa, Ann's Point Road, Box 398, Bass Harbor 04653.

Here is one of the more luxurious B&Bs to open in Down East Maine in years – a contemporary-style home at the end of its own peninsula, surrounded by the waters of Bass Harbor's back cove.

Lesley and Phil DiVirgilio pamper guests in four large and modern bed rooms, each with kingsize bed, TV, telephone, CD player and updated bath, all with glass showers and one with a whirlpool tub. But it's not so much the accommodations – comfortable as they are – that commend the place. It's the setting, a stone's throw from the ocean on a two-acre property with nearly 700 feet of shoreline. And the amenities: a 32-foot indoor pool, a six-person spa, a six-person Finnish sauna. The spa in its name comes from these features, plus the in-room massages and therapy offerings available upon request.

The DiVirgilios downsized for this venture after running for five years the Holbrook House, a twelve-room Victorian B&B in the heart of Bar Harbor – a proving ground that also launched Jack and Jeani Ochtera on the road to their Inn at Bay Ledge.

Phil and Lesley, who retains the accent of her native England, offer wine and cheese in the afternoon, and cookies and a glass of milk at nightly turndown. Morning brings a multi-course breakfast, and for long-term guests, Lesley never repeats a meal. It typically starts with her homemade granola and cranberry muffins or banana bread. Next comes what Phil calls "a dessert dish" – perhaps an apple crumble. The main course varies daily between sweet and savory, perhaps blueberry-stuffed french toast or Mexican eggs over tortillas, belgian waffles or eggs benedict.

(207) 244-9595. www.annspointinn.com. Four rooms with private baths. Doubles, $280 to $295 late June through mid-October, $150 to $225 rest of year.

Gourmet Treats

Potteries and crafts places abound in the vicinity of Blue Hill and Deer Isle. Foremost is **Rowantrees Pottery,** 9 Union St., Blue Hill, where Sheila Varnum and her associates continue the tradition launched in 1934 by Adelaide Pearson through her friend, Mahatma Gandhi. Named for the mountain ash tree above the green gate in front of the rambling house and barn, Rowantrees is especially known for its jam jar with a flat white lid covered with blueberries, as well as for unique glazes. **Rackliffe Pottery** on Route 172 also makes all kinds of handsome kitchenware.

Local farmers, food producers and artisans gather at the **Blue Hill Farmer's Market** at the Blue Hill Fair Grounds Saturday mornings in July and August to sell everything from fresh produce and goat cheese to handmade gifts and patterned sweaters. It's a fun event for local color and foods.

Pain de Famille, whose breads we enjoyed at its wholesale bakery in Castine, has a small bakery and café on Main Street in Blue Hill. Baker Kathleen McCloskey offers not only her specialty hearth breads but sandwiches, soups, salads, desserts and vegetarian and vegan entrées to go.

Organic food lovers head for the innovative **Four Season Farm** on Cape Rosier, which reopened its farm stand in 2005 after a 26-year hiatus. Noted organic gardeners Eliot Coleman and his wife, Barbara Damroach, offer not only the usual vegetables and fruits from fields and their year-round greenhouse but exotica like artichokes and bok choy. The stand is open Monday-Friday 1 to 5 and Saturday 10 to 5, July through September.

Nervous Nellie's Jams and Jellies, 598 Sunshine Road, Deer Isle, makes the products you see all over Maine the old-fashioned way. Founded by sculptor Peter Beerits, the business puts up 40,000 jars each year in a little house with a big kitchen. So many people were stopping in that Peter decided to serve refreshments as well. His **Mountainville Café** offers morning coffee and afternoon tea with homemade scones and breads (with plenty of jams). Included is a frozen drink called a Batido, a refreshing but caloric mix of cream cheese, freezer jam and crushed ice cubes. Besides all the wonderful jams (we especially like the wild Maine blueberry-ginger conserve and the hot tomato jelly), Peter's quirky sculptures on the grounds outside make this worth a visit. We were intrigued by a sculpture of a lobsterman with huge red wooden claws for arms. Lately, Peter has cleared the surrounding woods to be peopled with sculptures from his studio fashioned from an abandoned store he moved to the site. Look for witches, woodsmen and owls among the trees. Open daily 9 to 5, mid-May through Christmas; rest of year, by chance.

Stonington's Main Street has been enhanced by **The Clown,** a seasonal venture combining European antiques, fine art and Italian ceramics with Italian specialty foods and wines. The tramonti olive oil and chianti classico are produced in Tuscany on the farm of owners Kyle A. Wolfe and Martin Kolk, who opened a year-round offshoot of the same name in Portland and, in 2004, another offshoot in Belfast.

The hickory-smoked salmon at the **Stonington Sea Products** facility at 100 Route 15 outside Stonington has been rated the finest Scottish-style smoked salmon outside Scotland. General manager Richard Penfold, an émigré from the Shetland Islands of northeastern Scotland, smokes Bay of Fundy salmon slowly and naturally in a kiln imported from Glasgow. In addition to a variety of smoked seafood products, the retail shop in front offers fresh fish and lobster.

Maine stoneware pottery, cobalt blue songeware plates, hand-painted stoneware from Silesia and unusual candlesticks for the dinner table are among the design items of interest to cooks and hostesses at **Harbor Farm**, a store and showroom in an 1850 schoolhouse along the causeway on Little Deer Isle. It features unique, made-to-order home and kitchen accessories, from tinware and tiles to an apple peeler and a maker of toasted sandwiches with sealed edges.

Rooster Brother, 18 West Main St., Ellsworth, is an exceptional store for cooks, serious and otherwise. Occupying three floors of a large Victorian building, it has a specialty food and wine shop downstairs and a wide variety of cookware, china, linens, cookbooks and assorted kitchen equipment on the main floor. The Second Story now offers a seconds shop and sale items. More than 60 cheeses and an expanded wine selection known for good values are available. Lately, owners Pamela and George Elias have been concentrating on coffee roasting and an expanding bakery, which features its own French bread. We came away with four types of dried chile peppers we sometimes have trouble finding in the Northeast as well as a cookbook called *Hotter Than Hell.*

Little Notch Bakery in Southwest Harbor is a great bakery producing more than 4,500 loaves of bread weekly for avid customers, including some of Down East Maine's finest inns and restaurants. Specialties include Italian breads, focaccia, olive rolls and onion rolls. Owners Art and Kate Jacobs opened the year-round **Little Notch Café** and retail outlet at 340 Main St. in the center of town. Art said the bittersweet Belgian chocolate brownie he urged us to sample tastes like fudge, and it sure did. Had it been lunchtime, we'd have gone for the grilled flank steak sandwich with roasted peppers and onions on a baguette.

Little Notch Bakery products and Seal Cove goat cheese are hot numbers at

Sawyer's Market, the Southwest Harbor grocery with all the right stuff, including a rear deli case of fantastic-looking salads, marinated cooked salmon and other gourmet items prepared exclusively for Sawyer's. You could fashion yourself a delightful picnic here or at the Sawyers gourmet store selling wines, cheeses, pâtés and such just across Main Street.

The grocery store in Bar Harbor is the **J.H. Butterfield Co.,** a fixture since 1887 at 152 Main St. Catering to the upper crust, it has a fine supply of gourmet foods, chocolates, picnic items and luscious fruits, and there are good sandwiches to take out. Never have we seen so many varieties of Walker shortbreads and biscuits. There's also an extensive selection of beers and wines, including those from the nearby Bartlett Winery.

Not Quite the Corner Deli at 65 Main St. is the soup, salad and sandwich shop opened by Adeena and Chris Fisher, who ran George's restaurant across the way for several years until it closed in late 2005. The day's specials happened to include a couple of Greek specialties associated with George's. The deli is open daily 10 to 4 in summer, Monday-Friday in the off-season.

Fabulous entrées as well as salads, vegetables, sandwiches, specialty foods and more are offered seasonally at **Mano's Market,** 1517 Route 1, Hancock. It's the newest venture of Nicole Purslow, former owner of Le Domaine restaurant and inn next door, in partnership with Charlotte Humenuk. The pair put up lavish picnic baskets to go, or you can pick out items from the deli to enjoy at tables out back.

Worth a stop on the Schoodic Peninsula is the **Chickadee Creek Stillroom** on Route 186 in West Gouldsboro. Herbs and everlastings are charmingly displayed in a ramble of rustic little rooms. More than 300 varieties of herbs, spices and seasonings are sold by the ounce. Jeanie and Fred Cook grow some 40 varieties of herbs. They offer a potpourri called "Maine Woods, a walk through the pines and firs," for $3 a scoop, along with closet spices and bath herbs. They also sell garlic bread and logs of herbed goat's cheese. Jeanie will cut fresh herbs while you wait, $1 a bunch.

Award-Winning Fruit Wines

Bartlett Maine Estate Winery, 175 Chicken Mill Pond Road, Gouldsboro.

A winery in far Down East Maine? Yes, this with-it operation a half mile off Route 1 in Gouldsboro, east of Hancock, is in the forefront in producing premium fruit wines. Finding conditions unsuitable for grapes, winemakers Robert and Kathe Bartlett substituted local apples, pears, blackberries and blueberries, and pioneered in making fine wines that have won best-of-show awards in the East (including, in 1989, the most medals of any winery in the New England Wine Competition). They employ grape wine techniques in the production of 12,000 gallons annually, and the wines are aged in French and American oak.

A labor of love the couple built from the ground up, the winery occupies an unusual, hand-wrought stone building in the woods. The small tasting room offers more than twenty varieties, ranging from dry and semi-dry blueberry reds to refreshing pear-apple whites, sweet blackberry dessert wines and refreshing honey meads. When a friend shipped a few bottles of Bartlett's blueberry reserve to France, the recipients could not believe it was pressed from blueberries. We're partial to the nouveau blueberry, fit for the finest of gourmet dinners.

(207) 546-2408. Open Memorial Day through Columbus Day, Monday-Saturday 10 to 5; rest of year by appointment.

Index

A

B

H

I

J

K

L

M

N

O

P

T

U

V

W

X

Y

Z

Also by the Authors

The Ultimate New England Getaway Guide. The newest book by Nancy and Richard Woodworth describes where to go, stay, eat and play in New England's choicest areas. It reveals all the details on 30 getaway destinations that have the best of everything. Published in 2005. 490 pages of fresh ideas. $18.95.

Waterside Escapes in the Northeast. This new edition by Nancy and Richard Woodworth relates the best lodging, dining, attractions and activities in 36 great waterside vacation spots from the Chesapeake Bay to Cape Breton Island and from Lake Placid to Martha's Vineyard. First published in 1987; revised and expanded fifth edition in 2005. 490 pages to discover and enjoy. $18.95.

Inn Spots & Special Places in New England. The first in the series, this book by Nancy and Richard Woodworth tells you where to go, stay, eat and enjoy in New England's choicest areas. Focusing on 35 special places, it details the best inns and B&Bs, restaurants, sights to see and things to do. First published in 1986; fully revised and expanded seventh edition in 2004. 560 pages of great ideas. $18.95.

Inn Spots & Special Places / Mid-Atlantic. The second effort in the series, this new edition covers 35 favorite destinations from western New York through the Mid-Atlantic to southeastern Virginia. First published in 1992; fully revised and expanded fifth edition in 2003. 520 pages to enjoy. $18.95.

New England's Best. This new book by Nancy and Richard Woodworth is a comprehensive guide to the best lodging, dining and attractions around New England. It's the culmination of 30 years of living and traveling in New England by journalists who have seen them all and can recommend the best. Published in 2002. 602 pages of valuable information. $18.95.

Best Restaurants of New England. This new edition by Nancy and Richard Woodworth is the most comprehensive guide to great restaurants throughout New England. The authors detail the dining ambiance, menu offerings, hours and prices for more than 1,000 restaurants. First published in 1990; revised third edition in 2002. 474 pages of timely information. $16.95.

The Originals in Their Fields

These books may be ordered from your local bookstore, online or direct from the publisher, pre-paid, plus $2 shipping for each book. Connecticut residents add sales tax.

Wood Pond Press
365 Ridgewood Road
West Hartford, Conn. 06107
Tel: (860) 521-0389
Fax: (860) 313-0185
woodpond@ntplx.net
Web Site: www.getawayguides.com.

On the Web: Excerpts from these books may be found at **www.getawayguides.com.**